THE COMPLETE HANDBOOK OF
BASEBALL

Other Sports Books from SIGNET

☐ **INSTANT REPLAY: The Green Bay Diary of Jerry Kramer edited by Dick Schaap.** From the locker room to the goal line, from the training field to the Super Bowl, this is the inside story of a great pro-football team . . . "The best behind the scenes glimpse of pro football ever produced."—*The New York Times* (#E9657—$2.50)

☐ **PAPER LION by George Plimpton.** When a first-string writer suits-up to take his lumps as a last-string quarterback for the Detroit Lions, the result is "the best book ever about pro football!"—*Red Smith.* "A great book that makes football absolutely fascinating to fan and non-fan alike . . . a tale to gladden the envious heart of every weekend athlete."—*The New York Times* (#J7668—$1.95)

☐ **PLAYING PRO FOOTBALL TO WIN by John Unitas, with Harold Rosenthal.** A bruising inside look at the pro game by the greatest quarterback of them all. Revised and updated.
(#W7209—$1.50)

☐ **SCREWBALL by Tug McGraw and Joseph Durso.** "You gotta believe!" when baseball's star reliever and super flake rips the cover off the game he plays and life he's led . . . "It's the best!"—*Roger Kahn,* author of *The boys of Summer* in *The New York Times* Includes an action-packed photo insert. (#Y6421—$1.25)

☐ **THE PERFECT JUMP by Dick Schaap.** What happens to a world-record-breaking athlete when he's reached that once-in-a-lifetime perfection he can never achieve again? The glory and heartbreak of Bob Beamon, an athlete who reached the top and had nowhere left to go. With an exciting sports photo insert! (#E7248—$1.75)

1982 SEASON
THE COMPLETE HANDBOOK OF
BASEBALL

EDITED BY ZANDER HOLLANDER

A SIGNET BOOK
NEW AMERICAN LIBRARY

TIMES MIRROR

ACKNOWLEDGMENTS

Can Mike Schmidt make it three MVP awards in a row? Will Fernando Valenzuela be as fabulous in '82? Who will throw out the first ball in the next World Series? Our battery of experts can't possibly have the answers, but they've put everything else into this 12th edition of THE COMPLETE HANDBOOK OF BASEBALL. For their invaluable support, we acknowledge with appreciation contributing editors Eric Compton and Howard Blatt, and Nick Peters, Bill Madden, Mike Littwin, Frank Kelly, Phyllis Hollander, Lee Stowbridge, Curt Nichols, Beri Greenwald, Dot Gordineer, Seymour Siwoff, Bob Wirz, Chuck Adams, Vince Nauss, Bob Fishel, Phyllis Merhige, Bob Grim, Blake Cullen, Katy Feeney and the publicity directors of the 26 major-league teams.

Zander Hollander

PHOTO CREDITS: Covers—Rich Pilling. Inside: Malcolm Emmons, Nancy Hogue, Michael Homlitas, Mitchell B. Reibel/Fotosport, UPI.

SIGNET TRADEMARK REG. U.S. PAT. OFF. AND FOREIGN COUNTRIES
REGISTERED TRADEMARK—MARCA REGISTRADA
HECHO EN CHICAGO, U.S.A.

SIGNET, SIGNET CLASSICS, MENTOR, PLUME, MERIDIAN AND NAL BOOKS
are published by The New American Library Inc. 1633 Broadway
New York, New York 10019

First Printing, March, 1982

1 2 3 4 5 6 7 8 9

PRINTED IN THE UNITED STATES OF AMERICA

CONTENTS

Editor's Note: The material herein includes trades and rosters up to final printing deadline.

The Life and Times of Fabulous Fernando

By MIKE LITTWIN

Like Alexander before him, Fernando Valenzuela, at the tender age of 21, has few worlds left to conquer.

In his first full season in the major leagues, Fernando the Great was the best pitcher in the National League. He led his team, the Los Angeles Dodgers, to the World Championship. He was honored by the presidents of two nations. And he set about the business of becoming a millionaire.

His was a story you couldn't invent. Now all he has to do is top it.

What can he possibly do for an encore?

The Mexican national, who speaks no English but whose sensational performance of last season requires no translation, addressed the question at a Los Angeles press conference announcing his selection as winner of the Cy Young Award.

He smiled, thought for a moment, smiled again and shrugged.

"I don't know," said Valenzuela, the first rookie ever to win the Cy Young, through an interpreter.

One thing is sure, though, he won't worry much about it. Valenzuela doesn't worry much about anything. On the first day of the 1981 season, the then 20-year-old rookie was a last-minute selection to pitch before a full house at Dodger Stadium. An hour before the game, he was lying down in the training room—asleep.

He won Game 5 of the playoffs against Montreal to give the

Mike Littwin, author of the book "¡Fernando!," *has been an eyewitness to the Valenzuela experience as a sportswriter for the Los Angeles* Times.

Fernando plays catch before Series game at Yankee Stadium.

Dodgers the pennant. He won Game 3 of the World Series, with the Dodgers down by two to the Yankees, and turned the Series around.

Worry?

Valenzuela had lunch with President Reagan and Mexican President Jose Lopez Portillo at the White House. They wanted to have their picture taken with *him*.

He's quite a story, Fernando. And not just because of his tantalizing but mostly elusive screwball or his 13-7 record or his eight shutouts or 180 strikeouts, although they're part of it. A hero in the Latino community, the toast of two countries, Valenzuela transcends mere baseball. He is, to use an overworked word, a phenomenon. And he's a man of mystery, the private Fernando hidden to all but a few intimates. There is none other quite like him.

If he misses a parade, as he did following the World Series, it's a front-page story. There are records singing his praises, posters showing off his roundish form, a book recounting his brief life, a $20 silver medallion with his likeness imprinted on each side. His agent, Tony DeMarco, had lined up an estimated $500,000 in off-the-field benefits for Valenzuela and was pursuing a contract with the Dodgers that would make Fernando the highest-paid 21-year-old baseball player ever.

A non-charity appearance by Valenzuela costs a promoter $10,000. Over the winter, when Fernando wasn't pitching winter ball in Mexico, he was booked solid.

I remember Fernando when his life was much simpler. I first saw him in the fall of 1980 when he was called up to the Dodgers from their Double-A club in San Antonio. He was 19 then, had this fat and funny body, and everyone wondered what he was doing in a Dodger uniform.

He pitched 17⅔ innings, all in relief, and nearly saved the '80 season for the Dodgers. He was a curiosity piece then, and the butt of a few jokes from his teammates.

"He has to be at least 30," Jerry Reuss said.

"If he's 19, which I doubt," said Davey Lopes, "he's the most unbelievable 19 I've ever seen."

The Dodgers, to quiet the rumors, distributed his birth certificate to the local media.

The joke was that Fernando didn't know where he was or who he was pitching to as he busily struck out the likes of George Foster and Cesar Cedeno. Some joke. He was both happy and sad then. Happy to be in the big leagues. Sad to be there without a friend, knowing no one.

I've watched him since. I've seen him handle the media pres-

Tom Lasorda hugs his ace after his pennant-clinching win.

sure, handle situations that no youngster—much less one just a few years removed from a poor dirt farm in Etchohuaquila, Mexico—could be expected to endure. I saw his teammates shower him with respect and affection and love. I saw him grow up.

"You could see him change," said his manager, Tom Lasorda, "after a few months. He got more confidence in himself as a person. He was always confident in his pitching. But he made a few friends and he felt comfortable, he felt wanted."

Oh yes, the Dodgers wanted him. Everyone wanted a part of him. It got to be a little much after a while. Once, he had an interview set up with *Good Morning America*. Lasorda and Mike Brito, the man who discovered him and who was to become his protector, were scheduled to deliver him. He wouldn't go. Just didn't want to leave his hotel room. He'd had enough interviews. It was the same way with that World Series parade. Valenzuela still has so little perspective, so little ability to separate one event from another. He didn't understand the importance of a World Series victory parade.

Later, he would apologize. Brito would apologize, saying, "The next time, even if he's dying, we'll take him by the arms and legs and drag him there."

But there was nothing really to apologize for. He just didn't know any better.

"There are so many people pulling at him," said Reggie Smith, a teammate last year, "that sometimes he wants to be away from it all. Anybody could understand that. I don't know how he puts up with everything he does."

His teammates are protective of him, and so is Brito, a Dodger scout of Cuban birth who found Fernando pitching in the Mexican League. Dodgers vice-president Al Campanis flew to Yucatan, in the south of Mexico, to see Valenzuela pitch and struck a deal with the team owner. The Dodgers bought Fernando's contract for $120,000 in 1978. A year later they taught him the screwball and the rest is—well, you know what the rest is. At age 16 he had moved from the sandlots to the Mexican professional league and four years later he was the Cy Young winner.

Brito followed Valenzuela to Lodi, to San Antonio and even managed his team in the Mexican League. When Valenzuela was signed by the Dodgers, Brito promised Fernando's mother he would take care of her baby (Fernando is the youngest of 12 children) and he has.

When Valenzuela first came to Los Angeles, he moved to a hotel not far from Dodger Stadium. But his fame grew so quickly that soon Fernando could not leave his room without

facing a mob of fans. Brito, who lives in East Los Angeles, a predominantly Chicano section, offered Valenzuela the use of a
two-bedroom apartment behind his house. Soon Fernando became part of the Brito family.

And Brito, a portly man given to natty hats and fat cigars, has
become a celebrity. "I have to sign autographs now," he said.
"Did you ever hear of a scout signing autographs?"

So what's a typical Fernando day?

He likes to watch television, particularly cartoons. He swims in
the Brito swimming pool. Or plays pool. Maybe sees a movie. He
has no "civilian" friends, except a girlfriend from Yucatan who
often stays with the Britos. According to Brito, "They are very
much in love. I think they will be married."

Ask Fernando about it and he gets embarrassed and blushes.
"I don't talk about that," he said.

Still, he can't go out alone, not unless he's willing to be
mobbed. In East Los Angeles, he is a star among stars, bigger
than any Hollywood figure.

It is the same for him in Mexico, where they named a new stadium after him in Acapulco and where he has more keys to cities
than to hotel rooms. He has been the dinner guest of President
Portillo, who counts him as a friend. Any Mexican politician
would want to have Fernando as a friend. Brito tells this story:
Portillo was leaning out a window and kiddingly told Fernando,
"Don't put your face in front of mine. You'll take away all the
attention from me."

The life is one Valenzuela could never have envisioned as a
youngster. He grew up in an *ejido*, a communal farm of perhaps
200 people. There's no road sign pointing to Etchohuaquila, just
a dirt road leading to a farm without irrigation in the desert state
of Sonora, about 300 miles south of Arizona. The house he grew
up in is a four-room adobe with a mud-and-stick roof, a dirt
floor, windows without glass panes, no running water. There are
17 Valenzuelas living there now.

Four years removed from the *ejido*, Fernando has promised to
build his family a new house. He can afford it now, certainly. He
has spanned the great distance from a dirt-floor hut to $1,000-a-
day hotel rooms, such as the one where he once held a press conference in Chicago.

But he hasn't changed much. Not very much, anyway.

"I have learned much," he says. "I have seen so many things,
but I think that I am the same person."

He doesn't have superstar-itis. He always credits his teammates first. "That's why they love him," Lasorda said. "He's not
an 'I' player. Ordinarily, people would be jealous of someone

who has gotten the attention he has. But you don't see that on the Dodgers. They all love him."

His relationship with his teammates has grown and matured, just as Fernando has. A teammate of his in the Mexican League once said that Valenzuela spoke in sign language—a nod for yes, a shake of the head for no, and the appropriate hand movement for *mas o menos*, more or less. When he first became a Dodger, it was the same thing. But he made friends, especially with Pepe Frias. Some of the older Dodgers, particularly Reggie Smith, tried to look after him. He eventually started to joke around a little—his favorite being tapping a teammate on one shoulder while he stood on the other side.

"That's his joke," said teammate Jay Johnstone, "and we go along. It's his way of saying hello. There's still the language barrier and it's hard to get to know him. But he knows how we feel about him."

Valenzuela has learned some English and understands considerably more than he lets on, despite his insistent denials. Asked when he'll be able to speak English, Fernando says, "I'll keep talking Spanish. That way you can hear both languages." But Brito says that Fernando is simply too shy to speak what English he knows but that soon he'll surprise everyone.

"My daughters talk to him in Spanish and he answers them in English," Brito said. "One day he'll just start talking English. You wait."

He will, some day. But it will be too bad, in a way. Part of the beauty of Fernandomania is Valenzuela's innocence and naivete, the fact that we know so little of him and he so little of the world. That will change.

But will he?

Most don't think so. His body will stay round (the Dodgers have tried several diets but don't bother him much any more) and his screwball will stay elusive. How many games he can win, nobody knows.

Sandy Koufax, who should have some idea about pitching, said he couldn't remember seeing anything the equal of him.

A group of managers were standing around one day during the World Series in the lobby of a New York hotel. And Jim Fregosi was saying, "Nobody's ever done what Fernando has done at his age."

He didn't, like Joe Hardy, sell his soul to the devil; at least as far as we know, he didn't. Jay Johnstone had another idea. "It's like he was on Fantasy Island," Johnstone said. "This stuff doesn't happen in real life."

Except to Fernando.

Fabulous Fernando is the people's choice in Mexico City.

He doesn't know who Cy Young is, but some day they may be naming pitching awards after him.

Mike Schmidt tried to put the young pitcher into perspective after the Phillie slugger's home run last June helped hand Fernando his first defeat after eight victories. Someone asked Schmidt if he thought Fernando would remember his homer.

"Maybe some day when he's won his 39th Cy Young Award," Schmidt said, "if he can pronounce my name, maybe he'll tell someone while I'm sitting here in my easy chair watching him."

Maybe. The legend continues. His agent, DeMarco, was seeking $1-million a year for Valenzuela, who sold out every game but one he pitched at Dodger Stadium.

Los Angeles Times columnist Scott Ostler followed up that report by saying the Dodgers should pay Valenzuela whatever he wants. He's that rare. He even made up for the one mistake he made—missing that parade. A month later, he was the grand marshall of another.

It seems nothing he does is wrong. Does he have to worry about a sophomore jinx? Let's put it this way. You see the way he looks? *Playgirl* Magazine still named him one of America's 10 sexiest men. There's obviously nothing Fernando can't do.

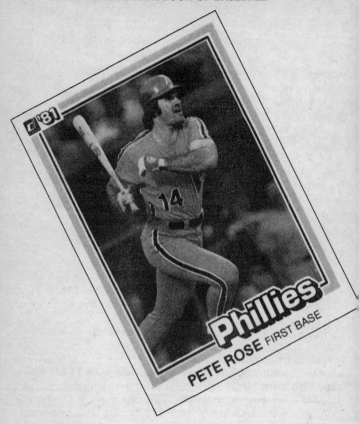

THE GREAT BASEBALL CARD WAR

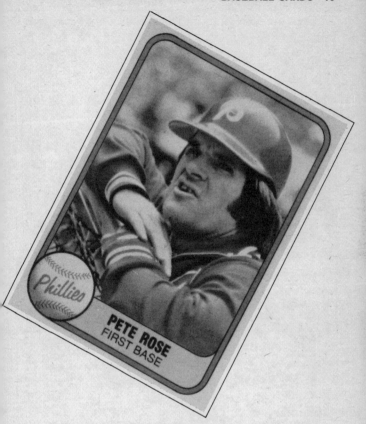

PETE ROSE
FIRST BASE

Phillies

By ERIC COMPTON

It is a war fought not with guns, but with lawsuits and appeals. It is a war fought over pieces of gum and pictures of baseball players. It is a war fought in the candy stores as well as the courts. It is the great baseball card war.

It erupted on all fronts in 1981 and, despite the latest court ruling, it may not be over. It involves three major companies—Topps, Fleer and Donruss—all of which are vying for the lion's

---

As boy and man, Eric Compton still collects baseball cards.

share of what is estimated to be a more than $10-million-a-year industry.

Until last year, Topps had the field to itself since 1956. That was the year Bowman, the major competition, dropped out. But the Fleer Corporation of Philadelphia, which boasts of having invented bubble gum in 1928, started legal action in 1975, seeking the right to package baseball cards with its gum.

The case finally came to court years later, and in July 1980, a federal court ruling in Philadelphia cleared the way for competition in cards. U.S. District Judge Clarence Newcomer ruled that Topps had conspired with the Major League Baseball Players Association to create a monopoly in the manufacture and sale of cards.

The ruling opened the door for Fleer and the Donruss Com-

pany, a subsidiary of General Mills. The two companies sought and received contracts from the players' association giving them the right—as Topps has that right—to reproduce photos of the players on cards.

So last year, youngsters had their choice among three sets of cards at the candy store. Topps came out about two weeks earlier than usual with its 726-card set. Fleer (660 cards) and Donruss

(605) soon followed. While no one at any of the companies would come out and say so, indications are that all three did well.

Fleer produced an impressive set, with clear, sharp pictures and an easy-to-read flip side containing the player's minor and major-league statistics. Donruss' first set contained many blurry photographs, but instead of filling the back side with mounds of statistics, Donruss listed career highlights of the player, which

JACK
PERCONTE
2nd BASE ☆

MIKE
SCIOSCIA
CATCHER ☆

FERNANDO
VALENZUELA
PITCHER

TOPPS DODGERS FUTURE STARS

made for interesting reading. Topps did its usual professional job and added some statistical categories to the flip side, perhaps in response to the competition. Topps also had a "Hit to Win" baseball game which offered a bat, a ball, a glove and a baseball book as prizes.

As usual when dealing with first sets, there were errors galore. In its first printing, Donruss spelled Graig Nettles "Craig" and listed Bobby Bonds' home-run total as 936, only 610 more than it should have been. And the Donruss card of Astro right-hander Frank LaCorte was actually a picture of Astro left-hander Rich Niemann.

Fleer's problems were mostly minor. The company misspelled Willie ("Willy") Montanez on his card, and also had him with the wrong team. Fleer also issued a card of Dick Howser as Yankee manager, even though Howser had been fired the previous November.

But Donruss and Fleer encountered more problems in the courts than they did with the selling of their cards. In late summer an Appeals Court in Philadelphia overturned the original ruling; it was a major victory for Topps.

In a legal sense, everything is back to pre-1981 status. But apparently that does not mean that signals are off for Fleer and Donruss. Fleer president Donald Peck has said his company plans to take the case to the Supreme Court, if necessary. Meanwhile, as this handbook went to press, both Fleer and Donruss

RON CEY
THIRD BASE

were making plans to issue 1982 cards.

According to a source close to the battlefront, Fleer was planning a 660-card set that would be sold with stick-on logos of the 26 major-league teams. Donruss was also preparing a 660-card set that would be marketed with a jigsaw-puzzle of a painting by noted sports artist Dick Perez. Topps, the only company authorized to distribute the cards with confectionaries (such as gum) or simply as cards without any product, would not reveal its plans.

"It's a fairly secretive business," admitted Topps spokesman Norman Liss. "You have to understand that cards compete with everything—movies, toys, comic books. We don't disclose what we're going to do."

It is safe to assume, however, that Topps will be swinging for the fences with its 1982 set.

In this competitive free-for-all, the serious collector stands to come out a winner. He'll be seeing more and better cards. But youngsters with limited funds will have their problems. They can't buy 'em all.

The Funniest Men
In the Game

By NICK PETERS

Baseball *isn't* such a funny game anymore.

The evolution of society and economic changes in the game have made the ballplayers more businesslike. They take themselves too seriously.

Some treat baseball like a 9-to-5 job. It is not unusual to see a ballplayer coming to work in a three-piece suit and carrying an attache case. The Dow Jones is his most important average.

Free agency has created more movement and modern times have brought about an independence which has affected camaraderie among teammates.

Seldom will you find ballplayers lingering in the clubhouse and discussing the intricacies of the game. Instead of conducting bull sessions at a nearby watering hole, they're rushing home in Mercedes and Rolls-Royces.

"The characters are starting to creep out of baseball," claims Giant manager Frank Robinson, whose career spans four decades.

But there is always room for free spirits, even if they are not named Lefty Gomez, Dizzy Dean or Casey Stengel. And the modern era is no exception.

Take the World Champion Los Angeles Dodgers, for example. They are a paradox. Despite the conservative image of their front office, the clubhouse is brimming with characters.

"Look who's managing them," says veteran pitcher Ken Brett, who had a brief stint in Los Angeles. "How can you take anything seriously with Tom Lasorda running the club?"

Indeed, the Dodgers seem to be the exception to the rule. With personalities like Jerry Reuss, Jay Johnstone and Rick Monday providing the laughs, the Dodgers also topped the majors in

As baseball writer for the Oakland Tribune, *Nick Peters keeps a close eye on the flakes.*

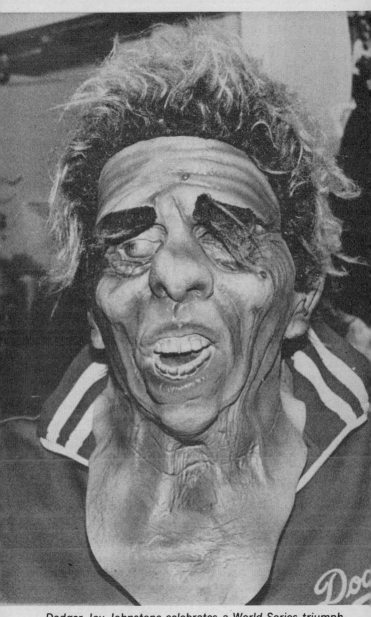

Dodger Jay Johnstone celebrates a World Series triumph.

pranks last year while becoming World Champions.

In a World Series dominated by George Steinbrenner's mega-lomaniacal manuevering, Johnstone provided much-needed relief after Game 4 by conducting interviews in a horror mask and a Star Patrol space helmet.

The impish Johnstone, in fact, ranks as the majors' No. 1 flake, keeping teammates in stitches. Tug McGraw and Bill Lee perhaps recieve more recognition, but they're in far different situations than Johnstone.

McGraw has been more visible because of World Series appearances, but his good nature is truly the exception on an otherwise very conservative Phillie organization. The witty Lee, on the other hand, has offended people with his hip nature and offbeat remarks. Like McGraw, he seems to please outsiders more than his teammates.

"I prefer the term free spirit to flake," Johnstone says. "Most of us are free spirits. Bill Lee is a flake. He's way out. I think we're an important influence on any ballclub. We keep things loose, make guys laugh. The stunts are mainly to pull guys together.

"I had some great teachers. When I reached the majors with the Angels, my roomie was Jim Piersall. Now there was a crazy guy. I saw him do all sorts of wild things. He said he did them to relieve the tension, to relax. We had guys like Bo Belinsky, Dean Chance, Leon Wagner and Jim Fregosi, so we were pretty loose. That was a good training ground for me.

"From there," Johnstone continues, "I went to the White Sox, who had weird guys like Bill Melton and Ed Herrmann. We did things to amuse ourselves. Baseball tends to drag in the dog days of August and September, so you do things to break the monotony. Then I joined Tug at Philadelphia and we were winning, so we could have more fun. It's tougher to be funny when you're losing."

Ozark, the Phillies manager at the time, recalled the Johnstone-McGraw act. "They're probably the two most offbeat guys in the game," Ozark says. "What makes them unusual is that they think they're normal and everyone else is nuts."

McGraw, when he was asked which he liked better, grass or artificial turf, once replied: "I don't know, I never smoked turf." That got Tug to thinking and he came up with a creative solution following a losing streak.

"I felt we were down after losing a couple of games," Tug said, "so I wanted to do something to get us high again. I tried sniffing a little coke . . . but I had to give it up when I couldn't get the Coke bottle in my nostril."

Johnstone considers McGraw's actions truly unique. "One time," Jay remembers, "Tug lost both ends of a doubleheader on the road and he decided to do some drinking. He had a few pops and then took himself to the nearest jail, demanding to be locked up.

"We had adjoining lockers in Philly and we were always thinking up things to do. Guys don't hang around as much now, but there always are opportunities in airplanes, buses, airports and hotels. I love instigating things and having someone else get the blame."

There was the time, for instance, when Johnstone placed a sticky brownie in Steve Garvey's first-base glove. Some chocolate remained on Jay's fingers and he casually rubbed it on Reuss' uniform. When Garvey noticed his gooey glove, he immediately began looking for a culprit. And there stood Reuss.

"You play one guy against another and 99 percent of the time the guys take it well," Johnstone says. "But you have to know who to pick on. There are some people who don't like fooling around. Most of the time, you leave them alone. On some occasions, however, the stunts are so far-fetched, the victim cannot help but laugh.

"One day," Johnstone recalls, "Bill Russell makes an error and he is really steaming when he comes back to the dugout. So while he went to bat, I took the glove and put iodine, tape and gauze on it. When he saw it, all he could do was laugh."

In a similar situation last season, the Giants' Darrell Evans was involved in a mild altercation at a San Francisco eatery and police were on the scene. After the next game, Evans returned to the Candlestick Park clubhouse only to find "prison bars" taped up and down his locker.

Rookies, of course, are always more vulnerable to clubhouse pranks, a hazing of sorts. Last year, Reuss nailed second baseman Steve Sax's shoes to his locker and Johnstone had some fun with Fernando Valenzuela, unaccustomed to such nonsense as a sandlotter in his native Mexico.

"Fernando was in the shower and he had his eyes closed while he was rinsing hair shampoo off his head," Johnstone proudly explains. "He couldn't see me, so I'd get some shampoo and pour it on his hair while he was rinsing. He kept rinsing and rinsing and there was still shampoo. He couldn't understand it."

But Johnstone isn't particular. He picks on veterans with equal abandon. Like the time he took some linament and casually lined Garvey's underwear with the hot stuff.

"Garv didn't realize it till he got on the freeway," Jay says, grinning. "By then it was too late . . . it wasn't a very comfortable 40-minute drive home."

The Johnstone-Reuss collaboration undeniably was the majors' No. 1 comedy act of 1981. Their best stunt took place in September when Jay and Jerry donned groundskeepers' uniforms and dragged the infield at Dodger Stadium before a game with the Pirates.

"We were fined ($200 each), but it was worth it because the fans got such a big kick out of it," says Johnstone. Adds Reuss: "We talked about it for some time and just picked our spot. That game with the Pirates was on TV, so we figured it would be a good time. I do things because I get bored. It also relieves the pressure because you concentrate so much when you're pitching."

Unfortunately for his teammates, Reuss has lots of idle time between starts and is always looking for ways to alleviate the pressure. There was the night, for instance, when the Dodgers were in a particularly tense game.

Lasorda, frequently the brunt of jokes, was sipping coffee in the dugout. He became involved in the proceedings and put his cup down. The alert Reuss seized upon the opportunity and dropped his slurpy chew of tobacco in the cup.

"At the end of the inning, Tommy picks up the cup and took a gulp," Reuss remembers. "All of a sudden, he was gasping. It was difficult to keep a straight face."

With the champion A's of the early Seventies, Catfish Hunter pulled the same stunt with teammate Dick Green. "Greenie was drinking a Coke and he set it down," Monday recalls. "Cat spit his chew into it and Greenie drank it down. He gagged for about half a minute . . . then threw up in the dugout."

Along those same lines, practical joker Bert Blyleven elicited the same result from John Milner when both were with the Pirates. Milner didn't relish the sight of blood, so Blyleven thought he'd have some fun.

"Bert got some red gum and mixed it with his chew," Reuss says. "We left just enough room on the bench so that Milner had to sit between us. Then Bert started coughing up what looked like his lungs and John lost his cookies.

"Blyleven is a master at making other guys throw up. He is just plain sick. A disgusting fellow. But a lot of fun. One time in Pittsburgh, it was Opening Day and about 40 degrees outside. He came by to pick me up around 8 A.M. and I took him a little by surprise by coming out of the house naked."

Steve Howe, who once had his streetclothes run up a flag pole by the mischievous Johnstone in spring training, also fell victim to Reuss' warped sense of humor. It happened after Howe had done something unmentionable in Reuss' shoe, so retaliation

Tug McGraw takes a ride on Phillie Phanatic in 1980.

was inevitable.

"We were on the road," Reuss says, "and I called room service at our hotel, identifying myself as Steve Howe. I said that my fiancee was coming to town and that I wanted it to be a special night. I asked them to send a bottle of their finest champagne, a dozen red roses and some steak and eggs. The bill came to $100."

Phone antics, of course, are simple to perform and common, but Moe Drabowsky altered the theme when he once telephoned Hong Kong from the bullpen and ordered takeout food for 40. Moe was a master at disguising his voice and having fun on the phone.

Rollie Fingers used to drive Charlie Finley up a wall at Oakland. It has been well-documented that Finley used the phone frequently for conversations with his managers, making dialing the dugout a daily chore.

Fingers enjoyed grabbing the phone when it rang and saying, "Hello, Charlie?" When it really was Finley on the other end, the owner would become enraged.

Fingers also enjoyed playing with matches, once burning Randy Jones' locker when both were with San Diego. Rollie's pyrotechnics started with the A's and the tradition has been carried on by the youthful and fun-loving Oakland players.

At Anaheim last spring, a reporter was interviewing Mike Norris when Dave Revering suddenly flicked his Bic. The fire spread to the scribe's pantscuff before Steve McCatty doused the flames with a beer.

McCatty is perhaps the prime prankster of the A's. After he was shelled at Texas in 1980, the pitcher climbed through a porthole and sat on the roof of the team bus as it made its way back to the hotel.

Manager Billy Martin insisted he was too alert to be trapped by the hot-footing McCatty, who waited until the final series of the 1980 season to prove his skipper wrong.

"Billy said that I could never get to him and he used to soak his shoestrings in water as a precaution," McCatty explains. "We were in Chicago for the final series and Billy was putting on the suicide squeeze and was all caught up in the game. He wasn't paying attention to anything else, so I got the fire going about two inches high up his laces.

"He looked down and started beating on it. Everybody was laughing and Billy was, too. Everyone thought he would start screaming and chewing me out, but he went along with it."

But Martin isn't one to forgive and forget. Revenge came quickly. The next day, the crotch was cut out of McCatty's slacks and the collar was shorn off his shirt. Nobody had to ask who had done the deed.

McCatty once placed shavings from a bar of soap on a teammate's hot dog. "It looked like onions," Cat points out. "Then the guy starts eating the dog and soap bubbles start coming out the corner of his mouth."

Teammate Norris drew the biggest chuckles during last year's strike when he came up with an unusual solution to the problem by checking into a Bay Area hotel. "I was so depressed," he explains, "I checked into the hotel so it would seem like being on a road trip."

What else would you expect from a pitcher? In fact, Johnstone seems to be an exception. Most of the cut-ups are pitchers, especially relievers. One explanation is that they have more time to kill between appearances and are isolated in the bullpen, away from the watchful eye of managers and coaches.

Drabowsky, after all, was a reliever. Likewise McGraw, Fingers, Lee, Sparky Lyle, Dan Quisenberry and Don Stanhouse. The latter was nicknamed Stan The Man Unusual by Oriole teammate Mike Flanagan.

Stanhouse not only had a comical appearance with his Harpo Marx hairstyle, but also was accompanied by a large stuffed gorilla which was doused with champagne when the O's won the 1979 AL pennant. Stanhouse, who once arrived at the ballpark in a hearse, was called Full Pack by Earl Weaver because that's how many cigarettes the manager would smoke while the reliever took his time on the mound.

Quisenberry, whose forte is offbeat remarks, last year described the seven-week strike layoff as "one-fifth of a pregnancy." As a collegian, Quiz was being taunted by a teammate, so he turned and fired into the dugout instead of to the plate.

"Humor is the best way to paralyze myself and prevent worrying," he says, describing himself as the Victor Borge of his profession. He concluded a magazine interview last year with: "I've seen the future and it's much like the present, only longer."

Kevin Saucier, who studied McGraw when both were with the Phillies, made quite a name for himself as a Tiger rookie last year. He earned the nickname Hot Sauce with his gyrations on the mound, making the fans recall similar antics by Mark (The Bird) Fidrych.

"So I'm a loony, what's wrong with that?" Saucier asks. "I do my best to hold my enthusiasm during a game, but when it's over and I've done a good job, it's time to let it out." His release includes pirouetting off the mound and vigorously grabbing for handshakes with as many teammates as he can.

But the master free spirit among relievers is the lovable

McGraw, who used to grow tomatoes in the Shea Stadium bullpen. During spring training, he removed his uniform on the mound, revealing green longjohns, a top hat and an ear-to-ear smile. What else did you expect on St. Patrick's Day?

Tug loves publicity and, appropriately, resides in Media, Pa. He has coined colorful names for some of his pitches: the Cutty Sark fastball ("It sails a little"); Bo Derek fastballs ("They have a little tail on them"); the John Jameson ("A straight shot"), and the Peggy Lee changeup ("The batter sees it and asks, 'Is that all there is?' ").

During a game with the Dodgers, McGraw struck Bill Russell on the shoulder with a pitch and a bench-clearing brawl ensued after Russell charged the mound. Tension was running high when the two clubs staged a rematch in Los Angeles. Tug broke it by walking out on the field wearing an olive-green combat jacket and a military helmet liner. He approached Russell to make peace and they both cracked up.

John Lowenstein of the Orioles also relied on great timing to bring the house down. He was on first base and heading for second on a grounder. The relay throw from second base struck him on the head and knocked him out. He lay motionless on the field and it was feared the injury was serious.

"He looked dead," said Frank Robinson, then a coach with the Orioles. "John had to be carried off the field on a stretcher. Everyone was worried because he wasn't moving. Suddenly, as the stretcher got near the dugout, he sits up, smiles and waves to the fans. Everyone roared."

Two of the newcomers in baseball, Joe Charboneau and Mickey Hatcher, are regarded as slightly unconventional. Shortly after being optioned to Charleston, W.Va., last year, Charboneau walked into a bank in his underwear.

Hatcher, a practical joker, used to sail smoke bombs on paper planes out of hotel windows until one landed on a roof and caught fire. The young practical joker was in his glory with the Dodgers, once throwing a live pig into Lasorda's office.

Lasorda frequently holds court in his Dodger Stadium quarters, where portions of the walls are dedicated to luminaries like Frank Sinatra. Stanhouse and Reuss once replaced all the entertainment stars' photos with those of the players. But that was a mild prank compared to what Monday instigated.

"Everyone knows how Tommy likes to pal around with Hollywood people," Monday says, "so a bunch of us got a makeup mirror, complete with all the lightbulbs, and we placed it in Tommy's office and took his desk out. Then we got some crayon and wrote on the mirror: 'Dear Tommy, You finally made it big in Hollywood. Love, Frank.' He went nuts."

Another manager who went nuts, but for a far different reason, was Kansas City's Jim Frey in a game at Seattle's Kingdome last May. Amos Otis was batting for the Royals and he hit a slow roller down the third-base line. The Mariners didn't have a chance to throw out the speedy Otis, so their only hope was to have the ball roll foul.

Third baseman Lenny Randle aided the process by landing on his stomach and blowing the ball foul. Catcher Terry Bulling grabbed the ball and plate umpire Larry McCoy signaled foul. A fuming Frey protested and Otis was awarded first base when it was ruled Randle had altered the course of the ball.

"The umpires didn't know what to do," says Seattle skipper Rene Lachemann. "Lenny said he only yelled at the ball . . . the breath from his yelling must have moved it." Adds Randle: "I didn't blow it. I used the power of suggestion. I yelled at it, 'Go foul, go foul!' How could they call it a hit? It was a foul."

Umpire Dave Phillips had an explanation. "None of us had ever seen anything like it," the ump admits. "I think Lenny did it to be funny. And it was funny, but you can't alter the course of the ball. You couldn't throw dirt at the ball and get away with it."

Lachemann, incidentally, is among the managers who aren't exactly run-of-the-mill. Rocky Bridges of the Triple-A Phoenix Giants is the most humorous of the pilots, but Lachemann raised some eyebrows after being hired by the Mariners when he requested living quarters in the Kingdome clubhouse instead of at a hotel.

"I usually spend 12 to 14 hours a day in the clubhouse, so why not?" Lachemann asks. "All I'd use an apartment or a hotel for is to sleep. Besides, the Kingdome isn't your average clubhouse. There are no smelly jocks and concrete floors. I have carpeting, a laundromat, a sauna, a whirlpool and maid service . . . and I can invite 60,000 for a party in my backyard."

Doug Rader was quick with the quip and the prank during his playing days. One such Houston caper involved Joe Pepitone shortly after he joined the Astros.

Pepitone went to his new teammates and told them he gladly would go along with clubhouse banter, but asked them to kindly keep away from his assortment of wigs because of their expense and the difficulty in trying to replace them.

The irreverent Rader found the situation irresistible. He snatched Pepitone's most expensive hairpiece, carried it to the toilet and soiled it. Pepi almost had heart failure when he came upon the ruined toupee, but the prank was a compulsion for Rader, who promptly left a blank check for his balding teammate.

A SIXTH NO-HITTER FOR NOLAN RYAN?

By ERIC COMPTON

The Dodgers' Dusty Baker leaned in at the plate while the tall, thin right-hander on the mound looked for the sign. The pitcher went into his delivery and sent a curve toward the plate. Baker, guessing that a curve was coming, deliberately swung under the ball a little, hoping to make solid contact. The ball bounced out to the third baseman, who calmly threw it to Houston's Cesar Cedeno at first. And all hell broke loose at the Astrodome.

The out completed one of baseball's rarest feats, a no-hitter, but it was nothing new for an Astro pitcher named Nolan Ryan. It was his fifth no-hitter, a 5-0 wipeout of the Dodgers last Sept. 26, and it meant an all-time record; Ryan and Sandy Koufax had previously shared the mark at four.

Will there be a sixth?

First off, Ryan's age may be of primary importance. The soft-spoken fireballer from Refugio, Tex., turned 35 years old in January. That would be approaching retirement time for most fastball pitchers, and one has to wonder just how long Ryan can keep throwing balls at speeds approaching 100 miles per hour.

But many baseball people argue that Ryan's age may not be as much of a factor as one might think. The reason for this is spelled C-U-R-V-E.

At age 34 last season, Ryan finally mastered the art of throwing his curve for strikes. In the no-hitter against the Dodgers, his fastest pitch was "only" 98 miles per hour, but he consistently got

---

Eric Compton, who pitches for the New York Daily News *sports department softball team and is a contributing editor of the Handbook, has never tossed a no-hitter.*

Nolan Ryan averages a no-hitter every 83 starts.

the curveball over the plate. The game was a microcosm of what Ryan had done all season, and the results showed in his statistics: an 11-5 record and an incredible 1.69 earned-run average—the second-lowest in the National League in 48 years. In 14 of his 21 starts in the regular season, Ryan allowed one earned run or less. It was a spectacular season.

But then, Ryan has always been spectacular. Drafted out of high school by the New York Mets, Nolan always had what you can't teach a pitcher: blazing speed. But the Mets rushed him to the major leagues and he never became a consistent winner in the Big Apple. A combination of Army reserve meetings, blisters on his fingers and a pitching staff that included names like Seaver and Koosman meant precious little work for a youngster who had trouble finding home plate.

But that all changed in 1972. In what may go down as the worst trade in the history of baseball, Ryan was traded to the California Angels in exchange for a washed-up Jim Fregosi. Finally getting a chance to pitch in a steady rotation, Ryan won 19 games and struck out a league-high 329 batters.

His first no-hitter came on May 15, 1973, when Ryan zipped the Royals, 3-0. Exactly two months later, he recorded No. 2, a 6-0 wipeout of Detroit. This was an incredible season for Ryan. Playing with a California team that batted a paltry .253 with only 93 homers, Ryan won 22 games, had a 2.28 ERA and struck out a record 383 batters. It is doubtful anyone will ever break that single-season strikeout mark.

In 1974, Ryan no-hit the Twins on Sept. 28, 4-0, for No. 3, and the following year, on June 1, he blanked Baltimore, 1-0, to tie Koufax' career record of four. Six years later he uncorked No. 5.

"It's hard to believe I got it," he said afterwards. "It's the one thing I wanted. I've had a shot at it for a long time. At my age, I didn't think I would get it."

As one considers Nolan's chances for another, a look at his past figures seems in order. He has had numerous near-misses (seven one-hitters, 14 two-hitters, 20 three-hitters) and still has averaged a no-hitter for every 83 starts. A check of the record book indicates that a no-hitter is pitched in one of every 574 games, so it is very unlikely that anyone will come along and top Ryan's record.

Though it is true that Ryan's age may be catching up to him, one has to feel that another no-hitter is a distinct possibility. He pitched better at age 34 than he ever had and he has the added advantage of pitching almost half his games in the Astrodome, a notoriously difficult park for hitters.

Sitting on his plateau of five no-hitters, Ryan could be content

Hall of Famer Sandy Koufax tossed four no-hitters.

to view some of the distinguished pitchers in his wake—Koufax with his four; Cy Young and Bob Feller, each of whom threw three; Warren Spahn, two, and Tom Seaver, one of Ryan's closest ballplayer friends, who has achieved one no-hitter. Walter Johnson, who until Ryan was considered the fastest pitcher of all, had only one. Robin Roberts, Steve Carlton and Ron Guidry have a combined total of zero.

If anyone is to challenge his record in the future, it will be someone with a blazing fastball. Junkball pitchers rarely throw no-hitters simply because they rely on getting ground balls and these grounders invariably find their way through the infield for hits. Fastball pitchers like Cleveland's Len Barker (who threw a perfect game last May against Toronto) and the Reds' Mario Soto or Bruce Berenyi would seem to have the speed to throw a no-hitter or two.

At age 35, Ryan should still have a few good years left in that miraculous right arm. And as long as he can throw the fastball at 90 or more mph and get his curve over, the sky's the limit for him.

A sixth no-hitter? Don't bet against it.

COMPLETE LIST OF NO-HITTERS

(Source: *The Book of Baseball Records* © 1981 by Seymour Siwoff)

NA—National Association	UA—Union Association
NL—National League	FL—Federal League
AA—American Association	AL—American League

*Perfect game
**First major-league start
***World Series (perfect game)

1875 Joseph Borden, Philadelphia vs. Chicago, NA, July 28 4-0
1876 George Washington Bradley, St. Louis vs. Hartford, NL,
     July 15 2-0
1880 *John Lee Richmond, Worcester vs. Cleveland, NL, June 12 .   1-0
     *John Montgomery Ward, Providence vs. Buffalo, NL,
     June 17 5-0
     Lawrence Corcoran, Chicago vs. Boston, NL, Aug. 19 6-0
     James Galvin, Buffalo vs. Worcester, NL, Aug. 20 1-0
1882 Anthony Mullane, Louisville vs. Cincinnati, AA, Sept. 11 2-0
     Guy Hecker, Louisville vs. Pittsburgh, AA, Sept. 19 3-1
     Lawrence Corcoran, Chicago vs. Worcester, NL, Sept. 20 5-0
1883 Charles Radbourne, Providence vs. Cleveland, NL, July 25 8-0

Hugh Dailey, Cleveland vs. Philadelphia, NL, Sept. 13 1-0
1884 Albert Atkisson, Philadelphia vs. Pittsburgh, AA, May 24 10-1
Edward Morris, Columbus vs. Pittsburgh, AA, May 29. 5-0
Frank Mountain, Columbus vs. Washington, AA, June 5. 12-0
Lawrence Corcoran, Chicago vs. Providence, NL, June 27 6-0
James Galvin, Buffalo vs. Detroit, NL, Aug. 4 18-0
Richard Burns, Cincinnati vs. Kansas City, UA, Aug. 26 3-1
Edward Cushman, Milwaukee vs. Washington, UA, Sept. 28 . 5-0
Edward Kimber, Brooklyn vs. Toledo, AA, Oct. 4 (10
innings). 0-0
1885 John Clarkson, Chicago vs. Providence, NL, July 27. 4-0
Charles Ferguson, Philadelphia vs. Providence, NL, Aug. 29. . 1-0
1886 Albert Atkisson, Philadelphia vs. New York, AA, May 1 3-2
William Terry, Brooklyn vs. St. Louis, AA, July 24. 1-0
Matthew Kilroy, Baltimore vs. Pittsburgh, AA, Oct. 6. 6-0
1888 William Terry, Brooklyn vs. Louisville, AA, May 27. 4-0
Henry Porter, Kansas City vs. Baltimore, AA, June 6. 4-0
Edward Seward, Philadelphia vs. Cincinnati, AA, July 26 12-2
August Weyhing, Philadelphia vs. Kansas City, AA, July 31. . . 4-0
1890 Ledell Titcomb, Rochester vs. Syracuse, AA, Sept. 15. 7-0
1891 Thomas Lovett, Brooklyn vs. New York, NL, June 22 4-0
Amos Rusie, New York vs. Brooklyn, NL, July 31 6-0
**Theodore Breitenstein, St. Louis vs. Louisville, AA, Oct. 4 . 8-0
1892 John Stivetts, Boston vs. Brooklyn, NL, Aug. 6. 11-0
Alex Sanders, Louisville vs. Baltimore, NL, Aug. 22 6-2
**Charles Jones, Cincinnati vs. Pittsburgh, NL, Oct. 15 7-1
1893 William Hawke, Baltimore vs. Washington, NL, Aug. 16. 5-0
1897 Denton (Cy) Young, Cleveland vs. Cincinnati, NL, Sept. 18 6-0
1898 Theodore Breitenstein, Cincinnati vs. Pittsburgh, NL,
April 22. 11-0
James Hughes, Baltimore vs. Boston, NL, April 22 8-0
Frank Donohue, Philadelphia vs. Boston, NL, July 8 5-0
Walter Thornton, Chicago vs. Brooklyn, NL, Aug. 21. 2-0
1899 Charles Phillippe, Louisville vs. New York, NL, May 25 7-0
Victor Willis, Boston vs. Washington, NL, Aug. 7 7-1
1900 Frank Hahn, Cincinnati vs. Philadelphia, NL, July 12 4-0
1901 Earl Moore, Cleveland vs. Chicago, AL, May 9 (Lost in 10). . . . 2-4
Christopher Mathewson, New York vs. St. Louis, NL,
July 15. 5-0
1902 James Callahan, Chicago vs. Detroit, AL, Sept. 20. 3-0
1903 Charles Fraser, Philadelphia vs. Chicago, NL, Sept. 18. 10-0
1904 *Denton (Cy) Young, Boston vs. Philadelphia, AL, May 5 3-0
Robert Wicker, Chicago vs. N.Y., NL, June 11 (Gave hit in
10th) 1-0
Jesse Tannehill, Boston vs. Chicago, AL, Aug. 17 6-0
1905 Christopher Mathewson, New York vs. Chicago, NL,
June 13 1-0
Weldon Henley, Philadelphia vs. St. Louis, AL, July 22. 6-0
Frank Smith, Chicago vs. Detroit, AL, Sept. 6 15-0
William Dineen, Boston vs. Chicago, AL, Sept. 27 2-0

1906 John Lush, Philadelphia vs. Brooklyn, NL, May 1 1-0
    Malcolm Eason, Brooklyn vs. St. Louis, NL, July 20 2-0
    Harry McIntire, Brooklyn vs. Pitt., NL, Aug. 1 (Lost in 13) 0-1
1907 Frank Pfeffer, Boston vs. Cincinnati, NL, May 8 6-0
    Nicholas Maddox, Pittsburgh vs. Brooklyn, NL, Sept. 20 2-1
1908 Denton (Cy) Young, Boston vs. New York, AL, June 30 8-0
    George Wiltse, N.Y. vs. Phil., NL, July 4 (10 innings) 1-0
    George Rucker, Brooklyn vs. Boston, NL, Sept. 5 6-0
    Robert Rhoades, Cleveland vs. Boston, AL, Sept. 18 2-1
    Frank Smith, Chicago vs. Philadelphia, AL, Sept. 20 1-0
    *Adrian Joss, Cleveland vs. Chicago, AL, Oct. 2 1-0
1909 Leon Ames, New York vs. Brooklyn, NL, April 15 (Lost in
    13) 0-3
1910 Adrian Joss, Cleveland vs. Chicago, AL, April 20 1-0
    Charles Bender, Philadelphia vs. Cleveland, AL, May 12 4-0
    Thomas Hughes, New York vs. Cleveland, AL, Aug. 30
    (Gave hit in 10th) 0-5
1911 Joseph Wood, Boston vs. St. Louis, AL, July 29 5-0
    Edward Walsh, Chicago vs. Boston, AL, Aug. 27 5-0
1912 George Mullin, Detroit vs. St. Louis, AL, July 4 7-0
    Earl Hamilton, St. Louis vs. Detroit, AL, Aug. 30 5-1
    Charles Tesreau, New York vs. Philadelphia, NL, Sept. 6 3-0
1914 James Scott, Chicago vs. Washington, AL, May 14 (Lost in
    10) 0-1
    Joseph Benz, Chicago vs. Cleveland, AL, May 31 6-1
    George Davis, Boston vs. Philadelphia, NL, Sept. 9 7-0
    Edward LaFitte, Brooklyn vs. Kansas City, FL, Sept. 19 6-2
1915 Richard Marquard, New York vs. Brooklyn, NL, April 15 2-0
    Frank Allen, Pittsburgh vs. St. Louis, FL, April 24 2-0
    Claude Hendrix, Chicago vs. Pittsburgh, FL, May 15 10-1
    Miles Main, Kansas City vs. Buffalo, FL, Aug. 16 5-0
    James Lavender, Chicago vs. New York, NL, Aug. 31 2-0
    Arthur Davenport, St. Louis vs. Chicago, FL, Sept. 7 3-0
1916 Thomas Hughes, Boston vs. Pittsburgh, NL, June 16 2-0
    George Foster, Boston vs. New York, AL, June 21 2-0
    Leslie Bush, Philadelphia vs. Cleveland, AL, Aug. 26 5-0
    Hubert Leonard, Boston vs. St. Louis, AL, Aug. 30 4-0
1917 Edward Cicotte, Chicago vs. St. Louis, AL, April 14 11-0
    George Mogridge, New York vs. Boston, AL, April 24 2-1
    Fred Toney, Cincinnati vs. Chicago, NL, May 2 (10 innings) . 1-0
    James Vaughn, Chicago vs. Cincinnati, NL, May 2, (Lost in
    10) 0-1
    Ernest Koob, St. Louis vs. Chicago, AL, May 5 1-0
    Robert Groom, St. Louis vs. Chicago, AL, May 6 3-0
    *Ernest Shore, Boston vs. Washington, AL, June 23 4-0
1918 Hubert Leonard, Boston vs. Detroit, AL, June 3 5-0
1919 Horace Eller, Cincinnati vs. St. Louis, NL, May 11 6-0
    Raymond Caldwell, Cleveland vs. New York, AL, Sept. 10 3-0
1920 Walter Johnson, Washington vs. Boston, AL, July 1 1-0
1922 *Charles Robertson, Chicago vs. Detroit, AL, April 30 2-0

Jesse Barnes, New York vs. Philadelphia, NL, May 7 6-0
1923 Samuel Jones, New York vs. Philadelphia, AL, Sept. 4 2-0
Howard Ehmke, Boston vs. Philadelphia, AL, Sept. 7 4-0
1924 Jesse Haines, St. Louis vs. Boston, NL, July 17 5-0
1925 Arthur (Dazzy) Vance, Brooklyn vs. Philadelphia, NL,
Sept. 13 10-1
1926 Theodore Lyons, Chicago vs. Boston, AL, Aug. 21 6-0
1929 Carl Hubbell, New York vs. Pittsburgh, NL, May 8 11-0
1931 Wesley Ferrell, Cleveland vs. St. Louis, AL, April 29 9-0
Robert Burke, Washington vs. Boston, AL, Aug. 8 5-0
1934 Louis Newsom, St. Louis vs. Boston, AL, Sept. 18 (Lost in
10) 1-2
Paul Dean, St. Louis vs. Brooklyn, NL, Sept. 21 3-0
1935 Vernon Kennedy, Chicago vs. Cleveland, AL, Aug. 31 5-0
1937 William Dietrich, Chicago vs. St. Louis, AL, June 1 8-0
1938 John Vander Meer, Cincinnati vs. Boston, NL, June 11 3-0
John Vander Meer, Cincinnati vs. Brooklyn, NL, June 15 6-0
Monte Pearson, New York vs. Cleveland, AL, Aug. 27 13-0
1940 Robert Feller, Cleveland vs. Chicago, AL, April 16 1-0
James Carleton, Brooklyn vs. Cincinnati, NL, April 30 3-0
1941 Lonnie Warneke, St. Louis vs. Cincinnati, NL, Aug. 30 2-0
1944 James Tobin, Boston vs. Brooklyn, NL, April 27 2-0
Clyde Shoun, Cincinnati vs. Boston, NL, May 15 1-0
1945 Richard Fowler, Philadelphia vs. St. Louis, AL, Sept. 9 1-0
1946 Edward Head, Brooklyn vs. Boston, NL, April 23 5-0
Robert Feller, Cleveland vs. New York, AL, April 30 1-0
1947 Ewell Blackwell, Cincinnati vs. Boston, NL, June 18 6-0
Donald Black, Cleveland vs. Philadelphia, AL, July 10 3-0
William McCahan, Philadelphia vs. Washington, AL, Sept. 3 . 3-0
1948 Robert Lemon, Cleveland vs. Detroit, AL, June 30 2-0
Rex Barney, Brooklyn vs. New York, NL, Sept. 9 2-0
1950 Vernon Bickford, Boston vs. Brooklyn, NL, Aug. 11 7-0
1951 Clifford Chambers, Pittsburgh vs. Boston, NL, May 6 3-0
Robert Feller, Cleveland vs. Detroit, AL, July 1 2-1
Allie Reynolds, New York vs. Cleveland, AL, July 12 1-0
Allie Reynolds, New York vs. Boston, AL, Sept. 28 8-0
1952 Carl Erskine, Brooklyn vs. Chicago, NL, June 19 5-0
Virgil Trucks, Detroit vs. Washington, AL, May 15 1-0
Virgil Trucks, Detroit vs. New York, AL, Aug. 25 1-0
1953 **Alva (Bobo) Holloman, St. Louis vs. Philadelphia, AL,
May 6 6-0
1954 James Wilson, Milwaukee vs. Philadelphia, NL, June 12 2-0
1955 Samuel Jones, Chicago vs. Pittsburgh, NL, May 12 4-0
1956 Carl Erskine, Brooklyn vs. New York, NL, May 12 3-0
Melvin Parnell, Boston vs. Chicago, AL, July 14 4-0
Salvatore Maglie, Brooklyn vs. Philadelphia, NL, Sept. 25 5-0
***Donald Larsen, New York, AL, vs. Brooklyn, NL, Oct. 8 . 2-0
1957 Robert Keegan, Chicago vs. Washington, AL, Aug. 20 6-0
1958 James Bunning, Detroit vs. Boston, AL, July 20 3-0
Hoyt Wilhelm, Baltimore vs. New York, AL, Sept. 20 1-0

1959 Harvey Haddix, Jr., Pittsburgh vs. Milwaukee, NL, May 26
     (Pitched 12 perfect innings, allowed hit in 13, lost) 0-1
1960 Donald Cardwell, Chicago vs. St. Louis, NL, May 15.......... 4-0
     Lou Burdette, Milwaukee vs. Philadelphia, NL, Aug. 18 1-0
     Warren Spahn, Milwaukee vs. Philadelphia, NL, Sept. 16......4-0
1961 Warren Spahn, Milwaukee vs. San Francisco, NL, April 28 1-0
1962 Robert (Bo) Belinsky, Los Angeles vs. Baltimore, AL, May 5 . 2-0
     Earl Wilson, Boston vs. Los Angeles, AL, June 26............. 2-0
     Sanford (Sandy) Koufax, Los Angeles vs. New York, NL,
         June 30 5-0
     William Monbouquette, Boston vs. Chicago, AL, Aug. 1.......1-0
     John Kralick, Minnesota vs. Kansas City, AL, Aug. 26 1-0
1963 Sanford (Sandy) Koufax, Los Angeles vs. San Francisco,
         NL, May 11 8-0
     Donald Nottebart, Houston vs. Philadelphia, NL, May 17......4-1
     Juan Marichal, San Francisco vs. Houston, NL, June 15 1-0
1964 Kenneth Johnson, Houston vs. Cincinnati, NL, April 23
         (Lost) 0-1
     Sanford (Sandy) Koufax, Los Angeles vs. Philadelphia, NL,
         June 4 3-0
     *James Bunning, Philadelphia vs. New York, NL, June 21 6-0
1965 James Maloney, Cincinnati vs. New York, NL, June 14 (10
         innings, gave two hits in 11th, lost) 0-1
     James Maloney, Cincinnati vs. Chicago, NL, Aug. 19 (10
         innings)... 1-0
     *Sanford (Sandy) Koufax, Los Angeles vs. Chicago, NL,
         Sept. 9.. 1-0
     David Morehead, Boston vs. Cleveland, AL, Sept. 16.......... 2-0
1966 Wilfred (Sonny) Siebert, Jr., Cleveland vs. Washington, AL,
         June 10 2-0
1967 Don Wilson, Houston vs. Atlanta, NL, June 18 2-0
     Dean Chance, Minnesota vs. Cleveland, AL, Aug. 25.......... 2-1
     Joe Horlen, Chicago vs. Detroit, AL, Sept. 10 6-0
1968 Thomas Phoebus, Baltimore vs. Boston, AL, April 27.......... 6-0
     *James Hunter, Oakland vs. Minnesota, AL, May 8 4-0
     George Culver, Cincinnati vs. Philadelphia, NL, July 29 6-1
     Gaylord Perry, San Francisco vs. St. Louis, NL, Sept. 17 1-0
     Ray Washburn, St. Louis vs. San Francisco, NL, Sept. 18...... 2-0
1969 William Stoneman, Montreal vs. Philadelphia, NL, April 17.... 7-0
     James Maloney, Cincinnati vs. Houston, NL, April 30 10-0
     Don Wilson, Houston vs. Cincinnati, NL, May 1.............. 4-0
     James Palmer, Baltimore vs. Oakland, AL, Aug. 13............ 8-0
     Ken Holtzman, Chicago vs. Atlanta, NL, Aug. 19............. 3-0
     Robert Moose, Pittsburgh vs. New York, NL, Sept. 20........ 4-0
1970 Dock Ellis, Pittsburgh vs. San Diego, NL, June 12 2-0
     Clyde Wright, California vs. Oakland, AL, July 3 4-0
     Bill Singer, Los Angeles vs. Philadelphia, NL, July 20 5-0
     Vida Blue, Oakland vs. Minnesota, AL, Sept. 21 6-0
1971 Ken Holtzman, Chicago vs. Cincinnati, NL, June 3............. 1-0
     Rick Wise, Philadelphia vs. Cincinnati, NL, June 23........... 4-0

Robert Gibson, St. Louis vs. Pittsburgh, NL, Aug. 14......... 11-0
1972 Burt Hooton, Chicago vs. Philadelphia, NL, April 16 4-0
Milton Pappas, Chicago vs. San Diego, NL, Sept. 2 8-0
William Stoneman, Montreal vs. New York, NL, Oct. 2 ......: 7-0
1973 Steven Busby, Kansas City vs. Detroit, AL, April 27...........3-0
Nolan Ryan, California vs. Kansas City, AL, May 15..........3-0
Nolan Ryan, California vs. Detroit, AL, July 15 6-0
James Bibby, Texas vs. Oakland, AL, July 30.................6-0
Philip Niekro, Atlanta vs. San Diego, NL, Aug. 5 9-0
1974 Steven Busby, Kansas City vs. Milwaukee, AL, June 19........2-0
Richard Bosman, Cleveland vs. Oakland, AL, July 19 4-0
Nolan Ryan, California vs. Minnesota, AL, Sept. 28..........4-0
1975 Nolan Ryan, California vs. Baltimore, AL, June 1.............1-0
Edward Halicki, San Francisco vs. New York, NL, Aug. 24.... 6-0
Vida Blue, William Abbott, Paul Lindblad and Roland Fin-
    gers, Oakland vs. California, AL, Sept. 28 (Blue went five
    innings, Abbott and Lindblad one each, and Fingers two
    innings)... 5-0
1976 Lawrence Dierker, Houston vs. Montreal, NL, July 9..........6-0
John Odom and Francisco Barrios, Chicago vs. Oakland,
    AL, July 28 (Odom pitched 5 innings, Barrios 4) 2-1
John Candelaria, Pittsburgh vs. Los Angeles, NL, Aug. 9 2-0
John Montefusco, San Francisco vs. Atlanta, NL, Sept. 29 9-0
1977 James Colborn, Kansas City vs. Texas, AL, May 14 6-0
Dennis Eckersley, Cleveland vs. California, AL, May 30 1-0
Bert Blyleven, Texas vs. California, AL, Sept. 22...............6-0
1978 Robert Forsch, St. Louis vs. Philadelphia, NL, April 16........5-0
Thomas Seaver, Cincinnati vs. St. Louis, NL, June 16 4-0
1979 Kenneth Forsch, Houston vs. Atlanta, NL, April 7 6-0
1980 Jerry Reuss, Los Angeles vs. San Francisco, NL, June 27 8-0
1981 Charlie Lea, Montreal vs. San Francisco, NL, May 10 4-0
*Len Barker, Cleveland vs. Toronto, AL, May 15 3-0
Nolan Ryan, Houston vs. Los Angeles, NL, Sept. 26 5-0

Ron Guidry fired best pitch at catcher George Steinbrenner.

The New Millionaires: VI

There's a new trend in the high-stakes world of the baseball marketplace. Apparently teams are beginning to adopt a charity-begins-at-home philosophy, locking up their own established talent to long-term deals before going on the lookout for new blood.

Among the players listed below who signed for more than $1 million this past off-season, most re-signed with their former clubs. The Pirates' Bill Madlock, the Reds' Dave Concepcion and the Yankees' Ron Guidry won't be changing their addresses.

Topping the list of free agents who flew the coop were Ken Griffey (dealt to the Yankees by the Reds when they couldn't come to terms); Reggie Jackson, the Yankee who became an Angel, and Dave Collins, another Red-turned-Yankee. Griffey made the biggest haul (if you don't count Mike Schmidt's extension) as George Steinbrenner dug into his bottomless pockets for a whopping $6 million for five years. Griffey's not the Yanks' best-paid outfielder, though, that distinction still belonging to last year's bank-breaker, Dave Winfield.

PLAYER	TEAM	YEARS	TOTAL
*Mike Schmidt	Phillies	6	$7,200,000
Ken Griffey	Yankees	5	6,000,000
Bill Madlock	Pirates	6	5,100,000
Dave Concepcion	Reds	5	4,630,000
Ron Guidry	Yankees	5	4,500,000
Reggie Jackson	Angels	4	4,000,000
Jerry Mumphrey	Yankees	6	3,970,000
Bobby Grich	Angels	4	3,300,000
Jerry Remy	Red Sox	5	2,800,000
Dave Collins	Yankees	3	2,500,000
Greg Luzinski	White Sox	3	2,250,000
Phil Garner	Astros	3	2,050,000
Ray Burris	Expos	3	1,800,000
Vern Ruhle	Astros	3	1,500,000
Amos Otis	Royals	2	1,270,000
Lou Piniella	Yankees	3	1,100,000
Bill Campbell	Cubs	3	1,050,000

*Contract torn up for '82 and extended through '87

INSIDE THE
AMERICAN LEAGUE

By BILL MADDEN
New York Daily News

PREDICTED ORDER OF FINISH	*East* Milwaukee Brewers Detroit Tigers New York Yankees Baltimore Orioles Cleveland Indians Boston Red Sox Toronto Blue Jays	*West* Oakland A's Kansas City Royals Chicago White Sox Texas Rangers California Angels Minnesota Twins Seattle Mariners

Playoff winner: Milwaukee

EAST DIVISION

		Owner		Morning Line Manager
1	**BREWERS** Navy, yellow & white Showed mettle in stretch last year	Bud Selig	1981 W 62 L 47	**9-5** Bob Rodgers
2	**TIGERS** Navy, orange & white Have lean and hungry look	John Fetzer	1981 W 60 L 49	**5-2** Sparky Anderson
3	**YANKEES** Navy blue pinstripes Beginning to show age	George Steinbrenner	1981 W 59 L 48	**4-1** Bob Lemon
4	**ORIOLES** Black, white & orange Falling back into the pack	Edward Bennett Williams	1981 W 59 L 46	**6-1** Earl Weaver
5	**INDIANS** Scarlet, white & blue Not enough speed for upset	Steve O'Neill	1981 W 52 L 50	**10-1** Dave Garcia
6	**RED SOX** Red, white & blue Pitching shorts hurts chances	Mrs. Tom Yawkey	1981 W 58 L 49	**10-1** Ralph Houk
7	**BLUE JAYS** Powder blue & white Not ready to move up in class	R. Howard Webster	1981 W 37 L 69	**100-1** Bobby Cox

BREWERS will stay close in early going, then make move at top of stretch. **TIGERS**, likely early leader, may not have staying power to hold off Brewers. **YANKEES** are showing age and will tire in backstretch. **ORIOLES** no longer have what it takes to finish in the money. **RED SOX** and **INDIANS** could surprise by finishing in top three. **BLUE JAYS** never a factor.

SUDS STAKES

82nd Running. American League Race. Distance, 162 games plus playoff. Purse (based on '81) $13,000 per winning player, division, up to $35,000 winning player total for World Championship. A field of 14 entered in two divisions.

Track Record 111 wins—Cleveland, 1954

WEST DIVISION	Owner		Morning Line Manager
1 **A'S** Forest green, gold & white The speed entry	Roy Eisenhardt	**1981** W 64 L 45	**2-1** Billy Martin
2 **ROYALS** Royal blue & white Been this route before	Ewing Kauffman	**1981** W 49 L 53	**3-1** Dick Howser
3 **WHITE SOX** Navy & white Defense weak down stretch	E. Einhorn/J. Reinsdorf	**1981** W 54 L 52	**4-1** Tony LaRussa
4 **RANGERS** Red, white & blue No staying power	Eddie Chiles	**1981** W 57 L 48	**6-1** Don Zimmer
5 **ANGELS** Red, white & navy Good jockey, but snakebitten	Gene Autry	**1981** W 51 L 59	**8-1** Gene Mauch
6 **TWINS** Scarlet, white & blue Untested but could surprise	Calvin Griffith	**1981** W 41 L 68	**8-1** Billy Gardner
7 **MARINERS** Blue & gold Not enough of a handicap here	George Argyros	**1981** W 44 L 65	**25-1** Rene Lachemann

A'S and **ROYALS** will run neck and neck from starting gate down stretch to finish line. **WHITE SOX** will need to run perfect race to pull upset. **RANGERS** will vie for lead early, then fade in stretch. **ANGELS** are unpredictable, but past performances indicate they won't be a factor. **TWINS** will show early speed, but lack staying power. **MARINERS** to trail the field.

BALTIMORE ORIOLES

TEAM DIRECTORY: Chairman of the Board: Edward Bennett Williams; Pres.: Jerold C. Hoffberger; Exec. VP-GM: Hank Peters; VP: Jack Dunn III; VP: Joseph P. Hamper, Jr.; Dir. Pub. Rel.: Bob Brown; Trav. Sec.: Philip Itzoe; Mgr.: Earl Weaver. Home: Memorial Stadium (52,696). Field distances: 309, l.f. line; 385, l.c.; 405, c.f.; 385, r.c., 309, r.f. line. Spring training: Miami, Fla.

SCOUTING REPORT

HITTING: A major concern of the Orioles last season was the puzzling second-half slump by Ken Singleton. After the strike, Singleton couldn't buy an extra-base hit and the Orioles paid dearly for that. Not surprisingly, their No. 1 objective of the off-season was to come up with another RBI man to back up Eddie Murray. They tried desperately to land Sixto Lezcano from the Cards—but he wound up in San Diego.

They also made a token effort to sign Reggie Jackson. Thus, the game plan in Baltimore to beef up the attack looks to be rid-

Earl Weaver can still argue with the best of 'em.

ing heavily on the abilities of Cal Ripken Jr., the much-touted rookie. Ripken may be tried in the outfield or at DH.

In the meantime, Orioles are counting on another big offensive year from third baseman Doug DeCinces (second on club in HR, RBI and gamers last year) as well as a comeback from Singleton. Fortunately, there is also Murray, fast emerging as the best hitter in baseball.

PITCHING: Last year everyone felt the Orioles were the team to beat because of their pitching. Instead, their major strength turned out to be a major weakness. Arm trouble cut Steve Stone's wins from 25 to four; Mike Flanagan had a second-straight so-so season after his Cy Young performance in '79; Jim Palmer ached and ached and may well be nearing the end of the line; Tim Stoddard was a bust in the bullpen, dropping from 26 saves to seven while his ERA ballooned from 2.51 to 3.89.

Had it not been for Sammy Stewart's yeoman job as long relief man, the Orioles might never have been a factor in the pennant race. That's why the best deal the Orioles made last winter may have been the one they DIDN'T make: Stewart and three rookies to the Cardinals for Garry Templeton and Lezcano. The Oriole pitching is just too fragile right now to sacrifice any quality such as Stewart, Scott McGregor or Dennis Martinez.

FIELDING: The Orioles have always prided themselves in defense and even though Brooks Robinson and Mark Belanger no longer hold forth at Memorial Stadium, the Birds are a steady lot in the field. Rich Dauer led all second basemen in fielding last year, Murray committed just one error at first and Sakata showed surprising range at short. Behind the plate, Dempsey is still regarded as the toughest catcher in the league to steal on. DeCinces has shown a tendency to be erratic at critical times at third, but is still better-than-adequate defensively. There is some concern about the outfield, where Al Bumbry and Singleton showed signs of slowing up a bit last year.

OUTLOOK: After so many years of being a pennant race fixture under Earl Weaver's feisty leadership, the Orioles appear to be slipping the other way now. The nucleus (Murray, Dauer, McGregor, the Martinez boys, Stewart and Singleton) is enough to keep them respectable. However, second-line pitching, bullpen and offensive outfield deficiencies were not rectified.

The Orioles, barring an unexpected infusion of help from the farm system, do not figure to hit or pitch enough to keep pace with Milwaukee, Detroit and New York. Underlying those problems is the growing suspicion that Weaver is losing his touch as manager.

BALTIMORE ORIOLES 1982 ROSTER

MANAGER Earl Weaver
Coaches—Elrod Hendricks, Ray Miller, Cal Ripken, Sr.,
Ralph Rowe, Jimmy Williams

PITCHERS

No.	Name	1981 Club	W-L	IP	SO	ERA	B-T	Ht.	Wt.	Born
52	Boddicker, Mike	Rochester	10-10	182	109	4.20	R-R	5-11	172	8/23/57 Cedar Rapids, IA
		Baltimore	0-0	6	2	4.50				
42	Carey, Brooks	Rochester	10-9	195	107	3.37	L-L	6-1½	185	3/18/56 Key West, FL
—	Davis, George	Charlotte	14-10	187	119	3.47	R-R	6-4	207	12/26/61 Dallas, TX
46	Flanagan, Mike	Baltimore	9-6	116	72	4.19	L-L	6-0	195	12/16/51 Manchester, NH
21	Ford, Dave	Baltimore	1-2	40	12	6.53	R-R	6-4	200	12/29/55 Cleveland, OH
		Rochester	1-0	6	1	1.50				
30	Martinez, Dennis	Baltimore	14-5	179	88	3.32	R-R	6-1	183	5/14/55 Nicaragua
23	Martinez, Tippy	Baltimore	3-3	59	50	2.90	L-L	5-10	175	5/31/50 LaJunta, CO
16	McGregor, Scott	Baltimore	13-5	160	82	3.26	B-L	6-1	190	1/18/54 Inglewood, CA
22	Palmer, Jim	Baltimore	7-8	127	35	3.76	R-R	6-3	194	10/15/45 New York, NY
—	Ramirez, Allan	Miami	0-1	13	10	2.77	R-R	5-10	190	5/1/57 Victoria, TX
		Rochester	1-3	41	26	4.17				
		Hagerstown	2-1	22	19	7.36				
57	Schneider, Jeff	Rochester	5-1	69	61	2.35	B-L	6-3	195	12/6/52 Bremerton, WA
		Baltimore	0-0	24	17	4.88				
53	Stewart, Sammy	Baltimore	4-8	112	57	2.33	R-R	6-3	208	10/28/54 Asheville, NC
49	Stoddard, Tim	Baltimore	4-2	37	32	3.89	R-R	6-7	250	1/24/53 East Chicago, IN
32	Stone, Steve	Baltimore	4-7	63	30	4.57	R-R	5-10	178	7/14/47 Cleveland, OH
—	Swaggerty, Bill	Charlotte	8-5	49	26	2.02	R-R	6-2	190	12/5/56 Sanford, FL
51	Welchel, Don	Charlotte	13-7	161	90	2.91	R-R	6-4	205	2/3/57 Atlanta, TX
		Rochester	1-1	12	7	2.25				

CATCHERS

No.	Name	1981 Club	H	HR	RBI	Pct.	B-T	Ht.	Wt.	Born
24	Dempsey, Rick	Baltimore	54	6	15	.215	R-R	6-0	184	9/13/49 Fayetteville, TN
41	Graham, Dan	Baltimore	25	2	11	.176	L-R	6-1	212	7/19/54 Ray, AZ
34	Morales, Jose	Baltimore	21	2	14	.244	R-R	6-0	195	12/30/44 Virgin Islands
59	Royster, Willie	Charlotte	149	31	88	.265	R-R	5-11	180	4/11/54 Clarksville, VA
		Baltimore	0	0	0	.000				
—	Stefero, John	Hagerstown	97	25	82	.287	L-R	5-8	185	9/22/59 Sumter, SC

INFIELDERS

No.	Name	1981 Club	H	HR	RBI	Pct.	B-T	Ht.	Wt.	Born
2	Bonner, Bob	Rochester	69	3	35	.229	R-R	6-0	185	8/12/56 Uvalde, TX
		Baltimore	8	0	2	.296				
10	Crowley, Terry	Baltimore	33	4	25	.246	L-L	6-0	182	2/16/47 Staten Island, NY
25	Dauer, Rich	Baltimore	97	4	38	.263	R-R	6-0	180	7/27/52 San Bernardino, CA
11	DeCinces, Doug	Baltimore	91	13	55	.263	R-R	6-2	194	8/29/50 Burbank, CA
6	Krenchicki, Wayne	Baltimore	12	0	6	.214	L-R	6-1	175	9/17/54 Trenton, NJ
		Rochester	10	0	4	.179				
33	Murray, Eddie	Baltimore	111	22	78	.294	B-R	6-2	200	2/24/56 Los Angeles, CA
8	Ripken, Cal Jr.	Rochester	126	23	75	.288	R-R	6-4	200	8/24/60 Havre de Grace, MD
		Baltimore	5	0	0	.128				
—	Rodriguez, Vic	Charlotte	168	9	65	.304	R-R	5-11	175	7/14/61 New York, NY
12	Sakata, Lenn	Baltimore	34	5	15	.227	R-R	5-9	160	6/8/53 Honolulu, HI

OUTFIELDERS

No.	Name	1981 Club	H	HR	RBI	Pct.	B-T	Ht.	Wt.	Born
27	Ayala, Benny	Baltimore	24	3	13	.279	R-R	6-1	195	2/7/51 Puerto Rico
1	Bumbry, Al	Baltimore	107	1	27	.273	L-R	5-8	175	4/21/47 Fredericksburg, VA
15	Corey, Mark	Rochester	16	1	5	.239	R-R	6-2	205	11/3/55 Tucumcari, NM
		Springfield	56	6	23	.304				
		Baltimore	0	0	0	.000				
28	Dwyer, Jim	Baltimore	30	3	10	.224	L-L	5-10	175	1/3/50 Evergreen, IL
—	Hazewood, Drungo	Rochester	6	1	6	.094	R-R	6-3	210	9/1/59 Mobile, AL
		Charlotte	96	19	55	.282				
38	Lowenstein, John	Baltimore	47	6	20	.249	L-R	6-1	180	1/27/47 Wolf Point, MT
35	Roenicke, Gary	Baltimore	59	3	20	.269	R-R	6-3	200	12/5/54 Covina, CA
37	Shelby, John	Charlotte	59	2	21	.235	B-R	6-1	175	2/23/58 Lexington, KY
		Rochester	86	3	32	.264				
		Baltimore	0	0	0	.000				
29	Singleton, Ken	Baltimore	101	13	49	.278	B-R	6-4	211	6/10/47 New York, NY
39	Williams, Dallas	Rochester	148	9	48	.283	L-L	5-11	165	2/28/58 Brooklyn, NY
		Baltimore	1	0	0	.500				

ORIOLE PROFILES

SCOTT McGREGOR 28 6-1 190   Bats S Throws L

Followed up his spectacular '80 season with another fine performance . . . Not an overpowering pitcher by any means, but maintains excellent control and mixes his pitches well . . . Was originally one of the "crown jewels" of the Yankee farm system whom Charlie Finley demanded as compensation for Yanks' trying to sign his manager, Dick Williams . . . Yanks wound up dealing him to Orioles and regretting it ever since . . . Born Jan. 18, 1954, in El Segundo, Calif. . . . Plagued by sore arm in 1978-79, but has shown no such symptoms since . . . Pitched Orioles' pennant clincher over Angels in 1979 . . . Was high school teammate of George Brett.

Year	Club	G	IP	W	L	Pct.	SO	BB	H	ERA
1976	Baltimore	3	15	0	1	.000	6	5	17	3.60
1977	Baltimore	29	114	3	5	.375	55	30	119	4.42
1978	Baltimore	35	233	15	13	.536	94	47	217	3.32
1979	Baltimore	27	175	13	6	.684	81	23	165	3.34
1980	Baltimore	36	252	20	8	.714	119	58	254	3.32
1981	Baltimore	24	160	13	5	.722	82	40	167	3.26
	Totals	154	949	64	38	.627	437	203	939	3.45

AL BUMBRY 34 5-8 175   Bats L Throws R

Still the key to the Orioles' attack with his team-leading base-stealing speed, but may be starting to decline . . . Led club in runs as well in '81 . . . Born April 21, 1947, in Fredericksburg, Va. . . . Career was almost ended by a broken ankle in 1978, but made fine recovery in '79 . . . Led Orioles in hitting in '80 and stole a career-high 44 bases . . . Among the best defensive center fielders in the game because of ability to cover a lot of ground . . . Was Rookie of the Year in 1973 when he hit .337 . . . Extremely active in community affairs for Orioles.

Year	Club	Pos.	G	AB	R	H	2B	3B	HR	RBI	SB	Avg.
1972	Baltimore	OF	9	11	5	4	0	1	0	0	1	.364
1973	Baltimore	OF	110	356	73	120	15	11	7	34	23	.337
1974	Baltimore	OF	94	270	35	63	10	3	1	19	12	.233
1975	Baltimore	OF-3B	114	349	47	94	19	4	2	32	16	.269
1976	Baltimore	OF	133	450	71	113	15	7	9	36	42	.251
1977	Baltimore	OF	133	518	74	164	31	3	4	41	19	.317
1978	Baltimore	OF	33	114	21	27	5	2	2	6	5	.237
1979	Baltimore	OF	148	569	80	162	29	1	7	49	37	.285
1980	Baltimore	OF	160	645	118	205	29	9	9	53	44	.318
1981	Baltimore	OF	101	392	61	107	18	2	1	27	22	.273
	Totals		1035	3674	585	1059	171	43	42	297	221	.288

JIM PALMER 36 6-3 194   Bats R Throws R

Suffered through first losing season since 1974, when his career was imperiled by arm trouble . . . But he had a great postseason behind the ABC microphones as media critics hailed the job he did as a World Series analyst . . . Not ready to devote full energies to TV and jockey shorts quite yet, though . . . Perfectionist on the mound . . . Three-time Cy Young Award winner ('73, '75, '76), making him one of four pitchers to have done it (Sandy Koufax, Steve Carlton and Tom Seaver are the others) . . . Born Oct. 15, 1945, in New York City, but grew up in California . . . He and manager Earl Weaver butt heads yearly . . . "See these gray hairs," said Weaver. "Every one of them has No. 22 on it." . . . Good bet to rebound from 7-8, 3.76 disappointment of last season, but winning 20 games in a season for the ninth time might be beyond his reach . . . Sorry, ladies, he's been married since 1964.

Year	Club	G	IP	W	L	Pct.	SO	BB	H	ERA
1965	Baltimore	27	92	5	4	.556	75	56	75	3.72
1966	Baltimore	30	208	15	10	.600	147	91	176	3.46
1967	Baltimore	9	49	3	1	.750	23	20	34	2.94
1969	Baltimore	26	181	16	4	.800	123	64	131	2.34
1970	Baltimore	39	305	20	10	.667	199	100	263	2.71
1971	Baltimore	37	282	20	9	.690	184	106	231	2.68
1972	Baltimore	36	274	21	10	.677	184	70	219	2.07
1973	Baltimore	38	296	22	9	.710	158	113	225	2.40
1974	Baltimore	26	179	7	12	.368	84	69	176	3.27
1975	Baltimore	39	323	23	11	.676	193	80	253	2.09
1976	Baltimore	40	315	22	13	.629	159	84	255	2.51
1977	Baltimore	39	319	20	11	.645	193	99	263	2.91
1978	Baltimore	38	296	21	12	.636	138	97	246	2.46
1979	Baltimore	23	156	10	6	.625	67	43	144	3.29
1980	Baltimore	34	224	16	10	.615	109	74	238	3.98
1981	Baltimore	22	127	7	8	.467	35	46	117	3.76
	Totals	503	3626	248	140	.639	2071	1212	3046	2.77

GARY ROENICKE 27 6-3 200   Bats R Throws R

Emerged as one of Orioles' most consistent hitters over second half of season last year after disappointing 1980 campaign . . . Is looked upon by many as the best defensive left fielder in Orioles' history . . . Born Dec. 5, 1954, in Covina, Calif. . . . Came to Orioles as the "throw-in" of the big deal that netted relievers Don Stanhouse and Joe Kerrigan from Expos in 1977 . . . Slump of 1980 was due a lot to injuries, and he underwent surgery on his right elbow after the season . . . His younger brother, Ron, plays outfield in the Dodger chain . . . Was a three-sport athlete in high school before signing with Expos as their No. 1 choice in the June 1973 draft.

Year	Club	Pos.	G	AB	R	H	2B	3B	HR	RBI	SB	Avg.
1976	Montreal	OF	29	90	9	20	3	1	2	5	0	.222
1978	Baltimore	OF	27	58	5	15	3	0	3	15	0	.259
1979	Baltimore	OF	133	376	60	98	16	1	25	64	1	.261
1980	Baltimore	OF	118	297	40	71	13	0	10	28	2	.239
1981	Baltimore	OF	85	219	31	59	16	0	3	20	1	.269
	Totals		392	1040	145	263	51	2	43	132	4	.253

KEN SINGLETON 34 6-4 211   Bats S Throws R

After carrying Orioles over first half of season, went into a puzzling second-half power slump in which he had no extra-base hits and four RBI all of August . . . Had back-to-back four-hit games in late April to lift his average temporarily to .512 . . . Born June 10, 1947, in Mount Vernon, N.Y. . . . Signed a five-year contract extension prior to last season which will make him an Oriole through '84 . . . Had elbow surgery in 1977 but has shown no after-effects . . . Was Mets' first pick in the January '67 draft, but they traded him to Montreal without ever really giving him a chance . . . Orioles got him in one of most one-sided deals in baseball history, sending Expos Dave McNally and Rich Coggins, both of whom were out of baseball in two years.

Year	Club	Pos.	G	AB	R	H	2B	3B	HR	RBI	SB	Avg.
1970	New York (NL)	OF	69	198	22	52	8	0	5	26	1	.263
1971	New York (NL)	OF	115	298	34	73	5	0	13	46	0	.245
1972	Montreal	OF	142	507	78	139	23	2	14	50	5	.274
1973	Montreal	OF	162	560	100	169	26	2	23	103	2	.302
1974	Montreal	OF	148	511	68	141	20	2	9	74	5	.276
1975	Baltimore	OF	155	586	88	176	37	4	15	55	3	.300
1976	Baltimore	OF	154	544	62	151	25	2	13	70	2	.278
1977	Baltimore	OF	152	536	90	176	24	0	24	99	0	.328
1978	Baltimore	OF	149	502	67	147	21	2	20	81	0	.293
1979	Baltimore	OF	159	570	93	168	29	1	35	111	3	.295
1980	Baltimore	OF	156	583	85	177	28	3	24	104	0	.304
1981	Baltimore	OF	103	363	48	101	16	1	13	49	0	.278
	Totals		1664	5758	834	1670	262	19	208	868	21	.290

RICH DAUER 29 6-0 180   Bats R Throws R

Had a dropoff in average after career-high .284 in 1980 . . . Biggest game came Aug. 24 when he drove in five runs vs. Seattle with his second and third HRs . . . Born July 27, 1952, in San Bernardino, Calif. . . . Struck out just 19 times in 618 plate appearances in '80, best in AL . . . Signed to a five-year contract through the 1985 season . . . Was Orioles' No. 1 selection in the secondary phase of June 1974 draft and two years later led International League in batting with .336 mark at Rochester . . . Set major-league record for most consecutive errorless games at second base (86) in 1978 . . . Not blessed with an abundance of speed, but has knack for getting in front of ball wherever it's hit.

Year	Club	Pos.	G	AB	R	H	2B	3B	HR	RBI	SB	Avg.
1976	Baltimore......	2B	11	39	0	4	0	0	0	3	0	.103
1977	Baltimore......	2B-3B	96	304	38	74	15	1	5	25	1	.243
1978	Baltimore......	2B-3B	133	459	57	121	23	0	6	46	0	.264
1979	Baltimore......	2B-3B	142	479	63	123	20	0	9	61	0	.257
1980	Baltimore......	2B-3B	152	557	71	158	32	0	2	63	3	.284
1981	Baltimore......	2B-3B	96	369	41	97	27	0	4	38	0	.263
	Totals..........		630	2207	270	577	117	1	26	236	4	.261

EDDIE MURRAY 26 6-2 200   Bats L-R Throws R

Got off to a slow start in first half of season, but carried Orioles the second half . . . "There have been so many non-contributors to this club the second half," O's GM Hank Peters said in early September. "There's a limit to what one man, Eddie Murray, can do." . . . Born Feb. 24, 1956, in Los Angeles . . . Signed a five-year, $1-million-per-season contract in December 1980 . . . Had a streak of 444 consecutive games played snapped in July 1980 . . . Same season became only the fifth switch-hitter in history to surpass 30 homers . . . Led Orioles in homers and RBI in 1980 and '81 . . . Knocked in six runs vs. Chisox on Aug. 16 with grand slam and two-run HR . . . One of 12 children. Brother Rich played with the Giants in recent years.

Year	Club	Pos.	G	AB	R	H	2B	3B	HR	RBI	SB	Avg.
1977	Baltimore......	OF-1B	160	611	81	173	29	2	27	88	0	.283
1978	Baltimore......	1B-3B	161	610	85	174	32	3	27	95	6	.285
1979	Baltimore......	1B	159	606	90	179	30	2	25	99	10	.295
1980	Baltimore......	1B	158	621	100	186	36	2	32	116	7	.300
1981	Baltimore......	1B	99	378	57	111	21	2	22	78	2	.294
	Totals..........		737	2826	413	823	148	11	133	476	25	.291

RICK DEMPSEY 32 6-0 184   Bats R Throws R

Fell off drastically with his bat, but his defensive skills still made him one of the Orioles' most indispensible people . . . Is one of the chief antagonists on the ballclub for Earl Weaver and yet the manager says of him: "He loves pain." . . . Originally signed by Twins and came to Orioles in big trade with Yankees that also brought Tippy Martinez and Scott McGregor to Baltimore . . . Born Sept. 13, 1949, in Fayetteville, Tenn. . . . Signed to a five-year contract through 1983 . . . Has been known to entertain fans during rain delays with famous "Baseball Soliloquy in Pantomime."

Year	Club	Pos.	G	AB	R	H	2B	3B	HR	RBI	SB	Avg.
1969	Minnesota	C	5	6	1	3	1	0	0	0	0	.500
1970	Minnesota	C	5	7	1	0	0	0	0	0	0	.000
1971	Minnesota	C	6	13	2	4	1	0	0	0	0	.308
1972	Minnesota	C	25	40	0	8	1	0	0	0	0	.200
1973	New York (AL) ..	C	6	11	0	2	0	0	0	0	0	.182
1974	New York (AL) ..	C-OF	43	109	12	26	3	0	2	12	1	.239
1975	New York (AL) ..	C-OF-3B	71	145	18	38	8	0	1	11	0	.262
1976	N.Y.-Balt. (AL) ..	C-OF	80	216	12	42	2	0	0	12	1	.194
1977	Baltimore.......	C	91	270	27	61	7	4	3	34	2	.226
1978	Baltimore.......	C	136	441	41	114	25	0	6	32	7	.259
1979	Baltimore.......	C	124	368	48	88	23	0	6	41	0	.239
1980	Baltimore.......	C-OF-1B	119	362	51	95	26	3	9	40	3	.262
1981	Baltimore.......	C	92	251	24	54	10	1	6	15	0	.215
	Totals..........		803	2239	237	535	107	8	33	197	14	.239

MIKE FLANAGAN 30 6-0 195   Bats L Throws L

Was again the iron man of Orioles' staff, continuing a streak of consecutive starts to 157 before developing tendinitis in September. "Just an oil change and a 30,000-inning checkup," he joked . . . Was hampered by a sore shoulder in '80, but pitched in spite of it, prompting O's pitching coach Ray Miller to say, "He's paying the price for being the defending Cy Young Award winner" . . . Born Dec. 16, 1951, in Manchester, N.H. . . . Led majors with 23 wins in '79 . . . Signed with Orioles out of U. of Massachusetts in 1973 after previously rejecting offer from Astros in '71 . . . His father, Edward, was a pitcher in the Red Sox' system in the late '40s.

Year	Club	G	IP	W	L	Pct.	SO	BB	H	ERA
1975	Baltimore................	2	10	0	1	.000	7	6	9	2.70
1976	Baltimore................	20	85	3	5	.375	56	33	83	4.13
1977	Baltimore................	36	235	15	10	.600	149	70	235	3.64
1978	Baltimore................	40	281	19	15	.559	167	87	271	4.04
1979	Baltimore................	39	266	23	9	.781	190	70	245	3.08
1980	Baltimore................	37	251	16	13	.552	128	71	278	4.12
1981	Baltimore................	20	116	9	6	.600	72	37	108	4.19
	Totals...................	194	1244	85	59	.590	769	374	1229	3.78

DOUG DeCINCES 31 6-2 194   Bats R Throws R

Put together one of his best seasons in the majors in the face of inevitable challenge from young Cal Ripken Jr. . . . Finished behind only Eddie Murray in RBI and gamers on the Orioles . . . Had spectacular streak of power in late May when he hit seven homers in a six-day spurt . . . Hit a pair of grand slams in August . . . Showed little hindrance from back problem that threatened his career after '80 season . . . Born Aug. 29, 1950, in Burbank, Calif. . . . Name is pronounced "Duh-SIN-say" . . . Very active in Special Olympics and brings underprivileged or handicapped kids to ballpark as his guests . . . Was one of the principal spokesmen for players during the strike of '81.

Year	Club	Pos.	G	AB	R	H	2B	3B	HR	RBI	SB	Avg.
1973	Baltimore.......	3B-2B-SS	10	18	2	2	0	0	0	3	0	.111
1974	Baltimore.......	3B	1	1	0	0	0	0	0	0	0	.000
1975	Baltimore.......	3B-SS-2B-1B	61	167	20	42	6	3	4	23	0	.251
1976	Baltimore.......	3B-2B-SS-1B	129	440	36	103	17	2	11	42	8	.234
1977	Baltimore.......	3B-2B-1B	150	522	63	135	28	3	19	69	8	.259
1978	Baltimore.......	3B-2B	142	511	72	146	37	1	28	80	7	.286
1979	Baltimore.......	3B	120	422	67	97	27	1	16	61	5	.230
1980	Baltimore.......	3B-1B	145	489	64	122	23	2	16	64	11	.249
1981	Baltimore.......	3B	100	346	49	91	23	2	13	55	0	.263
	Totals..........		858	2916	373	738	161	14	107	397	39	.253

DENNIS MARTINEZ 26 6-1 183   Bats R Throws R

The latest in a long line of Orioles' Cy Young-calibre pitchers . . . Took over as the club "ace" for at least the 1981 season when he paced club in wins, strikeouts and complete games . . . Hampered throughout 1980 season by two shoulder injuries, but regained form playing winter ball under O's pitching coach, Ray Miller. Was 6-1 with 1.39 ERA for Caguas of Puerto Rican League . . . "He has the best stuff on the ballclub," says Orioles' super scout Jim Russo . . . Problem in past has always been judgment of pitches and situations . . . Born May 14, 1955, in Granada, Nicaragua . . . Signed originally by Orioles as an undrafted free agent in 1973.

Year	Club	G	IP	W	L	Pct.	SO	BB	H	ERA
1976	Baltimore................	4	28	1	2	.333	18	8	23	2.57
1977	Baltimore................	42	167	14	7	.667	107	64	157	4.10
1978	Baltimore................	40	276	16	11	.593	142	93	257	3.52
1979	Baltimore................	40	292	15	16	.484	132	78	279	3.67
1980	Baltimore................	25	100	6	4	.600	42	44	103	3.96
1981	Baltimore................	25	179	14	5	.737	88	62	173	3.32
	Totals..................	176	1042	66	45	.595	529	349	992	3.64

TOP PROSPECTS

CAL RIPKEN JR. 21 6-4 200   Bats R Throws R

The most highly-touted prospect in Orioles' system since Eddie Murray . . . Batted .288 with 25 homers and 75 RBI for Roches-

ter before being called up at season's end . . . Son of Orioles'
third-base coach . . . Born Aug. 24, 1960, in Havre de Grace,
Md. . . . Can play shortstop as well as third base . . . Signed by
Orioles as second-round choice in June '78 draft . . . Has the
kind of power that Earl Weaver just loves.

BOB BONNER 26 6-0 185   **Bats R Throws R**

Orioles felt they could not wait for him to play out season at
Rochester and recalled him for second half of season . . . Saw
limited duty, but is expected to get a good shot at shortstop job
this spring . . . Hit just .229 at Rochester, his lowest average in
organized ball, but is rated major-league on his defense . . .
Contracted viral hepatitis last February, which may have had
something to do with low average . . . Born Aug. 12, 1956, in
Uvalde, Tex.

MANAGER EARL WEAVER: Has stayed with the same club
(13½ years) longer than any other manager in
baseball . . . Has reputation as the game's
smartest skipper as evidenced by six division
championships, four AL pennants and five
seasons of 100 or more victories . . . Plans to
manage Orioles through 1982 and then retire
. . . Born Aug. 14, 1930, in St. Louis . . . Is
20th in career wins . . . Champion umpire-
baiter, usually gets suspended once a year . . . Hobby is garden-
ing, which he had plenty of time to cultivate in '81 . . . Never
played in the majors.

GREATEST CATCHER

As far as the Orioles are concerned, their first catcher was their
best. When he was lured over from the White Sox to undertake
the rebuilding of the moribund 1954 Orioles, Paul Richards, an
ex-catcher, made it no secret what his first priority was. He immediately engineered the biggest trade in baseball history with
the Yankees—it involved 21 players—and, in it, he obtained not

one, but two top catching prospects. One was Hal Smith, who would later find fame with the Pirates as a World Series hero, and the other was Gus Triandos, who last year became the fifth member voted into the Baltimore Orioles' Hall of Fame.

Triandos spent eight productive seasons with the Orioles from 1955-62. He was the Orioles' first genuine long-ball threat, having hit 142 homers for the Birds. Thirty of them were hit in 1958, giving him a share (with Yogi Berra) of the AL record for most homers in a season by a catcher. Triandos was also a fine receiver and it was his honor to have caught the only no-hitter in the history of the Orioles' franchise—Hoyt Wilhelm's gem against the Yankees, Sept. 20, 1958. Oddly, it was in that game that Triandos hit his record-tying 30th homer, which accounted for the game's only run!

Triandos drove in 70 or more runs four different times for the Orioles and hit 20 or more homers in three seasons. He retired after 1965 with a lifetime .244 average, 167 homers and 608 RBI.

ALL-TIME ORIOLE SEASON RECORDS

BATTING: Ken Singleton, .328, 1977
HRs: Frank Robinson, 49, 1966
RBIs: Jim Gentile, 141, 1961
STEALS: Luis Aparicio, 57, 1964
WINS: Steve Stone, 25, 1980
STRIKEOUTS: Dave McNally, 202, 1968

BOSTON RED SOX

TEAM DIRECTORY: Pres.: Mrs. Thomas A. Yawkey; Exec. VP-GM: Haywood Sullivan; Exec. VP-Admin.: Edward (Buddy) LeRoux; Dir. Pub. Rel.: George Sullivan; Dir. Publ.: Dick Bresciani; Trav. Sec.: Jack Rogers; Mgr.: Ralph Houk. Home: Fenway Park (33,536). Field distances: 315, l.f. line; 390, c.f.; 420, r.c. corner; 380, r.c.; 302, r.f. line. Spring training: Winter Haven, Fla.

SCOUTING REPORT

HITTING: When have you ever known a Fenway Park ballclub that didn't hit? This one will be no different—especially now that Jerry Remy has been returned to the fold for a five-year, $2.8 million deal. Remy was the club's second-leading hitter at .307 and, over at third base, Carney Lansford led the league at .336. All told, the Bosox hit a league-leading .275. Dwight Evans is coming off his finest season ever in which he led the Red Sox in homers (22) and RBI (71) and led the league in total bases (215) and walks (85). All this and we still haven't gotten to Jim Rice, who had an off season and still hit .284 with 17 homers and 62 RBI.

Once again, Ralph Houk will have that pleasant problem of who NOT to play among Dave Stapleton (.285), Carl Yastrzemski (10 game-winning hits) or Tony Perez (the Bosox' hottest hitter in September). If the Red Sox have any offensive weakness it

Carney Lansford led AL with .336 average.

is at shortstop, where Glenn Hoffman (.231) was unable to fill Rick Burleson's shoes either with his bat or his glove.

PITCHING: Just as in past years, the Red Sox have their pitching problems. For as many runs as their hitters figure to get them, their pitching figures to give up just as many. Unless, that is, some surprises are in the offing. Last year, lefty Bob Ojeda showed promise of becoming the ace of the staff. This year, the Bosox are hoping that either Bruce Hurst or Chuck Rainey can nail down a place in the starting rotation and win consistently.

The Red Sox let Bill Campbell go in the free-agent sweepstakes last winter because they feel young Luis Aponte (7-5, 1.94 at Pawtucket) is ready to take his place in the bullpen alongside Mark Clear and Tom Burgmeier. What the Red Sox REALLY need in '82, though, is a return to form from Dennis Eckersley, the onetime ace of the staff who has mysteriously become a very mediocre pitcher.

FIELDING: Red Sox moved to shore up their defensive leak at third base last year when Lansford replaced scatter-armed Butch Hobson. They also did not lose all that much defense in center, where Rick Miller came back to replace Fred Lynn. And behind the plate, Rich Gedman was a pleasant surprise as Carlton Fisk's replacement.

Unfortunately, the Bosox haven't been able to replace Burleson at short and any place they put Stapleton they are sacrificing defense for offense. Remy is above average at second, but the first-base platoon of Perez, Yaz and Stapleton isn't going to dazzle anyone with footwork. Ditto Rice in left. Over in right, though, Evans won a Gold Glove and possesses the most lethal throwing arm of any right fielder in baseball. It's a sort of hodgepodge defense that, in the long run, should get the job done.

OUTLOOK: Call 'em the respectable Red Sox. Respectable is what they'll be. Any better than that will depend on people like Eckersley, Rice, Hoffman, Clear and Gedman. All of them need to have big seasons for the Red Sox to be a pennant contender. Gedman has to do it over a full season; Hoffman has to take charge at short; Rice and Eckersley have to regain their form of two-three seasons ago, and Clear has to pitch a full season like he did over the first half of last year.

Those are a lot of big ifs. Just the same, the cast of hitters, led by Lansford and Evans, plus the prodding and cajoling from Houk, the consummate "players manager," figures to keep the Red Sox a safe distance from the Blue Jays and still better than most of the Western Division clubs.

BOSTON RED SOX 1982 ROSTER

MANAGER Ralph Houk
Coaches—John Pesky, Eddie Yost, Walt Hriniak, Tommy Harper, Lee Stange

PITCHERS

No.	Name	1981 Club	W-L	IP	SO	ERA	B-T	Ht.	Wt.	Born
45	Aponte, Luis	Pawtucket	7-5	87	67	1.94	R-R	6-0	180	7/14/54 Venezuela
		Boston	1-0	16	11	0.57				
16	Burgmeier, Tom	Boston	4-5	60	35	2.85	L-L	5-11	180	8/2/43 St. Paul, MN.
—	Burtt, Dennis	Bristol	10-8	170	108	2.81	R-R	6-0	180	11/29/57 San Diego, CA
25	Clear, Mark	Boston	8-3	77	82	4.09	R-R	6-4	200	5/27/56 Los Angeles, CA
28	Crawford, Steve	Boston	0-5	58	29	4.97	R-R	6-5	225	4/29/58 Pryor, OK
—	Denman, Brian	Bristol	15-3	179	109	2.56	R-R	6-4	205	2/12/56 Minneapolis, MN
		Pawtucket	0-0	2	3	4.50				
43	Eckersley, Dennis	Boston	9-8	154	79	4.27	R-R	6-2	190	10/3/54 Oakland, CA
47	Hurst, Bruce	Pawtucket	12-7	157	99	2.87	L-L	6-3	185	3/24/58 St. George, UT
		Boston	2-0	23	11	4.30				
44	King, Jerry	Bristol	12-10	175	169	2.73	R-R	6-3	185	8/23/58 San Diego, CA
19	Ojeda, Bob	Pawtucket	12-9	173	119	2.13	L-L	6-1	185	12/17/57 Los Angeles, CA
		Boston	6-2	66	28	3.14				
—	Parks, Danny	Pawtucket	9-12	181	105	3.38	R-R	6-0	185	9/19/54 Huntsville, AL
42	Rainey, Chuck	Pawtucket	1-1	20	16	3.15	R-R	5-11	195	7/14/54 San Diego, CA
		Boston	0-1	40	20	2.70				
—	Schoppee, Dave	Bristol	8-3	92	70	1.76	R-R	6-3	190	4/24/57 Bangor, ME
48	Smithson, Mike	Pawtucket	2-4	91	82	3.86	L-R	6-8	200	1/1/55 Centerville, TN
46	Stanley, Bob	Boston	10-8	99	28	3.82	R-R	6-4	205	11/10/54 Portland, ME
21	Torrez, Mike	Boston	10-3	127	54	3.69	R-R	6-5	210	8/28/46 Topeka, KS
30	Tudor, John	Boston	4-3	79	44	4.56	L-L	6-0	185	2/2/54 Schenectady, NY

CATCHERS

No.	Name	1981 Club	H	HR	RBI	Pct.	B-T	Ht.	Wt.	Born
39	Allenson, Gary	Boston	31	5	25	.223	R-R	5-11	185	2/4/55 Culver City, CA
10	Gedman, Rich	Pawtucket	24	2	11	.296	L-R	6-0	210	9/26/59 Worcester, MA
		Boston	59	5	26	.288				
29	Lickert, John	Bristol	100	5	57	.270	R-R	5-11	175	4/4/60 Pittsburgh, PA
		Boston	0	0	0	.000				
—	Sullivan, Mark	Winston-Salem	109	14	64	.268	R-R	6-4	198	7/25/58 Quincy, MA

INFIELDERS

No.	Name	1981 Club	H	HR	RBI	Pct.	B-T	Ht.	Wt.	Born
—	Barrett, Marty	Pawtucket	91	1	28	.265	R-R	5-10	170	6/23/58 Arcadia, CA
—	Boggs, Wade	Pawtucket	167	5	60	.335	L-R	6-2	185	6/15/58 Omaha, NE
—	Guttierez, Jackie	Winston-Salem	126	1	45	.249	R-R	5-11	145	6/27/60 Colombia
18	Hoffman, Glenn	Boston	56	1	20	.231	R-R	6-2	175	7/7/58 Orange, CA
—	Jurak, Ed	Bristol	101	1	25	.340	R-R	6-2	165	10/24/57 Los Angeles, CA
		Pawtucket	27	1	9	.300				
4	Lansford, Carney	Boston	134	4	52	.336	R-R	6-2	195	2/5/57 San Jose, CA
24	Perez, Tony	Boston	77	9	39	.252	R-R	6-2	205	5/14/42 Cuba
2	Remy, Jerry	Boston	110	0	31	.307	L-R	5-9	165	11/8/52 Fall River, MA
11	Stapleton, Dave	Boston	101	10	42	.285	R-R	6-1	175	1/6/54 Fairhope, AL
12	Valdez, Julio	Pawtucket	99	6	27	.258	B-R	6-2	160	7/3/56 Dominican Republic
		Boston	5	0	3	.217				
1	Walker, Chico	Pawtucket	148	17	68	.277	B-R	5-9	170	11/25/57 Jackson, MS
		Boston	6	0	2	.353				
8	Yastrzemski, Carl	Boston	83	7	53	.246	L-R	5-11	185	8/22/39 Southampton, NY

OUTFIELDERS

No.	Name	1981 Club	H	HR	RBI	Pct.	B-T	Ht.	Wt.	Born
24	Evans, Dwight	Boston	122	22	71	.296	R-R	6-3	205	11/3/51 Santa Monica, CA
37	Hancock, Gary	Boston	7	0	3	.156	L-L	6-0	175	1/23/54 Tampa, FL
3	Miller, Rick	Boston	92	2	33	.291	L-L	6-0	185	4/19/48 Grand Rapids, MI
51	Nichols, Reid	Boston	9	0	3	.188	R-R	5-11	165	8/5/58 Ocala, FL
14	Rice, Jim	Boston	128	17	62	.284	R-R	6-2	205	3/8/53 Anderson, SC

RED SOX PROFILES

JIM RICE 29 6-2 205   Bats R Throws R

Got off to a slow start, but came on strong the second half of season when Red Sox most needed him . . . No question his productivity has suffered since the departure of Fred Lynn . . . Missed 31 games in 1980 with a fractured l 'c wrist and also got off to his worst start that year, hitting just .220 as of May 7 . . . Frequently at odds with the press because of his refusal to grant them interviews . . . Born March 8, 1953, in Anderson, S.C. . . . Had one of the greatest individual seasons any hitter could want in 1978 when he won MVP honors in AL by hitting .315 with 46 homers and 139 RBI . . . Is an avid golfer in off-season . . . Was Red Sox' No. 1 pick in 1971 June draft.

Year	Club	Pos.	G	AB	R	H	2B	3B	HR	RBI	SB	Avg.
1974	Boston	OF	24	67	6	18	2	1	1	13	0	.269
1975	Boston	OF	144	564	92	174	29	4	22	102	10	.309
1976	Boston	OF	153	581	75	164	25	8	25	85	8	.282
1977	Boston	OF	160	644	104	206	29	15	39	114	5	.320
1978	Boston	OF	163	677	121	213	25	15	46	139	7	.315
1979	Boston	OF	158	619	117	201	39	6	39	130	9	.325
1980	Boston	OF	124	504	81	148	22	6	24	86	8	.294
1981	Boston	OF	108	451	51	128	18	1	17	62	2	.284
	Totals		1034	4107	647	1252	189	56	213	731	49	.305

DAVE STAPLETON 28 6-1 175   Bats R Throws R

One of the Red Sox' most productive bats, but still a man without a position . . . Will likely wind up at first base once Carl Yastrzemski retires, but for now must be content shifting around the infield . . . Came up with a splash in 1980, batting .321 over the last 106 games after being called up May 30 . . . Had a 19-game hitting streak at Pawtucket earlier that year . . . Born Jan. 16, 1954, at Fairhope, Ala. . . . Was Red Sox' No. 10 pick in June 1975 draft . . . Played college ball at South Alabama U. under ex-major-league second baseman Eddie Stanky . . . An excellent all-around athlete in college where he lettered in football and basketball as well . . . Was co-MVP in International League in 1979.

Year	Club	Pos.	G	AB	R	H	2B	3B	HR	RBI	SB	Avg.
1980	Boston	INF-OF	106	449	61	144	33	5	7	45	3	.321
1981	Boston	INF-OF	93	355	45	101	17	1	10	42	0	.285
	Totals		199	804	106	245	50	6	17	87	3	.305

BOB OJEDA 24 6-1 185   Bats L Throws L

Looks to be one of the very few left-handers to have a future in Fenway Park . . . Called up by Red Sox after the strike and quickly became their most effective starting pitcher down the stretch run, once no-hitting the Yankees for eight innings . . . Doesn't overpower hitters, but has good command of his pitches and showed a lot of poise . . . Born Dec. 17, 1957, in Los Angeles . . . Name is pronounced "Oh-HEE-dah" . . . Was the top pitcher in the International League at time of his recall with 12-9 record, 2.13 ERA and 113 strikeouts in 173 innings at Pawtucket . . . Signed as an undrafted free agent out of College of the Sequoias in May 1978 by Red Sox . . . Played OF and 1B in college as well.

Year	Club	G	IP	W	L	Pct.	SO	BB	H	ERA
1980	Boston	7	26	1	1	.500	12	14	39	6.92
1981	Boston	10	66	6	2	.750	28	25	50	3.14
	Totals	17	92	7	3	.700	40	39	89	4.21

DWIGHT EVANS 30 6-3 205   Bats R Throws R

Finally burst into the stardom that has been predicted for him since 1973 when he first came up . . . With the aid of some tips from batting coach Walt Hrniak, he put together his best season as a major leaguer and was easily the Red Sox' Most Valuable Player, leading club in homers and RBI . . . Joined Babe Ruth, Ted Williams, Jimmie Foxx, and Mickey Mantle as the only players to ever lead AL in walks (85) and total bases (215) the same season . . . Hit .317 over his last 80 games of 1980 season which was sign of things to come . . . Was at .341 when the strike came . . . Has possibly the strongest throwing arm of any right fielder in the game . . . Missed most of 1977 season with knee injury . . . Born Nov. 3, 1951, in Santa Monica, Calif. . . . Owns three Gold Glove awards . . . Was Red Sox' No. 5 selection in June 1969 draft.

Year	Club	Pos.	G	AB	R	H	2B	3B	HR	RBI	SB	Avg.
1972	Boston	OF	18	57	2	15	3	1	1	6	0	.263
1973	Boston	OF	119	282	46	63	13	1	10	32	5	.223
1974	Boston	OF	133	463	60	130	19	8	10	70	4	.281
1975	Boston	OF	128	412	61	113	24	6	13	56	3	.274
1976	Boston	OF	146	501	61	121	34	5	17	62	6	.242
1977	Boston	OF	73	230	39	66	9	2	14	36	4	.287
1978	Boston	OF	147	497	75	123	24	2	24	63	8	.247
1979	Boston	OF	152	489	69	134	24	1	21	58	6	.274
1980	Boston	OF	148	463	72	123	37	5	18	60	3	.266
1981	Boston	OF	108	412	84	122	19	4	22	71	3	.296
	Totals		1172	3806	569	1010	206	35	150	514	42	.265

MARK CLEAR 25 6-4 200 Bats R Throws R

Another plus for Red Sox in deal with Angels in which they also got Carney Lansford and Rick Miller for Rick Burleson and Butch Hobson . . . Clear was their No. 1 relief man, leading club in saves . . . Born May 27, 1956, in Los Angeles . . . Made 110 appearances in two years with Angels, striking out 203 in 215 innings . . . Signed originally by Phillies in June 1974, but was released the following season at age 18 after going 0-7 with Pulaski of the rookie Appalachian League . . . Uncle is Bob Clear, Angels' bullpen coach in recent years . . . Made the jump from AA ball to Angels in 1979 and was the top rookie pitcher in AL with 11 wins and 14 saves . . . "He does tease you with his walks," says Ralph Houk, "but if he walks two, he'll strike out three."

Year	Club	G	IP	W	L	Pct.	SO	BB	H	ERA
1979	California	52	109	11	5	.688	98	68	87	3.63
1980	California	58	106	11	11	.500	105	65	82	3.31
1981	Boston	34	77	8	3	.727	82	51	69	4.09
	Totals	144	292	30	19	.612	285	184	238	3.64

DENNIS ECKERSLEY 27 6-2 190 Bats R Throws R

Is Red Sox' No. 1 pitcher, but has disappointed them with his inability to become a big winner the last couple of years . . . Has been bothered by a back problem which may be the root of his problems . . . Led club in complete games again last year . . . Came to Red Sox in spring trade of 1978 that sent catcher Bo Diaz to the Indians . . . Only Red Sox pitcher to win 20 games (in 1978) over the past five years . . . Was AL Rookie Pitcher of the Year in 1975 when he won 13 for Indians . . . In 1976 he became only eighth pitcher in history to strike out 200 in a season before reaching age of 22 . . . Born Oct. 3, 1954, in Oakland, Calif.

Year	Club	G	IP	W	L	Pct.	SO	BB	H	ERA
1975	Cleveland	34	187	13	7	.650	152	90	147	2.60
1976	Cleveland	36	199	13	12	.520	200	78	155	3.44
1977	Cleveland	33	247	14	13	.519	191	54	214	3.53
1978	Boston	35	268	20	8	.714	162	71	258	2.99
1979	Boston	33	247	17	10	.630	150	59	234	2.99
1980	Boston	30	198	12	14	.462	121	44	188	4.27
1981	Boston	23	154	9	8	.529	79	35	160	4.27
	Totals	224	1500	98	72	.576	1055	431	1356	3.39

RICH GEDMAN 22 6-0 210   Bats L Throws R

What a pleasant surprise he turned out to be for Red Sox! Was assured of getting a good look when Carlton Fisk became a free agent and signed with White Sox in spring, but did not take over as Bosox' No. 1 catcher until Gary Allenson went on disabled list in May . . . Between them, Allenson and Gedman had more RBI than Fisk . . . Started season at Pawtucket and was recalled June 16, presumably never to return . . . A local product born in Worcester, Mass. on Sept. 26, 1959, he signed with Red Sox as an undrafted free agent in August 1977 . . . Came up briefly to Red Sox at tail-end of 1980 but was hampered by a wrist injury . . . Has strong throwing arm and Red Sox like his defense behind plate.

Year	Club	Pos.	G	AB	R	H	2B	3B	HR	RBI	SB	Avg.
1980	Boston	C	9	24	2	5	0	0	0	1	0	.208
1981	Boston	C	62	205	22	59	15	0	5	26	0	.288
	Totals		71	229	24	64	15	0	5	27	0	.279

RICK MILLER 33 6-0 185   Bats L Throws L

Was big plus of the winter deals with California, doing an exceptional job as Fred Lynn's replacement in center field . . . Batted eighth or ninth in the lineup all year, but as Ralph Houk said: "He had so many big hits that started a rally or kept one going. That's the biggest contribution he's made to this team." . . . Defensively still has few superiors in AL and rarely gets bad jump on the ball . . . Was hampered by an eye infection in 1980 with Angels but still hit .274 despite 20-150 vision . . . Born April 19, 1948, in Grand Rapids, Mich. . . . Began career with Boston but skipped to Angels as a free agent in 1977 . . . Married to Carlton Fisk's sister . . . Lacks great speed.

Year	Club	Pos.	G	AB	R	H	2B	3B	HR	RBI	SB	Avg.
1971	Boston	OF	15	33	9	11	5	0	1	7	0	.333
1972	Boston	OF	89	98	13	21	4	1	3	15	0	.214
1973	Boston	OF	143	441	65	115	17	7	6	43	12	.261
1974	Boston	OF	114	280	41	73	8	1	5	22	13	.261
1975	Boston	OF	77	108	21	21	2	1	0	15	3	.194
1976	Boston	OF	105	269	40	76	15	3	0	27	11	.283
1977	Boston	OF	86	189	34	48	9	3	0	24	11	.254
1978	California	OF	132	475	66	125	25	4	1	37	3	.263
1979	California	OF	120	427	60	125	15	5	2	28	5	.293
1980	California	OF	129	412	52	113	14	3	2	38	7	.274
1981	Boston	OF	97	316	38	92	17	2	2	33	3	.291
	Totals		1107	3048	439	820	131	30	22	289	68	.269

CARL YASTRZEMSKI 42 5-11 185   Bats L Throws R

When asked why he wanted to come back for a 22nd season, Yaz replied: "Because I got only half of one this year and I feel like I got cheated." . . . Say this for Yastrzemski: he's never cheated the fans. Became only the fourth player in history to appear in over 3,000 games last season and, on Aug. 29, moved past Stan Musial into third place on the all-time games-played list . . . First AL player to achieve 400 homers and 3,000 hits in a career . . . Born Aug. 22, 1939, in Southampton, N.Y. . . . Red Sox still regard him as one of their most valued players in that he swings productive bat from first base, left field or DH . . . "Nobody on the club works harder," says Ralph Houk. "That's why Yaz is an inspiration to our young kids."

Year	Club	Pos.	G	AB	R	H	2B	3B	HR	RBI	SB	Avg.
1961	Boston	OF	148	583	71	155	31	6	11	80	6	.266
1962	Boston	OF	160	646	99	191	43	6	19	94	7	.296
1963	Boston	OF	151	570	91	183	40	3	14	68	8	.321
1964	Boston	OF-3B	151	567	77	164	29	9	15	67	6	.289
1965	Boston	OF	133	494	78	154	45	3	20	72	7	.312
1966	Boston	OF	160	594	81	165	39	2	16	80	8	.278
1967	Boston	OF	161	579	112	189	31	4	44	121	10	.326
1968	Boston	OF-1B	157	539	90	162	32	2	23	74	13	.301
1969	Boston	OF-1B	162	603	96	154	28	2	40	111	15	.255
1970	Boston	1B-OF	161	566	125	186	29	0	40	102	23	.329
1971	Boston	OF	148	508	75	129	21	2	15	70	8	.254
1972	Boston	OF-1B	125	455	70	120	18	2	12	68	5	.264
1973	Boston	1B-3B-OF	152	540	82	160	25	4	19	95	9	.296
1974	Boston	1B-OF	148	515	93	155	25	2	15	79	12	.301
1975	Boston	1B-OF	149	543	91	146	30	1	14	60	8	.269
1976	Boston	1B-OF	155	546	71	146	23	2	21	102	5	.267
1977	Boston	1B-OF	150	558	99	165	27	3	28	102	11	.296
1978	Boston	OF-1B	144	523	70	145	21	2	17	81	4	.277
1979	Boston	OF-1B	147	518	69	140	28	1	21	87	3	.270
1980	Boston	1B-OF	105	364	49	100	21	1	15	50	0	.275
1981	Boston	1B-OF	91	338	36	83	14	1	7	53	0	.246
	Totals		3058	11,149	1725	3192	600	58	426	1716	168	.286

CARNEY LANSFORD 24 6-2 195   Bats R Throws R

Became the Red Sox' top hitter and first right-handed hitter to win the AL batting title since 1970 . . . Wound up as key player in deal that sent Rick Burleson and Butch Hobson to Angels and considering accomplishments of other two players, Mark Clear and Rick Miller, Red Sox got a steal . . . Ironically, Angels refused to deal Lansford to Twins for Rod Carew in winter of '78 . . . Missed a month of 1978 season with torn ligaments in his left thumb . . . Born March 24, 1958, at St. George, Utah . . . Makes a cash donation to the boys baseball team in his home town of Santa Clara, Calif., every year . . . Was Angels' No. 3 pick in June '75 draft.

Year	Club	Pos.	G	AB	R	H	2B	3B	HR	RBI	SB	Avg.
1978	California	3B	121	453	63	133	23	2	8	52	20	.294
1979	California	3B	157	654	114	188	30	5	19	79	20	.287
1980	California	3B	151	602	87	157	27	3	15	80	14	.261
1981	Boston	3B	102	399	61	134	23	3	4	52	15	.336
	Totals		531	2108	325	612	103	13	46	263	69	.290

JERRY REMY 29 5-9 165   Bats L Throws R

Bounced back from two years of knee problems with .307 average in 88 games last year, the final season of his Red Sox contract . . . Only the second Boston player to steal 30 or more bases in the last 46 years (30 in 1978) . . . Called "Scoot" by his teammates . . . Drafted 453rd by Washington Senators in 1970 . . . Angels picked him up the following year, sent him to Boston for pitcher Don Aase in 1978 . . . Made all-star team in first season with Red Sox, but injuries limited him to total of 143 games in '79 and '80 . . . Born Nov. 8, 1952, in Fall River, Mass. . . . Averaged 35 stolen bases a season in his first four major-league years, but knee problems have taken their toll the last three years.

Year	Club	Pos.	G	AB	R	H	2B	3B	HR	RBI	SB	Avg.
1975	California	2B	147	569	82	147	17	5	1	46	34	.258
1976	California	2B	143	502	64	132	14	3	0	28	35	.263
1977	California	2B-3B	154	575	74	145	19	10	4	44	41	.252
1978	Boston	2B-SS	148	583	87	162	24	6	2	44	30	.278
1979	Boston	2B	80	306	49	91	11	2	0	29	14	.297
1980	Boston	2B-OF	63	230	24	72	7	2	0	9	14	.313
1981	Boston	2B	88	358	55	110	9	1	0	31	9	.307
	Totals		823	3123	435	859	101	29	7	231	177	.275

TOP PROSPECTS

BRUCE HURST 24 6-3 185   Bats L Throws L

Red Sox are hoping this left-hander can duplicate the promise Bob Ojeda showed last year . . . Hurst was 12-7 with 2.97 ERA at Pawtucket before earning September promotion to Red Sox . . . Biggest problem in past has always been control . . . Was Red Sox' first pick in June 1976 draft . . . Born March 24, 1958, in St. George, Utah . . . Will be given every chance to make 1982 starting rotation.

JULIO VALDEZ 25 6-2 160   **Bats S Throws R**

Could well be the Red Sox' shortstop of the future, although there is some concern as to whether he'll ever be a big-league hitter . . . Best minor-league average was .265 at Bristol in 1978 . . . Called up in August from Pawtucket, where he was hitting .260, and was used by Red Sox in spot situations . . . Born June 3, 1956, in San Cristobal, Dominican Republic.

MANAGER RALPH HOUK: Baseball's eternal optimist, Houk guided the Red Sox to heights no one felt possible last season . . . Granted, the split season didn't hurt, but Houk managed to get the utmost out of Red Sox' kids—Bob Ojeda, Rich Gedman, etc.—asked to fill in the big voids left by departures of Fred Lynn, Rick Burleson and Carlton Fisk . . . Called the ultimate "players' manager" . . . "If you can't play for Houk, you can't play for anyone" is a common compliment from his players . . . Ended two-year retirement to take over Red Sox last year . . . Won three pennants with Yankees (1961-63) before moving on to Tigers in the mid-'70s . . . Born Aug. 9, 1919, in Lawrence, Kan. . . . Known as "The Major", he was a battle-field hero in World War II.

GREATEST CATCHER

It is perhaps very painful to Red Sox fans knowing that the best catcher their team ever had is still playing baseball in the American League. That Carlton Fisk chose to change his "sox" from Red to White in the spring of '80 is still a source of great consternation in Beantown. After all, the man gave the Red Sox a decade of dedicated and tireless service and if there was anyone the Red Sox brass should have bent for in a contract dispute, it was Fisk.

Besides being one of baseball's real money players, Fisk

ranked eighth on the Red Sox' all-time home run list with 162; had a .284 lifetime batting average for 1,078 games; set club records for homers (26) and RBI (102) by a catcher in a season ('77); and is one of only six catchers to score 100 runs and drive in 100 runs in the same year ('77).

And who in Boston will ever forget Fisk's dramatic 12th-inning, game-winning homer that sent the 1975 World Series to a seventh game? The Red Sox signed Fisk as their No. 1 draft choice in June 1967, having scouted him at nearby U. of New Hampshire. Four years later, he was their No. 1 catcher and the American League's Rookie of the Year. Seven times he was named to the all-star team, five of them as a starter. Twice he overcame serious injury (knee in '74 and broken arm in '75) to do the job no one else could do behind the plate.

And then, in the spring of '81, he was gone. The Red Sox fans did get to see their greatest catcher in Fenway Park last year. On his first trip to Boston with the White Sox, he hit a three-run, eighth-inning homer on opening day to beat the Red Sox.

ALL-TIME RED SOX SEASON RECORDS

BATTING: Ted Williams, .406, 1941
HRs: Jimmy Foxx, 50, 1938
RBIs: Jimmy Foxx, 175, 1938
STEALS: Tommy Harper, 54, 1973
WINS: Joe Wood, 34, 1912
STRIKEOUTS: Joe Wood, 258, 1912

CLEVELAND INDIANS

TEAM DIRECTORY: Chairman of the Board: Steve O'Neill; Pres.: Gabe Paul; VP-GM: Phil Seghi; Treas.: Dudley S. Blossom; VP-Dir. Play. Dev.-Scouting: Bob Quinn; Dir. Pub. Rel.: Bob DiBiasio; Trav. Sec.: Mike Seghi; Mgr.: Dave Garcia. Home: Cleveland Municipal Stadium (74,208). Field distances: 320, l.f. line; 377, l.c.; 400, c.f.; 385, r.c.; 320, r.f. line. Spring training: Tucson, Ariz.

SCOUTING REPORT

HITTING: In their off-season scrambling to maintain a competitive position with the rest of the AL East, the Indians concentrated on getting more pitching. Fortunately, they were able to do that without weakening themselves too much on offense. True, they gave up their No. 2 hitter, Bo Diaz, but both Ron Hassey and Chris Bando are considered capable replacements with the bat. The Tribe's principal batting weakness last year was a woeful shortage of power. Their 39 homers ranked last in the AL. Two youngsters, one old, one new, could remedy that.

Joe Charboneau, who went from Rookie of the Year to Come-

Rick Manning is one of baseball's best outfielders.

down of the Year, will be given a new chance to regain his spot as DH. Von Hayes, a third baseman-outfielder, knocked in 73 runs in the International League while batting .316. He will be tried in right field. The trade of Duane Kuiper to the Giants leaves second base in the hands of either power hitter Alan Bannister or rookies Kevin Rhomberg and Jack Perconte. A full recovery from Andre Thornton (especially if Charboneau flops again) would also be a boon to the Tribe's power shortage.

PITCHING: The Indians held firm in the competitive AL East largely because of their pitching—a fact that was not lost on Gabe Paul. Faced with the prospect of losing two-fifths of his starting rotation (John Denny and Rick Waits) to free agency, Paul went out shopping over to the National League and picked up Rick Sutcliffe from the Dodgers, Ed Whitson from the Giants and Lary Sorensen from the Cardinals. All three look to be promising acquisitions very much capable of filling the void left by the Waits and Denny defections.

More importantly, Paul still has the heart of his starting rotation, Len (Perfect Game) Barker and Bert Blyleven, to team up with the three newcomers. There is, however, a problem in the bullpen, where not one Tribe reliever had more than three saves last year. Dan Spillner is the best of an uncertain lot.

FIELDING: What the Indians may lack in offense, they have been able to make up in defense. Mike Hargrove led the club in hitting and remained one of the best defensive first basemen in the league. Rick Manning in center, Toby Harrah at third and Tom Veryzer at short are above-average defensively. Second base figures to lose a little if either Bannister or the weak-armed Perconte wins the job. Overall, the Indians ranked 11th in defense last year, but they really weren't that bad.

OUTLOOK: Once again, the Tribe will ride on the arms of their starting pitching. That is Paul's gamble. The addition of three new starters plus the infusion of promising youngsters Hayes, Perconte, Bando and Rhomberg is what Indian fans must hope will be enough to keep their club in the thick of it this year.

If Sutcliffe can regain his 1979 Rookie-of-the-Year (17-10) form; if Sorensen can reverse a trend that has had him drop from 18 to 15 to 12 to seven wins over the past four years; if Hayes hits the way all the scouts predict he will, then perhaps the Indians can even contend. Otherwise, they'll probably be a .500 ballclub on the strength of either Barker and Blyleven pitching every other day.

CLEVELAND INDIANS 1982 ROSTER

MANAGER Dave Garcia
Coaches—Johnny Goryl, Tom McCraw, Mel Queen, Dennis
       Sommers

PITCHERS

No.	Name	1981 Club	W-L	IP	SO	ERA	B-T	Ht.	Wt.	Born
51	Anderson, Bud	Chattanooga	2-3	54	35	3.19	R-R	6-3	210	5/27/56 Rockville Center, NY
		Charleston	9-3	94	48	2.40				
39	Barker, Len	Cleveland	8-7	154	127	3.92	R-R	6-4	225	7/7/55 Ft. Knox, KY
28	Blyleven, Bert	Cleveland	11-7	159	107	2.89	R-R	6-3	205	4/6/51 Holland
63	Bohnet, John	Chattanooga	13-7	168	94	3.38	B-L	6-0	180	1/18/61 Pasadena, CA
45	Brennan, Tom	Charleston	11-8	156	62	3.92	R-R	6-1	180	10/30/52 Chicago, IL
		Cleveland	2-2	48	15	3.19				
17	Garland, Wayne	Cleveland	3-7	56	15	5.79	R-R	6-0	190	10/26/50 Nashville, TN
59	Glaser, Gordy	Charleston	9-10	164	48	4.60	R-R	6-3	185	11/19/57 Baton Rouge, LA
44	Glynn, Ed	Charleston	4-6	71	69	3.53	R-L	6-2	180	6/3/53 Flushing, NY
		Cleveland	0-0	8	4	1.13				
41	Lewallyn, Dennis	Wichita	8-5	68	45	3.42	R-R	6-4	195	8/11/53 Pensacola, FL
		Cleveland	0-0	13	11	5.54				
35	Martinez, Silvio	St. Louis	2-5	97	34	3.99	R-R	5-11	160	8/31/55 Dominican Republic
58	Nuismer, Jack	Chattanooga	5-5	79	55	4.56	R-R	6-2	180	9/20/57 Nashville, TN
		Charleston	5-4	91	62	2.99				
—	Sorenson, Lary	St. Louis	7-7	140	52	3.28	R-R	6-2	200	10/4/55 Detroit, MI
37	Spillner, Dan	Cleveland	4-4	97	59	3.15	R-R	6-1	190	11/27/51 Casper, WY
—	Sutcliffe, Rick	Los Angeles	2-2	47	16	4.02	L-R	6-6	225	6/21/56 Independence, MO
32	Whitson, Ed	San Francisco	6-9	123	65	4.02	R-R	6-3	200	5/19/55 Jefferson City, TN

CATCHERS

No.	Name	1981 Club	H	HR	RBI	Pct.	B-T	Ht.	Wt.	Born
23	Bando, Chris	Charleston	98	11	45	.306	B-R	6-0	195	2/4/56 Cleveland, OH
		Cleveland	10	0	6	.213				
9	Hassey, Ron	Cleveland	44	1	25	.232	L-R	6-2	195	2/27/53 Tucson, AZ
13	Pruitt, Ron	Charleston	31	3	14	.292	R-R	6-0	191	10/21/51 Flint, MI
		Cleveland	0	0	0	.000				

INFIELDERS

No.	Name	1981 Club	H	HR	RBI	Pct.	B-T	Ht.	Wt.	Born
7	Bannister, Alan	Cleveland	61	1	17	.263	R-R	5-11	175	9/3/51 Buena Park, CA
53	Cecchetti, George	Chattanooga	112	23	80	.255	L-L	5-11	185	7/31/60 Stockton, CA
10	Dybzinski, Jerry	Cleveland	17	0	6	.298	R-R	6-2	180	7/7/55 Cleveland, OH
22	Fischlin, Mike	Charleston	110	5	43	.238	R-R	6-1	165	9/13/55 Sacramento, CA
		Cleveland	10	0	5	.233				
21	Hargrove, Mike	Cleveland	102	2	49	.317	L-L	6-0	195	10/26/49 Perryton, TX
11	Harrah, Toby	Cleveland	105	5	44	.291	R-R	6-0	180	10/26/48 Sissonville, WVA
8	Hayes, Von	Charleston	120	10	73	.314	L-R	6-5	190	8/31/58 Stockton, CA
		Rich	28	1	17	.257				
57	LoGrande, Angelo	Charleston	135	13	66	.287	R-R	6-3	215	12/4/57 San Pedro, CA
—	Murray, Rich	Phoenix	117	12	69	.326	R-R	6-4	205	7/6/57 Los Angeles, CA
30	Pagel, Karl	Charleston	89	20	67	.272	L-L	6-2	185	3/29/55 Madison, WI
		Cleveland	4	1	4	.267				
—	Perconte, Jack	Albuquerque	155	1	58	.346	L-R	5-10	160	8/31/54 Joliet, IL
		Los Angeles	2	0	1	.222				
54	Rhomberg, Kevin	Chattanooga	187	1	56	.367	R-R	5-11	175	11/22/55 Dubuque, IA
12	Rosello, Dave	Cleveland	20	1	7	.238	R-R	5-11	160	6/26/50 Puerto Rico
29	Thornton, Andre	Cleveland	54	6	30	.239	R-R	6-2	205	8/13/49 Tuskegee, AL
15	Veryzer, Tom	Cleveland	54	0	14	.244	R-R	6-1	185	2/11/53 Port Jefferson, NY

OUTFIELDERS

No.	Name	1981 Club	H	HR	RBI	Pct.	B-T	Ht.	Wt.	Born
52	Castillo, Carmello	Chattanooga	125	11	57	.285	R-R	6-1	185	6/8/58 Dominican Republic
34	Charboneau, Joe	Cleveland	29	4	18	.210	R-R	6-2	200	6/17/55 Belevedere, IL
		Charleston	10	0	3	.217				
56	Craig, Rod	Charleston	20	2	6	.253	B-R	6-1	195	1/12/58 Los Angeles, CA
27	Dilone, Miguel	Cleveland	78	0	19	.290	B-R	5-11	160	11/1/54 Dominican Republic
25	Kelly, Pat	Cleveland	16	1	16	.213	L-L	6-1	195	7/30/44 Philadelphia, PA
20	Manning, Rick	Cleveland	88	4	33	.244	L-R	6-1	180	9/2/54 Niagara Falls, NY
55	Saavedra, Ed	Waterloo	151	19	85	.333	R-R	5-10	160	11/15/59 Panama

INDIAN PROFILES

LEN BARKER 26 6-4 225   Bats R Throws R

Pitched only the 12th perfect game in major-league history last May 15 when he beat Toronto, 3-0, striking out 11 in the process . . . Was the AL strikeout leader for the second straight season . . . Tied for Indians' club lead in complete games and shutouts . . . Born July 7, 1955, in Ft. Knox, Ky. . . . Indians acquired him from Texas in 1978 with Bobby Bonds in exchange for reliever Jim Kern . . . In '77 and '78 with Rangers, he was primarily a reliever . . . Switched to starting on a fulltime basis in '80, when he won more games than any Tribe pitcher since Gaylord Perry in '74 . . . Fastball has been clocked at 96 mph . . . Was football star as well as playing baseball in high school.

Year	Club	G	IP	W	L	Pct.	SO	BB	H	ERA
1976	Texas	2	15	1	0	1.000	7	6	7	2.40
1977	Texas	15	47	4	1	.800	51	24	36	2.68
1978	Texas	29	52	1	5	.167	33	29	63	4.85
1979	Cleveland	29	137	6	6	.500	93	70	146	4.93
1980	Cleveland	36	246	19	12	.613	187	92	237	4.17
1981	Cleveland	22	154	8	7	.533	127	46	150	3.92
	Totals	133	651	39	31	.557	498	267	639	4.18

MIGUEL DILONE 27 5-11 160   Bats S Throws R

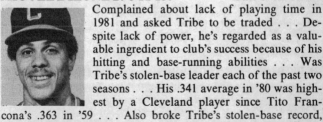

Complained about lack of playing time in 1981 and asked Tribe to be traded . . . Despite lack of power, he's regarded as a valuable ingredient to club's success because of his hitting and base-running abilities . . . Was Tribe's stolen-base leader each of the past two seasons . . . His .341 average in '80 was highest by a Cleveland player since Tito Francona's .363 in '59 . . . Also broke Tribe's stolen-base record, which had stood since 1917 . . . Born Nov. 1, 1954, in Santiago, Dominican Republic . . . Was purchased by Indians in May 1980 from Cubs' minor-league affiliate at Wichita . . . Is another product of the Harry Walker "hit-the-ball-to-all-fields" system that was taught in the Pirates' chain . . . Set an NL record in '77 for most stolen bases in a season without being caught (12).

Year	Club	Pos.	G	AB	R	H	2B	3B	HR	RBI	SB	Avg.
1974	Pittsburgh	OF	12	2	3	0	0	0	0	0	2	.000
1975	Pittsburgh	OF	18	6	8	0	0	0	0	0	2	.000
1976	Pittsburgh	OF	16	17	7	4	0	0	0	0	5	.235
1977	Pittsburgh	OF	29	44	5	6	0	0	0	0	12	.136
1978	Oakland	OF-3B	135	258	34	59	8	0	1	14	50	.229
1979	Oakland	OF	30	91	15	17	1	2	1	6	6	.187
1979	Chicago (NL)	OF	43	36	14	11	0	0	0	1	15	.306
1980	Cleveland	OF	132	528	82	180	30	9	0	40	61	.341
1981	Cleveland	OF	72	269	33	78	5	5	0	19	29	.290
	Totals		487	1251	201	355	44	16	2	80	182	.284

MIKE HARGROVE 32 6-0 195   Bats L Throws L

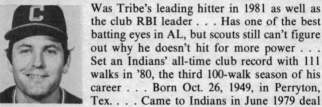

Was Tribe's leading hitter in 1981 as well as the club RBI leader . . . Has one of the best batting eyes in AL, but scouts still can't figure out why he doesn't hit for more power . . . Set an Indians' all-time club record with 111 walks in '80, the third 100-walk season of his career . . . Born Oct. 26, 1949, in Perryton, Tex. . . . Came to Indians in June 1979 deal with Padres for outfielder Paul Dade . . . Had a 23-game hitting streak in '80 . . . Began his career in Texas organization and was named AL Rookie of the Year in '74, when he hit .323 . . . Never played high-school baseball and only took it up in college (Northwestern Oklahoma State) at the insistence of his father . . . Texas made him 572nd overall pick in June 1972 draft.

Year	Club	Pos.	G	AB	R	H	2B	3B	HR	RBI	SB	Avg.
1974	Texas	1B-OF	131	415	57	134	18	6	4	66	0	.323
1975	Texas	1B-OF	145	519	82	157	22	2	11	62	4	.303
1976	Texas	1B	151	541	80	155	30	1	7	58	2	.287
1977	Texas	1B	153	525	98	160	28	4	18	69	2	.305
1978	Texas	1B	146	494	63	124	24	1	7	40	2	.251
1979	San Diego	1B	52	125	15	24	5	0	0	8	0	.192
1979	Cleveland	OF-1B	100	338	60	110	21	4	10	56	2	.325
1980	Cleveland	1B	160	589	86	179	22	2	11	85	4	.304
1981	Cleveland	1B	94	322	43	102	21	0	2	49	5	.317
	Totals		1132	3868	584	1145	191	20	70	493	21	.296

BERT BLYLEVEN 30 6-3 205   Bats R Throws R

Finished tied for third in AL in strikeouts . . . His nine complete games tied for club lead . . . Born April 6, 1951, in Zeist, Holland . . . Originally brought to the majors by the Twins, who traded him to Texas in 1976 when they could no longer afford to pay him top dollar . . . Had his lowest ERA in four seasons last year, but missed the last two weeks of the season with a sore elbow . . . Led the AL in shutouts in '73 with nine . . . Indians traded pitchers Victor Cruz and Bob Owchinko plus catcher Gary Alexander to get him from Pirates in December 1980 . . . Has won 13 games by 1-0 score, a feat bettered by only three pitchers in baseball history . . . Strikeout-walk ratio is among the very best in all of baseball.

Year	Club	G	IP	W	L	Pct.	SO	BB	H	ERA
1970	Minnesota	27	164	10	9	.526	135	47	143	3.18
1971	Minnesota	38	278	16	15	.516	224	59	267	2.82
1972	Minnesota	39	287	17	17	.500	228	69	247	2.73
1973	Minnesota	40	325	20	17	.541	258	67	296	2.52
1974	Minnesota	37	281	17	17	.500	249	77	244	2.66
1975	Minnesota	35	276	15	10	.600	233	84	219	3.00
1976	Minn.-Tex.	36	298	13	16	.448	219	81	283	2.87
1977	Texas	30	235	14	12	.538	182	69	181	2.72
1978	Pittsburgh	34	244	14	10	.583	182	66	217	3.02
1979	Pittsburgh	37	237	12	5	.706	172	92	238	3.61
1980	Pittsburgh	34	217	8	13	.381	168	59	219	3.82
1981	Cleveland	20	159	11	7	.611	107	40	145	2.89
	Totals	407	3001	167	148	.530	2357	810	2699	2.95

TOBY HARRAH 33 6-0 180   Bats R Throws R

Popped off at his teammates late last season out of frustration at never having played on a pennant-winning ballclub . . . Played in every Tribe game for the second straight year . . . Born Oct. 26, 1948, in Sissonville, West Va. . . . Was traded to Indians in December 1978 for Buddy Bell in straight-up swap of third basemen . . . Has led Indians in runs scored each of the past three seasons . . . His nine game-winning RBI were tops on the Cleveland club last year . . . Originally signed by Phillies organization and is one of the last remaining major leaguers to have played in Washington . . . Among the better defensive third basemen in AL . . . Attended Ohio Northern U. on a football scholarship . . . Has been an AL all-star three times, all as a shortstop . . . Made the switch to third in '77.

Year	Club	Pos.	G	AB	R	H	2B	3B	HR	RBI	SB	Avg.
1969	Washington	SS	8	1	4	0	0	0	0	0	0	.000
1971	Washington	SS-3B	127	383	45	88	11	3	2	22	10	.230
1972	Texas	SS	116	374	47	97	14	3	1	31	16	.259
1973	Texas	3B-SS	118	461	64	120	16	1	10	50	10	.260
1974	Texas	SS-3B	161	573	79	149	23	2	21	74	15	.260
1975	Texas	SS-3B-2B	151	522	81	153	24	1	20	93	23	.293
1976	Texas	SS-3B	155	584	64	152	21	1	15	67	8	.260
1977	Texas	3B-SS	159	539	90	142	25	5	27	87	27	.263
1978	Texas	SS-3B	139	450	56	103	17	3	12	59	31	.229
1979	Cleveland	3B-SS	149	527	99	147	25	1	20	77	20	.279
1980	Cleveland	3B-SS	160	561	100	150	22	4	11	72	17	.267
1981	Cleveland	3B-SS	103	361	64	105	12	4	5	44	12	.291
	Totals		1546	5336	793	1406	210	28	144	676	189	.263

RICK MANNING 27 6-1 180   Bats L Throws R

Still among the most gifted defensive outfielders in baseball . . . Is also one of the game's best base runners . . . Tribe officials wish he would hit more and explored trade offers for him last winter . . . Was Indians' No. 1 selection in the 1972 amateur draft . . . Played football, baseball and basketball in high school . . . Born Sept. 2, 1954, in Niagara Falls, N.Y. . . . Was originally a shortstop and switched to center field while in the minors . . . Is in third year of a five-year, $1.4-million contract . . . Shelved by a back injury most of the '77 season . . . Was second on club in stolen bases in '81 and third in runs . . . Has a base-stealing success ratio of nearly 80 percent.

Year	Club	Pos.	G	AB	R	H	2B	3B	HR	RBI	SB	Avg.
1975	Cleveland......	OF	120	480	69	137	16	5	3	35	19	.285
1976	Cleveland......	OF	138	552	73	161	24	7	6	43	16	.292
1977	Cleveland......	OF	68	252	33	57	7	3	5	18	9	.226
1978	Cleveland......	OF	148	566	65	149	27	3	3	50	12	.263
1979	Cleveland......	OF	144	560	67	145	12	2	3	51	30	.259
1980	Cleveland......	OF	140	471	55	110	17	4	3	52	12	.234
1981	Cleveland......	OF	103	360	47	88	15	3	4	33	25	.244
	Totals..........		861	3241	409	847	118	27	27	282	123	.261

Len Barker pitched a perfect game against Toronto in 1981.

RON HASSEY 29 6-2 195   Bats L Throws R

Trade of Bo Diaz assures him of regaining his No. 1 catching job with Tribe . . . Injured his left knee April 15 in home-plate collision with Rangers' Bump Wills and was out of action three weeks . . . Also bothered by bruised right elbow . . . Born Feb. 27, 1953, at Tucson, Ariz. . . . Was Indians' No. 18 selection in June 1976 amateur draft after achieving All-America honors at U. of Arizona . . . Paced Arizona to '76 NCAA championship . . . Led all major-league catchers in hitting in '80 and committed just four errors behind the plate . . . Was also Indians' top clutch hitter in '80 when he hit .379 with men in scoring position . . . Father played in the Yankee organization.

Year	Club	Pos.	G	AB	R	H	2B	3B	HR	RBI	SB	Avg.
1978	Cleveland.......	C	25	74	5	15	0	0	2	9	2	.203
1979	Cleveland.......	C-1B	75	223	20	64	14	0	4	32	1	.287
1980	Cleveland.......	C-1B	130	390	43	124	18	4	8	65	0	.318
1981	Cleveland.......	C-1B	61	190	8	44	4	0	1	25	0	.232
	Totals..........		291	877	76	247	36	4	15	131	3	.282

ED WHITSON 26 6-3 200   Bats R Throws R

Tribe is counting on him to help fill starting pitching void left by defection of John Denny . . . Was a bit of a disappointment to Giants last year after achieving all-star honors in '80 . . . Became exclusively a starter in '80 . . . Born May 19, 1955, in Johnson City, Tenn. . . . Came up originally with the Pirates in '77 and was used mostly as a reliever with them . . . Indians surrendered their team captain, Duane Kuiper, to acquire him after last season . . . Was part of the package the Giants acquired from Pittsburgh in June 1979 for Bill Madlock . . . No-hit the Expos over 5⅔ innings Aug. 27, 1980, before leaving game with a leg injury . . . Was named to 1980 all-star team as a replacement for Vida Blue but did not pitch.

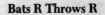

Year	Club	G	IP	W	L	Pct.	SO	BB	H	ERA
1977	Pittsburgh	5	16	1	0	1.000	10	9	11	3.38
1978	Pittsburgh	43	74	5	6	.455	64	37	66	3.28
1979	Pitt.-S.F.	37	158	7	11	.389	93	75	151	4.10
1980	San Francisco	34	212	11	13	.458	90	56	222	3.10
1981	San Francisco	22	123	6	9	.400	65	47	130	4.02
	Totals..................	141	583	30	39	.435	322	224	580	3.60

TOP PROSPECTS

CHRIS BANDO 26 6-0 195   **Bats S Throws R**
Had the misfortune of being a catcher in the most catching-rich
organization in AL . . . Finished sixth in the International
League batting race last year with .306 average for Charleston
. . . Had 11 homers and 45 RBI as well . . . Brother of Sal
Bando . . . Born Feb. 4, 1956, in Cleveland . . . Was Indians'
No. 2 pick in June 1978 amateur draft after achieving All-Amer-
ica honors and leading Arizona State to the NCAA champion-
ship . . . Was the all-star catcher in Southern League in '80,
when he hit .349 at Chattanooga.

KEVIN RHOMBERG 26 5-11 175   **Bats R Throws R**
Had a banner year at Chattanooga last season after being de-
moted to AA ball to learn second base . . . Will battle Alan Bannister and Jack Perconte for Indians' 2B job . . . Named Southern League all-star in '81 when he led circuit in hitting (.366),
hits (187), triples (14) and stolen bases (74) . . . Born Nov. 22,
1955, in Dubuque, Iowa.

MANAGER DAVE GARCIA: Honest, hard-working and knowl-
edgeable baseball man who has the misfor-
tune of managing in the most competitive division in baseball . . . Is second-oldest skipper
in the AL . . . Took over Tribe reins from
Jeff Torborg in July 1979 . . . Previously
managed Angels and coached for Indians
(1975-76) and Padres (1970-73) . . . Was fired
as Angels manager in 1978 because he was too
quiet . . . Spent 20 years as a minor-league infielder but never
made it to the majors . . . Born Sept. 15, 1920, in East St. Louis
. . . Was a player-manager in minors until '58, when he finally
hung up his glove . . . Managed in minors a total of 14 seasons.

GREATEST CATCHER

He never hit much, but with his club, he really didn't have to.
Jim Hegan's main concern, in his 10 years as the Indians'

catcher, was to handle with care the finest pitching staff in baseball. He did that with excellence.

It is no coincidence that the only pennants won by the Indians in the last 62 years came in 1948 and 1954. Jim Hegan was the catcher on both those clubs.

In '48, Hegan handled a pitching staff that included 20-game winners Bob Lemon and Gene Bearden, plus Bob Feller (19-15), Steve Gromek (9-3) and a promising young southpaw named Sam Zoldak (9-6). Hegan hit .248 that year, but drove in a career-high 61 runs. Hegan continued as the Indians' mainstay behind the plate through the early '50s and the Korean War, and in 1954, he found himself playing in another World Series for Cleveland. This time he was entrusted with handling what many baseball people consider to be the greatest pitching staff of all time: Early Wynn (23-11), Lemon (23-7), Mike Garcia (19-8), Art Houtteman (15-7) and, of course, the great Feller (13-3).

Bob Lemon has often said, "The heart of those great Cleveland teams was my old roomie, Jim Hegan. He was the guy who guided us all through."

And he was the guy who, despite a lifetime .228 average, was the greatest catcher in Cleveland history.

ALL-TIME INDIAN SEASON RECORDS

BATTING: Joe Jackson, .408, 1911
HRs: Al Rosen, 43, 1953
RBIs: Hal Trosky, 162, 1936
STEALS: Miguel Dilone, 61, 1980
WINS: Jim Bagby, 31, 1920
STRIKEOUTS: Bob Feller, 348, 1946

DETROIT TIGERS

TEAM DIRECTORY: Owner-Chairman of the Board: John Fetzer; Pres.-GM: Jim Campbell; VP-Operations: William Haase; VP-Baseball: William Lajoie; VP-Finance: Alex Callam; Dir. Pub. Rel.: Dan Ewald; Trav. Sec.: Bill Brown; Mgr.: Sparky Anderson. Home: Tiger Stadium (54,226). Field distances: 340, l.f. line; 365, l.c.; 440, c.f.; 370, r.c.; 325, r.f. line. Spring training: Lakeland, Fla.

SCOUTING REPORT

HITTING: The Tigers, who possess plenty of speed on the base-paths, may be hard-pressed to take full advantage of the short right-field porch in Tiger Stadium this year. They will miss the bat of Steve Kemp, traded to the White Sox for Chet Lemon. However, if Kirk Gibson stays healthy and Lance Parrish rebounds from a sub-par year with the bat, the Tigers should hit their share of home runs. More importantly, they have the nucleus of a consistent attack with Lemon, Gibson, Lou Whitaker, Alan Trammell and Parrish.

What would make the Tigers a genuine threat to take it all in '82 would be a big power year from among Champ Summers, Rick Leach, John Wockenfuss or Richie Hebner, the principal reserves. The Tigers' biggest weakness appears to be at the corners of the infield where Tom Brookens (at third) and a platoon at first do not come close to matching up with the firepower of the Yanks and Brewers at those positions. The Tigers did not seem too concerned about that last winter, however, as evidenced by their efforts to trade a surplus of outfield reserves for another starting pitcher.

PITCHING: In Jack Morris and Dan Petry, the Tigers have two of the most promising young right-handers in the American League. Unfortunately, the talent falls off sharply in the rotation after them—especially if Milt Wilcox does not come all the way back from his off-season basketball injury. It would seem the Tigers are going to need a lift from some of their youngsters—Larry Rothschild (8-5 at Evansville), George Cappuzello or Howard Bailey. A bright spot is Kevin Saucier, who emerged as the stopper in the bullpen last year with 13 saves, four wins and a 1.65 ERA.

The Tigers also have some quality middle relief men in Aurelio Lopez, Dave Rozema (who threw two shutouts in spot starting assignments) and Dave Tobik. It is not an imposing staff, but

Powerful Kirk Gibson does it all, including bunting.

there is promise here and if Wilcox is okay so, too, could be the Tiger pitching.

FIELDING: Here is one of the Tigers' principal strongpoints. The DP combo of Trammell and Whitaker is about the best there is in the AL. Gibson will probably move to right, with Lemon taking over in center. Both are fleet afoot with good throwing arms. Lemon, though spectacular at times, was guilty of frequent mental mistakes with Chisox, which led to his departure. Parrish is one of the best young catchers in the game. Thus, the Tigers are strong defensively up the middle—where it counts most. In addition, newcomer Larry Herndon will be a defensive asset in left field.

OUTLOOK: The Tigers have been a team that is coming for three seasons now. Every year they keep getting a little better. Gibson's breakthrough last year may be the key. He has all the tools to be a genuine superstar, capable of carrying a team by himself. What you have to like about the Tigers is their strength up the middle: Parrish, Trammell, Whitaker and Gibson (or Lemon). They will also come at you with an abundance of speed and defense, two key ingredients for any pennant contender.

Three major questions must be answered however, before you make any bold predictions about the Tigers: The first-base job remained unsettled through the winter, the starting pitching after Morris and Petry was a genuine concern, and Saucier has to prove last year wasn't a one-shot fluke.

DETROIT TIGERS 1982 ROSTER

MANAGER Sparky Anderson
Coaches—Gates Brown, Billy Consolo, Roger Craig, Alex
       Grammas, Dick Tracewski

PITCHERS

No.	Name	1981 Club	W-L	IP	SO	ERA	B-T	Ht.	Wt.	Born
60	Bailey, Howard	Detroit	1-4	37	17	7.30	R-L	6-3	185	7/31/58 Grand Haven, MI
		Evansville	2-7	86	56	5.02				
41	Cappuzzello, George	Evansville	4-0	46	27	1.76	R-L	6-0	195	1/15/54 Youngstown, OH
		Detroit	1-1	34	19	3.44				
21	Kinney, Dennis	Evansville	6-4	71	45	2.03	L-L	6-1	195	2/26/52 Toledo, OH
		Detroit	0-0	4	3	9.00				
29	Lopez, Aurelio	Detroit	5-2	82	53	3.62	R-R	6-0	215	10/5/48 Mexico
47	Morris, Jack	Detroit	14-7	198	97	3.05	R-R	6-3	190	5/16/55 St. Paul, MN
22	Pashnick, Larry	Evansville	9-10	165	64	2.89	R-R	6-2	195	4/25/56 Lincoln Park, MI
46	Petry, Dan	Detroit	10-9	141	79	3.00	R-R	6-4	200	11/13/58 Palo Alto, CA
48	Robbins, Bruce	Birmingham	3-2	57	60	3.79	L-L	6-2	190	9/10/59 Dunkirk, NY
42	Rothschild, Larry	Evansville	8-5	77	81	3.27	L-R	6-2	180	3/12/54 Chicago, IL
		Detroit	0-0	6	1	1.50				
19	Rozema, Dave	Detroit	5-5	104	46	3.63	R-R	6-4	200	8/5/56 Grand Rapids, MI
49	Rucker, Dave	Detroit	0-0	4	2	6.75	L-L	6-1	190	9/1/58 San Bernardino, CA
		Evansville	7-4	67	36	3.76				
30	Ruiz, Augie	Birmingham	5-3	123	106	3.15	L-L	6-1	190	2/12/57 Honolulu, HI
31	Saucier, Kevin	Detroit	4-2	49	23	1.65	R-L	6-1	195	8/9/56 Pensacola, FL
45	Tobik, Dave	Detroit	2-2	60	32	2.70	R-R	6-1	190	3/2/53 Euclid, OH
28	Ujdur, Jerry	Evansville	7-10	163	88	4.09	R-R	6-1	195	3/5/57 Duluth, MN
		Detroit	0-0	14	5	6.43				
40	Underwood, Pat	Evansville	9-8	165	90	3.98	L-L	6-0	180	2/9/57 Kokomo, IN
44	Weaver, Roger	Evansville	11-7	138	69	3.85	R-R	6-3	200	10/6/54 Amsterdam, NY
39	Wilcox, Milt	Detroit	12-9	166	79	3.04	R-R	6-2	215	4/20/50 Honolulu, HI

CATCHERS

No.	Name	1981 Club	H	HR	RBI	Pct.	B-T	Ht.	Wt.	Born
8	Castillo, Marty	Evansville	105	17	68	.265	R-R	6-1	205	1/16/57 Long Beach, CA
		Detroit	1	0	0	.125				
17	Fahey, Bill	Detroit	17	1	9	.254	L-R	6-0	195	6/14/50 Detroit, MI
13	Parrish, Lance	Detroit	85	10	46	.244	R-R	6-3	210	6/15/56 Clairton, PA
14	Wockenfuss, John	Detroit	37	9	25	.215	R-R	6-0	190	2/27/49 Welch, WV

INFIELDERS

No.	Name	1981 Club	H	HR	RBI	Pct.	B-T	Ht.	Wt.	Born
16	Brookens, Tom	Detroit	58	4	25	.243	R-R	5-10	170	8/10/53 Chambersburg, PA
25	DeJohn, Mark	Evansville	94	5	43	.238	B-R	5-11	175	9/18/53 Middletown, CT
2	Hebner, Richie	Detroit	51	5	28	.226	L-R	6-1	195	11/26/47 Boston, MA
5	Johnson, Howard	Birmingham	130	27	83	.266	B-R	6-0	180	11/29/60 Clearwater, FL
12	Kelleher, Mick	Detroit	17	0	6	.221	R-R	5-9	165	7/25/47 Seattle, WA
7	Leach, Rick	Evansville	18	2	16	.409	L-L	6-0	195	5/4/57 Ann Arbor, MI
		Detroit	16	1	11	.193				
9	Papi, Stan	Detroit	19	3	12	.204	R-R	6-0	175	5/14/51 Fresno, CA
3	Trammell, Alan	Detroit	101	2	31	.258	R-R	6-0	170	2/21/58 Garden Grove, CA
1	Whitaker, Lou	Detroit	88	5	36	.263	L-L	5-11	160	5/12/57 New York, NY

OUTFIELDERS

No.	Name	1981 Club	H	HR	RBI	Pct.	B-T	Ht.	Wt.	Born
10	Cowens, Al	Detroit	66	1	18	.261	R-R	6-2	200	10/25/51 Los Angeles, CA
37	Filkins, Les	Evansville	82	10	55	.287	L-L	5-11	185	9/14/56 Chicago, IL
23	Gibson, Kirk	Detroit	95	9	40	.328	L-L	6-3	210	5/28/57 Pontiac, MI
—	Herndon, Larry	San Francisco	105	5	41	.288	R-R	6-3	190	11/3/53 Sunflower, MS
35	Jones, Lynn	Detroit	45	2	19	.259	R-R	5-9	165	1/1/53 Meadville, PA
—	Lemon, Chet	Chicago (AL)	99	9	50	.302	R-R	6-0	190	2/12/55 Jackson, MS
32	Peters, Rick	Detroit	53	0	15	.256	B-R	5-10	160	11/21/55 Lynnwood, WA
24	Summers, Champ	Detroit	42	3	21	.255	L-R	6-2	210	6/15/48 Bremerton, WA

TIGER PROFILES

JACK MORRIS 26 6-3 190   Bats R Throws R

Led the Tiger staff in victories for third straight year in 1981 . . . Had a sensational first half, winning honors as the All-Star Game starter, but then faltered in second half while Tigers were battling for their first division title since '72 . . . Finished second in AL in innings pitched . . . Fastball has been clocked at 94 mph . . . Pitched a one-hitter vs. Twins, Aug. 21, 1980 . . . Born May 16, 1955, in St. Paul, Minn. . . . Was Tigers' No. 5 selection in June 1976 draft after collegiate career at Brigham Young . . . His 15 complete games in '81 ranked third in AL.

Year	Club	G	IP	W	L	Pct.	SO	BB	H	ERA
1977	Detroit	7	46	1	1	.500	28	23	38	3.72
1978	Detroit	28	106	3	5	.375	48	49	107	4.33
1979	Detroit	27	198	17	7	.708	113	59	179	3.27
1980	Detroit	36	250	16	15	.516	112	87	252	4.18
1981	Detroit	25	198	14	7	.667	97	78	153	3.05
	Totals	123	798	51	35	.593	398	296	729	3.67

LANCE PARRISH 25 6-3 210   Bats R Throws R

Became highest-paid Tiger in history when he signed a six-year, $3.7-million contract last April . . . Led the Tigers in homers last year . . . Is regarded as one of the best young catchers in baseball . . . Was Tigers' No. 1 pick in June 1974 draft and spurned a football scholarship from UCLA to play baseball . . . Born June 15, 1956, in Clairton, Pa. . . . Was originally signed as a third baseman, but switched to catching in '75 . . . Spent part of one offseason as a bodyguard for rock star Tina Turner . . . Had seven game-winning RBI in '81, second on the Tigers . . . In '79, twice collected four hits in one game . . . Showed no signs of being a major-league hitting prospect until his fourth year in the minors, when he hit .279 at Evansville.

Year	Club	Pos.	G	AB	R	H	2B	3B	HR	RBI	SB	Avg.
1977	Detroit	C	12	46	10	9	2	0	3	7	0	.196
1978	Detroit	C	85	288	37	63	11	3	14	41	0	.219
1979	Detroit	C	143	493	65	136	26	3	19	65	6	.276
1980	Detroit	C-1B-OF	144	553	79	158	34	6	24	82	6	.286
1981	Detroit	C	96	348	39	85	18	2	10	46	2	.244
	Totals		480	1728	230	451	91	14	70	241	14	.261

ALAN TRAMMELL 24 6-0 170   Bats R Throws R

Prompted previously conservative Tigers to revamp their salary structure when he signed a 7-year, $2.8-million contract, longest in the club's history . . . "If any player on our club deserves that kind of money, he does," said Tigers' GM Jim Campbell . . . Was second on Tigers in hits and stolen bases in 1981 . . . Has excellent range and arm at short and is probably among the three best at his position in the league . . . Won Gold Glove in '80 . . . Born Feb. 21, 1958, in Garden Grove, Calif. . . . Tigers selected him No. 2 in the '76 amateur draft . . . His 107 runs in '80 tied for fifth-best in club history . . . Was Southern League MVP in '77, when he hit .291 at Montgomery.

Year	Club	Pos.	G	AB	R	H	2B	3B	HR	RBI	SB	Avg.
1977	Detroit	SS	19	43	6	8	0	0	0	0	0	.186
1978	Detroit	SS	139	448	49	120	14	6	2	34	3	.268
1979	Detroit	SS	142	460	68	127	11	4	6	50	17	.276
1980	Detroit	SS	146	560	107	168	21	5	9	65	12	.300
1981	Detroit	SS	105	392	52	101	15	3	2	31	10	.258
	Totals		551	1903	282	524	61	18	19	180	42	.275

CHET LEMON 27 6-0 196   Bats R Throws R

Enjoyed one of his better seasons in '81, getting his average over .300 again . . . Seems to be a much better hitter when surrounded with more prolific long-ball sluggers . . . Traded to Tigers for Steve Kemp last November . . . Is a crowd-pleaser with his outfield speed, arm and overall defensive excellence . . . One major weakness is his base-running ability–or lack of it . . . Born Feb. 12, 1955, at Jackson, Miss. . . . Led White Sox in doubles and triples last year . . . Was tried with some success in the leadoff spot toward end of '80 season, but was happy to go back to the No. 6 spot last year . . . Came to White Sox in 1975 in one of the few bad deals made by Charlie Finley. A's got pitchers Stan Bahnsen and Skip Pitlock. White Sox got one of the best center fielders in baseball.

Year	Club	Pos.	G	AB	R	H	2B	3B	HR	RBI	SB	Avg.
1975	Chicago (AL)	3B-OF	9	35	2	9	2	0	0	1	1	.257
1976	Chicago (AL)	OF	132	451	46	111	15	5	4	38	13	.246
1977	Chicago (AL)	OF	150	553	99	151	38	4	19	67	8	.273
1978	Chicago (AL)	OF	105	357	51	107	24	6	13	55	5	.300
1979	Chicago (AL)	OF	148	556	79	177	44	2	17	86	7	.318
1980	Chicago (AL)	OF	147	514	76	150	32	6	11	51	6	.292
1981	Chicago (AL)	OF	94	328	50	99	23	6	9	50	5	.302
	Totals		785	2794	403	804	178	29	73	348	45	.288

KIRK GIBSON 24 6-3 210　　　　　　**Bats L Throws L**

Has been considered one of the most exciting prospects to come along since Mickey Mantle and last year he finally lived up to that billing . . . Was Tigers' MVP down the stretch run with his clutch hitting . . . Led club in average and stolen bases and probably would have added the power categories, too, had his playing time not been limited early in the year . . . Born June 28, 1957, in Pontiac, Mich. . . . Was Tigers' No. 1 selection in June 1978 amateur draft . . . Career was almost ended by a wrist injury in '80 that severely curtailed his ability to swing a bat . . . Was a football flanker as well as center fielder at Michigan State.

Year	Club	Pos.	G	AB	R	H	2B	3B	HR	RBI	SB	Avg.
1979	Detroit.........	OF	12	38	3	9	3	0	1	4	3	.237
1980	Detroit.........	OF	51	175	23	46	2	1	9	16	4	.263
1981	Detroit.........	OF	83	290	41	95	11	3	9	40	17	.328
	Totals.........		146	503	67	150	16	4	19	60	24	.298

MILT WILCOX 31 6-2 215　　　　　　**Bats R Throws R**

Continues to defy his critics by being a consistent winner despite having been a salvage project by Tigers . . . Had a lot of arm trouble early in his career and was ready to quit when Tigers rescued him from Cubs' organization in 1976 . . . Was second on Tiger staff in strikeouts and complete games in '81 . . . Born April 20, 1950, in Honolulu and still keeps a pair of Hawaiian war god statues for good luck . . . Signed originally by the Reds and pitched for Sparky Anderson in '70 and '71 . . . Serves as Tigers' player rep . . . Used to raise chinchillas during the offseason . . . Jammed index finger on pitching hand playing basketball in November and needed surgery, a cause for some concern.

Year	Club	G	IP	W	L	Pct.	SO	BB	H	ERA
1970	Cincinnati	5	22	3	1	.750	13	7	19	2.45
1971	Cincinnati	18	43	2	2	.500	21	17	43	3.35
1972	Cleveland...............	32	156	7	14	.333	90	72	145	3.40
1973	Cleveland...............	26	134	8	10	.444	82	68	143	5.84
1974	Cleveland...............	41	71	2	2	.500	33	24	74	4.69
1975	Chicago (NL).............	25	38	0	1	.000	21	17	50	5.68
1977	Detroit.................	20	106	6	2	.750	82	37	96	3.65
1978	Detroit.................	29	215	13	12	.520	132	68	208	3.77
1979	Detroit.................	33	196	12	10	.545	109	73	201	4.36
1980	Detroit.................	32	199	13	11	.542	97	68	201	4.48
1981	Detroit.................	24	166	12	9	.571	79	52	152	3.04
	Totals.................	285	1346	78	74	.513	759	503	1332	4.09

DAN PETRY 23 6-4 200   **Bats R Throws R**

Came on as Tigers' top pitcher in second half of '81, when they led AL East most of the way . . . Tied for club lead in shutouts and was third on staff in complete games . . . Is still learning, but scouts like his chances to be a big winner . . . Born Nov. 13, 1958, in Palo Alto, Calif. . . . Was Tigers' fourth selection in the June 1976 draft . . . Had three shutouts in '80, which also led Tiger staff . . . Pitched two complete games in his first four major-league starts in '79 . . . Has had the lowest ERA of Tiger starters for the past two seasons . . . Was tied for second on Tiger staff in strikeouts last year.

Year	Club	G	IP	W	L	Pct.	SO	BB	H	ERA
1979	Detroit	15	98	6	5	.545	43	33	90	3.95
1980	Detroit	27	165	10	9	.526	88	83	156	3.93
1981	Detroit	23	141	10	9	.526	79	57	115	3.00
	Totals	65	404	26	23	.531	210	173	361	3.61

TOM BROOKENS 28 5-10 170   **Bats R Throws R**

Began '81 season on disabled list with pulled hamstring, then in his first day back, injured his ankle taking infield practice and did not get his season started until May 4 . . . Slow start was probably most to blame for subpar overall season . . . Became Tigers' regular third baseman in May, 1980, when Richie Hebner was moved to first . . . Born Aug. 10, 1953, in Chambersburg, Pa. . . . Was Tigers' No. 1 selection in June 1975 amateur draft . . . Singled in his first major-league at-bat off Geoff Zahn in 1979 . . . Had greatest day Sept. 20, 1980, when he went 5-for-5 and took part in a triple play.

Year	Club	Pos.	G	AB	R	H	2B	3B	HR	RBI	SB	Avg.
1979	Detroit	3B-2B	60	190	23	50	5	2	4	21	10	.263
1980	Detroit	3B-2B-SS	151	509	64	140	25	9	10	66	13	.275
1981	Detroit	3B-2B-SS	71	239	19	58	10	1	4	25	5	.243
	Totals		282	938	106	248	40	12	18	112	28	.264

LOU WHITAKER 24 5-11 160   **Bats L Throws R**

Made a fine comeback from puzzling off year in 1980 . . . Slump in '80 may have been caused by Tigers' insistence that he draw more walks. Some felt he had lost his aggressiveness at the plate . . . Excellent defensive second baseman who has been Alan Trammell's keystone partner since both were at Montgomery in 1977 . . . Born May 12, 1957, in New York

. . . Tigers made him their No. 5 choice in June 1975 amateur draft . . . Was named AL Rookie of the Year in '78 . . . Missed 20 games of '79 season due to back and finger injuries . . . Was originally a third baseman, but was switched to second in '76 . . . Soft-spoken and introverted, can be moody at times.

Year	Club	Pos.	G	AB	R	H	2B	3B	HR	RBI	SB	Avg.
1977	Detroit.........	2B	11	32	5	8	1	0	0	2	0	.250
1978	Detroit.........	2B	139	484	71	138	12	7	3	58	7	.285
1979	Detroit.........	2B	127	423	75	121	14	8	3	42	20	.286
1980	Detroit.........	2B	145	477	68	111	19	1	1	45	8	.233
1981	Detroit.........	2B	109	335	48	88	14	4	5	36	5	.263
	Totals..........		531	1751	267	466	60	20	12	183	40	.266

AL COWENS 30 6-2 200   Bats R Throws R

Appears to be on the slide since his big years with the Royals, but is still a good defensive outfielder with occasional pop . . . Came on strong for Tigers in 1980 after being traded from the Angels for first baseman Jason Thompson . . . Sees less and less action vs. right-handed pitching . . . Big year was '77, when he finished second in AL MVP vote . . . Was suspended seven games and fined by AL in '80 for engaging in a fight with White Sox reliever Ed Farmer, whom he charged in retaliation for a Farmer pitch that had broken his jaw a year earlier.

Year	Club	Pos.	G	AB	R	H	2B	3B	HR	RBI	SB	Avg.
1974	Kansas City.....	OF-3B	110	269	28	65	7	1	1	25	5	.242
1975	Kansas City.....	OF	120	328	44	91	13	8	4	42	12	.277
1976	Kansas City.....	OF	152	581	71	154	23	6	3	59	23	.265
1977	Kansas City.....	OF	162	606	98	189	32	14	23	112	16	.312
1978	Kansas City.....	OF-3B	132	485	63	133	24	8	5	63	14	.274
1979	Kansas City.....	OF	136	516	69	152	18	7	9	73	10	.295
1980	Cal.-Detroit	OF	142	522	69	140	20	3	6	59	6	.268
1981	Detroit.........	OF	85	253	27	66	11	4	1	18	3	.261
	Totals..........		1039	3560	469	990	148	51	52	451	89	.278

LARRY HERNDON 28 6-3 190   Bats R Throws R

An early-season sensation, batted .419 in April and .308 in May, entering strike with a .300 average . . . Tailed off in second half, batting .273 . . . Topped Giants with 105 hits and belted eight triples for two-year total of 19 . . . Traded to the Tigers for pitchers Dan Schatzeder and Mike Chris last winter . . . Almost was sent to Astros for Ken Forsch the previous winter, but Forsch refused to accept trade . . . Born Nov. 3, 1953, in Sunflower, Miss. . . . Has taken time to blossom

following sensational rookie campaign in 1976 . . . Hit safely in
24 of first 26 games after being promoted from Triple-A.

Year	Club	Pos.	G	AB	R	H	2B	3B	HR	RBI	SB	Avg.
1974	St. Louis	OF	12	1	3	1	0	0	0	0	0	1.000
1976	San Francisco ...	OF	115	337	42	97	11	3	2	23	12	.288
1977	San Francisco ...	OF	49	109	13	26	4	3	1	5	4	.239
1978	San Francisco ...	OF	151	471	52	122	15	9	1	32	13	.259
1979	San Francisco ...	OF	132	354	35	91	14	5	7	36	8	.257
1980	San Francisco ...	OF	139	493	54	127	17	11	8	49	8	.258
1981	San Francisco ...	OF	96	364	48	105	15	8	5	41	15	.288
	Totals..........		694	2129	247	569	76	39	24	186	60	.267

TOP PROSPECTS

LARRY ROTHSCHILD 28 6-2 180   **Bats L Throws R**
Brought up to Tigers late last season after compiling 8-5 record
with 3.26 ERA and 129 strikeouts in 171 innings at Evansville
. . . Born March 12, 1954, in Chicago . . . Signed originally by
Reds and drafted by Tigers off the Indianapolis roster in 1980
. . . Pitched college ball at Florida State and was primarily a
reliever.

DARRELL BROWN 26 6-0 180   **Bats R Throws R**
Has very limited power . . . Brought up from Evansville in Sep-
tember of last year, having hit .270 in American Association . . .
Born Oct. 29, 1955, in Oklahoma City, Okla. . . . Was Tigers'
No. 3 selection in June '77 amateur draft . . . Could stick with
Tigers because of his base-stealing ability . . . Has excellent
speed and a good throwing arm.

MANAGER SPARKY ANDERSON: Took over the Tiger helm
from Les Moss in June 1979 and has a contract
through 1984 . . . Managed Tigers to their
best finish last year since they won the AL
East in 1972 . . . Prior to piloting Tigers, won
five division titles and two World Series as
manager of the Reds from 1970-78 . . . Ranks
sixth all-time in winning percentage among
managers with 10 or more years experience
. . . Named Manager of the Year in 1972 and 1975 . . . Credits
the late Charlie Dressen for having the most influence on his

career . . . Came up through the Dodger chain as a player when
Dressen was their manager . . . Played only one season of major-league ball, 1959, when he hit .219 in 152 games as the Phillies' shortstop . . . Born Feb. 22, 1934, in Bridgewater, S.D.

GREATEST CATCHER

When defining greatness, one must take longevity and consistency into utmost consideration. They are perhaps the hallmarks
of what makes a person great at his profession. When the histori-
ans look back on the American League in the 1960s, they will
find one catcher who epitomized consistency: Bill Freehan.

Freehan caught for the Tigers from 1962 until 1976. He was
there when the Tigers were a struggling middle-of-the-road out-
fit in the early '60s. He was there when they won it all in 1968.
And he was there when they "stole" a divisional title under Billy
Martin in '72. He was the American League's all-star catcher in
1967, '68, '69 and '71.

Among Freehan's records are: Highest fielding percentage
lifetime by a catcher (.993), most putouts lifetime by a catcher
(9,941), most chances lifetime by a catcher (10,662). In addition,
Freehan holds the American League records for most putouts in
a game by a catcher (19), most putouts in a season by a catcher
(971) and most chances in a season by a catcher (1,044).

He was pretty fair hitter, too. His best year came the year the
Tigers won the championship, 1968. Freehan had a career-high
25 homers and 84 RBI that season and led the AL in putouts
with 1,133. He finished in 1976 after 1,774 games—all with the
Tigers—200 homers, 758 RBI and a lifetime batting average of
.262. Throw in his five Gold Gloves and you have the most consistent catcher in the American League for over a decade.

ALL-TIME TIGER SEASON RECORDS

BATTING: Ty Cobb, .420, 1911
HRs: Hank Greenberg, 58, 1938
RBIs: Hank Greenberg, 183, 1937
STEALS: Ty Cobb, 96, 1915
WINS: Denny McLain, 31, 1968
STRIKEOUTS: Mickey Lolich, 308, 1971

MILWAUKEE BREWERS

TEAM DIRECTORY: Chairman of the Board: Edmund Fitzgerald; Pres.: Bud Selig; Exec. VP-GM: Harry Dalton; Asst. to GM: Sal Bando; VP-Marketing: Dick Hackett; VP-Stadium Oper.: Gabe Paul, Jr.; VP-Admin.: Tom Ferguson; VP-Fin.: Dick Hoffman; VP-Broadcast Oper.: William Haig; Coordinator of Minor Leagues: Bruce Manno; Dir. Publ.: Tom Skibosh; Mgr.: Buck Rodgers. Home: Milwaukee County Stadium (53,-192). Field distances: 315, l.f. line, 362, l.f.; 392, l.c.; 402, c.f.; 392, r.c.; 362, r.f.; 315, r.f. line. Spring training: Sun City, Ariz.

SCOUTING REPORT

HITTING: The Brewers, on paper, are the best-balanced hitting team in the American League. They have power in the middle of the order (Gorman Thomas, Ben Oglivie, Cecil Cooper and Ted Simmons) plus a pair of excellent "table setters" in Robin Yount and Paul Molitor. Molitor was bothered by injuries last year and the Brewers have been unable to find a regular position for him, but if he hits near his potential, the Brewers' hitting can be even better.

Yount, with a steady spray of extra-base hits, is finally winning recognition as one of the most valuable players in the game. Cooper is one of the five best "pure hitters" in the league. Looking down the Brewer lineup, there is nary a batting weakness. Designated hitter Charlie Moore (.301) might be switched to the outfield if Molitor can make the conversion to third base and

Rollie Fingers was a rare double winner: Cy Young and MVP.

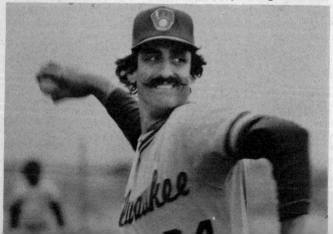

Larry Hisle is able to come back from a two-year shoulder injury. But even if those proposed changes don't work out, Brewers will have little trouble scoring runs again in '82.

PITCHING: Alas, that pitching. Brewers helped themselves considerably last year when they acquired Rollie Fingers and Pete Vuckovich from the Cardinals—yet they still finished 12th overall in team ERA with a 3.91 mark. Only the Twins' and Mariners' staffs gave up more runs per game. For that reason, the Brewers sought to add another quality starter over the winter but failed in their efforts. Thus, they will go into 1982 with Vuckovich as their ace and Mike Caldwell (11-9, 3.94), Moose Haas (11-7, 4.47) and Randy Lerch (7-9, 4.30) as the rest of the rotation.

This could well prove to be the Brewers' Achilles heel in their efforts to overtake the Yankees. Fortunately for Brewer manager Buck Rodgers, the bullpen is as deep and talented as the Yankees', with Fingers coming off his MVP season of 6-3, 1.04 ERA and league-leading 28 saves. Besides Fingers, southpaws Bob McClure and Jamie Easterly provide better-than-adequate middle-inning insurance.

FIELDING: The sign of a good team is a solid defense up the middle and the Brewers have it. The DP team of Jim Gantner at second and Yount at short, backed up by Thomas in center, is as sound as any in the league. Cooper is likewise an excellent defensive first baseman, while Simmons is adequate behind the plate, making up for whatever deficiencies he has with savvy. Both Thomas and Oglivie possess above-average throwing arms and opposing clubs have learned not to try to take that extra base on the Brewer outfielders. Third base and right field remain to be settled in the wake of the Molitor experiment, but either way, the Brewers' defense is sound in the important places.

OUTLOOK: In the opinion of many observers, the Brewers were the best team in baseball in the month of October last year. The Yankees especially conceded the Brewers had been tougher than the Dodgers—even though they lost to LA. Fingers, of course, is the key to the Brewers' success, but they also support him with a solid hitting attack and a sound defense. Only a worse failure from the starting pitching could short-circuit the first pennant in Milwaukee since the late '50s. That is a legitimate concern, though, since Caldwell, now 33, has gone steadily downhill since winning 22 in '78, and Lerch has yet to prove he can be a big winner, even with a team that backs him with runs. Overall, the Brewers seem to have enough hitting, defense and bullpen to take them to the wire.

MILWAUKEE BREWERS 1982 ROSTER

MANAGER Bob Rodgers
Coaches—Larry Haney, Ron Hansen, Harvey Kuenn,
Harry Warner, Cal McLish

PITCHERS

No.	Name	1981 Club	W-L	IP	SO	ERA	B-T	Ht.	Wt.	Born
46	Augustine, Jerry	Milwaukee	2-2	61	26	4.28	L-L	6-0	185	7/24/52 Kewaunee, WI
47	Bernard, Dwight	Milwaukee	0-0	5	1	3.60	R-R	6-2	170	5/31/52 Mt. Vernon, IL
		Vancouver	3-5	51	42	3.35				
48	Caldwell, Mike	Milwaukee	11-9	144	41	3.94	R-L	6-0	185	1/22/49 Tarboro, NC
25	Cleveland, Reggie	Milwaukee	2-3	65	18	5.12	R-R	6-4	200	5/23/48 Canada
42	Cocanower, Jaime	Vancouver	6-12	137	78	5.65	R-R	6-4	200	2/14/57 Canal Zone
49	DiPino, Frank	Milwaukee	0-0	2	3	0.00	L-L	5-10	175	10/22/56 Camillus, NY
		Vancouver	3-5	81	81	4.33				
28	Easterly, Jamie	Milwaukee	3-3	62	31	3.19	L-L	5-10	180	2/17/53 Houston, TX
34	Fingers, Rollie	Milwaukee	6-3	78	61	1.04	R-R	6-4	195	8/25/46 Steubenville, CA
30	Haas, Moose	Milwaukee	11-7	137	64	4.47	R-R	6-0	170	4/22/56 Baltimore, MD
54	Jones, Doug	Vancouver	5-3	80	38	3.04	R-R	6-2	170	6/24/57 Lebanon, IN
		El Paso	5-7	90	62	5.80				
35	Lerch, Randy	Milwaukee	7-9	111	53	4.30	L-L	6-3	190	10/9/54 Sacramento, CA
10	Madden, Mike	El Paso	6-8	125	140	5.67	L-L	6-1	185	1/13/58 Denver, CO
10	McClure, Bob	Milwaukee	0-0	8	6	3.38	B-L	5-11	170	4/29/53 Oakland, CA
26	Moore, Donnie	Milwaukee	0-0	4	2	6.75	L-R	6-0	170	2/13/54 Lubbock, TX
40	Mueller, Willie	Milwaukee	0-0	2	1	4.50	R-R	6-4	220	8/30/56 West Bend, WI
		Vancouver	5-3	81	52	1.78				
55	Olsen, Rich	Vancouver	9-7	146	67	3.51	R-R	6-0	180	6/1/57 Kailua, HI
43	Porter, Chuck	Milwaukee	0-0	4	1	4.50	R-R	6-3	188	1/12/56 Baltimore, MD
		Vancouver	7-10	140	54	3.79				
41	Slaton, Jim	Milwaukee	5-7	117	47	4.38	R-R	6-0	185	6/19/50 Long Beach, CA
—	Torres, Tony	El Paso	5-7	122	110	4.34	R-R	6-1	195	7/7/59
50	Vuckovich, Pete	Milwaukee	14-4	150	84	3.54	R-R	6-4	220	10/27/52 Johnstown, PA

CATCHERS

No.	Name	1981 Club	H	HR	RBI	Pct.	B-T	Ht.	Wt.	Born
59	Lake, Steve	Vancouver	80	2	38	.230	R-R	6-1	180	3/14/57 Redondo Beach, CA
22	Moore, Charlie	Milwaukee	47	1	9	.301	R-R	5-11	180	6/21/53 Birmingham, AL
23	Simmons, Ted	Milwaukee	82	14	61	.216	B-R	6-0	200	8/1/49 Highland Park, MI
5	Yost, Ned	Milwaukee	6	3	3	.222	R-R	6-1	185	8/19/55 Eureka, CA

INFIELDERS

15	Cooper, Cecil	Milwaukee	133	12	60	.320	L-L	6-2	190	12/20/49 Brenham, TX
17	Gantner, Jim	Milwaukee	94	2	33	.267	L-R	5-11	175	1/5/54 Eden, WI
13	Howell, Roy	Milwaukee	58	6	33	.238	L-R	6-1	195	12/18/53 Lompoc, CA
7	Money, Don	Milwaukee	40	2	14	.216	R-R	6-1	190	6/7/47 Washington, DC
11	Romero, Ed	Milwaukee	18	1	10	.198	R-R	5-11	150	12/9/57 Puerto Rico
—	Rush, Lawrence	Vancouver	80	2	38	.230	R-R	6-2	195	10/25/56 Los Angeles, CA
19	Yount, Robin	Milwaukee	103	10	49	.273	R-R	6-0	170	9/16/55 Danville, IL

OUTFIELDERS

57	Bass, Kevin	Vancouver	87	2	30	.257	B-R	6-0	180	5/12/59 Menlo Park, CA
27	Bosley, Thad	Milwaukee	24	0	3	.229	L-L	6-3	174	9/17/56 Oceanside, CA
		Vancouver	19	0	3	.373				
29	Brouhard, Mark	Milwaukee	51	2	20	.274	R-R	6-1	210	5/22/56 Burbank, CA
		Vancouver	39	0	14	.320				
16	Edwards, Marshall	Milwaukee	14	0	4	.241	L-L	5-9	157	8/27/52 Los Angeles, CA
		Vancouver	19	0	3	.373				
9	Hisle, Larry	Milwaukee	20	4	11	.230	R-R	6-2	195	5/5/47 Portsmouth, OH
4	Molitor, Paul	Milwaukee	67	2	19	.267	R-R	6-0	175	8/22/56 St. Paul, MN
42	Oglivie, Ben	Milwaukee	97	14	72	.243	L-L	6-2	170	2/11/49 Panama
—	Skube, Bob	El Paso	113	18	59	.284	L-L	6-0	182	10/8/57 Northridge, CA
20	Thomas, Gorman	Milwaukee	94	21	65	.259	R-R	6-3	200	12/12/50 Charleston, SC

BREWER PROFILES

ROLLIE FINGERS 35 6-4 200   Bats R Throws R

Was the reason the Brewers went as far as they did in 1981, having a part in more than half of their victories and earning MVP award . . . Also became third reliever in history to win Cy Young . . . His 1.04 ERA was lowest of his career . . . Led the league in saves for third time with 28 . . . Born Aug. 25, 1946, in Steubenville, Cal. . . . Came to Brewers with Ted Simmons and Pete Vuckovich for Lary Sorenson, Dave La-Point, Sixto Lezcano and David Green in December 1980 swap with Cardinals . . . Pitched previous four years in San Diego after playing out his option with A's and becoming free agent . . . "San Diego was a place I just had to get out of," he said. "I never realized how being with clubs that don't win can take your enthusiasm out of the game. They were talking about 1984, but I couldn't wait that long."

Year	Club	G	IP	W	L	Pct.	SO	BB	H	ERA
1968	Oakland	1	1	0	0	.000	0	1	4	36.00
1969	Oakland	60	119	6	7	.462	61	41	116	3.71
1970	Oakland	45	148	7	9	.438	79	48	137	3.65
1971	Oakland	48	129	4	6	.400	98	30	94	3.00
1972	Oakland	65	111	11	9	.550	113	33	85	2.51
1973	Oakland	62	127	7	8	.467	110	39	107	1.91
1974	Oakland	76	119	9	5	.643	95	29	104	2.65
1975	Oakland	75	127	10	6	.625	115	33	95	2.98
1976	Oakland	70	135	13	11	.542	113	40	118	2.47
1977	San Diego	78	132	8	9	.471	113	36	123	3.00
1978	San Diego	67	107	6	13	.316	72	29	84	2.52
1979	San Diego	54	84	9	9	.500	65	37	91	4.50
1980	San Diego	66	103	11	9	.550	69	32	101	2.80
1981	Milwaukee	47	78	6	3	.667	61	13	55	1.04
	Totals	814	1520	107	104	.507	1164	440	1314	2.87

CECIL COOPER 32 6-2 190   Bats L Throws L

Was once again Brewers' leading hitter, finishing fourth overall in AL with .320 average . . . Led the league in doubles with 35 and tied for third in hits. Was third also in runs . . . Born Dec. 20, 1949, in Brenham, Tex. . . . Had his best all-around season in 1980 when only George Brett's assault on .400 could overshadow his stats that included a .352 average, 25 homers, 96 runs and a league-leading 122 RBI

. . . Set Brewer club records of 335 total bases and 219 hits that year . . . Came over to Milwaukee from Red Sox in December 1976 for George Scott and Bernie Carbo . . . Has hit .300 or better in each of the last five seasons . . . Attended Prairie View A&M and was drafted sixth by the Red Sox in 1968 draft . . . Scout who signed him was ex-big-league, pinch-hit champ Dave Philley.

Year	Club	Pos.	G	AB	R	H	2B	3B	HR	RBI	SB	Avg.
1971	Boston	1B	14	42	9	13	4	1	0	3	1	.310
1972	Boston	1B	12	17	0	4	1	0	0	2	0	.235
1973	Boston	1B	30	101	12	24	2	0	3	11	1	.238
1974	Boston	1B	121	414	55	114	24	1	8	43	2	.275
1975	Boston	1B	106	305	49	95	17	6	14	44	1	.311
1976	Boston	1B	123	451	66	127	22	6	15	78	7	.282
1977	Milwaukee	1B	160	643	86	193	31	7	20	78	13	.300
1978	Milwaukee	1B	107	407	60	127	23	2	13	54	3	.312
1979	Milwaukee	1B	150	590	83	182	44	1	24	106	15	.308
1980	Milwaukee	1B	153	622	96	219	33	4	25	122	17	.352
1981	Milwaukee	1B	106	416	70	133	35	1	12	60	5	.320
	Totals		1082	4008	586	1231	236	29	134	601	65	.307

PETE VUCKOVICH 29 6-4 220   Bats R Throws R

Was the extra bonus of the Ted Simmons-Rollie Fingers deal with the Cardinals in December 1980, emerging as Brewers' top winner . . . Tied for the AL lead in wins and was all alone at the top in winning percentage . . . Cards were fearful of losing him to free agency, but Brewers signed him to a long-term deal early in the season . . . Came off his sickbed to beat the Yankees in the fourth game of the AL East playoffs . . . Born Oct. 27, 1952, in Johnstown, Pa. . . . Originally signed by the White Sox as a third-round pick in the June 1974 draft . . . Spent just two seasons in the minors before coming to big leagues for keeps . . . Has been in double figures for victories the last four seasons . . . Topped Brewers in strikeouts in 1981 and pitched the club's only shutout . . . Was Cardinals' strikeout leader in all three of his seasons with them.

Year	Club	G	IP	W	L	Pct.	SO	BB	H	ERA
1975	Chicago (AL)	4	10	0	1	.000	5	7	17	13.50
1976	Chicago (AL)	33	110	7	4	.636	62	60	122	4.66
1977	Toronto	53	148	7	7	.500	123	59	143	3.47
1978	St. Louis	45	198	12	12	.500	149	59	187	2.55
1979	St. Louis	34	233	15	10	.600	145	64	229	3.59
1980	St. Louis	32	222	12	9	.571	132	68	203	3.41
1981	Milwaukee	24	150	14	4	.778	84	57	137	3.54
	Totals	225	1071	67	47	.588	700	374	1038	3.54

ROBIN YOUNT 26 6-0 170

Bats R Throws R

He's been around so long, it's hard to believe he's still only 26 . . . Played only 64 games in minor leagues before making his big-league debut in 1974 at age 18 . . . Born Sept. 16, 1955, in Danville, Ill. . . . Collected his 1,000th career hit in 1980, becoming one of the youngest players to do so . . . Really came into his own the last couple of years by steadying himself in the field and maturing as a hitter with surprising power . . . Brewer opponents will tell you he's their MVP, the guy you have to keep under control if you want to beat them . . . Led the AL in doubles with 49 in 1980. Also became the first shortstop in 15 years to reach the 300 total-bases plateau that year . . . Is Brewers' all-time club leader in hits, doubles, triples and at-bats.

Year	Club	Pos.	G	AB	R	H	2B	3B	HR	RBI	SB	Avg.
1974	Milwaukee......	SS	107	344	48	86	14	5	3	26	7	.250
1975	Milwaukee......	SS	147	558	67	149	28	2	8	52	12	.267
1976	Milwaukee......	SS-OF	161	638	59	161	19	3	2	54	16	.252
1977	Milwaukee......	SS	154	605	66	174	34	4	4	49	16	.288
1978	Milwaukee......	SS	127	502	66	147	23	9	9	71	16	.293
1979	Milwaukee......	SS	149	577	72	154	26	5	8	51	11	.267
1980	Milwaukee......	SS	143	611	121	179	49	10	23	87	20	.293
1981	Milwaukee......	SS	96	377	50	103	15	5	10	49	4	.273
	Totals..........		1084	4212	549	1153	208	43	67	439	102	.274

TED SIMMONS 32 6-0 200

Bats S Throws R

Despite hitting for the lowest average in his career, had a productive first season in the American League, finishing third on Brewers in RBI and tied for second on club in homers . . . Also had 12 game-winning RBI, which was tops on Brewers and third best in the AL . . . Came to Brewers with Rollie Fingers and Pete Vuckovich in deal with Cardinals . . . St. Louis fans protested loud and long about his departure, but he had refused to move to first base when Cards signed Darrell Porter . . . Showed last year he's still a good catcher with better-than-average throwing arm . . . Born Aug. 9, 1949, in Highland Park, Mich. . . . Spent 11 seasons with Cardinals, hitting over .300 in six of them . . . Became a switch-hitter at age 13 . . . Was a fullback in high school and had football scholarship offers from Ohio State, Michigan, Michigan St. and Colorado . . . Is still working toward a speech degree in college . . . Has NL record for most homers by a switch-hitter (172).

Year	Club	Pos.	G	AB	R	H	2B	3B	HR	RBI	SB	Avg.
1968	St. Louis	C	2	3	0	1	0	0	0	0	0	.333
1969	St. Louis	C	5	14	0	3	0	1	0	3	0	.214
1970	St. Louis	C	82	284	29	69	8	2	3	24	2	.243
1971	St. Louis	C	133	510	64	155	32	4	7	77	1	.304
1972	St. Louis	C-1B	152	594	70	180	36	6	16	96	1	.303
1973	St. Louis	C-1B-OF	161	619	62	192	36	2	13	91	2	.310
1974	St. Louis	C-1B	152	599	66	163	33	6	20	103	0	.272
1975	St. Louis	C-1B-OF	157	581	80	193	32	3	18	100	1	.332
1976	St. Louis	C-1B-OF-3B	150	546	60	159	35	3	5	75	0	.291
1977	St. Louis	C-OF	150	516	82	164	25	3	21	95	2	.318
1978	St. Louis	C-OF	152	516	71	148	40	5	22	80	1	.287
1979	St. Louis	C	123	448	68	127	22	0	26	87	0	.283
1980	St. Louis	C-OF	145	495	84	150	33	2	21	98	1	.303
1981	Milwaukee	C	100	380	45	82	13	3	14	61	0	.216
	Totals		1664	6105	781	1786	345	40	186	990	11	.293

BEN OGLIVIE 33 6-2 170   Bats L Throws L

Got off to a slow start last year, but finished strong to rank third in AL in RBI . . . Broke through with his biggest season in 1980, hitting a career-high .304 with league-leading 41 HR and 118 RBI that was second-best in AL . . . Had 11 game-winning RBI for Brewers last year . . . Born Feb. 11, 1949, in Colon, Panama . . . Was an outstanding soccer player as well as baseball player growing up in New York City . . . Red Sox originally signed him as their seventh-round pick in June 1968 draft . . . Was later traded to Detroit and Brewers obtained him from Tigers for pitcher Jim Slaton and Rich Folkers in December 1977 . . . Possesses perhaps the strongest throwing arm of any left fielder in the AL . . . Has averaged nearly 90 RBI in four seasons with the Brewers . . . Hobbies include swimming, backgammon and electronics.

Year	Club	Pos.	G	AB	R	H	2B	3B	HR	RBI	SB	Avg.
1971	Boston	OF	14	38	2	10	3	0	0	4	0	.263
1972	Boston	OF	94	253	27	61	10	2	8	30	1	.241
1973	Boston	OF	58	147	16	32	9	1	2	9	1	.218
1974	Detroit	OF-1B	92	252	28	68	11	3	4	29	12	.270
1975	Detroit	OF-1B	100	332	45	95	14	1	9	36	11	.286
1976	Detroit	OF-1B	115	305	36	87	12	3	15	47	9	.285
1977	Detroit	OF	132	450	63	118	24	2	21	61	9	.262
1978	Milwaukee	OF-1B	128	469	71	142	29	4	18	72	11	.303
1979	Milwaukee	OF-1B	139	514	88	145	30	4	29	81	12	.282
1980	Milwaukee	OF	156	592	94	180	26	2	41	118	11	.304
1981	Milwaukee	OF	107	400	53	97	15	2	14	72	2	.243
	Totals		1135	3752	523	1035	183	24	161	559	79	.276

PAUL MOLITOR 25 6-0 175 Bats R Throws R

Was sidelined from May 3 into second half of last season with badly sprained ankle that curtailed his productivity. However, he had a good playoff against Yankees . . . Originally a second baseman, was switched to the outfield in 1981 so Brewers could get Jim Gantner into the lineup on an everyday basis . . . Had big season in 1980 when he set personal one-season highs in doubles (29) and stolen bases (34) . . . Hit .309 in clutch situations in '80, but missed 43 games due to injury . . . Earned several rookie honors in 1978 when he filled in at shortstop for injured Robin Yount and hit .273 . . . Born Aug. 22, 1956, in St. Paul, Minn. . . . Played only one year of minor-league ball and hit .346 with Burlington . . . Brewers signed him out of U. of Minnesota, where he was All-Big Ten three years and an All-American two years.

Year	Club	Pos.	G	AB	R	H	2B	3B	HR	RBI	SB	Avg.
1978	Milwaukee......	2B-SS-3B	125	521	73	142	26	4	6	45	30	.273
1979	Milwaukee......	2B-SS	140	584	88	188	27	16	9	62	33	.322
1980	Milwaukee......	2B-SS-3B	111	450	81	137	29	2	9	37	34	.304
1981	Milwaukee......	OF-2B	64	251	45	67	11	0	2	19	10	.267
	Totals..........		440	1806	287	534	93	22	26	163	107	.296

JIM GANTNER 28 5-11 175 Bats L Throws R

Had second straight productive season as a Brewer regular in '81 . . . Is not a power-hitting second baseman, but on Brewers, he doesn't have to be . . . Scouts love his gung-ho attitude. A "gamer" who makes the best of average tools . . . A tough strikeout . . . In 1980, his best all-around season in majors, he hit .282 overall, .295 with men on base and .350 with men in scoring position . . . Born Jan. 5, 1954, at Eden, Wis. . . . Was Brewers' 12th pick in the June 1974 draft . . . Went to college at University of Wisconsin-Oshkosh and twice participated in NAIA World Series . . . Came up for good in '78 and showed versatility by playing all four infield positions.

Year	Club	Pos.	G	AB	R	H	2B	3B	HR	RBI	SB	Avg.
1976	Milwaukee......	3B	26	69	6	17	1	0	0	7	1	.246
1977	Milwaukee......	3B	14	47	4	14	1	0	1	2	2	.298
1978	Milwaukee......	INF	43	97	14	21	1	0	1	8	2	.216
1979	Milwaukee......	INF-P	70	208	29	59	10	3	2	22	3	.284
1980	Milwaukee......	3B-2B-SS	132	415	47	117	21	3	4	40	11	.282
1981	Milwaukee......	2B-3B-SS	107	352	35	94	14	1	2	33	3	.267
	Totals..........		392	1188	135	322	48	7	10	112	22	.271

GORMAN THOMAS 31 6-3 200   Bats R Throws R

Was second in the AL in homers with 21 . . . Batting average was his highest in the majors . . . A durable player who comes to play and seldom misses a game . . . Born Dec. 12, 1950, at Charleston, S.C. . . . Took awhile before developing into the major-league slugger he is now . . . After seven seasons up and down in majors and minors, seemed to put it all together at Spokane in '77 when he hit 36 homers and drove in 114 runs . . . He had 32 homers with Brewers in 1978, then led the AL with 45 in '79 . . . Was a first-round pick of the Seattle Pilots in the June 1969 draft . . . Hobbies include music, golf, cars and billiards . . . Has the most homers (158) of any Brewer in the history of the club.

Year	Club	Pos.	G	AB	R	H	2B	3B	HR	RBI	SB	Avg.
1973	Milwaukee......	OF-3B	59	155	16	29	7	1	2	11	5	.187
1974	Milwaukee......	OF	17	46	10	12	4	0	2	11	4	.261
1975	Milwaukee......	OF	121	240	34	43	12	2	10	28	4	.179
1976	Milwaukee......	OF-3B	99	227	27	45	9	2	8	36	2	.198
1978	Milwaukee......	OF	137	452	70	111	24	1	32	86	3	.246
1979	Milwaukee......	OF	156	557	97	136	29	0	45	123	1	.244
1980	Milwaukee......	OF	162	628	78	150	26	3	38	105	8	.239
1981	Milwaukee......	OF	103	363	54	94	22	0	21	65	4	.259
	Totals..........		854	2668	386	620	133	9	158	465	31	.232

MIKE CALDWELL 33 6-0 185   Bats R Throws L

Is still Brewers' No. 1 left-handed starter, but looks as if he might be in decline. Had second straight so-so season after brilliant '78 and '79 campaigns . . . Pitched well against Yankees in playoffs, however, proving he can still do the job in critical situations . . . Was second on Brewer staff in complete games in '81, but had no shutouts for first time since '77 . . . Born Jan. 22, 1949, in Tarboro, N.C. . . . Brewers obtained him from Reds in June 1977 in one of their best deals ever. Brewers yielded only a pair of minor leaguers who never made it . . . Began his career with the Padres, then went to Giants, where he won 14 in '74 before developing arm trouble . . . Is suspected of throwing an occasional spitter . . . Went to North Carolina State and holds school records for most victories in a season (9) and career (32).

Year	Club	G	IP	W	L	Pct.	SO	BB	H	ERA
1971	San Diego	6	7	1	0	1.000	5	3	4	0.00
1972	San Diego	42	164	7	11	.389	102	49	183	4.01
1973	San Diego	55	149	5	14	.263	86	53	146	3.74
1974	San Francisco	31	189	14	5	.737	83	63	176	2.95
1975	San Francisco	38	163	7	13	.350	57	48	194	4.80
1976	San Francisco	50	107	1	7	.125	55	20	145	4.88
1977	Cincinnati	14	25	0	0	.000	11	8	25	3.96
1977	Milwaukee	21	94	5	8	.385	38	36	101	4.60
1978	Milwaukee	37	293	22	9	.710	131	54	258	2.37
1979	Milwaukee	30	235	16	6	.727	89	39	252	3.29
1980	Milwaukee	34	225	13	11	.542	74	56	248	4.04
1981	Milwaukee	24	144	11	9	.550	41	38	151	3.94
	Totals...................	382	1795	102	93	.523	772	467	1883	3.65

TOP PROSPECT

RICH OLSEN 24 6-0 180   Bats R Throws R

Doesn't overwhelm you with his stuff, but could crack the Brewer staff if one of the veteran starters falter . . . Was 9-7 with 3.51 ERA in heavy-hitting Pacific Coast League last year . . . Born June 1, 1957, in Honolulu and still lives there . . . Played three years for U. of Hawaii baseball team . . . Was Brewers' fourth pick in June 1978 amateur draft . . . A starter throughout his career.

MANAGER BOB (BUCK) RODGERS: Was rumored to be in trouble late last year when Brewers showed signs of faltering down the stretch and George Bamberger was ready to come back to managing . . . Saved his job, though, with excellent maneuvering of his personnel through the playoffs, extending Yankees to a hard-fought five games . . . Born Aug. 16, 1938, in Delaware, Ohio . . . Attended Ohio Wesleyan and Ohio Northern Universities . . . Beginning his fifth season with the Brewers, the first three having been spent as a coach under Bamberger . . . Was interim manager in 1980 when Bamberger had heart problems . . . Previous managerial experience was in minor leagues in Angels' chain . . . Spent his entire major-league playing career with Angels, compiling .232 average for nine seasons. Was Angels' first-string catcher from 1962-67.

GREATEST CATCHER

In assessing the Brewers' catching situation since 1969, when the club was initially formed as the ill-fated Seattle Pilots, it is difficult to argue that any of their catchers were better than their present one, Ted Simmons. True, the Brewers had Darrell Porter for awhile and Charlie Moore has done a yeoman job behind the plate for them since he came up in '74. But didn't Brewers GM Harry Dalton say, when he made the deal, "Getting Ted Simmons ends one of the longest searches in the history of this franchise"?

Oddly, in his first year as an American Leaguer, Simmons did not have one of his best years with the bat, hitting some 75 points below his lifetime average. Yet, it was no coincidence that the Brewers rose to their greatest heights in '81, Ted Simmons' first year on the job for them behind the plate. Indeed, Simmons led the team with 12 game-winning RBI and was an instant leader on the field. Leadership is something that comes from already having proven yourself.

Prior to coming over to the Brewers in the big December 1980 deal with Rollie Fingers and Pete Vuckovich, Simmons had been the Cardinals' mainstay catcher for a decade. Six times he hit over .300 and five times he was voted to the NL all-star team. And when Whitey Herzog, the Cards' GM-manager, announced he was trading Simmons, the fans of St. Louis rebelled. The switchboards at Busch Stadium lit up in protest and the telegrams came in waves. The people in St. Louis were well aware the Brewers had just acquired their best catcher ever.

ALL-TIME BREWER SEASON RECORDS

BATTING: Cecil Cooper, .352, 1980
HRs: Gorman Thomas, 45, 1979
RBIs: Gorman Thomas, 123, 1979
STEALS: Tommy Harper, 73, 1969
WINS: Mike Caldwell, 22, 1978
STRIKEOUTS: Marty Pattin, 161, 1971

NEW YORK YANKEES

TEAM DIRECTORY: Prin. Owner: George Steinbrenner, III; Pres.: Lou Saban; Exec. VP: Cedric Tallis; VP-Baseball Oper.: Bill Bergesch; Dir. Pub. Rel.: Irv Kaze; Trav. Sec.: Bill Kane; Mgr.: Bob Lemon. Home: Yankee Stadium (57,545). Field distances: 312, l.f. line; 387, l.f.; 430, l.c.; 417, c.f.; 385, r.c.; 353, r.f.; 310, r.f. line. Spring training: Fort Lauderdale, Fla.

SCOUTING REPORT

HITTING: If there has been one major deficiency evident about the Yankees since they last won it all in '78, it is hitting. Surprisingly, the additions of Ken Griffey and Dave Collins do not appear to strengthen the Yankees significantly here.

Their prime weakness has been at cleanup, where Reggie Jackson suffered through his worst season. The Yankees no longer have the long-ball potential to merely crush their opposition. There is also some question now as to whether Dave Winfield can be a .300, 100-RBI hitter without a cleanup hitter to back him up.

Goose Gossage saved 20 games in only 32 appearances.

The Yankees will rely more on timely hitting and speed, but somehow that pattern doesn't fit their image. Graig Nettles, at age 37, is suddenly Yankees' chief home-run threat. Further, they got little production out of their first-base unit of Bob Watson and Dave Revering. It also remains to be seen how the defection of hitting coach Charlie Lau will affect Rick Cerone and Bucky Dent, his prize pupils.

PITCHING: Once again the Yankees' strong point and the reason they should hang close all year. The re-signing of Ron Guidry was a must, though, in that Tommy John (39 in May) and Rudy May (38 in July) are getting along in age. The Yankees may finally have to let youngsters Gene Nelson and Andy McGaffigan prove their worth a la Dave Righetti in '81.

The Yankees' biggest plus, of course, is the bullpen of Rich Gossage, Ron Davis, George Frazier and, possibly, veteran lefty Bob Sykes. With the virtually unhittable Gossage holding forth as the cleanup man, the Yankees need only to forge an early lead and take it into the seventh inning. That was their formula last year and it took them right into the World Series.

FIELDING: Always and still a Yankee strength. They seldom if ever beat themselves in the field. Bucky Dent and Willie Randolph are a sure-handed DP combo and Nettles is without question the master of his craft at third. Winfield, Griffey and Jerry Mumphrey comprise one of the fastest outfields in baseball. Cerone is solid defensively behind the plate.

The Yankees finished fourth in fielding overall and figure to do as well or better. No longer do opposing baserunners dare to take liberties on the Yankee outfield. If there is any weakness in defense it is at first, where Bob Watson covers little ground. Collins will get a shot here.

OUTLOOK: When the Yankees collapsed in the World Series, George Steinbrenner promised wholesale changes. The Yankee boss cited age and lack of speed as the prime reasons for his team's breakdown. In Griffey and Collins, Stenbrenner has added speed and Griffey should do a lot for the defense in the outfield.

But despite the presence of the Great Gossage in the bullpen and the expected base-stealing boom from Griffey, Collins, Jerry Mumphrey and Willie Randolph, there is a lot of age here. Among the candidates for the starting lineup opening day are Watson (36 in April), Nettles (37) and designated hitters Lou Piniella (38) and Oscar Gamble (33). Even Griffey will be 32 in April.

NEW YORK YANKEES 1982 ROSTER

MANAGER Bob Lemon
Coaches—Joe Altobelli, Yogi Berra, Mike Ferraro, Clyde King, Jeff Torborg

PITCHERS

No.	Name	1981 Club	W-L	IP	SO	ERA	B-T	Ht.	Wt.	Born
39	Davis, Ron	New York (AL)	4-5	73	83	2.71	R-R	6-4	205	8/6/55 Houston, TX
—	Filson, Pete	Ft. Lauderdale	7-1	68	68	1.99	L-L	6-2	175	9/28/58 Darby, PA
		Nashville	10-2	99	71	1.82				
43	Frazier, George	Springfield	1-2	31	28	3.19	R-R	6-5	205	10/13/54 Oklahoma City, OK
		Columbus	4-1	58	49	3.10				
		New York (AL)	0-1	28	17	1.61				
54	Gossage, Rich	New York (AL)	3-2	47	48	0.77	R-R	6-3	217	7/5/51 Colorado Springs, CO
49	Guidry, Ron	New York (AL)	11-5	1217	104	2.76	L-L	5-11	160	8/28/50 Lafayette, LA
25	John, Tommy	New York (AL)	9-8	140	50	2.64	R-L	6-3	203	5/22/43 Terre Haute, IN
45	May, Rudy	New York (AL)	6-11	148	79	4.14	L-L	6-2	205	7/18/44 Coffeyville, KS
58	McGaffigan, Andy	Columbus	8-6	103	57	3.23	R-R	6-3	195	10/25/56 West Palm Beach, FL
		New York (AL)	0-0	7	2	2.57				
—	Morgan, Mike	Nashville	8-7	169	100	4.42	R-R	6-3	195	10/8/59 Tulare, CA
46	Nelson, Gene	Ft. Lauderdale	1-0	10	8	4.50	R-R	6-1	180	12/3/60 Tampa, FL
		Columbus	4-0	32	37	2.53				
		New York (AL)	3-1	39	16	4.85				
—	Pacella, John	Columbus	11-9	155	135	4.47	R-R	6-2	184	9/15/56 Brooklyn, NY
36	Reuschel, Rick	Chicago (NL)	4-7	86	53	3.45	R-R	6-3	230	5/16/49 Quincy, IL
		New York (AL)	4-4	71	22	2.66				
19	Righetti, Dave	Columbus	5-0	45	50	1.00	L-L	6-3	198	11/29/58 San Jose, CA
		New York (AL)	8-4	105	89	2.06				
—	Sykes, Bob	St. Louis	2-0	37	14	4.62	B-L	6-2	200	12/11/54 Neptune, NJ
—	Werly, Jamie	Nashville	13-11	222	193	2.59	R-R	6-2	185	9/7/56 Elmhurst, IL

CATCHERS

No.	Name	1981 Club	H	HR	RBI	Pct.	B-T	Ht.	Wt.	Born
10	Cerone, Rick	New York (AL)	57	2	21	.244	R-R	5-11	185	5/19/54 Newark, NJ
23	Foote, Barry	Chicago (NL)	0	0	1	.000	R-R	6-3	215	2/16/52 Smithfield, NC
		New York (AL)	26	6	10	.208				
38	Gulden, Brad	Spokane	14	2	9	.275	L-R	5-10	175	6/10/56 New Ulm, MN
		Seattle	3	0	1	.188				
		Columbus	70	17	42	.295				

INFIELDERS

No.	Name	1981 Club	H	HR	RBI	Pct.	B-T	Ht.	Wt.	Born
57	Ashford, Tucker	Columbus	151	17	86	.300	R-R	6-1	190	12/14/54 Memphis, TN
		New York (AL)	0	0	0	.000				
66	Balboni, Steve	Columbus	107	33	98	.247	R-R	6-6	225	1/16/57 Brockton, MA
		New York (AL)	2	0	2	.286				
20	Dent, Bucky	New York (AL)	54	7	27	.238	R-R	5-11	182	11/25/51 Savannah, GA
—	Mattingly, Don	Nashville	172	7	98	.314	L-L	6-0	175	4/20/61 Evansville, IN
18	Milbourne, Larry	New York (AL)	51	1	12	.313	B-R	6-0	165	2/14/51 Port Norris, NJ
9	Nettles, Graig	New York (AL)	85	15	46	.244	L-R	6-0	185	8/20/44 San Diego, CA
—	Nixon, Otis	Nashville	102	0	20	.251	R-R	6-2	180	1/9/59 Columbus Co., NC
30	Randolph, Willie	New York (NL)	83	2	24	.232	R-R	5-11	166	7/6/54 Holly Hill, SC
12	Revering, Dave	Oak-NY (AL)	48	4	17	.233	L-R	6-4	205	2/12/53 Roseville, CA
55	Robertson, Andre	Columbus	104	9	49	.259	R-R	5-10	155	10/2/57 Orange, TX
		New York (AL)	5	0	0	.263				
28	Watson, Bob	New York (AL)	33	6	12	.212	R-R	6-2	210	4/10/46 Los Angeles, CA

OUTFIELDERS

No.	Name	1981 Club	H	HR	RBI	Pct.	B-T	Ht.	Wt.	Born
13	Brown, Bobby	Columbus	50	6	27	.329	B-R	6-1	207	5/24/54 Norfolk, VA
		New York (AL)	14	0	6	.226				
29	Collins, Dave	Cincinnati	98	3	23	.272	S-L	5-10	175	10/20/52 Rapid City, SD
17	Gamble, Oscar	New York (AL)	45	10	27	.238	L-R	5-11	175	12/20/49 Ramer, AL
—	Griffey, Ken	Cincinnati	123	2	34	.311	L-L	5-11	200	4/10/50 Donora, PA
22	Mumphrey, Jerry	New York (AL)	98	6	32	.307	B-R	6-2	185	9/9/52 Tyler, TX
56	Patterson, Mike	Columbus	81	15	54	.253	L-R	5-10	190	1/26/58 Los Angeles, CA
		Oak-NY (AL)	10	0	1	.313				
14	Piniella, Lou	New York (AL)	44	5	18	.277	R-R	6-2	200	8/28/43 Tampa, FL
—	Wilborn, Ted	Nashville	164	9	86	.297	B-R	6-0	170	12/16/58 Waco, TX
31	Winfield, Dave	New York (AL)	114	13	68	.294	R-R	6-6	220	10/3/51 St. Paul, MN

YANKEE PROFILES

RICH GOSSAGE 30 6-3 217   Bats R Throws R

Still without question the most feared pitcher in baseball; the principal reason Yankees will always be contenders—as long as he's sound . . . In the final year of $2.75-million contract he signed with Yanks as a free agent in '77 . . . Born July 5, 1951, in Colorado Springs, Colo. . . . Thrives on pressure and hitters quake at facing his fastball, which is clocked regularly at 96 mph . . . Friends and foes call him "Goose" . . . Prior to coming to Yanks from Pirates' bullpen, he had been undistinguished starter with White Sox . . . Progressed through Chisox' minor-league system with Bucky Dent and they wound up in World Series together with Yanks . . . Was well on his way to eclipsing John Hiller's major-league record for saves (38 in 1977) when strike came, and still wound up with 20 in '81.

Year	Club	G	IP	W	L	Pct.	SO	BB	H	ERA
1972	Chicago (AL)	36	80	7	1	.875	57	44	72	4.28
1973	Chicago (AL)	20	50	0	4	.000	33	37	57	7.38
1974	Chicago (AL)	39	89	4	6	.400	64	47	92	4.15
1975	Chicago (AL)	62	142	9	8	.529	130	70	99	1.84
1976	Chicago (AL)	31	224	9	17	.346	135	90	214	3.94
1977	Pittsburgh	72	133	11	9	.550	151	49	78	1.62
1978	New York (AL)	63	134	10	11	.476	122	59	87	2.01
1979	New York (AL)	36	58	5	3	.625	41	19	48	2.64
1980	New York (AL)	64	99	6	2	.750	103	37	74	2.27
1981	New York (AL)	32	47	3	2	.600	48	14	22	0.77
	Totals	455	1056	64	63	.504	884	366	843	2.96

DAVE WINFIELD 30 6-6 220   Bats R Throws R

Paid big first dividends on his 10-year, $15-million contract with Yanks, leading club in RBI and providing some exceptional outfield defense . . . Made what many observers consider the greatest catch ever Sept. 25, 1981, when he climbed leftfield wall and reached nearly four rows deep with his long arms to haul in drive by Orioles' Doug DeCinces . . . Was easily Yanks' Most Valuable Player . . . Doesn't like to sit . . . Born Oct. 3, 1951—the same day Bobby Thomson hit his "Shot Heard 'Round the World" to beat Dodgers in playoff—in St. Paul, Minn. . . . Played on U. of Minnesota basketball team as well as being MVP of College Baseball World Series . . . Very active in charitable work for underprivileged youngsters

. . . Last season ended on a very disappointing note when he went 1-for-22 in World Series.

Year	Club	Pos.	G	AB	R	H	2B	3B	HR	RBI	SB	Avg.
1973	San Diego	OF-1B	56	141	9	39	4	1	3	12	0	.277
1974	San Diego	OF	145	498	57	132	18	4	20	75	9	.265
1975	San Diego	OF	143	509	74	136	20	2	15	76	23	.267
1976	San Diego	OF	137	492	81	139	26	4	13	69	26	.283
1977	San Diego	OF	157	615	104	169	29	7	25	92	16	.275
1978	San Diego	OF-1B	158	587	88	181	30	5	24	97	21	.308
1979	San Diego	OF	159	597	97	184	27	10	34	118	15	.308
1980	San Diego	OF	162	558	89	154	25	6	20	87	23	.276
1981	New York (AL)	OF	105	388	52	114	25	1	13	68	11	.294
	Totals		1222	4385	651	1248	204	40	167	694	144	.285

KEN GRIFFEY 31 5-11 200   Bats L Throws L

Just when it seemed injuries might retard his skills, veteran outfielder bounced back with strong season . . . Batted .300 in first half and only Pete Rose had more hits . . . Improved to .324 second half, including a .357 August . . . Finished sixth in NL batting race and is among active leaders with .307 lifetime average . . . Born April 19, 1950, in Donora, Pa., also birthplace of Stan Musial . . . Over .300 in five of last seven years . . . Career interrupted by knee injury in '79 . . . Has .313 average in nine playoff games . . . All-Star Game MVP in 1980 . . . Acquired from Reds for pair of minor-leaguers when it was apparent he'd be lost to free agency and signed multi-year, $1.2-million-a-year pact.

Year	Club	Pos.	G	AB	R	H	2B	3B	HR	RBI	SB	Avg.
1974	Cincinnati	OF	88	227	24	57	9	5	2	19	9	.251
1975	Cincinnati	OF	132	463	95	141	15	9	4	46	16	.305
1976	Cincinnati	OF	148	562	111	189	28	9	6	74	34	.336
1977	Cincinnati	OF	154	585	117	186	35	8	12	57	17	.318
1978	Cincinnati	OF	158	614	90	177	33	8	10	63	23	.288
1979	Cincinnati	OF	95	380	62	120	27	4	8	32	12	.316
1980	Cincinnati	OF	146	544	89	160	28	10	13	85	23	.294
1981	Cincinnati	OF	101	396	65	123	21	6	2	34	12	.311
	Totals		1047	3857	672	1186	201	60	60	424	150	.307

TOMMY JOHN 38 6-3 203   Bats R Throws R

Enjoyed another banner season in '81 despite being engulfed in tragedy for part of it when his infant son, Travis, fell out of a window and suffered serious head injuries . . . Travis recovered and John again led Yanks in complete games (7) . . . Strike may have ended any hopes he had of one day achieving 300 wins, however . . . Born May 5, 1943, in Terre Haute, Ind. . . . Possesses probably the best sinker ball in the league, though some suggest he adds a little "extra" to it . . .

"The Bionic Man" . . . His career almost ended when doctors had to transplant a tendon from his right elbow to left elbow in 1974 . . . In final year of his free-agent Yankee contract, although that was expected to be rectified before start of '82 season . . . A Steinbrenner favorite, he won support from Yankee boss when he protested being lifted for a pinch-hitter in fourth inning of final World Series game.

Year	Club	G	IP	W	L	Pct.	SO	BB	H	ERA
1963	Cleveland	6	20	0	2	.000	9	6	23	2.25
1964	Cleveland	25	94	2	9	.182	65	35	97	3.93
1965	Chicago (AL)	39	184	14	7	.667	126	58	162	3.03
1966	Chicago (AL)	34	223	14	11	.560	138	57	195	2.62
1967	Chicago (AL)	31	178	10	13	.435	110	47	143	2.48
1968	Chicago (AL)	25	177	10	5	.667	117	49	135	1.98
1969	Chicago (AL)	33	232	9	11	.450	128	90	230	3.26
1970	Chicago (AL)	37	269	12	17	.414	138	101	253	3.28
1971	Chicago (AL)	38	229	13	16	.448	131	58	244	3.62
1972	Los Angeles	29	187	11	5	.688	117	40	172	2.89
1973	Los Angeles	36	218	16	7	.696	116	50	202	3.10
1974	Los Angeles	22	153	13	3	.813	78	42	133	2.59
1975	Los Angeles					Did Not Play				
1976	Los Angeles	31	207	10	10	.500	91	61	207	3.09
1977	Los Angeles	31	220	20	7	.741	123	50	225	2.78
1978	Los Angeles	33	213	17	10	.630	124	53	230	3.30
1979	New York (AL)	37	276	21	9	.700	111	65	268	2.97
1980	New York (AL)	36	265	22	9	.710	78	56	270	3.43
1981	New York (AL)	20	140	9	8	.529	50	39	135	2.64
	Totals	543	3485	223	159	.584	1850	957	3324	3.01

JERRY MUMPHREY 29 6-2 185   Bats S Throws R

A key acquisition by the Yankees in late spring, he provided them a steady .300 bat and much-needed speed on the basepaths. Led club in hitting and stolen bases . . . Felled by an ankle injury late in the season, but it wasn't serious . . . Despite great speed, had problems defensively in Yankee Stadium's spacious center field and seemed uncertain at times . . . Yanks gave up Ruppert Jones, their previous starting center fielder, plus three prospects—Joe Lefebvre, Tim Lollar and Chris Welsh—to get him and John Pacella . . . Signed six-year, $3.9-million contract, passing up 1981 free-agent draft . . . Born Sept. 9, 1952, in Tyler, Tex.

Year	Club	Pos.	G	AB	R	H	2B	3B	HR	RBI	SB	Avg.
1974	St. Louis	OF	5	2	2	0	0	0	0	0	0	.000
1975	St. Louis	OF	11	16	2	6	2	0	0	1	0	.375
1976	St. Louis	OF	112	384	51	99	15	5	1	26	22	.258
1977	St. Louis	OF	145	463	73	133	20	10	2	38	22	.287
1978	St. Louis	OF	125	367	41	96	13	4	2	37	14	.262
1979	St. Louis	OF	124	339	53	100	10	3	3	32	8	.295
1980	San Diego	OF	160	564	61	168	24	3	4	59	52	.298
1981	New York (AL)	OF	80	319	44	98	11	5	6	32	13	.307
	Totals		762	2454	327	700	95	30	18	225	131	.285

GRAIG NETTLES 37 6-0 185   Bats L Throws L

Answered critics who questioned if he could come back from hepatitis that limited him to under 100 games in 1980 for first time since '69 . . . Won praise even from George Steinbrenner, often his sharpest critic, who said, "Nettles is one of the few guys earning his money on this club this year." That was during one of Steinbrenner's "rap sessions" and Nettles, in fact, had a typical power year, finishing third on club in RBI . . . In the field, he made his customary spectacular plays almost daily and restaked claim to being one of the great defensive third basemen in history . . . Only seven players in Yankee history have hit more homers than he has . . . Broke bone in his thumb in the World Series of '81 and was limited to just three games . . . Born Aug. 20, 1944, in San Diego . . . Had his contract extended by Steinbrenner through 1983.

Year	Club	Pos.	G	AB	R	H	2B	3B	HR	RBI	SB	Avg.
1967	Minnesota	PH	3	3	0	1	1	0	0	0	0	.333
1968	Minnesota	OF-3B-1B	22	76	13	17	2	1	5	8	0	.224
1969	Minnesota	OF-3B	96	225	27	50	9	2	7	26	1	.222
1970	Cleveland	3B-OF	157	549	81	129	13	1	26	62	3	.235
1971	Cleveland	3B	158	598	78	156	18	1	28	86	7	.261
1972	Cleveland	3B	150	557	65	141	28	0	17	70	2	.253
1973	New York (AL) . .	3B	160	552	65	129	18	0	22	81	0	.234
1974	New York (AL) . .	3B-SS	155	566	74	139	21	1	22	75	1	.246
1975	New York (AL) . .	3B	157	581	71	155	24	4	21	91	1	.267
1976	New York (AL) . .	3B	158	583	88	148	29	2	32	93	11	.254
1977	New York (AL) . .	3B	158	589	99	150	23	4	37	107	2	.255
1978	New York (AL) . .	3B-SS	159	587	81	162	23	2	27	93	1	.276
1979	New York (AL) . .	3B	145	521	71	132	15	1	20	73	1	.253
1980	New York (AL) . .	3B-SS	89	324	52	79	14	0	16	45	0	.244
1981	New York (AL) . .	3B	103	349	46	85	7	1	15	46	0	.244
	Totals		1870	6660	911	1673	245	20	295	956	30	.251

BUCKY DENT 30 5-11 182   Bats R Throws R

Although average dropped somewhat, he was enjoying one of his more productive seasons and, at one point in August, had more home runs than Reggie Jackson . . . Tore ligaments in his hand sliding into second against Chicago in late August and was through for the season . . . Yanks missed his steady hand at shortstop as he hasn't lost anything in the field . . . Born Nov. 25, 1951, in Savannah, Ga. . . . Grew up in Maimi area and signed with White Sox out of Miami Dade J.C. . . . Will always be remembered for his autumn of 1978, when his home run beat Red Sox in AL East playoff and his .417 average against Dodgers won him World Series MVP honors . . .

One deficiency is his lack of speed, but you'd never know it by the way he covers shortstop.

Year	Club	Pos.	G	AB	R	H	2B	3B	HR	RBI	SB	Avg.
1973	Chicago (AL)....	2B-3B-SS	40	117	17	29	2	0	0	10	2	.248
1974	Chicago (AL)....	SS	154	496	55	136	15	3	5	45	3	.274
1975	Chicago (AL)....	SS	157	602	52	159	29	4	3	58	2	.264
1976	Chicago (AL)....	SS	158	562	44	138	18	4	2	52	3	.246
1977	New York (AL) ..	SS	158	477	54	118	18	4	8	49	1	.247
1978	New York (AL) ..	SS	123	379	40	92	11	1	5	40	3	.243
1979	New York (AL) ..	SS	141	431	47	99	14	2	2	32	0	.230
1980	New York (AL) ..	SS	141	489	57	128	26	2	5	52	0	.262
1981	New York (AL) ..	SS	73	227	20	54	11	0	7	27	0	.238
	Totals..........		1145	3780	386	953	144	20	37	365	14	.252

RICK CERONE 27 5-11 185   Bats R Throws R

Incurred the wrath of owner George Steinbrenner by winning $440,00 salary arbitration after 1980 season, and never heard the end of it as his average took a tumble last year . . . Nevertheless, trade rumors must be discounted since he gave Yanks excellent defense behind the plate . . . Bat needs another look in season not interrupted by strike . . . Was also sidelined for a month between April and May with broken thumb . . . Born May 19, 1954, in Newark, N.J. . . . Wants to be in there every day . . . Was Indians' No. 1 draft pick in 1974 . . . Yanks got him in steal of deal with Toronto, which got Chris Chambliss then traded him away . . . Took more heat from Steinbrenner during World Series, but afterward, Yankee boss said, "I know Rick Cerone never failed to give me his all."

Year	Club	Pos.	G	AB	R	H	2B	3B	HR	RBI	SB	Avg.
1975	Cleveland.......	C	7	12	1	3	1	0	0	0	0	.250
1976	Cleveland.......	C	7	16	1	2	0	0	0	1	0	.125
1977	Toronto	C	31	100	7	20	4	1	1	10	0	.200
1978	Toronto	C	88	282	25	63	8	2	3	20	0	.223
1979	Toronto	C	136	469	47	112	27	4	7	61	1	.239
1980	New York (AL) ..	C	147	519	70	144	30	4	14	85	1	.277
1981	New York (AL) ..	C	71	234	23	57	13	2	2	21	0	.244
	Totals..........		487	1632	174	401	83	12	27	198	2	.246

WILLIE RANDOLPH 27 5-11 163   Bats R Throws R

Fell off with the bat last season, but was again among Yanks' top base-stealing threats . . . Best season was 1980, when he led AL in walks and finished second to MVP George Brett in on-base percentage with .429 . . . Solid defensively and latest in long line of all-star caliber Yank second basemen that includes Tony Lazzeri, Joe Gordon and Bobby

Richardson . . . Came over from the Pirates in 1975 deal that ranks as one of Yanks' best. He was just minor-league prospect then and they gave up pitcher Doc Medich . . . Ideal leadoff man . . . Born July 6, 1954, in Holly Hill, S.C. . . . Hopes one day to steal 50 bases. Yanks would like that, too . . . Earned a new lease on life with Yankee boss George Steinbrenner for his World Series play, in which he hit .278 with double, triple and two homers.

Year	Club	Pos.	G	AB	R	H	2B	3B	HR	RBI	SB	Avg.
1975	Pittsburgh......	2B-3B	30	61	9	10	1	0	0	3	1	.164
1976	New York (AL) ..	2B	125	430	59	115	15	4	1	40	37	.267
1977	New York (AL) ..	2B	147	551	91	151	28	11	4	40	13	.274
1978	New York (AL) ..	2B	134	499	87	139	18	6	3	42	36	.279
1979	New York (AL) ..	2B	153	574	98	155	15	13	5	61	33	.270
1980	New York (AL) ..	2B	138	513	99	151	23	7	7	46	30	.294
1981	New York (AL) ..	2B	93	357	59	83	14	3	2	24	14	.232
	Totals..........		720	2985	502	804	114	44	22	256	164	.269

RON GUIDRY 31 5-11 160   Bats L Throws L

Bothered by a bone bruise on his right foot first half of the season, but re-emerged as the best pitcher on Yanks' staff—if not in the league—the second half . . . Put together string of 20 straight scoreless innings at one point . . . Credited the development of a change-up to go with his fastball and slider as the prime reason for his regained dominance . . . Born Aug. 28, 1950, in Lafayette, La. . . . Says his toughest opponent remains George Brett . . . Owns best slider in the AL . . . Was unanimous Cy Young Award winner in 1978, when he was 25-3 with a 1.74 ERA . . . After intensive negotiations between agent John Schneider and George Steinbrenner, Guidry accepted a contract ranging from $4 to $5 million, depending on whether he pitches the next four or five seasons.

Year	Club	G	IP	W	L	Pct.	SO	BB	H	ERA
1975	New York (AL)...........	10	16	0	1	.000	15	9	15	3.38
1976	New York (AL)...........	20	16	0	0	.000	12	4	20	5.63
1977	New York (AL)...........	31	211	16	7	.696	176	65	174	2.82
1978	New York (AL)...........	35	274	25	3	.893	248	72	187	1.74
1979	New York (AL)...........	33	236	18	8	.692	201	71	203	2.78
1980	New York (AL)...........	37	220	17	10	.630	166	80	215	3.56
1981	New York (AL).........	23	127	11	5	.688	104	26	100	2.76
	Totals..................	189	1100	87	34	.719	922	327	914	2.73

DAVE RIGHETTI 23 6-3 198   Bats L Throws L

Named AL Rookie of the Year for '81 but fell just shy of enough innings to qualify for the ERA crown . . . Was the last pitcher cut in spring training, but was called up May 20 after compiling a 5-0 record and 1.00 ERA for Clippers . . . Credits Columbus pitching coach Sammy Ellis for his development. "He taught me to grow up," he says . . . Born Nov. 28, 1958, in San Jose, Calif. . . . His father, Pinky Righetti, was a minor-league shortstop in the Braves' organization . . . Yankees acquired him from Texas in deal that sent Sparky Lyle to Rangers . . . Had been scouted by Yankees' Jerry Walker, who told then-Yankee President Al Rosen: "This kid can be another Ron Guidry and if you ever have the chance to get him, do it."

Year	Club	G	IP	W	L	Pct.	SO	BB	H	ERA
1979	New York (AL)	3	17	0	1	.000	13	10	10	3.71
1981	New York (AL)	15	105	8	4	.667	89	38	75	2.06
	Totals	18	122	8	5	.615	102	48	85	2.29

DAVE COLLINS 29 5-10 175   Bats S Throws L

Ex-Red snared as free agent for three-year contract worth at least $2.5 million . . . Last year he had contrasting seasons as one of players hurt most by the strike . . . Batted .312 in first half and led league with 44 runs scored . . . Tailed off to .214 in second half . . . Player of Week, April 13-19, batting .421 . . . Batted .406 in April . . . Among fastest players in majors, but stolen bases dipped from club-record 79 in 1980 to 26 . . . Born Oct. 20, 1952, in Rapid City, S.D. . . . Failed to impress in AL stints with Angels and Mariners, but made best of opportunity with Reds as fill-in for injured Foster and Griffey and batted .318 in 1979 . . . Batted .357 in playoffs that season . . . Stole 22 bases in a row in 1980.

Year	Club	Pos.	G	AB	R	H	2B	3B	HR	RBI	SB	Avg.
1975	California	OF	93	319	41	85	13	4	3	29	24	.266
1976	California	OF	99	365	45	96	12	1	4	28	32	.263
1977	Seattle	OF	120	402	46	96	9	3	5	28	25	.239
1978	Cincinnati	OF	102	102	13	22	1	0	0	7	7	.216
1979	Cincinnati	OF-1B	122	396	59	126	16	4	3	35	16	.318
1980	Cincinnati	OF	144	551	94	167	20	4	3	35	79	.303
1981	Cincinnati	OF	95	360	63	98	18	6	3	23	26	.272
	Totals		775	2495	361	690	89	22	21	185	209	.277

TOP PROSPECTS

STEVE BALBONI 25 6-6 225   **Bats R Throws R**
Has already become a legend with his minor-league, power-hitting feats . . . Last year led International League in homers (33) and RBI (98) before getting September recall from Yanks . . . In 1980, he led Southern League in same departments with 34 HR and 122 RBI . . . Still, there is some doubt if he can hit major-league pitching consistently. Has trouble with fastball across the letters . . . Will be given shot as right-handed-hitting first baseman this spring . . . Born Jan. 16, 1957, in Brockton, Mass.

ANDY McGAFFIGAN 25 6-3 195   **Bats R Throws R**
Emerged as the best of the Yankees' young pitchers not yet traded away . . . Was 8-6 with 3.23 ERA at Columbus last year and impressed with his poise and command of pitches during September look-see . . . Faces a big challenge to crack Yankee rotation this spring, but most scouts agree he's not far away from being a bonafide major league pitcher—for someone . . . Born Oct. 25, 1956, in West Palm Beach, Fla.

MANAGER BOB LEMON: Took over the Yankee helm in mid-season for second time, this time from Gene Michael, and led them into World Series for second time . . . On this occasion, however, Yankees lost in six games to the Dodgers, whom they beat under his direction in 1978. And this time, Lemon's decision to pinch-hit for veteran Tommy John in the fourth inning of a tied Game 6 was one of several Lemon moves that were widely criticized . . . In '78, he took over for Billy Martin and led Yanks to one of the greatest comebacks in baseball history, storming back from 14 games behind the Red Sox as late as July 19 . . . An easy-going "players' manager" who had few rules . . . Hall of Fame pitcher during his playing days with Indians, he was 207-128 from 1946-58 . . . Previously managed Royals and White Sox, winning Manager of the Year honors with both clubs . . . Born Sept. 22, 1920, in San Bernardino, Calif.

GREATEST CATCHER

The No. 8 is retired by the Yankees in honor of the greatest catcher they ever had. His name is Bill Dickey/Yogi Berra. Indeed, both Dickey and Berra wore No. 8 and to honor one and not the other would be a great injustice. The fact is, both were the greatest catcher the Yankees ever had—Dickey for the '30s and '40s and Berra for the '50s and '60s. Between them, the two catchers were key contributors to 18 Yankee championship teams from 1932-63.

Dickey was first. He came up in 1928 and before he turned over the catching chores to Berra in 1946, he (1) caught 100 or more games for 13 consecutive seasons (2) drove in 100 or more runs four straight seasons; (3) was named outstanding American League catcher six times; (4) hit over .300 ten times; and (5) hit 20 or more homers four straight seasons.

Berra learned the catching trade from Dickey and took over as the Yankees' No. 1 catcher in 1947 after a year of apprenticeship. When he retired in 1963 to become the Yankee manager, his list of accomplishments were as long as Dickey's. Berra holds the AL record for most homers in a season by a catcher (30, set in '52 and '56). He also holds the AL records for putouts (8,696) and chances by a catcher lifetime (9,493). There are 12 World Series records that belong to Berra and, of course, there are those three Most Valuable Player Awards he won in '51, '54 and '55. Like Dickey, Yogi had four straight years with 100 or more RBI.

Dickey finished with a lifetime batting average of .313, 202 homers and 1,209 RBI. Berra's lifetime totals show a .285 average, 358 homers and 1,430 RBI. Any team would have loved to have either. The Yankees had both.

ALL-TIME YANKEE SEASON RECORDS

BATTING: Babe Ruth, .393, 1923
HRs: Roger Maris, 61, 1961
RBIs: Lou Gehrig, 184, 1931
STEALS: Fred Maisel, 74, 1914
WINS: Jack Chesbro, 41, 1904
STRIKEOUTS: Ron Guidry, 248, 1978

TORONTO BLUE JAYS

TEAM DIRECTORY: Chairman of the Board: R. Howard Webster; Vice Chairman: N.E. Peter Hardy; VP-Baseball Oper.: Pat Gillick; VP-Bus. Oper.: Paul Beeston; Dir. Pub. Rel.: Howard Starkman; Trav. Sec.: Ken Carson; Mgr.: Bobby Cox. Home: Exhibition Stadium (43,737). Field distances: 330, l.f. line; 375, l.c.; 400, c.f.; 375, r.c.; 330, r.f. line. Spring training: Dunedin, Fla.

SCOUTING REPORT

HITTING: The Blue Jays in 1981 established themselves as one of the worst hitting teams of all time. They were shut out 20 times and had they kept that pace over a full season, would have broken the all-time record. Their overall team batting average was .226. They scored just 329 runs in 106 games.

Worst of all, however, is the sad fact that they have made no significant changes to improve this sorry situation. Instead, the Blue Jays, who have been serving as a minor-league team for

Woeful Blue Jays got 11 wins from Dave Stieb.

their youngsters on a major-league level, are hopeful that such prospects as Lloyd Moseby (.233), Jorge Bell (.233) and Jesse Barfield (.232) will continue to show improvement in '82. It is on these young hitters that the Blue Jays and new manager Bobby Cox are pinning their hopes. Those hopes, however, are geared toward 1984 and beyond.

PITCHING: Just because the Jays finished last didn't mean nobody was interested in talking to them at the winter meetings. Talk was cheap—and it always centered around pitching, the one area in which the Blue Jays have some quality. Specifically, there is Dave Stieb, the most impressive young right-hander in the AL. Stieb somehow managed a winning record (11-10) and an ERA under 3.50 (3.18). He did it by completing 11 games and not letting the bullpen get its hand in his business.

There was some ability after Stieb, too, although No. 2 starter Jim Clancy was a major disappointment, dropping from 13-16 and 3.30 to 6-12 and 4.19. Luis Leal picked up a lot for Clancy with seven wins. Roy Lee Jackson, picked up from the Mets, was a pleasant surprise, posting a 2.61 ERA and seven saves in 39 games. The other half of the Blue Jay relief corps, Joey McLaughlin, also had an excellent year in '81 with 10 saves. Otherwise, the Jays will scramble with a pile of retreads to put together a respectable staff behind Stieb. We're talking here about people like Mark Bomback, Juan Berenguer and Nino Espinosa.

FIELDING: The Blue Jays didn't field too well in 1981, either. Here, too, they finished dead last in the American League, committing 105 errors in 106 games. Perhaps the worst culprit was shortstop Alfredo Griffin, whose stock has dropped greatly since winning Rookie-of-the-Year honors in '79. Griffin led the league in errors at shortstop for the second straight year. The situation got so bad that Blue Jay officials are thinking of shifting Griffin over to third for '82 and giving 19-year-old Tony Fernandez a chance to jump all the way from A ball to the majors. Otherwise, ex-Yankee Aurelio Rodriguez and his fine glove might replace the departed Danny Ainge at third.

OUTLOOK: Dim. The Blue Jays have no hope of escaping the cellar this year unless, miraculously, all their kids—Moseby, Bell, Barfield, etc.—blossom at once. No one expects that to happen. About the only sunlight on the horizon is the fact that the Blue Jays continue to get top picks in the free agent amateur drafts and may one day at last have a nucleus of young, homegrown talent capable of contending. By then, though, Stieb should hope he's long since been traded.

TORONTO BLUE JAYS 1982 ROSTER

MANAGER Bobby Cox
Coaches—Cito Gaston, John Sullivan, Al Widmar, Jimmy Williams

PITCHERS

No.	Name	1981 Club	W-L	IP	SO	ERA	B-T	Ht.	Wt.	Born
30	Berenguer, Juan	KC-Toronto	2-13	91	49	5.24	R-R	5-11	186	11/30/54 Panama
45	Bomback, Mark	Syracuse	1-0	9	8	3.00	R-R	5-11	170	4/14/53 Portsmouth, VA
		Toronto	5-5	90	33	3.90				
—	Choi, Dong Won	not available					R-R	5-10	175	N/A Seoul, South Korea
18	Clancy, Jim	Toronto	6-12	125	56	4.90	R-R	6-4	202	12/18/55 Chicago, IL
—	Eichhorn, Mark	Knoxville	10-14	192	99	3.98	R-R	6-3	185	11/21/60 San Jose, CA
38	Espinosa, Nino	Philadelphia	2-5	74	22	6.08	R-R	6-1	186	8/15/53 Dominican Republic
		Toronto	0-0	1	0	9.00				
36	Garvin, Jerry	Toronto	1-2	53	25	3.40	L-L	6-3	195	10/21/55 Oakland, CA
25	Jackson, Roy Lee	Toronto	1-2	62	27	2.61	R-R	6-2	195	5/1/54 Opelika, AL
48	Leal, Luis	Toronto	7-13	130	71	3.67	R-R	6-3	205	3/21/57 Venezuela
50	McLaughlin, Joey	Toronto	1-5	60	38	2.85	R-R	6-2	205	7/11/56 Tulsa, OK
33	Murray, Dale	Syracuse	5-4	78	57	1.85	R-R	6-4	205	2/2/50 Cuero, TX
		Toronto	1-0	15	12	1.20				
—	Senteney, Steve	Knoxville	10-5	106	89	3.14	R-R	6-2	205	8/7/57 Indianapolis, IN
37	Stieb, Dave	Toronto	11-10	184	89	3.18	R-R	6-1	185	7/22/57 Santa Ana, CA
40	Todd, Jackson	Toronto	2-7	98	41	3.95	R-R	6-2	190	11/20/51 Tulsa, OK

CATCHERS

No.	Name	1981 Club	H	HR	RBI	Pct.	B-T	Ht.	Wt.	Born
13	Martinez, Buck	Toronto	29	4	21	.227	R-R	5-11	200	11/7/48 Redding, CA
5	Milner, Brian	Knoxville	89	2	35	.231	R-R	6-2	200	11/17/59 Fort Worth, TX
27	Petralli, Gene	Syracuse	40	0	16	.265	B-R	6-1	180	9/25/59 Sacramento, CA
12	Whitt, Ernie	Toronto	46	1	16	.236	L-R	6-2	200	6/13/52 Detroit, MI

INFIELDERS

No.	Name	1981 Club	H	HR	RBI	Pct.	B-T	Ht.	Wt.	Born
34	Cox, Ted	Spokane	13	0	8	.149	R-R	6-3	205	1/24/53 Midwest City, OK
		Knoxville	59	11	50	.306				
		Toronto	15	2	9	.300				
7	Garcia, Damaso	Toronto	63	1	13	.252	R-R	6-0	165	2/7/57 Dominican Republic
4	Griffin, Alfredo	Toronto	81	0	21	.209	B-R	5-11	160	3/6/57 Dominican Republic
39	Hernandez, Pedro	Syracuse	67	1	28	.256	R-R	6-1	160	4/4/59 Dominican Republic
49	Hodgson, Paul	Knoxville	96	7	40	.286	R-R	6-2	190	4/14/60 Canada
8	Iorg, Garth	Toronto	52	0	10	.242	R-R	5-11	165	10/12/54 Arcata, CA
2	Manrique, Fred	Knoxville	131	5	42	.279	R-R	6-1	175	11/5/61 Venezuela
		Toronto	4	0	1	.143				
10	Mayberry, John	Toronto	72	17	43	.248	L-L	6-3	220	2/18/50 Detroit, MI
—	Rodriguez, Aurelio	New York (AL)	18	2	8	.346	R-R	5-11	175	12/28/47 Mexico
26	Upshaw, Willie	Toronto	19	4	10	.171	L-L	6-0	185	4/27/57 Blanco, TX

OUTFIELDERS

No.	Name	1981 Club	H	HR	RBI	Pct.	B-T	Ht.	Wt.	Born
29	Barfield, Jesse	Knoxville	137	16	70	.261	R-R	6-1	170	10/29/59 Joliet, IL
		Toronto	22	2	9	.232				
11	Bell, Jorge	Toronto	38	5	12	.233	R-R	6-1	190	10/21/59 Dominican Republic
9	Bonnell, Barry	Toronto	50	4	28	.220	R-R	6-3	200	10/27/53 Milford, OH
7	Moseby, Lloyd	Toronto	88	9	43	.233	L-R	6-3	200	11/5/59 Portland, AR
—	Powell, Hosken	Minnesota	63	2	25	.239	L-L	6-1	185	5/14/55 Selma, AL
—	Schroeder, Jay	Florence	85	10	47	.203	R-R	6-4	198	6/28/61 Milwaukee, WI
—	Shepherd, Ron	Kinston	114	16	66	.235	R-R	6-4	180	10/27/60 Longview, TX
19	Velez, Otto	Toronto	51	11	28	.213	R-R	6-0	195	11/29/50 Puerto Rico
—	Webster, Mitch	Knoxville	163	1	42	.294	B-L	6-1	180	5/16/59 Larned, KS
20	Woods, Al	Toronto	71	1	21	.247	L-L	6-3	200	8/8/53 Oakland, CA

BLUE JAY PROFILES

DAVE STIEB 24 6-1 185   Bats R Throws R

Had another standout season as one of the most-coveted pitchers in AL . . . Blue Jays not likely to deal him away, though. Led club in wins, complete games, shutouts, strikeouts and innings pitched. His two shutouts were the only ones turned in by the Toronto staff in '81 . . . An excellent fielding pitcher as well . . . Born July 22, 1957, in Santa Ana, Calif. . . . Was Blue Jays' fifth-round pick in June 1978 draft . . . Attended Southern Illinois U., where he also played outfield . . . Pitched and served as DH in his first season as a Blue Jay farmhand . . . Last season he became first starter in Blue Jays' history to have a winning record.

Year	Club	G	IP	W	L	Pct.	SO	BB	H	ERA
1979	Toronto	18	129	8	8	.500	52	48	139	4.33
1980	Toronto	34	243	12	15	.444	108	83	232	3.70
1981	Toronto	25	184	11	10	.524	89	61	148	3.18
	Totals	77	556	31	33	.484	249	192	519	3.67

OTTO VELEZ 31 6-0 195   Bats R Throws R

In his year of free agency, did not hit for as high an average as he probably would have preferred, but finished second on Blue Jays in home runs . . . Blue Jays took him from the Yankees in the 1976 expansion draft and he has rewarded them with five fairly productive years . . . Best season was 1980 when he hit 20 HR in 104 games . . . Born Nov. 29, 1950, in Ponce, Puerto Rico . . . Was once one of the farmhands whom Yankees refused to give A's as compensation for signing Dick Williams as their manager back in 1973 . . . In his major-league debut, went 3-for-4 against Tigers' Mickey Lolich.

Year	Club	Pos.	G	AB	R	H	2B	3B	HR	RBI	SB	Avg.
1973	New York (AL)	OF	23	77	9	15	4	0	2	7	0	.195
1974	New York (AL)	1B-OF-3B	27	67	9	14	1	1	2	10	0	.209
1975	New York (AL)	1B	6	8	0	2	0	0	0	1	0	.250
1976	New York (AL)	1B-OF-3B	49	94	11	25	6	0	2	10	0	.266
1977	Toronto	OF	120	360	50	92	19	3	16	62	4	.256
1978	Toronto	OF-1B	91	248	29	66	14	2	9	38	1	.266
1979	Toronto	OF-1B	99	274	45	79	21	0	15	48	0	.288
1980	Toronto	1B	104	357	54	96	12	3	20	62	0	.269
1981	Toronto	OF-1B	80	240	32	51	9	2	11	28	0	.213
	Totals		599	1725	239	440	86	11	77	266	5	.255

JOHN MAYBERRY 32 6-3 220   Bats L Throws L

Did not have a good average in '81, but was again Blue Jays' most productive and dangerous hitter, leading club in homers and RBI . . . Had an excellent season in '80 when he hit 30 homers and knocked in 82 runs . . . Blue Jays got him from Royals for "future considerations" in April 1978 . . . Born Feb. 18, 1950, in Detroit . . . Originally signed by the Astros, the scout being Pat Gillick, who now serves as Blue Jays' vice president . . . Royals acquired him in '71 and he played an integral part on their 1976 and '77 AL West champs . . . Would probably be even more dangerous if Blue Jays had some quality hitters to protect him.

Year	Club	Pos.	G	AB	R	H	2B	3B	HR	RBI	SB	Avg.
1968	Houston........	1B	4	9	0	0	0	0	0	0	0	.000
1969	Houston........	PH	5	4	0	0	0	0	0	0	0	.000
1970	Houston........	1B	50	148	23	32	3	2	5	14	1	.216
1971	Houston........	1B	46	137	16	25	0	1	7	14	0	.182
1972	Kansas City.....	1B	149	503	65	150	24	3	25	100	0	.298
1973	Kansas City.....	1B	152	510	87	142	20	2	26	100	3	.278
1974	Kansas City.....	1B	126	427	63	100	13	1	22	69	4	.234
1975	Kansas City.....	1B	156	554	95	161	38	1	34	106	5	.291
1976	Kansas City.....	1B	161	594	76	138	22	2	13	95	3	.232
1977	Kansas City.....	1B	153	543	73	125	22	1	23	82	1	.230
1978	Toronto	1B	152	515	51	129	15	2	22	70	1	.250
1979	Toronto	1B	137	464	61	127	22	1	21	74	1	.274
1980	Toronto	1B	149	501	62	124	19	2	30	82	0	.248
1981	Toronto	1B	94	290	34	72	6	1	17	43	1	.248
	Totals..........		1534	5199	706	1325	204	19	245	849	20	.255

JORGE BELL 22 6-1 190   Bats R Throws R

Despite modest stats in his rookie season, Jays feel he's a genuine prospect and their left fielder of the future . . . Was brought along slowly, often sitting against right-handers . . . Was drafted from the Phillies' organization in December 1980. Phils had tried to cover him up when he was placed on disabled list most of '80 with a stress fracture in his shoulder . . . Hit .305 for Phils' Spartanburg farm in '79 . . . Born Oct. 21, 1959, in San Pedro, Dominican Republic . . . Has extra-base power . . . Is one of a half-dozen Dominican players on Blue Jay roster.

Year	Club	Pos.	G	AB	R	H	2B	3B	HR	RBI	SB	Avg.
1981	Toronto	OF	60	163	19	38	2	1	5	12	3	.233

DAMASO GARCIA 25 6-0 165   Bats R Throws R

Gave Blue Jays another productive year at second base, leading club in stolen bases . . . Was acquired by them in November 1979 deal that sent Rick Cerone to the Yankees . . . In rookie season of 1980, finished second on Jays in hitting and helped club set AL record with 206 double plays . . . Born Feb. 7, 1957, in Moca, Dominican Republic . . . His idol is Rod Carew . . . Played both second and shortstop in Yankees' minor-league system . . . Cracked a bone in his right hand when hit by a pitch Aug. 21 and missed final six weeks of '81 season.

Year	Club	Pos.	G	AB	R	H	2B	3B	HR	RBI	SB	Avg.
1978	New York (AL) ..	SS-2B	18	41	5	8	0	0	0	1	1	.195
1979	New York (AL) ..	SS-3B	11	38	3	10	1	0	0	4	2	.263
1980	Toronto	2B	140	543	50	151	30	7	4	46	13	.278
1981	Toronto	2B	64	250	24	63	8	1	1	13	13	.252
	Totals..........		233	872	82	232	39	8	5	64	29	.266

JESSE BARFIELD 22 6-1 170   Bats R Throws R

Took over as Blue Jays' right fielder in September and showed promise that he would be there a long while . . . Was their No. 9 pick in June 1977 free-agent draft . . . Born Oct. 29, 1959, in Joliet, Ill. . . . Did not show a lot of hitting potential in his first three years in the minors, but Blue Jays wrote that off to inexperience and youth . . . Attended high school outside Chicago where Blue Jays discovered him . . . Sent to Florida Instructional League in 1977 and '78 . . . Hit .261 with 16 HR and 72 RBI in 141 games for Jays' Knoxville farm last year . . . Is an excellent defensive outfielder with strong throwing arm.

Year	Club	Pos.	G	AB	R	H	2B	3B	HR	RBI	SB	Avg.
1981	Toronto	OF	25	95	7	22	3	2	2	9	4	.232

ERNIE WHITT 29 6-2 200   Bats L Throws R

Has become Jays' No. 1 catcher almost by default what with the trades that have sent Alan Ashby and Rick Cerone away in recent years . . . Does not appear that he'll ever be a great hitter, but is regarded as an excellent handler of pitchers . . . Born June 13, 1952, in Detroit . . . Blue Jays took him from Red Sox in the 1976 expansion draft . . . Spent the better part of eight years in the minors before finally reaching big time to stay in '80 . . . Played first base and outfield as well in the minors.

Year	Club	Pos.	G	AB	R	H	2B	3B	HR	RBI	SB	Avg.
1976	Boston.........	C	8	18	4	4	2	0	1	3	0	.222
1977	Toronto	C	23	41	4	7	3	0	0	6	0	.171
1978	Toronto	C	2	4	0	0	0	0	0	0	0	.000
1980	Toronto	C	106	295	23	70	12	2	6	34	1	.237
1981	Toronto	C	74	195	16	46	9	0	1	16	5	.236
	Totals..........		213	553	47	127	26	2	8	59	6	.230

JIM CLANCY 26 6-4 202   Bats R Throws R

Slipped a bit from his excellent 1980 showing last year as his complete games dropped from 15 to two and his ERA increased by over a run per game . . . Blue Jays still regard him highly, though . . . Came off a pair of tendon operations in his heel in '79 to become one of Blue Jays' most reliable starters in '80, establishing a club record for strikeouts (152) as well as leading club in wins and complete games . . . Born Dec. 18, 1955, in Chicago . . . Came to Blue Jays from Texas in the 1976 expansion draft.

Year	Club	G	IP	W	L	Pct.	SO	BB	H	ERA
1977	Toronto	13	77	4	9	.308	44	47	80	5.03
1978	Toronto	31	194	10	12	.455	106	91	199	4.08
1979	Toronto	12	64	2	7	.222	33	31	65	5.48
1980	Toronto	34	251	13	16	.448	152	128	217	3.30
1981	Toronto	22	125	6	12	.333	56	64	126	4.90
	Totals...................	112	711	35	56	.385	391	361	687	4.18

LLOYD MOSEBY 22 6-3 200   Bats L Throws L

Started to show signs of becoming a quality big-league hitter last year after winning Blue Jays' center-field job . . . Led the Blue Jays in RBI and was second on the club in stolen bases . . . Was Blue Jays' No. 2 selection in June 1978 draft, with only Atlanta's Bob Horner being picked ahead of him . . . Born Nov. 5, 1959, in Portland, Ark., but grew up in Oakland, Calif., where he was a high-school baseball and basketball All-America selection . . . Started out as a catcher in Little League ball and was cut from the team. Credits his high school coach for making him a quality outfielder . . . Has four brothers and three sisters.

Year	Club	Pos.	G	AB	R	H	2B	3B	HR	RBI	SB	Avg.
1980	Toronto	OF	114	389	44	89	24	1	9	46	4	.229
1981	Toronto	OF	100	378	36	88	16	2	9	43	11	.233
	Totals..........		214	767	80	177	40	3	18	89	15	.231

ALFREDO GRIFFIN 25 5-11 160   Bats S Throws R

Was a major disappointment to Blue Jays last year, his average having declined to its lowest ebb since his rookie season of '79 . . . His two-year decline had club seriously considering trade offers for him this winter . . . Was Rookie of the Year in 1979 when he hit .287 with 21 stolen bases . . . Average was tops among AL shortstops that year . . . Began career in Cleveland farm system and was obtained by Blue Jays in December 1978 trade for reliever Victor Cruz . . . Born March 6, 1957, in Santo Domingo, Dominican Republic . . . Went to same high school as Rico Carty . . . Shared AL lead in triples in '80 with 15 . . . Had only 17 walks in 388 at-bats in '81 and committed an alarming total of 31 errors.

Year	Club	Pos.	G	AB	R	H	2B	3B	HR	RBI	SB	Avg.
1976	Cleveland.......	SS	12	4	0	1	0	0	0	0	0	.250
1977	Cleveland.......	SS	14	41	5	6	1	0	0	3	2	.146
1978	Cleveland.......	SS	5	4	1	2	1	0	0	0	0	.500
1979	Toronto	SS	153	624	81	179	22	10	2	31	20	.287
1980	Toronto	SS	155	653	63	166	26	15	2	41	18	.254
1981	Toronto	SS-3B	101	388	30	81	19	6	0	21	8	.209
	Totals..........		440	1714	180	435	69	31	4	96	48	.254

TOP PROSPECTS

TONY FERNANDEZ 19 6-1 160   Bats S Throws R

Regarded as possibly the best prospect in the Blue Jays' system. Despite his youth, Jays were prepared to give him a baptism under fire last September, but he pulled a rib muscle while at Syracuse and was through for the season . . . Hit a club-leading .318 for Blue Jays' Kinston farm last year and was promoted to Syracuse, where he hit .276 over last 31 games . . . Has excellent base-running speed . . . Born Aug. 6, 1962, in San Pedro, Dominican Republic.

GREG WELLS 27 6-6 225   Bats R Throws R

Was the leading hitter for Blue Jays' Syracuse farm last year, batting .292 with 20 HR and 71 RBI . . . Is primarily a DH, but can play first base . . . This will likely be his last look this spring, but could catch on with big club because of his bat . . . Born April 25, 1954, in McIntosh, Ala.

MANAGER BOBBY COX: Was the front-runner for the Blue

Jays' job from the very beginning because of his close ties with Toronto Director of Player Personnel Pat Gillick . . . Worked with Gillick when both were with the Yankee organization a few years back . . . Braves' owner Ted Turner refused to criticize him when he fired him last fall and, in fact, went so far to say, "Bobby would be a candidate for the job if he wasn't the guy I was firing." . . . Born May 21, 1941, in Tulsa, Okla. . . . Had a brief major-league playing career (1968-69) as a third baseman with the Yanks . . . Bad knees ended his playing days and Yanks sent him to Ft. Lauderdale in '71 to begin his managing career . . . Managed six years in Yankee farm system, winning two pennants, before Braves tapped him in 1978 . . . Coached under Billy Martin with Yanks in '77.

GREATEST CATCHER

In their five-year history, the Blue Jays have had two all-star-caliber catchers. Unfortunately, both of them are playing for other teams now and both of them reached all-star status *after* leaving Toronto.

Their names are Alan Ashby, generally believed to have the best throwing arm of any catcher in the National League, and Rick Cerone, generally regarded as being one of the best clutch hitters in the American League. Cerone and Ashby actually have a lot in common. They were both with the Indians in 1976 and they were both with the Blue Jays in '77 and '78. Coincidentally, they were both traded by the Blue Jays in the month of November, one year apart.

For their time in Toronto, however, Cerone must be given the highest points. He spent '77, '78 and '79 with the Blue Jays and, while he never hit better than .239 (in his final year), he showed enough to impress the Yankees to part with Chris Chambliss in order to get him. Ashby spent two years in Toronto, hit .210 and .261, and was traded away to the Astros for a lot less than what was secured for Cerone—pitcher Mark Lemongello, whose greatest claim to fame was his brother, a singing sensation whose career never got past TV ads.

Cerone, on the other hand, knocked in 61 runs for the lowly Blue Jays in 1979 after getting off to a bad start. He hit .261 after the All-Star break. In 1977, he was the Blue Jays' opening-day catcher (over Ashby), but broke his thumb five days into the season and didn't get his job back until '79.

ALL-TIME BLUE JAY SEASON RECORDS

BATTING: Bob Bailor, .310, 1977
HRs: John Mayberry, 30, 1980
RBIs: John Mayberry, 82, 1980
STEALS: Alfredo Griffin, 20, 1979
WINS: Dave Lemanczyk, 13, 1977
        Jim Clancy, 13, 1980
STRIKEOUTS: Jim Clancy, 152, 1980

CALIFORNIA ANGELS

TEAM DIRECTORY: Chairman of the Board-Pres.: Gene Autry; VP-GM: Buzzie Bavasi; VP-Chief Admin. Officer: Mike Port; Asst. Chairman of the Board: Red Patterson; Dir. Pub. Rel.: Tom Seeberg; Mgr.: Gene Mauch. Home: Anaheim Stadium (65,158). Field distances: 333, l.f. line; 386, l.c.; 404, c.f.; 386, r.c.; 333, r.f. line; Spring training: Casa Grande, Ariz., Palm Springs, Calif.

SCOUTING REPORT

HITTING: A lot will depend on how completely Fred Lynn comes back from off-season knee surgery. If Lynn hits the way he did in Boston, then a lot of pressure will be taken off the rest of the Angel lineup. Just the same, the Angels should not have trouble scoring runs. Bobby Grich, coming off one of his finest years in which he tied for the AL home-run lead, is the best hitting second baseman in the league. The same can be said for Rick Burleson among the shortstops. Don Baylor drove in more runs (64) than any other designated hitter. And now the Angels have added the game-breaking bat of Reggie Jackson.

The Angels also got another productive season from Disco Dan Ford (.277, 15, 48) in right field. There are some holes, though. Veteran Bob Boone, picked up from the Phillies to han-

Fred Lynn hopes to return to form he showed in Boston.

dle the bulk of the catching, is past his prime with the bat. And third base, which will be battled over by newcomer Tim Foli and holdover Butch Hobson, remains a very big question mark. One place the Angels have no problem getting base hits is first base where Rod Carew (.305) is keeping hot-shot rookie Daryl Sconiers (.354 at Salt Lake City) cooling his heels at Triple A.

PITCHING: In attempting to determine the source of the Angels' collapse last year, one really doesn't have to look much farther than the pitching staff. In an effort to rectify his colossal blunder of letting Nolan Ryan get away, Angels' general manager Buzzie Bavasi went around signing every available pitcher last year. What he wound up with was a collection of sore arms and washouts. Bill Travers came up lame, John D'Acquisto went to the minors, Jesse Jefferson and Luis Sanchez were of little help and Doug Rau showed scant hope of recovering from a rotator cuff injury. Only Ken Forsch, who emerged as the ace of the staff with 11 wins and a 2.94 ERA, and Geoff Zahn, who had his typical 10-11 season, justified Bavasi's scrambling for arms.

This year, the Angels are hoping for a further comeback from Bruce Kison as well as a possible switch from relieving to starting by Don Aase. It is still a staff in disarray and the foremost problem for Gene Mauch.

FIELDING: When healthy, the Angels could be one of the top defensive clubs in baseball. Boone behind the plate still possesses a strong throwing arm. Grich and Burleson at second and short are both former Gold Glove winners, and Lynn in center is one of the best outfielders in the business. That's strength up the middle, provided Lynn is able to play.

At the corners of the infield, the Angels have big weaknesses. Hobson was the worst defensive third baseman in the league last year and Carew has never overwhelmed anyone with his footwork and glove at first. Last year only the Blue Jays finished lower than the Angels in team defense.

OUTLOOK: They have come to call the Angels "Baseball's Bermuda Triangle" and for good reason. Nothing seems to go right for this team, which has endured enough injuries in the past three years to qualify as central casting for "General Hospital." It really has been a soap opera out there in Disneyland with Lynn, Travers, Kison, Brian Downing, etc., being struck down with serious injuries after signing for big bundles of Gene Autry's money. Only if most of them can return to form—and Jackson justifies the money they're paying him—can the Angels hope to erase their star-crossed image and reach for the stars.

CALIFORNIA ANGELS 1982 ROSTER

MANAGER Gene Mauch
Coaches—Bob Clear, Preston Gomez, Bobby Knoop, Tom Morgan, Jimmy Reese, Merv Rettenmund

PITCHERS

No.	Name	1981 Club	W-L	IP	SO	ERA	B-T	Ht.	Wt.	Born
46	Aase, Don	California	4-4	65	38	2.35	R-R	6-3	195	9/8/54 Orange, CA
—	Brown, Curt	Holyoke	5-3	66	31	1.48	R-R	6-3	170	1/15/60 Ft. Lauderdale, FL
		Redwood	1-0	9	2	6.00				
—	Brown, Steve	Salt Lake City	11-13	187	78	4.58	R-R	6-5	200	2/12/57 San Francisco, CA
—	Buckley, Brian	Redwood	9-5	87	93	3.10	R-R	6-2	210	4/23/58 Santa Monica, CA
28	D'Acquisto, John	California	0-0	19	8	10.89	R-R	6-2	195	12/25/51 San Diego, CA
		S. Lake City	5-10	92	66	8.32				
43	Forsch, Ken	California	11-7	153	55	2.94	R-R	6-4	215	9/8/46 Sacramento, CA
37	Frost, Dave	S. Lake City	1-2	23	14	8.61	R-R	6-6	235	11/17/52 Long Beach, CA
		California	1-8	47	16	5.55				
41	Hassler, Andy	California	4-3	76	44	3.20	L-L	6-5	215	10/18/51 Texas City, TX
34	Jefferson, Jesse	California	2-4	77	27	3.62	R-R	6-3	214	3/3/50 Midlothian, VA
24	Kison, Bruce	California	1-1	44	19	3.48	R-R	6-4	173	2/18/50 Pasca, WA
22	Mahler, Mickey	S. Lake City	10-4	127	63	4.96	B-L	6-3	190	7/30/52 Montgomery, AL
		California	0-0	6	5	0.00				
21	Moreno, Angel	S. Lake City	1-0	17	14	4.76	L-L	5-9	165	6/6/56 Mexico
		California	1-3	31	12	2.90				
45	Renko, Steve	California	8-4	102	50	3.44	R-R	6-6	225	12/10/44 Kansas City, KS
40	Sanchez, Luis	California	0-2	34	13	2.91	R-R	6-2	170	8/24/53 Venezuela
		S. Lake City	0-0	8	7	7.88				
26	Travers, Bill	California	0-1	10	5	8.10	L-L	6-6	200	10/27/52 Norwood, MA
—	Walters, Mike	S. Lake City	7-6	79	52	2.85	R-R	6-5	195	10/18/57 St. Louis, MO
39	Witt, Mike	California	8-9	129	75	3.28	R-R	6-7	185	8/20/60 Fullerton, CA
38	Zahn, Geoff	California	10-11	161	52	4.42	L-L	6-1	185	12/19/46 Baltimore, MD

CATCHERS

No.	Name	1981 Club	H	HR	RBI	Pct.	B-T	Ht.	Wt.	Born
—	Boone, Bob	Philadelphia	48	4	24	.211	R-R	6-2	202	11/19/47 San Diego, CA
5	Downing, Brian	California	79	9	41	.249	R-R	5-10	200	10/9/50 Los Angeles, CA
11	Ferguson, Joe	Los Angeles	2	0	1	.143	R-R	6-2	215	9/19/46 San Francisco, CA
		California	7	1	5	.233				

INFIELDERS

No.	Name	1981 Club	H	HR	RBI	Pct.	B-T	Ht.	Wt.	Born
—	Bishop, Mike	S. Lake City	129	15	91	.274	R-R	6-2	188	11/5/58 Santa Maria, CA
7	Burleson, Rick	California	126	5	33	.293	R-R	5-10	160	4/29/51 Lynwood, CA
19	Campaneris, Bert	California	21	1	10	.256	R-R	5-10	160	3/9/42 Cuba
24	Carew, Rod	California	111	2	21	.305	L-R	6-0	182	10/1/45 Panama
—	Foli, Tim	Pittsburgh	78	0	20	.247	R-R	6-0	175	12/8/50 Culver City, CA
4	Grich, Bobby	California	107	22	61	.304	R-R	6-2	190	1/15/49 Muskegon, MI
13	Harris, John	S. Lake City	15	1	11	.306	L-L	6-3	215	9/13/54 Portland, OR
		California	19	3	9	.247				
10	Hobson, Butch	California	63	4	36	.235	R-R	6-1	190	8/17/51 Tuscaloosa, AL
21	Lubratich, Steve	S. Lake City	164	13	68	.298	R-R	6-0	170	5/1/55 Oakland, CA
		California	3	0	1	.143				
—	Moreno, Jose	Hawaii	120	11	70	.305	R-L	6-0	175	11/2/57 Dominican Republic
		San Diego	11	0	6	.229				
2	Patek, Fred	California	11	0	5	.234	R-R	5-5	150	10/9/44 Oklahoma City, OK
—	Pettis, Gary	Holyoke	112	3	36	.266	B-R	6-1	155	4/3/58 Oakland, CA
6	Sconiers, Daryl	S. Lake City	145	13	74	.354	L-L	6-2	185	10/3/58 San Bernardino, CA
		California	14	1	7	.269				

OUTFIELDERS

No.	Name	1981 Club	H	HR	RBI	Pct.	B-T	Ht.	Wt.	Born
25	Baylor, Don	California	90	17	66	.239	R-R	6-1	210	6/28/49 Austin, TX
25	Beniquez, Juan	California	30	3	13	.181	R-R	5-11	165	5/13/50 Puerto Rico
30	Brunansky, Tom	California	5	3	6	.152	R-R	6-4	205	8/20/60 Covina, CA
		S. Lake City	114	22	81	.332				
32	Clark, Bobby	California	22	4	19	.250	R-R	6-0	190	6/13/55 Sacramento, CA
15	Ford, Dan	California	104	15	48	.277	R-R	6-1	185	5/19/52 Los Angeles, CA
20	Harlow, Larry	California	17	0	4	.207	L-L	6-2	176	11/13/51 Colorado Springs, CO
44	Jackson, Reggie	New York (AL)	79	15	54	.237	L-L	6-0	206	5/18/46 Wyncote, PA
8	Lynn, Fred	California	56	5	31	.219	L-L	6-1	190	2/3/52 Chicago, IL

ANGEL PROFILES

KEN FORSCH 35 6-4 215   Bats R Throws R

Proved to be one of the few productive acquisitions made by the Angels in '81, leading the team in victories, complete games, shutouts and ERA for a starter . . . Came over from Astros for infielder Dickie Thon. Astros had originally traded him to Giants, but he had right of refusal—and used it . . . Born Sept. 8, 1946, in Sacramento, Calif. . . .
Brother Bob pitches for Cards and they are the only brothers to have each pitched no-hitters in the majors . . . Was Astros' top reliever in mid-'70s, but switched to starter's role late in 1978 . . . Set Astros' club record with 70 appearances in 1974.

Year	Club	G	IP	W	L	Pct.	SO	BB	H	ERA
1970	Houston	4	24	1	2	.333	13	5	28	5.63
1971	Houston	33	188	8	8	.500	131	53	162	2.54
1972	Houston	30	156	6	8	.429	113	62	163	3.92
1973	Houston	46	201	9	12	.429	149	74	197	4.21
1974	Houston	70	103	8	7	.533	48	37	98	2.80
1975	Houston	34	109	4	8	.333	54	30	114	3.22
1976	Houston	52	92	4	3	.571	49	26	76	2.15
1977	Houston	42	86	5	8	.385	45	28	80	2.72
1978	Houston	52	133	10	6	.625	71	37	135	2.71
1979	Houston	26	178	11	6	.647	58	35	155	3.03
1980	Houston	32	222	12	13	.480	84	41	230	3.20
1981	California	20	153	11	7	.611	55	27	143	2.94
	Totals	441	1645	89	88	.503	870	455	1582	3.16

GEOFF ZAHN 35 6-1 185   Bats L Throws L

One of the few Angel free-agent pickups who earned his pay in 1981 . . . Was second on club in victories and complete games . . . Played out option with Twins and signed three-year, free-agent pact with Angels in December 1980 . . . A workhorse, he averaged 13 wins and 213 innings from 1977-80 . . . Born Dec. 19, 1946, in Baltimore . . .
Originally a Dodger, he went to the Cubs in '75 and was released a year later when his arm went bad . . . Twins signed him after a spring trial in '76 on recommendation of Gene Mauch . . . "I thank Gene Mauch for reviving my career," he says. "I'm no longer a power pitcher, but since I've learned to use more changeups, I'm more effective and consistent."

Year	Club	G	IP	W	L	Pct.	SO	BB	H	ERA
1973	Los Angeles	6	13	1	0	1.000	9	2	5	1.38
1974	Los Angeles	21	80	3	5	.375	33	16	78	2.03
1975	L.A.-Chi. (NL)	18	66	2	8	.200	22	31	69	4.64
1976	Chicago (NL)	3	8	0	1	.000	4	2	16	11.25
1977	Minnesota	34	198	12	14	.462	88	66	234	4.68
1978	Minnesota	35	252	14	14	.500	106	81	260	3.04
1979	Minnesota	26	169	13	7	.650	58	41	181	3.57
1980	Minnesota	38	233	14	18	.438	96	66	273	4.40
1981	California	25	161	10	11	.476	52	43	181	4.42
	Totals	206	1180	69	78	.469	468	348	1297	3.91

DAN FORD 29 6-1 185 — Bats R Throws R

Made excellent comeback from knee injury that required off-season surgery in '80 . . . Was third on Angels in homers and RBI . . . Came to the Angels from Twins in December 1978 for first basemen Ron Jackson and Dan Goodwin . . . Responded to change of scenery with his finest season in '79, scoring 100 runs and knocking in 101 . . . Homered in his first at-bat in each of the first two AL playoff games of '79 vs. Orioles . . . Born May 19, 1952, in Los Angeles . . . "I love pressure situations," he says. "When someone asks a lot of me, it makes me drive myself a little more." . . . Nicknamed "Disco."

Year	Club	Pos.	G	AB	R	H	2B	3B	HR	RBI	SB	Avg.
1975	Minnesota	OF	130	440	72	123	21	1	15	59	6	.280
1976	Minnesota	OF	145	514	87	137	24	7	20	86	17	.267
1977	Minnesota	OF	144	453	66	121	25	7	11	60	6	.267
1978	Minnesota	OF	151	592	78	162	36	10	11	82	7	.274
1979	California	OF	142	569	100	165	26	5	21	101	8	.290
1980	California	OF	65	226	22	63	11	0	7	25	0	.279
1981	California	OF	97	375	53	104	14	1	15	48	2	.277
	Totals		874	3169	478	875	157	31	100	462	46	.276

FRED LYNN 30 6-1 190 — Bats L Throws L

Suffered through the most frustrating year of his career last year after coming over to Angels from Red Sox in December . . . Was hampered by a bad knee, but Angels would not allow him to get it operated on until September. As a result, he hit 80 points below his career average and was blamed for the overall collapse of the Angels . . . Born Feb. 3, 1952, in Chicago . . . Has won three Gold Gloves . . . Pulled off the rarest of doubles when he won both Rookie of the Year and MVP honors in the AL in 1975 . . . Was the first rookie to ever lead the league in slugging percentage (.566) . . . Going into last year, had lifetime average of .338 with men on base . . . Had 10 RBI in a game, June 18, 1975.

Year	Club	Pos.	G	AB	R	H	2B	3B	HR	RBI	SB	Avg.
1974	Boston.........	OF	15	43	5	18	2	2	2	10	0	.419
1975	Boston.........	OF	145	528	103	175	47	7	21	105	10	.331
1976	Boston.........	OF	132	507	76	159	32	8	10	65	14	.314
1977	Boston.........	OF	129	497	81	129	29	5	18	76	2	.260
1978	Boston.........	OF	150	541	75	161	33	3	22	82	3	.298
1979	Boston.........	OF	147	531	116	177	42	1	39	122	2	.333
1980	Boston.........	OF	110	415	67	125	32	3	12	61	12	.301
1981	California.......	OF	76	256	28	56	8	1	5	31	1	.219
	Totals..........		904	3318	551	1000	225	30	129	552	44	.301

RICK BURLESON 30 5-10 160   Bats R Throws R

Was one of the Angels' few bright spots in dismal '81 season . . . Led the club in hits and was again the AL's best all-around shortstop . . . Nicknamed "Rooster" for his combative spirit on the field, he came over from Red Sox after winning his right to become free agent in a contract hassle. Angels gave up Carney Lansford, Mark Clear and Rick Miller to get him and Butch Hobson . . . Was named Most Valuable Red Sox player in both 1979 and 1980 . . . Born April 29, 1951, in Lynwood, Calif. . . . "I would like to be remembered as a winner and a guy who played this game well," he said, "but most of all I'd like to be remembered as a guy who came to play."

Year	Club	Pos.	G	AB	R	H	2B	3B	HR	RBI	SB	Avg.
1974	Boston.........	SS-2B-3B	114	384	36	109	22	0	4	44	3	.284
1975	Boston.........	SS	158	580	66	146	25	1	6	62	8	.252
1976	Boston.........	SS	152	540	75	157	27	1	7	42	14	.291
1977	Boston.........	SS	154	663	80	194	36	7	3	52	13	.293
1978	Boston.........	SS	145	626	75	155	32	5	5	49	8	.248
1979	Boston.........	SS	153	627	93	174	32	5	5	60	9	.278
1980	Boston.........	SS	155	644	89	179	29	2	8	51	12	.278
1981	California.......	SS	109	430	53	126	17	1	5	33	4	.293
	Totals..........		1140	4494	567	1240	220	22	43	393	71	.276

ROD CAREW 36 6-0 182   Bats L Throws R

Owns highest lifetime batting average of all active players . . . A seven-time American League batting champ . . . Bothered by numerous injuries last year, including a partially separated left shoulder and a concussion . . . One thing that has eluded him in his long and distinguished career is the opportunity to play in a World Series . . . Came to Angels from Twins in February 1979 for outfielders Ken Landreaux and

Dave Engle and pitcher Brad Havens. Twins, who were about to lose him to free agency, feel they got the best of the deal . . . Is active in charity work with the Multiple Sclerosis Foundation, March of Dimes and Society for the Blind . . . Born Oct. 1, 1945, in Gatun, Panama Canal Zone, but grew up in New York City.

Year	Club	Pos.	G	AB	R	H	2B	3B	HR	RBI	SB	Avg.
1967	Minnesota......	2B	137	514	66	150	22	7	8	51	5	.292
1968	Minnesota......	2B-SS	127	461	46	126	27	2	1	42	12	.273
1969	Minnesota......	2B	123	458	79	152	30	4	8	56	19	.332
1970	Minnesota......	2B-1B	51	191	27	70	12	3	4	28	4	.366
1971	Minnesota......	2B-3B	147	577	88	177	16	10	2	48	6	.307
1972	Minnesota......	2B	142	535	61	170	21	6	0	51	12	.318
1973	Minnesota......	2B	149	580	98	203	30	11	6	62	41	.350
1974	Minnesota......	2B	153	599	86	218	30	5	3	55	38	.364
1975	Minnesota......	2B-1B	143	535	89	192	24	4	14	80	35	.359
1976	Minnesota......	1B-2B	156	605	97	200	29	12	9	90	49	.331
1977	Minnesota......	1B-2B	155	616	128	239	38	16	14	100	23	.388
1978	Minnesota......	1B-2B-OF	152	564	85	188	26	10	5	70	27	.333
1979	California......	1B	110	409	78	130	15	3	3	44	18	.318
1980	California......	1B	144	540	74	179	34	7	3	59	23	.331
1981	California......	1B	93	364	57	111	17	1	2	21	16	.305
	Totals..........		1982	7548	1159	2505	371	101	82	857	328	.332

BOBBY GRICH 33 6-2 190   Bats R Throws R

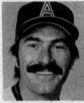

Passed up second shot at free-agent draft to re-sign with Angels, accepting four-year pact for $3.3 million in November . . . Became the first second baseman since Rogers Hornsby in 1925 to have a piece of the home run title when he finished in a four-way tie. Also had a 21-game hitting streak, longest by an Angel in '81 . . . Was second on the Angels in RBI and gamers . . . Signed originally with the Angels as a free agent in 1976 and after being sidelined much of 1977 with a herniated disc, came back to play a major role in their '79 AL West title drive with 30 HR and 101 RBI . . . Orioles were his first team and in 1973 he set major-league record for second basemen with .995 fielding percentage . . . Born Jan. 15, 1949, in Muskegon, Mich.

Year	Club	Pos.	G	AB	R	H	2B	3B	HR	RBI	SB	Avg.
1970	Baltimore.......	SS-2B-3B	30	95	11	20	1	3	0	8	1	.211
1971	Baltimore.......	SS-2B	7	30	3	9	0	0	1	6	1	.300
1972	Baltimore.......	SS-2B-1B-3B	133	460	66	128	21	3	12	50	13	.278
1973	Baltimore.......	2B	162	581	82	146	29	7	12	50	17	.251
1974	Baltimore.......	2B	160	582	92	153	29	6	19	82	17	.263
1975	Baltimore.......	2B	150	524	81	136	26	4	13	57	14	.262
1976	Baltimore.......	2B-3B	144	518	93	138	31	4	13	54	14	.266
1977	California......	SS	52	181	24	44	6	0	7	23	6	.243
1978	California......	2B	144	487	68	122	16	2	6	42	4	.251
1979	California......	2B	153	534	78	157	30	5	30	101	1	.294
1980	California......	2B-1B	150	498	60	135	22	2	14	62	3	.271
1981	California......	2B	100	352	56	107	14	2	22	61	2	.304
	Totals..........		1385	4842	719	1295	225	38	149	595	93	.267

DON BAYLOR 32 6-1 210   Bats R Throws R

Might well have been the most productive .220 hitter in baseball last year, leading the Angels in RBI and gamers . . . Is strictly a DH now despite immense pride in his outfielding . . . Always was hampered by a weak arm . . . An outspoken leader on the Angels, he once said: "I don't believe in waiting until the next day to say something. I'm a veteran and that gives me the right to say some things." . . . Is among Angels' Top 10 in nine offensive categories . . . Was overwhelming choice for AL Most Valuable Player in '79 . . . Born June 28, 1949, in Austin, Tex. . . . Active in the campaign to raise funds for Cystic Fibrosis.

Year	Club	Pos.	G	AB	R	H	2B	3B	HR	RBI	SB	Avg.
1970	Baltimore.......	OF	8	17	4	4	0	0	0	4	1	.235
1971	Baltimore.......	OF	1	2	0	0	0	0	0	1	0	.000
1972	Baltimore.......	OF-1B	102	319	33	81	13	3	11	38	24	.254
1973	Baltimore.......	OF-1B	118	405	64	116	20	4	11	51	32	.286
1974	Baltimore.......	OF-1B	137	489	66	133	22	1	10	59	29	.272
1975	Baltimore.......	OF-1B	145	524	79	148	21	6	25	76	32	.282
1976	Oakland........	OF-1B	157	595	85	147	25	1	15	68	52	.247
1977	California......	OF-1B	154	561	87	141	27	0	25	75	26	.251
1978	California......	OF-1B	158	591	103	151	26	0	34	99	22	.255
1979	California......	OF-1B	162	628	120	186	33	3	36	139	22	.296
1980	California......	OF	90	340	39	85	12	2	5	51	6	.250
1981	California......	OF	103	377	52	90	18	1	17	66	3	.239
	Totals..........		1355	4849	732	1282	217	21	189	727	249	.264

LARRY HARLOW 30 6-2 176   Bats L Throws L

Is a better hitter than his average of '81 showed—at least in the opinion of Yankees' batting coach Charlie Lau, who says: "Given the chance, Harlow could hit .300. He has all the tools." . . . May get that chance in '82 if Angel youngsters don't beat him to it . . . Born Nov. 13, 1951, in Colorado Springs, Colo. . . . Wound up playing regularly in right field at tailend of '81 season, hitting leadoff . . . Came to Angels from Orioles' organization in exchange for infielder Floyd Rayford in June '79 . . . Orioles signed him as an undrafted free agent out of the Connie Mack baseball tourney in Farmington, N.M.

Year	Club	Pos.	G	AB	R	H	2B	3B	HR	RBI	SB	Avg.
1975	Baltimore.......	OF	4	3	1	1	0	0	0	0	0	.333
1977	Baltimore.......	OF	46	48	4	10	0	1	0	0	6	.208
1978	Baltimore.......	OF	147	460	67	112	25	1	8	26	14	.243
1979	Balt.-Cal.......	OF	100	200	27	48	9	2	0	15	2	.240
1980	California......	OF-1B	109	301	47	83	13	4	4	27	3	.276
1981	California......	OF	43	82	13	17	1	0	0	4	1	.207
	Totals..........		449	1094	159	271	48	8	12	72	26	.248

REGGIE JACKSON 35 6-0 206   Bats L Throws L

Last season was a mixed bag . . . Began it on disabled list with tendon injury in his leg, then could not seem to rid his mind of contract hassle with George Steinbrenner . . . But in second half, he suddenly regained his old power —and flair for the dramatic—as evidenced by his home run and ensuing brawl with Indians' John Denny, who had decked him Sept. 23 . . . Previously had gone from May 25 to Aug. 29 without a home run . . . Born May 18, 1946, in Wyncote, Pa. . . . No. 1 goal is to achieve 500 homers and, thus, a sure ticket to the Hall of Fame . . . He begins a new life as an Angel with a $4-million, four-year contract.

Year	Club	Pos.	G	AB	R	H	2B	3B	HR	RBI	SB	Avg.
1967	Kansas City.....	OF	35	118	13	21	4	4	1	6	1	.178
1968	Oakland........	OF	154	553	82	138	13	6	29	74	14	.250
1969	Oakland........	OF	152	549	123	151	36	3	47	118	13	.275
1970	Oakland........	OF	149	426	57	101	21	2	23	66	26	.237
1971	Oakland........	OF	150	567	87	157	29	3	32	80	16	.277
1972	Oakland........	OF	135	499	72	132	25	2	25	75	9	.265
1973	Oakland........	OF	151	539	99	158	28	2	32	117	22	.293
1974	Oakland........	OF	148	506	90	146	25	1	29	93	25	.289
1975	Oakland........	OF	157	593	91	150	39	3	36	104	17	.253
1976	Baltimore.......	OF	134	498	84	138	27	2	27	91	28	.277
1977	New York (AL)..	OF	146	525	93	150	39	2	32	110	17	.286
1978	New York (AL)..	OF	139	511	82	140	13	5	27	97	14	.274
1979	New York (AL)..	OF	131	465	78	138	24	2	29	89	9	.297
1980	New York (AL)..	OF	143	514	94	154	22	4	41	111	1	.300
1981	New York (AL)..	OF	94	334	33	79	17	1	15	54	0	.237
	Totals..........		2018	7197	1178	1953	362	42	425	1285	212	.271

TOP PROSPECTS

DARYL SCONIERS 23 6-2 185   Bats L Throws L

Called up from Salt Lake City in September last year after finishing third in Pacific Coast League batting race at .354 . . . Has a good chance to stick as a back-up to Rod Carew and lefty DH . . . Won Texas League batting crown in 1980, hitting .370 . . . Born Oct. 3, 1958, in San Bernardino, Cal.

TOM BRUNANSKY 21 6-4 205   Bats R Throws R

Angels tried to rush him last year and wound up sending him back to Salt Lake City where he hit .332 with 22 homers and 81 RBI . . . May now be ready to step in to take a regular job in the outfield . . . Born Aug. 20, 1960, in Covina, Calif. . . . Was Angels' No. 1 pick in June 1978 draft and is regarded as the best all-around hitter in their farm system.

MANAGER GENE MAUCH: Has dubious record of having  managed most years without having won any kind of title: 22. Took over Angels from Jim Fregosi at midseason last year and watched them sink even further into the depths of the AL West the second half . . . Injury to Fred Lynn didn't help . . . Began '81 season as Angels' director of player personnel after resigning the year before as Twins' manager in second year of three-season pact . . . Named Manager of the Year on three occasions . . . Was a shortstop during his playing days, mostly with the Dodgers in the '40s . . . Born Nov. 18, 1925, in Salina, Kan.

GREATEST CATCHER

The best catcher ever to don the uniform of the California/LA Angels is managing in Milwaukee. Buck Rodgers spent nine seasons behind the plate in Anaheim, unfortunately most of them while the Angels were languishing near the bottom of the standings.

They were a floundering expansion franchise in 1962, searching frantically for the right pieces to make a contender. They struck it rich when they selected Rodgers from the Tiger roster in the 1960 expansion draft. Rodgers hit .258 in '62 and was a top candidate for Rookie-of-the-Year honors. With the exception of 1963, when he broke his finger, Rodgers averaged over 130 games per season for the Angels through 1967, and was always one of the club's steadiest run producers.

In the Angels' all-time top 10 lists, Rodgers ranks third in at-bats (3,033), second in games (932), sixth in runs (259), third in hits (704), third in total bases (947), third in RBI (288), and third in extra-base hits (163).

After the 1968 season, the Angels, recognizing the leadership qualities Rodgers had demonstrated as the cornerstone to their early franchise, put him to work as a manager in their minor-league system. But someone along the way forgot just how important a role he had played in the franchise's history. Otherwise, why is the best catcher the Angels ever had managing in Milwaukee?

ALL-TIME ANGEL SEASON RECORDS

BATTING: Rod Carew, .331, 1980
HRs: Leon Wagner, 37, 1962
　　　　Bobby Bonds, 37, 1977
RBIs: Don Baylor, 139, 1979
STEALS: Mickey Rivers, 70, 1975
WINS: Clyde Wright, 22, 1970
　　　　Nolan Ryan, 22, 1974
STRIKEOUTS: Nolan Ryan, 383, 1973

Rod Carew is all-time Angel batting leader.

CHICAGO WHITE SOX

TEAM DIRECTORY: Pres.: Eddie Einhorn; Chairman of the Board: Jerry Reinsdorf; VP-GM: Roland Hemond; Dir. Play. Dev.: Bobby Winkles; Dir. Pub. Rel.: Chuck Shriver; Trav. Sec.: Glen Rosenbaum; Mgr.: Tony LaRussa. Home: Comiskey Park (44,492). Field distances: 352, l.f. line; 375, l.c.; 405, c.f.; 375, r.c.; 352, r.f. line. Spring training: Sarasota, Fla.

SCOUTING REPORT

HITTING: By going after "the best available players" in the off-season trade market, the White Sox may not have strengthened themselves where they needed strengthening most, but they almost surely have improved their hitting attack. Specifically, Steve Kemp, obtained from the Tigers for Chet Lemon, gives the Chisox the left-handed power hitter they have long sought. And

Steve Kemp brings a .277 average to the Windy City.

from Seattle, the White Sox picked up Tom Paciorek, who had his finest season last year, leading the Mariners in almost every offensive category.

Along with Greg Luzinski (21 homers), Harold Baines (.286, 10 homers), Carlton Fisk and, at times, Wayne Nordhagen (.308), Paciorek and Kemp comprise one of the most potent attacks in the AL. Paciorek will play first base and Kemp will go to left field. The White Sox also got unexpected punch out of their double-play combo of Bill Almon (.301) and Tony Bernazard (.276) last year, but there is some question about their ability to do it again.

PITCHING: The White Sox pitching will probably be the most telling factor about their club this year. Most observers believe Britt Burns is on the verge of becoming the premier left-hander in the AL. There were high expectations for right-hander Richard Dotson until he inexplicably went into a second-half fizzle last season. Steve Trout, the No. 3 pitcher, has a lot of ability, but some question his mental approach.

Dennis Lamp posted the third-best ERA in the league last year (2.41) after coming over from the Cubs, but, like Almon and Bernazard, scouts want to see him do it again. The White Sox bullpen is also suspect with 38-year-old Jerry Koosman and Lamarr Hoyt (neither a flamethrower) the top two firemen on call.

FIELDING: A White Sox' weak point for over a decade now and '82 figures to be no different. Many observers felt that Almon and Bernazard played over their heads defensively and offensively last year. Almon particularly broke down in the field the latter half of the season. Similarly, Ron LeFlore, who possesses one of the weakest throwing arms in baseball, is penciled in to replace Lemon as the Chisox' center fielder. That means a lot of defensive questions right up the middle, where it usually counts the most.

OUTLOOK: The White Sox are probably the hardest team to figure in the AL West. All logic tells you they will have problems winning close games because of their spotty defense and suspect pitching. Yet, there are an abundance of quality players—gamers if you will—on this team. Fisk, Luzinski, Kemp, Paciorek and Baines pose a formidable middle of the order for opposing pitchers to deal with. Quite possibly, if Dotson and Trout can pitch up to their capabilities and the Chisox can swing a deal for a little more infield and bullpen help, they can mount a serious challenge to Oakland and Kansas City.

CHICAGO WHITE SOX 1982 ROSTER

MANAGER Tony LaRussa
Coaches—Art Kusnyer, Charlie Lau, Jim Leyland, Dave Nelson, Ron Schueler

PITCHERS

No.	Name	1981 Club	W-L	IP	SO	ERA	B-T	Ht.	Wt.	Born
50	Agosto, Juan	Edmonton	7-10	120	55	4.11	L-L	6-0	175	2/23/58 Puerto Rico
		Chicago (AL)	0-0	6	3	4.50				
52	Barnes, Richard	Edmonton	13-8	163	80	4.74	R-L	6-4	186	7/11/59 Palm Beach, FL
30	Baumgarten, Ross	Chicago (AL)	5-9	102	52	4.06	L-L	6-1	183	9/27/55 Highland Park, IL
40	Burns, Britt	Chicago (AL)	10-6	157	108	2.64	L-L	6-5	215	6/8/59 Houston, TX
43	Desjarlais, Keith	Appleton	3-6	78	50	3.12	R-R	6-3	215	7/4/59 Dearborn, MI
		Glens Falls	8-3	92	52	3.42				
49	Dotson, Richard	Chicago (AL)	9-8	141	73	3.77	R-R	6-0	185	1/10/59 Cincinnati, OH
45	Hickey, Kevin	Chicago (AL)	0-2	44	17	3.68	L-L	6-1	170	2/25/57 Chicago, IL
31	Hoyt, Lamarr	Chicago (AL)	9-3	91	60	3.56	R-R	6-1	222	1/1/59 Columbia, SC
36	Koosman, Jerry	Minn-Chi (AL)	4-13	121	76	4.02	R-L	6-2	225	12/23/43 Appleton, MN
53	Lamp, Dennis	Chicago (AL)	7-6	127	71	2.41	R-R	6-3	210	9/23/52 Los Angeles, CA
27	McGlothen, Lynn	Chicago (NL)	1-4	55	26	4.75	L-R	6-2	215	3/27/50 Monroe, LA
		Chicago (AL)	0-0	22	12	4.09				
51	Patterson, Reggie	Edmonton	10-8	136	79	3.31	R-R	6-4	180	11/7/58 Birmingham, AL
		Appleton	0-0	5	2	1.80				
		Chicago (AL)	0-1	7	2	14.14				
33	Trout, Steve	Chicago (AL)	8-7	125	54	3.46	L-L	6-4	189	7/20/57 Detroit, MI

CATCHERS

No.	Name	1981 Club	H	HR	RBI	Pct.	B-T	Ht.	Wt.	Born
72	Fisk, Carlton	Chicago (AL)	89	7	46	.263	R-R	6-2	220	12/26/47 Bellows Falls, VT
7	Hill, Marc	Chicago (AL)	0	0	0	.000	R-R	6-3	215	2/18/52 Elsberry, MO
		Glens Falls	3	0	3	.429				
18	Seilheimer, Ricky	Glens Falls	68	7	25	.259	L-R	5-11	179	7/30/60 Brenham, TX

INFIELDERS

No.	Name	1981 Club	H	HR	RBI	Pct.	B-T	Ht.	Wt.	Born
34	Almon, Bill	Chicago (AL)	105	4	41	.301	R-R	6-3	170	11/21/52 Providence, RI
14	Bernazard, Tony	Chicago (AL)	106	6	34	.276	B-R	5-9	160	8/24/56 Puerto Rico
32	Castro, Jose	Oklahoma City	123	11	76	.303	R-R	5-9	155	5/5/58 Cuba
1	Loviglio, Jay	Edmonton	138	11	57	.298	R-R	5-9	160	5/30/56 Freeport, NY
		Chicago (AL)	4	0	2	.267				
12	Morrison, Jim	Chicago (AL)	68	10	34	.234	R-R	5-11	182	9/23/52 Pensacola, FL
26	Mullins, Francis	Edmonton	59	8	28	.248	R-R	6-0	182	5/14/57 Oakland, CA
11	Pryor, Greg	Chicago (AL)	17	0	6	.224	R-R	6-0	186	10/2/49 Marietta, OH
25	Squires, Mike	Chicago (AL)	78	0	25	.265	L-L	5-11	198	3/5/52 Kalamazoo, MI
27	Walker, Greg	Glens Falls	163	22	86	.321	L-R	6-3	205	10/6/59 Douglas, GA

OUTFIELDERS

No.	Name	1981 Club	H	HR	RBI	Pct.	B-T	Ht.	Wt.	Born
3	Baines, Harold	Chicago (AL)	80	10	41	.286	L-L	6-2	175	3/15/59 Easton, MD
17	Hairston, Jerry	Mexico City	118	7	73	.296	B-R	5-10	180	2/16/52 Birmingham, AL
		Chicago (AL)	7	1	6	.280				
—	Kemp, Steve	Detroit	103	9	49	.277	L-L	6-0	190	8/7/54 San Angelo, TX
42	Kittle, Ron	Glens Falls	126	40	103	.324	R-R	6-4	200	1/5/58 Gary, IN
47	Kuntz, Rusty	Chicago (AL)	14	0	4	.255	R-R	6-3	190	2/4/55 Orange, CA
6	LeFlore, Ron	Chicago (AL)	83	0	24	.246	R-R	6-0	200	6/16/52 Detroit, MI
19	Luzinski, Greg	Chicago (AL)	100	21	62	.265	R-R	6-1	225	11/22/51 Chicago, IL
5	Molinaro, Bob	Chicago (AL)	11	1	9	.262	L-R	6-0	177	5/21/50 Newark, NJ
20	Nordhagen, Wayne	Chicago (AL)	64	6	33	.308	R-R	6-2	210	7/4/48 Thief River Falls, MN
—	Paciorek, Tom	Seattle	132	14	66	.326	R-R	6-4	210	11/2/46 Detroit, MI
48	Sutherland, Leo	Edmonton	127	1	42	.273	L-L	5-10	171	4/6/58 Cuba
		Chicago (AL)	2	0	0	.167				

WHITE SOX PROFILES

STEVE KEMP 27 6-0 190   Bats L Throws L

After winning second straight salary arbitration squabble with Tiger management last year, he fell into disfavor with Detroit fans, many of whom were laid-off auto workers . . . Showed signs of his unhappiness as power stats dropped off . . . Tigers entertained trade offers for him for the first time this winter, since he would have become a free agent after 1982, and they traded him to the White Sox for outfielder Chet Lemon . . . Was first player selected in January 1976 amateur draft after winning All-America honors at Southern California . . . A gamer who gives it his all on offense and defense . . . Holds Southern Cal batting record of .435 in his sophomore year . . . Born Aug. 7, 1954, in San Angelo, Tex.

Year	Club	Pos.	G	AB	R	H	2B	3B	HR	RBI	SB	Avg.
1977	Detroit	OF	151	552	75	142	29	4	18	88	3	.257
1978	Detroit	OF	159	582	75	161	18	4	15	79	2	.277
1979	Detroit	OF	134	490	88	156	26	3	26	105	5	.318
1980	Detroit	OF	135	508	88	149	23	3	21	101	5	.293
1981	Detroit	OF	105	372	52	103	18	4	9	49	9	.277
	Totals		684	2504	378	711	114	18	89	422	24	.284

RON LeFLORE 33 6-0 200   Bats R Throws R

Gave the White Sox the much-needed speed on the bases they were looking for when they signed him for big bucks as a free agent in November 1980 . . . Disappointed them with his overall hitting as average hovered in the .250s—40 points below his career mark—for the second straight year . . . Was a pleasant surprise defensively, making numerous big catches in left field . . . Arm is still among the weakest in baseball, though . . . Born June 16, 1948, in Detroit, but lists himself as being four years younger . . . Considered a problem player by former Expos manager Dick Williams, but had no problems with Tony LaRussa last year . . . Spent time in Southern Michigan

State Prison, where he was discovered by the Tigers in 1973 . . . Never played high school ball.

Year	Club	Pos.	G	AB	R	H	2B	3B	HR	RBI	SB	Avg.
1974	Detroit	OF	59	254	37	66	8	1	2	13	23	.260
1975	Detroit	OF	136	550	66	142	13	6	8	37	28	.258
1976	Detroit	OF	135	544	93	172	23	8	4	39	58	.316
1977	Detroit	OF	154	652	100	212	30	10	16	57	39	.325
1978	Detroit	OF	155	666	126	198	30	3	12	62	68	.297
1979	Detroit	OF	148	600	110	180	22	10	9	57	78	.300
1980	Montreal	OF	139	521	95	134	21	11	4	39	97	.257
1981	Chicago (AL)	OF	82	337	46	83	10	4	0	24	36	.246
	Totals		1008	4124	673	1187	157	53	55	328	427	.288

TOM PACIOREK 35 6-4 210   Bats R Throws R

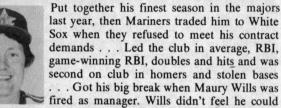

Put together his finest season in the majors last year, then Mariners traded him to White Sox when they refused to meet his contract demands . . . Led the club in average, RBI, game-winning RBI, doubles and hits and was second on club in homers and stolen bases . . . Got his big break when Maury Wills was fired as manager. Wills didn't feel he could contribute as a regular and tried to trade him to the Royals . . . Low point in his career came when Braves released him in 1978 . . . Born Nov. 2, 1946, in Detroit.

Year	Club	Pos.	G	AB	R	H	2B	3B	HR	RBI	SB	Avg.
1970	Los Angeles	OF	8	9	2	2	1	0	0	0	0	.222
1971	Los Angeles	OF	2	2	0	1	0	0	0	1	0	.500
1972	Los Angeles	OF-1B	11	47	4	12	4	0	1	6	1	.255
1973	Los Angeles	OF-1B	96	195	26	51	8	0	5	18	3	.262
1974	Los Angeles	OF-1B	85	175	23	42	8	6	1	24	1	.240
1975	Los Angeles	OF	62	145	14	28	8	0	1	5	4	.193
1976	Atlanta	OF-1B-3B	111	324	39	94	10	4	4	36	2	.290
1977	Atlanta	1B-OF-3B	72	155	20	37	8	0	3	15	1	.239
1978	Atlanta	1B	5	9	2	3	0	0	0	0	0	.333
1978	Seattle	OF-1B	70	251	32	75	20	3	4	30	2	.299
1979	Seattle	OF-1B	103	310	38	89	23	4	6	42	6	.287
1980	Seattle	OF-1B	126	418	44	114	19	1	15	59	3	.273
1981	Seattle	OF-1B	104	405	50	132	28	2	14	66	13	.326
	Totals		855	2445	294	680	137	20	54	302	36	.278

TONY BERNAZARD 25 5-9 160   Bats S Throws R

Another pleasant surprise for White Sox last season. Took over as their second baseman after being acquired in a trade with Expos . . . Was strictly a utility player with the Expos, but was an everyday performer with Chisox . . . Hits Orioles like he owns them . . . Was some question as to whether he will be the answer at second for White Sox in the long run. Hitting and defense tailed off second half and Sox also expected more speed on the basepaths from him . . . Born Aug. 24, 1956, at Caguas, P.R. . . . Signed originally by Expos in 1973.

Year	Club	Pos.	G	AB	R	H	2B	3B	HR	RBI	SB	Avg.
1979	Montreal.......	2B	22	40	11	12	2	0	1	8	1	.300
1980	Montreal.......	2B-SS	82	183	26	41	7	1	5	18	9	.224
1981	Chicago (AL)....	2B	106	384	53	106	14	4	6	34	4	.276
	Totals..........		210	607	90	159	23	5	12	60	14	.262

BILL ALMON 29 6-3 170　　　　　　Bats R Throws R

Turned out to be the biggest surprise of the 1981 season after coming to White Sox' spring camp as a virtual "walk-on" and walking off with the starting shortstop job . . . Fooled all his skeptics by maintaining .300 average all season long and doing the job defensively for Chisox . . . Was released by Mets at Christmas and contacted by White Sox general manager Roland Hemond, who lived nearby in Rhode Island. Hemond offered only a minor-league contract and a chance to make big club in spring . . . Was previously a No. 1 draft pick of Padres out of Brown University, but was beaten out for their SS job by Ozzie Smith in 1978 . . . Born Nov. 21, 1952, in Providence, R.I.

Year	Club	Pos.	G	AB	R	H	2B	3B	HR	RBI	SB	Avg.
1974	San Diego......	SS	16	38	4	12	1	0	0	3	1	.316
1975	San Diego......	SS	6	10	0	4	0	0	0	0	0	.400
1976	San Diego......	SS	14	57	6	14	3	0	1	6	3	.246
1977	San Diego......	SS	155	613	75	160	18	11	2	43	20	.261
1978	San Diego......	3B-SS-2B	138	405	39	102	19	2	0	21	17	.252
1979	San Diego......	SS-2B-OF	100	198	20	45	3	0	1	8	6	.227
1980	Mont-N.Y. (NL)..	SS-2B-3B	66	150	15	29	4	3	0	7	2	.193
1981	Chicago (AL)....	SS-3B	103	349	46	105	10	2	4	41	16	.301
	Totals..........		598	1820	205	471	58	18	8	129	65	.259

RICHARD DOTSON 23 6-0 185　　　　　Bats R Throws R

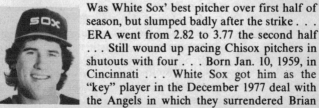

Was White Sox' best pitcher over first half of season, but slumped badly after the strike . . . ERA went from 2.82 to 3.77 the second half . . . Still wound up pacing Chisox pitchers in shutouts with four . . . Born Jan. 10, 1959, in Cincinnati . . . White Sox got him as the "key" player in the December 1977 deal with the Angels in which they surrendered Brian Downing, Chris Knapp and David Frost for Dotson and Bobby Bonds . . . Had problems with his control, but made the big breakthrough in 1980 when he mastered the changeup . . . Prefers to be called Richard . . . White Sox hoping a fresh start this year will enable him to regain the form that prompted the "Datsun Saves But Dotson Wins" posters in Comiskey Park.

Year	Club	G	IP	W	L	Pct.	SO	BB	H	ERA
1979	Chicago (AL)	5	24	2	0	1.000	13	6	28	3.75
1980	Chicago (AL)	33	198	12	10	.545	109	87	185	4.27
1981	Chicago (AL)	24	141	9	8	.529	73	49	145	3.77
	Totals	62	363	23	18	.561	195	142	358	4.04

BRITT BURNS 22 6-5 215   Bats R Throws L

Took command as ace of White Sox' staff over otherwise dismal second half for club . . . Despite death of his father, who was struck by a car just prior to resumption of season, Burns went on to pace White Sox in victories, strikeouts and complete games . . . Born June 8, 1959, in Houston . . . Was Rookie Pitcher of the Year in 1980 when he led team in wins, complete games and strikeouts and ranked third in AL in ERA . . . Must be regarded as one of the best young left-handers in baseball . . . Was discovered by a former book critic for Chicago Tribune, who read about him in the paper while passing through Birmingham, Ala., and passed the clip along to then-White Sox owner Bill Veeck.

Year	Club	G	IP	W	L	Pct.	SO	BB	H	ERA
1978	Chicago (AL)	2	8	0	2	.000	3	3	14	12.38
1979	Chicago (AL)	6	5	0	0	.000	2	1	10	5.40
1980	Chicago (AL)	34	238	15	13	.536	133	63	213	2.84
1981	Chicago (AL)	24	157	10	6	.625	108	49	139	2.64
	Totals	66	408	25	21	.543	246	116	376	2.98

CARLTON FISK 34 6-2 220   Bats R Throws R

Was White Sox' MVP over the first half of the season, then went into a puzzling slump the second half . . . Hit only two homers after the strike and average dropped nearly 40 points . . . He blamed slump on the long inactivity of the strike which caused him to lose weight while sapping his strength . . . Signed with White Sox as a free agent, March 10, 1981, after bitter contract dispute with Red Sox . . . Will forever be remembered for his dramatic homer that won Game 6 of the 1975 Red Sox-Reds World Series . . . Red Sox' Rick Miller is his brother-in-law, while Giants' punter Dave Jennings is a cousin . . . Active in the National Easter Seals program . . . Born Dec. 26, 1947, at Bellows Falls, Vt.

Year	Club	Pos.	G	AB	R	H	2B	3B	HR	RBI	SB	Avg.
1969	Boston	C	2	5	0	0	0	0	0	0	0	.000
1971	Boston	C	14	48	7	15	2	1	2	6	0	.313
1972	Boston	C	131	457	74	134	28	9	22	61	5	.293
1973	Boston	C	135	508	65	125	21	0	26	71	7	.246
1974	Boston	C	52	187	36	56	12	1	11	26	5	.299
1975	Boston	C	79	263	47	87	14	4	10	52	4	.331
1976	Boston	C	134	487	76	124	17	5	17	58	12	.255
1977	Boston	C	152	536	106	169	26	3	26	102	7	.315
1978	Boston	C-OF	157	571	94	162	39	5	20	88	7	.284
1979	Boston	C-OF	91	320	49	87	23	2	10	42	3	.272
1980	Boston	C-OF-1B-3B	131	478	73	138	25	3	18	62	11	.289
1981	Chicago (AL)	C	96	338	44	89	12	0	7	46	3	.263
	Totals		1174	4198	671	1186	219	33	169	614	64	.283

GREG LUZINSKI 31 6-1 225   Bats R Throws R

Proved to be the most valuable of all cele-
brated off-season pickups by White Sox, leading the club in homers, RBI and gamers . . .
Born Nov. 22, 1950, in Chicago . . . Spurned
free-agent draft to sign three-year,
$2.25-million contract . . . Sold to White Sox
from Phillies in the spring of '81 . . . Left
Phillies bitter, having had many run-ins with
manager Dallas Green . . . Bothered by bad knee, had lowest
average of his career in 1980, and was a virtually forgotten man
in the World Series . . . Provides $20,000 in tickets for under-
privileged kids each season . . . Has lifetime .310 average for
four NL playoffs.

Year	Club	Pos.	G	AB	R	H	2B	3B	HR	RBI	SB	Avg.
1970	Philadelphia	1B	8	12	0	2	0	0	0	0	0	.167
1971	Philadelphia	1B	28	100	13	30	8	0	3	15	2	.300
1972	Philadelphia	OF-1B	150	563	66	158	33	5	18	68	0	.281
1973	Philadelphia	OF	161	610	76	174	26	4	29	97	3	.285
1974	Philadelphia	OF	85	302	29	82	14	1	7	48	3	.272
1975	Philadelphia	OF	161	596	85	179	35	3	34	120	3	.300
1976	Philadelphia	OF	149	533	74	162	28	1	21	95	1	.304
1977	Philadelphia	OF	149	544	99	171	35	3	39	130	3	.309
1978	Philadelphia	OF	155	540	85	143	32	2	35	101	8	.265
1979	Philadelphia	OF	137	452	47	114	23	1	18	81	3	.252
1980	Philadelphia	OF	106	368	44	84	19	1	19	56	3	.228
1981	Chicago (AL)	DH	104	378	55	100	15	1	21	62	0	.265
	Totals		1393	4998	673	1399	268	22	244	873	29	.280

HAROLD BAINES 23 6-2 175   Bats L Throws L

Scouts predict he will be the White Sox'
best all-around player in the very near future . . .
Improved noticeably last year from very
promising rookie season . . . Platoons against
right-handed pitchers, but will likely hit more
and more vs. lefties, too . . . Possesses good
speed and excellent throwing arm . . . Born
March 15, 1959, at St. Michaels, Md. . . . Was

discovered by ex-White Sox owner Bill Veeck when he was playing Little League ball in the same town on Maryland's Eastern Shore that Veeck was living in . . . Veeck later insisted White Sox draft him first in 1977 June draft over Paul Molitor and Terry Kennedy.

Year	Club	Pos.	G	AB	R	H	2B	3B	HR	RBI	SB	Avg.
1980	Chicago (AL)....	OF	141	491	55	125	23	6	13	49	2	.255
1981	Chicago (AL)....	OF	82	280	42	80	11	7	10	41	6	.286
	Totals..........		223	771	97	205	34	13	23	90	8	.266

TOP PROSPECTS

RON KITTLE 24 6-4 200   Bats R Throws R
Came on as the No. 1 surprise of the White Sox farm system last year, tearing apart the Eastern League with a .324 average, 40 HR and 103 RBI, the latter two league-leading figures . . . Was Eastern League MVP . . . Reason he was surprise was that White Sox signed him in September 1978 after he had been released by Dodgers because of a neck injury . . . Will likely wind up at Triple A this year, but Chisox now regard his bat highly . . . Born Jan. 5, 1958, at Gary, Ind.

JAY LOVIGLIO 25 5-9 160   Bats R Throws R
Scrappy little infielder whom Chisox acquired from Phillies last spring for reliever Mike Proly . . . Can play second or third and White Sox will give him every opportunity to stick this spring . . . Born May 30, 1956, in Freeport, N.Y. . . . Batted .299 with 11 HR and 57 RBI for White Sox' Edmonton (PCL) farm last year and was recalled in September for a look.

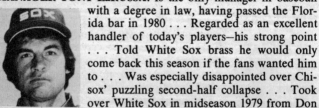

MANAGER TONY LaRUSSA: Is the only manager in baseball with a degree in law, having passed the Florida bar in 1980 . . . Regarded as an excellent handler of today's players—his strong point . . . Told White Sox brass he would only come back this season if the fans wanted him to . . . Was especially disappointed over Chisox' puzzling second-half collapse . . . Took over White Sox in midseason 1979 from Don Kessinger . . . Spent majority of his playing career with A's and was roommate of Mariner manager Rene Lachemann when both labored in A's farm system . . . Was born Oct. 4, 1944, in Tampa, Fla.

GREATEST CATCHER

The White Sox are one of the few teams in baseball to have a catcher who is a member of the Hall of Fame. His name is Ray Schalk. While he is generally reputed to be one of the best defensive catchers of his time (1912-1929), he is *not* the greatest catcher the White Sox have ever had. *That* man is Sherman Lollar who, in the same number of years (18), hit 155 homers to Schalk's 12 and drove in 808 runs to Schalk's 594. True, they belong to different eras, but somehow, Ray Schalk must have had some friends on that Veterans Committee that voted him into the Hall of Fame. If Schalk's there, Sherm Lollar surely deserves to be, too.

Schalk and Lollar have one thing in common. They caught for the only two White Sox pennant-winners in the last 62 years. Schalk caught for the ill-fated 1919 Black Sox team that threw the World Series to the Reds, and Lollar caught for the 1959 White Sox team that put the "Go Go" back into baseball. Lollar was not part of that "Go Go." He was the brawn that balanced the rabbit attack, contributing 22 home runs and 84 RBI in '59. That was the extent of the White Sox power. He remained the most dangerous long-ball bat in the Sox' attack until 1963, when he announced his retirement.

The White Sox acquired Lollar from the Browns after the 1951 season, but he got his start with the Yankees and Cleveland before that. But the Indians had Jim Hegan and the Yanks had Yogi Berra, so Sherm Lollar went on to Chicago where, despite the myth of Ray Schalk, he was able to become the greatest catcher in his team's history.

ALL-TIME WHITE SOX SEASON RECORDS

BATTING: Luke Appling, .388, 1936
HRs: Dick Allen, 37, 1972
RBIs: Zeke Bonura, 138, 1936
STEALS: Wally Moses, 56, 1943
          Luis Aparicio, 56, 1959
WINS: Ed Walsh, 40, 1908
STRIKEOUTS: Ed Walsh, 269, 1908

KANSAS CITY ROYALS

TEAM DIRECTORY: Chairman of the Board: Ewing Kauffman; Pres.: Joe Burke; Exec. VP-GM: John Schuerholz; Exec. VP-Administration: Spencer Robinson; VP-Controller: Dale Rohr; Dir. Pub. Rel.: Dean Vogelaar; Trav. Sec.: Bill Beck; Mgr.: Dick Howser. Home: Royals Stadium (40,628). Field distances: 330, l.f. line; 385, l.c.; 410, c.f.; 385, r.c.; 330, r.f. line. Spring training: Fort Myers, Fla.

SCOUTING REPORT

HITTING: You have to like the Royals' hitting attack if for no other reason than the fact they finished fourth overall in the AL last season despite admitted off seasons from George Brett, Hal McRae, Willie Wilson and U. L. Washington. Given a clean start with a new manager they apparently like playing for, the Royals figure to resemble the kind of offensive team that was the scourge of the AL in 1980. An interesting development may be the proposed shift of Brett to left field. That would free Brett from the encumbrances of third base and enable him to concentrate more on his hitting—which he does better than anyone in baseball.

Manager Dick Howser has made it plain he plans to restore the go-go in the Royals' attack and take the reins off Wilson, Frank White and Washington. Howser also figures to have a better bench this season with outfielder Jerry Martin from the Giants. An added bonus would be the development of rookie catcher Don Slaught (out last year with a broken leg). That would free John Wathan to return to the role of backup first baseman, outfielder and catcher, in which he prospered in '80.

PITCHING: The Royal pitching for 1982 will have much the same look as in previous years: Larry Gura and Dennis Leonard anchoring the starting rotation and sidearming Dan Quisenberry taking charge in the bullpen. Quisenberry recovered from the roughing up the Phillies gave him in the '80 World Series and came on strong down the stretch last year to finish with 18 saves. This year Howser hopes he'll get some help from Jeff Schattinger (8-4 with a 2.65 ERA at Omaha) and Reds' farmhand Scott Brown (6-5, 2.28 at Indianapolis).

Mike Jones, a 6-5, 226-pound left-hander, was impressive as the No. 3 starter last year, but an off-season auto accident could shelve him for the season. Jim Wright, Paul Splittorff and rookie Bill Paschall are other likely starters.

He's known for his bat, but George Brett can field, too.

FIELDING: One of the Royals' strengths in recent years has been their defense, particularly up the middle, and this season should be no different. White is a Gold Glover at second, Washington is above average at short and Amos Otis or Willie Wilson can do the job in center. One major drawback in the KC defense, though, is the catching. Wathan committed seven errors last season, but more telling was the freedom enemy base runners enjoyed with him.

OUTLOOK: The Royals did some minor tinkering over the winter, but, like the A's, they are counting on their farm system to provide the necessary improvements to get them over the top. Because there is no clear-cut favorite in the rag-tag West, the Royals have the nucleus to win it. However, their task would be made a lot easier if a couple of the rookie pitchers come through. Ditto catcher Slaught or infielder Onix Concepcion. Otherwise, the expected bat revival from Brett, base-running revival from Wilson and improved bench should keep the Royals in the fight right to the end.

KANSAS CITY ROYALS 1982 ROSTER

MANAGER Dick Howser
Coaches—Cloyd Boyer, Jose Martinez, Joe Nossek, Jim
        Schaffer, Rocky Colavito

PITCHERS

No.	Name	1981 Club	W-L	IP	SO	ERA	B-T	Ht.	Wt.	Born
—	Brown, Scott	Indianapolis	6-5	87	86	2.28	R-R	6-6	225	8/31/56 DeQuincy, LA
		Cincinnati	1-0	13	7	2.77				
28	Chamberlain, C.	Omaha	6-7	133	58	3.72	R-R	6-1	190	2/2/57 Hollywood, CA
32	Gura, Larry	Kansas City	11-8	172	61	2.72	L-L	6-1	185	11/26/47 Joliet, IL
33	Hammaker, Atlee	Omaha	11-5	146	63	3.64	B-L	6-3	200	1/24/58 Carmel, CA
		Kansas City	1-3	39	11	5.31				
40	Jones, Mike	Omaha	11-7	134	101	2.98	L-L	6-5	226	7/30/59 Rochester, NY
		Kansas City	6-3	76	29	3.20				
22	Leonard, Dennis	Kansas City	13-11	202	107	2.99	R-R	6-1	190	5/8/51 Brooklyn, NY
27	Martin, Renie	Kansas City	4-5	62	25	2.76	R-R	6-4	184	8/30/55 Dover, DE
29	Quisenberry, Dan	Kansas City	1-4	62	20	1.74	R-R	6-2	180	2/7/54 Santa Monica, CA
31	Schattinger, J.	Omaha	8-4	78	40	2.65	—	6-5	194	— Fresno, CA
34	Splittorff, Paul	Kansas City	5-5	99	48	4.36	L-L	6-3	210	10/8/46 Evansville, IN
—	Wills, Frank	Jacksonville	9-14	192	170	3.98				
35	Wright, Jim	Kansas City	2-3	52	27	3.46	R-R	6-6	220	3/3/55 St. Joseph, MO

CATCHERS

No.	Name	1981 Club	H	HR	RBI	Pct.	B-T	Ht.	Wt.	Born
—	Keatley, Greg	Omaha	57	5	21	.237				
9	Quirk, Jamie	Kansas City	25	0	10	.250	L-R	6-4	200	10/22/54 Whittier, CA
12	Wathan, John	Kansas City	76	1	19	.252	R-R	6-2	205	10/4/49 Cedar Rapids, IA

INFIELDERS

No.	Name	1981 Club	H	HR	RBI	Pct.	B-T	Ht.	Wt.	Born
24	Aikens, Willie	Kansas City	93	17	53	.266	L-R	6-2	220	10/14/54 Seneca, SC
—	Biancalana, Bud	Jacksonville	81	2	27	.210				
5	Brett, George	Kansas City	109	6	43	.314	L-R	6-0	200	5/15/53 Glendale, WV
7	Chalk, Dave	Kansas City	11	0	5	.224	R-R	5-10	170	8/30/50 Del Rio, TX
2	Concepcion, Onix	Omaha	112	6	57	.256	R-R	5-6	160	10/5/58 Dorado, PR
		Kansas City	0	0	0	.000				
51	Heath, Kelly	Omaha	93	3	37	.240	R-R	5-7	155	9/4/57 Plattsburg, NY
17	Ireland, Tim	Omaha	117	7	59	.260	R-R	6-0	180	3/14/53 Oakland, CA
		Kansas City	0	0	0	.000				
14	May, Lee	Kansas City	16	0	8	.291	R-R	6-3	225	3/23/43 Birmingham, AL
16	Phelps, Ken	Kansas City	3	0	1	.136	L-L	6-1	209	8/6/54 Seattle, WA
		Omaha	22	5	21	.333				
18	Mulliniks, Rance	Kansas City	10	0	5	.227	L-R	6-0	170	1/15/56 Tulare, CA
30	Washington, U.L.	Kansas City	77	2	29	.227	B-R	5-11	175	10/27/53 Otoka, OK
—	Wellman, Brad	Jacksonville	131	6	47	.263				
20	White, Frank	Kansas City	91	9	38	.250	R-R	5-11	170	9/4/50 Greenville, MS

OUTFIELDERS

No.	Name	1981 Club	H	HR	RBI	Pct.	B-T	Ht.	Wt.	Born
—	Brewer, Mike	Ft. Myers	132	16	84	.288				
23	Geronimo, Cesar	Kansas City	29	2	13	.246	L-L	6-2	175	3/11/48 Dominican Republic
—	Martin, Jerry	San Francisco	58	4	25	.241	R-R	6-3	195	5/11/49 Columbia, SC
11	McRae, Hal	Kansas City	106	7	36	.272	R-R	5-11	180	7/10/46 Avon Park, FL
4	Motley, Darryl	Omaha	118	18	64	.288	R-R	5-9	196	1/21/60 Muskogee, OK
		Kansas City	29	2	8	.232				
26	Otis, Amos	Kansas City	100	9	57	.269	R-R	5-11	166	4/26/47 Mobile, AL
—	Ryal, Mark	Jacksonville	121	14	69	.267				
		Omaha	4	0	1	.211				
37	Sheridan, Pat	Omaha	94	5	31	.298	L-R	6-3	175	12/4/57 Ann Arbor, MI
		Kansas City	0	0	0	.000				
6	Wilson, Willie	Kansas City	133	1	32	.303	B-R	6-3	190	7/9/55 Montgomery, AL

ROYAL PROFILES

GEORGE BRETT 28 6-0 200   Bats L Throws R

Suffered through the most frustrating season of his career last season, one year after captivating all of baseball with his assault on .400 . . . Besides being bothered by assorted nagging injuries, he became embroiled in separate fights with a local writer and a photographer, and at one time took out his frustrations by smashing up a bathroom with his bat at Metropolitan Stadium in Minnesota . . . Despite all these woes, he still wound up ninth in the AL batting race . . . Was named MVP in 1980, when he led Royals to their first AL pennant with an incredible season that had him at or above .400 nearly all year . . . His .390 equalled the highest average ever recorded by a third baseman and he also became only 17th player in history to eclipse 100-RBI plateau and average at least one RBI per game . . . Born May 15, 1953, in Glendale, W. Va.

Year	Club	Pos.	G	AB	R	H	2B	3B	HR	RBI	SB	Avg.
1973	Kansas City.....	3B	13	40	2	5	2	0	0	0	0	.125
1974	Kansas City.....	3B-SS	133	457	49	129	21	5	2	47	8	.282
1975	Kansas City.....	3B-SS	159	634	84	195	35	13	11	89	13	.308
1976	Kansas City.....	3B-SS	159	645	94	215	34	14	7	67	21	.333
1977	Kansas City.....	3B-SS	139	564	105	176	32	13	22	88	14	.312
1978	Kansas City.....	3B-SS	128	510	79	150	45	8	9	62	23	.294
1979	Kansas City.....	3B-1B	154	645	119	212	42	20	23	107	17	.329
1980	Kansas City.....	3B-1B	117	449	87	175	33	9	24	118	15	.390
1981	Kansas City.....	3B	89	347	42	109	27	7	6	43	14	.314
	Totals.........		1091	4291	661	1366	271	89	104	621	125	.318

WILLIE AIKENS 27 6-2 220   Bats L Throws R

Was about the Royals' only bonafide home run threat last year . . . Lacks range at first base and is a defensive liability at times . . . Born Oct. 14, 1954, in Seneca, S.C. . . . Was 1980 World Series hero in Royals' losing effort vs. Phillies, hammering four home runs in the six games . . . Only man ever to hit two homers in two different games of the same Series . . . Full name is Willie Mays Aikens, so named because he was born shortly after Mays' great catch in '54 World Series . . . Suffers from a speech impediment which was a detriment to him in his youth . . . Came to Royals from Angels in trade for Al

Cowens in December 1979 . . . Was Angels' No. 1 choice in January 1975 amateur draft.

Year	Club	Pos.	G	AB	R	H	2B	3B	HR	RBI	SB	Avg.
1977	California......	1B	42	91	5	18	4	0	0	6	1	.198
1979	California......	1B	116	379	59	106	18	0	11	81	1	.280
1980	Kansas City.....	1B	151	543	70	151	24	0	20	98	1	.278
1981	Kansas City.....	1B	101	349	45	93	16	0	17	53	0	.266
	Totals..........		410	1362	179	368	62	0	58	238	3	.270

LARRY GURA 34 6-1 185   Bats L Throws L

Had another outstanding year in 1981, overcoming bone chips in his finger, suffered while fielding a ball Sept. 9 . . . Showed no ill effects from that injury and wound up leading Royals' staff with 12 complete games . . . Born Nov. 26, 1947, in Joliet, Ill. . . . Was acquired by Royals from Yankees in 1976 for catcher Fran Healy and ever since has been the target of uncomplimentary remarks by his ex-manager, Billy Martin . . . Played collegiate baseball at Arizona State and was Cubs' No. 2 pick in June 1969 amateur draft . . . Was 19-1 with 1.73 ERA as a senior in college . . . Has occasionally been used in relief by Royals.

Year	Club	G	IP	W	L	Pct.	SO	BB	H	ERA
1970	Chicago (NL)............	20	38	1	3	.250	21	23	35	3.79
1971	Chicago (NL)............	6	3	0	0	.000	2	1	6	6.00
1972	Chicago (NL)............	7	12	0	0	.000	13	3	11	3.75
1973	Chicago (NL)............	21	65	2	4	.333	43	11	79	4.85
1974	New York (AL)...........	8	56	5	1	.833	17	12	54	2.41
1975	New York (AL)..........	26	151	7	8	.467	65	41	173	3.52
1976	Kansas City.............	20	63	4	0	1.000	22	20	47	2.29
1977	Kansas City.............	52	106	8	5	.615	46	28	108	3.14
1978	Kansas City.............	35	222	16	4	.800	81	60	183	2.72
1979	Kansas City.............	39	234	13	12	.520	85	73	226	4.46
1980	Kansas City.............	36	283	18	10	.643	113	76	272	2.96
1981	Kansas City.............	23	172	11	8	.579	61	35	139	2.72
	Totals..................	293	1405	85	55	.607	569	383	1333	3.29

DENNIS LEONARD 30 6-1 190   Bats R Throws R

Was Royals' top winner in 1981 for the seventh straight year . . . His 88 wins over the last five years is the highest total of any right-hander in the AL . . . Is the only Royal pitcher to post 20 or more victories in more than one season . . . Born May 8, 1951, in Brooklyn, N.Y. . . . Finished tied for third in AL last year in strikeouts . . . Had his lowest ERA as a major leaguer last season . . . Is the hardest thrower among the Royals' pitchers and mixes fastball well with a curve and slider . . . Is 3-4 in postseason pitching . . . Led the AL in starts in '78, '80 and '81 . . . Had a streak of 23 scoreless innings during 1980.

Year	Club	G	IP	W	L	Pct.	SO	BB	H	ERA
1974	Kansas City.............	5	22	0	4	.000	8	12	28	5.32
1975	Kansas City.............	32	212	15	7	.682	146	90	212	3.78
1976	Kansas City.............	35	259	17	10	.630	150	70	247	3.51
1977	Kansas City.............	38	293	20	12	.625	244	79	246	3.04
1978	Kansas City.............	40	295	21	17	.553	183	78	283	3.33
1979	Kansas City.............	32	236	14	12	.538	126	56	226	4.08
1980	Kansas City.............	38	280	20	11	.645	155	80	271	3.79
1981	Kansas City.............	26	202	13	11	.542	107	41	202	2.99
	Totals..................	246	1799	120	84	.588	1119	506	1715	3.52

JOHN WATHAN 32 6-2 205   Bats R Throws R

Suffered at the bat last year, probably because he was asked to shoulder the first-string catching load in the wake of Darrell Porter's defection and the club's refusal to find a suitable replacement . . . Wathan's strength was as a utility man who could pick his spots; Royals suffered when he was taken out of that role . . . Is below-average defensively behind the plate and opposing runners were able to take many liberties on him last year . . . Has good speed . . . Born Oct. 4, 1949, in Cedar Rapids, Iowa . . . Was Royals' No. 1 pick in the January 1971 amateur draft . . . Would likely benefit from a return to DH and utility duties.

Year	Club	Pos.	G	AB	R	H	2B	3B	HR	RBI	SB	Avg.
1976	Kansas City.....	C-1B	27	42	5	12	1	0	0	5	0	.286
1977	Kansas City.....	C-1B	55	119	18	39	5	3	2	21	2	.328
1978	Kansas City.....	1B-C	67	190	19	57	10	1	2	28	2	.300
1979	Kansas City.....	1B-C-OF	90	199	26	41	7	3	2	28	2	.206
1980	Kansas City.....	1B-OF-C	126	453	57	138	14	7	6	58	17	.305
1981	Kansas City.....	1B-OF-C	89	301	24	76	9	3	1	19	11	.252
	Totals..........		454	1304	149	363	46	17	13	159	34	.278

HAL McRAE 35 5-11 180   Bats R Throws R

Was thought to be slowing up last year, but he had a big turnaround with the bat after the Royals changed managers . . . Despite McRae's advancing age, Dick Howser said he wants and needs him in 1982 . . . Is considered one of baseball's real "gamers" . . . Born July 10, 1946, in Avon Park, Fla. . . . One of 11 children . . . Royals got him from Reds in December 1972 in four-player trade . . . Testament to his big-game ability is his lifetime .409 average for three World Series . . . Spends most of the game in clubhouse concentrating when he's the DH . . . Has had salary squabbles with Royals' brass the last couple of years.

Year	Club	Pos.	G	AB	R	H	2B	3B	HR	RBI	SB	Avg.
1968	Cincinnati	2B	17	51	1	10	1	0	0	2	1	.196
1970	Cincinnati	OF-3B-2B	70	165	18	41	6	1	8	23	0	.248
1971	Cincinnati	OF	99	337	39	89	24	2	9	34	3	.264
1972	Cincinnati	OF-3B	62	97	9	27	4	0	5	26	0	.278
1973	Kansas City	OF-3B	106	338	36	79	18	3	9	50	2	.234
1974	Kansas City	OF-3B	148	539	71	167	36	4	15	88	11	.310
1975	Kansas City	OF-3B	126	480	58	147	38	6	5	71	11	.306
1976	Kansas City	OF	149	527	75	175	34	5	8	73	22	.332
1977	Kansas City	OF	162	641	104	191	54	11	21	92	18	.298
1978	Kansas City	OF	156	623	90	170	39	5	16	72	17	.273
1979	Kansas City	DH	101	393	55	113	32	4	10	74	5	.288
1980	Kansas City	OF	124	489	73	145	39	5	14	83	10	.297
1981	Kansas City	OF	101	389	38	106	23	2	7	36	3	.272
	Totals		1420	5069	667	1460	348	48	127	722	103	.288

DAN QUISENBERRY 28 6-2 180   Bats R Throws R

Began last season much like he ended 1980 in the World Series—being hit hard and regularly . . . But got his act together and finished with the third-highest save total in the league (18) . . . His ERA was the lowest of his big-league career . . . The Royals' resident flake, he is seldom without a funny line or quip for quote-hungry reporters . . . Born Feb. 7, 1954, in Santa Monica, Calif. . . . Throws submarine style, like Pittsburgh's Kent Tekulve . . . Gets his outs through ground balls, not strikeouts . . . Signed by Royals in 1975 as an undrafted amateur free agent . . . Threw overhand until late in his college career . . . Learned a lot from Tekulve, "especially to keep my body down and my weight on my back foot."

Year	Club	G	IP	W	L	Pct.	SO	BB	H	ERA
1979	Kansas City	32	40	3	2	.600	13	7	42	3.15
1980	Kansas City	75	128	12	7	.632	37	27	129	3.09
1981	Kansas City	40	62	1	4	.200	20	15	59	1.74
	Totals	147	230	16	13	.552	70	49	230	2.74

AMOS OTIS 34 5-11 166   Bats R Throws R

Was eligible to become a free agent after last season, but surprised many by electing to stay with Royals on a new two-year, $1.27-million contract . . . "I might have gotten more money elsewhere," he said, "but I really didn't want to leave here." . . . May yet have to switch to left to make room for the faster Willie Wilson in center . . . His 16 stolen bases were second only to Wilson on the Royals last year . . . Born April 26, 1947, in Mobile, Ala. . . . Royals obtained him from the Mets in 1969 for third baseman Joe Foy . . . His desire has been questioned frequently in his career, but he's been among the most consistent run producers for KC . . . Sign that he's not through was his RBI total last season as compared to 1980.

Year	Club	Pos.	G	AB	R	H	2B	3B	HR	RBI	SB	Avg.
1967	New York (NL)..	OF-3B	19	59	6	13	2	0	0	1	0	.220
1969	New York (NL)..	OF-3B	48	93	6	14	3	1	0	4	1	.151
1970	Kansas City.....	OF	159	620	91	176	36	9	11	58	33	.284
1971	Kansas City.....	OF	147	555	80	167	26	4	15	79	52	.301
1972	Kansas City.....	OF	143	540	75	158	28	2	11	54	28	.293
1973	Kansas City.....	OF	148	583	89	175	21	4	26	93	13	.300
1974	Kansas City.....	OF	146	552	87	157	31	9	12	73	18	.284
1975	Kansas City.....	OF	132	470	87	116	26	6	9	46	39	.247
1976	Kansas City.....	OF	153	592	93	165	40	2	18	86	26	.279
1977	Kansas City.....	OF	142	478	85	120	20	8	17	78	23	.251
1978	Kansas City.....	OF	141	486	74	145	30	7	22	96	32	.298
1979	Kansas City.....	OF	151	577	100	170	28	2	18	90	30	.295
1980	Kansas City.....	OF	107	394	56	99	16	3	10	53	16	.251
1981	Kansas City.....	OF	99	372	49	100	22	3	9	57	16	.269
	Totals..........		1735	6371	978	1775	329	60	178	868	327	.279

U. L. WASHINGTON 28 5-11 175   Bats S Throws R

Like many of the Royals last year, he tailed off dramatically from his 1980 stats . . . Never quite got his bat untracked despite discarding his famous toothpick early in the year . . . Has good speed and is a better-than-average shortstop . . . Born Oct. 27, 1953, in Otoka, Oklahoma . . . Like his keystone mate, Frank White, he got his start with Royals in their ill-fated academy . . . Became a switch-hitter in 1975 while at Omaha . . . Played both baseball and basketball in high school and attended Murray State one year . . . Strikes out a lot more than you would expect from a contact hitter of his caliber . . . Assumed role of KC's everyday shortstop in 1980.

Year	Club	Pos.	G	AB	R	H	2B	3B	HR	RBI	SB	Avg.
1977	Kansas City.....	SS	10	20	0	4	1	1	0	1	1	.200
1978	Kansas City.....	SS-2B	69	129	10	34	2	1	0	9	12	.264
1979	Kansas City.....	SS-2B-3B	101	268	32	68	12	5	2	25	10	.254
1980	Kansas City.....	SS	153	549	79	150	16	11	6	53	20	.273
1981	Kansas City.....	SS	98	339	40	77	19	1	2	29	10	.227
	Totals..........		431	1305	161	333	50	19	10	117	53	.255

FRANK WHITE 31 5-11 170   Bats R Throws R

Remains the defensive hub of the Royals' infield, a perennial Gold Glover who has superior range and arm . . . Discovered by Royals in a tryout and is the first graduate from their ill-fated baseball academy . . . Born Sept. 4, 1950, in Greenville, Miss. . . . Had a rather surprising dropoff in stolen bases last year, but still has excellent speed . . . Didn't play baseball in high school because there was no team . . . Has appeared in two All-Star Games . . . Holds Royals' club record of 62 consecutive games without an error at second base . . . Missed a month of 1979 season with broken hand, but still recorded career highs for homers, doubles and runs.

Year	Club	Pos.	G	AB	R	H	2B	3B	HR	RBI	SB	Avg.
1973	Kansas City.....	SS-2B	51	139	20	31	6	1	0	5	3	.223
1974	Kansas City.....	2B-SS-3B	99	204	19	45	6	3	1	18	3	.221
1975	Kansas City.....	2B-3B-SS-C	111	304	43	76	10	2	7	36	11	.250
1976	Kansas City.....	2B-SS	152	446	39	102	17	6	2	46	20	.229
1977	Kansas City.....	2B-SS	152	474	59	116	21	5	5	50	23	.245
1978	Kansas City.....	2B	143	461	66	127	24	6	7	50	13	.275
1979	Kansas City.....	2B	127	467	73	124	26	4	10	48	28	.266
1980	Kansas City.....	2B	154	560	70	148	22	5	7	60	19	.264
1981	Kansas City.....	2B	94	364	35	91	17	1	9	38	4	.250
	Totals.........		1083	3419	424	860	149	33	48	351	124	.252

TOP PROSPECTS

JEFF SCHATTINGER 26 6-5 194   Bats L Throws R
Compiled an 8-4 record at Omaha last year with a 2.65 ERA and 23 saves . . . Has good chance to stick as a backup to Quisenberry in the bullpen . . . Signed by Royals in January 1979 after a collegiate career at U. of California . . . Was originally a starter, but was converted to relief once he turned pro . . . Born Oct. 25, 1955, in Fresno, Calif.

SCOTT BROWN 25 6-6 225   Bats R Throws R
Became a Royal in trade that sent Clint Hurdle to the Reds . . . Was 6-5 with a 2.28 ERA at Indianapolis and 1-0 with 2.77 in 10 games with the Reds . . . Born Aug. 31, 1956, in DeQuincy, La.

MANAGER DICK HOWSER: Took over Kansas City reins from Jim Frey in September and guided club to AL West second-half title . . . In his first season as a big-league manager, he piloted Yankees to AL East flag in 1980 with 103 wins, only to be fired when club lost three straight to Royals in playoffs . . . Born May 14, 1937, in Miami, Fla. . . . Compiled lifetime average of .248 in eight big-league seasons as a second baseman-shortstop for A's, Indians and Yankees . . . Before assuming reins as Yankee manager in 1980, he was club's third-base coach from 1969-78 . . . Coached one year at Florida State, compiling 43-17-1 record.

GREATEST CATCHER

For the Kansas City Royals, the best catcher in the franchise's history is the one who got away—Darrell Porter. It is hard to deny the "greatest catcher" tag to the guy who brought them into their only World Series.

Actually Porter had his best year in 1979, when he hit .291 for the Royals and knocked in 112 runs, a club record for catchers and the second-best RBI total in the team's history. The Royals acquired Porter from the Brewers after the 1976 season in hopes of coming up with the "missing link" that would take them that extra yard to the American League pennant. When they failed to get by the Yankees in the AL Championship Series of '77 and '78, it wasn't Porter's fault. He hit .333 in the '77 playoffs and .357 in the '78 encounter.

In '79, the year the Royals didn't win the AL West, Porter had his finest year in baseball and his manager, Whitey Herzog, said Porter should have been voted the AL's Most Valuable Player. It was no surprise then that, when Herzog went over to the Cardinals, one of his first transactions was to sign free agent Darrell Porter to a five-year megabuck contract. No fool, Herzog knew he was getting the best catcher he'd ever managed.

ALL-TIME ROYAL SEASON RECORDS

BATTING: George Brett, .390, 1980
HRs: John Mayberry, 34, 1975
RBIs: George Brett, 118, 1980
STEALS: Willie Wilson, 83, 1979
WINS: Steve Busby, 22, 1974
STRIKEOUTS: Dennis Leonard, 244, 1977

MINNESOTA TWINS

TEAM DIRECTORY: Chairman of the Board-Pres.: Calvin Griffith; VP-Asst. Treas.: Thelma Griffith Hayes; VP-Sec. Treas.: Clark Griffith; VP: Bruce Haynes; VP: James Robertson; VP: George Brophy; VP-Trav. Sec.: Howard T. Fox, Jr.; Dir. Pub. Rel.: Tom Mee; Mgr.: Billy Gardner. Home: Hubert H. Humphrey Metrodome (54,000). Field distances: 346, l.f. line; 400, c.f.; 326, r.f. line. Spring training: Orlando, Fla.

SCOUTING REPORT

HITTING: You can't really judge the Twins by what they hit last year (.240), 13th in the American League. Only the Blue Jays had a lower average and only the Indians hit fewer home runs. Specifically because of that offensive futility, the Twins plan to embark on a youth movement in 1982. As a result, youngsters Kent Hrbek (first base), Lenny Faedo (shortstop), Gary Gaetti (third base) and possibly Mark Funderburk (outfield) and Tim Laudner (catcher) will be given a chance to prove their worth.

Manager Billy Gardner was particularly impressed with Hrbek and Gaetti at the end of last season, and the Twins made serious efforts to trade two of their previous offensive threats,

John Castino comes back from back surgery.

Roy Smalley and Butch Wynegar, over the winter. But even if the rookie crop comes through, the Twins do not figure to hit many home runs in their new home under the Metrodome. Smalley, who was bothered by a bad back most of the second half, led the Twins in homers last year with seven.

PITCHING: The Minnesota pitching, like its hitting, ranked next-to-last in the AL last year. There are no aces here where Roger Erickson (3-8, 3.86), Fernando Arroyo (7-10, 3.94), Pete Redfern (9-8, 4.06), Al Williams (6-10, 4.08) and Brad Havens (3-6, 3.58) comprise the starting rotation. Of the five, Havens showed the most long-range promise last year. Fortunately, there is Doug Corbett (2.56, 17 saves), the top-rated relief pitcher in the AL, manning the bullpen. The Twins, for the third straight year, also are gambling on help from the minor-league draft. This time it's Paul Boris, a 26-year-old Rutgers graduate who was 10-6 at Columbus in '81.

FIELDING: One reason the Twins want to give a full shot to Faedo and Gaetti is that they feel it will tighten up their defense. Smalley, who has never had much range at short, will serve mostly as a DH in '82 unless he's traded. John Castino, who underwent back surgery over the winter, will move from third to second if recovered in time for spring training. Possibly because they are concerned about Laudner's defensive ability behind the plate, the Twins were asking a lot for Wynegar, a sound defensive receiver. Another defensive problem is where to play Mickey Hatcher. The Twins still hold out hope he'll develop into a good major-league hitter, but they were not satisfied with him as a center fielder. That's where they had their biggest need going into spring training.

OUTLOOK: The Twins will either be one of the most exciting and interesting teams in the AL this year or one of the absolute worst. It all depends on the kids. There are times when you could see as many as six rookies on the field at the same time for the Twins. It may be asking a little too much, however, to expect Faedo, Gaetti, Hrbek, Laudner, Boris and Funderburk to all make the grade together. If just a couple of them do, the Twins should be satisfied.

This is a club that has always kept a steady stream of talent coming up through the farm system. It appears they are once again on the rise—through their own means. The Twins will probably finish in the middle of the pack, but keep an eye on them for awhile anyway.

MINNESOTA TWINS 1982 ROSTER

MANAGER Billy Gardner
Coaches—Karl Kuehl, Jim Lemon, Johnny Podres, Rick
       Stelmaszek

PITCHERS

No.	Name	1981 Club	W-L	IP	SO	ERA	B-T	Ht.	Wt.	Born
—	Arrington, Sam	Visalia	12-7	168	98	3.64	R-R	6-5	225	2/11/61 —
30	Arroyo, Fernando	Minnesota	7-10	128	39	3.94	R-R	6-2	190	3/21/52 Sacramento, CA
—	Boris, Paul	Columbus	10-6	131	102	3.37	R-R	6-2	200	12/13/55 Irvington, NJ
34	Cooper, Don	Minnesota	1-5	59	33	4.27	R-R	6-1	177	2/15/57 New York, NY
23	Corbett, Doug	Minnesota	2-6	88	60	2.56	R-R	6-1	185	11/4/52 Sarasota, FL
19	Erickson, Roger	Minnesota	3-8	91	44	3.86	R-R	6-3	190	8/30/56 Springfield, IL
—	Everett, Smokey	Wis. Rapids	5-2	45	63	1.40	L-R	5-10	185	9/14/57 —
37	Felton, Terry	Toledo	7-11	131	99	4.19	R-R	6-2	185	10/29/57 Texarkana, TX
		Minnesota	0-0	1	1	54.00				
39	Havens, Brad	Orlando	6-2	74	58	3.53	L-L	6-1	180	11/17/59 Highland Park, MI
		Minnesota	3-6	78	43	3.58				
—	Hobbs, Jack	Orlando	11-7	139	116	4.08	L-L	6-2	190	11/11/56 —
		Minnesota	0-0	6	1	3.00				
—	Hodge, Eddie	Toledo	8-17	163	84	4.53	L-L	6-2	185	4/19/58 —
31	Jackson, Darrell	Toledo	0-0	8	6	2.25	L-L	5-10	151	4/3/56 Los Angeles, CA
		Minnesota	3-3	33	26	4.36				
33	O'Connor, Jack	Minnesota	3-2	35	16	5.91	L-L	6-3	203	6/2/58 Yucca Valley, CA
17	Redfern, Pete	Minnesota	9-8	142	77	4.06	R-R	6-2	190	8/25/54 Glendale, CA
20	Veselic, Bob	Toledo	11-11	171	94	4.16	R-R	6-0	182	9/27/55 Pittsburgh, PA
		Minnesota	1-1	23	13	3.13				
28	Williams, Al	Minnesota	6-10	150	76	4.08	R-R	6-4	190	5/7/54 Nicaragua

CATCHERS

No.	Name	1981 Club	H	HR	RBI	Pct.	B-T	Ht.	Wt.	Born
—	Austin, Rick	Visalia	116	5	57	.297	R-R	5-11	185	8/5/59 —
11	Butera, Sal	Minnesota	40	0	18	.240	R-R	6-0	189	9/25/52 Richmond Hill, NY
—	Laudner, Tim	Orlando	123	42	104	.284	R-R	6-3	212	6/7/58 —
		Minnesota	7	2	5	.163				
48	Smith, Ray	Minnesota	8	1	1	.200	R-R	6-1	185	9/18/55 Glendale, CA
16	Wynegar, Butch	Minnesota	37	0	10	.247	B-R	6-0	195	3/14/56 York, PA

INFIELDERS

No.	Name	1981 Club	H	HR	RBI	Pct.	B-T	Ht.	Wt.	Born
2	Castino, John	Minnesota	102	6	36	.268	R-R	5-11	175	10/23/54 Evanston, IL
—	Corcoran, Tim	Evansville	100	8	63	.298	L-L	5-11	175	3/19/53 Glendale, CA
		Minnesota	9	0	4	.176				
21	Faedo, Lenny	Char-Toledo	87	7	44	.250	R-R	6-0	170	5/13/60 Tampa, FL
		Minnesota	8	0	6	.195				
—	Gaetti, Gary	Orlando	137	30	93	.277	R-R	6-0	180	8/19/58 —
		Minnesota	5	2	3	.192				
25	Goodwin, Danny	Minnesota	34	2	17	.225	L-R	6-1	209	9/2/53 St. Louis, MO
—	Hrbek, Kent	Visalia	175	27	111	.379	L-R	6-4	200	5/21/60 —
		Minnesota	16	1	7	.239				
—	Mesa, Ivan	Glens Falls	109	3	24	.236	R-R	6-0	175	5/4/61 —
5	Smalley, Roy	Minnesota	44	7	22	.263	B-R	6-1	190	10/25/52 Los Angeles, CA
1	Vega, Jesus	Tol-Tide.	99	6	35	.258	R-R	6-1	190	10/14/55 Puerto Rico
50	Washington, Ron	Toledo	157	15	55"	.289	R-R	5-11	160	4/29/52 New Orleans, LA
		Minnesota	19	0	5	.226				
7	Wilfong, Rob	Minnesota	75	3	19	.246	L-R	6-1	185	9/1/53 Pasadena, CA

OUTFIELDERS

No.	Name	1981 Club	H	HR	RBI	Pct.	B-T	Ht.	Wt.	Born
—	Bush, Randy	Orlando	140	22	94	.290	L-L	6-1	190	10/5/58 —
—	Douglas, Steve	Orlando	151	7	54	.294	R-R	5-11	180	1/17/57 —
51	Engle, Dave	Minnesota	64	5	32	.258	R-R	6-3	210	11/30/56 San Diego, CA
52	Funderburk, Mark	Toledo	88	18	52	.223	R-R	6-4	226	5/16/57 Charlotte, NC
		Minnesota	3	0	2	.200				
—	Hatcher, Mickey	Minnesota	96	3	37	.255	R-R	6-2	195	3/15/55 Cleveland, OH
—	Johnson, Randy	Glens Falls	102	32	98	.255	L-L	6-2	189	8/15/58 —
32	Ward, Gary	Minnesota	78	3	29	.264	R-R	6-2	207	12/6/53 Los Angeles, CA

TWIN PROFILES

GARY WARD 28 6-2 207   Bats R Throws R

Was one of the Twins' most pleasant surprises
of '81, leading the club in hitting his rookie
season . . . Figures to be their left fielder for
a long time to come . . . Born Dec. 6, 1953, in
Los Angeles . . . First caught Twins' attention
in September 1980, when he came up from
Toledo and hit .463 with 10 RBI over the
Twins' final 13 games . . . Was sent to the
Venezuelan Winter League to further his development and it
paid off last year . . . Twins feel he can be an 85-100 RBI producer over a full season . . . On Sept. 18, 1980, he became only the
sixth Twin ever to hit for the cycle . . . Combines excellent
speed with a strong throwing arm in the outfield.

Year	Club	Pos.	G	AB	R	H	2B	3B	HR	RBI	SB	Avg.
1979	Minnesota......	DH	10	14	2	4	0	0	0	1	0	.286
1980	Minnesota......	OF	13	41	11	19	6	2	1	10	0	.463
1981	Minnesota......	OF	85	295	42	78	7	6	3	29	5	.264
	Totals..........		108	350	55	101	13	8	4	40	5	.289

ROB WILFONG 28 6-1 185   Bats L Throws R

Though he faced a fight for his second-base
job this spring, Twins concede they need his
lefty bat in their predominantly right-handed
lineup . . . Does not hit left-handed pitching
well, but will play the majority of the Twins'
games at 2B this year, especially if John Castino can't come back from spinal disc surgery
. . . Best year was 1979 when he hit .313 . . .
In 1980, he set a league record for fielding percentage by a second baseman, .9948 . . . Born Sept. 1, 1953, in Pasadena, Calif.
. . . An excellent bunter . . . Younger brother, Jim, was once an
outfielder in Tigers' system.

Year	Club	Pos.	G	AB	R	H	2B	3B	HR	RBI	SB	Avg.
1977	Minnesota......	2B	73	171	22	42	1	1	1	13	10	.246
1978	Minnesota......	2B	92	199	23	53	8	0	1	11	8	.266
1979	Minnesota......	2B-OF	140	419	71	131	22	6	9	59	11	.313
1980	Minnesota......	2B-OF	131	416	55	103	16	5	8	45	10	.248
1981	Minnesota......	2B-OF	93	305	32	75	11	3	3	19	2	.246
	Totals..........		529	1510	203	404	58	15	22	147	41	.268

MICKEY HATCHER 27 6-2 195   Bats R Throws R

About as fierce a competitor as you will find. Problem is, Twins can't decide where to play him . . . Did a creditable job as their center fielder in '81, but will likely wind up as DH this year . . . A consistent .300 hitter in his three minor-league seasons in the Dodger chain, and Twins feel he will hit more this year with a full season under his belt . . . Born March 15, 1955, in Cleveland . . . Was a third baseman with the Dodgers, but couldn't beat out Ron Cey, prompting trade to Twins for Ken Landreaux . . . Won the Pacific Coast League batting title with .371 average for Albuquerque in '79 . . . Led the Twins in RBI and doubles last year . . . Played college baseball at Oklahoma and was also a wide receiver/punter for Sooner football team.

Year	Club	Pos.	G	AB	R	H	2B	3B	HR	RBI	SB	Avg.
1979	Los Angeles.....	3B-OF	33	93	9	25	4	1	1	5	1	.269
1980	Los Angeles.....	OF-3B	57	84	4	19	2	0	1	5	0	.226
1981	Minnesota......	OF-3B	99	377	36	96	23	2	3	37	3	.255
	Totals..........		189	554	49	140	29	3	5	47	4	.253

AL WILLIAMS 27 6-4 190   Bats R Throws R

Overcame a slow start to emerge as Twins' most dependable starter in the "second season" of '81 . . . Led club in strikeouts and complete games . . . Born May 7, 1954, in Pearl Lagoon, Nicaragua . . . Originally signed by Pirates but was released after two seasons in their minor-league system when Nicaraguan government would not grant him a visa to play for the 1977 season . . . That prompted him to join guerrilla forces in Nicaragua and he spent next 16 months engaged in jungle fighting against the forces of Anastasio Somoza . . . Got back into baseball in 1979 and was strikeout leader of the Inter-American League where he caught the eyes of Twins' scouts . . . Never threw a baseball until he was 17 years old . . . Earliest ambition was to be a rodeo rider.

Year	Club	G	IP	W	L	Pct.	SO	BB	H	ERA
1980	Minnesota...............	18	77	6	2	.750	35	30	73	3.51
1981	Minnesota...............	23	150	6	10	.375	76	52	160	4.08
	Totals..................	41	227	12	12	.500	111	82	232	3.89

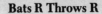

DOUG CORBETT 29 6-1 185   Bats R Throws R

Had a second straight banner season, finishing fourth in AL in saves . . . Can't judge his effectiveness by his won-lost record . . . Appeared in twice as many games as any other Twins' hurler . . . Born Nov. 14, 1952, in Sarasota, Fla. . . . Spent five years buried in the Reds' minor-league system until rescued by Twins in the winter draft of 1979 . . . Twins claimed him for $25,000, one of the best bargains ever . . . Rarely blows a lead and has the ability to get batters out via the ground ball or the strikeout . . . Has been a reliever all through his career and pitched college ball at U. of Florida . . . Only once, in his first year, has he ever had an ERA of over 3.00 as a professional.

Year	Club	G	IP	W	L	Pct.	SO	BB	H	ERA
1980	Minnesota	73	136	8	6	.571	89	42	102	1.99
1981	Minnesota	54	88	2	6	.250	60	34	80	2.56
	Totals	127	224	10	12	.455	149	76	182	2.21

BUTCH WYNEGAR 26 6-0 195   Bats S Throws R

Began 1981 season on the disabled list after undergoing surgery for bone chips in his right elbow and was not activated until May 16 . . . Was on disabled list again in August with a shoulder injury . . . Was overall a very disappointing season—especially after he had signed the longest (five years) contract ever offered by the Twins the previous winter . . . Twins' owner Calvin Griffith talked about trading him in September, but conceded there was no catcher in Twins' system who could match his defensive abilities . . . Had a solid 39 percent success ratio of throwing out base runners prior to injury-plagued '81 season . . . Had previously been the most durable catcher in baseball, averaging over 140 games per season . . . Born March 14, 1956, in York, Pa. . . . Began switch-hitting at age nine to imitate his idol, Mickey Mantle.

Year	Club	Pos.	G	AB	R	H	2B	3B	HR	RBI	SB	Avg.
1976	Minnesota	C	149	534	58	139	21	2	10	69	0	.260
1977	Minnesota	C-3B	144	532	76	139	22	3	10	79	2	.261
1978	Minnesota	C-3B	135	454	36	104	22	1	4	45	1	.229
1979	Minnesota	C	149	504	74	136	20	0	7	57	2	.270
1980	Minnesota	C	146	486	61	124	18	3	5	57	3	.255
1981	Minnesota	C	47	150	11	37	5	0	0	10	0	.247
	Totals		770	2660	316	679	108	9	36	317	8	.255

ROGER ERICKSON 25 6-3 190   Bats R Throws R

Slumped a bit after "comeback" season in 1980 . . . Had only one complete game . . . In '80, he had seven complete games, but lost five of them . . . Born Aug. 30, 1956, in Springfield, Ill. . . . Underwent elbow surgery after 1979 season . . . Twins' catcher Butch Wynegar reported in '80 that Erickson had lost none of the zip on his fastball . . . As his ERA indicated again last year, he is still the victim of little support from his light-hitting mates . . . Made big jump from Class AA ball to Twins in 1978 after just one season in minor leagues.

Year	Club	G	IP	W	L	Pct.	SO	BB	H	ERA
1978	Minnesota	37	266	14	13	.519	121	79	268	3.96
1979	Minnesota	24	123	3	10	.231	47	48	154	5.63
1980	Minnesota	32	191	7	13	.350	97	56	198	3.25
1981	Minnesota	14	91	3	8	.273	44	31	93	3.86
	Totals	107	671	27	44	.380	309	214	713	4.05

DAVE ENGLE 25 6-3 210   Bats R Throws R

Despite low average as a rookie last year, Twins are confident Engle is their right fielder of the future . . . Was a consistent high-average hitter in his three previous years in minors, winning the International League batting title in 1980 at Toledo . . . Played third base his first two minor-league seasons, but was switched to right field because of his excellent throwing arm . . . Born Nov. 30, 1956, in San Diego . . . Came over to Twins as part of the Rod Carew trade with the Angels in 1978 after having been Angels' No. 2 pick in the June draft that year . . . Played collegiate ball at Southern Cal. . . . Twins would like to see a little more power from his bat considering his size.

Year	Club	Pos.	G	AB	R	H	2B	3B	HR	RBI	SB	Avg.
1981	Minnesota	OF	82	248	29	64	14	4	5	32	0	.258

JOHN CASTINO 27 5-11 175   Bats R Throws R

Tailed off with the bat in '81 after outstanding freshman and sophomore seasons, but was bothered by a bad back through much of "second season" and underwent spinal fusion operation . . . Twins plan to move him to second this year, (if healthy) to make room for rookie Gary Gaeti at third . . . Healthy, Castino must still be regarded among the best defensive infielders in baseball . . . Born Oct. 23, 1954, in Evanston, Ill. . . . A hustler with a feisty, combative nature on the field . . . Shared Rookie-of-the Year honors in 1979 . . . Played college ball at Rollins in Florida . . . Was Twins' third pick in the June 1976 free-agent draft . . . Made jump from AA ball to the Twins after just two-and-a-half years of minor-league experience.

Year	Club	Pos.	G	AB	R	H	2B	3B	HR	RBI	SB	Avg.
1979	Minnesota	3B-SS	148	393	49	112	13	8	5	52	5	.285
1980	Minnesota	3B-SS	150	546	67	165	17	7	13	64	7	.302
1981	Minnesota	3B-SS	101	381	41	102	13	9	6	36	4	.268
	Totals		399	1320	157	379	43	24	24	152	16	.287

ROY SMALLEY 29 6-1 190   Bats S Throws R

Was a major disappointment to Twins last year after signing four-year, $2.4-million contract—the largest ever given out by Calvin Griffith . . . In Smalley's defense, he was bothered by a bad back during second season and was second on Twins in game-winning hits . . . Born Oct. 25, 1952, in Los Angeles . . . Is Gene Mauch's nephew and had his best years playing for "Unc" in 1978 and '79 . . . Oversized for a shortstop and consensus is beginning to form that he is better suited for third base . . . Does not possess great range although he did set an AL record for assists with 572 in 1979 . . . Was the No. 1 pick of the January 1974 free-agent draft—by Texas . . . His father, Roy Sr., was a shortstop with the Cubs and Phillies.

Year	Club	Pos.	G	AB	R	H	2B	3B	HR	RBI	SB	Avg.
1975	Texas	SS-2B-C	78	250	22	57	8	0	3	33	4	.228
1976	Texas-Minnesota	SS-2B	144	513	61	133	18	3	3	44	2	.259
1977	Minnesota	SS	150	584	93	135	21	5	6	56	5	.231
1978	Minnesota	SS	158	586	80	160	31	3	19	77	2	.273
1979	Minnesota	SS-1B	162	621	94	168	28	3	24	95	2	.271
1980	Minnesota	SS-1B	133	486	64	135	24	1	12	63	3	.278
1981	Minnesota	SS	56	167	24	44	7	1	7	22	0	.263
	Totals		881	3207	438	832	137	16	74	390	18	.259

TOP PROSPECTS

KENT HRBEK 21 6-4 200   Bats L Throws L

Recalled by Twins from Class A ball in August and, in his very first big-league game, hit a home run to beat Yankees . . . Was MVP of the California League in '81, hitting a league-leading .379 for Visalia with 27 HR and 111 RBI in 121 games . . . Signed by Twins in '78, but missed most of '79 season with a knee injury . . . Born May 21, 1960, in Minneapolis, he grew up just a few miles from Metropolitan Stadium . . . Has good chance to stick as Twins' first baseman in '82.

LENNY FAEDO 21 6-0 170　　　　　　　　**Bats R Throws R**
Came up at end of last season and impressed with his defense, pesky hitting and speed on the basepaths until cut down by injury . . . Shortstop job is his until he loses it . . . Hit .250 at Toledo last year with seven HR and 44 RBI . . . Was Twins' No. 1 pick in the June 1978 draft out of Tampa's Jefferson H.S., where he once hit four consecutive home runs and was walked intentionally with bases loaded to force in tying run . . . Born May 13, 1960, in Tampa, Fla.

MANAGER BILLY GARDNER: Took over Twins' pilot's job from Johnny Goryl at midseason last year and was rewarded with a contract extension through 1982 . . . Twins responded to his firm but enthusiastic approach and remained in contention for AL West "second season" flag until final week of season . . . Elected to go with youngsters the second half of the season . . . Was Twins' third-base coach prior to being named manager . . . A second baseman in his playing days, he hit .237 in 10 big-league seasons with Giants, Orioles, Twins, Yankees and Red Sox . . . Coached two seasons with Boston, then embarked on a managerial career in the minors. Won five pennants in 12 minor-league seasons as a manager and was named Manager of the Year three times . . . Born July 19, 1927, in New London, Conn.

GREATEST CATCHER

One important question in assessing the best catcher in a club's history is "Who was behind the plate in the years the club won?" The Twins have won only one American League pennant since coming to Minnesota—in 1965—and the catcher on that club was Earl Battey. He hit .297 that season and knocked in 60 runs. In the World Series against the Dodgers that fall, Battey had a homer and two RBI, but there was some doubt on the Twins' part that he was playing at full strength after suffering a severely bruised neck when he crashed into the roof of the dugout pursuing a foul ball hit by Willie Davis in Game 3.

The fact is, few, if any, clubs have ever won a pennant without a good man behind the plate. In '65, the Twins had Battey. They obtained him prior to the 1960 season from the White Sox in exchange for one of their greatest slugging stars, Roy Sievers. It was a deal they never regretted as Battey served the next seven seasons as the Twins' first-string catcher, hitting .270, .302, .280, .285, .272, .297 and .255. In that same time, he was also a three-time recipient of the Gold Glove for defensive excellence and was chosen to four all-star teams.

Battey also hit in double figures for homers five times, reaching a one-season high of 26 in 1963. Coming to the Twins was the best thing that ever happened to him in baseball. When he was with the White Sox, he was playing behind Sherm Lollar, *their* greatest catcher.

ALL-TIME TWIN SEASON RECORDS

BATTING: Rod Carew, .388, 1977
HRs: Harmon Killebrew, 49, 1964, 1969
RBIs: Harmon Killebrew, 140, 1969
STEALS: Rod Carew, 49, 1976
WINS: Jim Kaat, 25, 1966
STRIKEOUTS: Bert Blyleven, 258, 1973

OAKLAND A's

TEAM DIRECTORY: Pres.: Roy Eisenhardt; Exec. VP: Wally Haas; VP: Carl Finley; Dir. Minor League Operations: Walt Jocketty; Dir. Publ.-Trav. Sec.: Mickey Morabito; Mgr.: Billy Martin. Home: Oakland Coliseum (50,000). Field distances: 330, l.f. line; 375, l.c.; 400, c.f.; 375, r.c.; 330, r.f. line. Spring training: Scottsdale, Ariz.

SCOUTING REPORT

HITTING: The A's do not overwhelm you with their hitting attack—especially when you get past their gifted outfield. But as per the style of all Billy Martin teams, they bear the mark of opportunists. Best example of that is Dwayne Murphy, who hit just .251 last year, but led the league with 15 game-winning RBI. The A's outfield was surely a versatile one on offense. Tony Armas tied for the league lead in homers (22) and was second in RBI (72). Rickey Henderson, on the other hand, led the league in runs (89), hits (135) and stolen bases (56). Henderson and Murphy combined to rank fourth and second, respectively in walks.

The rest of the A's lineup did not contribute nearly as much as the outfield last year, although Cliff Johnson proved to be a most valuable off-season pickup, ranking sixth among designated hitters with a .273 average, 14 homers and 53 RBI. Martin hopes to get some added production from rookie first baseman Kelvin Moore (.327, 31 homers and 109 RBI at Tacoma). The A's major weakness continues to be their infield where second baseman Dave McKay, shortstop Rob Picciolo and third baseman Wayne Gross were all found wanting last year, particularly on offense. Martin will take a long look at shortstop Jimmy Sexton, an ex-Astro and Pirate. Sexton seemed to at last find his niche in the Pacific Coast League last season when he hit .319 and stole 56 bases. Dan Meyer and Joe Rudi, obtained over the winter, bolster the A's bench.

PITCHING: Just like their starting lineup, the A's pitching staff must be divided into two parts: good and bad. The starters are second to none in the AL and helped the staff rank second overall in ERA. Steve McCatty won the ERA title (2.32) and was second in the Cy Young voting with his 14-7 mark. Rick Langford led the AL in complete games (18) for the second straight year, and Mike Norris (12-9) is still considered the A's ace. Throw in Matt Keough (10-6) and Brian Kingman (who most scouts still feel has the best stuff on the staff) and the A's almost don't need a bullpen. Which is fortunate since they don't have one.

Martin is banking on Dave Beard, a 6-5 fireballer who was 11-11 at Tacoma, to master his control and emerge as the missing link in the bullpen. Martin likens Beard's fastball to that of Goose Gossage.

FIELDING: Once again, you have to divide the A's in half. Taking their better half first, the Oakland outfield is second to none defensively. Henderson and Murphy each won Gold Gloves last year and Armas, whose throwing arm is on a par with anyone's, could have won one, too. The infield, however, is weak. Martin liked to say how his shortstops, Picciolo and Chicken Stanley committed only eight errors all year last season. He does not tell you how many balls they never got to. The A's also ranked last in the AL in double plays.

OUTLOOK: The Athletics failed to bolster themselves in the critical middle-infield positions over the winter. They similarly did little to strengthen their bullpen. Martin is gambling that Tacoma graduates Beard, Moore and Sexton will provide enough help to keep the A's on top. He may be right, since the Royals and Rangers didn't make any significant off-season changes, either. Indeed, the formula of solid starting pitching, speed, power and defense from the outfield, plus an occasional pop from Cliff Johnson in the DH role, may well be enough to again bring Martin's A's home first.

A's Rickey Henderson narrowly missed winning MVP honors.

OAKLAND A'S 1982 ROSTER

MANAGER Billy Martin
Coaches—Clete Boyer, Art Fowler, Charlie Metro, George
Mitterwald, Jackie Moore

PITCHERS

No.	Name	1981 Club	W-L	IP	SO	ERA	B-T	Ht.	Wt.	Born
—	Atherton, Keith	West Haven	11-13	175	116	3.60	R-R	6-3	190	2/19/59 Mathews, VA
33	Beard, Dave	Tacoma	11-11	129	114	4.26	L-R	6-5	190	10/2/59 Atlanta, GA
		Oakland	1-1	13	15	2.77				
38	Jones, Jeff	Oakland	4-1	61	43	3.39	R-R	6-3	210	7/29/56 Detroit, MI
27	Keough, Matt	Oakland	10-6	140	60	3.41	R-R	6-2	175	7/3/55 Pomona, CA
50	Kingman, Brian	Oakland	3-6	100	52	3.96	R-R	6-1	190	7/27/54 Los Angeles, CA
22	Langford, Rick	Oakland	12-10	195	84	3.00	R-R	6-0	180	3/20/52 Farmville, VA
54	McCatty, Steve	Oakland	14-7	186	91	2.32	R-R	6-3	205	3/20/54 Detroit, MI
17	Norris, Mike	Oakland	12-9	173	78	3.75	R-R	6-2	172	3/19/55 San Francisco, CA
51	Owchinko, Bob	Oakland	4-3	39	26	3.23	L-L	6-2	195	1/1/55 San Diego, CA
31	Underwood, Tom	NY(AL)-Oak	4-6	84	75	3.64	R-L	5-11	177	12/22/53 Kokomo, IN

CATCHERS

No.	Name	1981 Club	H	HR	RBI	Pct.	B-T	Ht.	Wt.	Born
24	Dempsey, Pat	Tacoma	29	0	8	.209	R-R	6-4	185	10/23/56 Encino, CA
		West Haven	38	0	21	.297				
2	Heath, Mike	Oakland	71	8	30	.236	R-R	5-11	176	2/5/56 Tampa, FL
44	Johnson, Cliff	Oakland	71	17	59	.260	R-R	6-5	225	7/22/47 San Antonio, TX
30	Kearney, Robert	Tacoma	70	3	29	.252	R-R	6-0	180	10/3/56 San Antonio, TX
5	Newman, Jeff	Oakland	50	3	15	.231	R-R	6-2	215	9/11/48 Ft. Worth, TX

INFIELDERS

No.	Name	1981 Club	H	HR	RBI	Pct.	B-T	Ht.	Wt.	Born
3	Babitt, Mack	Oakland	40	0	14	.256	R-R	5-8	174	3/9/59 Oakland, CA
14	Drumright, Keith	Tacoma	18	0	7	.228	L-R	5-10	160	10/21/54 Springfield, MO
		Oakland	25	0	11	.291				
10	Gross, Wayne	Oakland	50	10	31	.206	L-R	5-10	162	1/14/52 Riverside, CA
9	Klutts, Mickey	Tacoma	11	1	4	.393	R-R	5-11	189	9/30/54 Montebello, CA
		Oakland	17	5	11	.370				
39	McKay, Dave	Oakland	59	4	21	.263	B-R	6-1	195	3/14/50 Vancouver, BC
—	Meyer, Dan	Seattle	66	3	22	.261	L-R	5-11	180	8/3/52 Hamilton, OH
26	Moore, Kelvin	Tacoma	166	31	109	.327	R-L	6-1	190	9/26/57 Leroy, AL
		Oakland	12	1	3	.255				
—	Phillips, Tony	West Haven	114	9	64	.247	B-R	5-10	160	11/9/59 Atlanta, GA
		Tacoma	4	0	2	.364				
8	Picciolo, Rob	Oakland	48	4	13	.268	R-R	6-2	185	2/4/53 Santa Monica, CA
15	Sexton, Jimmy	Tacoma	123	4	35	.319	R-R	5-11	175	12/15/51 Mobile, AL
		Oakland	0	0	0	.000				
12	Spencer, Jim	NY(AL)-Oak	44	4	13	.188	L-L	6-2	205	7/30/47 Hanover, PA
11	Stanley, Fred	Oakland	28	0	7	.193	R-R	5-11	167	8/13/47 Lake City, IA

OUTFIELDERS

No.	Name	1981 Club	H	HR	RBI	Pct.	B-T	Ht.	Wt.	Born
20	Armas, Tony	Oakland	115	22	76	.261	R-R	6-1	192	7/12/53 Venezuela
7	Bosetti, Rick	Tor-Oak	13	0	5	.197	R-R	5-11	185	8/5/53 Redding, CA
16	Davis, Michael	Tacoma	148	6	71	.287	L-L	6-2	165	6/11/59 San Diego, CA
		Oakland	1	0	0	.050				
—	Grandas, Bob	Tacoma			Disabled List		R-R	6-1	190	4/4/57 Flint, MI
35	Henderson, Rickey	Oakland	135	6	35	.319	R-L	5-10	180	12/25/58 Chicago, IL
21	Murphy, Dwayne	Oakland	98	15	60	.251	L-R	6-1	180	3/18/55 Merced, CA
6	Page, Mitchell	Oakland	13	4	13	.141	L-R	6-2	205	3/1/53 Compton, CA
		Tacoma	82	17	68	.328				
—	Rudi, Joe	Boston	22	6	24	.180	R-R	6-2	200	9/7/46 Modesto, CA

A's PROFILES

RICKEY HENDERSON 23 5-10 180   Bats R Throws L

Did it all for the A's in 1981, leading club in hits, average, runs, stolen bases and on-base percentage . . . Says Billy Martin, "Rickey Henderson is the best player in baseball." . . . His great promise was spelled out in 1980, when he became the first American Leaguer in history to steal 100 bases, while hitting .303 and scoring 111 runs . . . A gifted defensive outfielder, he has been among the leaders in assists each of the last two years . . . Born Dec. 25, 1958, in Chicago . . . Graduated from Oakland Technical High in 1976 and was A's No. 4 selection in the June draft that year . . . Also rushed for 1,100 yards in football his senior year in high school.

Year	Club	Pos.	G	AB	R	H	2B	3B	HR	RBI	SB	Avg.
1979	Oakland........	OF	89	351	49	96	13	3	1	26	33	.274
1980	Oakland........	OF	158	591	111	179	22	4	9	53	100	.303
1981	Oakland........	OF	108	423	89	135	18	7	6	35	56	.319
	Totals..........		355	1365	249	410	53	14	16	114	189	.300

MIKE NORRIS 27 6-2 172   Bats R Throws R

Numbers dropped off after sensational 1980 season as he had problems with his control . . . Went from No. 1 to No. 3 on A's staff . . . 1980 was going to be hard to top, though, as he was second in AL in ERA (2.53), complete games (24) and won 22 games, only to be denied Cy Young Award . . . Signed a megabuck five-year contract over the winter of 1980-81 . . . Signed as Oakland's No. 1 selection in January 1973 draft, but career was quickly in jeopardy when he underwent elbow surgery in 1975 . . . Struck out 287 batters in 288 minor-league innings . . . Born March 19, 1955, in San Francisco.

Year	Club	G	IP	W	L	Pct.	SO	BB	H	ERA
1975	Oakland.................	4	17	1	0	1.000	5	8	6	0.00
1976	Oakland.................	24	96	4	5	.444	44	56	91	4.78
1977	Oakland.................	16	77	2	7	.222	35	31	77	4.79
1978	Oakland.................	14	49	0	5	.000	36	35	46	5.51
1979	Oakland.................	29	146	5	8	.385	96	94	146	4.81
1980	Oakland.................	33	284	22	9	.710	180	83	215	2.54
1981	Oakland.................	23	173	12	9	.571	78	63	145	3.75
	Totals..................	143	842	46	43	.517	474	370	726	3.76

MATT KEOUGH 26 6-2 175   Bats R Throws R

Continued to enjoy renewed prosperity under the guidance of Billy Martin and Art Fowler . . . Was second on A's talented staff in shut-outs . . . Big turnabout, of course, came in 1980, when he went from 2-17 to 16-13 . . . His ERA in 1980 (2.92) was fourth-best in AL . . . Tied a major-league mark by losing his first 14 decisions of 1979, but the next year Billy Martin said, "He has too much ability not to be a winning pitcher in the majors." . . . Originally an infielder when drafted by the A's in 1973 . . . Converted to pitcher in 1976 . . . Born July 3, 1955, in Pomona, Cal. . . . Father, Marty, was an out-fielder with Red Sox and Reds . . . Attended UCLA as a pre-law major.

Year	Club	G	IP	W	L	Pct.	SO	BB	H	ERA
1977	Oakland	7	43	1	3	.250	23	22	39	4.81
1978	Oakland	32	197	8	15	.348	108	85	178	3.24
1979	Oakland	30	177	2	17	.105	95	78	220	5.03
1980	Oakland	34	250	16	13	.552	121	94	218	2.92
1981	Oakland	19	140	10	6	.625	60	45	125	3.41
	Totals	122	807	37	54	.407	407	324	780	3.65

RICK LANGFORD 30 6-0 180   Bats R Throws R

Was once again team and league leader in complete games in 1981, but slipped a bit in overall effectiveness . . . Had a pair of shut-outs and was third overall in AL in innings pitched . . . Born March 20, 1952, in Farm-ville, Va. . . . A's got him in one of their best deals of the Charlie Finley regime, sending Phil Garner to Pirates for Langford, Tony Armas, Mitchell Page and Doc Medich in March 1977 . . . Really reached full bloom as a pitcher under the tutelage of Billy Martin and Art Fowler, winning 43 games over the past three years while, at the same time, putting the bullpen out of work . . . In 1981, he completed 85 percent of his starts, the best percentage since Bob Feller in 1948 . . . Attended Florida State for one year and played outfield on baseball team . . . Hit a double in his first major-league at-bat with Pirates in '76.

Year	Club	G	IP	W	L	Pct.	SO	BB	H	ERA
1976	Pittsburgh	12	23	0	1	.000	17	14	27	6.26
1977	Oakland	37	208	8	19	.296	141	73	223	4.02
1978	Oakland	37	176	7	13	.350	92	56	169	3.43
1979	Oakland	34	219	12	16	.429	101	57	233	4.27
1980	Oakland	35	290	19	12	.613	102	64	276	3.26
1981	Oakland	24	195	12	10	.545	84	58	190	3.00
	Totals	179	1111	58	71	.450	537	322	1118	3.65

TONY ARMAS 28 6-1 192   Bats R Throws R

Carried the A's to their first-half "pennant" with his home-run bat . . . Had 13 homers and 41 RBI in first 60 games . . . Many scouts rate his throwing arm the best in all of baseball . . . Born July 12, 1953, in Anzoatequi, Venezuela . . . Came to A's from Pirates in 1977 in Phil Garner deal . . . Bothered by injuries his first three years with the A's, he spent a month each season on the disabled list with assorted knee and shoulder problems . . . Big breakthrough came in 1980 when, injury-free, he hit solid .279 with 35 homers and 109 RBI.

Year	Club	Pos.	G	AB	R	H	2B	3B	HR	RBI	SB	Avg.
1976	Pittsburgh	OF	4	6	0	2	0	0	0	1	0	.333
1977	Oakland	OF-SS	118	363	26	87	8	2	13	53	1	.240
1978	Oakland	OF	91	239	17	51	6	1	2	13	1	.213
1979	Oakland	OF	80	278	29	69	9	3	11	34	1	.248
1980	Oakland	OF	158	628	87	175	18	8	35	109	5	.279
1981	Oakland	OF	109	440	51	115	24	3	22	76	5	.261
	Totals		560	1954	210	499	65	17	83	286	13	.255

STEVE McCATTY 28 6-3 205   Bats R Throws R

"I'd like to have 10 pitchers on this team with the same attitude that he's got," A's pitching coach Art Fowler says of McCatty . . . At one point in 1981, he recorded 22 straight scoreless innings, tops by any pitcher on the talented Oakland staff . . . Criticized for his portly stature, McCatty is defended again by Fowler, who says, "Charles Atlas couldn't play ball and he had the most perfect body in the world." . . . Signed by A's out of McComb Community College (Mich.) in June 1973 . . . Was originally an outfielder-first baseman . . . Led A's in shutouts last year . . . Born March 20, 1954, in Detroit . . . Credits his success in '81 to "hard work and following Fowler's advice to 'Throw the ball hard and over the plate; don't aim it.'"

Year	Club	G	IP	W	L	Pct.	SO	BB	H	ERA
1977	Oakland	4	14	0	0	.000	9	7	16	5.14
1978	Oakland	9	20	0	0	.000	10	9	26	4.50
1979	Oakland	31	186	11	12	.478	87	80	207	4.21
1980	Oakland	33	222	14	14	.500	114	99	202	3.85
1981	Oakland	22	186	14	7	.667	91	61	140	2.32
	Totals	99	628	39	33	.542	311	256	591	3.55

DWAYNE MURPHY 27 6-1 180   Bats L Throws R

Perhaps the most underrated player in baseball because he has the misfortune of playing between Tony Armas and Rickey Henderson . . . But while Armas led A's in RBI last year and Henderson led in hits and runs, Murphy led league in game-winning hits . . . Like Henderson, he has great speed afoot and is an excellent defensive outfielder . . . Born March 18, 1955, in Merced, Calif. . . . Was A's No. 12 pick in the June 1973 draft and he finally made it to big club in 1978 . . . His career was threatened in 1974, when he spent seven weeks on the disabled list with a broken bone in his foot . . . Was a three-sport athlete in high school . . . Studies martial arts in off season.

Year	Club	Pos.	G	AB	R	H	2B	3B	HR	RBI	SB	Avg.
1978	Oakland	OF	60	52	15	10	2	0	0	5	0	.192
1979	Oakland	OF	121	388	57	99	10	4	11	40	15	.255
1980	Oakland	OF	159	573	86	157	18	2	13	68	26	.274
1981	Oakland	OF	107	390	58	98	10	3	15	60	10	.251
	Totals		447	1403	216	364	40	9	39	173	51	.259

MIKE HEATH 27 5-11 176   Bats R Throws R

Is one of the most underrated catchers in American League and, despite his low average, delivered some big hits to the A's last year . . . Scouts rate him in the top five defensively in AL and he has an above-average throwing arm . . . Born Feb. 5, 1955, in Tampa, Fla. . . . Prior to 1981, saw a lot of action in a utility role, filling in at DH, right field and left field . . . One of many ex-Yankees playing for Billy Martin on the A's . . . A's got him from Texas in 1979 for pitcher John Henry Johnson . . . Was an all-state football player as well as an All-America baseball star in high school . . . During the offseason, he enjoys racquetball and hunting . . . Was originally a shortstop when Yanks made him their No. 2 pick in June 1973 free-agent draft.

Year	Club	Pos.	G	AB	R	H	2B	3B	HR	RBI	SB	Avg.
1978	New York (AL)	C	33	92	6	21	3	1	0	8	0	.228
1979	Oakland	OF-C-3B	74	258	19	66	8	0	3	27	1	.256
1980	Oakland	C-OF	92	305	27	74	10	2	1	33	3	.243
1981	Oakland	C-OF	84	301	26	71	7	1	8	30	3	.236
	Totals		283	956	78	232	28	4	12	98	7	.243

CLIFF JOHNSON 34 6-5 225   **Bats R Throws R**

In the year that "Billy Ball" reached its greatest heights, few contributed more than Johnson . . . Picked up in the off-season from the Cubs, he wound up second on A's in homers and RBI . . . Played mostly as a DH, but can still fill in at first base and behind the plate . . . Was reunited with Martin, having played under him with the Yankees in '77 and '78 . . . His exit was sealed with Yanks when he became involved in a shower-room scuffle with Goose Gossage that resulted in Gossage breaking his thumb and missing most of 1979 season . . . Born July 27, 1947, in San Antonio, Tex. . . . Was fifth choice of Astros in June 1966 free-agent draft . . . Batted third in A's lineup last year.

Year	Club	Pos.	G	AB	R	H	2B	3B	HR	RBI	SB	Avg.
1972	Houston	C	5	4	0	1	0	0	0	0	0	.250
1973	Houston	1B	7	20	6	6	2	0	2	6	0	.300
1974	Houston	C-1B	83	171	26	39	4	1	10	29	0	.228
1975	Houston	1B-C-OF	122	340	52	94	16	1	20	65	1	.276
1976	Houston	C-OF-1B	108	318	36	72	21	2	10	49	0	.226
1977	Houston	OF-1B	51	144	22	43	8	0	10	23	0	.299
1977	New York (AL)	C-1B	56	142	24	42	8	0	12	31	0	.296
1978	New York (AL)	C-1B	76	174	20	32	9	1	6	19	0	.184
1979	N.Y.-Clev. (AL)	C	100	304	48	82	16	0	20	67	2	.270
1980	Cleveland	DH	54	174	25	40	3	1	6	28	0	.230
1980	Chicago (NL)	1B-OF-C	68	196	28	46	8	0	10	34	0	.235
1981	Oakland	DH	84	273	40	71	8	0	17	59	5	.260
	Totals		814	2260	327	568	103	6	123	410	8	.251

DAVE McKAY 32 6-1 195   **Bats S Throws R**

In the much-maligned A's infield of 1981, McKay earned raves from his teammates and Billy Martin's staff. "In many ways," said Martin, "Dave was our MVP. He proved to me he's a winner." . . . Took over the second-base job for keeps in the second half of '81 season after Martin decided youngsters Shooty Babbitt and Keith Drumright weren't the answer over the long haul . . . Came to A's on a look-see basis in spring training of '80 and impressed Martin for the first time by hitting .286 in camp and showing versatility . . . Born March 14, 1950, in Vancouver, B.C. . . . Tied a major-league record by hitting a home run in his first big league at-bat, Aug. 22, 1975 . . . Originally the property of the Twins and hit safely in 21 of his first 22 games for them in '75 . . . A's got him when Blue Jays gave up on him and released him after '79 season . . .

Played soccer, rugby and basketball in high school and later attended Creighton.

Year	Club	Pos.	G	AB	R	H	2B	3B	HR	RBI	SB	Avg.
1975	Minnesota......	3B	33	125	8	32	4	1	2	16	1	.256
1976	Minnesota......	3B-SS	45	138	8	28	2	0	-0	8	1	.203
1977	Toronto........	2B-3B-SS	95	274	18	54	4	3	3	22	2	.197
1978	Toronto........	2B-SS-3B	145	504	59	120	20	-8	7	45	4	.238
1979	Toronto........	2B-3B	47	156	19	34	9	0	0	12	1	.218
1980	Oakland........	2B-3B-SS	123	295	29	72	16	1	1	29	1	.244
1981	Oakland........	2B-3B	79	224	25	59	11	1	4	21	4	.263
	Totals..........		567	1716	166	399	66	14	17	153	14	.233

TOP PROSPECTS

KELVIN MOORE 24 6-1 197　　　　　　**Bats R Throws L**
The best young power hitter to come out of A's farm system since Reggie Jackson . . . Hit .327 with 31 homers and 109 RBI in rarified air of Pacific Coast League . . . Good bet to stick as Oakland's No. 1 first baseman against left-handed pitching . . . Born Sept. 26, 1957, in Leroy, Ala. . . . Had 25 HR and 100 RBI in PCL in 1980.

DAVE BEARD 22 6-5 190　　　　　　**Bats R Throws L**
A's are hoping he could be their answer to Goose Gossage . . . A big strong kid with 95 mph speed, but he's had control problems in past . . . Was 11-11 with 4.26 ERA and 114 strikeouts in 129 innings for A's Tacoma farm in Pacific Coast League last year before being promoted in September . . . Born Oct. 2, 1959, in Atlanta, Ga.

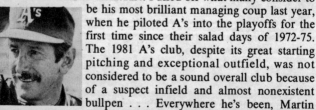

MANAGER BILLY MARTIN: Pulled off what many consider to be his most brilliant managing coup last year, when he piloted A's into the playoffs for the first time since their salad days of 1972-75. The 1981 A's club, despite its great starting pitching and exceptional outfield, was not considered to be a sound overall club because of a suspect infield and almost nonexistent bullpen . . . Everywhere he's been, Martin has been a winner, going all the way back to his playing days when he played a key role on seven Yankee World Series clubs . . . Born May 16, 1928, in Berkeley, Calif. . . . Won division titles with Twins in 1969 and Tigers in 1972 before winning AL pennants with Yankees in '76 and '77. His '77 club won World Series over Dodgers in six games . . . Batted .257 lifetime for 12-year career, but owns a .333 mark in World Series play . . . Always a tough and fiery competitor, he was suspended last year for bumping and throwing dirt on umpire Terry Cooney.

GREATEST CATCHER

To find the greatest catcher in the history of the Athletics' franchise, you have to go back through two cities, two franchise shifts and nearly 50 years. But if you are to determine the finest catcher ever to wear the big "A" on his chest, then you have no choice but to go with the great Mickey Cochrane. He played for Connie Mack's great Athletics teams of the '20s and '30s, but there can be no question that no subsequent A's catcher—in either Kansas City or Oakland—could have carried his glove or bat.

Mickey Cochrane, "Iron Mike" as he was called, was maybe the greatest of all time. From 1927-33, he hit .338, .293, .331, .357, .349, .293 and .322 respectively for Mack's A's and was behind the plate for three World Series clubs. In that same span, he led AL catchers in putouts six different times, and in fielding average and assists twice. Cochrane was also named the AL's Most Valuable Player in 1928 and 1934 when, oddly enough, the A's did *not* win pennants.

When Mack reluctantly decided to break up those great Athletics teams, he traded Cochrane to the Tigers in December 1933. It was the end of a great era, the last great era for the A's in Philadelphia. Mickey Cochrane was the heart of it. Cochrane was elected to the Hall of Fame in 1947.

ALL-TIME A's SEASON RECORDS

BATTING: Napoleon Lajoie, .422, 1901
HRs: Jimmie Foxx, 58, 1932
RBIs: Jimmie Foxx, 169, 1932
STEALS: Rickey Henderson, 100, 1980
WINS: John Coombs, 31, 1910
       Lefty Grove, 31, 1931
STRIKEOUTS: Rube Waddell, 349, 1904

SEATTLE MARINERS

TEAM DIRECTORY: Owner: George Argyros; Pres.: Dan O'Brien; VP/Sales-Marketing: Bill Long; Dir. Marketing: Jeff Odenwald; Mgr. Broadcast Services: Melody Tucker; Dir. Pub. Rel.: Randy Adamack; Mgr.: Rene Lachemann. Home: Kingdome (59,438). Field distances: 316, l.f. line; 365, l.c.; 410, c.f.; 365, r.c.; 316, r.f. line. Spring training: Tempe, Ariz.

SCOUTING REPORT

HITTING: The best of it is gone. Mariner owner George Argyros played games with outfielder Tom Paciorek too long last winter and, as a result, had to trade his leading hitter (.326, 14 homers, 66 RBI, 13 gamers) to the White Sox. In return the Mariners were able to bolster their offense at catcher with Jim Essian (.308 in 27 games last year for the White Sox).

But the bulk of the Seattle attack will fall on the shoulders of Richie Zisk (.311, 16, 43) and perhaps journeyman Gary Gray, who surprised by hitting 13 home runs in 69 games. For the most part, the Mariners are playing a waiting game for some of their prize draft choices to mature. They include outfielder Al Chambers and infielder Darnell Coles, both at least two years away.

PITCHING: If there was anything for rookie manager Rene Lachemann to be hopeful about with the Mariners last year, it was their pitching. At season's end Jim Beattie looked as if he might finally be ready to assume the front-line starter's role the Yankees expected of him after the '78 World Series. In addition, Floyd Bannister was the most sought-after pitcher of the winter meetings. Lachemann also liked what he saw of rookie Bob Stoddard (10-4, 2.90 at Spokane) and Jerry Don Gleaton.

The Mariners have also not yet given up on Ken Clay, who was a better pitcher than his 2-7 record indicated. Most encouraging to Lachemann, however, has to be his bullpen, where right-hander Larry Andersen suddenly blossomed with three wins, five saves and a 2.65 ERA, and lefty Shane Rawley won four while saving eight. Rawley was the second-most sought-after Mariner at the winter meetings.

FIELDING: One of the more interesting facets of the 1982 season will be how the Mariner broadcast crew keeps the "Cruz Connection" unconfused. The Mariners picked up troubled

Richie Zisk (16 homers) is a king in the Kingdome.

Todd Cruz from the White Sox and he will team up with hold-over second baseman Julio Cruz to form the double-play combo at the Kingdome.

Todd Cruz is regarded as a flashy fielder who has mental lapses and has yet to prove he can go the distance. In addition, he has had a few brushes with the law and the White Sox were happy to get rid of him. The rest of the Mariner defense is shaky, too. Essian should provide some stability behind the plate, but third base (probably rookie Paul Serna) and the outfield (a free-for-all among youngsters Dave Henderson, Rod Allen or veteran Joe Simpson) are very unsettled.

OUTLOOK: The Mariners are still a long way from assuming a contender's role. There is simply no offense here and the defense isn't so hot, either. But there are some good young arms and Lachemann is a good, young manager who deserves a chance to build and grow with this team. If the young pitchers continue to develop, maybe the wait won't be so long. Right now, however, you have to pencil the Mariners in for last in the West.

SEATTLE MARINERS 1982 ROSTER

MANAGER Rene Lachemann
Coaches—Dave Duncan, Vada Pinson, Bill Plummer

PITCHERS

No.	Name	1981 Club	W-L	IP	SO	ERA	B-T	Ht.	Wt.	Born
31	Allard, Brian	Spokane	1-1	14	11	1.29	R-R	6-1	175	1/3/58 Spring Valley, IL
		Seattle	3-2	48	20	3.75				
39	Andersen, Larry	Seattle	3-3	68	40	2.65	R-R	6-3	180	5/16/53 Portland, OR
38	Bannister, Floyd	Seattle	9-9	121	85	4.46	L-L	6-1	195	6/10/55 Pierre, SD
45	Beattie, Jim	Spokane	6-9	120	70	3.15	R-R	6-6	210	7/4/54 Hampton, VA
		Seattle	3-2	67	36	2.96				
—	Best, Karl	Lynn	4-4	71	50	3.80	R-R	6-4	190	3/6/59 Aberdeen, WA
—	Black, Bud	Lynn	2-6	87	86	3.00	L-L	6-2	180	6/30/57 San Mateo, CA
		Spokane	1-0	8	4	4.50				
		Seattle	0-0	1	0	0.00				
—	Bordi, Richard	Tacoma	9-11	191	101	3.68	R-R	6-7	210	4/18/59 S. San Francisco, CA
		Oakland	0-0	2	0	0.00				
48	Clark, Bryan	Seattle	2-5	93	52	4.35	L-L	6-2	185	7/12/56 Madera, CA
49	Clay, Ken	Seattle	2-7	101	32	4.63	R-R	6-3	195	4/6/54 Lynchburg, VA
—	Drago, Dick	Seattle	4-6	54	27	5.50	R-R	6-1	200	6/25/45 Toledo, OH
13	Finch, Steve	Spokane	6-9	107	66	5.05	R-R	6-3	160	3/9/58 Escondido, CA
28	Gleaton, Jerry Don	Spokane	5-7	91	57	4.15	L-L	6-3	215	9/14/57 Brownwood, TX
		Seattle	4-7	85	31	4.76				
—	Musselman, Ron	Spokane	1-8	67	25	3.76	R-R	6-1	185	11/11/54 Wilmington, NC
—	Nunez, Edwin	Wausau	16-3	185	205	2.48	R-R	6-5	220	5/27/63 Puerto Rico
20	Parrott, Mike	Seattle	3-6	85	43	5.08	R-R	6-4	205	12/6/54 Oxnard, CA
41	Rawley, Shane	Spokane	0-0	6	3	0.00	L-L	6-0	175	7/27/55 Racine, WI
		Seattle	4-6	68	35	3.97				
34	Stoddard, Bob	Spokane	10-4	121	27	2.90	R-R	6-1	190	3/8/58 San Jose, CA
		Seattle	2-1	35	22	2.57				
—	Welborn, Sammye	Spokane	3-3	82	52	5.93	L-R	6-4	205	6/16/56 Wichita Falls, TX

CATCHERS

No.	Name	1981 Club	H	HR	RBI	Pct.	B-T	Ht.	Wt.	Born
—	Bulling, Terry	Seattle	38	2	15	.247	R-R	6-0	210	12/15/52 Lynwood, CA
—	Essian, Jim	Chicago (AL)	16	0	5	.308	R-R	6-1	187	1/2/51 Detroit, MI
—	Firova, Dan	Nuevo Laredo	69	3	38	.237	R-R	6-0	185	10/16/56 Refugio, TX
		Seattle	0	0	0	.000				
36	Mercado, Orlando	Spokane	67	4	31	.215	R-R	6-0	180	11/7/61 Puerto Rico
3	Narron, Jerry	Seattle	45	3	17	.222	L-R	6-3	205	1/15/56 Goldsboro, NC
37	Valle, Dave	Lynn	81	11	54	.258	R-R	6-2	200	10/30/60 Bayside, NY

INFIELDERS

No.	Name	1981 Club	H	HR	RBI	Pct.	B-T	Ht.	Wt.	Born
4	Anderson, Jim	Seattle	33	2	19	.204	R-R	6-0	180	2/23/57 Los Angeles, CA
23	Bochte, Bruce	Seattle	87	6	30	.260	L-L	6-3	200	11/12/50 Pasadena, CA
—	Castillo, Manny	Omaha	182	10	91	.335	B-R	5-9	160	4/1/57 Dominican Republic
6	Cruz, Julio	Seattle	90	2	24	.256	B-R	5-9	160	12/2/54 Brooklyn, NY
—	Cruz, Todd	Edmonton	7	1	2	.269	R-R	5-10	185	11/12/55 Highland Park, MI
15	Edler, Dave	Seattle	11	0	5	.141	R-R	6-1	190	8/5/56 Sioux City, IA
		Spokane	57	6	30	.254				
29	Gray, Gary	Seattle	51	13	31	.245	R-R	6-0	215	9/21/52 New Orleans, LA
40	Maler, Jim	Spokane	158	19	99	.305	R-R	6-4	230	8/16/58 New York, NY
		Seattle	8	0	2	.348				
—	Presley, Jim	Wausau	58	12	53	.283	R-R	6-1	180	10/23/61 Pensacola, FL
		Lynn	55	8	36	.257				
—	Ramos, Domingo	Syracuse	82	0	31	.256	R-R	5-10	154	3/29/58 Dominican Republic
—	Randle, Lenny	Seattle	63	4	25	.231	B-R	5-10	170	2/12/49 Long Beach, CA
—	Serna, Paul	Lynn	13	0	3	.255	R-R	5-8	170	11/16/58 El Centro, CA
		Nuevo Laredo	82	2	31	.291				
		Seattle	24	4	9	.255				

OUTFIELDERS

No.	Name	1981 Club	H	HR	RBI	Pct.	B-T	Ht.	Wt.	Born
—	Allen, Rod	Edmonton	114	11	53	.294	R-R	6-1	185	10/5/59 Los Angeles, CA
—	Chambers, Al	Lynn	120	20	77	.269	L-L	6-4	217	3/24/61 Harrisburg, PA
42	Henderson, Dave	Seattle	21	6	13	.167	R-R	6-2	210	7/21/58 Dos Palos, CA
		Spokane	76	12	50	.279				
54	Nanni, Tito	Lynn	90	7	40	.249	L-L	6-4	220	12/3/59 Philadelphia, PA
18	Simpson, Joe	Seattle	64	2	30	.222	L-L	6-3	180	12/31/51 Purcell, OK
22	Zisk, Richie	Seattle	111	16	43	.311	R-R	6-1	205	2/6/49 Brooklyn, NY

MARINER PROFILES

JULIO CRUZ 27 5-9 160   **Bats S Throws R**

Once again was among the Mariners' most valuable players in '81, finishing second in the AL in stolen bases . . . Led Mariners in runs scored and triples as well . . . Is considered to be possibly the best defensive second baseman in AL when it comes to turning the double play . . . Born Dec. 2, 1954, in Brooklyn . . . Has speed, agility, quickness and strength . . . Was passed up completely in the 1974 amateur draft and was signed by the Angels . . . Learned to switch-hit under tutelage of Angel coaches Del Crandall and Bob Clear in 1974 . . . Mariners got him via the expansion draft . . . Ranked third in AL with 49 stolen bases in 1979 despite missing 54 games with a torn ligament in his thumb.

Year	Club	Pos.	G	AB	R	H	2B	3B	HR	RBI	SB	Avg.
1977	Seattle.........	2B	60	199	25	51	3	1	1	7	15	.256
1978	Seattle.........	2B-SS	147	550	77	129	14	1	1	25	59	.235
1979	Seattle.........	2B	107	414	70	112	16	2	1	29	49	.271
1980	Seattle.........	2B	119	422	66	88	9	3	2	16	45	.209
1981	Seattle.........	2B	94	352	57	90	12	3	2	24	43	.256
	Totals..........		527	1937	295	470	54	10	7	101	211	.243

GARY GRAY 29 6-0 215   **Bats R Throws R**

Was finally given a chance to play regularly in '81 and proved what many suspected all along: he can hit big-league pitching . . . Was the biggest surprise of the first season, leading AL in homers for quite awhile, but cooled off a bit after strike . . . Originally signed by Texas and came to Seattle via the minor-league draft after being sent to the Yucatan club of the Mexican League by Cleveland after the '80 season . . . Proved to be a valued pickup for M's . . . Never hit below .300 in seven full minor-league seasons . . . Born Sept. 21, 1952, in New Orleans . . . Hit .335 for Indians' Tacoma farm in 1980, which was prime reason M's drafted him.

Year	Club	Pos.	G	AB	R	H	2B	3B	HR	RBI	SB	Avg.
1977	Texas..........	OF	1	2	0	0	0	0	0	0	0	.000
1978	Texas..........	DH	17	50	4	12	1	0	2	6	1	.240
1979	Texas..........	DH	16	42	4	10	0	0	0	1	0	.238
1980	Cleveland......	1B-OF	28	54	4	8	1	0	2	4	0	.148
1981	Seattle.........	1B-OF	69	208	27	51	7	1	13	31	2	.245
	Totals..........		131	356	39	81	9	1	17	42	3	.228

SHANE RAWLEY 26 6-0 175   Bats L Throws L

Did not have one of his better seasons in '81, but still led Mariner staff in saves and appearances . . . Biggest problem was his control . . . Born July 27, 1955, in Racine, Wis. . . . Obtained from Reds in trade for Dave Collins . . . Originally signed by Expos as their No. 2 draft choice in June 1974 . . . Doesn't yield many home runs . . . Despite off season, must be considered a valuable performer because of the shortage of left-handed bullpen stoppers.

Year	Club	G	IP	W	L	Pct.	SO	BB	H	ERA
1978	Seattle	52	111	4	9	.308	66	51	114	4.14
1979	Seattle	48	84	5	9	.357	48	40	88	3.86
1980	Seattle	59	114	7	7	.500	68	63	103	3.32
1981	Seattle	46	68	4	6	.400	35	38	64	3.97
	Totals	205	377	20	31	.392	217	192	369	3.80

TERRY BULLING 29 6-0 210   Bats R Throws R

Was the big surprise of Mariners' spring camp in '81, winding up with the first-string catching job . . . Was acquired by Mariners in a straight cash deal with Twins in 1979 . . . Is considered an excellent defensive catcher and gave indication he might become a decent hitter, although with limited power . . . In first two pro seasons in Twins' organization, he was the Midwest League's all-star catcher . . . Born Dec. 15, 1952, in Lynwood, Calif. . . . Graduated from California State University at Los Angeles in 1974.

Year	Club	Pos.	G	AB	R	H	2B	3B	HR	RBI	SB	Avg.
1977	Minnesota	C	15	32	2	5	1	0	0	5	0	.156
1981	Seattle	C	62	154	15	38	3	0	2	15	0	.247
	Totals		77	186	17	43	4	0	2	20	0	.231

BRUCE BOCHTE 31 6-3 200   Bats L Throws L

Once again one of the Mariners' more consistent hitters in '81 although his average slipped under .300 for first time in three years . . . Will likely platoon again at first base . . . Selected as Mariners' Most Valuable Player in 1980 when he led club in hitting, games, doubles, RBI and walks . . . Born Nov. 12, 1950, in Pasadena, Calif. . . . Signed with Mariners as a free agent in 1977 . . . Has better speed than his limited stolen-base totals indicate . . . Holds Mariner club record for fielding percentage by a first baseman (.996 in 1980) . . . Played two seasons of college baseball and basketball at Santa Clara before signing with Angels in June 1972.

Year	Club	Pos.	G	AB	R	H	2B	3B	HR	RBI	SB	Avg.
1974	California......	OF-1B	57	196	24	53	4	1	5	26	6	.270
1975	California......	1B	107	375	41	107	19	3	3	48	3	.285
1976	California......	OF-1B	146	466	53	120	17	1	2	49	4	.258
1977	Cal.-Cle........	OF-1B	137	492	64	148	23	1	7	51	6	.301
1978	Seattle.........	OF-1B	140	486	58	128	25	3	11	51	3	.263
1979	Seattle.........	1B	150	554	81	175	38	6	16	100	2	.316
1980	Seattle.........	1B	148	520	62	156	34	4	13	78	2	.300
1981	Seattle.........	1B-OF	99	335	39	87	16	0	6	30	1	.260
	Totals..........		984	3424	422	974	176	19	63	433	27	.284

Bruce Bochte: Only Mariner at '79 All-Star Game in Seattle.

JIM ESSIAN 31 6-1 190   Bats R Throws R

Victim of circumstances with White Sox last season after signing four-year, $1-million-plus contract as free agent in fall 1980 . . . Chicago subsequently landed Carlton Fisk, leaving Essian in the role of bit player . . . Hit a career-high .308, but had just 52 at-bats last season . . . Obtained by Mariners along with Todd Cruz and Rod Allen in Tom Paciorek deal . . . Still has reputation as one of the league's best defensive catchers and can also play third and first in a pinch . . . Born Jan. 2, 1951, in Detroit.

Year	Club	Pos.	G	AB	R	H	2B	3B	HR	RBI	SB	Avg.
1973	Philadelphia.....	C	2	3	0	0	0	0	0	0	0	.000
1974	Philadelphia.....	C-1B-3B	17	20	1	2	0	0	0	0	0	.100
1975	Philadelphia.....	C	2	1	1	1	0	0	0	1	0	1.000
1976	Chicago (AL)....	C-1B-3B	78	199	20	49	7	0	0	21	2	.246
1977	Chicago (AL)....	C-3B	114	322	50	88	18	2	10	44	1	.273
1978	Oakland........	C-1B-2B	126	278	21	62	9	1	3	26	2	.223
1979	Oakland........	C-1B-3B	98	313	34	76	16	0	8	40	0	.243
1980	Oakland........	C-1B-3B	87	285	19	66	11	0	5	29	1	.232
1981	Chicago (AL)....	C	27	52	6	16	3	0	0	5	0	.308
	Totals.........		551	1473	152	358	64	3	26	166	6	.243

RICHIE ZISK 33 6-1 205   Bats R Throws R

Credit the Mariners for getting the first big dividends from Zisk's 10-year megabuck contract signed with Texas in 1977 . . . Coming over from Rangers, he found a home to his liking in the Kingdome with his highest average since 1974 . . . Led the Mariners in homers . . . Is now almost a fulltime DH . . . Had best season with White Sox in '77 with career highs in homers and RBI. Then went into the free-agent draft . . . Played basketball and soccer as well in high school and attended Seton Hall (N.J.) College before signing with the Pirates in 1967 . . . Had a four-year National League average of .299 . . . In 1978 with Texas, he had 17 game-winning hits.

Year	Club	Pos.	G	AB	R	H	2B	3B	HR	RBI	SB	Avg.
1971	Pittsburgh......	OF	7	15	2	3	1	0	1	2	0	.200
1972	Pittsburgh......	OF	17	37	4	7	3	0	0	4	0	.189
1973	Pittsburgh......	OF	103	333	44	108	23	7	10	54	0	.324
1974	Pittsburgh......	OF	149	536	75	168	30	3	17	100	1	.313
1975	Pittsburgh......	OF	147	504	69	146	27	3	20	75	0	.290
1976	Pittsburgh......	OF	155	581	91	168	35	2	21	89	1	.289
1977	Chicago (AL)....	OF	141	531	78	154	17	6	30	101	0	.290
1978	Texas..........	OF	140	511	68	134	19	1	22	85	3	.262
1979	Texas..........	OF	144	503	69	132	21	1	18	64	1	.262
1980	Texas..........	OF	135	448	48	130	17	1	19	77	0	.290
1981	Seattle.........	OF	94	357	42	111	12	1	16	43	0	.311
	Totals.........		1232	4356	590	1261	205	25	174	694	6	.289

FLOYD BANNISTER 26 6-1 195   Bats L Throws L

Has yet to really break out with that "big" season everyone has been expecting of him since Astros made him nation's No. 1 pick out of Arizona State in June '76 draft . . . Had the only two shutouts on the Mariner staff in '81 . . . Born June 10, 1955, in Pierre, S.D. . . . Pitched just seven games in Houston farm system before Astros brought him to the big leagues to stay in 1977 . . . Mariners got him in trade for SS Craig Reynolds . . . Friends and family live in Seattle, which should give him incentive to put it all together soon . . . Was selected to pitch on all-star team that toured Japan in 1979 . . . Has led Mariners in strikeouts all three seasons he's been with them.

Year	Club	G	IP	W	L	Pct.	SO	BB	H	ERA
1977	Houston	24	143	8	9	.471	112	68	138	4.03
1978	Houston	28	110	3	9	.250	94	63	120	4.83
1979	Seattle	30	182	10	15	.400	115	68	185	4.05
1980	Seattle	32	218	9	13	.409	155	66	200	3.47
1981	Seattle	21	121	9	9	.500	85	39	128	4.46
	Totals	135	774	39	55	.415	561	304	771	4.06

TOP PROSPECTS

BOB STODDARD 25 6-1 190   Bats R Throws R

Was the first pitcher ever signed and developed by Mariners and, based on showing in his September call-up last year, he is ready to take a spot in Seattle's starting rotation . . . Led Pacific Coast League with 2.90 ERA while winning 10 of 14 decisions for Spokane . . . Was out of action three times, however, with tendinitis in his right elbow . . . Born March 8, 1958, in San Jose, Calif.

DAVE HENDERSON 23 6-2 210   Bats R Throws R

Disregard the meager average he had in limited play for Mariners last year . . . M's like his power numbers (12 HR and 50 RBI) at Spokane and feel it's just a matter of time when he arrives as an outfield regular for them . . . Suffered an Achilles tendon injury in 1978 which hampered his progress . . . Was Mariners' first choice in June 1977 free-agent draft and is rated an excellent defensive outfielder with fine throwing arm . . . Born July 21, 1958, in Dos Palos, Calif.

MANAGER RENE LACHEMANN: Took over as Mariners' manager from Maury Wills on May 6 of last year with team mired at 6-18. Club finished up at 38-47 and he was rewarded with a three-year contract, the Mariners having the option of renewing the second two years . . . Ironically he began his major-league career as a batboy with the Dodgers in 1959—the same year Maury Wills was a rookie shortstop . . . Played briefly as a catcher for the A's in 1965, '66 and '68, batting just .210 in 118 total games . . . Brother Marcel was a pitcher in the A's system at the same time and is now a pitching instructor in the Angels' system . . . Lach's career as a player ended in 1972 and the following year he became manager of A's Burlington, Iowa, farm . . . Managed nine years in the minors with an overall 509-598 mark with perennially weak A's and Mariners' farm clubs . . . At 36, he is the youngest manager in the big leagues . . . He was born in Los Angeles on May 4, 1945.

GREATEST CATCHER

The first few years of the Seattle Mariner franchise have been, well, difficult. There hasn't been a whole lot to cheer about in the great northwest other than maybe the arrival of the King-dome and its short power alleys. There have not been too many players of significance in the Mariners' history, but one, Bob Stinson, deserves a call for sheer perseverence.

It was Stinson's unfortunate duty to handle such fledgling pitching arms as Gary Wheelock, Rick Jones, Bill Laxton, Frank MacCormack, Paul Mitchell and Rob Dressler. He did it and still managed to keep both his head and batting average above water.

Stinson lasted as the Mariners' catcher from 1977, when he was selected off the Royals' roster in the expansion draft, until 1980, when he was finally released after suffering a knee injury two years earlier.

In his and the Mariners' first year in the AL, Stinson hit .269 in 105 games. The following season, though disabled from Aug. 21

to Sept. 7, he hit .258 in 124 games, smacked a career-high 11 homers and drove in 55 runs. After the '78 season, Stinson's playing time became limited as the Mariners sought to bring in younger faces. He got into just 95 games in '79 and had his playing time cut to 48 games in '80. To this date, however, no catcher has lasted four years on the Mariners' major-league roster. In terms of an expansion team, that feat is sufficient to earn Stinson the mantle of Mariner greatness.

ALL-TIME MARINER SEASON RECORDS

BATTING: Tom Paciorek, .326, 1981
HRs: Willie Horton, 29, 1979
RBIs: Willie Horton, 106, 1979
STEALS: Julio Cruz, 59, 1978
WINS: Mike Parrott, 14, 1979
STRIKEOUTS: Floyd Bannister, 155, 1980

TEXAS RANGERS

TEAM DIRECTORY: Chairman of the Board: Eddie Chiles; Exec. VP: Eddie Robinson; Exec. VP: Samuel G. Meason; Farm Dir.: Joe Klein; News Media Dir.: Burt Hawkins; Trav. Sec.: Dan Schimek; Mgr.: Don Zimmer. Home: Arlington Stadium (41,284). Field distances: 330, l.f. line; 380, l.c.; 400, c.f.; 380, r.c.; 330, r.f. line. Spring training: Pompano Beach, Fla.

SCOUTING REPORT

HITTING: The Rangers were a two-man offense last year and therein lies the root of their problems. While they hit .270 as a team, only Buddy Bell (.294, 10, 64) and Al Oliver (.309, 4, 55) could be considered consistent run-producers. What it came down to was this: the Rangers had an awful lot of very light .260-.270 hitters. Bell led the club in homers and RBI and if the Rangers are to make a run for the top this year, he's going to have to get a lot more help from among Pat Putnam (.266, 8, 35), Billy Sample (.283, 3, 25), Leon Roberts (.279, 4, 31) or perhaps rookie Mike Richardt, who won the American Association batting title at Wichita last year with a .354 mark.

The Rangers also could use a comeback of sorts from Mickey Rivers, who dropped from .333 and 18 stolen bases in '80 to .286 and nine steals. Besides Richardt (who will be given a long look

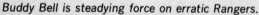

Buddy Bell is steadying force on erratic Rangers.

at second base), Rangers' manager Don Zimmer will also watch first baseman Bob Jones (.315, 72 RBI at Wichita). Regardless, the Rangers do not appear to be a team that is going to overwhelm anyone this season with their hitting attack.

PITCHING: As of now, the Rangers do not boast of any future Hall of Famers on their pitching staff. Nevertheless, you'd have never guessed that, considering the flock of offers they entertained this past winter for Danny Darwin (9-9, 3.64) and Rick Honeycutt (11-6, 3.30). Zimmer will build his hopes around that lefty-righty tandem this year. Doc Medich (10-6, 3.08) is as good a No. 3 starter as you could find, and Zimmer is hopeful that knuckleballer Charlie Hough's surprising performance down the stretch last year (4-1, 2.96, two complete games) was no fluke. If not, the Rangers should be in good shape pitching-wise.

They sacrificed Jim Kern in order to get Flynn, but the bullpen should be better than adequate with Steve Comer (8-2, six saves) and lefty John Henry Johnson. Zimmer also plans to give rookie John Butcher a full shot to make the starting rotation. If Butcher succeeds—or if Jon Matlack ever pitches up to his potential—Zimmer might move Darwin back to the bullpen.

FIELDING: The Rangers tightened up their infield defense last year when they acquired Mario Mendoza to play shortstop. By season's end, however, they were thinking in terms of Mark Wagner at short for '82; he shouldn't be much of a defensive fall-off. Of larger concern was Bump Wills at second. Wills just never has impressed anyone with his ground-covering ability. Thus, the Rangers picked up Doug Flynn from the Mets. Flynn is a Gold Glove second baseman who can also play short. Over at third, Buddy Bell also possesses a Gold Glove, as does Jim Sundberg behind the plate. The outfield of Rivers, Sample, Roberts or Johnny Grubb is fleet afoot but there are no "cannons".

OUTLOOK: Zimmer somehow had coaxed more runs out of the Rangers than any other team in baseball scored until the strike last year. Then, when everyone came back, the Rangers went flat. Unless a bonafide run producer can be picked up, the Rangers will have their problems staying with the Royals, A's and probably White Sox, too.

There are also too many questions about the pitching. If Darwin goes back to the bullpen, the Rangers are going to need big years from Hough, Medich and Honeycutt. Sample, Rivers and Putnam were also big disappointments last year and the Rangers must get better, more productive seasons from all of them.

TEXAS RANGERS 1982 ROSTER

MANAGER Don Zimmer
Coaches—Jackie Brown, Tommy Helms, Darrell Johnson,
Fred Koenig, Wayne Terwilliger

PITCHERS

No.	Name	1981 Club	W-L	IP	SO	ERA	B-T	Ht.	Wt.	Born
39	Babcock, Bob	Texas	1-1	29	18	2.17	R-R	6-5	201	8/25/49 New Castle, PA
29	Butcher, John	Wichita	8-10	136	87	5.61	R-R	6-4	190	3/8/57 Glendale, CA
		Texas	1-2	28	19	1.61				
11	Comer, Steve	Texas	8-2	77	22	2.57	B-R	6-3	205	1/13/54 Minneapolis, MN
44	Darwin, Danny	Texas	9-9	146	98	3.64	R-R	6-3	190	10/25/55 Bonham, TX
40	Honeycutt, Rick	Texas	11-6	128	40	3.30	L-L	6-1	190	6/29/54 Chattanooga, TN
49	Hough, Charlie	Texas	4-1	82	69	2.96	R-R	6-2	190	1/5/48 Honolulu, HI
38	Johnson, John Henry	Texas	3-1	24	8	2.63	L-L	6-2	190	8/21/56 Houston, TX
35	Lacey, Bob	Cleveland-Texas	0-0	22	11	7.77	R-L	6-5	207	8/25/53 Fredericksburg, VA
—	Lazorko, Jack	Tulsa	4-8	67	36	3.36	R-R	5-11	195	3/30/56 Hoboken, NJ
		Wichita	1-0	13	9	2.70				
32	Matlack, John	Texas	4-7	104	43	4.15	L-L	6-3	200	1/19/50 West Chester, PA
33	Medich, Doc	Texas	10-6	143	65	3.08	R-R	6-5	227	12/9/48 Aliquippa, PA
53	Mercer, Mark	Wichita	10-8	101	60	5.27	L-L	6-5	220	5/22/54 Fort Bragg, NC
		Texas	0-1	8	8	4.50				
24	Schmidt, Dave	Tulsa	1-1	24	17	1.88	R-R	6-1	185	4/22/57 Niles, MI
		Wichita	2-5	87	49	4.88				
		Texas	0-1	32	13	3.09				
12	Whitehouse, Len	Wichita	6-5	105	58	3.87	L-L	5-11	175	9/10/57 Burlington, VT
		Texas	0-1	3	2	18.00				

CATCHERS

No.	Name	1981 Club	H	HR	RBI	Pct.	B-T	Ht.	Wt.	Born
9	Ellis, John	Texas	8	1	7	.138	R-R	6-2	210	8/21/48 New London, CT
8	Johnson, Bobby	Wichita	93	20	57	.263	R-R	6-3	195	7/31/59 Dallas, TX
		Texas	5	2	4	.278				
—	Scott, Don	Tulsa	91	5	41	.236	B-R	5-11	185	8/16/61 Dunedin, FL
10	Sundberg, Jim	Texas	94	3	28	.277	R-R	6-0	195	5/18/51 Galesburg, IL

INFIELDERS

No.	Name	1981 Club	H	HR	RBI	Pct.	B-T	Ht.	Wt.	Born
—	Aviles, Ramon	Philadelphia	6	0	3	.214	R-R	5-9	155	1/22/52 Dominican Republic
25	Bell, Buddy	Texas	106	10	64	.294	R-R	6-2	185	8/27/51 Pittsburgh, PA
23	Flynn, Doug	New York (NL)	72	1	20	.222	R-R	5-11	165	4/18/51 Lexington, KY
—	Holt, Roger	Wichita	110	4	49	.262	B-R	5-11	165	4/8/56 Daytona Beach, FL
14	Mendoza, Mario	Texas	53	0	22	.231	R-R	5-11	185	12/26/50 Mexico
4	Norman, Nelson	Wichita	86	0	31	.246	B-R	6-2	160	5/23/58 Puerto Rico
		Texas	3	0	2	.231				
—	O'Brien, Peter	Tulsa	109	17	78	.285	L-L	6-1	185	2/9/58 Santa Monica, CA
18	Putnam, Pat	Texas	79	8	35	.266	L-R	6-1	214	12/3/53 Bethel, VT
—	Richardt, Mike	Wichita	124	8	60	.354	R-R	6-0	170	5/24/58 Los Angeles, CA
13	Stein, Bill	Texas	38	2	22	.330	R-R	5-10	170	1/21/47 Battle Creek, MI
—	Tolleson, Wayne	Wichita	98	3	38	.261	B-R	5-9	160	11/22/55 Spartanburg, SC
		Texas	4	0	1	.167				
30	Wagner, Mark	Texas	22	1	14	.259	R-R	6-1	175	3/4/54 Conneaut, OH
1	Wills, Bump	Texas	103	2	41	.251	B-R	5-9	177	7/27/52 Washington, DC

OUTFIELDERS

No.	Name	1981 Club	H	HR	RBI	Pct.	B-T	Ht.	Wt.	Born
—	Capra, Nick	Wichita	104	4	38	.261	R-R	5-8	165	3/8/58 Denver, CO
6	Grubb, John	Texas	46	3	26	.231	L-R	6-3	180	8/4/48 Richmond, VA
—	Jones, Bob	Wichita	111	20	72	.315	L-L	6-1	170	10/11/49 Elkton, MD
		Texas	9	3	7	.265				
0	Oliver, Al	Texas	130	4	55	.309	L-L	6-1	203	10/14/46 Portsmouth, OH
17	Rivers, Mickey	Texas	114	3	26	.286	L-L	5-10	162	10/30/48 Miami, FL
16	Roberts, Leon	Texas	65	4	31	.279	R-R	6-3	200	1/22/51 Vicksburg, MS
5	Sample, Billy	Texas	65	3	25	.283	R-R	5-9	175	4/2/55 Roanoke, VA
—	Wright, George	Tulsa	127	11	58	.260	R-R	5-11	180	12/12/58 Oklahoma, OK

RANGER PROFILES

AL OLIVER 35 6-1 203   Bats L Throws L

Paced the Rangers' regular batsmen for the fourth straight year and has not hit under .300 since 1975 . . . Has become a full-time DH . . . Was second on Rangers in RBI and games . . . Big year was 1980 when he played every game, was second in AL in doubles, fourth in RBI and hits, fifth in total bases . . . Born Oct. 14, 1946, at Portsmouth, Ohio . . .
Rangers obtained him from Pirates for Bert Blyleven in December 1977 . . . Plays with enthusiasm, but also has a Rodney Dangerfield "I-get-no-respect" complex . . . Attended Kent State University.

Year	Club	Pos.	G	AB	R	H	2B	3B	HR	RBI	SB	Avg.
1968	Pittsburgh	OF	4	8	1	1	0	0	0	0	0	.125
1969	Pittsburgh	1B-OF	129	463	55	132	19	2	17	70	8	.285
1970	Pittsburgh	OF-1B	151	551	63	149	33	5	12	83	1	.270
1971	Pittsburgh	OF-1B	143	529	69	149	31	7	14	64	4	.282
1972	Pittsburgh	OF-1B	140	565	88	176	27	4	12	89	2	.312
1973	Pittsburgh	OF-1B	158	654	90	191	38	7	20	99	6	.292
1974	Pittsburgh	OF-1B	147	617	96	198	38	12	11	85	10	.321
1975	Pittsburgh	OF-1B	155	628	90	176	39	8	18	84	4	.280
1976	Pittsburgh	OF-1B	121	443	62	143	22	5	12	61	6	.323
1977	Pittsburgh	OF	154	568	75	175	29	6	19	82	13	.308
1978	Texas	OF	133	525	65	170	35	5	14	89	8	.324
1979	Texas	OF	136	492	69	159	28	4	12	76	4	.323
1980	Texas	OF-1B	163	656	96	209	43	3	19	117	5	.319
1981	Texas	OF-1B	102	421	53	130	29	1	4	55	3	.309
	Totals		1836	7120	972	2158	411	69	184	1054	74	.303

MARIO MENDOZA 31 5-11 185   Bats R Throws R

In Mendoza, the Rangers got what they wanted last year—excellent defense at short. However, they also felt they could not carry his light bat and were back to experimenting with others at season's end . . . Came to Rangers from Seattle along with Rick Honeycutt in December 1980 . . . Maury Wills, his former manager at Seattle, called him "the best defensive shortstop in the major leagues" . . . Born Dec. 26, 1950, in Chihuahua, Mexico . . . Originally property of the Pirates, who bought his contract from Mexican League in 1972

. . . Was a base-stealing threat in the minors, but never showed it in the big leagues.

Year	Club	Pos.	G	AB	R	H	2B	3B	HR	RBI	SB	Avg.
1974	Pittsburgh	SS	91	163	10	36	1	2	0	15	1	.221
1975	Pittsburgh	SS-3B	56	50	8	9	1	0	0	2	0	.180
1976	Pittsburgh	SS-3B-2B	50	92	6	17	5	0	0	12	0	.185
1977	Pittsburgh	SS-3B-P	70	81	5	16	3	0	0	4	0	.198
1978	Pittsburgh	2B-3B-SS	57	55	5	12	1	0	1	3	3	.218
1979	Seattle	SS	148	373	26	74	10	3	1	29	3	.198
1980	Seattle	SS	114	277	27	68	6	3	2	14	3	.245
1981	Texas	SS	88	229	18	53	6	1	0	22	2	.231
	Totals		674	1320	105	285	33	9	4	101	12	.216

JIM SUNDBERG 30 6-0 195   Bats R Throws R

Regarded around the league as the No. 1 defensive catcher . . . Got off to a slow start with the bat, but at season's end he was hitting his customary solid .270 . . . In '80 he established a career high for homers with 10 . . . The most durable catcher in baseball as well . . . Has won six Gold Gloves . . . Born May 18, 1951, in Galesburg, Ill. . . . Signed by Rangers out of U. of Iowa and played only one year of AA ball before jumping to majors to stay in '74 . . . Holds AL record for most seasons leading the league in assists . . . Shares AL record for fewest errors in a season by a catcher with four in 1979.

Year	Club	Pos.	G	AB	R	H	2B	3B	HR	RBI	SB	Avg.
1974	Texas	C	132	368	45	91	13	3	3	36	2	.247
1975	Texas	C	155	472	45	94	9	0	6	36	3	.199
1976	Texas	C	140	448	33	102	24	2	3	34	0	.228
1977	Texas	C	149	453	61	132	20	3	6	65	2	.291
1978	Texas	C	149	518	54	144	23	6	6	58	2	.278
1979	Texas	C	150	495	50	136	23	4	5	64	3	.275
1980	Texas	C	151	505	59	138	24	1	10	63	2	.273
1981	Texas	C	102	339	42	94	17	2	3	28	2	.277
	Totals		1128	3598	389	931	153	21	42	384	16	.259

PAT PUTNAM 28 6-1 214   Bats L Throws R

Has still not delivered consistently with the extra-base power he showed in minor leagues . . . Rangers will likely continue to platoon him against right-handers . . . Despite low average, was second on the club in homers in '81 . . . Named Sporting News' AL Rookie of the Year in '79 when he hit .277 . . . Born Dec. 3, 1953, in Bethel, Vt. . . . Showed his great promise in 1978 at Tucson when he hit .309 with 21 HR and 96 RBI. Two years earlier, he knocked in 142 runs for Asheville and was named Minor League Player of the Year . . . Played college ball under Eddie Stanky at South Alabama.

Year	Club	Pos.	G	AB	R	H	2B	3B	HR	RBI	SB	Avg.
1977	Texas..........	1B	11	26	3	8	4	0	0	3	0	.308
1978	Texas..........	1B	20	46	4	7	1	0	1	2	0	.152
1979	Texas..........	1B	139	426	57	118	19	2	18	64	1	.277
1980	Texas..........	1B-3B	147	410	42	108	16	2	13	55	0	.263
1981	Texas..........	1B	95	297	33	79	17	2	8	35	4	.266
	Totals..........		412	1205	139	320	57	6	40	159	5	.266

LEON ROBERTS 31 6-3 200   Bats R Throws R

He's one Ranger who shouldn't be blamed for club's annual collapse last year . . . Had to play his way into the starting lineup and over one-third of his hits were for extra bases . . . Proved to be a valuable pickup despite apparently being an afterthought in the huge deal with Seattle that brought him to Texas in December 1980. Rangers sent Richie Zisk to Seattle, while Rick Honeycutt was their prime goal . . . Signed originally with Detroit, but did not blossom until '78 when he was named Seattle's MVP off his .302, 22 HR and 92 RBI . . . Born Jan. 22, 1951, in Vicksburg, Miss.

Year	Club	Pos.	G	AB	R	H	2B	3B	HR	RBI	SB	Avg.
1974	Detroit.........	OF	17	63	5	17	3	2	0	7	0	.270
1975	Detroit.........	OF	129	447	51	115	17	5	10	38	3	.257
1976	Houston.........	OF	87	235	31	68	11	2	7	33	1	.289
1977	Houston.........	OF	19	27	1	2	0	0	0	2	0	.074
1978	Seattle.........	OF	134	472	78	142	21	7	22	92	6	.301
1979	Seattle.........	OF	140	450	61	122	24	6	15	54	3	.271
1980	Seattle.........	OF	119	374	48	94	18	3	10	33	8	.251
1981	Texas..........	OF	72	233	26	65	17	2	4	31	3	.279
	Totals..........		717	2301	301	625	111	27	68	290	24	.272

DOC MEDICH 33 6-5 227   Bats R Throws R

Unexpectedly emerged as the right-handed ace of the Ranger staff last year, leading the staff with four shutouts . . . In 1980 he led the Ranger staff in victories, but got very little recognition for it . . . A resident in general surgery at Pittsburgh's Allegheny General Hospital, he has twice been forced into practice, saving the lives of heart-attack victims before games . . . Born Dec. 9, 1948, in Aliquippa, Pa. . . . Began career with Yankees and was a consistent double-figure winner for them until traded to Pirates in '76 for Willie Randolph . . . Rangers signed him as a free agent in November 1977.

Year	Club	G	IP	W	L	Pct.	SO	BB	H	ERA
1972	New York (AL)	1	0	0	0	.000	0	2	2	
1973	New York (AL)	34	235	14	9	.609	145	74	217	2.95
1974	New York (AL)	38	280	19	15	.559	154	91	275	3.60
1975	New York (AL)	38	272	16	16	.500	132	72	271	3.51
1976	Pittsburgh	29	179	8	11	.421	86	48	193	3.52
1977	Oak.-Sea.	29	170	12	6	.667	77	53	181	4.55
1977	New York (NL)	1	7	0	1	.000	3	1	6	3.86
1978	Texas	28	171	9	8	.529	71	52	166	3.74
1979	Texas	29	149	10	7	.588	58	49	156	4.17
1980	Texas	34	204	14	11	.560	91	56	230	3.93
1981	Texas	20	143	10	6	.625	65	33	136	3.08
	Totals	281	1810	112	90	.554	882	531	1833	3.65

RICK HONEYCUTT 27 6-1 190   Bats L Throws L

Came back strong from embarrassing suspension in 1980. Was caught taping a tack to his glove Sept. 30, 1980 and was suspended rest of season and five days into 1981 . . . Was top winner on Texas staff in '81 and also led club in complete games . . . Rangers acquired him from Seattle in big off-season deal of 1980 winter meetings . . . Born June 29, 1954, in Chattanooga, Tenn. . . . Attended U. of Tennessee and was originally signed by Pirates in June 1976 . . . Played first base when not pitching during his first year in the minors.

Year	Club	G	IP	W	L	Pct.	SO	BB	H	ERA
1977	Seattle	10	29	0	1	.000	17	11	26	4.34
1978	Seattle	26	134	5	11	.313	50	49	150	4.90
1979	Seattle	33	194	11	12	.478	83	67	201	4.04
1980	Seattle	30	203	10	17	.370	79	60	221	3.95
1981	Texas	20	128	11	6	.647	40	17	120	3.30
	Totals	119	688	37	47	.440	269	204	718	4.06

DOUG FLYNN 31 5-11 165   Bats R Throws R

Weak bat prompted Mets to give him up in trade for reliever Jim Kern . . . Slumped at plate after a .388 April . . . Batted .239 in the first half and dipped to .201 after strike . . . Came to Mets in Tom Seaver swap . . . Won Gold Glove for first time in 1980, fielding .991 . . . Many regarded him as finest second baseman in league . . . Born April 18, 1951, in Lexington, Ky. . . . Belted three triples in a game in '80, tying major-league mark . . . Played basketball and baseball at Kentucky . . . Nephew of legendary Adolph Rupp . . . Became a country and western singer in winter of 1980-81 . . . Father, Robert, played in Dodgers' organization.

Year	Club	Pos.	G	AB	R	H	2B	3B	HR	RBI	SB	Avg.
1975	Cincinnati	3B-2B-SS	89	127	17	34	7	0	1	20	3	.268
1976	Cincinnati	2B-3B-SS	93	219	20	62	5	2	1	20	2	.283
1977	Cin.-N.Y. (NL)...	SS-2B-3B	126	314	14	62	7	2	0	19	1	.197
1978	New York (NL)..	SS-2B	156	532	37	126	12	8	0	36	3	.237
1979	New York (NL)..	2B-SS	157	555	35	135	19	5	4	61	0	.243
1980	New York (NL)..	2B-SS	128	443	46	113	9	8	0	24	2	.255
1981	New York (NL)..	2B-SS	105	325	24	72	12	4	1	20	1	.222
	Totals..........		854	2515	193	604	71	29	7	200	12	.240

MICKEY RIVERS 33 5-10 162   Bats L Throws L

Failed to hit .300 for the first time since coming to the Rangers from Yankees in '79 . . . Is stealing fewer and fewer bases each season, which is an indication he may be fading as a productive player . . . Born Oct. 30, 1948, in Miami . . . Had his best seasons with the Yankees in the mid-'70s and was considered the catalyst on their 1977-78 world championship clubs . . . Rangers got him in midseason 1979 deal for Oscar Gamble . . . Had vintage 1980 season for Rangers and was named club's Player of the Year by the writers.

Year	Club	Pos.	G	AB	R	H	2B	3B	HR	RBI	SB	Avg.
1970	California.......	OF	17	25	6	8	2	0	0	3	1	.320
1971	California.......	OF	78	268	31	71	12	2	1	12	13	.265
1972	California.......	OF	58	159	18	34	6	2	0	7	4	.214
1973	California.......	OF	30	129	26	45	6	4	0	16	8	.349
1974	California.......	OF	118	466	69	133	19	11	3	31	30	.285
1975	California.......	OF	155	615	70	175	17	13	1	53	70	.285
1976	New York (AL)..	OF	137	590	95	184	31	8	8	67	43	.312
1977	New York (AL)..	OF	138	565	79	184	18	5	12	69	22	.326
1978	New York (AL)..	OF	141	559	78	148	25	8	11	48	25	.265
1979	NY (AL)-Texas...	OF	132	533	72	156	27	8	9	50	10	.293
1980	Texas..........	OF	147	630	96	210	32	6	7	60	18	.333
1981	Texas..........	OF	99	399	62	114	21	2	3	26	9	.286
	Totals..........		1250	4938	702	1462	216	69	55	442	253	.296

BUDDY BELL 30 6-2 185   Bats R Throws R

The best player on the Rangers, as evidenced by his team-leading HR, RBI and gamer statistics last year . . . Has few peers defensively at third, too . . . Rangers got him in straight-up deal with Indians for Toby Harrah in December 1978 . . . Born Aug. 27, 1951, in Pittsburgh . . . Father, Gus, played outfield with Pirates, Reds, Braves and Mets . . . Rangers have occasionally moved him over to shortstop where he's played well, but third is where he belongs . . . Earned a

Gold Glove in '79 . . . Originally came up as an outfielder with Indians . . . Has played on three all-star teams so far.

Year	Club	Pos.	G	AB	R	H	2B	3B	HR	RBI	SB	Avg.
1972	Cleveland.......	OF-3B	132	466	49	119	21	1	9	36	5	.255
1973	Cleveland.......	3B-OF	156	631	86	169	23	7	14	59	7	.268
1974	Cleveland.......	3B	116	423	51	111	15	1	7	46	1	.262
1975	Cleveland.......	3B	153	553	66	150	20	4	10	59	6	.271
1976	Cleveland.......	3B-1B	159	604	75	170	26	2	7	60	3	.281
1977	Cleveland.......	3B-OF	129	479	64	140	23	4	11	64	1	.292
1978	Cleveland.......	3B	142	556	71	157	27	8	6	62	1	.282
1979	Texas..........	3B-SS	162	670	89	200	42	3	18	101	5	.299
1980	Texas..........	3B-SS	129	490	76	161	24	4	17	83	3	.329
1981	Texas..........	3B-SS	97	360	44	106	16	1	10	64	3	.294
	Totals..........		1375	5232	671	1483	237	35	109	634	35	.283

TOP PROSPECTS

JOHN BUTCHER 25 6-4 190   **Bats R Throws R**
Showed his promise with a 1-0, five-hit shutout of Angels on next-to-last day of '81 season. Struck out eight in the game and walked only one . . . In '80, he led International League with 14 complete games . . . Has excellent control, which could be his ticket to stay this year . . . Born March 8, 1957, in Glendale, Cal.

MIKE RICHARDT 23 6-0 170   **Bats R Throws R**
Was the American Association batting champion with a .354 mark at Wichita last year and Rangers plan to give him a long look at second base this spring . . . Good contact hitter and considered an excellent fielder . . . Was Rangers' Minor League Player of the Year in 1980 when he hit .279 at Charleston of the International League . . . Born May 24, 1958, in Los Angeles.

MANAGER DON ZIMMER: Discovered the same fate as all his predecessors in Texas last year. That is, the Rangers just don't play as well as they look . . . Had the club in contention just before the strike, then watched them collapse the second half as pitching fell off . . . Signed as Rangers' manager Nov. 12, 1980, after being let go by Boston earlier in the year . . . Made his big-league managerial debut in '72 with the

Padres . . . Was a scrappy infielder in his playing days with Dodgers, Cubs, Mets, Reds and Senators . . . Career was nearly ended in 1953 when he was struck in the head by a pitch and missed rest of season. Has a plate in his head from incident . . . Born Jan. 17, 1931, in Cincinnati.

GREATEST CATCHER

Somehow it is difficult to associate the Texas Rangers with Washington. But if you look back a few years in the baseball record books, you will discover that the present Texas franchise was, in fact, the Washington Senators in its 1961 conception. The Washington Senators, old or new, never had a catcher of Hall-of-Fame potential. The closest might have been Muddy Ruel, who caught for the World Champion 1924 Senators and had a lifetime batting average of .275 for 19 years.

So if you're looking for a great catcher here, you've got to go to the present—and Jim Sundberg. Whose work could compare to the steady, efficient, potential Hall-of-Fame job Jim Sundberg has done behind the plate for the Rangers since 1974? He came up to the majors with just one year of minor-league experience and has averaged 145 games per season since (strike year not included). In that time, Sundberg has won five Gold Gloves for defensive excellence. In '78, he batted safely in 22 straight games and in '79 he established the AL record for highest-fielding percentage by a catcher (.995). In addition, Sundberg now holds the AL record for most seasons leading the league in assists (five). He has twice been selected an AL all-star.

ALL-TIME RANGER SEASON RECORDS

BATTING: Mickey Rivers, .333, 1980
HRs: Jeff Burroughs, 30, 1973
RBIs: Jeff Burroughs, 118, 1974
STEALS: Bump Wills, 52, 1978
WINS: Ferguson Jenkins, 25, 1974
STRIKEOUTS: Gaylord Perry, 233, 1975

INSIDE THE
NATIONAL LEAGUE

By NICK PETERS
Oakland Tribune

	West	*East*
PREDICTED ORDER OF FINISH	Houston Astros	Montreal Expos
	Los Angeles Dodgers	Philadelphia Phillies
	Cincinnati Reds	St. Louis Cardinals
	San Francisco Giants	Pittsburgh Pirates
	San Diego Padres	New York Mets
	Atlanta Braves	Chicago Cubs

Playoff winner: Houston

WEST DIVISION	Owner		Morning Line Manager
1 ASTROS Orange & white Ready to go all the way	John McMullen	1981 W 61 L 49	**3-2** Bill Virdon
2 DODGERS Royal blue & white Lots of changes, confusion	Peter O'Malley	1981 W 63 L 47	**3-2** Tommy Lasorda
3 REDS Red & white Always in contention	J.R. and W.J. Williams	1981 W 66 L 42	**4-1** John McNamara
4 GIANTS White, orange & black Something missing	Bob Lurie	1981 W 56 L 55	**20-1** Frank Robinson
5 PADRES Brown, gold & white Best chance for improvement	Ray Kroc	1981 W 41 L 69	**50-1** Dick Williams
6 BRAVES Royal blue & white Same old act	Ted Turner	1981 W 50 L 56	**100-1** Joe Torre

Another three-team race, with **ASTROS** prevailing because of strength down the stretch. **DODGERS** could stumble at the gate with a new look and **REDS** will always make it close. **GIANTS** interesting, but too many weaknesses. New jockey perks **PADRES**, but **BRAVES** heading for a fall.

THE OIL WELL HANDICAP

106th Running. National League Race. Distance, 162 games plus playoff. Purse (based on '81) $13,000 per winning player, division, up to $35,000 winning player total for World Championship. A field of 12 entered in two divisions.

Track Record 116 wins—Chicago, 1906

EAST DIVISION	Owner		Morning Line Manager
1 **EXPOS** Scarlet, white & royal blue Class of the field	Charles Bronfman	1981 W 60 L 48	**3-2** Jim Fanning
2 **PHILLIES** Crimson & white A little too old	Bill Giles	1981 W 59 L 48	**5-1** Pat Corrales
3 **CARDINALS** Red & white Not well armed for race	August A. Busch	1981 W 59 L 43	**10-1** Whitey Herzog
4 **PIRATES** Old gold, white & black Ready for pasture	John Galbreath	1981 W 46 L 56	**25-1** Chuck Tanner
5 **METS** Orange, white & blue A frisky young colt	N. Doubleday-F. Wilpon	1981 W 41 L 62	**50-1** George Bamberger
6 **CUBS** Royal blue & white New look, no talent	Tribune Co.-A.J. McKenna	1981 W 38 L 65	**75-1** Lee Elia

Basically a three-horse race with **EXPOS** gaining an edge following last year's win. **PHILLIES** will be hard-pressed to place because of age, but **CARDINALS'** lack of power could be detrimental to fast finish. **PIRATES** running on memories, but still strong enough to stave off steadily-improving **METS**. As usual, green **CUBS** hold up rear.

ATLANTA BRAVES

TEAM DIRECTORY: Chairman of the Board: Bill Bartholomay; Pres.: Ted Turner; VP-GM: John Mullen; Dir. Play. Dev.: Hank Aaron; Trav. Sec.: Bill Acree; Dir. Pub. Rel.: Wayne Minshew; Mgr.: Joe Torre. Home: Atlanta Stadium (52,791). Field distances: 330, l.f. line; 402, c.f.; 330, r.f. line. Spring training: West Palm Beach, Fla.

SCOUTING REPORT

HITTING: A mystery team in 1981, explaining the change in managers. The Braves play in one of baseball's best parks for hitters, right? So how could they merely bat .243, 11th in the league, and finish behind 10 clubs in slugging percentage? That's the question new skipper Joe Torre must answer, because nobody else could figure out why the lights went out in Georgia last season. Whatever the reason, Claudell Washington was the batting leader at .291 and Bob Horner led the home-run parade with 15.

It was a sorry attack and there is no reasonable excuse. The offense unquestionably suffered when Gary Matthews went to Philly, but Washington helped to heal that wound. What is difficult to understand is why Dale Murphy slumped to .247 or why Horner hasn't become the superstar everyone expected. You can chalk it up as an off year, but the club was dormant over the winter, so the same cast must try again. The only consistent hitter, though, is the unspectacularly efficient Chris Chambliss. So Horner and Murphy must improve or the team won't.

PITCHING: Surprisingly effective last year considering the ballpark and the patchwork rotation. The Braves had a 3.45 team ERA, so they stayed in more games with their pitching than with their overrated offense. None of the pitchers ranked among the leaders, but Rick Mahler blossomed into a success (8-6, 2.81) and Phil Niekro will never hurt you.

The glue, however, was an excellent bullpen headed by Rick Camp (9-3, 1.78, 17 saves), Al Hrabosky (1.06) and Gene Garber (2.59). They turned the narrow defeats of the past into victories, as a 10-4 record in extra-inning games and an 18-10 mark in one-run decisions would attest.

FIELDING: Not good. Last year the club had a .976 percentage, 10th in the league, and only first baseman Chambliss, second baseman Glenn Hubbard and Washington were reliable fielders. Chambliss led the loop in assists and chances, Hubbard's .991

Bob Horner had "off" year, clubbing 15 homers.

percentage was .001 behind the leader and Washington surprised with only one error in 151 chances. Rafael Ramirez' 30 errors were the most by a shortstop. Bruce Benedict shows promise behind the plate, leading the league in assists. The big weakness is on the left side, where third baseman Horner and Ramirez don't do the pitchers any favors.

OUTLOOK: Not encouraging considering the strength of the division and the club's inactive winter. There simply are too many question marks for a club destined to have difficulty breaking .500. If Murphy, Horner, Chambliss and Washington all have that big year together, something could happen. But that's highly unlikely, especially since the club competes in a pitching-rich division that can make any lineup look bad. The pitching doesn't seem as good as the ERA suggests and the defense is shaky, so this obviously is a team closer to the bottom than the top.

ATLANTA BRAVES 1982 ROSTER

MANAGER Joe Torre
Coaches—Tommie Aaron, Bob Gibson, Dal Maxvill, Joe Pignatano, Rube Walker

PITCHERS

No.	Name	1981 Club	W-L	IP	SO	ERA	B-T	Ht.	Wt.	Born
50	Alvarez, Jose	Richmond	7-5	71	61	2.15	R-R	5-11	175	4/12/56 Tampa, FL
		Atlanta	0-0	2	2	0.00				
32	Bedrosian, Steve	Richmond	10-10	184	144	2.69	R-R	6-3	200	12/6/57 Methuen, MA
		Atlanta	1-2	24	9	4.50				
40	Boggs, Tom	Atlanta	3-13	143	81	4.09	R-R	6-2	200	10/25/55 Poughkeepsie, NY
34	Bradford, Larry	Atlanta	2-0	27	14	3.67	R-L	6-1	205	2/21/51 Chicago, IL
37	Camp, Rick	Atlanta	9-3	76	47	1.78	R-R	6-1	198	6/10/53 Trion, GA
38	Cowley, Joe	Savannah	6-0	69	56	2.74	R-R	6-5	220	8/15/58 Lexington, KY
		Richmond	3-2	45	39	2.80				
36	Diaz, Carlos	Richmond	3-3	48	29	2.81	R-L	6-0	170	1/7/58 Honolulu, HI
26	Garber, Gene	Atlanta	4-6	59	34	2.59	R-R	5-10	175	11/13/47 Lancaster, PA
49	Hanna, Preston	Atlanta	2-1	35	22	6.43	R-R	6-1	185	9/10/54 Pensacola, FL
39	Hrabosky, Al	Atlanta	1-1	34	13	1.06	R-L	5-10	180	7/21/49 Oakland, CA
42	Mahler, Rick	Atlanta	8-6	112	54	2.81	R-R	6-1	190	8/5/53 Austin, TX
29	Matula, Rick	Richmond	7-4	94	37	2.97	R-R	6-0	195	11/22/53 Wharton, TX
		Atlanta	0-0	7	0	6.43				
27	McWilliams, Larry	Richmond	13-10	178	157	4.35	L-L	6-5	175	2/10/54 Wichita, KS
		Atlanta	2-1	38	23	3.08				
35	Niekro, Phil	Atlanta	7-7	139	62	3.11	R-R	6-1	180	4/1/39 Blaine, OH
43	Walk, Bob	Richmond	2-1	22	13	2.45	R-R	6-3	195	11/26/56 Van Nuys, CA
		Atlanta	1-4	43	16	4.60				

CATCHERS

No.	Name	1981 Club	H	HR	RBI	Pct.	B-T	Ht.	Wt.	Born
20	Benedict, Bruce	Atlanta	78	5	35	.264	R-R	6-1	185	8/18/55 Birmingham, AL
4	Pocoroba, Biff	Atlanta	22	0	8	.180	L-R	5-10	180	7/25/53 Burbank, CA
14	Sinatro, Matt	Richmond	101	6	53	.235	R-R	5-9	174	3/22/60 Hartford, CT
		Atlanta	9	0	4	.281				

INFIELDERS

No.	Name	1981 Club	H	HR	RBI	Pct.	B-T	Ht.	Wt.	Born
10	Chambliss, Chris	Atlanta	110	8	51	.272	L-R	6-1	215	12/26/48 Dayton, OH
2	Gomez, Luis	Atlanta	7	0	1	.200	R-R	5-9	150	8/19/51 Mexico
5	Horner, Bob	Atlanta	83	15	42	.277	R-R	5-11	195	8/6/57 Junction City, KS
17	Hubbard, Glen	Atlanta	85	6	33	.235	R-R	5-9	160	9/25/57 Germany
47	Jacoby, Brook	Savannah	148	24	81	.292	R-R	5-11	175	11/23/59 Philadelphia, PA
		Atlanta	2	0	1	.200				
6	Johnson, Randy	Richmond	132	12	72	.281	R-R	6-1	185	6/10/56 Escondido, CA
51	Perry, Gerald	Savannah	132	19	83	.277	L-R	5-11	180	10/30/60 Savannah, GA
16	Ramirez, Rafael	Atlanta	67	2	20	.218	R-R	6-0	170	2/18/59 Dominican Republic
15	Runge, Paul	Richmond	98	9	41	.230	R-R	6-0	165	5/21/58 Kingston, NY
		Atlanta	7	0	2	.259				
11	Smith, Ken	Richmond	128	11	60	.268	L-R	6-1	195	2/12/58 Youngstown, OH
		Atlanta	1	0	0	.333				

OUTFIELDERS

No.	Name	1981 Club	H	HR	RBI	Pct.	B-T	Ht.	Wt.	Born
30	Asselstine, Brian	Atlanta	22	2	10	.256	L-R	6-1	190	9/23/53 Santa Barbara, CA
22	Butler, Brett	Richmond	156	3	36	.335	L-L	5-10	160	6/15/57 Los Angeles, CA
		Atlanta	32	0	4	.254				
31	Hall, Albert	Savannah	150	5	27	.308	B-R	5-11	155	3/7/59 Birmingham, AL
		Atlanta	0	0	0	.000				
19	Harper, Terry	Richmond	10	2	4	.227	R-R	6-1	195	8/19/55 Douglasville, GA
		Atlanta	19	2	8	.260				
24	Kominsk, Brad	Durham	148	33	104	.322	R-R	6-2	185	4/4/61 Lima, OH
25	Linares, Rufino	Atlanta	67	5	25	.265	R-R	6-0	170	2/28/55 Dominican Republic
48	Miller, Ed	Atlanta	31	0	7	.231	B-R	5-9	165	6/29/57 San Pablo, CA
3	Murphy, Dale	Atlanta	91	13	50	.247	R-R	6-4	185	3/12/56 Portland, OR
1	Royster, Jerry	Atlanta	19	0	9	.204	R-R	6-0	165	10/18/52 Sacramento, CA
18	Washington, Claudell	Atlanta	93	5	37	.291	L-L	6-0	190	8/31/54 Los Angeles, CA
28	Whisenton, Larry	Richmond	121	13	72	.271	L-L	6-1	190	7/3/56 St. Louis, MO
		Atlanta	1	0	0	.200				

BRAVE PROFILES

CLAUDELL WASHINGTON 27 6-0 190 Bats L Throws L

Under considerable pressure after signing fat contract as a free agent . . . Silenced some skeptics by leading Braves in hitting at .291 . . . Batted .294 in first half and .288 after strike . . . Was at his best in August, batting .343 . . . Surprising that more of his power didn't surface in cozy Fulton County Stadium . . . Has unique distinction of being one of only three players to blast three homers in a game in each league . . . Did it for White Sox against Tigers in '79 and for Mets against Dodgers in '80 . . . Babe Ruth and Johnny Mize are others to turn trick . . . Born Aug. 31, 1954, in Los Angeles . . . Didn't play as a prep, but was signed off sandlots and batted .308 in his first full year with A's in 1975.

Year	Club	Pos.	G	AB	R	H	2B	3B	HR	RBI	SB	Avg.
1974	Oakland	OF	73	221	16	63	10	5	0	19	6	.285
1975	Oakland	OF	148	590	86	182	24	7	10	48	40	.308
1976	Oakland	OF	134	490	65	126	20	6	5	53	37	.257
1977	Texas	OF	129	521	63	148	31	2	12	68	21	.284
1978	Texas-Chi (AL)	OF	98	356	34	90	16	5	6	33	5	.253
1979	Chicago (AL)	OF	131	471	79	132	33	5	13	66	19	.280
1980	Chicago (AL)	OF	32	90	15	26	4	2	1	12	4	.289
1980	New York (NL)	OF	79	284	38	78	16	4	10	42	17	.275
1981	Atlanta	OF	85	320	37	93	22	3	5	37	12	.291
	Totals		909	3343	433	938	176	39	62	407	161	.281

CHRIS CHAMBLISS 33 6-1 215　　　　Bats L Throws R

Another Brave who suffered a power shortage last year . . . Hit five of his eight home runs in August, batting .317 . . . Showed consistency by batting .271-.273 in the two halves . . . Made a big splash in his NL debut in 1980, tying Henry Aaron's club record of 37 doubles . . . Born Dec. 26, 1948, in Dayton, Ohio . . . Quiet, solid performer who has been underrated . . . Became an overnight celebrity when his ninth-inning homer against the Royals placed Yankees in 1976 World Series . . . Batted .524 against the Reds in Series and is a .340 hitter in 14 postseason games . . . After All-American career at UCLA, batted .342 at Wichita in 1970, becoming the first rookie to win a Triple-A batting title.

Year	Club	Pos.	G	AB	R	H	2B	3B	HR	RBI	SB	Avg.
1971	Cleveland.......	1B	111	415	49	114	20	4	9	48	2	.275
1972	Cleveland.......	1B	121	466	51	136	27	2	6	44	3	.292
1973	Cleveland.......	1B	155	572	70	156	30	2	11	53	4	.273
1974	Cleve.-N.Y. (AL) .	1B	127	467	46	119	20	3	6	50	0	.255
1975	New York (AL) ..	1B	150	562	66	171	38	4	9	72	0	.304
1976	New York (AL) ..	1B	156	641	79	188	32	6	17	96	1	.293
1977	New York (AL) ..	1B	157	600	90	172	32	6	17	90	4	.287
1978	New York (AL) ..	1B	162	625	81	171	26	3	12	90	2	.274
1979	New York (AL) ..	1B	149	554	61	155	27	3	18	63	3	.280
1980	Atlanta.........	1B	158	602	83	170	37	2	18	72	7	.282
1981	Atlanta.........	1B	107	404	44	110	25	2	8	51	4	.272
	Totals..........		1553	5908	720	1662	324	37	131	729	30	.281

DALE MURPHY 26 6-4 185   Bats R Throws R

Somewhat disappointing year at the plate, batting .250 in first half and .242 thereafter . . . Made switch from catcher to center field two years ago and was an immediate success . . . Belted three homers against Giants in '79 . . . Had 13 homers and 36 RBI after six weeks of that season before tearing up a knee . . . Bounced back with a great year in 1980 . . . Born March 12, 1956, in Portland, Ore. . . . Only Mike Schmidt and Bob Horner hit more homers in NL in 1980 . . . Made NL All-Star squad that season . . . Good speed for big man, was No. 2 on club with 14 steals last year . . . Attended Brigham Young University.

Year	Club	Pos.	G	AB	R	H	2B	3B	HR	RBI	SB	Avg.
1976	Atlanta.........	C	19	65	3	17	6	0	0	9	0	.262
1977	Atlanta.........	C	18	76	5	24	8	1	2	14	0	.316
1978	Atlanta.........	C-1B	151	530	66	120	14	3	23	79	11	.226
1979	Atlanta.........	1B-C	104	384	53	106	7	2	21	57	6	.276
1980	Atlanta.........	OF-1B	156	569	98	160	27	2	33	89	9	.281
1981	Atlanta.........	OF	104	369	43	91	12	1	13	50	14	.247
	Totals..........		552	1993	268	518	74	9	92	298	40	.260

BOB HORNER 24 6-1 195   Bats R Throws R

Greatest young slugger in game had a disappointing power season despite team-leading 15 homers . . . For second straight season he got off to slow start, connecting for only four homers in first half while batting .287 . . . Erupted for 11 homers after strike, batting .270 . . . In 1980, belted 25 of his 35 homers after the All-Star break . . . Born Aug. 1, 1957, in Junction City, Kan. . . . His 15 homers for season paled in comparison to the 14 he whacked in July 1980 . . . That season, he refused Ted Turner's option to Triple-A and showed up boss with .302 average, 30 homers and 76 RBI over final 90 games . . . Tremendous potential as power hitter . . . Belted NCAA-record 58 career homers at Arizona State, including season mark of 25 his final year.

Year	Club	Pos.	G	AB	R	H	2B	3B	HR	RBI	SB	Avg.
1978	Atlanta.........	3B	89	323	50	86	17	1	23	63	0	.266
1979	Atlanta.........	3B-1B	121	487	66	153	15	1	33	98	0	.314
1980	Atlanta.........	3B-1B	124	463	81	124	14	1	35	89	3	.268
1981	Atlanta.........	3B	79	300	42	83	10	0	15	42	2	.277
	Totals.........		413	1573	239	446	56	3	106	292	5	.284

GLENN HUBBARD 24 5-9 160   Bats R Throws R

Like most of his teammates, tailed off at the dish last year . . . At least showed consistency, batting .236 first half and .235 second . . . Scrappy play and solid glove were instrumental in club's 1980 rise . . . Joined Braves in June and they went 65-54 with him at second base . . . Flashed good power with compact swing, belting 15 homers over last two seasons . . . Born Sept. 25, 1957, in Hann Air Force Base, West Germany . . . A standout prep wrestler in Utah . . . Batted at least .315 in last five minor-league seasons before joining parent club to stay . . . Had identical .336 Triple-A averages at Richmond in '78 and '79 . . . Regarded as one of best hustlers in majors.

Year	Club	Pos.	G	AB	R	H	2B	3B	HR	RBI	SB	Avg.
1978	Atlanta.........	2B	44	163	15	42	4	0	2	13	2	.258
1979	Atlanta.........	2B	97	325	34	75	12	0	3	29	0	.231
1980	Atlanta.........	2B	117	431	55	107	21	3	9	43	7	.248
1981	Atlanta.........	2B	99	361	39	85	13	5	6	33	4	.235
	Totals.........		357	1280	143	309	50	8	20	118	13	.241

RUFINO LINARES 27 6-0 170   Bats R Throws R

A potentially solid hitter if his minor-league statistics and 78 games with 1981 Braves are indicative . . . Batted .319 in May and had a .258 average in first half before improving to .270 after the strike . . . Outfielder was born Feb. 28, 1955, in San Pedro de Macoris, Dominican Republic . . . Earned promotion with tremendous success in 1980, batting .425 in 51 games at Savannah and .329 at Richmond, but lacked sufficient at-bats to win batting titles . . . Only Savannah player to ever average above .300 over an entire season, batting .303 in '78 . . . Hit safely in 56 of 63 games played at Richmond in 1980.

Year	Club	Pos.	G	AB	R	H	2B	3B	HR	RBI	SB	Avg.
1981	Atlanta........	OF	78	253	27	67	9	2	5	25	8	.265

PHIL NIEKRO 43 6-1 180   Bats R Throws R

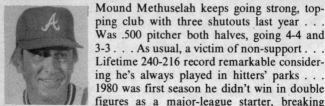

Mound Methuselah keeps going strong, topping club with three shutouts last year . . . Was .500 pitcher both halves, going 4-4 and 3-3 . . . As usual, a victim of non-support . . . Lifetime 240-216 record remarkable considering he's always played in hitters' parks . . . 1980 was first season he didn't win in double figures as a major-league starter, breaking string of 14 straight with at least 11 victories . . . Born April 1, 1939, in Lansing, Ohio . . . One of few pitchers in history to win 20 and lose 20 the same season, going 21-20 in '79 . . . A workhorse, topped NL in innings pitched 1977-79 . . . Also league ERA leader with a 1.87 in 1967, when he had nine saves to go with 11 wins . . . Fired no-hitter against San Diego, Aug. 5, 1973 . . . Prep teammate of John Havlicek.

Year	Club	G	IP	W	L	Pct.	SO	BB	H	ERA
1964	Milwaukee...............	10	15	0	0	.000	8	7	15	4.80
1965	Milwaukee...............	41	75	2	3	.400	40	26	73	2.88
1966	Atlanta..................	28	50	4	3	.571	17	23	48	4.14
1967	Atlanta..................	46	207	11	9	.550	129	55	164	1.87
1968	Atlanta..................	37	257	14	12	.538	140	45	228	2.50
1969	Atlanta..................	40	284	23	13	.639	193	57	235	2.57
1970	Atlanta..................	34	230	12	18	.400	168	68	222	4.27
1971	Atlanta..................	42	269	15	14	.517	173	70	248	2.98
1972	Atlanta..................	38	282	16	12	.571	164	53	254	3.06
1973	Atlanta..................	42	245	13	10	.565	131	89	214	3.31
1974	Atlanta..................	41	302	20	13	.606	195	88	249	2.38
1975	Atlanta..................	39	276	15	15	.500	144	72	285	3.20
1976	Atlanta..................	38	271	17	11	.607	173	101	249	3.29
1977	Atlanta..................	44	330	16	20	.444	262	164	315	4.04
1978	Atlanta..................	44	334	19	18	.514	248	102	295	2.88
1979	Atlanta..................	44	342	21	20	.512	208	113	311	3.39
1980	Atlanta..................	40	275	15	18	.455	176	85	256	3.63
1981	Atlanta..................	22	139	7	7	.500	62	56	120	3.11
	Totals..................	670	4183	240	216	.526	2640	1274	3781	3.13

BRUCE BENEDICT 26 6-1 185   Bats R Throws R

His first full season as a big leaguer was the best for this strong-armed catcher . . . Off to a good start, batted .287 in first half . . . Hit .234 after the strike . . . Has shown gradual improvement in three years as a big leaguer . . . Born Aug. 18, 1955, in Birmingham, Ala. . . . Used weight program to strengthen arm and is adroit at cutting down base runners

. . . Also able to handle Phil Niekro's flutterball with minimal difficulty . . . Named male Athlete of the Year at Nebraska-Omaha in 1975 . . . Nicknamed "Eggs," naturally . . . Father played pro ball with Yankees and Cardinals farm clubs.

Year	Club	Pos.	G	AB	R	H	2B	3B	HR	RBI	SB	Avg.
1978	Atlanta.........	C	22	52	3	13	2	0	0	1	0	.250
1979	Atlanta.........	C	76	204	14	46	11	0	0	15	1	.225
1980	Atlanta.........	C	120	359	18	91	14	1	2	34	3	.253
1981	Atlanta.........	C	90	295	26	78	12	1	5	35	1	.264
	Totals..........		308	910	61	228	39	2	7	85	5	.251

RICK CAMP 28 6-1 198   Bats R Throws R

One of majors' finest relievers, has kept ERA below 2.00 two years in a row . . . Was 5-1 with 1.38 ERA and eight saves the first half . . . Had 4-2 record and nine saves after the strike . . . Shared NL Pitcher of the Month honors in August for 2-0 record and five saves . . . NL Pitcher of Week, Aug. 17-23, with four saves in four games . . . Born June 10, 1953, in Trion, Ga. . . . Remarkable comeback story . . . Arm trouble had him on verge of being washed up, but he made squad as non-roster player in spring training of 1980 . . . Was voted Braves' MVP by teammates following sensational second half during which he saved 19 games after the All-Star break . . . Attended West Georgia College.

Year	Club	G	IP	W	L	Pct.	SO	BB	H	ERA
1976	Atlanta.................	5	11	0	1	.000	6	2	13	6.55
1977	Atlanta.................	54	79	6	3	.667	51	47	89	3.99
1978	Atlanta.................	42	74	2	4	.333	23	32	99	3.77
1980	Atlanta.................	77	108	6	4	.600	33	29	92	1.92
1981	Atlanta.................	48	76	9	3	.750	47	12	68	1.78
	Totals.................	226	348	23	15	.605	160	122	361	2.90

TOP PROSPECTS

BRETT BUTLER 24 5-10 160   Bats L Throws L

This outfielder's name is a natural for Dixie and his swift rise through the Braves' system suggests stardom may be on the way . . . Batted .366 for Durham in 1980 and was promoted to Triple-A, where he was named International League MVP last year after batting .335 with 44 steals and 103 walks in 125 games . . . In a brief trial with Atlanta, he batted .254 in 40 games . . . Born June 15, 1957, in Los Angeles . . . Club also high on catcher Matt Sinatro, who batted .281 in 12 games after recall from Richmond.

MANAGER JOE TORRE: Had a year to go on his contract when

Mets dumped him at end of last season . . .
Immediately snatched by Atlanta . . . Should
be a hit . . . Was on first Atlanta club, batting
.315 with 36 homers and 101 RBI in 1966 . . .
Spent 10 years with Milwaukee and Atlanta,
but had best year in 1973, winning MVP and
batting honors with a .363 average for the
Cardinals . . . Born July 18, 1940, in Brooklyn
. . . Nine-time NL All-Star at first, third and catcher . . . Regarded a very patient manager, but Mets wanted a change after
he failed to produce a winner in five seasons . . . Succeeded Joe
Frazier as Mets' manager May 31, 1977, and soon after retired as
active player . . . Batted .297 lifetime with 252 homers and 1,185
RBI.

GREATEST CATCHER

A two-way tie between two moderns, Del Crandall ranking as
the best in Milwaukee history and new manager Joe Torre quali-
fying as Atlanta's finest receiver.

Crandall, who played with the Braves from 1949 to 1963,
posted a .254 lifetime average, five times topped NL catchers in
games played and was the man behind the success of Warren
Spahn and Lew Burdette.

Torre provided more sock, averaging .294 in his Braves career
from 1961-67. He batted .321 in '64 and had his finest Atlanta
season in '66, batting .315 with 36 homers and 101 RBI.

ALL-TIME BRAVE SEASON RECORDS

BATTING: Rogers Hornsby, .387, 1928
HRs: Eddie Mathews, 47, 1953
    Hank Aaron, 47, 1971
RBIs: Eddie Mathews, 135, 1953
STEALS: Ralph Meyers, 57, 1913
WINS: Vic Willis, 27, 1902
    Charles Pittinger, 27, 1902
    Dick Rudolph, 27, 1914
STRIKEOUTS: Phil Niekro, 262, 1977

Knuckleballing Phil Niekro is club leader in strikeouts.

CINCINNATI REDS

TEAM DIRECTORY: Chairmen of the Board: James R. Williams, William J. Williams; Pres.: Dick Wagner; VP-Scouting Dir.: Joe Bowen; VP-Play. Per.: Sheldon Bender; Dir. Publ.: Jim Ferguson; Trav. Sec.: Doug Bureman; Mgr.: John McNamara. Home: Riverfront Stadium (52,392). Field distances: 330, l.f. line; 404, c.f.; 330, r.f. line. Spring training: Tampa, Fla.

SCOUTING REPORT

HITTING: With Dave Collins gone via free agency and Ken Griffey traded to the Yankees, the Reds are minus 38 of their 58 stolen bases and two forces at the top of the batting order, so it's difficult to envision the club being better offensively. Last year, only the Phillies had a higher average than Cincy's .267 and only

At age 36, Tom Seaver had fine 14-2 record and 2.55 ERA.

Philly scored more runs. Without Collins and Griffey, it's doubtful the club can maintain those high standards.

But don't weep for manager John McNamara. Anyone who has Dave Concepcion, John Bench, George Foster, ex-Astro Cesar Cedeno, ex-Royal Clint Hurdle and the ever-improving Joe Nolan will score some runs. The question is how many runs the Reds will need to offset so-so pitching. Also, it remains to be seen how the RBI figures of Concepcion (67) and Foster (90) are affected by Collins' and Griffey's absence. But the Reds are a resilient lot. They didn't crumble when Tony Perez, Joe Morgan and Pete Rose left, so they may find a way again.

PITCHING: Nothing to rave about (3.73 last year), but the one-two starting punch of Tom Seaver (14-2, 2.55) and Mario Soto (12-9, 3.29) ranks with the best and they're backed by a stout bullpen. Joe Price and Tom Hume had to be doing something right last year, because Cincy topped the league with a 23-10 mark in one-run decisions. The second-line pitching could blossom, improving the staff. Bruce Berenyi, Frank Pastore and Charlie Leibrandt are brimming with potential and could make this a powerful staff if Seaver can put together another great year.

FIELDING: The Reds tied with the Cardinals as the best in the league with a .981 mark and made the fewest errors (80). The Reds had no individual leaders, except catcher Nolan, so it's a solid team defense and could improve with Collins gone and Cedeno's excellent glove in center in place of Griffey's. Concepcion remains the nonpareil shortstop. Foster made only two errors in left and Nolan justified Bench's request to do less catching by topping NL catchers with a .995 percentage. Bench handled himself well at first, but not as well as Dan Driessen.

OUTLOOK: Hard to figure. The Reds won more games than anyone (66) in the league last year, but they're not likely to improve with Collins and Griffey gone. It looks like a transitional year, with some new faces, like prospect Paul Householder, Cedeno and Hurdle, trying to pick up the slack. How the newcomers respond could determine where the club will finish. The Reds surprised by doing so well in 1981 and could do it again because other clubs like the Dodgers and the Giants also are experiencing changes. There is a nucleus of proven veterans to insure a smooth transition and—who knows?—if the Astros falter, this is a team which could sneak in. The Reds, more than anything else, know how to win. Players like Foster, Bench, Concepcion and Seaver won't let them forget.

CINCINNATI REDS 1982 ROSTER

MANAGER John McNamara
Coaches—Joe Amalfitano, Harry Dunlop, Bill Fischer,
Russ Nixon, Ron Plaza

PITCHERS

No.	Name	1981 Club	W-L	IP	SO	ERA	B-T	Ht.	Wt.	Born
38	Berenyi, Bruce	Cincinnati	9-6	126	106	3.50	R-R	6-3	215	8/21/54 Bryan, OH
54	Brito, Jose	Indianapolis	6-11	116	91	4.89	R-R	6-2	160	10/28/59 Dominican Republic
37	Combe, Geoff	Indianapolis	0-2	19	10	1.89	R-R	6-1	190	2/1/56 Melrose, MA
		Cincinnati	1-0	18	9	7.50				
—	Dowless, Mike	Waterbury	6-13	150	98	5.28	R-R	6-6	235	12/13/60 Bethesda, MD
40	Edelen, Joe	Springfield	9-1	96	45	3.56	R-R	6-0	180	9/16/55 Durant, OK
		St. L-Cin	2-0	30	15	5.70				
47	Hume, Tom	Cincinnati	9-4	68	27	3.44	R-R	6-1	180	3/29/53 Cincinnati, OH
51	LaCoss, Mike	Cincinnati	4-7	78	22	6.12	R-R	6-4	190	5/30/56 Glendale, CA
48	Lahti, Jeff	Indianapolis	6-6	100	70	2.97	R-R	6-0	180	10/8/56 Oregon City, OR
44	Leibrandt, Charlie	Indianapolis	9-7	169	101	2.93	R-L	6-4	200	10/4/56 Chicago, IL
		Cincinnati	1-1	30	9	3.60				
—	Lesley, Brad	Cedar Rapids	4-1	34	51	0.79	R-R	6-6	220	9/11/58 Turlock, CA
		Waterbury	4-1	45	37	2.60				
31	Moskau, Paul	Cincinnati	2-1	55	32	4.91	R-R	6-2	205	12/20/53 St. Joseph, MO
35	Pastore, Frank	Cincinnati	4-9	132	81	4.02	R-R	6-3	205	8/21/57 Alhambra, CA
49	Price, Joe	Cincinnati	6-1	54	41	2.50	R-L	6-4	210	11/29/56 Inglewood, CA
—	Ryder, Brian	Columbus	8-7	157	113	4.93	R-R	6-6	220	2/13/60 Worcester, MA
41	Seaver, Tom	Cincinnati	14-2	166	87	2.55	R-R	6-1	208	11/17/44 Fresno, CA
36	Soto, Mario	Cincinnati	12-9	175	151	3.29	R-R	6-0	185	7/12/56 Dominican Republic

CATCHERS

No.	Name	1981 Club	H	HR	RBI	Pct.	B-T	Ht.	Wt.	Born
5	Bench, John	Cincinnati	55	8	25	.309	R-R	6-1	215	12/7/47 Oklahoma City, OK
17	Nolan, Joe	Cincinnati	73	1	26	.309	L-R	6-0	190	5/12/51 St. Louis, MO
9	O'Berry, Mike	Cincinnati	20	1	5	.180	R-R	6-2	195	4/20/54 Birmingham, AL
60	Van Gorder, Dave	Indianapolis	108	15	66	.250	R-R	6-2	205	3/27/57 Los Angeles, CA

INFIELDERS

No.	Name	1981 Club	H	HR	RBI	Pct.	B-T	Ht.	Wt.	Born
12	Barranca, German	Indianapolis	137	5	34	.284	L-R	6-0	170	10/19/56 Mexico
		Cincinnati	2	0	1	.333				
28	Cedeno, Cesar	Houston	83	5	34	.271	R-R	6-2	190	2/25/51 Dominican Republic
13	Concepcion, Dave	Cincinnati	129	5	67	.306	R-R	6-2	175	6/17/48 Venezuela
22	Driessen, Dan	Cincinnati	55	7	33	.236	L-R	5-11	200	7/29/51 Hilton Head, SC
55	Esasky, Nick	Indianapolis	112	17	62	.265	R-R	6-3	200	2/24/60 Hialeah, FL
59	Foley, Tom	Indianapolis	81	6	27	.233	L-R	6-1	160	9/9/59 Columbus, GA
7	Landestoy, Rafael	Hou-Cin	13	0	5	.153	B-R	5-9	165	5/28/53 Dominican Republic
56	Lawless, Tom	Waterbury	152	8	50	.291	R-R	5-11	170	12/19/56 Erie, PA
16	Oester, Ron	Cincinnati	96	5	42	.271	B-R	6-2	185	5/5/56 Cincinnati, OH

OUTFIELDERS

No.	Name	1981 Club	H	HR	RBI	Pct.	B-T	Ht.	Wt.	Born
33	Biittner, Larry	Cincinnati	13	0	8	.213	L-L	6-2	200	7/27/47 Pocahontas, IA
15	Foster, George	Cincinnati	122	22	90	.295	R-R	6-1	185	12/1/48 Tuscaloosa, AL
—	Hurdle, Clint	Kansas City	25	4	15	.329	L-R	6-3	195	7/30/57 Big Rapids, MI
21	Householder, Paul	Indianapolis	136	19	77	.300	B-R	6-0	180	9/4/58 Columbus, OH
		Cincinnati	19	2	9	.275				
—	Little, Ron	Tampa	120	2	59	.262	B-L	6-2	200	2/8/61 Asheboro, NC
28	Mejias, Sam	Cincinnati	14	0	7	.286	R-R	6-0	170	5/9/52 Dominican Republic
20	Milner, Eddie	Indianapolis	130	3	42	.287	L-L	5-11	170	5/21/55 Columbus, OH
		Cincinnati	1	0	1	.200				
61	Redus, Gary	Waterbury	119	20	75	.249	R-R	6-1	180	11/1/56 Limestone Co., AL
—	Vail, Mike	Cincinnati	5	0	3	.161	R-R	6-0	185	11/10/51 San Francisco, CA
58	Walker, Duane	Indianapolis	127	19	80	.282	L-L	6-0	185	3/13/57 Pasadena, TX

RED PROFILES

GEORGE FOSTER 33 6-1 185   Bats R Throws R

Bounced back from off year and registered statistics (22 homers, 90 RBI) which would have been respectable for a full season . . . Belted eight homers and totaled 27 RBI in May . . . Topped NL with 14 homers and 49 RBI in first half, batting .297 . . . Batted .292 when season resumed . . . Missed RBI title by one . . . Born Dec. 1, 1948, in Ralph, Ala. . . . Had 13 game-winning RBI and played in all 108 Cincinnati games . . . Averaged 130 RBI per season and won three straight crowns 1976-78 . . . Blasted 52 home runs in 1977 . . . Waves a menacing black bat . . . A steal for the Reds, who obtained him from Giants for Frank Duffy and Vern Geishert in 1971.

Year	Club	Pos.	G	AB	R	H	2B	3B	HR	RBI	SB	Avg.
1969	San Francisco ...	OF	9	5	1	2	0	0	0	1	0	.400
1970	San Francisco ...	OF	9	19	2	6	1	1	1	4	0	.316
1971	S.F.-Cin.	OF	140	473	50	114	23	4	13	58	7	.241
1972	Cincinnati	OF	59	145	15	29	4	1	2	12	2	.200
1973	Cincinnati	OF	17	39	6	11	3	0	4	9	0	.282
1974	Cincinnati	OF	106	276	31	73	18	0	7	41	3	.264
1975	Cincinnati	OF-1B	134	463	71	139	24	4	23	78	2	.300
1976	Cincinnati	OF-1B	144	562	86	172	21	9	29	121	17	.306
1977	Cincinnati	OF	158	615	124	197	31	2	52	149	6	.320
1978	Cincinnati	OF	158	604	97	170	26	7	40	120	4	.281
1979	Cincinnati	OF	121	440	68	133	18	3	30	98	0	.302
1980	Cincinnati	OF	144	528	79	144	21	5	25	93	1	.273
1981	Cincinnati	OF	108	414	64	122	23	2	22	90	4	.295
	Totals..........		1307	4583	694	1312	213	38	248	874	46	.286

DAVE CONCEPCION 33 6-2 175   Bats R Throws R

Threatened to enter free agency, but was signed to five-year, $4.63-million contract by Reds at conclusion of 1981 season . . . Named Player of the Month for April after .364 average and 21 RBI . . . Collected 1,500th major-league hit in August . . . Primarily known for Gold Glove fielding in '70s, he shouldered more of the offensive load as Big Red Machine cogs gradually were phased out . . . Born June 17, 1948, in Aragua, Venezuela . . . Batted .306 with nine game-winning RBI first half, .307 with five game-winners after the strike . . . His 14 game-winning RBI topped NL . . . 67 RBI impressive considering only five homers . . . Has .351 playoffs average . . . Winner of five Gold Gloves.

Year	Club	Pos.	G	AB	R	H	2B	3B	HR	RBI	SB	Avg.
1970	Cincinnati	SS-2B	101	265	38	69	6	3	1	19	10	.260
1971	Cincinnati	SS-2B-3B-OF	130	327	24	67	4	4	1	20	9	.205
1972	Cincinnati	SS	119	378	40	79	13	2	2	29	13	.209
1973	Cincinnati	SS-OF	89	328	39	94	18	3	8	46	22	.287
1974	Cincinnati	SS-OF	160	594	70	167	25	1	14	82	41	.281
1975	Cincinnati	SS-3B	140	507	62	139	23	1	5	49	33	.274
1976	Cincinnati	SS	152	576	74	162	28	7	9	69	21	.281
1977	Cincinnati	SS	156	572	59	155	26	3	8	64	29	.271
1978	Cincinnati	SS	153	565	75	170	33	4	6	67	23	.301
1979	Cincinnati	SS	149	590	91	166	25	3	16	84	19	.281
1980	Cincinnati	SS-2B	156	622	72	162	31	8	5	77	12	.260
1981	Cincinnati	SS	106	421	57	129	28	0	5	67	4	.306
	Totals		1611	5745	701	1559	260	39	80	673	236	.271

RON OESTER 25 6-2 185   Bats S Throws R

Not affected by so-called sophomore jinx, the second baseman supplied even more punch during the strike-interrupted season than he did as a rookie in 1980 . . . Batted .292 in the first half, .248 in the second . . . Junior Kennedy was groomed to replace Joe Morgan in '80, winning the job in the spring . . . When Kennedy slumped, Oester made most of opportunity and has held job ever since . . . Batted .450 in first 10 games as a regular . . . Born May 6, 1956, in Cincinnati . . . Originally developed as a shortstop, but has shown Gold Glove ability at second and appears to be a fixture in club's future plans.

Year	Club	Pos.	G	AB	R	H	2B	3B	HR	RBI	SB	Avg.
1978	Cincinnati	SS	6	8	1	3	0	0	0	1	0	.375
1979	Cincinnati	SS	6	3	0	0	0	0	0	0	0	.000
1980	Cincinnati	2B-SS-3B	100	303	40	84	16	2	2	20	6	.277
1981	Cincinnati	2B-SS	105	354	45	96	16	7	5	42	2	.271
	Totals		217	668	86	183	32	9	7	63	8	.274

JOHNNY BENCH 34 6-1 215   Bats R Throws R

Has been replaced by Gary Carter as finest catcher in NL, but he prefers it that way while playing more first base in an effort to prolong career . . . Limited to 52 games by injury last year, yet was productive . . . Batted .343 first half and .266 with six homers the second half . . . Born Dec. 7, 1947, in Oklahoma City, Okla. . . . Set career home run record for catchers in 1980, passing Yogi Berra . . . Catcher of '70s, a decade in which his 1,013 RBI topped the majors . . . Pushed

Dan Driessen out of first-base picture until he broke an ankle against Giants . . . Two-time NL MVP.

Year	Club	Pos.	G	AB	R	H	2B	3B	HR	RBI	SB	Avg.
1967	Cincinnati	C	26	86	7	14	3	1	1	6	0	.163
1968	Cincinnati	C	154	564	67	155	40	2	15	82	1	.275
1969	Cincinnati	C	148	532	83	156	23	1	26	90	6	.293
1970	Cincinnati	C-OF-1B-3B	158	605	97	177	35	4	45	148	5	.293
1971	Cincinnati	C-1B-OF-3B	149	562	80	134	19	2	27	61	2	.238
1972	Cincinnati	C-OF-1B-3B	147	538	87	145	22	2	40	125	6	.270
1973	Cincinnati	C-OF-1B-3B	152	557	83	141	17	3	25	104	4	.253
1974	Cincinnati	C-3B-1B	160	621	108	174	38	2	33	129	5	.280
1975	Cincinnati	C-OF-1B	142	530	83	150	39	1	28	110	11	.283
1976	Cincinnati	C-OF-1B	135	465	62	109	24	1	16	74	13	.234
1977	Cincinnati	C-OF-1B-3B	142	494	67	136	34	2	31	109	2	.275
1978	Cincinnati	C-OF-1B	120	393	52	102	17	1	23	73	4	.260
1979	Cincinnati	C-1B	130	464	73	128	19	0	22	80	4	.276
1980	Cincinnati	C	114	360	52	90	12	0	24	68	4	.250
1981	Cincinnati	1B-C	52	178	14	55	8	0	8	25	0	.309
	Totals		1929	6949	1015	1866	350	22	364	1284	67	.269

TOM SEAVER 37 6-1 208   Bats R Throws R

Tom Terrific was just that last season, demonstrating remarkable consistency by going 7-1 in each half . . . Was 3-0 with a 1.97 ERA in May, recording 250th career victory . . . Named NL Pitcher of the Month in September after posting 5-0 record . . . Hiked strikeout total to 3,075, but dropped from fifth to sixth on all-time list . . . Born Nov. 17, 1944, in Fresno, Calif. . . . Always a fast finisher . . . Was 14-1 down stretch in '79 and 4-1 in September 1980 . . . Only Walter Johnson and Grover Cleveland Alexander have better career ERAs among pitchers with more than 3,000 innings . . . Has 259-143 lifetime record . . . Has won three Cy Young Awards, all with Mets ('69, '73 and '75) . . . Finished three points behind L.A.'s Fernando Valenzuela in last year's Cy Young balloting.

Year	Club	G	IP	W	L	Pct.	SO	BB	H	ERA
1967	New York (NL)	35	251	16	13	.552	170	78	224	2.76
1968	New York (NL)	36	278	16	12	.571	205	48	224	2.20
1969	New York (NL)	36	273	25	7	.781	208	82	202	2.21
1970	New York (NL)	37	291	18	12	.600	283	83	230	2.81
1971	New York (NL)	36	286	20	10	.667	289	61	210	1.76
1972	New York (NL)	35	262	21	12	.636	249	77	215	2.92
1973	New York (NL)	36	290	19	10	.655	251	64	219	2.07
1974	New York (NL)	32	236	11	11	.500	201	75	199	3.20
1975	New York (NL)	36	280	22	9	.710	243	88	217	2.38
1976	New York (NL)	35	271	14	11	.560	235	77	211	2.59
1977	New York (NL)-Cincinnati	33	261	21	6	.778	196	66	199	2.59
1978	Cincinnati	36	260	16	14	.533	226	89	218	2.87
1979	Cincinnati	32	215	16	6	.727	131	61	187	3.14
1980	Cincinnati	26	168	10	8	.556	101	59	140	3.64
1981	Cincinnati	23	166	14	2	.875	87	66	120	2.55
	Totals	504	3788	259	143	.644	3075	1074	3015	2.60

MARIO SOTO 25 6-0 185   Bats R Throws R

Had second consecutive outstanding season in 1981, overshadowed only by Seaver's accomplishments . . . Was 6-6 the first half; 6-3 after the strike . . . Reds' best pitcher in 1980 . . . Pitched three shutouts last year . . . Well represented among NL leaders in '81 . . . Only Valenzuela and Carlton had more innings and strikeouts and 10 complete games was second to Fernando's 11 . . . Born July 12, 1956, in Bani, Dominican Republic . . . Blossomed at midseason 1980 and was 9-5 with 2.29 ERA and four saves after the All-Star break . . . He's 21-14 since that time and is pitching with poise and confidence, surpassing Frank Pastore as staff's best bet for stardom.

Year	Club	G	IP	W	L	Pct.	SO	BB	H	ERA
1977	Cincinnati	12	61	2	6	.250	44	26	60	5.31
1978	Cincinnati	5	18	1	0	1.000	13	13	13	2.50
1979	Cincinnati	25	37	3	2	.600	32	30	33	5.35
1980	Cincinnati	53	190	10	8	.556	182	84	126	3.08
1981	Cincinnati	25	175	12	9	.571	151	61	142	3.29
	Totals	120	481	28	25	.528	422	214	374	3.59

CLINT HURDLE 24 6-3 195   Bats L Throws R

Acquired from Royals in exchange for right-hander Scott Brown, a promising young reliever . . . Spent a month on the disabled list in each half of split season last year with lower back problem, but hit a career-high .328 in the 28 games he did play . . . Was under a lot of pressure as 19-year-old rookie phenom in 1977 and was booed his first two seasons in KC . . . Hit .375 during 1980 playoff sweep of Yankees . . . Born July 30, 1957, in Big Rapids, Mich. . . . Royals' top pick in 1975 draft . . . Strong and accurate arm . . . Cocky, gregarious guy.

Year	Club	Pos.	G	AB	R	H	2B	3B	HR	RBI	SB	Avg.
1977	Kansas City	OF	9	26	5	8	0	0	2	7	0	.308
1978	Kansas City	OF-3B-1B	133	417	48	110	25	5	7	56	1	.264
1979	Kansas City	OF-3B	59	171	16	41	10	3	3	30	0	.240
1980	Kansas City	OF	130	395	50	116	31	2	10	60	0	.294
1981	Kansas City	OF	28	76	12	25	3	1	4	15	0	.329
	Totals		359	1085	131	300	69	11	26	168	1	.276

CESAR CEDENO 31 6-2 190   Bats R Throws R

Slipped last season while troubled with injuries and Astros dealt him for Ray Knight . . . Batted .305 in the first half, but tailed off to .230 after the strike . . . Like most of his teammates, he failed to provide punch in division playoffs as Houston blew 2-0 lead . . . Enjoyed best season in seven years in 1980 . . . Born Feb. 25, 1951, in Santo Domingo . . . Suffered dislocated ankle in '80 Championship Series and required surgery, perhaps explaining '81 slump . . . Won five straight Gold Gloves, 1972-76.

Year	Club	Pos.	G	AB	R	H	2B	3B	HR	RBI	SB	Avg.
1970	Houston	OF	90	355	46	110	21	4	7	42	17	.310
1971	Houston	OF-1B	161	611	85	161	40	6	10	81	20	.264
1972	Houston	OF	139	559	103	179	39	8	22	82	55	.320
1973	Houston	OF	139	525	86	168	35	2	25	70	56	.320
1974	Houston	OF	160	610	95	164	29	5	26	102	57	.269
1975	Houston	OF	131	500	93	144	31	3	13	63	50	.288
1976	Houston	OF	150	575	89	171	26	5	18	83	58	.297
1977	Houston	OF	141	530	92	148	36	8	14	71	61	.279
1978	Houston	OF	50	192	31	54	8	2	7	23	23	.281
1979	Houston	OF-1B	132	470	57	123	27	4	6	54	30	.262
1980	Houston	OF	137	499	71	154	32	8	10	73	48	.309
1981	Houston	OF	82	306	42	83	19	0	5	34	12	.271
	Totals		1512	5732	890	1659	343	55	163	778	487	.289

TOM HUME 28 6-1 180   Bats R Throws R

Another excellent season for the bullpen stopper . . . Was the beneficiary of several late-inning victories . . . Went 4-2 in the first half and 5-2 after the strike . . . Made Doug Bair expendable with stout relief performances in '79 and '80, totaling 42 saves those two years . . . Born March 29, 1953, in Cincinnati . . . Joins with Joe Price to give Reds one of best left-right bullpen combos, the pair combining for 15-5 record and 17 saves . . . Was nondescript spot starter until he found his niche as bullpen ace . . . Had a scare during winter of 1980-81 when he, teammate Bill Bonham and their wives were trapped in Las Vegas hotel inferno and had to be rescued from roof.

Year	Club	G	IP	W	L	Pct.	SO	BB	H	ERA
1977	Cincinnati	14	43	3	3	.500	22	17	54	7.12
1978	Cincinnati	42	174	8	11	.421	90	50	198	4.14
1979	Cincinnati	57	163	10	9	.526	80	33	162	2.76
1980	Cincinnati	78	137	9	10	.474	68	38	121	2.56
1981	Cincinnati	51	68	9	4	.692	27	31	63	3.44
	Totals	242	585	39	37	.513	287	169	598	3.52

TOP PROSPECT

PAUL HOUSEHOLDER 23 6-0 180   **Bats S Throws R**
Also regarded as best bet to make grade last year, but saw only
limited duty down the stretch, batting .275 in 23 games . . . Outfielder batted .300 with 19 homers and 77 RBI at Indianapolis
after .295 mark with same club in '80 . . . Born Sept. 4, 1958, in
Columbus, Ohio.

MANAGER JOHN McNAMARA: Was fit to be tied last year
when the Reds posted baseball's best overall
record, 66-42, and had to stay home instead of
advancing to the playoffs . . . "We were
cheated and we were deprived and we're
walking away with nothing to show for it,"
said McNamara, whose Reds fell behind the
Dodgers in the first half and the Astros in the
second half . . . Had standings been com-
puted combining both halves, Cincy would have won by four
games, speaking well for Mac's direction . . . Born June 4, 1932,
in Sacramento, Calif. . . . Began managerial career at age 26,
won first pennant at 29 . . . Won flag in first crack with Reds in
'79, slipped to third in last week of 1980 and had a winner in vain
last year . . . People tend to underestimate Mac and his club and
he has a way of proving them wrong, the split-season format
notwithstanding.

GREATEST CATCHER

Who else but John Bench? A standout ever since his Rookie-
of-the-Year performance of 1968, and many regard him as the
greatest catcher of all-time. Surely, none ever hit with more
power. In 1980, he passed Yogi Berra as the most prolific home-
run hitter among catchers, belting 323 while at that position.

Bench, a two-time MVP, led the league with 45 homers and
148 RBI in 1970, setting a single-season homer mark for catchers.
He also posted a 40-125 double in '72 and won his third RBI

crown with 129 in '74. He was also considered the best fielding backstop in the NL 10 different years.

Cincy has had its share of good ones, though. Bubble Hargrave batted .353 in '26 and Ernie Lombardi won the batting title with a .342 mark in '38.

ALL-TIME RED SEASON RECORDS

BATTING: Cy Seymour, .377, 1905
HRs: George Foster, 52, 1977
RBIs: George Foster, 149, 1977
STEALS: Bob Bescher, 80, 1911
WINS: Adolfo Luque, 27, 1923
       Bucky Walters, 27, 1939
STRIKEOUTS: Jim Maloney, 265, 1963

Johnny Bench catches less but enjoys it more in Cincinnati.

HOUSTON ASTROS

TEAM DIRECTORY: Exec. Comm.: John J. McMullen, Jack Trotter, Herb Neyland; Pres.-GM: Al Rosen; Asst. GM: Tony Siegle; Admin. Asst.-Trav. Sec.: Donald Davidson; Dir. Minor Leagues: Bill Wood; Dir. Scouting: Lynwood Stallings; Dir. Publ.: Mike Ryan; Mgr.: Bill Virdon. Home: Astrodome (45,-000). Field distances: 340, l.f. line; 390, l.c.; 406, c.f.; 390, r.c.; 340, r.f. line. Spring training: Cocoa, Fla.

SCOUTING REPORT

HITTING: So who needs great hitting when the pitching is so good? Everyone pokes fun at the Astros' allegedly anemic batting order, but somehow Houston gets the job done. Besides, Houston's .257 team average last year displayed more punch than clubs like Atlanta and Montreal, which supposedly have more hitters. So much for stereotypes.

The club isn't devoid of competent batters. Art Howe had the highest first-half average last season before settling for a team-leading .296. Joe Pittman batted at a .281 clip, Alan Ashby checked in at .271 and Jose Cruz was the best .267 hitter in baseball, collecting 12 game-winning RBI and 13 homers, eight more than any other Astro. Add former Red Ray Knight (.277 career) and the hitting's plenty good behind such parsimonious pitching.

PITCHING: The best in baseball last year, as a nifty 2.66 team ERA proves, and it could improve if Don Sutton stitches two good halves together, if Joe Niekro (9-9) and Vern Ruhle (4-6) become winners and if J.R. Richard can come back. Now for the good news: Nolan Ryan (1.69) and Bob Knepper (2.18) were one-two in the ERA race and Sutton (2.60) and Niekro (2.82) gave the staff four of the top 12 spots.

Quality and depth abound, keeping the club in virtually every game. There simply isn't a weak link in the rotation and one shudders to think what will happen if Richard resumes his winning ways. And to think, the Astros were thinking about signing Ron Guidry over the winter! The stingy staff fired 19 shutouts last year, including another Ryan no-hitter, and when the starters got in trouble, Joe Sambito, Dave Smith and Frank LaCorte usually worked out of it. Simply stupendous.

FIELDING: No individual standouts, but solid defensive excellence in support of the pitching. The Astros fielded at a .980 clip, .001 behind the leaders. They could improve as Art Howe shifts from third to first to make room for Knight. Phil Garner and Pittman are adequate at second. Craig Reynolds may have lost a step at shortstop, but he's still tough. Ashby and Luis Pujols handle themselves well behind the plate and Terry Puhl is one of two regular outfielders not to make an error last season, handling 190 chances. Fielding is particularly critical to this club because it plays so many close games and cannot afford errors.

OUTLOOK: The Astros may not be denied this time around, especially if internal problems anchor the Dodgers. Houston simply has to find a way to hit better in the playoffs. Their pitchers limited the Dodgers to 13 runs in five games, but the futile Astros mustered only six, further enhancing the club's no-hit image. An added stick in the lineup—Dave Parker's, perhaps—would go a long way in making the club whole. If the Astros don't do it this season, it may be their last strong shot because age is creeping up on them, while other division clubs are emphasizing youth. It would be a bonus if Mike Ivie adds the sock, but don't count on it.

Heart of the Astro attack: Jose Cruz had 12 "gamers".

HOUSTON ASTROS 1982 ROSTER

MANAGER Bill Virdon
Coaches—Deacon Jones, Don Leppert, Bob Lillis, Mel
Wright

PITCHERS

No.	Name	1981 Club	W-L	IP	SO	ERA	B-T	Ht.	Wt.	Born
39	Knepper, Bob	Houston	9-5	157	75	2.18	L-L	6-2	200	5/25/54 Akron, OH
31	LaCorte, Frank	Houston	4-2	42	40	3.64	R-R	6-1	180	10/13/51 San Jose, CA
36	Niekro, Joe	Houston	9-9	166	77	2.82	R-R	6-1	190	11/7/44 Martins Ferry, OH
51	Paris, Zacarias	Columbus	11-9	190	166	4.36	R-R	6-1	150	9/9/57 Dominican Republic
44	Pladson, Gordie	Tucson	3-12	101	55	6.77	R-R	6-4	210	7/31/56 Canada
		Houston	0-0	4	3	9.00				
50	Richard, J.R.	Houston		Did not play			R-R	6-8	237	3/7/50 Vienna, LA
42	Roberge, Bert	Tucson	5-4	87	62	3.62	R-R	6-4	190	10/3/53 Lewiston, ME
47	Ross, Mark	Columbus	8-10	116	70	2.17	R-R	6-0	195	8/8/54 Galveston, TX
48	Ruhle, Vern	Houston	4-6	102	39	2.91	R-R	6-1	187	1/25/51 Coleman, MI
34	Ryan, Nolan	Houston	11-5	149	140	1.69	R-R	6-2	195	1/31/47 Refugio, TX
35	Sambito, Joe	Houston	5-5	64	41	1.83	L-L	6-1	190	6/28/52 Brooklyn, NY
27	Smith, Billy	Tucson	5-2	76	27	2.96	R-R	6-7	225	9/13/54 LaMarque, TX
		Houston	1-1	21	3	3.00				
45	Smith, Dave	Houston	5-3	75	52	2.76	R-R	6-1	195	1/21/55 San Francisco, CA
41	Sprowl, Bobby	Houston	0-1	29	18	5.90	L-L	6-2	190	4/14/56 Sandusky, OH
20	Sutton, Don	Houston	11-9	159	104	2.60	R-R	6-1	185	4/2/45 Clio, AL

CATCHERS

No.	Name	1981 Club	H	HR	RBI	Pct.	B-T	Ht.	Wt.	Born
14	Ashby, Alan	Houston	69	4	33	.271	B-R	6-2	190	7/8/51 Long Beach, CA
11	Knicely, Alan	Tucson	150	18	96	.306	R-R	6-1	205	5/19/55 Harrisonburg, VA
		Houston	4	2	2	.571				
6	Pujols, Luis	Houston	28	1	14	.239	R-R	6-1	195	11/18/55 Dominican Republic

INFIELDERS

No.	Name	1981 Club	H	HR	RBI	Pct.	B-T	Ht.	Wt.	Born
17	Doran, Bill	Columbus	117	5	56	.278	R-R	5-11	175	5/28/58 Cincinnati, OH
23	Garcia, Kiko	Houston	37	0	15	.272	R-R	5-11	178	10/14/53 Martinez, CA
3	Garner, Phil	Pitt-Hou	73	1	26	.248	R-R	5-10	177	4/30/49 Jefferson City, TN
24	Heep, Danny	Tucson	96	11	60	.337	L-L	5-11	185	7/3/57 San Antonio, TX
		Houston	24	0	11	.250				
18	Howe, Art	Houston	107	3	36	.296	R-R	6-1	185	12/15/46 Pittsburgh, PA
15	Ivie, Mike	SF-Hou	15	0	9	.254	R-R	6-4	215	8/8/52 Decatur, GA
–	Knight, Ray	Cincinnati	100	6	34	.259	R-R	6-2	185	12/28/52 Albany, GA
1	Pena, Bert	Tucson	122	7	66	.261	R-R	5-11	165	7/11/59 Puerto Rico
		Houston	1	0	0	.500				
9	Pittman, Joe	Tucson	8	1	5	.348	R-R	6-1	180	1/1/54 Houston, TX
		Houston	38	0	7	.281				
12	Reynolds, Craig	Houston	84	4	31	.260	L-R	6-1	175	12/27/52 Houston, TX
8	Roberts, Dave	Houston	13	1	5	.241	R-R	6-4	200	2/17/51 Lebanon, OR
16	Spilman, Harry	Cin-Hou	14	0	4	.241	L-R	6-1	190	7/18/54 Albany, GA
10	Thon, Dickie	Houston	26	0	3	.274	R-R	5-11	150	6/20/58 South Bend, IN
38	Tolman, Tim	Tucson	154	14	99	.322	R-R	6-0	190	4/20/56 Santa Monica, CA
		Houston	1	0	0	.125				
29	Walling, Denny	Houston	37	5	23	.234	L-R	6-1	185	4/17/54 Neptune, NJ

OUTFIELDERS

No.	Name	1981 Club	H	HR	RBI	Pct.	B-T	Ht.	Wt.	Born
25	Cruz, Jose	Houston	109	13	55	.267	L-L	6-0	175	8/8/47 Puerto Rico
26	Loucks, Scott	Tucson	92	3	22	.271	R-R	6-0	178	11/11/56 Anchorage, AK
		Houston	4	0	0	.571				
21	Puhl, Terry	Houston	88	3	28	.251	L-R	6-1	190	7/8/56 Canada
37	Ray, Larry	Columbus	128	21	106	.253	L-R	6-0	190	3/11/58 Madison, IN
46	Robles, Ruben	Daytona Beach	96	5	39	.283	R-R	6-2	190	8/13/59 Dominican Republic

ASTRO PROFILES

JOSE CRUZ 34 6-0 175   Bats L Throws L

Average dropped, but he remained club's best clutch hitter last year . . . Had eight more homers than closest teammate and his 12 game-winning RBI easily topped club . . . Batted .278 with 11 homers in the first half, .251 with two homers after the strike . . . Batted .300 in division playoffs . . . Born Aug. 8, 1947, in Arroyo, Puerto Rico . . . The best of the baseball-playing Cruz brothers . . . Batted .400 in '80 Championship Series . . . Roberto Clemente Award winner in Puerto Rico, 1979-80 . . . One of game's most underrated players . . . Overshadowed by Astros' pitching prominence . . . Houston MVP in 1979 . . . Stole only five bases last year after averaging 36 in previous five years.

Year	Club	Pos.	G	AB	R	H	2B	3B	HR	RBI	SB	Avg.
1970	St. Louis	OF	6	17	2	6	1	0	0	1	0	.353
1971	St. Louis	OF	83	292	46	80	13	2	9	27	6	.274
1972	St. Louis	OF	117	332	33	78	14	4	2	23	9	.235
1973	St. Louis	OF	132	406	51	92	22	5	10	57	10	.227
1974	St. Louis	OF-1B	107	161	24	42	4	3	5	20	4	.261
1975	Houston	OF	120	315	44	81	15	2	9	49	6	.257
1976	Houston	OF	133	439	49	133	21	5	4	61	28	.303
1977	Houston	OF	157	579	87	173	31	10	17	87	44	.299
1978	Houston	OF-1B	153	565	79	178	34	9	10	83	37	.315
1979	Houston	OF	157	558	73	161	33	7	9	72	36	.289
1980	Houston	OF	160	612	79	185	29	7	11	91	36	.302
1981	Houston	OF	107	409	53	109	16	5	13	55	5	.267
	Totals		1432	4685	620	1318	233	59	99	626	221	.281

RAY KNIGHT 29 6-2 185   Bats R Throws R

Continued to slip after .318 surprise as Pete Rose's successor in 1979 . . . Astros acquired him from Reds for Cesar Cedeno after Knight hit .250 in first half and .269 following strike last year . . . Was third on the Reds in game-winning RBI with seven . . . Belted three grand-slam homers in 1980, equaling Reds' single-season mark set by Frank Robinson and Lee May . . . Also became 20th player in majors to hit two homers in one inning, against Mets in 1980 . . . Born Dec. 28, 1952, in Albany, Ga. . . . Made it easier for fans to accept Rose's departure when he stepped in and had third highest average in NL in '79, also belting 37 doubles and knocking in 79 runs . . .

May have been a fluke, because nothing in his minor-league career suggested such productivity.

Year	Club	Pos.	G	AB	R	H	2B	3B	HR	RBI	SB	Avg.
1974	Cincinnati	3B	14	11	1	2	1	0	0	2	0	.182
1977	Cincinnati	3B-2B-OF-SS	80	92	8	24	5	1	1	13	1	.261
1978	Cincinnati	3B-2B-OF-SS	83	65	7	13	3	0	1	4	0	.200
1979	Cincinnati	3B	150	551	64	175	37	4	10	79	4	.318
1980	Cincinnati	3B	162	618	71	163	39	7	14	78	1	.264
1981	Cincinnati	3B	106	386	43	100	23	1	6	34	2	.259
	Totals..........		595	1723	194	477	108	13	32	210	8	.277

TERRY PUHL 25 6-1 190   Bats L Throws R

Also tailed off sharply, though leading club in stolen bases . . . Entered season with .288 lifetime average, but batted .269 in the first half and .225 down the stretch . . . Committed no errors as Cedeno's center-field replacement in 1979, but is the right fielder now . . . Set record for hits in Championship Series with 10 in 1980, batting .526 against Phillies . . . Born July 8, 1956, in Melville, Sask., Canada . . . His high school didn't field a baseball team and he was rejected by Expos in a tryout . . . Signed as a free agent by Houston in '73 . . . Enjoyed 18-game batting streak in '78 . . . Collected seven hits in doubleheader against Braves in 1980.

Year	Club	Pos.	G	AB	R	H	2B	3B	HR	RBI	SB	Avg.
1977	Houston........	OF	60	229	40	69	13	5	0	10	10	.301
1978	Houston........	OF	149	585	87	169	25	6	3	35	32	.289
1979	Houston........	OF	157	600	87	172	22	4	8	49	30	.287
1980	Houston........	OF	141	535	75	151	24	5	13	55	27	.282
1981	Houston........	OF	96	350	43	88	19	4	3	28	22	.251
	Totals..........		603	2299	332	649	103	24	27	177	121	.282

ART HOWE 35 6-1 185   Bats R Throws R

Irate over All-Star Game snub last year . . . With good reason, because he was leading NL with .344 average in first half . . . Slipped to .244 second half . . . NL Player of the Month in May with .432 average . . . Set Astros' club record with 23-game batting streak that month . . . Settled into third-base job after swap of Enos Cabell . . . One of best "players to be named later," joining Houston in 1975 swap for Tommy Helms of Pittsburgh . . . Didn't reach majors to stay until he was 29

. . . Born Dec. 15, 1946, in Pittsburgh . . . A quarterback at Wyoming until back injury ended grid career . . . Was a computer programmer until he signed with Bucs at age 24 in '71.

Year	Club	Pos.	G	AB	R	H	2B	3B	HR	RBI	SB	Avg.
1974	Pittsburgh	3B-SS	29	74	10	18	4	1	1	5	0	.243
1975	Pittsburgh	3B-SS	63	146	13	25	9	0	1	10	1	.171
1976	Houston	3B-2B	21	29	0	4	1	0	0	0	0	.138
1977	Houston	2B-3B-SS	125	413	44	109	23	7	8	58	0	.264
1978	Houston	2B-3B-1B	119	420	46	123	33	3	7	55	2	.293
1979	Houston	2B-3B-1B	118	355	32	88	15	2	6	33	3	.248
1980	Houston	INF	110	321	34	91	12	5	10	46	1	.283
1981	Houston	1B-3B	103	361	43	107	22	4	3	36	1	.296
	Totals		688	2119	222	565	119	22	36	243	8	.267

ALAN ASHBY 30 6-2 190   Bats S Throws R

Enjoyed one of postseason's most dramatic moments when his two-run homer off Dave Stewart in the ninth inning downed the Dodgers in opener of division series . . . That was his only hit of the series, however . . . Divided catching chores with Luis Pujols at start of season but he's more or less a regular now after blossoming as a hitter . . . Entered 1981 with .229 lifetime average, and hit 42 points better than that last season . . . Born July 8, 1951, in Long Beach, Calif. . . . Played high-school ball with Garry Maddox as a teammate . . . A strong-armed catcher who handles the club's array of mound talent well . . . Batted career-high .293 for Reno in '71 and had .284 mark at Oklahoma City in '74.

Year	Club	Pos.	G	AB	R	H	2B	3B	HR	RBI	SB	Avg.
1973	Cleveland	C	11	29	4	5	1	0	1	3	0	.172
1974	Cleveland	C	10	7	1	1	0	0	0	0	0	.143
1975	Cleveland	C-1B-3B	90	254	32	57	10	1	5	32	0	.224
1976	Cleveland	C-1B-3B	89	247	26	59	5	1	4	32	0	.239
1977	Toronto	C	124	396	25	83	16	3	2	29	0	.210
1978	Toronto	C	81	264	27	69	15	0	9	29	1	.261
1979	Houston	C	108	336	25	68	15	2	2	35	0	.202
1980	Houston	C	116	352	30	90	19	2	3	48	0	.256
1981	Houston	C	83	255	20	69	13	0	4	33	0	.271
	Totals		712	2140	190	501	94	9	30	241	4	.234

NOLAN RYAN 35 6-2 195   Bats R Throws R

Recaptured his old intimidating form last season, posting best ERA in NL . . . Hurled record fifth no-hitter against Dodgers, Sept. 26 . . . Also had no-hitter snapped in seventh inning by Expos, Sept. 4 . . . Blanked Mets June 5, but in the process walked two batters to surpass Early Wynn as majors' all-time leader in bases on balls . . . Third on all-time

strikeout list with 3,249 . . . Born Jan. 31, 1947, in Refugio, Tex.
. . . Was 5-3 with a 1.37 ERA in first half, improving record to
6-2 after the strike . . . Holds major-league mark of 135 games
with 10 or more strikeouts . . . Fired two-hitter to win division
playoff opener, but was blanked in deciding game . . . Was 7-9
after joining Astros as free agent in 1980 before going 4-1 down
the stretch to help win the pennant . . . Has thrown seven one-
hitters.

Year	Club	G	IP	W	L	Pct.	SO	BB	H	ERA
1966	New York (NL)	2	3	0	1	.000	6	3	5	15.00
1968	New York (NL)	21	134	6	9	.400	133	75	93	3.09
1969	New York (NL)	25	89	6	3	.667	92	53	60	3.54
1970	New York (NL)	27	132	7	11	.389	125	97	86	3.41
1971	New York (NL)	30	152	10	14	.417	137	116	125	3.97
1972	California	39	284	19	16	.543	329	157	166	2.28
1973	California	41	326	21	16	.568	383	162	238	2.87
1974	California	42	333	22	16	.578	367	202	221	2.89
1975	California	28	198	14	12	.538	186	132	152	3.45
1976	California	39	284	17	18	.486	327	183	193	3.36
1977	California	37	299	19	16	.543	341	204	198	2.77
1978	California	31	235	10	13	.435	260	148	183	3.71
1979	California	34	223	16	14	.533	223	114	169	3.59
1980	Houston	35	234	11	10	.524	200	98	205	3.35
1981	Houston	21	149	11	5	.688	140	68	99	1.69
	Totals	452	3075	189	174	.521	3249	1812	2193	3.11

BOB KNEPPER 27 6-2 200   Bats L Throws L

Impressive debut with Astros after two
straight losing seasons with Giants . . . Won
first five decisions . . . Was 2-0 with a 0.43
ERA in April . . . NL Player of the Week,
April 20-26, for two shutouts; he doubled and
scored the only run in one of the wins . . . 3-0
with a 1.29 ERA and two more shutouts in
May . . . 5-1 with a 1.15 ERA in the first half,
4-4 down the stretch . . . Born May 25, 1954, in Akron, Ohio
. . . In only playoff appearance, he lost to Dodgers in third game
. . . Posted 20-5 record at Fresno in 1974 . . . Struggling at
Phoenix in '77, he was promoted to Giants because of injuries
and he stayed after posting 11-9 rookie record . . . Started '79
with 6-2 record, but loss of confidence affected pitching until last
season.

Year	Club	G	IP	W	L	Pct.	SO	BB	H	ERA
1976	San Francisco	4	25	1	2	.333	11	7	26	3.24
1977	San Francisco	27	166	11	9	.550	100	72	151	3.36
1978	San Francisco	36	260	17	11	.607	147	85	218	2.63
1979	San Francisco	34	207	9	12	.429	123	77	241	4.65
1980	San Francisco	35	215	9	16	.360	103	61	242	4.10
1981	Houston	22	157	9	5	.643	75	38	128	2.18
	Totals	158	1030	56	55	.505	559	340	1006	3.41

JOE NIEKRO 37 6-1 190   Bats R Throws R

Unsung hero of the majors' finest starting rotation . . . Was 4-0 with a 2.00 ERA in May en route to a 6-5, 2.84 first half . . . Slipped to 3-4 after the strike, but bounced back in division playoffs . . . Blanked Dodgers for eight innings in second game and Astros won in 11th . . . Is 0-0 in postseason play, but has not allowed a run in 18 innings . . . Born Nov. 7, 1944, in Martins Ferry, Ohio . . . Brother of Braves' Phil . . . Turned 6-0 start in '79 into first 20-win season and made it two in a row in '80 . . . One of the few pitchers who has mastered the knuckler . . . Beat Dodgers on a six-hitter in one-game playoff to decide 1980 division race . . . Holds club record of nine straight wins.

Year	Club	G	IP	W	L	Pct.	SO	BB	H	ERA
1967	Chicago (NL)	35	170	10	7	.588	77	32	171	3.34
1968	Chicago (NL)	34	177	14	10	.583	65	59	204	4.32
1969	Chi. (NL)-S.D.	41	221	8	18	.308	62	51	237	3.71
1970	Detroit	38	213	12	13	.480	101	72	221	4.06
1971	Detroit	31	122	6	7	.462	43	49	136	4.50
1972	Detroit	18	47	3	2	.600	24	8	62	3.83
1973	Atlanta	20	24	2	4	.333	12	11	23	4.13
1974	Atlanta	27	43	3	2	.600	31	18	36	3.56
1975	Houston	40	88	6	4	.600	54	39	79	3.07
1976	Houston	36	118	4	8	.333	77	56	107	3.36
1977	Houston	44	181	13	8	.619	101	64	155	3.03
1978	Houston	35	203	14	14	.500	97	73	190	3.86
1979	Houston	38	264	21	11	.656	119	107	221	3.00
1980	Houston	37	256	20	12	.625	127	79	268	3.55
1981	Houston	24	166	9	9	.500	77	47	150	2.82
	Totals	499	2293	145	129	.529	1067	765	2260	3.56

DON SUTTON 36 6-2 185   Bats R Throws R

Disappointing 4-7 first half with 3.40 ERA, but club's biggest winner down the stretch, going 7-2 after the strike before cracking a kneecap on a pitch thrown by Jerry Reuss . . . How he responds from surgery could determine his future . . . Won ERA crown in 1980, but Dodgers still let him get away . . . Holds most of Dodgers' pitching records following 15 consecutive years with at least 11 victories for them . . . Yankees bid for his free-agent services, too, but Sutton wanted to prove that George Steinbrenner can't buy everything . . . Born May 2, 1945, in Clio, Ala. . . . Abandoned idea of TV film on illegal pitches when he was unmasked at St. Louis and his identity

was divulged . . . He's 3-1 in Championship Series, 2-2 in World Series and 1-0 in All-Star Games.

Year	Club	G	IP	W	L	Pct.	SO	BB	H	ERA
1966	Los Angeles	37	226	12	12	.500	209	52	192	2.99
1967	Los Angeles	37	233	11	15	.423	169	57	223	3.94
1968	Los Angeles	35	208	11	15	.423	162	59	179	2.60
1969	Los Angeles	41	293	17	18	.486	217	91	269	3.47
1970	Los Angeles	38	260	15	13	.536	201	78	251	4.08
1971	Los Angeles	38	265	17	12	.586	194	55	231	2.55
1972	Los Angeles	33	273	19	9	.679	207	63	186	2.08
1973	Los Angeles	33	256	18	10	.643	200	56	196	2.43
1974	Los Angeles	40	276	19	9	.679	179	80	241	3.23
1975	Los Angeles	35	254	16	13	.552	175	62	202	2.87
1976	Los Angeles	35	268	21	10	.677	161	82	231	3.06
1977	Los Angeles	33	240	14	8	.636	150	69	207	3.19.
1978	Los Angeles	34	238	15	11	.577	154	54	228	3.55
1979	Los Angeles	33	226	12	15	.444	146	61	201	3.82
1980	Los Angeles	32	212	13	5	.722	128	47	163	2.21
1981	Houston	23	159	11	9	.550	104	29	132	2.60
	Totals	557	3887	241	184	.567	2756	995	3332	3.05

JOE SAMBITO 29 6-1 190   Bats L Throws L

Astros' toughest reliever posted 1.59 ERA and six saves in first half and a 4-2 record with four saves after the strike . . . Won the second game of the division playoffs on Dennis Walling's pinch-hit in the 11th . . . Blossomed as a fireman in 1979, not allowing an earned run in 27 consecutive appearances over a span of 40⅔ innings . . . Had a 13-game scoreless streak in '78 and an eight-gamer in '80 . . . Born June 28, 1952, in Brooklyn . . . Came to majors as a starter in '76 after combining for an 11-2 mark at Columbus and Memphis . . . Made four starts for Astros, pitched a shutout and was switched to bullpen in '77 . . . Played baseball and football at Adelphi (N.Y.) University.

Year	Club	G	IP	W	L	Pct.	SO	BB	H	ERA
1976	Houston	20	53	3	2	.600	26	14	45	3.57
1977	Houston	54	89	5	5	.500	67	24	77	2.33
1978	Houston	62	88	4	9	.308	96	32	85	3.07
1979	Houston	63	91	8	7	.533	83	23	80	1.78
1980	Houston	64	90	8	4	.667	75	22	65	2.20
1981	Houston	49	64	5	5	.500	41	22	43	1.83
	Totals	312	475	33	32	.508	388	137	395	2.41

TOP PROSPECTS

ALAN KNICELY 26 6-1 205   Bats R Throws R

Two outstanding Triple-A seasons back to back at Tucson (PCL), batting .318 with 22 homers in 1980 and .306 with 18 homers last year . . . Played three games with Astros at end of season and rapped two homers, raising eyebrows on powerless team . . . Born May 19, 1955, in Harrisonburg, Va. . . . Began career as pitcher and switched to catcher . . . PCL champ with 105 RBI in '80 . . . Tucson teammates Danny Heep (first baseman) and Scott Loucks (outfielder) also merit watching.

MANAGER BILL VIRDON: Strictly vanilla in a profession of

rocky roads . . . Doesn't have any flair, but gets job done with patience and a great pitching staff . . . Job rumored on the line at times because Astros haven't gone all the way, but plenty of clubs would love to have him . . . Has been a winner everywhere, but seems to come up one game short in playoffs, losing three of them, three games to two . . . Born June 9, 1931, in Hazel Park, Mich. . . . As rookie skipper in '72, won division title with Pittsburgh . . . Held club together despite some grumbling by veterans and injury to J.R. Richard in 1980 . . . Club won a record 93 games that year and won the second half in '81 . . . Former major-league outfielder, batting .319 in '56 after winning Rookie-of-the-Year honors in 1955 with Cardinals.

GREATEST CATCHER

John Bateman was the best in the early days of the franchise, but the club didn't have a truly solid catcher until John Bench chased Johnny Edwards out of Cincinnati. Edwards played for Houston in 1969-74 and set defensive standards with his new club.

Edwards, a decent hitter, set records with 138 consecutive errorless games and 805 chances without an error in 1970-71. His 1,214 chances in '69 are a record and his 9,628 lifetime chances are a league mark.

ALL-TIME ASTRO SEASON RECORDS

BATTING: Rusty Staub, .333, 1967
HRs: Jimmy Wynn, 37, 1967
RBIs: Bob Watson, 110, 1977
STEALS: Cesar Cedeno, 61, 1977
WINS: Joe Niekro, 21, 1979
STRIKEOUTS: J.R. Richard, 313, 1979

LOS ANGELES DODGERS

TEAM DIRECTORY: Pres.: Peter O'Malley; VP-Player Personnel: Al Campanis; VP-Public Relations: Fred Claire; VP-Minor Leagues: Bill Schweppe; Dir. Publ.: Steve Brener; Trav. Sec.: Bill DeLury; Mgr.: Tom Lasorda. Home: Dodger Stadium (56,000). Field distances: 330, l.f. line; 370, l.c.; 395, c.f.; 370, r.c.; 330, r.f. line. Spring training: Vero Beach, Fla.

SCOUTING REPORT

HITTING: The Dodgers always hit, a fact frequently guised by their annual pitching success. The club batted .262 last year and appears to have some solid young hitters ready to take over for veterans with diminishing skills. Dusty Baker, Ron Cey and Steve Garvey, however, don't belong in the Over-the-Hill Gang. The trio formed the heart of the batting order last year and again figures to be instrumental in any success the Dodgers may achieve.

Garvey is Mr. Consistency and the National League's Mr. October. Just wind him up and he hits. Ditto Cey, who led the club with 13 homers despite playing only 85 games. Baker's power

The Dodgers celebrate their World Championship.

lessened, but he batted .320. The newcomer to make the biggest impact one year ago was Pedro Guerrero (.300, 12 homers) and a rookie or newcomer Jorge Orta could fill the bill this summer. The club is loaded with punch, including Rick Monday and Jay Johnstone off the bench.

PITCHING: Despite their hitting prowess, it's pitching that is the Dodgers' trademark and 1981 was no exception. Few teams could overcome the loss of a Don Sutton, but the Dodgers merely unveiled Fernando Valenzuela. The Mexican lefty captivated baseball, earned a Cy Young Award and was the main thrust behind a long-awaited World Championship. What Valenzuela did defies description, but he had plenty of help.

In fact, teammates Burt Hooton (2.28) and Jerry Reuss (2.29) registered lower ERAs than Valenzuela's 2.48, and the trio enabled the staff to post a collective 3.01. Bob Welch is a reliable fourth starter and the bullpen is sound, with Steve Howe the prime stopper. But the L.A. starters are so good, a great bullpen isn't necessary for this staff to flourish.

FIELDING: The defense is more than adequate despite frequent criticism of aging DP combo Bill Russell and Davey Lopes, who may be phased out this year in favor of Steve Sax. Lopes made only two errors during the regular season, helping the club to a .980 percentage. Russell, battling injuries, was less impressive, but now ex-Oriole Mark Belanger brings his glove for late-inning rescues. Garvey was the first-base leader, showing one error in 1,075 chances. Cey slipped at third, but Baker and Ken Landreaux were solid in the outfield—Landreaux made no errors—and catchers Mike Scioscia and Steve Yeager are above average defensively.

OUTLOOK: Whenever the Dodgers go with an influx of young talent, as may be the case this year, they temporarily fall back and regroup to form another dynasty. This state of change could weaken the club's pennant chances, but some new faces must be moved in to insure future success. How well the Albuquerque grads adjust could determine immediate success in what surely will be a dogfight with prime nemesis Houston. So many constants—like the pitching and the hitting—remain, it's difficult to envision this club having a poor year. The season, however, figures to test Tom Lasorda's managerial skills and how he blends the old with the new will have a bearing on what the Dodgers do. Uneasy rests the head that wears the crown, a fact never more evident than in the Dodgers' 1982 pursuit of a repeat.

LOS ANGELES DODGERS 1982 ROSTER

MANAGER Tom Lasorda
Coaches—Monty Basgall, Mark Cresse, Manny Mota,
Danny Ozark, Ron Perranoski

PITCHERS

No.	Name	1981 Club	W-L	IP	SO	ERA	B-T	Ht.	Wt.	Born
27	Beckwith, Joe	Los Angeles				Disabled List	L-R	6-3	2001/28/55 Auburn, AL
37	Castillo, Robert	Los Angeles	2-4	51	35	5.29	R-R	5-10	170	4/18/55 Los Angeles, CA
51	Forster, Terry	Los Angeles	0-1	31	17	4.06	L-L	6-4	210	1/14/52 Sioux Falls, SD
38	Goltz, Dave	Los Angeles	2-7	77	48	4.09	R-R	6-4	215	6/23/49 Pelican Rapids, MN
55	Holton, Brian	Albuquerque	16-6	191	73	3.44	R-R	6-2	180	11/29/59 McKeesport, PA
46	Hooton, Burt	Los Angeles	11-6	142	74	2.28	R-R	6-1	200	2/7/50 Greenville, TX
49	Howe, Steve	Los Angeles	5-3	54	32	2.50	L-L	6-1	180	3/10/58 Pontiac, MI
49	Niedenfuer, Tom	San Antonio	13-3	90	95	1.80	R-R	6-5	225	8/13/59 St. Louis Park, MN
		Los Angeles	3-1	26	12	3.81				
26	Pena, Alejandro	Albuquerque	2-5	56	40	1.61	R-R	6-3	200	6/25/59 Dominican Republic
		Los Angeles	1-1	25	14	2.88				
25	Power, Ted	Albuquerque	18-3	187	111	3.56	R-R	6-4	220	1/31/55 Guthrie, OK
		Los Angeles	1-3	14	7	3.21				
41	Reuss, Jerry	Los Angeles	10-4	153	51	2.29	L-L	6-5	217	6/19/49 St. Louis, MO
56	Rodas, Rich	San Antonio	14-6	176	148	4.34	L-L	6-3	170	11/7/59 Roseville, CA
39	Shirley, Steve	Albuquerque	5-3	57	36	2.37	L-L	6-0	185	10/12/56 San Francisco, CA
48	Stewart, Dave	Los Angeles	4-3	43	29	2.51	R-R	6-2	200	2/19/57 Oakland, CA
34	Valenzuela, Fernando	Los Angeles	13-7	192	180	2.48	L-L	5-11	200	11/1/60 Mexico
35	Welch, Bob	Los Angeles	9-5	141	88	3.45	R-R	6-3	190	11/3/56 Detroit, MI
—	White, Larry	Chattanooga	10-12	172	100	3.51	R-R	6-5	190	9/24/58 San Fernando, CA

CATCHERS

No.	Name	1981 Club	H	HR	RBI	Pct.	B-T	Ht.	Wt.	Born
9	Crow, Don	Albuquerque	94	0	54	.286	R-R	6-4	195	8/18/58 Yakima, WA
14	Scioscia, Mike	Los Angeles	80	2	29	.276	L-R	6-2	220	11/27/58 Upper Darby, CA
7	Yeager, Steve	Los Angeles	18	3	7	.209	R-R	6-0	205	11/24/48 Huntington, WV

INFIELDERS

No.	Name	1981 Club	H	HR	RBI	Pct.	B-T	Ht.	Wt.	Born
—	Belanger, Mark	Baltimore	23	1	10	.165	R-R	6-2	170	6/8/44 Pittsfield, MA
47	Brock, Greg	San Antonio	147	32	106	.295	R-L	6-3	200	6/14/57 McMinnville, OR
10	Cey, Ron	Los Angeles	90	13	50	.288	R-R	5-10	185	2/15/48 Tacoma, WA
6	Garvey, Steve	Los Angeles	122	10	64	.283	R-R	5-10	190	12/22/48 Tampa, FL
15	Lopes, Dave	Los Angeles	44	5	17	.206	R-R	5-9	175	5/3/46 E. Providence, RI
5	Marshall, Mike	Albuquerque	174	34	137	.370	R-R	6-5	220	1/12/60 Libertyville, IL
		Los Angeles	5	0	1	.200				
18	Russell, Bill	Los Angeles	61	0	22	.233	R-R	6-0	180	10/21/48 Pittsburg, KS
52	Sax, Steve	San Antonio	168	8	52	.346	R-R	5-11	175	1/29/60 Sacramento, CA
		Los Angeles	33	2	9	.277				

OUTFIELDERS

No.	Name	1981 Club	H	HR	RBI	Pct.	B-T	Ht.	Wt.	Born
12	Baker, Dusty	Los Angeles	128	9	49	.320	R-R	6-2	195	6/15/49 Riverside, CA
22	Bradley, Mark	San Antonio	149	20	89	.316	R-R	6-1	185	12/3/56 Elizabethtown, KY
		Los Angeles	1	0	0	.167				
28	Guerrero, Pedro	Los Angeles	104	12	48	.300	R-R	5-11	176	6/29/56 Dominican Republic
21	Johnstone, Jay	Los Angeles	17	3	6	.205	L-R	6-1	190	11/20/46 Manchester, CT
44	Landreaux, Ken	Los Angeles	98	7	41	.251	L-R	5-11	170	12/22/54 Los Angeles, CA
3	Law, Rudy	Albuquerque	133	0	39	.335	L-L	6-1	165	10/7/56 Waco, TX
20	Maldonado, Candy	Albuquerque	154	21	104	.335	R-R	6-0	190	9/5/60 Puerto Rico
		Los Angeles	1	0	0	.083				
17	Mitchell, Bobby	Albuquerque	106	1	63	.311	L-L	5-10	170	4/7/55 Salt Lake City, UT
		Los Angeles	1	0	0	.125				
16	Monday, Rick	Los Angeles	41	11	25	.315	L-L	6-3	200	11/20/45 Batesville, AR
—	Orta, Jorge	Cleveland	92	5	34	.272	L-R	5-10	175	11/26/50 Mexico
50	Roenicke, Ron	Albuquerque	130	15	94	.316	B-L	6-0	180	8/19/56 Covina, CA
		Los Angeles	11	0	0	.234				
30	Thomas, Derrel	Los Angeles	54	4	24	.248	B-R	6-0	160	1/14/51 Los Angeles, CA

DODGER PROFILES

STEVE GARVEY 33 5-10 190   Bats R Throws R

A model of consistency . . . Dipped at the plate during regular season, but picked up slack in playoffs and World Series . . . Batted .359 in 16 postseason games while teammates were struggling . . . National League's version of Mr. October . . . Including division playoffs, he has .346 average in 45 postseason games . . . His total of seven homers is a Championship Series career mark . . . Born Dec. 22, 1948, in Tampa . . . Batted .279-288 in the two halves last season . . . Started Dodger comeback in division series against Astros with two-run homer in Game 3 . . . His two-run homer in Game 4 of Championship Series downed Expos . . . Played in all 110 games to move into second place on NL consecutive-games list with 945 . . . Billy Williams is tops with 1,117 . . . Six 200-hit seasons . . . Former Michigan State star . . . Nice-guy image rankles some people.

Year	Club	Pos.	G	AB	R	H	2B	3B	HR	RBI	SB	Avg.
1969	Los Angeles.....	3B	3	3	0	1	0	0	0	0	0	.333
1970	Los Angeles.....	3B-2B	34	93	8	25	5	0	1	6	1	.269
1971	Los Angeles.....	3B	81	225	27	51	12	1	7	26	1	.227
1972	Los Angeles.....	3B-1B	96	294	36	79	14	2	9	30	4	.269
1973	Los Angeles.....	1B-OF	114	349	37	106	17	3	8	50	0	.304
1974	Los Angeles.....	1B	156	642	95	200	32	3	21	111	5	.312
1975	Los Angeles.....	1B	160	659	85	210	38	6	18	95	11	.319
1976	Los Angeles.....	1B	162	631	85	200	37	4	13	80	19	.317
1977	Los Angeles.....	1B	162	646	91	192	25	3	33	115	9	.297
1978	Los Angeles.....	1B	162	639	89	202	36	9	21	113	10	.316
1979	Los Angeles.....	1B	162	648	92	204	32	1	28	110	3	.315
1980	Los Angeles.....	1B	163	658	77	200	27	1	26	106	6	.304
1981	Los Angeles.....	1B	110	431	63	122	23	1	10	64	3	.283
	Totals..........		1565	5918	785	1792	298	34	195	906	72	.303

DUSTY BAKER 32 6-2 195   Bats R Throws R

Registered best batting average among Dodgers during season, but slumped in playoffs and Series . . . Struggled with .213 average and five RBI—three in one game—during 16 postseason contests . . . Batted .303 in first half and improved to .341 after the strike . . . Hit .316 in Championship Series and has .375 lifetime average in 13 NLCS games . . . Born June 15, 1949, in Riverside, Calif. . . . Unappreciated as a member of Braves . . . Finally made it to All-Star Game last year, getting one hit in two trips, after previous snubs . . . Batted .399

in '77 World Series . . . Had two 15-game batting streaks last season . . . A 25th-round draft pick who fooled the experts . . . Wears No. 12 because his hero, Tommy Davis, wore that number for Dodgers . . . Seemingly sacrificed power for average last year.

Year	Club	Pos.	G	AB	R	H	2B	3B	HR	RBI	SB	Avg.
1968	Atlanta.........	OF	6	5	0	2	0	0	0	0	0	.400
1969	Atlanta.........	OF	3	7	0	0	0	0	0	0	0	.000
1970	Atlanta.........	OF	13	24	3	7	0	0	0	4	0	.292
1971	Atlanta.........	OF	29	62	2	14	2	0	0	4	0	.226
1972	Atlanta.........	OF	127	446	62	143	27	2	17	76	4	.321
1973	Atlanta.........	OF	159	604	101	174	29	4	21	99	24	.288
1974	Atlanta.........	OF	149	574	80	147	35	0	20	69	18	.256
1975	Atlanta.........	OF	142	494	63	129	18	2	19	72	12	.261
1976	Los Angeles.....	OF	112	384	36	93	13	0	4	39	2	.242
1977	Los Angeles.....	OF	153	533	86	155	26	1	30	86	2	.291
1978	Los Angeles.....	OF	149	522	62	137	24	1	11	66	12	.262
1979	Los Angeles.....	OF	151	554	86	152	29	1	23	88	11	.274
1980	Los Angeles.....	OF	153	579	80	170	26	4	29	97	12	.294
1981	Los Angeles.....	OF	103	400	48	128	17	3	9	49	10	.320
	Totals..........		1451	5188	709	1451	246	18	183	749	107	.280

RON CEY 34 5-10 185   **Bats R Throws R**

Outstanding season despite missing four weeks with fractured bone above left wrist . . . Didn't play any regular-season games after Sept. 9, yet still topped club with 13 homers and nine game-winning RBI . . . Made a dramatic return for NL Championship Series and paced victory over Expos in Game 1 with two runs scored . . . Batted .350 with six RBI in World Series . . . Born Feb. 15, 1948, in Tacoma, Wash. . . . Batted .274 with nine homers in first half and .315 after the strike . . . Belted nine of his homers in May . . . NL Player of Week, May 11-17, for .462 average, five homers, 12 RBI and three game-winning RBI . . . Hit .346 in August . . . His 204 career homers are L.A. record . . . Inducted into Washington State U. Hall of Fame . . . Nicknamed "Penguin."

Year	Club	Pos.	G	AB	R	H	2B	3B	HR	RBI	SB	Avg.
1971	Los Angeles.....	PH	2	2	0	0	0	0	0	0	0	.000
1972	Los Angeles.....	3B	11	37	3	10	1	0	1	3	0	.270
1973	Los Angeles.....	3B	152	507	60	124	18	4	15	80	1	.245
1974	Los Angeles.....	3B	159	577	88	151	20	2	18	97	1	.262
1975	Los Angeles.....	3B	158	566	72	160	29	2	25	101	5	.283
1976	Los Angeles.....	3B	145	502	69	139	18	3	23	80	0	.277
1977	Los Angeles.....	3B	153	564	77	136	22	3	30	110	3	.241
1978	Los Angeles.....	3B	159	555	84	150	32	0	23	84	2	.270
1979	Los Angeles.....	3B	150	487	77	137	20	1	28	81	3	.281
1980	Los Angeles.....	3B	157	551	81	140	25	0	28	77	2	.254
1981	Los Angeles.....	3B	85	312	42	90	15	2	13	50	0	.288
	Totals..........		1331	4660	653	1237	200	17	204	763	17	.265

PEDRO GUERRERO 25 5-11 176   Bats R Throws R

They're no longer saying Pedro Who? . . . A big hit in World Series, batting .333 with two homers and seven RBI . . . Did most of his damage in decisive Game 6, knocking in five runs with a homer, triple and single . . . Won job in outfield over injured Reggie Smith and kept it with .325 first half, including 10 homers . . . Batted .269 in second half . . . Played third base when Cey was injured . . . Born June 29, 1956, in San Pedro de Macoris, Dominican Republic . . . Had best month in May with .361 average and seven homers . . . Homered in Dodgers' 2-1 victory over Houston in Game 4 of division play-offs . . . Also homered in NLCS and totaled four homers in postseason play . . . A prodigious minor-league hitter.

Year	Club	Pos.	G	AB	R	H	2B	3B	HR	RBI	SB	Avg.
1978	Los Angeles.....	1B	5	8	3	5	0	1	0	1	0	.625
1979	Los Angeles.....	OF-1B-3B	25	62	7	15	2	0	2	9	2	.242
1980	Los Angeles.....	OF-INF	75	183	27	59	9	1	7	31	2	.322
1981	Los Angeles.....	OF-3B	98	347	46	104	17	2	12	48	5	.300
	Totals..........		203	600	83	183	28	4	21	89	9	.305

JORGE ORTA 31 5-10 175   Bats L Throws R

Traded by Cleveland to Los Angeles after slipping with the bat, but was still a tough out . . . Is in third year of a five-year, $1.5-million contract signed with Indians as a free agent . . . With White Sox he played mostly second, but was always being shifted to new positions, which affected his hitting . . . His father was an outstanding baseball player in Cuba . . . Finished second to Rod Carew in 1974 batting race . . . Born Nov. 26, 1950, in Mazatian, Mexico . . . Had six hits in one game June 15, 1980, vs. Twins . . . Named to the Mexican Hall of Fame in 1976 . . . Discovered in Mexican Leagues by White Sox general manager Roland Hemond in 1969.

Year	Club	Pos.	G	AB	R	H	2B	3B	HR	RBI	SB	Avg.
1972	Chicago (AL)....	SS-2B-3B	51	124	20	25	3	1	3	11	1	.202
1973	Chicago (AL)....	2B-SS	128	425	46	113	9	10	6	40	8	.266
1974	Chicago (AL)....	2B-SS	139	525	73	166	31	2	10	67	9	.316
1975	Chicago (AL)....	2B	140	542	64	165	26	10	11	83	16	.304
1976	Chicago (AL)....	OF-3B	158	636	74	174	29	8	14	72	24	.274
1977	Chicago (AL)....	2B	144	564	71	159	27	8	11	84	4	.282
1978	Chicago (AL)....	2B	117	420	45	115	19	2	13	53	1	.274
1979	Chicago (AL)....	2B	113	325	49	85	18	3	11	46	1	.262
1980	Cleveland.......	OF-2B	129	481	78	140	18	3	10	64	6	.291
1981	Cleveland.......	OF-2B	88	338	50	92	14	3	5	34	4	.272
	Totals..........		1207	4380	570	1234	194	50	94	554	74	.282

BURT HOOTON 32 6-1 200   Bats R Throws R

Finding it difficult to keep a low profile after pitching spectacularly in postseason . . . Was 4-1 in playoffs and World Series, never allowing more than one run in a game . . . Nicknamed "Happy" because he never looks it . . . They say he smiles at home . . . Posted best ERA on staff and lowest of his major-league career . . . Was 7-3 with a 2.96 ERA in the first half, 4-3 after the strike . . . Born Feb. 7, 1950, in Greenville, Tex. . . . With Dodgers down 0-2 in division playoffs, he beat Astros in Game 3 and triggered turnaround . . . Won Games 1 and 4 in NLCS, yielding no earned runs in 14⅔ innings . . . Winning pitcher in World Series clincher . . . His knuckle curve is rated best in bigs . . . Former All-American at Texas, posting 35-3 career record.

Year	Club	G	IP	W	L	Pct.	SO	BB	H	ERA
1971	Chicago (NL)	3	21	2	0	1.000	22	10	8	2.14
1972	Chicago (NL)	33	218	11	14	.440	132	81	201	2.81
1973	Chicago (NL)	42	240	14	17	.452	134	73	248	3.68
1974	Chicago (NL)	48	176	7	11	.389	94	51	214	4.81
1975	Chi. (NL)-LA	34	235	18	9	.667	153	68	190	3.06
1976	Los Angeles	33	227	11	15	.423	116	60	203	3.25
1977	Los Angeles	32	223	12	7	.632	153	60	184	2.62
1978	Los Angeles	32	236	19	10	.655	104	61	196	2.71
1979	Los Angeles	29	212	11	10	.524	129	63	191	2.97
1980	Los Angeles	34	207	14	8	.636	118	64	194	3.65
1981	Los Angeles	23	142	11	6	.647	74	33	124	2.28
	Totals	343	2137	130	107	.549	1229	624	1953	3.17

FERNANDO VALENZUELA 21 5-11 200 Bats L Throws R

Amazing debut season brought him double honors—as Cy Young and Rookie-of-the-Year Award winner . . . Won first eight starts, five of them shutouts . . . Was 9-4 with a 2.45 ERA in the first half and 4-3 thereafter . . . Pitcher of the Month in April for 5-0 record, four shutouts, 43 strikeouts and one run allowed in 45 innings . . . Eight straight wins to start the season tied major-league record . . . On Sept. 17, he tied major-league record of eight shutouts by a rookie . . . Born Nov. 1, 1960, in Navajoa, Sonora, Mexico . . . Four-hit, 2-1 victory in Game 4 squared division playoffs . . . Won NLCS clincher in Game 5, yielding only one run . . . Struggled for 5-4 complete-game victory in Game 3 of World Series, beginning L.A. comeback . . . Fernandomania gripped NL, boosting at-

tendance whenever he pitched . . . Through it all, he remained humble and level-headed . . . Screwball is his best pitch.

Year	Club	G	IP	W	L	Pct.	SO	BB	H	ERA
1980	Los Angeles	10	18	2	0	1.000	16	5	8	0.00
1981	Los Angeles	25	192	13	7	.650	180	61	140	2.48
	Totals	35	210	15	7	.682	196	66	148	2.27

JERRY REUSS 32 6-5 217   Bats L Throws L

Best winning percentage on club . . . Was the epitome of consistency, going 5-2 in each half . . . No runs and only 10 hits allowed in 18 innings of division playoffs . . . Won clincher, 4-0, in Game 5 over Nolan Ryan . . . Pitched five-hit, 2-1 victory in Game 5 of World Series . . . Born June 19, 1949, in St. Louis . . . Slow start with Dodgers in '79 before notching his best season in '80 . . . It included a no-hitter against Giants and a league-leading six shutouts . . . A cut-up who keeps others loose . . . Finished second to Phils' Steve Carlton in Cy Young voting in '80 . . . Won nine of his last 12 decisions last year . . . Comeback Player of the Year in 1980.

Year	Club	G	IP	W	L	Pct.	SO	BB	H	ERA
1969	St. Louis	1	7	1	0	1.000	3	3	2	0.00
1970	St. Louis	20	127	7	8	.467	74	49	132	4.11
1971	St. Louis	36	211	14	14	.500	131	109	228	4.78
1972	Houston	33	192	9	13	.409	174	83	177	4.17
1973	Houston	41	279	16	13	.552	177	117	271	3.74
1974	Pittsburgh	35	260	16	11	.593	105	101	259	3.50
1975	Pittsburgh	32	237	18	11	.621	131	78	224	2.54
1976	Pittsburgh	31	209	14	9	.609	108	51	209	3.53
1977	Pittsburgh	33	208	10	13	.435	116	71	225	4.11
1978	Pittsburgh	23	83	3	2	.600	42	23	97	4.88
1979	Los Angeles	39	160	7	14	.333	83	60	178	3.54
1980	Los Angeles	37	229	18	6	.750	111	40	193	2.52
1981	Los Angeles	22	153	10	4	.714	51	27	138	2.29
	Totals	383	2355	143	118	.548	1306	812	2333	3.56

BOB WELCH 25 6-3 190   Bats R Throws R

A mainstay during regular season who was not prominent in postseason play . . . Posted 4-3 record with 3.22 ERA in the first half and improved to 5-2 after the strike . . . Accustomed to comebacks . . . Before 1980 season he won his battle over the bottle and responded with solid year . . . Hurled one-hitter against Braves, facing minimum 27 batters . . . Born Nov. 3, 1956, in Detroit . . . Had to fight to enter rotation last year after developing bone spur in right elbow during spring training . . . Had career-high 11 strikeouts against Cubs

. . . First gained fame with memorable strikeout of Reggie Jackson in 1978 World Series . . . All-American at Eastern Michigan.

Year	Club	G	IP	W	L	Pct.	SO	BB	H	ERA
1978	Los Angeles	23	111	7	4	.636	66	26	92	2.03
1979	Los Angeles	25	81	5	6	.455	64	32	82	4.00
1980	Los Angeles	32	214	14	9	.609	141	79	190	3.28
1981	Los Angeles	23	141	9	5	.643	88	41	141	3.45
	Totals	103	547	35	24	.593	359	178	505	3.18

STEVE HOWE 24 6-1 180 　　　　Bats L Throws L

Proved 1980 rookie season was no fluke by repeating stinginess in relief last year . . . Was 4-2 with a 2.08 ERA and five saves in the first half . . . Worked two scoreless innings in division playoffs . . . Ditto in NLCS . . . Even better in World Series, winning Game 4 and saving clincher . . . Born March 10, 1958, in Pontiac, Mich. . . . All-time winningest pitcher as Michigan All-American, posting 27-8 college record . . . No. 1 draft choice in 1979 . . . Only one year of minors, going 6-2 with 3.13 ERA for Albuquerque . . . NL Rookie of the Year in 1980, figuring in 24 L.A. victories . . . Got chance when injuries shelved Terry Forster and Don Stanhouse . . . Set L.A. rookie record for saves.

Year	Club	G	IP	W	L	Pct.	SO	BB	H	ERA
1980	Los Angeles	59	85	7	9	.438	39	22	83	2.65
1981	Los Angeles	41	54	5	3	.625	32	18	51	2.50
	Totals	100	139	12	12	.500	71	40	134	2.59

TOP PROSPECTS

ALBUQUERQUE DUKES 　　　　Won 94 Lost 38

Countless standouts from a Triple-A team, which batted a collective .325, should help the Dodgers immediately . . . First baseman Mike Marshall won PCL Triple Crown with .373 average, 34 homers and 137 RBI . . . Second baseman Jack Perconte batted .346 but the Dodgers sent him to Cleveland in the trade for the Indians' Jorge Orta . . . Outfielder Candy Maldonado batted .335 with 21 homers and 104 RBI . . . Outfielder Ron Roenicke had .316 average and 94 RBI . . . Shortstop Gary Weiss batted .294 . . . Top pitchers were Ted Power (18-3), Brian Holton (16-6), Rick Wright (14-6) and Dave Moore (12-5) . . . Take your pick . . . This is regarded as one of the best minor-league teams of all time, reminiscent of the old Newark teams; many of the players are can't-miss prospects.

MANAGER TOM LASORDA: Waved his magic wand and the Dodgers responded with three miraculous comebacks to reward skipper with his first World Series championship . . . Club won first half by one-half game over Cincy with 36-21 record, but hardly looked like champs in 27-26 second half, finishing fourth . . . Club was down 0-2 to Astros and 1-2 to Expos before winning each series and advancing to World Series, where they lost first two games before winning four in a row . . . Every time you turned around, animated Lasorda was rushing mound, jaws and arms flapping . . . Born Sept. 22, 1927, in Norristown, Pa. . . . A born ham, quick with the one-liners . . . Only thing he likes better than baseball is food . . . His office, brimming with show-biz people and autographed photos, resembles Sardi's . . . Makes friends and enemies with equal abandon . . . Truly bleeds Dodger Blue.

GREATEST CATCHER

The finest L.A. receiver is John Roseboro, but the Dodgers' all-time greatest catcher is a cinch. Roy Campanella, a Hall of Famer, destroys the competition as he did NL pitching from 1948 until a broken spine tragically ended his career in '57.

Campy was a three-time MVP (1951-53-55) and would have been even more heralded if he weren't sharing New York headlines with Yogi Berra. Campanella set a record (since broken) with 41 homers for a catcher in '53, the same year he topped the league with 142 RBI in 144 games. He finished with 242 homers in parts of 10 years.

ALL-TIME DODGER SEASON RECORDS

BATTING: Babe Herman, .393, 1930
HRs: Duke Snider, 43, 1956
RBIs: Tommy Davis, 153, 1962
STEALS: Maury Wills, 104, 1962
WINS: Joe McGinnity, 29, 1900
STRIKEOUTS: Sandy Koufax, 382, 1965

SAN DIEGO PADRES

(At press time, Templeton-Smith deal awaited Smith's signing.)

TEAM DIRECTORY: Owner: Ray Kroc; Pres.: Ballard Smith; VP-Baseball Oper.: Jack McKeon; Senior VP: Elton Schiller; Dir. Play. Dev.: Bob Cluck; Admin. Minor Leagues-Scouting: Tom Romenesko; Dir. Pub. Rel.: Bob Chandler; Trav. Sec.: John Mattei; Mgr.: Dick Williams. Home: San Diego Stadium (51,362). Field distances: 330, l.f. line; 420, c.f.; 330, r.f. line. Spring training: Yuma, Ariz.

SCOUTING REPORT

HITTING: One is to assume San Diego's attack will continue to improve. Not only does a flock of promising young hitters have one more year of experience, but the addition of Garry Templeton and Sixto Lezcano figures to give new skipper Dick Williams a fairly solid lineup from top to bottom. The Padres batted .256 last year, but sharply reduced their base-stealing under Frank Howard, dipping from a league-leading 239 steals in 1980 to a

High-flying Juan Bonilla hit and fielded well in NL debut.

paltry 83. Williams likes the running game, so the San Diego base-runners will cause more problems for pitchers now.

Luis Salazar (.303), Terry Kennedy (.301) and Juan Bonilla (.290) all proved they could hit last year and they figure to get much better. Veterans Gene Richards and Broderick Perkins already are proven hitters and Ruppert Jones should improve following an adjustment to the NL. Ditto Lezcano, who is a far better power hitter than his St. Louis production suggested last year. Templeton simply is the best hitting shortstop in the league when he's in the right frame of mind. If he is, the NL West may no longer have a patsy.

PITCHING: Well, nobody's perfect. Except for some late-season flashes, the staff was inconsistent and unimpressive last year. The prospects don't look much better and there's one less veteran arm with Steve Mura gone. A lot hinges on what youngsters like Fred Kuhaulua, Steve Fireovid and Chris Welch do, and whether aging John Curtis and Rick Wise can make comebacks. Juan Eichelberger has developed into a quality starter and Gary Lucas (2.00, 13 saves) is powerful out of the bullpen, but there are too many ifs on the rest of the staff.

FIELDING: The club doesn't figure to be any stronger afield without the dazzling Ozzie Smith, who was the best defensive shortstop in the league. He fielded .976, as compared to Templeton's .960, yet 1981 must be regarded as an off year for the former Cardinal. Perkins is solid at first, Bonilla shows signs of becoming one of the best at second and Salazar should settle down at third after also being used as an outfielder. Richards' 14 assists topped NL outfielders, Jones is a class act in center and Lezcano was a crack fielder with the Brewers before his 1981 adjustment problems. Kennedy figures to improve following a rugged debut (20 errors) as a regular catcher.

OUTLOOK: Fairly encouraging because the club has an abundance of young talent and a manager who might be able to do something with it. The brass was criticized for drastically cleaning house one year ago, but the pieces are beginning to fit and this won't be an easy lineup for any pitcher. Williams should get the Padres running again, which will help. The big drawback, however, is pitching. This club seems capable of scoring four or five runs per game, but giving up six or seven. It doesn't add up to a winner, but the Padres likely will field their most potent lineup ever. If everything comes together, this could be the league's surprise team of 1982.

SAN DIEGO PADRES 1982 ROSTER

MANAGER Dick Williams
Coaches—Jack Krol, Norm Sherry, Bobby Tolan, Ozzie Virgil

PITCHERS

No.	Name	1981 Club	W-L	IP	SO	ERA	B-T	Ht.	Wt.	Born
30	Boone, Dan	San Diego	1-0	63	43	2.86	L-L	5-8	131	1/14/54 Long Beach, CA
39	Chiffer, Floyd	Hawaii	4-5	68	51	3.44	R-R	6-2	180	4/20/56 Long Island City, NY
51	Curtis, John	San Diego	2-6	67	31	5.10	L-L	6-2	185	3/9/48 Newton, MA
43	Dravecky, Dave	Amarillo	15-5	172	141	2.67	L-L	6-1	195	2/14/56 Youngstown, OH
13	Eichelberger, Juan	San Diego	8-8	141	81	3.51	R-R	6-3	205	10/21/53 St. Louis, MO
62	Fireovid, Steve	Hawaii	11-7	162	57	3.17	B-R	6-2	195	6/6/57 Bryan, OH
		San Diego	0-1	26	11	2.77				
59	Hamm, Tim	Amarillo	9-6	123	78	2.27	R-R	6-4	200	8/8/60 Santa Cruz, CA
		Hawaii	3-3	75	40	3.60				
63	Hawkins, Andy	Amarillo	11-10	200	144	4.19	R-R	6-3	200	1/21/60 Waco, TX
41	Kuhaulua, Fred	Hawaii	10-10	162	85	4.17	L-L	5-11	175	2/23/53 Honolulu, HI
		San Diego	1-0	29	16	2.48				
50	Littlefield, John	San Diego	2-3	64	21	3.66	R-R	6-2	200	1/5/54 Covina, CA
48	Lollar, Tim	San Diego	2-8	77	38	6.08	L-L	6-3	195	3/17/56 Poplar Bluff, MO
43	Lucas, Gary	San Diego	7-7	90	53	2.00	L-L	6-5	200	11/8/54 Colton, CA
54	Seaman, Kim	Hawaii	6-8	114	79	5.29	L-L	6-3	205	5/6/57 Pascagoula, MS
44	Show, Eric	Hawaii	7-3	85	70	2.54	R-R	6-1	185	5/19/56 Riverside, CA
		San Diego	1-3	23	22	3.13				
42	Stablein, George	Hawaii	3-4	91	51	3.76	R-R	6-4	185	10/29/57 Inglewood, CA
49	Tellman, Tom	Hawaii	12-11	176	67	3.63	R-R	6-4	185	3/29/54 Warren, PA
58	Thurmond, Mark	Amarillo	12-5	193	128	3.26	L-L	6-0	180	9/12/56 Houston, TX
38	Urrea, John	San Diego	2-2	49	19	2.39	R-R	6-3	205	2/9/55 Los Angeles, CA
26	Welsh, Chris	San Diego	6-7	124	51	3.77	L-L	6-2	185	4/15/55 Wilmington, DE
40	Wise, Rick	San Diego	4-8	98	27	3.77	R-R	6-2	195	9/13/45 Jackson, MI

CATCHERS

No.	Name	1981 Club	H	HR	RBI	Pct.	B-T	Ht.	Wt.	Born
10	Gwosdz, Doug	Hawaii	53	8	28	.264	R-R	5-11	180	6/20/60 Houston, TX
		San Diego	4	0	3	.167				
16	Kennedy, Terry	San Diego	115	2	41	.301	L-R	6-4	220	6/4/56 Euclid, OH
9	Swisher, Steve	San Diego	4	0	0	.143	R-R	6-2	205	8/9/51 Parkersburg, WV
47	Tingley, Ron	Amarillo	109	13	60	.288	R-R	6-2	160	5/27/59 Presque Isle, ME

INFIELDERS

No.	Name	1981 Club	H	HR	RBI	Pct.	B-T	Ht.	Wt.	Born
5	Bass, Randy	San Diego	37	4	20	.210	L-R	6-1	210	3/13/54 Lawton, OK
3	Bonilla, Juan	San Diego	107	1	25	.290	R-R	5-9	170	1/12/56 Puerto Rico
8	Evans, Barry	San Diego	30	0	7	.323	R-R	6-1	180	11/30/56 Atlanta, GA
6	Flannery, Tim	Hawaii	22	0	10	.282	L-R	5-11	170	9/29/57 Tulsa, OK
		San Diego	17	0	6	.254				
35	Lansford, Joe	Amarillo	110	25	86	.237	R-R	6-5	225	1/15/61 San Jose, CA
15	Perkins, Broderick	San Diego	71	2	40	.280	L-L	5-10	180	11/23/54 Pittsburg, CA
12	Ramirez, Mario	Hawaii	103	5	49	.251	R-R	5-9	159	9/12/57 Puerto Rico
		San Diego	1	0	1	.077				
4	Salazar, Luis	San Diego	121	3	38	.303	R-R	5-9	180	5/19/56 Venezuela
1	Templeton, Garry	St. Louis	96	1	33	.288	B-R	5-11	170	3/24/56 Lockey, TX

OUTFIELDERS

No.	Name	1981 Club	H	HR	RBI	Pct.	B-T	Ht.	Wt.	Born
24	Edwards, Dave	San Diego	24	2	13	.214	R-R	6-0	177	2/24/54 Los Angeles, CA
22	Jones, Ruppert	San Diego	99	4	39	.249	L-L	5-10	175	3/12/55 Dallas, TX
18	Lefebvre, Joe	San Diego	63	8	31	.256	L-R	5-10	175	2/22/56 Concord, NH
—	Lezcano, Sixto	St. Louis	57	5	28	.266	R-R	5-10	175	11/28/53 Puerto Rico
17	Richards, Gene	San Diego	113	3	42	.288	L-L	6-0	175	9/29/53 Monticello, SC
2	Wiggins, Alan	Hawaii	155	0	33	.302	B-R	6-2	160	2/17/58 Los Angeles
		San Diego	5	0	0	.357				

PADRE PROFILES

GENE RICHARDS 28 6-0 175   Bats L Throws L

Flashed speed by tying for NL lead with 12 triples, but stolen bases dropped from club-record 61 in 1980 to 20 . . . Prominent in trade talk involving Yankees during World Series . . . Batted .266 in first half, but finished strong with a .314 mark after the strike . . . Shaky as a fielder during early years in bigs, but no longer a liability . . . Set club record with 21 outfield assists in 1980 . . . Born Sept. 12, 1953, in Monticello, S.C. . . . Played at South Carolina State until school dropped baseball . . . A California League standout with Reno is 1975, batting .381 and stealing 85 bases . . . Set major-league mark for a rookie with 56 steals in '77, topped by Tim Raines last year.

Year	Club	Pos.	G	AB	R	H	2B	3B	HR	RBI	SB	Avg.
1977	San Diego	OF-1B	146	525	79	152	16	11	5	32	56	.290
1978	San Diego	OF-1B	154	555	90	171	26	12	4	45	37	.308
1979	San Diego	OF	150	545	77	152	17	9	4	41	24	.279
1980	San Diego	OF	158	642	91	193	26	8	4	41	61	.301
1981	San Diego	OF	104	393	47	113	14	12	3	42	20	.288
	Totals		712	2660	384	781	99	52	20	201	198	.294

GARRY TEMPLETON 26 5-11 170   Bats S Throws R

Shortstop swap for Padres' Ozzie Smith followed troubled season as a Cardinal in which he still finished with respectable figures . . . Suspended and fined $5,000 after making obscene gestures to fans in St. Louis, Aug. 26 . . . Pulled into dugout by manager Whitey Herzog . . . Later apologized to fans and teammates and finished strong . . . Batted .265 in first half and overcame problems for .323 second half . . . Born March 24, 1956, in Lockey, Tex. . . . Considered one of premier athletes in game but wore out welcome with Cards . . . Became first switch-hitter to collect 100 hits from each side in '79.

Year	Club	Pos.	G	AB	R	H	2B	3B	HR	RBI	SB	Avg.
1976	St. Louis	SS	53	213	32	62	8	2	1	17	11	.291
1977	St. Louis	SS	153	621	94	200	19	18	8	79	28	.322
1978	St. Louis	SS	155	647	82	181	31	13	2	47	34	.280
1979	St. Louis	SS	154	672	105	211	32	19	9	62	26	.314
1980	St. Louis	SS	118	504	83	161	19	9	4	43	31	.319
1981	St. Louis	SS	80	333	47	96	16	8	1	33	8	.288
	Totals		713	2990	443	911	125	69	25	281	138	.305

BRODERICK PERKINS 27 5-10 180   Bats L Throws L

Created a mild stir by predicting he could hit .400 following a quick start . . . Fell short by .120 . . . But was batting .422 on May 12 after a 15-game batting streak . . . Batted .330 in May and was a .314 hitter prior to the strike . . . Slipped badly thereafter, hitting only .234 in the second half . . . Born Nov. 23, 1954, in Pittsburg, Cal. . . . Flexed hitting muscles in 1980 . . . After batting .312 at Hawaii, he hit .370 down the stretch for San Diego, including a 13-game batting streak . . . Withstood challenge of Randy Bass for first-base job . . . Conference MVP as a slugger at St. Mary's (Calif.) College . . . Batted .355 and .345 in first two years of pro ball.

Year	Club	Pos.	G	AB	R	H	2B	3B	HR	RBI	SB	Avg.
1978	San Diego	1B	62	217	14	52	14	1	2	33	4	.240
1979	San Diego	1B	57	87	8	23	0	0	0	8	0	.264
1980	San Diego	1B-OF	43	100	18	37	9	0	2	14	2	.370
1981	San Diego	1B-OF	92	254	27	71	18	3	2	40	0	.280
	Totals		254	658	67	183	41	4	6	95	6	.278

RUPPERT JONES 27 5-10 175   Bats L Throws L

Blasted career-high 34 doubles, second best in the league . . . Made adjustment to NL after four years in AL . . . Started slowly, but batted .275 after May 13 . . . A .242 hitter in the first half, .256 thereafter . . . Earned reputation as a slugger after belting 24 homers for first-year Mariners in 1977, most homers by an AL center fielder that year . . . Born March 12, 1955, in Dallas . . . Reared in Berkeley, where he was a prep superstar, turning down a chance to play college football . . . Came up through K.C. system and was first player selected in expansion draft . . . A favorite of Seattle fans who chanted "Roop, Roop, Roop" . . . Plagued by injuries throughout career.

Year	Club	Pos.	G	AB	R	H	2B	3B	HR	RBI	SB	Avg.
1976	Kansas City	OF	28	51	9	11	1	1	1	7	0	.216
1977	Seattle	OF	160	597	85	157	26	8	24	76	13	.263
1978	Seattle	OF	129	472	48	111	24	3	6	46	22	.235
1979	Seattle	OF	162	622	109	166	29	9	21	78	33	.267
1980	New York (AL)	OF	83	328	38	73	11	3	9	42	18	.223
1981	San Diego	OF	105	397	53	99	34	1	4	39	7	.249
	Totals		667	2467	342	617	125	25	65	288	93	.250

TERRY KENNEDY 25 6-4 220   **Bats L Throws R**

Lived up to expectations in first full season as a regular catcher . . . Collected two hits against Giants on final day to finish above .300 . . . A .333 May enabled him to bat .308 in the first half . . . A .294 post-strike hitter . . . Defensive shortcomings attributed to inexperience . . . Born June 4, 1956, in Mesa, Ariz. . . . Son of former major-league player and executive Bob Kennedy . . . Named to NL All-Star Game squad . . . Overshadowed by Ted Simmons at St. Louis and joined Padres in 11-player swap involving Rollie Fingers . . . College Player of the Year at Florida State . . . Needs to improve fielding to become a superstar.

Year	Club	Pos.	G	AB	R	H	2B	3B	HR	RBI	SB	Avg.
1978	St. Louis	C	10	29	0	5	0	0	0	2	0	.172
1979	St. Louis	C	33	109	11	31	7	0	2	17	0	.284
1980	St. Louis	C-OF	84	248	28	63	12	3	4	34	0	.254
1981	San Diego	C	101	382	32	115	24	1	2	41	0	.301
	Totals		228	768	71	214	43	4	8	94	0	.279

JUAN BONILLA 26 5-9 170   **Bats R Throws R**

A spring-training steal for GM Jack McKeon, who sent Bob Lacey to Cleveland for this standout second baseman . . . Had 23-game errorless string and appears to have a bright future . . . Can hit, too, as evidenced by .284 first half and .294 mark after the strike . . . Erupted for a .348 average in August . . . Born Feb. 12, 1956, in Santurce, Puerto Rico . . . Like Kennedy, attended Florida State, where he was an All-American third baseman . . . Has Gold Glove potential . . . Showed promise in minors, topped by a .303 average for Tacoma in 1980 . . . Also was the best fielder in the PCL.

Year	Club	Pos.	G	AB	R	H	2B	3B	HR	RBI	SB	Avg.
1981	San Diego	2B	99	369	30	107	13	2	1	25	4	.290

LUIS SALAZAR 25 5-9 180   **Bats R Throws R**

Made a sparkling debut with .337 average in 44 games in 1980 and proved that was no fluke last season . . . Playing third base and the outfield, he batted .294 in the first half and .312 after the strike to finish above .300 . . . Was at his best in August, batting above .350 . . . Belted four hits in a doubleheader in major-league debut, Aug. 17, 1980 . . . Born

May 19, 1956, in Puerto LaCruz, Venezuela . . . Outstanding hitter in Pirates system before coming to Padres in a trade . . . Batted .323 with 27 homers at Buffalo in 1979 . . . Stole 41 bases in the PCL in 1979 and 43 in the same league the next year.

Year	Club	Pos.	G	AB	R	H	2B	3B	HR	RBI	SB	Avg.
1980	San Diego	3B-OF	44	169	28	57	4	7	1	25	11	.337
1981	San Diego	3B-OF	109	400	37	121	19	6	3	38	11	.303
	Totals		153	569	65	178	23	13	4	63	22	.313

JUAN EICHELBERGER 28 6-3 205   Bats R Throws R

First full season in the majors was a rousing success . . . Blossomed into Padres' ace . . . Got going with a 4-2 May and was 6-3 when strike hit before slumping to 2-5 down stretch . . . Rallied in September for six-hit victory over Reds and a 10-strikeout win against Dodgers . . . Born Oct. 21, 1953, in St. Louis . . . Reared in San Francisco and pitched for U. of California at Berkeley . . . Had brief major-league flings in '78 and '79 before joining Padres to stay in 1980 . . . Started that season 7-3 for Hawaii and was 4-2 with San Diego despite emergency appendectomy which shelved him three weeks . . . Potentially outstanding if he improves control.

Year	Club	G	IP	W	L	Pct.	SO	BB	H	ERA
1978	San Diego	3	3	0	0	.000	2	2	4	12.00
1979	San Diego	3	21	1	1	.500	12	11	15	3.43
1980	San Diego	15	89	4	2	.667	43	55	73	3.64
1981	San Diego	25	141	8	8	.500	81	74	136	3.51
	Totals	46	254	13	11	.542	138	142	228	3.65

GARY LUCAS 27 6-5 200   Bats L Throws L

Justified trading of Rollie Fingers by becoming a standout reliever . . . Led NL with 57 appearances and was fifth in saves with 13 . . . Also won seven games to figure in 20 of the club's 41 victories . . . Posted 3-5, 2.44 stats in first half with 10 saves and was 4-2 after the strike . . . Born Nov. 8, 1954, in Riverside, Calif. . . . Gave club a hint of what was to come with incredible stretch drive in 1980 . . . In final 25 appearances, he gave up five runs and catcher Gene Tenace called him "a left-handed Fingers" . . . Began 1980 season as a starter before conversion to relief . . . A 19th-round selection out of Chapman College (Calif.).

Year	Club	G	IP	W	L	Pct.	SO	BB	H	ERA
1980	San Diego	46	150	5	8	.385	85	43	138	3.24
1981	San Diego	57	90	7	7	.500	53	36	78	2.00
	Totals	103	240	12	15	.444	138	79	216	2.78

CHRIS WELSH 26 6-2 185   Bats L Throws L

Obtained in a swap with the Yankees, he was a solid starter in his first taste of major-league ball . . . Inherited Randy Jones' tough-luck label after losing three games, 2-1, 2-1 and 1-0 . . . Could have been 9-4 instead of 6-7 . . . Topped squad with four complete games and two shutouts, including a three-hitter over the Reds . . . Born April 14, 1955, in Wilmington, Del. . . . Reared in Cincinnati, where he was a fan of Reds and Pete Rose . . . Graduated from South Florida . . . Posted 3-4 record with 2.88 ERA first half and was 3-3 in final half . . . Was 2-0 in playoffs for Columbus in 1980, including Governor's Cup clincher over Toledo.

Year	Club	G	IP	W	L	Pct.	SO	BB	H	ERA
1981	San Diego	22	124	6	7	.462	51	41	122	3.77

TOP PROSPECTS

STEVE FIREOVID 24-6-2 195   Bats S Throws R

Fireovid was 45-24 in four minor-league seasons in the Padres system before his recall from Hawaii, where he was 11-7 with a 3.17 ERA last year . . . Didn't win a game for San Diego, but looked sharp in four starts, posting a 2.77 ERA . . . Born June 6, 1957, in Bryan, Ohio . . . Attended Miami of Ohio.

ALAN WIGGINS 24 6-2 160   Bats S Throws R

Swift outfielder drafted out of the Dodgers organization . . . Set an all-time pro record of 120 steals in 135 games for Lodi of the California League in 1980 . . . Topped PCL with 73 steals for Hawaii in '81, batting .302 . . . In 15 games with the Padres, he batted .357 with two steals . . . Born Jan. 17, 1958, in Los Angeles . . . Fred Kuhaulua (1-0 in September after a 10-10 season at Hawaii) and reliever Eric Show also figure in Padres' future plans.

MANAGER DICK WILLIAMS: Highest-paid manager in the history of the Padres . . . Was rumored to be headed to the Yankees, but he signed three-year, $450,000 contract with San Diego last November . . . Fired by Expos Sept. 8 when team was floundering . . . Then Expos went on to Eastern title under Jim Fanning . . . Guided Oakland to three straight division titles and two World Series crowns from 1971-73 . . . Three-time Manager of the Year . . . A stern, no-nonsense disciplinarian who is not overly popular with his players . . . Born May 7, 1929, in St. Louis . . . As rookie manager in 1967, he piloted Red Sox into World Series . . . Almost took over as Yankee manager in 1974, but Charlie Finley wouldn't let him escape from contract . . . A journeyman throughout his 13-year playing career, he has enjoyed much more success as a manager, with almost 1,100 wins . . . Sixth Padre manager in the last five years.

GREATEST CATCHER

Slim pickings here because there simply isn't much to choose from on an expansion franchise. Gene Tenace wins by default, though his four years with the club, 1977-80, were hardly memorable.

Tenace, who gained notoriety with the A's, at least provided some punch for the Padres, averaging 17 homers and 60 RBI in his four-year stint. Before long, however, Terry Kennedy is destined to emerge as No. 1. In his first year with San Diego, Kennedy batted .301 and will only get better.

ALL-TIME PADRE SEASON RECORDS

BATTING: Clarence Gaston, .318, 1970
HRs: Nate Colbert, 38, 1970
RBIs: Dave Winfield, 118, 1979
STEALS: Gene Richards, 61, 1980
WINS: Randy Jones, 22, 1976
STRIKEOUTS: Clay Kirby, 231, 1971

SAN FRANCISCO GIANTS

TEAM DIRECTORY: Pres.: Bob Lurie; VP-Baseball Oper.: Tom Haller; VP-Bus. Oper.: Pat Gallagher; VP-Administration: Corey Busch; Dir. Play. Per. and Development: Bob Fontaine; Dir. Scouting-Minor League Oper.: Jack Schwarz; Dir. Publ.: Duffy Jennings; Community and PR Dir.: Stu Smith; Asst. VP-Baseball Oper.-Trav. Sec.: Ralph Nelson; Mgr.: Frank Robinson. Home: Candlestick Park (58,000). Field distances: 335, l.f. line; 365, l.c.; 410, c.f.; 365, r.c.; 335, r.f. line. Spring training: Scottsdale, Ariz.

SCOUTING REPORT

HITTING: The Giants improved to .250 last season and got a boost from Joe Morgan's presence, but there won't be a drastic improvement this year unless young outfielders Chili Davis and Jeff Leonard come through. The swaps of veteran outfielders Larry Herndon and Jerry Martin have made it a necessity for the youngsters to develop rapidly. Leonard, the former Astro, showed signs by batting .307 in the second half following .401 success at Phoenix (PCL).

The old reliables are Morgan, Darrell Evans, Jack Clark and Milt May, whose .310 topped the club. Clark has MVP potential and a fat contract, so he may be ready to bust out with a dynamite season. Morgan, who may be pushed by ex-Indian Duane Kuiper, could improve on .240 in his leadoff role. A bonus down low in the order comes from the revived batting of Johnnie Le-Master, who transformed himself from a nothing at the dish to a respectable .253 hitter.

PITCHING: The Giants are in a division dominated by pitching, so there's no mistaking their top priority. The winter meetings stocked the roster with five new pitchers and the Giants apparently will continue to do it with numbers instead of names. They do not have an abundance of pitching standouts, as do the Astros and the Dodgers, but they do get results. The Giants' 3.28 ERA was third best in the NL even though it seemed the club was doing it with mirrors.

Vida Blue and Doyle Alexander are dependable starters and former Tiger Dan Schatzeder and former Royal Rich Gale will join the rotation. Al Holland may also get a starting shot, but that would weaken a tremendous one-two bullpen punch with Greg Minton (2.89, 21 saves). Gary Lavelle adds quality and depth to a bullpen which was the key to the club's 1981 success.

Giants are hoping for giant performance from Jack Clark.

FIELDING: Not good, but getting better. The addition of Morgan tightened the defense considerably, helping LeMaster blossom at short. The pair formed a solid double-play combination and center fielder Leonard added strength up the middle, making no errors. Evans was solid, if unspectacular, at third and Clark's 14 assists in right topped NL outfielders. May takes a lot of heat behind the plate because of his arm, but he's respectable in other phases of the job. Wherever Enos Cabell plays is a problem, presumably because of eye trouble.

OUTLOOK: A strange club to figure. The Giants finished strong last year and manager Frank Robinson, with the help of Morgan, has developed a winning attitude. It's the bullpen, however, which carried the club and Robinson was smart enough to take advantage of it. There are enough new arms to suggest the club will continue to get five or six innings from the starters before Robby calls for help. If Clark, Evans and Morgan can avoid early-season slumps and Leonard and Davis play as expected, this team could surprise. But things have to break just right, because the Astros and the Dodgers definitely have the edge on paper.

SAN FRANCISCO GIANTS 1982 ROSTER

MANAGER Frank Robinson
Coaches—Don Buford, Jim Davenport, Jim Lefebvre, Don
McMahon, John Van Ornum

PITCHERS

No.	Name	1981 Club	W-L	IP	SO	ERA	B-T	Ht.	Wt.	Born
33	Alexander, Doyle	San Francisco	11-7	152	77	2.90	R-R	6-3	205	9/4/50 Cordova, AL
14	Blue, Vida	San Francisco	8-6	125	63	2.45	B-L	6-0	192	7/28/49 Mansfield, LA
34	Bordley, Bill	San Francisco		disabled list			L-L	6-2	200	1/9/58 Los Angeles, CA
48	Breining, Fred	San Francisco	5-2	78	37	2.54	R-R	6-4	185	11/15/55 San Francisco, CA
—	Chris, Mike	Evansville	2-2	39	21	6.46	L-L	6-2	185	10/8/57 Santa Monica, CA
		Birmingham	5-5	89	77	4.15				
—	Calvert, Mark	Phoenix	7-4	101	31	4.46	R-R	6-1	195	9/29/56 Tulsa, OK
—	Capilla, Doug	Chicago (NL)	1-0	51	28	3.18	L-L	5-8	175	1/7/52 Honolulu, HI
—	Garrelts, Scott	Shreveport	3-8	71	73	4.44	R-R	6-4	195	10/30/61 Urbana, IL
—	Gale, Rich	Kansas City	6-6	102	47	5.38	R-R	6-7	225	1/19/54 Littleton, NH
40	Hargesheimer, Al	Phoenix	6-8	118	64	3.66	R-R	6-3	200	11/21/56 Chicago, IL
		San Francisco	1-2	19	6	4.26				
19	Holland, Al	San Francisco	7-5	101	78	2.41	R-L	5-11	213	8/16/52 Roanoke, VA
—	Laskey, Bill	Omaha	10-8	138	87	3.91	R-R	6-5	190	12/20/57 Toledo, OH
46	Lavelle, Gary	San Francisco	2-6	66	45	3.82	B-L	6-2	205	1/3/49 Scranton, PA
38	Minton, Greg	San Francisco	4-5	84	29	2.89	R-R	6-2	194	7/29/51 Lubbock, TX
28	Rowland, Mike	Phoenix	15-7	176	84	3.99	R-R	6-3	205	1/31/53 Chicago, IL
		San Francisco	0-1	16	8	3.38				
—	Schatzeder, Dan	Detroit	6-8	71	20	6.08	L-L	6-0	195	12/1/54 Elmhurst, IL
50	Stember, Jeff	Phoenix	7-9	116	63	6.44	R-R	6-5	220	3/2/58 Elizabeth, NJ
17	Tufts, Bob	Phoenix	9-2	69	38	1.70	L-L	6-5	210	11/2/55 Medford, MA
		San Francisco	0-0	15	12	3.60				

CATCHERS

No.	Name	1981 Club	H	HR	RBI	Pct.	B-T	Ht.	Wt.	Born
15	Brenly, Bob	Phoenix	.75	7	41	.292	R-R	6-2	210	2/25/54 Coshocton, OH
		San Francisco	15	1	4	.333				
37	Cummings, Bob	Shreveport	55	4	22	.228	R-R	6-2	185	9/8/60 Chicago, IL
7	May, Milt	San Francisco	98	2	33	.310	L-R	6-0	190	8/1/50 Gary, IN
18	Rabb, John	Shreveport	98	16	58	.276	R-R	6-1	179	6/23/60 Los Angeles, CA
3	Ransom, Jeff	Phoenix	83	3	39	.232	R-R	5-11	185	11/11/60 Fresno, CA
		San Francisco	4	0	0	.267				

INFIELDERS

No.	Name	1981 Club	H	HR	RBI	Pct.	B-T	Ht.	Wt.	Born
16	Bergman, Dave	Houston-SF	38	4	14	.252	L-L	6-2	180	6/6/53 Evanston, IL
—	Boyland, Dorian	Portland	65	2	28	.310	L-L	6-4	204	1/6/55 Chicago, IL
		Pittsburgh	0	0	0	.000				
—	Brown, Chris	Fresno	84	8	44	.255	R-R	6-0	185	8/15/61 Jackson, MS
23	Cabell, Enos	San Francisco	101	2	36	.255	R-R	6-5	185	10/8/49 Ft. Riley, KS
41	Evans, Darrell	San Francisco	92	12	48	.258	L-R	6-2	200	5/26/47 Pasadena, CA
24	Kuiper, Duane	Cleveland	53	0	14	.257	L-R	6-0	175	6/19/50 Racine, WI
10	LeMaster, Johnnie	San Francisco	82	0	28	.253	R-R	6-2	165	6/19/54 Portsmouth, OH
8	Morgan, Joe	San Francisco	74	8	31	.240	L-R	5-7	160	9/19/43 Bonham, TX
—	O'Malley, Tom	Shreveport	135	6	53	.289	L-R	6-0	178	12/25/60 Orange, NJ
2	Pettini, Joe	Phoenix	21	0	5	.244	R-R	5-9	165	1/26/55 Wheeling, WV
		San Francisco	2	0	2	.069				
6	Stennett, Rennie	San Francisco	20	1	7	.230	R-R	5-11	185	4/5/51 Panama
21	Sularz, Guy	Phoenix	167	2	56	.324	R-R	5-11	165	11/7/55 Minneapolis, MN
		San Francisco	4	0	2	.200				

OUTFIELDERS

No.	Name	1981 Club	H	HR	RBI	Pct.	B-T	Ht.	Wt.	Born
22	Clark, Jack	San Francisco	103	17	53	.268	R-R	6-3	205	11/10/55 New Brighton, PA
30	Davis, Chili	Phoenix	117	19	75	.350	B-R	6-3	195	1/17/60 Jamaica
		San Francisco	2	0	0	.133				
—	Deer, Rob	Fresno	137	33	107	.286	R-R	6-3	210	9/29/60 Orange, CA
26	Leonard, Jeff	Houston-SF	42	4	29	.290	R-R	6-4	200	9/22/55 Philadelphia, PA
		Phoenix	75	7	45	.401				
49	Venable, Max	Phoenix	122	8	48	.285	L-R	5-10	185	6/6/57 Phoenix, AZ
		San Francisco	6	0	1	.188				
1	Wohlford, Jim	San Francisco	11	1	7	.162	R-R	5-11	175	2/28/51 Visalia, CA

GIANT PROFILES

JACK CLARK 26 6-3 205   **Bats R Throws R**

Made drastic improvement following strike and finished with respectable statistics . . . Batted .224 with six homers in first half; .315 with 11 homers in second half . . . Flourished in August with .365 average and .649 slugging percentage . . . Emerging as club leader . . . Topped team with 11 game-winning RBI after leading NL with 18 in 1980 . . . Outspoken young veteran blasted manager Frank Robinson in late August after producing game-winning, extra-inning homer . . . Potential superstar if he puts everything together . . . Born Nov. 10, 1955, in New Brighton, Pa. . . . Became a father for the second time during the season . . . Set all-time Giants marks in 1978 with a 26-game hitting streak and 46 doubles.

Year	Club	Pos.	G	AB	R	H	2B	3B	HR	RBI	SB	Avg.
1975	San Francisco ...	OF-3B	8	17	3	4	0	0	0	2	1	.235
1976	San Francisco ...	OF	26	102	14	23	6	2	2	10	6	.225
1977	San Francisco ...	OF	136	413	64	104	17	4	13	51	12	.252
1978	San Francisco ...	OF	156	592	90	181	46	8	25	98	15	.306
1979	San Francisco ...	OF-3B	143	527	84	144	25	2	26	86	11	.273
1980	San Francisco ...	OF	127	437	77	124	20	8	22	82	2	.284
1981	San Francisco ...	OF	99	385	60	103	19	2	17	53	1	.268
	Totals..........		695	2473	392	683	133	26	105	382	48	.276

DARRELL EVANS 34 6-2 200   **Bats L Throws R**

Veteran slugger had contrasting half seasons . . . Totaled nine homers and 29 RBI in first half, but batted only .223 after traditional slow start . . . Improved to .300 in second half, but hit only three homers . . . Constantly frustrated by Candlestick Park, where wind holds up his long drives and rough infield contributes to his error total . . . Born May 26, 1947, in Pasadena, Calif. . . . Was junior-college basketball star . . . Steady, if not spectacular, fielder who is rankled by constant talk of switching positions . . . Had to win third-base job last spring from newcomer Enos Cabell and was told to bring first-baseman's glove to 1982 camp . . . Belted 41 homers for 1973 Braves, joining Henry Aaron and Dave Johnson as only trio to hit 40 or more for one team in same season.

Year	Club	Pos.	G	AB	R	H	2B	3B	HR	RBI	SB	Avg.
1971	Atlanta.........	3B-OF	89	260	42	63	11	1	12	38	2	.242
1972	Atlanta	3B	125	418	67	106	12	0	19	71	4	.254
1973	Atlanta.........	3B-1B	161	595	114	167	25	8	41	104	6	.281
1974	Atlanta	3B	160	571	99	137	21	3	25	79	4	.240
1975	Atlanta	3B-1B	156	567	82	138	22	2	22	73	12	.243
1976	Atl.-S.F.	1B-3B	136	396	53	81	9	1	11	46	9	.205
1977	San Francisco ...	OF-1B-3B	144	461	64	117	18	3	17	72	9	.254
1978	San Francisco ...	3B	159	547	82	133	24	2	20	78	4	.243
1979	San Francisco ...	3B	160	562	68	142	23	2	17	70	6	.253
1980	San Francisco ...	3B-1B	154	556	69	147	23	0	20	78	17	.264
1981	San Francisco ...	3B-1B	102	357	51	92	13	4	12	48	2	.258
	Totals..........		1570	5360	798	1343	202	27	216	767	75	.251

DAN SCHATZEDER 27 6-0 195   Bats L Throws L

Returns to National League after two largely unproductive seasons in Detroit . . . Came to Giants in deal that sent Larry Herndon to the Motor City . . . Was originally Expos' property and had fine 10-5 record in Montreal in 1979 . . . But Expos traded him to Tigers in Ron LeFlore deal that winter . . . Had fine second half in 1980 and was counted on as Tigers' top southpaw last year. He failed, to put it mildly . . . Allowed 74 hits and 29 walks in 71 innings and had sky-high 6.08 ERA . . . Born Dec. 1, 1954, in Elmhurst, Ill. . . . Has done some of his best work as a long relief man and may be used in that role here . . . A graduate of Denver University.

Year	Club	G	IP	W	L	Pct.	SO	BB	H	ERA
1977	Montreal	6	22	2	1	.667	14	13	16	2.45
1978	Montreal	29	144	7	7	.500	69	68	108	3.06
1979	Montreal	32	162	10	5	.667	106	59	136	2.83
1980	Detroit	32	193	11	13	.458	94	58	178	4.01
1981	Detroit	17	71	6	8	.429	20	29	74	6.08
	Totals	116	592	36	34	.514	303	227	512	3.65

MILT MAY 31 6-0 190   Bats L Throws R

His .310 average was the highest ever by a San Francisco catcher, topping Dick Dietz' .300 in 1970 . . . Batted .308 first half, .313 after the strike in a show of consistency . . . Improved behind the plate as well after throwing problems in 1980 which earned him the nickname "Venus de Milo" . . . Arm merely average, but booming bat can't keep him out of lineup . . . Would be a great DH . . . Born Aug. 1, 1950, in Gary, Ind.

. . . Son of Pinky May, former Phillies infielder . . . Belted game-winning hit as pinch-batter for Pirates against Orioles in Game 4 of 1971 World Series . . . Coming off best season in major-league career, which has been plagued by injuries that retarded his progress.

Year	Club	Pos.	G	AB	R	H	2B	3B	HR	RBI	SB	Avg.
1970	Pittsburgh	PH	5	4	1	2	1	0	0	2	0	.500
1971	Pittsburgh	C	49	126	15	35	1	0	6	25	0	.278
1972	Pittsburgh	C	57	139	12	39	10	0	0	14	0	.281
1973	Pittsburgh	C	101	283	29	76	8	1	7	31	0	.269
1974	Houston	C	127	405	47	117	17	4	7	54	0	.289
1975	Houston	C	111	386	29	93	15	1	4	52	1	.241
1976	Detroit	C	6	25	2	7	1	0	0	1	0	.280
1977	Detroit	C	115	397	32	99	9	3	12	46	0	.249
1978	Detroit	C	105	352	24	88	9	0	10	37	0	.250
1979	Det.-Chi. (AL)	C	71	213	24	54	15	0	7	31	0	.254
1980	San Francisco	C	111	358	27	93	16	2	6	50	0	.260
1981	San Francisco	C	97	316	20	98	17	0	2	33	1	.310
	Totals		955	3004	262	801	119	11	61	376	2	.267

VIDA BLUE 32 6-0 192   Bats S Throws L

Became first pitcher to win an All-Star Game for both leagues when he earned the NL decision at Cleveland . . . Curiously, he was the last AL pitcher to win the All-Star Game, doing so in 1971 . . . Had 3-1 record with a 1.13 ERA in May and entered strike at 5-5 with a 2.22 ERA . . . Won three out of four second-half decisions before being shelved by a hand injury, reportedly suffered in a domestic altercation . . . Born July 28, 1949, in Mansfield, La. . . . Made a sensational splash as an A's rookie, firing no-hitter against Twins in 1970 . . . Encore was even better, winning MVP and Cy Young Awards in 1971, his first full season in the bigs . . . Came to Giants in blockbuster swap with Oakland and promptly earned NL Pitcher-of-the-Year honors.

Year	Club	G	IP	W	L	Pct.	SO	BB	H	ERA
1969	Oakland	12	41	1	1	.500	24	18	49	6.21
1970	Oakland	6	39	2	0	1.000	35	12	20	2.08
1971	Oakland	39	312	24	8	.750	301	88	209	1.82
1972	Oakland	25	151	6	10	.375	111	48	117	2.80
1973	Oakland	37	264	20	9	.690	158	105	214	3.27
1974	Oakland	40	282	17	15	.531	174	98	246	3.26
1975	Oakland	39	278	22	11	.667	189	99	243	3.01
1976	Oakland	37	298	18	13	.581	166	63	268	2.35
1977	Oakland	38	280	14	19	.424	157	86	284	3.83
1978	San Francisco	35	258	18	10	.643	171	70	233	2.79
1979	San Francisco	34	237	14	14	.500	138	111	246	5.01
1980	San Francisco	31	224	14	10	.583	129	61	202	2.97
1981	San Francisco	18	125	8	6	.571	63	54	97	2.45
	Totals	391	2790	178	126	.586	1816	913	2428	3.09

JOHNNIE LeMASTER 27 6-2 165   Bats R Throws R

"Bones" enjoyed his finest big-league season in 1981, justifying Giants' faith in him . . . Entered season with .221 career average, but batted .252 in first half and .255 in second half . . . Credits working with Harry Walker prior to season for his batting rise . . . Offense considered a bonus because of his glove . . . Vastly underrated, according to manager Frank Robinson, and has great range . . . Born June 19, 1954, in Portsmouth, Ohio . . . Took awhile for S.F. fans to accept the slender shortstop, often a target of criticism . . . Once stitched BOO to the back of his jersey, drawing laughs from fans and teammates—and a fine from the front office . . . Plans on becoming switch-hitter.

Year	Club	Pos.	G	AB	R	H	2B	3B	HR	RBI	SB	Avg.
1975	San Francisco ...	SS	22	74	4	14	4	0	2	9	2	.189
1976	San Francisco ...	SS	33	100	9	21	3	2	0	9	2	.210
1977	San Francisco ...	SS-3B	68	134	13	20	5	1	0	8	2	.149
1978	San Francisco ...	SS-2B	101	272	23	64	18	3	1	14	6	.235
1979	San Francisco ...	SS	108	343	42	87	11	2	3	29	9	.254
1980	San Francisco ...	SS	135	405	33	87	16	6	3	31	0	.215
1981	San Francisco ...	SS	104	324	27	82	9	1	0	28	3	.253
	Totals..........		571	1652	151	375	66	15	9	128	24	.227

GREG MINTON 30 6-2 194   Bats R Throws R

Enjoyed remarkable season, setting club saves record with his 21st on final day . . . Did not yield a home run entire year, extending string to 255 innings, a major-league record . . . Joe Ferguson of Dodgers was last to homer off him, Sept. 6, 1978 . . . Sinkerball specialist who insists he's trying to live down image which has earned him nickname "Moon Man" . . . Born July 29, 1951, in Lubbock, Tex. . . . Replaced ailing Randy Moffitt as club's right-handed bullpen ace in 1979, fashioning 1.80 ERA . . . Came to Giants in one of club's better swaps of 1970s, one which sent catcher Fran Healy to Kansas City . . . Reared in San Diego area, where he was an avid surfer.

Year	Club	G	IP	W	L	Pct.	SO	BB	H	ERA
1975	San Francisco	4	17	1	1	.500	6	11	19	6.88
1976	San Francisco	10	26	0	3	.000	7	12	32	4.85
1977	San Francisco	2	14	1	1	.500	5	4	14	4.50
1978	San Francisco	11	16	0	1	.000	6	8	22	7.88
1979	San Francisco	46	80	4	3	.571	33	27	59	1.80
1980	San Francisco	68	91	4	6	.400	42	34	81	2.47
1981	San Francisco	55	84	4	5	.444	29	36	84	2.89
	Totals..................	196	328	14	20	.412	128	132	311	3.18

AL HOLLAND 29 5-11 213   Bats R Throws L

Stocky southpaw may be the Fernando Valen-zuela of 1982 . . . Came out of bullpen in September and made three impressive starts to figure in starting plans for the future . . . Was 3-2 with a 3.07 ERA in the first half and 4-3 record following strike doesn't reflect his effectiveness down the stretch . . . Born Aug. 16, 1952, in Roanoke, Va. . . . Obtained from Pirates in Bill Madlock deal and fired seven scoreless innings in his Giant debut late in '79 . . . Became one of premier left-handed relievers in league as rookie in 1980 and replaced Gary Lavelle as No. 1 lefty out of bullpen . . . Played football at North Carolina A&T.

Year	Club	G	IP	W	L	Pct.	SO	BB	H	ERA
1977	Pittsburgh	2	2	0	0	.000	1	0	4	9.00
1979	San Francisco	3	7	0	0	.000	7	5	3	0.00
1980	San Francisco	54	82	5	3	.625	65	34	71	1.76
1981	San Francisco	47	101	7	5	.583	78	44	87	2.41
	Totals	106	192	12	8	.600	151	83	165	2.11

DOYLE ALEXANDER 31 6-3 205   Bats R Throws R

Club's most effective and dependable starter following a steal of a swap with Atlanta for John Montefusco . . . Beat Cincinnati to become one of four active major-leaguers to defeat all 26 major-league teams . . . Made a sensational debut with Giants, going 3-1 with a 1.29 ERA in April . . . Was 5-4 with a 2.69 ERA before strike; 6-3 thereafter . . . Born Sept. 4, 1950, in Cordova, Ala. . . . Dissatisfaction over Giants' reluctance to extend contract had "Alex" threatening retirement at season's end, so a trade was possible . . . Was Braves' top starter in 1980, but contract squabble with Ted Turner led to trade.

Year	Club	G	IP	W	L	Pct.	SO	BB	H	ERA
1971	Los Angeles	17	92	6	6	.500	30	18	105	3.82
1972	Baltimore	35	106	6	8	.429	49	30	78	2.46
1973	Baltimore	29	175	12	8	.600	63	52	169	3.84
1974	Baltimore	30	114	6	9	.400	40	43	127	4.03
1975	Baltimore	32	133	8	6	.500	46	47	127	3.05
1976	Balt.-N.Y. (AL)	30	201	13	9	.591	58	63	172	3.36
1977	Texas	34	237	17	11	.607	82	82	221	3.65
1978	Texas	31	191	9	10	.474	81	71	198	3.86
1979	Texas	23	113	5	7	.417	50	69	114	4.46
1980	Atlanta	35	232	14	11	.560	114	74	227	4.19
1981	San Francisco	24	152	11	7	.611	77	44	156	2.90
	Totals	320	1746	107	94	.532	690	593	1694	3.63

TOP PROSPECTS

CHARLES DAVIS 22 6-3 195   Bats S Throws R
Being groomed for an outfield berth . . . Was spring training
sensation of 1981 and went north with club . . . Farmed out for
more seasoning, he was a PCL rookie standout . . . "Chili" batted .350 in 88 games with 19 homers, 75 RBI and club-record 41
stolen bases . . . Born Jan. 17, 1960, in Kingston, Jamaica . . .
Only Jeff Leonard was more impressive at Phoenix, batting .401
before joining Giants for second half . . . Club also likes second
baseman Mike Rex (.323 at Phoenix); reliever Bob Tufts (9-2,
1.70 at Phoenix) and Alan Fowlkes (14-10, 2.84 as Texas League
Pitcher of Year at Shreveport).

DOE BOYLAND 27 6-4 204   Bats L Throws L
Time may be running out for this first baseman-outfielder who
was regarded as Pirates' top prospect in '79 . . . Became a Giant
in trade for pitcher Tom Griffin . . . Enjoyed best hitting success
at Triple-A level with .310 at Portland last year . . . Born Jan. 6,
1955, in Chicago.

MANAGER FRANK ROBINSON: Rewarded with a two-year
contract extension through 1984 after guiding
club to 56-55 record . . . Big improvement
considering 75-86 finish in 1980 under Dave
Bristol and sluggish, 27-32 first half in 1981
. . . Upset players on occasion with candid
criticism of frequent mental blunders . . .
Deft handler of bullpen . . . Realized early
that he had no nine-inning pitchers, so he
didn't hesitate going to one of the finest bullpens in the majors
. . . Became first black manager with the Indians in 1975 and
first man of his race to manage in NL with Giants last year . . .
Plays down significance of achievements, except those as a
player . . . They include 586 homers, a Triple Crown at Baltimore and the distinction of being the only man to win MVP
awards in both leagues . . . Born Aug. 31, 1935, in Beaumont,
Tex., but was reared in Oakland.

GREATEST CATCHER

No superstars here, but some decent candidates. Present GM Tom Haller was the best of the San Francisco catchers and Walker Cooper, in a brief stint with the Giants, belted 35 homers and drove in 122 runs in '47, but they merely battle for third on the list.

Wes Westrum had to be a great catcher, or else he wouldn't have played so long with a .217 lifetime average. Wes set a fielding mark for NL catchers with only one error in 139 games in 1950, a .998 percentage. But he's not the best, either.

That distinction goes to Harry Danning, who caught Carl Hubbell's scroogie from 1933 through 1942. Harry The Horse had a .285 lifetime average and batted .306, .313 and .300 in 1938-40.

ALL-TIME GIANT SEASON RECORDS

BATTING: Bill Terry, .401, 1930
HRs: Willie Mays, 52, 1965
RBIs: Mel Ott, 151, 1929
STEALS: George Burns, 62, 1914
WINS: Christy Mathewson, 37, 1908
STRIKEOUTS: Christy Mathewson, 267, 1903

CHICAGO CUBS

TEAM DIRECTORY: Chairman of the Board: Andrew J. Mc-Kenna; VP-GM: Dallas Green; Dir. Scouting/Minor Leagues: Gordon Goldsberry; Dir. Pub. Rel.: Peter Mead; Mgr.: Lee Elia. Home: Wrigley Field (37,471). Field distances: 355, l.f. line; 400, c.f.; 353, r.f. line. Spring training: Mesa, Ariz.

SCOUTING REPORT

HITTING: Dead last in 1981 and not much hope for a drastic improvement if Bill Buckner is traded away before opening day. Buck, the NL batting champ in 1980, enjoyed a solid .311 season for an encore. Imagine what it would have been like without him. The Cubs batted .236, which was .007 below any other team in the league. Of the newcomers, former Phils' catcher Keith Moreland should add some punch, but it's obvious hitting won't be the club's strength.

There is sock in the outfield, however, with Steve Henderson (.293), Leon Durham (.290) and Jerry Morales (.286). Henderson

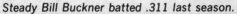

Steady Bill Buckner batted .311 last season.

and Durham figure to improve with age, especially after they become better accustomed to the nuances of Wrigley. Discounting Buckner, however, there is no punch in the infield. Ken Reitz (.215) and Ivan DeJesus (.194) were major disappointments and no second baseman batted above .218, explaining the acquisition of Junior Kennedy from Cincinnati. Jody Davis showed promise as a rookie catcher last year, but it remains to be seen where he fits in with Moreland in the fold.

PITCHING: It's no secret what GM Dallas Green regarded as his top priority when he took over. The Cubs' pitching staff has been drastically revamped, and it's no wonder considering last year's 4.01 team ERA, which was better, incidentally, only than Philadelphia's 4.05.

That suggests the former Phils' manager may not know that much about pitching, but at least he's trying to make things better. Off-season mound acquisitions include Dickie Noles, Dan Larson, Allen Ripley, Fergie Jenkins and Bill Campbell. They all will have an ample opportunity to aid the salvage operation because holdover talent isn't plentiful, with the best of them being Randy Martz, Doug Bird and Dick Tidrow (if he re-signs).

FIELDING: Another weakness in 1981—and what wasn't? Only the Mets showed a lower fielding percentage than the Cubs' .974. DeJesus topped NL shortstops in putouts and double plays, and Reitz' .977 percentage was the best among regular third basemen, but that's where the positive figures end. Buckner made more errors than any first baseman and ditto Henderson in the outfield. On the bright side, Moreland is considered a decent receiver and rookie Pat Tabler displayed some fancy glove work at second after coming from the Yankees' system last summer.

OUTLOOK: The Cubs sorely needed a change in ownership and direction, and they got both last year. The Chicago Tribune acquired the club from the Wrigley family, Green was snatched from the Phillies to be general manager, and brought his third-base coach, Lee Elia, with him to manage. At least they're trying, making some off-season deals and bringing back an old favorite, Jenkins, in an effort to change their losing image. But it's not going to happen overnight, so the Cubs' best hope is to edge the Pirates and the Mets for fourth place. It could happen if a couple of the new pitchers come through and if youngsters like Henderson and Durham continue to improve. But, as former manager Joe Amalfitano sadly discovered last year, there no longer is a Bruce Sutter around to partially disguise the club's myriad flaws.

CHICAGO CUBS 1982 ROSTER

MANAGER Lee Elia
Coaches—Billy Connors, Gordy MacKenzie, John
Vukovich, Billy Williams

PITCHERS

No.	Name	1981 Club	W-L	IP	SO	ERA	B-T	Ht.	Wt.	Born
—	Bird, Doug	New York (AL)	5-1	53	28	2.72	R-R	6-4	189	3/5/50 Corona, CA
		Chicago (NL)	4-5	75	34	3.60				
—	Campbell, Bill	Boston	1-1	48	37	3.19	R-R	6-3	190	8/9/48 Highland Park, MI
36	Caudill, Bill	Chicago (NL)	1-5	71	45	5.83	R-R	6-1	175	7/13/56 Santa Monica, CA
—	Eastwick, Rawly	Chicago (NL)	0-1	43	24	2.30	R-R	6-3	172	10/24/50 Camden, NJ
—	Geisel, Dave	Iowa	1-2	38	43	4.50	L-L	6-3	205	1/18/51 Windber, PA
		Chicago (NL)	2-0	16	7	0.56				
—	Griffin, Mike	Columbus	3-1	48	33	2.42	R-R	6-5	196	6/26/57 Colusa, CA
		New York (AL)	0-0	4	4	2.25				
		Chicago (NL)	2-5	52	20	4.50				
38	Hernandez, Willie	Iowa	4-5	74	41	3.91	L-L	6-2	180	11/14/55 Puerto Rico
		Chicago (NL)	0-0	14	13	3.86				
54	Howell, Jay	Iowa	5-10	144	90	3.76	R-R	6-3	205	11/26/55 Miami, FL
		Chicago (NL)	2-0	22	10	4.91				
—	Jenkins, Ferguson	Texas	5-8	106	63	4.50	R-R	6-5	210	12/13/43 Canada
—	Kravec, Ken	Chicago (NL)	1-6	78	50	5.08	L-L	6-0	180	7/29/51 Cleveland, OH
—	Larson, Dan	Okla. City	14-7	178	112	3.49	R-R	6-1	180	7/4/54 Los Angeles, CA
		Philadelphia	3-0	28	15	4.18				
34	Martz, Randy	Chicago (NL)	5-7	108	32	3.67	R-R	6-4	215	5/28/56 Harrisburg, PA
—	McClain, Joe	Iowa	6-7	111	82	5.37	R-R	6-2	200	1/25/56 Johnson City, TN
—	Noles, Dickie	Okla. City	6-6	104	82	3.29	R-R	6-2	178	11/19/56 Charlotte, NC
		Philadelphia	2-2	58	34	4.19				
—	Ripley, Al	San Francisco	4-4	91	47	4.05	R-R	6-3	200	10/18/52 Norwood, MA
43	Segelke, Herman	Iowa	5-7	107	65	5.97	R-R	6-4	200	4/24/58 San Mateo, CA
—	Semall, Paul	Iowa	8-6	93	65	3.00	R-R	6-4	205	7/16/55 Cleveland, OH
46	Smith, Lee	Chicago (NL)	3-6	67	50	3.49	R-R	6-5	220	12/4/57 Jamestown, LA

CATCHERS

No.	Name	1981 Club	H	HR	RBI	Pct.	B-T	Ht.	Wt.	Born
7	Davis, Jody	Chicago (NL)	46	4	21	.256	R-R	6-4	200	11/12/56 Gainesville, GA
—	Diaz, Michael	Midland	101	10	60	.267	R-R	6-2	195	4/15/60 San Francisco, CA
16	Hayes, Bill	Iowa	66	10	42	.247	R-R	6-0	195	10/24/57 Cheverly, MD
—	Moreland, Keith	Philadelphia	50	6	37	.255	R-R	6-0	200	5/2/54 Dallas, TX

INFIELDERS

No.	Name	1981 Club	H	HR	RBI	Pct.	B-T	Ht.	Wt.	Born
22	Buckner, Bill	Chicago (NL)	131	10	75	.311	L-L	6-1	185	12/14/49 Vallejo, CA
11	DeJesus, Ivan	Chicago (NL)	78	0	13	.194	R-R	5-11	175	1/9/53 Puerto Rico
—	Fletcher, Scott	Iowa	117	4	33	.255	R-R	5-11	168	7/30/58 Ft. Walton, FL
		Chicago (NL)	10	0	1	.217				
—	Kennedy, Junior	Cincinnati	11	0	5	.250	R-R	6-0	185	8/9/50 Gibson, OK
—	Martinez, Carmelo	Midland	111	20	81	.295	R-R	6-1	190	7/28/60 Puerto Rico
44	Reitz, Ken	Chicago (NL)	56	2	28	.215	R-R	6-0	185	6/24/51 San Francisco, CA
—	Tabler, Pat	Columbus	53	11	33	.296	R-R	6-2	195	2/2/58 Hamilton, OH
		Iowa	68	6	37	.306				
		Chicago (NL)	19	1	5	.188				
18	Tyson, Mike	Chicago (NL)	17	2	8	.185	R-R	5-9	170	1/13/50 Rocky Mount, NC
21	Waller, Ty	Iowa	56	6	29	.263	R-R	6-0	180	3/14/57 Fresno, CA
		Chicago (NL)	19	3	13	.268				

OUTFIELDERS

No.	Name	1981 Club	H	HR	RBI	Pct.	B-T	Ht.	Wt.	Born
28	Durham, Leon	Chicago (NL)	95	10	35	.290	L-L	6-2	210	7/31/57 Cincinnati, OH
—	Grant, Tom	Iowa	81	6	39	.272	L-R	6-2	190	5/28/57 Worcester, MA
32	Hall, Mel	Midland	165	24	93	.321	L-L	6-0	185	9/16/60 Lyons, NY
		Chicago (NL)	1	1	2	.091				
—	Henderson, Steve	Chicago (NL)	84	5	35	.293	R-R	6-1	197	11/18/52 Houston, TX
30	Lezcano, Carlos	Iowa	38	2	18	.217	R-R	6-2	185	9/30/55 Puerto Rico
—	Morales, Jerry	Chicago (NL)	70	1	25	.286	R-R	5-10	175	2/18/49 Puerto Rico
25	Thompson, Scot	Iowa	74	2	29	.267	L-L	6-3	175	12/7/55 Grove City, PA
		Chicago (NL)	19	0	8	.165				

CUB PROFILES

BILL BUCKNER 32 6-1 185   Bats L Throws L

A bright beacon on a fog-shrouded team . . . "Buck" had another superb season in '81 after winning first batting title the year before . . . Constantly mentioned in trade talks because he's club's most valuable property since Bruce Sutter's departure . . . Player of the Week in NL, April 27-May 3, after batting .450 with five doubles . . . Batted .360 in May with 24 RBI . . . Repeated as Player of Week, Sept. 7-13, with .500 average, five doubles, nine RBI and three game-winners . . . Born Dec. 14, 1949, in Vallejo, Calif. . . . Led league with 35 doubles . . . Among top six in five other categories . . . Only Pete Rose had more hits . . . One of toughest batters to strike out . . . An All-American high-school gridder . . . Consistent, batting .313 first half, .310 second.

Year	Club	Pos.	G	AB	R	H	2B	3B	HR	RBI	SB	Avg.
1969	Los Angeles.....	PH	1	1	0	0	0	0	0	0	0	.000
1970	Los Angeles.....	OF-1B	28	68	6	13	3	1	0	4	0	.191
1971	Los Angeles.....	OF-1B	108	358	37	99	15	1	5	41	4	.277
1972	Los Angeles.....	OF-1B	105	383	47	122	14	3	5	37	10	.319
1973	Los Angeles.....	1B-OF	140	575	68	158	20	0	8	46	12	.275
1974	Los Angeles.....	OF-1B	145	580	83	182	30	3	7	58	31	.314
1975	Los Angeles.....	OF	92	288	30	70	11	2	6	31	8	.243
1976	Los Angeles.....	1B-OF	154	642	76	193	28	4	7	60	28	.301
1977	Chicago (NL)....	1B	122	426	40	121	27	0	11	60	7	.284
1978	Chicago (NL)....	1B	117	446	47	144	26	1	5	74	7	.323
1979	Chicago (NL)....	1B	149	591	72	168	34	2	14	66	9	.284
1980	Chicago (NL)....	1B-OF	145	578	69	187	41	3	10	68	1	.324
1981	Chicago (NL)....	1B-OF	106	421	45	131	35	3	10	75	5	.311
	Totals..........		1412	5357	620	1588	284	28	88	620	122	.296

STEVE HENDERSON 29 6-1 197   Bats R Throws R

Had solid season with Cubs after swap coming from Mets in trade for Dave Kingman . . . Batted .289 first half and improved to .297 after strike . . . Joined Mets from Reds in Tom Seaver trade and batted .297, missing Rookie-of-the-Year honors by one vote . . . Suffered serious ankle injury in 1979, but bounced back strong to become club batting leader in 1980 . . . Born Nov. 18, 1952, in Houston . . . An NAIA superstar at Prairie View, batting .488 and .525 . . . Has hit below .290 only once in five major-league seasons . . . Drafted by

Reds and was batting .326 at Indianapolis in '77 before joining Mets after midseason deal.

Year	Club	Pos.	G	AB	R	H	2B	3B	HR	RBI	SB	Avg.
1977	New York (NL)..	OF	99	350	67	104	16	6	12	65	6	.297
1978	New York (NL)..	OF	157	587	83	156	30	9	10	65	13	.266
1979	New York (NL)..	OF	98	350	42	107	16	8	5	39	13	.306
1980	New York (NL)..	OF	143	513	75	149	17	8	8	58	23	.290
1981	Chicago (NL)....	OF	82	287	32	84	9	5	5	35	5	.293
	Totals..........		579	2087	299	600	88	36	40	262	60	.287

IVAN DeJESUS 29 5-11 175   Bats R Throws R

Horrible first half had him batting .160 at time of strike . . . Rallied to bat .227 in second half, but fell off sharply at plate after entering season with .267 lifetime average . . . Stolen bases dropped from 44 to 21 . . . But continued to show durability, playing in all 106 games after averaging 157 in previous four seasons . . . Born Jan. 9, 1953, in Santurce, Puerto Rico . . . Joined Cubs in 1977 after being groomed as Bill Russell's successor with Dodgers . . . Led league with 104 runs his second full season in 1978 . . . A steady and underrated fielder . . . His 44 steals in 1980 were most by a Cub since the '20s.

Year	Club	Pos.	G	AB	R	H	2B	3B	HR	RBI	SB	Avg.
1974	Los Angeles.....	SS	3	3	1	1	0	0	0	0	0	.333
1975	Los Angeles.....	SS	63	87	10	16	2	1	0	2	1	.184
1976	Los Angeles.....	SS-3B	22	41	4	7	2	1	0	2	0	.171
1977	Chicago (NL)....	SS	155	624	91	166	31	7	3	40	24	.266
1978	Chicago (NL)....	SS	160	619	104	172	24	7	3	35	41	.278
1979	Chicago (NL)....	SS	160	636	92	180	26	10	5	52	24	.283
1980	Chicago (NL)....	SS	157	618	78	160	26	3	3	33	44	.259
1981	Chicago (NL)....	SS	106	403	49	78	8	4	0	13	21	.194
	Totals..........		826	3031	429	780	119	33	14	177	155	.257

KEN REITZ 30 6-0 185   Bats R Throws R

Hardly a smashing success in his debut with Cubs . . . Batted 48 points below his lifetime .263 average and didn't produce anticipated power at Wrigley . . . Batted a poor .234 first half and it got worse . . . Hit .189 when season resumed . . . Still valuable for his glove . . . Won Gold Glove in 1975 and 1980 . . . Set major-league mark with only nine errors in '77 and lowered it by making only eight in 1980 . . . Born June 24, 1951, in San Francisco . . . Vetoed swap to Cubs after

1980 season, but relented and deal was completed few weeks later . . . Collected 1,000th hit in '79, but Lou Brock belted No. 3,000 the same game . . . Regarded as best fielding third baseman in NL.

Year	Club	Pos.	G	AB	R	H	2B	3B	HR	RBI	SB	Avg.
1972	St. Louis	3B	21	78	5	28	4	0	0	10	0	.359
1973	St. Louis	SS-3B	147	426	40	100	20	2	6	42	0	.235
1974	St. Louis	3B-SS-2B	154	579	48	157	28	2	7	54	0	.271
1975	St. Louis	3B	161	592	43	159	25	1	5	63	1	.269
1976	San Francisco	3B-SS	155	577	40	154	21	1	5	66	5	.267
1977	St. Louis	3B	157	587	58	153	36	1	17	79	2	.261
1978	St. Louis	3B	150	540	41	133	26	2	10	75	1	.246
1979	St. Louis	3B	159	605	42	162	41	2	8	73	1	.268
1980	St. Louis	3B	151	523	39	141	33	0	8	58	0	.270
1981	Chicago (NL)	3B	82	260	10	56	9	1	2	28	0	.215
	Totals		1337	4767	366	1243	243	12	68	548	10	.261

LEON DURHAM 24 6-2 210   Bats L Throws L

Key man in swap with Cardinals involving Bruce Sutter . . . Didn't disappoint in first full major-league campaign, batting .312 in first half and .269 after the strike . . . Batted .358 with 15 of team-high 25 steals in May . . . Was a .339 hitter in August . . . Born July 31, 1957, in Cincinnati . . . Cardinals' first selection in June 1976 draft after three-sport stardom as prep . . . Regarded as top prospect after landing all-star honors in Texas League in '78 and American Association in '79 . . . Showed good power in minors and hopefully will be able to take advantage of friendly confines of Wrigley Field.

Year	Club	Pos.	G	AB	R	H	2B	3B	HR	RBI	SB	Avg.
1980	St. Louis	OF-1B	96	303	42	82	15	4	8	42	8	.271
1981	Chicago (NL)	OF-1B	87	328	42	95	14	6	10	35	25	.290
	Totals		183	631	84	177	29	10	18	77	33	.281

JERRY MORALES 33 5-10 175   Bats R Throws R

Old reliable, returned to club as free agent in 1980 and picked up where he left off in '77, before swap to St. Louis . . . Batted .302 in first half and .264 thereafter . . . Averaged 13.5 homers and 77 RBI in four years with Cubs, 1974-77 . . . Slipped with Cardinals, Tigers and Mets before regaining batting eye with Cubs . . . Born Feb. 18, 1949, in Yabucoa, Puerto Rico . . . Selected by Padres from Mets in 1969 expansion draft . . . Played in 1977 All-Star Game . . . Batted .345

in pro debut in 1966 and hasn't been above .290 since . . . Originally joined Cubs in '73 in deal involving Glenn Beckert.

Year	Club	Pos.	G	AB	R	H	2B	3B	HR	RBI	SB	Avg.
1969	San Diego	OF	19	41	5	8	2	0	1	6	0	.195
1970	San Diego	OF	28	58	6	9	0	1	1	4	0	.155
1971	San Diego	OF	12	17	1	2	0	0	0	1	1	.118
1972	San Diego	OF-3B	115	347	38	83	15	7	4	18	4	.239
1973	San Diego	OF	122	388	47	109	23	2	9	34	6	.281
1974	Chicago (NL)	OF	151	534	70	146	21	7	15	82	2	.273
1975	Chicago (NL)	OF	153	578	62	156	21	0	12	91	3	.270
1976	Chicago (NL)	OF	140	537	66	147	17	0	16	67	3	.274
1977	Chicago (NL)	OF	136	490	56	142	34	5	11	69	0	.290
1978	St. Louis	OF	130	457	44	109	19	8	4	46	4	.239
1979	Detroit	OF	129	440	50	93	23	1	14	56	10	.211
1980	New York (NL)	OF	94	193	19	49	7	1	3	30	2	.254
1981	Chicago (NL)	OF	84	245	27	70	6	2	1	25	1	.286
	Totals		1313	4325	491	1123	188	34	91	529	36	.260

JODY DAVIS 25 6-4 200  Bats R Throws R

Cubs' best newcomer last year, seeing more time behind the plate than incumbent catcher Tim Blackwell . . . Solid and consistent rookie season, batting .256 and .255 in the two halves . . . Hailed for defensive play . . . Solid minor-league hitter . . . Had 94 RBI in '78 and 21 homers and 91 RBI in '78 . . . Developed ulcers during 1980 season and dropped 50 pounds, but recovered to enjoy a good spring with Cubs in first taste of bigs . . . Born Nov. 12, 1956, in Gainesville, Ga. . . . Attended Middle Georgia College . . . Good clutch hitter, topped Texas League with 16 game-winning RBI in '79 . . . Drafted from Cardinals' Triple-A club in winter of 1980.

Year	Club	Pos.	G	AB	R	H	2B	3B	HR	RBI	SB	Avg.
1981	Chicago (NL)	C	56	180	14	46	5	1	4	21	0	.256

BILL CAMPBELL 33 6-3 190 Bats R Throws R

Gambling Cubs signed him to three-year, $1.1 million pact in December . . . It's a gamble because Campbell has been plagued with shoulder problems over parts of last three years . . . Has parlayed free-agency into two megabuck contracts . . . Left Twins to sign with Red Sox in 1977 and had outstanding first season in Boston, recording 31 saves . . . It's been downhill since . . . Was 1-1 with seven saves in 30 appearances last year and pushed career save total over the 100 mark . . . Born Aug. 9, 1948, in Highland Park, Mich. . . . An outfielder from Little League through high-school ball, he turned to pitching fulltime at Mt. San Antonio Junior College in 1966.

Year	Club	G	IP	W	L	Pct.	SO	BB	H	ERA
1973	Minnesota	28	52	3	3	.500	42	20	44	3.12
1974	Minnesota	63	120	8	7	.533	89	55	109	2.63
1975	Minnesota	47	121	4	6	.400	76	46	119	3.79
1976	Minnesota	78	168	17	5	.773	115	62	145	3.30
1977	Boston	69	140	13	9	.591	114	60	112	2.96
1978	Boston	29	51	7	5	.583	47	17	62	3.88
1979	Boston	41	55	3	4	.429	25	23	55	4.25
1980	Boston	23	41	4	0	1.000	17	22	44	4.83
1981	Boston	30	48	1	1	.500	37	20	45	3.19
	Totals	408	796	60	40	.600	562	325	735	3.31

DOUG BIRD 32 6-4 189   Bats R Throws R

Went from penthouse to outhouse in same season . . . Started with Yankees and was 5-1 with a 2.72 ERA in first half . . . Joined Cubs in Rick Reuschel swap and was off to a sensational start (3-1), blanking Dodgers . . . Had a combined 9-6 record . . . Born March 3, 1950, in Corona, Calif. . . . Released by Phillies after '79 season and signed as free agent by Yankees' Triple-A club . . . Was 6-0 with Columbus and was purchased by Yankees, going 3-0 for an unbeaten season in 1980 . . . Gained most notoriety as reliever for Royals, registering 20 saves as rookie in '73 . . . Thrust into starting role with K.C. in '76 and went 12-10.

Year	Club	G	IP	W	L	Pct.	SO	BB	H	ERA
1973	Kansas City	54	102	4	4	.500	83	30	81	3.00
1974	Kansas City	55	92	7	6	.538	62	27	100	2.74
1975	Kansas City	51	105	9	6	.600	81	40	100	3.26
1976	Kansas City	39	198	12	10	.545	107	31	191	3.36
1977	Kansas City	53	118	11	4	.733	83	29	120	3.89
1978	Kansas City	40	99	6	6	.500	48	31	110	5.27
1979	Philadelphia	32	61	2	0	1.000	33	16	73	5.16
1980	New York (AL)	22	51	3	0	1.000	17	14	47	2.65
1981	New York (AL)	17	53	5	1	.833	28	16	58	2.72
1981	Chicago (NL)	12	75	4	5	.444	34	16	72	3.60
	Totals	375	954	63	42	.600	576	250	952	3.58

RANDY MARTZ 25 6-4 215   Bats L Throws R

Blossomed into club's most effective reliever upon departure of Bruce Sutter . . . Was 3-5 first half, 2-2 thereafter . . . Had no professional saves until he registered six last season . . . Cubs' first selection in June 1977 draft . . . Born May 28, 1956, in Harrisburg, Pa., attended U. of South Carolina on a football scholarship and didn't play baseball for two years . . . Had only one collegiate season and it was a gem . . . Was 14-0 with a 1.98 ERA and named MVP by "Collegiate Baseball," earning Lefty Gomez Plate . . . Was 32-36 in minors before joining Cubs in 1980 . . . Has a bright future if development continues.

Year	Club	G	IP	W	L	Pct.	SO	BB	H	ERA
1980	Chicago (NL)	6	30	1	2	.333	5	11	28	2.10
1981	Chicago (NL)	33	108	5	7	.412	32	49	103	3.67
	Totals	39	138	6	9	.400	37	60	131	3.33

TOP PROSPECT

PAT TABLER 24 6-2 195　　　　　　　**Bats R Throws R**
Former No. 1 draft choice of Yankees (1976) is the Cubs' second baseman of the future . . . Batted only .188 in 35 games with Chicago, but sparkled in Triple-A, batting .306 for Iowa . . . Born Feb. 2, 1958, in Hamilton, Ohio . . . Solid minor-league credentials . . . At Nashville in 1980, led Southern League with 13 game-winning RBI and set club record with 38 doubles . . . A slick fielder.

MANAGER LEE ELIA: Almost a foregone conclusion that new general manager Dallas Green would bring Elia with him from Philadelphia, where he was a coach . . . Born July 16, 1937, in Philadelphia . . . Former infielder who had brief trials with White Sox in '66 and Cubs in 1968 . . . Once belted 29 homers for Indianapolis (AAA) in '65 . . . Nicknamed "Banty Rooster" as player . . . Successful minor-league skipper in Phils' system . . . Won pennant in 1975 (Spartanburg) and division titles in '78 (Reading) and '79 (Oklahoma City) . . . Was Phillies' third-base coach in 1980-81 . . . Attended U. of Delaware, same as Green.

GREATEST CATCHER

This one is easy. Hall of Famer Gabby Hartnett ranks with the best of all-time and no other Cubs catcher comes close. Gabby was with Chicago from 1922 through 1940, posting a .297 life-time average, playing in four World Series and seven times topping the NL backstops in fielding percentage.

But he was better known for his slugging. Though overshadowed by teammate Hack Wilson's 56 homers and 190 RBI when the baseball was juiced in 1930, Hartnett made it an awesome one-two punch by belting 37 homers, knocking in 122 runs and batting .339. In '35, he batted .344; two years later he posted a career-high .354.

ALL-TIME CUB SEASON RECORDS

BATTING: Rogers Hornsby, .380, 1929
HRs: Hack Wilson, 56, 1930
RBIs: Hack Wilson, 190, 1930
STEALS: Frank Chance, 67, 1903
WINS: Mordecai Brown, 29, 1908
STRIKEOUTS: Ferguson Jenkins, 274, 1970

MONTREAL EXPOS

TEAM DIRECTORY: Chairman of the Board: Charles Bronfman; Pres.-Chief Exec. Off.: John McHale; VP-Mgr: Jim Fanning; VP-Baseball Oper.: Bing Devine; Dir. Scouting: Danny Menendez; Dir. Fin.: Dennis Bodin; Dir. Marketing: Rene Guimond; Dirs. Publ.: Monique Giroux, Richard Griffin; Trav. Sec.: Peter Durso. Home: Olympic Stadium (58,838). Field distances: 325, l.f. line; 375, l.c.; 404, c.f.; 375, r.c.; 325, r.f. line. Spring training: West Palm Beach, Fla.

SCOUTING REPORT

HITTING: Despite a trio of .300 hitters in Andre Dawson, Warren Cromartie and Tim Raines, the Expos batted a paltry .246 last season, obviously a deceptive figure. Montreal makes things happen offensively, thanks to the on-base prowess of Raines, whose rookie heroics (.304 and 71 steals in 88 games) were overshadowed only by Fernando Valenzuela's. Raines' artistry enabled the Expos to finish fifth in runs scored while ranking only 10th in batting.

Dawson developed into a solid MVP candidate, blending speed (26), power (24 homers) and average (.302) to fuel the at-

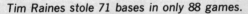

Tim Raines stole 71 bases in only 88 games.

tack. Gary Carter makes it a solid one-two punch and he definitely has the ability to improve on a .251 average. Cromartie is the most underrated player on the club and outstanding in the clutch, notching eight game-winning RBI to Dawson's team-leading nine. The club would have even more sock if Larry Parrish regains his previous touch and if Tim Wallach and Terry Francona develop as expected.

PITCHING: It came together nicely last year, as heretofore journeyman Ray Burris added depth and quality to the starting rotation down the stretch and newcomer Jeff Reardon fortified the bullpen, once a club weakness. The staff ERA of 3.30 was fourth-best in the league and topped the hitting-oriented NL East and there's no reason to believe youngsters like Bill Gullickson, Scott Sanderson and perhaps Charlie Lea won't continue to improve.

Steve Rogers, impeccable in the NL East Division playoffs, is the mainstay and Woodie Fryman (5-3, 1.88) somehow keeps rolling along in the bullpen. This is a fine staff, perfectly blending youth and experience. Burris and Reardon made the difference one year ago and they could play the same role this season.

FIELDING: Strength down the middle, especially behind the plate and in center. Dawson can play with the best, handling the most outfield chances in the league last year and showing a strong arm. Carter has the same distinction and ranks as the finest all-around catcher in the game. Cromartie does a solid job whether he's at first or in the outfield. Though Chris Speier was outstanding down the stretch at shortstop last year, error-prone former Met Frank Taveras could challenge for his job. Collectively, Montreal fielded .980, a mere .001 behind the league-leaders.

OUTLOOK: A lot depends on Jim Fanning's development as a skipper. He improved the club attitude in September-October, but didn't exhibit the tactical skill of his predecessor, Dick Williams, so it remains to be seen how he'll do over the long haul. This club has enough tools to win by accident, but in a tight race, a manager could make a difference. Position switches also bear watching. If Raines moves to second so Francona can play regularly in the outfield, the team might miss Rodney Scott's solid glove and his speed on the bases. But the overall prospects for a second straight pennant are solid simply because top contenders Philadelphia and St. Louis don't look improved and the Expos should be better.

MONTREAL EXPOS 1982 ROSTER

MANAGER Jim Fanning
Coaches—Steve Boros, Galen Cisco, Pat Mullin, Vern Rapp

PITCHERS

No.	Name	1981 Club	W-L	IP	SO	ERA	B-T	Ht.	Wt.	Born
22	Bahnsen, Stan	Montreal	2-1	49	28	4.96	R-R	6-3	198	12/15/44 Council Bluffs, IA
48	Burris, Ray	Montreal	9-7	136	52	3.04	R-R	6-5	200	8/22/50 Idabel, OK
51	Engle, Rick	Montreal	0-0	2	2	18.00	L-L	5-11	180	4/7/57 Corbin, KY
		Denver	6-7	154	78	4.74				
35	Fryman, Woodie	Montreal	5-3	43	25	1.88	R-L	6-2	215	4/12/40 Ewing, KY
32	Gorman, Tom	Montreal	0-0	15	13	4.20	L-L	6-4	195	12/12/57 Woodburn, OR
		Memphis	12-9	91	94	3.07				
34	Gullickson, Bill	Montreal	7-9	157	115	2.81	R-R	6-3	198	2/20/59 Marshall, MN
23	Jackson, Grant	Pitt-Mont	2-2	43	21	3.77	B-L	6-0	204	9/28/42 Fostoria, OH
20	James, Bob	Denver	1-2	57	46	5.68	R-R	6-4	215	8/15/58 Glendale, CA
53	Lea, Charlie	Montreal	5-4	64	31	4.64	R-R	6-4	194	12/25/56 France
37	Lee, Bill	Montreal	5-6	89	34	2.93	L-L	6-3	190	12/28/46 Burbank, CA
46	Palmer, David	Memphis	0-0	0	0	0.00	R-R	6-1	205	10/19/57 Glens Falls, NY
		W. Palm Beach	0-0	11	7	0.82				
31	Reardon, Jeff	NY (NL)-Mont	3-0	70	49	2.19	R-R	6-1	190	10/1/55 Dalton, MA
45	Rogers, Steve	Montreal	12-8	161	87	3.41	R-R	6-1	177	10/26/49 Jefferson City, MO
21	Sanderson, Scott	Montreal	9-7	137	77	2.96	R-R	6-5	195	7/22/56 Dearborn, MI
—	Sattler, Bill	Memphis	11-6	163	93	2.76	R-R	6-0	165	8/19/57 Youngstown, OH
66	Smith, Bryn	Montreal	1-0	13	9	2.77	R-R	6-2	200	8/11/55 Marrietta, GA
		Denver	15-5	181	127	3.09				
27	Sosa, Elias	Montreal	1-2	39	18	3.69	R-R	6-2	205	6/10/50 Dominican Republic
—	Taylor, Jeff	W. Palm Beach	8-10	152	140	4.50	L-L	6-3	190	12/11/59 Ravenna, OH

CATCHERS

No.	Name	1981 Club	H	HR	RBI	Pct.	B-T	Ht.	Wt.	Born
8	Carter, Gary	Montreal	94	16	68	.251	R-R	6-2	215	4/8/54 Culver City, CA
44	Ramos, Bobby	Montreal	8	1	3	.195	R-R	5-11	208	11/5/55 Cuba
50	Wieghaus, Tom	Montreal	0	0	0	.000	R-R	6-0	195	2/1/57 Chicago Heights, IL
		Denver	83	4	50	.239				

INFIELDERS

No.	Name	1981 Club	H	HR	RBI	Pct.	B-T	Ht.	Wt.	Born
49	Cromartie, Warren	Montreal	109	6	42	.304	L-L	6-0	200	9/29/53 Miami, FL
19	Gates, Mike	Montreal	1	0	0	.500	L-R	6-0	165	9/20/56 Culver City, CA
		Denver	154	3	57	.309				
55	Hostetler, Dave	Montreal	3	1	1	.500	R-R	6-4	215	3/27/56 Pasadena, CA
		Denver	140	27	103	.318				
62	Johnson, Wallace	Montreal	2	0	3	.222	B-R	6-0	173	12/25/56 Gary, IN
		Denver	64	0	16	.298				
		Memphis	37	1	18	.363				
43	Manuel, Jerry	Montreal	11	3	10	.200	R-R	6-0	155	12/23/53 Hahira, GA
2	Mills, Brad	Montreal	5	0	1	.238	L-R	6-0	195	1/19/57 Lemon Cove, CA
		Denver	134	12	66	.314				
5	Milner, John	Pitt.-Mont	32	5	18	.237	L-L	6-0	183	12/28/49 Atlanta, GA
15	Parrish, Larry	Montreal	85	8	44	.244	R-R	6-3	215	11/10/53 Winter Haven, FL
12	Phillips, Mike	S.D.-Mont.	18	0	4	.214	L-R	6-1	185	8/19/50 Beaumont, TX
3	Scott, Rodney	Montreal	69	0	26	.205	B-R	6-0	155	10/16/53 Indianapolis, IN
4	Speier, Chris	Montreal	69	2	25	.225	R-R	6-1	175	6/28/50 Alameda, CA
—	Taveras, Frank	New York (NL)	65	0	11	.230	R-R	6-0	170	12/24/50 Dominican Republic

OUTFIELDERS

No.	Name	1981 Club	H	HR	RBI	Pct.	B-T	Ht.	Wt.	Born
33	Briggs, Dan	Montreal	1	0	0	.091	L-L	6-0	180	11/18/52 Scotia, CA
		Denver	155	22	110	.314				
10	Dawson, Andre	Montreal	119	24	64	.302	R-R	6-3	180	7/10/54 Miami, FL
16	Francona, Terry	Montreal	26	1	8	.274	L-L	6-1	190	4/22/59 Aberdeen, SD
		Denver	125	1	58	.352				
		Memphis	56	0	18	.348				
25	Office, Rowland	Montreal	7	0	0	.175	L-L	6-0	170	10/25/52 Sacramento, CA
30	Raines, Tim	Montreal	95	5	37	.304	B-R	5-8	165	9/16/59 Sanford, FL
56	Rooney, Pat	Montreal	0	0	0	.000	R-R	6-1	190	11/28/57 Chicago, IL
		Denver	38	8	29	.212				
		Memphis	11	2	6	.306				
29	Wallach, Tim	Montreal	50	4	13	.236	R-R	6-3	220	9/14/58 Huntington Park, CA
18	White, Jerry	Montreal	26	3	11	.218	B-R	5-11	172	8/23/52 Shirley, MA

EXPO PROFILES

ANDRE DAWSON 27 6-3 180   Bats R Throws R

Became a solid MVP candidate, with only Phillies' Mike Schmidt being more of an offensive force in NL . . . Batted .325 with 13 homers in the first half and .280 with 11 homers after the strike . . . Batted .339 in April, .317 in May and .329 in August before tailing off in September . . . Batted .245 with no RBI in 10 postseason games . . . Born July 10, 1954, in Miami . . . Topped club with nine game-winning RBI after ranking second in NL with 17 in '80 . . . Best blend of speed and power in majors today . . . Rookie of the Year in 1977 . . . Won Gold Glove and Silver Bat in '80 . . . Tied club record with 19-game hitting streak in 1980 . . . Had a career slugging percentage of .612 in minors . . . Attended Florida A&M.

Year	Club	Pos.	G	AB	R	H	2B	3B	HR	RBI	SB	Avg.
1976	Montreal	OF	24	85	9	20	4	1	0	7	1	.235
1977	Montreal	OF	139	525	64	148	26	9	19	65	21	.282
1978	Montreal	OF	157	609	84	154	24	8	25	72	28	.253
1979	Montreal	OF	155	639	90	176	24	12	25	92	35	.275
1980	Montreal	OF	151	577	96	178	41	7	17	87	34	.308
1981	Montreal	OF	103	394	71	119	21	3	24	64	26	.302
	Totals		705	2744	405	775	136	39	110	380	144	.282

TIM RAINES 22 5-8 165   Bats S Throws R

An incredible rookie season for fleet outfielder . . . Topped majors in steals and also batted above .300 . . . Heading for 100-steal season when strike hit . . . Batted .322 with 50 steals in first half and dipped to .270-21 after strike due in part to hand injury that shelved him until NLCS . . . Born Sept. 16, 1959, in Sanford, Fla. . . . First player in history to steal 30 bases in 30 or less games . . . Batted .355 with 16 steals in April and added 24 thefts with .308 average in May . . . Can also play the infield . . . Batted .354 with 77 steals at Denver in '80, prompting promotion . . . All-star second baseman in minors.

Year	Club	Pos.	G	AB	R	H	2B	3B	HR	RBI	SB	Avg.
1979	Montreal	PR	6	0	3	0	0	0	0	0	2	.000
1980	Montreal	2B-OF	15	20	5	1	0	0	0	0	5	.050
1981	Montreal	OF	88	313	61	95	13	7	5	37	71	.304
	Totals		109	333	69	96	13	7	5	37	78	.288

GARY CARTER 27 6-2 210   Bats R Throws R

Game's finest catcher had another banner season in '81, though his average wasn't up to snuff . . . Batted .245 and .258 in the two halves . . . Started strong with .327 in April before slumping rest of first half . . . Recharged batteries during layoff and won All-Star Game MVP honors with two home runs . . . That triggered a five-homer, 20-RBI August . . . NL Player of the Week, Aug. 24-30, with three homers, including fifth career grand slam, 13 RBI and .444 average . . . Born April 8, 1954, in Culver City, Cal. . . . Likely to enter free-agent draft after '81 . . . Batted .421 with .684 slugging percentage in division playoffs, winning second game with a two-run homer . . . Batted .438 in Championship Series, but had no RBI . . . Rookie of the Year in '75 . . . Collects baseball cards.

Year	Club	Pos.	G	AB	R	H	2B	3B	HR	RBI	SB	Avg.
1974	Montreal	C-OF	9	27	5	11	0	1	1	6	2	.407
1975	Montreal	OF-C-3B	144	503	58	136	20	1	17	68	5	.270
1976	Montreal	C-OF	91	311	31	68	8	1	6	38	0	.219
1977	Montreal	C-OF	154	522	86	148	29	2	31	84	5	.284
1978	Montreal	C-1B	157	533	76	136	27	1	20	72	10	.255
1979	Montreal	C	140	505	74	143	26	5	22	75	3	.283
1980	Montreal	C	154	549	76	145	25	5	29	101	3	.264
1981	Montreal	C	100	374	48	94	20	2	16	68	1	.251
	Totals..........		949	3324	454	881	155	18	142	512	29	.265

WARREN CROMARTIE 28 6-0 190   Bats L Throws L

Least heralded of the Montreal stars . . . Batted .300 for the first time as a major leaguer . . . Plays outfield and first base . . . Batted .282 in the first half, but zoomed to .328 down the stretch to pick up slumping teammates . . . Also filled in capably as lead-off batter when Raines missed 20 games in September . . . Batted .338 in August . . . Set club record with 19-game batting streak in '79, later equaled by Dawson . . . Born Sept. 29, 1953, in Miami . . . A junior-college superstar at Miami Dade . . . First-round draft choice of Expos in '73 . . . Batted .336 at Quebec City in '74 in first pro season and .337 with Denver in '76 before joining Expos to stay.

Year	Club	Pos.	G	AB	R	H	2B	3B	HR	RBI	SB	Avg.
1974	Montreal	OF	8	17	2	3	0	0	0	0	1	.176
1976	Montreal	OF	33	81	8	17	1	0	0	2	1	.210
1977	Montreal	OF	155	620	64	175	41	7	5	50	10	.282
1978	Montreal	OF-1B	159	607	77	180	32	6	10	56	8	.297
1979	Montreal	OF	158	659	84	181	45	5	8	46	8	.275
1980	Montreal	1B-OF	162	597	74	172	33	5	14	70	8	.288
1981	Montreal	1B-OF	99	358	41	109	19	2	6	42	2	.304
	Totals..........		774	2939	350	837	172	25	43	266	38	.285

CHRIS SPEIER 31 6-1 175   Bats R Throws R

Late-season surge salvaged a poor year at the plate . . . Batted .256 in the first half and .156 after the strike, but he had key hits in final weeks on march to division title . . . Good year afield, accented by postseason performance . . . Batted .400 with four runs scored in division playoffs . . . Born June 28, 1950, in Alameda, Calif. . . . No team drafted him as free agent last fall . . . Played for Cal Santa Barbara before signing with Giants . . . Played only one year of pro ball before making the Giants in 1971 . . . Batted .357 in Championship Series against Pirates that year . . . Three-time all-star, 1972-74 . . . Swapped to Expos for Tim Foli in 1977.

Year	Club	Pos.	G	AB	R	H	2B	3B	HR	RBI	SB	Avg.
1971	San Francisco ...	SS	157	601	74	141	17	6	8	46	4	.235
1972	San Francisco ...	SS	150	562	74	151	25	2	15	71	9	.269
1973	San Francisco ...	SS-2B	153	542	58	135	17	4	11	71	4	.249
1974	San Francisco ...	SS-2B	141	501	55	125	19	5	9	53	3	.250
1975	San Francisco ...	SS-3B	141	487	60	132	30	5	10	69	4	.271
1976	San Francisco ...	INF	145	495	51	112	18	4	3	40	2	.226
1977	S.F.-Mtl.........	SS	145	548	59	128	31	6	5	38	1	.234
1978	Montreal	SS	150	501	47	126	18	3	5	51	1	.251
1979	Montreal	SS	113	344	31	78	13	1	7	26	0	.227
1980	Montreal	SS-3B	128	388	35	103	14	4	1	32	0	.265
1981	Montreal	SS-3B	96	307	33	69	10	2	2	25	1	.225
	Totals..........		1519	5276	577	1300	212	42	76	522	29	.246

LARRY PARRISH 28 6-3 205   Bats R Throws R

Continued to drop off at the plate after being Expos' MVP with .307, 30-homer season of '79 . . . On verge of losing job after .220 first half . . . Recovered to bat .265 with 33 RBI in the second half . . . Belted three homers and knocked in seven runs against Braves, April 25, 1980 . . . One week later, he was struck on wrist by an Ed Whitson fastball; he hasn't been the same since . . . Montreal's all-time leader in games played with 967 . . . Born Nov. 30, 1953, in Winter Haven, Fla. . . . Has trio of three-homer games . . . Florida State League MVP in '73 . . . Set Expo record with 71 extra-base hits and 300 total bases in '79 . . . Had top slugging percentage of .551, too, until Dawson's .553 broke it last year.

Year	Club	Pos.	G	AB	R	H	2B	3B	HR	RBI	SB	Avg.
1974	Montreal	3B	25	69	9	14	5	0	0	4	0	.203
1975	Montreal	3B-2B-SS	145	532	50	146	32	5	10	65	4	.274
1976	Montreal	3B	154	543	65	126	28	5	11	61	2	.232
1977	Montreal	3B	123	402	50	99	19	2	11	46	2	.246
1978	Montreal	3B	144	520	68	144	39	4	15	70	2	.277
1979	Montreal	3B	153	544	83	167	39	2	30	82	5	.307
1980	Montreal	3B	126	452	55	115	27	3	15	72	2	.254
1981	Montreal	3B	97	349	42	85	19	3	8	44	0	.244
	Totals..........		967	3411	422	896	218	24	100	444	17	.263

STEVE ROGERS 32 6-1 177   Bats R Throws R

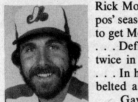

Rick Monday's homer off him ended the Expos' season, but Rogers did as much as anyone to get Montreal into the Championship Series . . . Defied the odds by beating Steve Carlton twice in NL East Division playoff matchups . . . In his 3-0 shutout in the clincher, he also belted a two-run single off the Phillies' ace . . . Gave Expos a 2-1 Championship Series edge by beating Dodgers, 4-1, in third game . . . Born Oct. 27, 1949, in Jefferson City, Mo. . . . Was 7-4 in first half, 4-4 thereafter . . . Finally raised lifetime record above .500 after a career of tough-luck defeats . . . All-American at Tulsa U., where he was 31-5 . . . Never allowed more than three runs in first 21 starts of '78, yet he won only 13 games all season.

Year	Club	G	IP	W	L	Pct.	SO	BB	H	ERA
1973	Montreal	17	134	10	5	.667	64	49	93	1.54
1974	Montreal	38	254	15	22	.405	154	80	225	4.46
1975	Montreal	35	252	11	12	.478	137	88	248	3.29
1976	Montreal	33	230	7	17	.292	150	69	212	3.21
1977	Montreal	40	302	17	16	.515	206	81	272	3.10
1978	Montreal	30	219	13	10	.565	126	64	186	2.47
1979	Montreal	37	249	13	12	.520	143	78	232	3.00
1980	Montreal	37	281	16	11	.593	147	85	247	2.98
1981	Montreal	22	161	12	8	.600	87	41	149	3.41
	Totals..................	289	2082	114	113	.502	1214	635	1894	3.13

SCOTT SANDERSON 25 6-5 195   Bats R Throws R

Club's most effective starter in the first half, going 6-2 with a 2.15 ERA . . . Was 3-0, 1.35 in April . . . Only 3-5 in the second half . . . He's been a winner every year in pro ball . . . Attracted attention after joining club in '78 and going 4-0 in September . . . Hurled a one-hitter against the Giants in '79 . . . Born July 22, 1956, in Dearborn, Mich. . . . Figured in six shutout victories in 1980, his best season in majors . . . Played for Vanderbilt . . . Stamina was questioned until he logged 211 innings in 1980 . . . Reached majors after only working in 28 minor-league games and posting 14-7 record in 1977-78.

Year	Club	G	IP	W	L	Pct.	SO	BB	H	ERA
1978	Montreal	10	61	4	2	.667	50	21	52	2.51
1979	Montreal	34	168	9	8	.529	138	54	148	3.43
1980	Montreal	33	211	16	11	.593	125	56	206	3.11
1981	Montreal	22	137	9	7	.563	77	31	122	2.96
	Totals	99	577	38	28	.576	390	162	528	3.10

BILL GULLICKSON 23 6-3 198   Bats R Throws R

Pitched better than 7-9 record would suggest . . . Rallied from 3-6 record and 3.43 ERA in first half to go 4-3 down the stretch . . . Fanned 13 Cubs Sept. 20 of last year after striking out 18 Chicago batters in 1980 game . . . NL Rookie Pitcher of the Year in '80 . . . Beat Phillies, 3-1, in second game of division playoffs . . . Had only two runs of support in a pair of Championship Series losses . . . Born Feb. 20, 1959, in Marshall, Minn. . . . No. 2 pick in nation, behind White Sox' Harold Baines, in 1977 draft . . . Posted 1.82 ERA for West Palm Beach in second pro season . . . Was 10-3 at Memphis in '79 and 6-2 at Denver in '80 before reaching Expos to stay.

Year	Club	G	IP	W	L	Pct.	SO	BB	H	ERA
1979	Montreal	1	1	0	0	.000	0	0	2	0.00
1980	Montreal	24	141	10	5	.667	120	50	127	3.00
1981	Montreal	22	157	7	9	.438	115	34	142	2.81
	Totals	47	299	17	14	.548	235	84	271	2.89

RAY BURRIS 31 6-5 200   Bats R Throws R

Marvelous reclamation project after signing with Expos as free agent during spring training . . . Couldn't win with the Mets, but was the pitching ace for Montreal down the stretch . . . Posted most wins since '77 and got big chance only because Expos' phenom Charlie Lea developed elbow trouble . . . Replaced Lea in rotation after Lea was NL Pitcher of the Month in May, firing a no-hitter . . . Burris was 3-5 in the first half and 6-2 after the strike . . . Born Aug. 22, 1950, in Idabel, Okla. . . . Lost third game of division playoffs, but was sensational against Dodgers in Championship Series . . . Pitched five-hitter to beat Fernando Valenzuela in Game 2 and allowed only one run in eight innings of Game 5 before giving way to Rogers . . . Spurned free-agent draft to re-sign with Expos.

Year	Club	G	IP	W	L	Pct.	SO	BB	H	ERA
1973	Chicago (NL).............	31	65	1	1	.500	57	27	65	2.91
1974	Chicago (NL).............	40	75	3	5	.375	40	26	91	6.60
1975	Chicago (NL).............	36	238	15	10	.600	108	73	259	4.12
1976	Chicago (NL).............	37	249	15	13	.536	112	70	251	3.11
1977	Chicago (NL).............	39	221	14	16	.467	105	67	270	4.72
1978	Chicago (NL).............	40	199	7	13	.350	94	79	210	4.75
1979	Chi.-N.Y. (NL)...........	18	43	0	2	.000	24	21	44	4.81
1979	New York (AL)	15	28	1	3	.250	19	10	40	6.11
1980	New York (NL)	29	170	7	13	.350	83	54	181	4.02
1981	Montreal	22	136	9	7	.563	52	41	117	3.04
	Totals..................	307	1424	72	83	.465	694	468	1528	4.15

TOP PROSPECTS

TERRY FRANCONA 22 6-1 190   **Bats L Throws L**
Outfielder batted .352 with American Association champion Denver and finished with .274 mark in 34 games with Expos . . . All-American at U. of Arizona . . . Batted .300 in only previous pro season in '80 . . . Son of former major leaguer Tito . . . Born April 22, 1959, in New Brighton, Pa.

DAVE HOSTETLER 26 6-4 215   **Bats R Throws R**
First baseman batted .318 with 27 homers and 103 RBI at Denver . . . Added three hits, including homer, in six trips with Expos . . . Former Southern Cal star, setting single-season record of 16 homers . . . Born March 27, 1956, in Pasadena, Calif.

MANAGER JIM FANNING: Just missed becoming first manager in major-league history to win a pennant after taking a club over in September . . . Succeeded Dick Williams on Sept. 8, with Expos mired in a 3-7 slump that made them 14-12 in the second half . . . Club won 16 of its last 27 games and then edged the Phillies, 3-2, in the NL East playoffs . . . Born Sept. 14, 1927, in Chicago . . . Criticized for replacing Ray Burris with Steve Rogers in ninth inning of final game in NLCS, since Rick Monday's homer off Rogers gave Dodgers the pennant . . . Has been with Expos since their birth . . . Named general manager in 1968 and promoted to vice president in 1973 . . . Hadn't managed since 1962, in Braves system, before last September . . . A former catcher in the Cubs' organization . . . Loyal company man . . . Looked out of place in baseball uniform after so many years in three-piece suits . . . Well-liked.

GREATEST CATCHER

Absolutely no contest. Gary Carter has been the club's best backstop ever since he stepped behind the plate in 1974 and became the NL Rookie of the Year. He's supplanted John Bench as the best in the league and, with Thurman Munson's death, has no peers in the majors.

Carter can do it all: Hit for a respectable average, knock in runs, provide the long ball and field. He topped NL catchers in assists in '77 and '80 and with a .993 fielding percentage in '80. That also was his most productive year at the dish, including 29 homers and 101 RBI.

Also an outstanding pressure player, he thrived down the stretch as the Expos won their first NL East title last year. He also performed well in the NLCS against the Dodgers, belting seven hits in 16 trips. He has a brilliant future, though it may not be with Montreal.

ALL-TIME EXPO SEASON RECORDS

BATTING: Rusty Staub, .311, 1971
HRs: Gary Carter, 31, 1977
RBIs: Ken Singleton, 103, 1973
STEALS: Ron LeFlore, 97, 1980
WINS: Ross Grimsley, 20, 1978
STRIKEOUTS: Bill Stoneman, 251, 1971

NEW YORK METS

TEAM DIRECTORY: Chairman of the Board: Nelson Double-
day; Pres.: Fred Wilpon; Exec. VP-GM: Frank Cashen;
VP-Baseball Oper.: Lou Gorman; Dir. Scouting: Joe McIlvaine;
Dir. Minor Leagues: Steve Schryver; Dir. Pub. Rel.: Jay Hor-
witz; Mgr.: George Bamberger. Home: Shea Stadium (55,300).
Field distances: 338, l.f. line; 371, l.c.; 410, c.f.; 371, r.c.; 338, r.f.
line. Spring training: St. Petersburg, Fla.

SCOUTING REPORT

HITTING: Good and getting better. The infusion of youngsters
Hubie Brooks (.307) and Mookie Wilson (.271, 24 steals) gave
the lineup some spark last season and they both are stamped as
future stars. One would also expect Ellis Valentine to recapture
his batting form following a sickly .208 debut with the Mets.
That trio immediately makes the club more formidable than it
was one year ago at this time.

Dave Kingman still has some good years left after adding
some punch (22 homers, 59 RBI) to the lineup last year and he
surely is capable of another big home-run season. Catchers John
Stearns and Alex Trevino are both solid, if unspectacular, hitters.
Youngsters Ron Gardenhire, Wally Backman and Brian Giles
will be given a chance to fill the middle-infield spots vacated by
the trading of the light-hitting Frank Taveras and Doug Flynn.

Hubie Brooks looks for glove to match his bat.

Lee Mazzilli is coming off a horrible year (.228) at the plate; Joel Youngblood hit .350, but missed more than half the season with a knee injury and, with Kingman at first, Rusty Staub's productive bat (.317) was often used only in pinch-hitting roles.

PITCHING: Figures to be the most improved area on the club under Professor George Bamberger's guidance. The Mets were sixth in team ERA (3.55) and should do a lot better if a couple of young arms develop as expected and Craig Swan makes a strong comeback following some encouraging winter work.

Pat Zachry (7-14) and Mike Scott (5-10) will be prime Bamberger reclamation projects. Two 1981 surprises, Pete Falcone (5-3, 2.56) and Ed Lynch (4-5, 2.93), have tasted success and may be ready for a big breakthrough. Greg Harris and Terry Leach looked good last year and youngsters Tim Leary, Charles Puleo and Jesse Orosco may be ready to stick. Neil Allen (2.96, 18 saves) already ranks with the best relievers in baseball. Injury-plagued Jim Kern, obtained from Texas, could also help in the pen.

FIELDING: Absolutely the pits and a top priority for Bambi if he is to get the most of his pitching talent. The Mets were by far the worst defensive team in the league last year. Their 130 errors were 17 more than any other team and their .968 fielding percentage was .006 lower than any other club's. Taveras (.931) was the chief offender, committing 24 errors, and he was sent away. But the Mets may miss Flynn's Gold Glove at second. Brooks was as rough at third base (21 errors, .924) as he was smooth at the plate. Kingman, a liability in the outfield, was only slightly better at first and the 38-year-old Staub lacks range at that position. Valentine has a strong arm, Mazzilli a weak one.

OUTLOOK: There are some signs of encouragement that the youth movement is paying off, but the club has a long way to go to reach the level of the three contenders. Bamberger's presence inevitably will help the pitchers, but it remains to be seen how effective they can be if the defense isn't shored up. The club wasn't very active during the winter months, which suggests contentment. That could be dangerous if some prospects don't continue to improve and some veterans don't bounce back to previously successful form. This is a team which seems capable of either showing a significant improvement, or falling flat on its face. All the pitching in the world won't help if the fielders flop or if players like Valentine, Kingman, Wilson and Brooks aren't solid at the plate.

NEW YORK METS 1982 ROSTER

MANAGER George Bamberger
Coaches—Jim Frey, Bud Harrelson, Frank Howard, Bill
         Monbouquette

PITCHERS

No.	Name	1981 Club	W-L	IP	SO	ERA	B-T	Ht.	Wt.	Born
13	Allen, Neil	New York (NL)	7-6	67	50	2.96	R-R	6-2	195	1/24/58 Kansas City, KS
33	Falcone, Pete	New York (NL)	5-3	95	56	2.56	L-L	6-2	185	10/1/53 Brooklyn, NY
45	Gaff, Brent	Jackson	5-1	57	27	2.53	R-R	6-2	185	10/5/58 Fort Wayne, IN
		Tidewater	9-5	147	59	2.94				
20	Harris, Greg	Tidewater	4-0	48	26	2.06	B-R	6-0	165	11/2/55 Lynwood, CA
		New York (NL)	3-5	69	54	4.43				
32	Hausman, Tom	New York (NL)	0-1	33	13	2.18	R-R	6-5	200	3/31/53 Mobridge, SD
28	Holman, Scott	Jackson	4-9	110	43	3.85	R-R	6-0	190	9/18/58 Santa Paula, CA
35	Jones, Randy	New York (NL)	1-8	59	14	4.88	R-L	6-0	180	1/12/50 Fullerton, CA
—	Kern, Jim	Texas	1-2	30	20	2.70	R-R	6-5	205	3/15/49 Gladwin, MI
43	Leach, Terry	Jackson	5-1	58	43	1.71	R-R	6-0	215	3/13/54 Selma, AL
		Tidewater	5-2	76	42	2.72				
		New York (NL)	1-1	35	16	2.57				
38	Leary, Tim	New York (NL)	0-0	2	3	0.00	R-R	6-3	195	12/23/58 Santa Monica, CA
		Tidewater	1-3	34	15	3.71				
34	Lynch, Ed	Tidewater	7-6	99	54	3.91	R-R	6-5	210	2/25/56 Brooklyn, NY
		New York (NL)	4-5	80	27	2.93				
47	Orosco, Jesse	Tidewater	9-5	87	81	3.31	R-L	6-2	174	4/21/57 Santa Barbara, CA
		New York (NL)	0-1	17	18	1.59				
25	Puleo, Charlie	Tidewater	12-9	169	133	3.46	R-R	6-3	190	2/7/55 Glen Ridge, NJ
		New York (NL)	0-0	13	8	0.00				
30	Scott, Mike	New York (NL)	5-10	136	54	3.90	R-R	6-3	215	4/26/55 Santa Monica, CA
44	Searage, Ray	Tidewater	2-0	27	23	2.33	L-L	6-1	180	5/1/55 Freeport, NY
		New York (NL)	1-0	37	16	3.65				
27	Swan, Craig	New York (NL)	0-2	14	9	3.21	R-R	6-3	215	11/30/50 Van Nuys, CA
40	Zachry, Pat	New York (NL)	7-14	139	76	4.14	R-R	6-5	175	4/24/52 Richmond, TX

CATCHERS

No.	Name	1981 Club	H	HR	RBI	Pct.	B-T	Ht.	Wt.	Born
42	Hodges, Ron	New York (NL)	13	1	6	.302	L-R	6-1	185	6/22/49 Franklin Co., VA
12	Stearns, John	New York (NL)	74	1	24	.271	R-R	6-0	185	8/21/51 Denver, CO
29	Trevino, Alex	New York (NL)	39	0	10	.262	R-R	5-10	165	8/26/57 Mexico

INFIELDERS

No.	Name	1981 Club	H	HR	RBI	Pct.	B-T	Ht.	Wt.	Born
6	Backman, Wally	New York (NL)	10	0	0	.278	B-R	5-9	160	9/22/59 Hillsboro, OR
		Tidewater	9	0	6	.153				
7	Brooks, Hubie	New York (NL)	110	4	38	.307	R-R	6-0	180	9/24/56 Los Angeles, CA
3	Cubbage, Mike	New York (NL)	17	1	4	.213	L-R	6-0	180	7/21/50 Charlottesville, VA
19	Gardenhire, Ron	Tidewater	105	2	40	.254	R-R	6-0	175	10/24/57 Germany
		New York (NL)	13	0	3	.271				
15	Giles, Brian	Tidewater	107	1	40	.268	R-R	6-1	165	4/27/60 Manhattan, KS
		New York (NL)	0	0	0	.000				
26	Kingman, Dave	New York (NL)	78	22	59	.221	R-R	6-6	210	12/21/48 Pendleton, OR
2	Oquendo, Jose	Lynchburg	98	0	38	.249	R-R	5-10	148	7/4/63 Puerto Rico
21	Rajsich, Gary	Tidewater	70	24	56	.277	L-L	6-2	205	10/28/54 Youngstown, OH
10	Staub, Rusty	New York (NL)	51	5	21	.317	L-R	6-2	215	4/1/44 New Orleans, LA

OUTFIELDERS

No.	Name	1981 Club	H	HR	RBI	Pct.	B-T	Ht.	Wt.	Born
4	Bailor, Bob	New York (NL)	23	0	8	.284	R-R	5-10	160	7/10/51 Connellsville, PA
5	Howard, Mike	Tidewater	116	6	33	.278	B-R	6-2	185	4/2/58 Seattle, WA
		New York (NL)	4	0	3	.167				
22	Jorgensen, Mike	New York (NL)	25	3	15	.205	L-L	6-0	192	8/16/48 Passaic, NJ
16	Mazzilli, Lee	New York (NL)	74	6	34	.228	B-R	6-1	180	3/25/55 New York, NY
17	Valentine, Ellis	Mont-NY (NL)	51	8	36	.208	R-R	6-4	205	7/30/54 Helena, AR
1	Wilson, Mookie	New York (NL)	89	3	14	.271	B-R	5-10	170	2/9/56 Bamberg, SC
8	Wynne, Marvell	Jackson	142	4	50	.286	L-L	5-11	170	12/17/59 Chicago, IL
18	Youngblood, Joel	New York (NL)	50	4	25	.350	R-R	5-11	175	8/28/51 Houston, TX

MET PROFILES

HUBIE BROOKS 25 6-0 180   Bats R Throws R

Sensational rookie season at third base, ranking among NL batting leaders . . . Batted .344 in May and .302 in first half . . . .310 hitter in August . . . Player of the Week, Sept. 14-20, after batting .500 . . . A .312 hitter in the second half . . . Tied record with three errors in an inning during loss to Dodgers . . . Born Sept. 24, 1956, in Compton, Cal. . . . Has hit successfully at all levels . . . Showed .309 mark in 24 games with Mets in 1980 was no fluke . . . Two-time All-American at Arizona State . . . Batted .364 for 1977 national champs . . . Set NCAA record with 126 hits as a senior in '78, leading nation with .424 average . . . Career .396 average an ASU record . . . College teammate of Bob Horner.

Year	Club	Pos.	G	AB	R	H	2B	3B	HR	RBI	SB	Avg.
1980	New York (NL)..	3B	24	81	8	25	2	1	1	10	1	.309
1981	New York (NL)..	3B-OF	98	358	34	110	21	2	4	38	9	.307
	Totals..........		122	439	42	135	23	3	5	48	10	.308

JOEL YOUNGBLOOD 30 5-11 175   Bats R Throws R

Used a .396 May to bat .359 in the first half, getting 128 at-bats . . . Can't crack lineup, so may not figure in future New York plans . . . Second-best pinch-batter in NL with .538 mark in 1980 . . . Born Aug. 28, 1951, in Houston . . . Injuries limited him to 15 plate appearances in second half . . . Spent five years in Reds' minor-league system, batting .317 at Indianapolis (AAA) in '73 . . . Has improved average every season in bigs, beginning with .193 in '76 . . . Development of Wilson and Brooks and acquisition of Valentine seemingly makes Joel expendable . . . Had 18 outfield assists in '79 and batted .316 on postseason NL tour of Japan.

Year	Club	Pos.	G	AB	R	H	2B	3B	HR	RBI	SB	Avg.
1976	Cincinnati	OF-3B-2B-C	55	57	8	11	1	1	0	1	1	.193
1977	St.L.-N.Y. (NL) ..	2B-OF-3B	95	209	17	51	13	1	0	12	1	.244
1978	New York (NL)..	OF-2B-3B-SS	113	266	40	67	12	8	7	30	4	.252
1979	New York (NL)..	OF-3B-2B	158	590	90	162	37	5	16	60	18	.275
1980	New York (NL)..	OF-2B-3B	146	514	58	142	26	2	8	69	14	.276
1981	New York (NL)..	OF-3B	43	143	16	50	10	2	4	25	2	.350
	Totals..........		630	1779	229	483	99	19	35	197	40	.272

MOOKIE WILSON 26 5-10 170   **Bats S Throws R**

Another outstanding rookie, fleet outfielder topped Mets with 24 steals in first full season . . . Batted .288 in first half and .259 after the strike . . . Rookie of the Year at Tidewater in 1979, stealing 49 bases . . . Followed with 50 thefts and .295 average with same club in '80 prior to promotion to Mets . . . Born Feb. 9, 1956, in Bamberg, S.C. . . . Star at U. of South Carolina . . . Led club to runner-up finish in 1977 College World Series (against Brooks and ASU) by batting .357 . . . Considering he's from Bamberg, it's only natural that he plays for a Bamberger . . . Turned to switch-hitting in spring of 1980 to make better use of speed.

Year	Club	Pos.	G	AB	R	H	2B	3B	HR	RBI	SB	Avg.
1980	New York (NL)..	OF	27	105	16	26	5	3	0	4	7	.248
1981	New York (NL)..	OF	92	328	49	89	8	8	3	14	24	.271
	Totals..........		119	433	65	115	13	11	3	18	31	.266

DAVE KINGMAN 33 6-6 210   **Bats R Throws R**

Kong improved his press relations and his home-run total with return to Mets . . . Injury-free, played in 100 games and belted 22 homers, four more than in troubled 1980 . . . Batted .220 with 14 homers in first half, .222 in second half . . . NL Player of the Week, May 26-31, for .412 average and four homers . . . Belted 11th grand slam Aug. 22, tying Johnny Bench and Willie Stargell for most slams by an active player . . . Born Dec. 21, 1948, in Pendleton, Ore. . . . Played at Southern Cal, where he also was a pitching standout . . . Signed with Giants and belted a grand slam off Pirates' Dave Giusti in first game . . . 48 homers in '79 were most by a Cubs slugger since Hack Wilson set NL record with 56 in 1930.

Year	Club	Pos.	G	AB	R	H	2B	3B	HR	RBI	SB	Avg.
1971	San Francisco ...	1B-OF	41	115	17	32	10	2	6	24	5	.278
1972	San Francisco ...	3B-1B-OF	135	472	65	106	17	4	29	83	16	.225
1973	San Francisco ...	3B-1B-P	112	305	54	62	10	1	24	55	8	.203
1974	San Francisco ...	1B-3B-OF	121	350	41	78	18	2	18	55	8	.223
1975	New York (NL)..	OF-1B-3B	134	502	65	116	22	1	36	88	7	.231
1976	New York (NL)..	OF-1B	123	474	70	113	14	1	37	86	7	.238
1977	NY (NL)-SD.....	OF-1B	114	379	38	84	16	0	20	67	5	.222
1977	Calif-NY (AL)...	1B-DH-OF	18	60	9	13	4	0	6	11	0	.217
1978	Chicago (NL)...	OF-1B	119	395	65	105	17	4	28	79	3	.266
1979	Chicago (NL)....	OF	145	532	97	153	19	5	48	115	4	.288
1980	Chicago (NL)....	1B-OF	81	255	31	71	8	0	18	57	2	.278
1981	New York (NL)..	1B-OF	100	353	40	78	11	3	22	59	6	.221
	Totals..........		1243	4192	592	1011	166	23	292	779	71	.241

JOHN STEARNS 30 6-0 185   Bats R Throws R

Won battle with Alex Trevino for catching job, but also can play first base . . . Batted .267 in first half, improving to .275 after layoff . . . Bounced back strong after 1980 surgery on right index finger . . . Had 25 doubles in 91 games prior to injury . . . Born Aug. 21, 1951, in Denver . . . Set modern major-league mark with 25 steals by a catcher in '78 . . . An outstanding defensive back at Colorado, he made All-Big Eight squad as a senior . . . Played in three bowls with Buffs and drafted in 17th round by Bills in 1973 . . . All-American in baseball after topping NCAA with 15 homers and .819 slugging percentage as a senior . . . Only one homer in last two seasons with Mets, however.

Year	Club	Pos.	G	AB	R	H	2B	3B	HR	RBI	SB	Avg.
1974	Philadelphia.....	C	1	2	0	1	0	0	0	0	0	.500
1975	New York (NL)..	C	59	169	25	32	5	1	3	10	4	.189
1976	New York (NL)..	C-3B	32	103	13	27	6	0	2	10	1	.262
1977	New York (NL)..	C-1B	139	431	52	108	25	1	12	55	9	.251
1978	New York (NL)..	C-3B	143	477	65	126	24	1	15	73	25	.264
1979	New York (NL)..	C-3B-1B-OF	155	538	58	131	29	2	9	66	15	.243
1980	New York (NL)..	C-1B-3B	91	319	42	91	25	1	0	45	7	.285
1981	New York (NL)..	C-3B	80	273	25	74	12	1	1	24	12	.271
	Totals..........		699	2312	280	590	127	7	42	283	73	.255

LEE MAZZILLI 27 6-1 180   Bats S Throws R

Former idol of fans has lost some of its luster, batting almost 50 points below his lifetime average last season . . . Maz hit .215 in the first half and .242 down stretch . . . Career marked by inconsistency . . . Teases Mets with some hot streaks . . . Batted .303 in '79 with 79 RBI as budding superstar . . . Slow start in '80 before an 11-homer, 25-RBI July . . . Born March 25, 1955, in New York City, so a natural favorite of home crowd until things go bad . . . Has homered from both sides of plate in same game . . . In 1979 All-Star Game, he belted pinch-homer in eighth for tie and walked with bases loaded in ninth to force in winning run . . . Champion speed skater in his youth.

Year	Club	Pos.	G	AB	R	H	2B	3B	HR	RBI	SB	Avg.
1976	New York (NL)..	OF	24	77	9	15	2	0	2	7	5	.195
1977	New York (NL)..	OF	159	537	66	134	24	3	6	46	22	.250
1978	New York (NL)..	OF	148	542	78	148	28	5	16	61	20	.273
1979	New York (NL)..	OF-1B	158	597	78	181	34	4	15	79	34	.303
1980	New York (NL)..	1B-OF	152	578	82	162	31	4	16	76	41	.280
1981	New York (NL)..	OF-1B	95	324	36	74	14	5	6	34	17	.228
	Totals..........		736	2655	349	714	133	21	61	303	139	.269

MIKE SCOTT 26 6-3 215   Bats R Throws R

Don't let the 5-10 won-lost, 3.90 ERA fool you: Scott has a big future with the Mets, especially now that George Bamberger's around to teach the young staff his Staten Island sinker . . . Was hard-luck pitcher last year, losing bundle of low-run games, including a 1-0 complete-game loss to Fernando Valenzuela and the Dodgers early in the season . . . Born April 26, 1955, in Hawthorne, Calif. . . . Led Pepperdine to three straight conference titles . . . Still a California boy at heart, he programs Beach Boys surfing sound over public-address system between innings of the games he pitches. Says it relaxes him.

Year	Club	G	IP	W	L	Pct.	SO	BB	H	ERA
1979	New York (NL)	18	52	1	3	.250	21	20	59	5.37
1980	New York (NL)	6	29	1	1	.500	13	8	40	4.34
1981	New York (NL)	23	136	5	10	.333	54	34	130	3.90
	Totals	47	217	7	14	.333	88	62	229	4.31

ELLIS VALENTINE 27 6-4 205   Bats R Throws R

Trying hard to recapture old magic after escaping Dick Williams' doghouse at Montreal . . . Good gamble for Mets because he can play when healthy . . . Batted .200 in first half, improving to .213 after strike . . . Despite problems, still tied for club lead in game-winning RBI (six), was second in homers and third in RBI . . . Born July 30, 1954, in Helena, Ark. . . . Played only 86 games because of injuries in 1980, yet had 67 RBI . . . Has yet to put all the tools together . . . Can run, throw and field . . . Once stole 14 consecutive bases for Montreal . . . Gold Glove outfielder in 1978 with club-record 24 assists . . . Entered 1981 with .290 lifetime average and should bounce back this year if 1980 beaning hasn't taken a permanent toll on his performance as hitter.

Year	Club	Pos.	G	AB	R	H	2B	3B	HR	RBI	SB	Avg.
1975	Montreal	OF	12	33	2	12	4	0	1	3	0	.364
1976	Montreal	OF	94	305	36	85	15	2	7	39	14	.279
1977	Montreal	OF	127	508	63	149	28	2	25	76	13	.293
1978	Montreal	OF	151	570	75	165	35	2	25	76	13	.289
1979	Montreal	OF	146	548	73	151	39	3	21	82	11	.276
1980	Montreal	OF	86	311	40	98	22	2	13	67	5	.315
1981	Mont-N.Y. (NL)	OF	70	245	23	51	11	1	8	36	0	.208
	Totals		686	2520	312	711	144	12	100	379	56	.282

NEIL ALLEN 24 6-2 195   Bats R Throws R

Registered 18 of club's 22 saves and has 40 over last two years on a club that doesn't win many . . . With seven wins, he figured in 25 of 41 Mets' victories . . . Brilliant start, not allowing a run in April . . . Was 1-0 with two saves, yielding three hits in 11 innings . . . 3-3 with six saves first half, doubling saves with 4-3 mark after strike . . . NL Player of the Week, Aug. 17-23, for two saves and a victory . . . Was 2-1 with seven saves in August . . . Born Jan. 24, 1958, in Kansas City, Kan. . . . Switched to bullpen after losing four of first five starts in '79 . . . Football scholarship offers from all Big Eight schools . . . Was heading to Kansas State as a QB, but signed with Mets instead.

Year	Club	G	IP	W	L	Pct.	SO	BB	H	ERA
1979	New York (NL)	50	99	6	10	.375	65	47	100	3.55
1980	New York (NL)	59	97	7	10	.412	79	40	87	3.71
1981	New York (NL)	43	67	7	6	.538	50	26	64	2.96
	Totals	152	263	20	26	.435	194	113	251	3.46

PETE FALCONE 28 6-2 185   Bats L Throws L

A pleasant surprise for Mets . . . Turned in lowest ERA after seven big-league seasons . . . Used as spot starter and in long relief, posted team-leading three complete games . . . First sub-3.00 ERA and only second time under 4.00 . . . Key was mastering control . . . Born Oct. 1, 1953, in Brooklyn . . . Long road back after solid rookie season with Giants in 1975, when he and roomie John Montefusco were bright spots in S.F. . . . Then had five straight losing seasons before turning it around last year . . . Cousin of former catcher Joe Pignatano . . . Equaled modern major-league mark by striking out first six batters of game against Phillies in 1980.

Year	Club	G	IP	W	L	Pct.	SO	BB	H	ERA
1975	San Francisco	34	190	12	11	.522	131	111	171	4.17
1976	St. Louis	32	212	12	16	.429	138	93	173	3.23
1977	St. Louis	27	124	4	8	.333	75	61	130	5.44
1978	St. Louis	19	75	2	7	.222	28	48	94	5.76
1979	New York (NL)	33	184	6	14	.300	113	76	194	4.16
1980	New York (NL)	37	157	7	10	.412	109	58	163	4.53
1981	New York (NL)	35	95	5	3	.625	56	36	84	2.56
	Totals	217	1037	48	69	.410	650	483	1009	4.15

TOP PROSPECTS

ED LYNCH 26 6-5 210   Bats R Throws R
Finished with Mets after starting in Triple-A and impressed with
2.93 ERA . . . More effective in bigs after posting 3.91 ERA at
Tidewater . . . Born Feb. 12, 1956, in Miami . . . Teammate of
Mookie Wilson at South Carolina, going 15-2 in two years . . .
Studying for a Master's Degree in business . . . Tim Leary, who
came up with a sore arm in first major-league start, was only 1-3,
with 3.71 ERA at Tidewater, but is highly-touted . . . Outfielder
Gary Rajsich (24 HRs, 56 RBI, .277 at Tidewater) is top hitting
prospect . . . Second baseman Wally Backman (.278 in 26 games
with Mets last year) will finally get his chance, with the departure of Doug Flynn.

Rookie Mookie Wilson stole 24 bases for the Mets.

MANAGER GEORGE BAMBERGER: Became game's highest-paid skipper when he signed a one-year, $200,000 contract . . . A homecoming of sorts for Staten Island-born Bamberger . . . Born Aug. 1, 1925 . . . Former Orioles pitching coach hired basically to develop young Mets' arms . . . Made great strides as Milwaukee manager before slowed by a heart attack in 1980 . . . Took over Brewers in '78 and they became a winner for the first time, improving by 26 games to 93 wins . . . They were 95-66 in '79 . . . Had bypass surgery after heart attack and resumed job before giving way to Bob Rodgers Sept. 6 . . . Has been handling special assignments for Brewers and insists heart problem was exaggerated . . . Pitched briefly with New York Giants . . . A famous minor-league pitcher, winning 213 games, mostly with Oakland and Vancouver in Pacific Coast League.

GREATEST CATCHER

Only two candidates: Jerry Grote and John Stearns. The latter is a better hitter, but Grote was no slouch at the plate and was far better behind it as the man who handled the pitching stars of two World Series squads in '69 and '73.

Grote, who also played in two series with Dodgers and in two All-Star Games, set numerous fielding standards and topped the NL catchers with a .995 fielding percentage in '75. He only made one error in 450 chances in '72 and posted a .251 lifetime average.

ALL-TIME MET SEASON RECORDS

BATTING: Cleon Jones, .340, 1969
HRs: Dave Kingman, 37, 1976
RBIs: Rusty Staub, 105, 1975
STEALS: Frank Taveras, 42, 1979
WINS: Tom Seaver, 25, 1969
STRIKEOUTS: Tom Seaver, 289, 1971

PHILADELPHIA PHILLIES

TEAM DIRECTORY: Pres.: William Y. Giles; Exec. VP: David Montgomery; VP-Dir. Play. Per.: Paul Owens; VP-Dir. Fin.: George F.H. Harrison; Adm. Scouting: Jack Pastore; Dir. Pub. Rel.: Larry Shenk; Trav. Sec.: Ed Ferenz; Mgr.: Pat Corrales. Home: Veterans Stadium (65,454). Field distances: 330, l.f. line; 408, c.f.; 330, r.f. line. Spring training: Clearwater, Fla.

SCOUTING REPORT

HITTING: When you start with a Pete Rose and clean up with a Mike Schmidt, things can't be too tough. The club had its problems last year, but hitting wasn't among them. In fact, they led the league with a .273 average and scored 27 more runs than anyone else. There shouldn't be a significant dropoff. Lonnie Smith and his .324 average are gone, but newcomer Bo Diaz is expected to compensate by adding punch behind the plate.

MVP Mike Schmidt powered Phils into the playoffs.

It all begins with Rose and Schmidt, however, and what else is there to say about the prolific pair? Rose, showing no signs of slowing down, batted .325 and belted more hits than anyone in the league. Schmidt, the MVP, made a shambles of the power derby by blasting 31 homers in a shortened season in which nobody else could hit more than 24. Gary Matthews (.301) and Manny Trillo (.287) complemented them and even Larry Bowa (.283) hit with vigor. Hitting definitely is not a problem.

PITCHING: This is another story. The Phillies disproved the theory that pitching is the name of the game by reaching the playoffs with the worst ERA (4.05) in the league. They've added Mike Krukow, who was 9-9 with the Cubs, but that won't help if Larry Christenson is lost to free agency.

Dick Ruthven (12-7, 5.14) pitched much worse than his record shows and it remains to be seen how much longer aging Steve Carlton, Tug McGraw and Sparky Lyle can work at peak efficiency. Carlton lost twice in the division playoffs, marring an otherwise outstanding 13-4, 2.42 campaign. There's a big dropoff after him in the rotation, however, and the club will be hard-pressed to improve its shabby pitching.

FIELDING: It's more than adequate with Schmidt, Bowa and Trillo forming a web around the infield. Schmidt led the league in assists and total chances at third base, Bowa missed by a hair in leading the shortstops in fielding percentage by a hair and Trillo topped the circuit in putouts and made only seven errors at second base. Diaz will improve the catching with his rifle arm and Bake McBride and Garry Maddox are solid outfielders, even though Maddox has slipped a notch from his Gold Glove days. Defense doesn't seem to be a major problem following a .980 season which fell only .001 shy of the league lead. If there is a crack, it will be at short, because Bowa isn't getting any younger.

OUTLOOK: Solid hitting and fielding make the Phils a contender, but pitching problems likely will keep them out of the playoffs. Unless they're careful, they may suffer from the same aging problems that sapped the Pirates. As a result, they have been replaced by the Cardinals as the prime threat to a Montreal repeat. But you cannot count a team out when it has Schmidt, Rose and Carlton. The Phils no longer are the best, but they have enough firepower to make things interesting, plus they're in a weak division, so anything can happen. Pat Corrales has some tools as a rookie NL skipper, but he also has enough problems to keep him from getting overconfident.

PHILADELPHIA PHILLIES 1982 ROSTER

MANAGER Pat Corrales
Coaches—Dave Bristol, Deron Johnson, Claude Osteen,
Mike Ryan, Bobby Wine

PITCHERS

No.	Name	1981 Club	W-L	IP	SO	ERA	B-T	Ht.	Wt.	Born
—	Baller, Jay	Peninsula	9-14	147	166	3.92	R-R	6-6	215	10/6/60 Stayton, OH
40	Brusstar, Warren	Oklahoma City	3-2	93	47	2.81	R-R	6-3	200	2/2/52 Oakland, CA
		Philadelphia	0-1	12	8	4.50				
50	Bystrom, Marty	Philadelphia	4-3	54	24	3.33	R-R	6-5	200	7/26/58 Coral Gables, FL
		Reading	0-0	4	2	4.50				
32	Carlton, Steve	Philadelphia	13-4	190	119	2.42	L-L	6-5	210	12/22/44 Miami, FL
—	Carman, Don	Reading	12-13	176	103	4.04	L-L	6-3	190	8/14/59 Oklahoma City, OK
43	Davis, Mark	Oklahoma City	5-2	65	56	3.88	L-L	6-3	180	10/19/60 Livermore, CA
		Philadelphia	1-4	43	29	7.74				
—	Krukow, Mike	Chicago (NL)	9-9	144	101	3.69	R-R	6-4	195	1/21/52 Long Beach, CA
28	Lyle, Sparky	Philadelphia	9-6	75	29	4.44	L-L	6-1	195	7/22/44 Reynoldsville, PA
45	McGraw, Tug	Philadelphia	2-4	44	26	2.66	R-L	6-0	186	8/30/44 Martinez, CA
30	Proly, Mike	Philadelphia	2-1	63	19	3.86	R-R	5-10	184	12/15/50 Jamaica, NY
—	Rajsich, Dave	Wichita	6-5	85	60	4.24	L-L	6-5	180	9/28/51 Youngstown, OH
35	Reed, Jerry	Reading	5-4	79	62	3.30	R-R	6-1	190	10/8/55 Bryson City, NC
		Philadelphia	0-1	5	5	7.20				
44	Ruthven, Dick	Philadelphia	12-7	147	80	5.14	R-R	6-3	190	3/27/51 Sacramento, CA
—	Smith, Roy	Reading	11-8	161	117	4.42	R-R	6-3	195	9/6/61 Mt. Vernon, NY

CATCHERS

No.	Name	1981 Club	H	HR	RBI	Pct.	B-T	Ht.	Wt.	Born
—	Diaz, Bo	Cleveland	57	7	38	.313	R-R	5-11	190	3/23/53 Venezuela
17	McCormack, Don	Oklahoma City	92	11	75	.229	R-R	6-3	205	9/18/55 Omak, WA
		Philadelphia	1	0	0	.250				
11	Virgil, Ozzie	Oklahoma City	63	11	44	.229	R-R	6-1	195	12/7/56 Puerto Rico
		Philadelphia	0	0	0	.000				

INFIELDERS

No.	Name	1981 Club	H	HR	RBI	Pct.	B-T	Ht.	Wt.	Born
16	Aguayo, Luis	Philadelphia	18	1	7	.214	R-R	5-9	173	3/13/59 Puerto Rico
10	Bowa, Larry	Philadelphia	102	0	31	.283	B-R	5-10	155	12/6/45 Sacramento, CA
—	Franco, Julio	Reading	160	8	74	.301	R-R	5-11	155	8/23/58 Dominican Republic
—	Hamric, Rusty	Reading	162	5	67	.309	R-R	6-0	175	2/6/58 Abilene, TX
24	Matuszek, Len	Okla. City	146	21	91	.315	L-R	6-2	190	9/27/54 Toledo, OH
		Philadelphia	3	0	1	.273				
14	Rose, Pete	Philadelphia	140	0	33	.325	B-R	5-11	200	4/14/41 Cincinnati, OH
37	Sandberg, Ryne	Okla. City	152	9	62	.293	R-R	6-1	175	9/18/59 Spokane, WA
		Philadelphia	1	0	0	.167				
20	Schmidt, Mike	Philadelphia	112	31	91	.316	R-R	6-2	198	9/27/49 Dayton, OH
9	Trillo, Manny	Philadelphia	100	6	36	.287	R-R	6-1	164	12/25/50 Venezuela

OUTFIELDERS

No.	Name	1981 Club	H	HR	RBI	Pct.	B-T	Ht.	Wt.	Born
—	Culmer, Wil	Reading	116	10	53	.282	R-R	6-4	210	11/11/58 Bahamas
26	Davis, Dick	Philadelphia	32	2	19	.333	R-R	6-3	185	9/25/53 Long Beach, CA
22	Dernier, Bob	Okla. City	150	5	34	.302	R-R	6-0	160	1/5/57 Kansas City, MO
		Philadelphia	3	0	0	.750				
23	Gross, Greg	Philadelphia	23	0	7	.225	L-L	5-11	175	8/1/52 York, PA
31	Maddox, Garry	Philadelphia	85	5	40	.263	R-R	6-3	185	9/1/49 Cincinnati, OH
34	Matthews, Gary	Philadelphia	108	9	67	.301	R-R	6-3	180	7/5/50 San Fernando, CA
21	McBride, Bake	Philadelphia	60	2	21	.271	L-R	6-2	190	2/3/49 Fulton, MO
—	Sanchez, Alejandro	Reading	136	13	76	.275	R-R	6-0	175	2/26/59 Dominican Republic
25	Unser, Del	Philadelphia	9	0	6	.153	L-L	5-11	180	12/9/44 Decatur, IL
29	Vukovich, George	Oklahoma City	70	8	48	.302	L-R	6-0	198	6/24/56 Chicago, IL
		Philadelphia	10	1	4	.385				

PHILLIE PROFILES

PETE ROSE 40 5-11 200
Bats S Throws R

No signs of slowing down for Charlie Hustle . . . All-time great led the majors with 140 hits and was runnerup in NL batting race . . . Lifetime average of .310 . . . In the eighth inning Aug. 10, he belted a single off St. Louis reliever Mark Littell for his 3,631st hit, breaking Stan Musial's NL record . . . Only Ty Cobb (4,191) and Henry Aaron (3,771) have more hits than Pete's 3,697 . . . Born April 4, 1941, in Cincinnati . . . Only Cobb has more singles . . . Second to Mike Schmidt in runs scored in 1981 . . . NL Player of the Week, Aug. 10-16 . . . Started with a bang, batting .382 in April . . . Hit .330 in the first half, .319 in the second half . . . Holds major-league mark with 10 200-hit seasons . . . Just missed becoming only player to win batting titles in three different decades . . . Rookie of the Year in '63 and MVP in '73 . . . 44-game hitting streak set NL record in 1978.

Year	Club	Pos.	G	AB	R	H	2B	3B	HR	RBI	SB	Avg.
1963	Cincinnati	2B-OF	157	623	101	170	25	9	6	41	13	.273
1964	Cincinnati	2B	136	516	64	139	13	2	4	34	4	.269
1965	Cincinnati	2B	162	670	117	209	35	11	11	81	8	.312
1966	Cincinnati	2B-3B	156	654	97	205	38	5	16	70	4	.313
1967	Cincinnati	OF-2B	148	585	86	176	32	8	12	76	11	.301
1968	Cincinnati	OF-2B-1B	149	626	94	210	42	6	10	49	3	.335
1969	Cincinnati	OF-2B	156	627	120	218	33	11	16	82	7	.348
1970	Cincinnati	OF	159	649	120	205	37	9	15	52	12	.316
1971	Cincinnati	OF	160	632	86	192	27	4	13	44	13	.304
1972	Cincinnati	OF	154	645	107	198	31	11	6	57	10	.307
1973	Cincinnati	OF	160	680	115	230	36	8	5	64	10	.338
1974	Cincinnati	OF	163	652	110	185	45	7	3	51	2	.284
1975	Cincinnati	3B-OF	162	662	112	210	47	4	7	74	0	.317
1976	Cincinnati	3B-OF	162	665	130	215	42	6	10	63	9	.323
1977	Cincinnati	3B	162	655	95	204	38	7	9	64	16	.311
1978	Cincinnati	3B-OF-1B	159	655	103	198	51	3	7	52	13	.302
1979	Philadelphia	1B-3B-2B	163	628	90	208	40	5	4	59	20	.331
1980	Philadelphia	1B	162	655	96	185	42	1	1	64	12	.282
1981	Philadelphia	1B	107	431	73	140	18	5	0	33	4	.325
	Totals		2937	11,910	1916	3697	672	122	155	1110	171	.310

MIKE SCHMIDT 32 6-2 198
Bats R Throws R

Nobody does it better when it comes to power . . . Had seven more homers than anyone else while defending major-league home-run title . . . Topped majors with 91 RBI and batted above .300 for the first time, giving him most pleasure . . . Led league in four offensive categories, including runs, walks (73), on-base average (.435) and slugging percentage (.644)

. . . Born Sept. 27, 1949, in Dayton, Ohio . . . Batted .284 with 14 homers and 41 RBI in first half . . . Improved to .356, 17, 50 after the strike . . . Hit nine homers in May and August . . . NL Player of the Month in August for .380 average and .817 slugging percentage . . . Streaky tendencies . . . Four homers in one game at Wrigley Field in '76 . . . Seven homers in five games in '79 . . . Eight homers in last 16 games in '80 . . . Five NL home-run crowns . . . NL and World Series MVP in '80 . . . MVP repeater in '81 . . . Signed for six years for over $7 million.

Year	Club	Pos.	G	AB	R	H	2B	3B	HR	RBI	SB	Avg.
1972	Philadelphia.....	3B-2B	13	34	2	7	0	0	1	3	0	.206
1973	Philadelphia.....	3B-2B-1B-SS	132	367	43	72	11	0	18	52	8	.196
1974	Philadelphia.....	3B	162	568	108	160	28	7	36	116	23	.282
1975	Philadelphia.....	3B-SS	158	562	93	140	34	3	38	95	29	.249
1976	Philadelphia.....	3B	160	584	112	153	31	4	38	107	14	.262
1977	Philadelphia.....	3B-SS-2B	154	544	114	149	27	11	38	101	15	.274
1978	Philadelphia.....	3B-SS	145	513	93	129	27	2	21	78	19	.251
1979	Philadelphia.....	3B-SS	160	541	109	137	25	4	45	114	9	.253
1980	Philadelphia.....	3B	150	548	104	157	25	8	48	121	12	.286
1981	Philadelphia.....	3B	102	354	78	112	19	2	31	91	12	.316
	Totals..........		1336	4615	856	1216	227	41	314	878	141	.263

GARY MATTHEWS 31 6-3 180 Bats R Throws R

Bargain for Phillies after escaping Ted Turner's doghouse . . . Made immediate hit by batting .340 in April and .324 in May . . . Entered strike batting .317 and hit .283 thereafter . . . NL Player of the Month for September, batting .330 with seven homers and 31 RBI in 28 games . . . Club's leading hitter in play-offs, batting .400 against Expos . . . Born July 5, 1950, in San Fernando, Calif. . . . Promising outfielder with Giants, but they let him get away over a contract hassle . . . Rookie of the Year in '73 . . . Aggressive and underrated . . . Benched after 10 games following slow start in 1980, but bounced back with 13 game-winning RBI.

Year	Club	Pos.	G	AB	R	H	2B	3B	HR	RBI	SB	Avg.
1972	San Francisco ...	OF	20	62	11	18	1	1	4	14	0	.290
1973	San Francisco ...	OF	148	540	74	162	22	10	12	58	17	.300
1974	San Francisco ...	OF	154	561	87	161	27	6	16	82	11	.287
1975	San Francisco ...	OF	116	425	67	119	22	3	12	58	13	.280
1976	San Francisco ...	OF	156	587	79	164	28	4	20	84	12	.279
1977	Atlanta.........	OF	148	555	89	157	25	5	17	64	22	.283
1978	Atlanta.........	OF	129	474	75	135	20	5	18	62	8	.285
1979	Atlanta.........	OF	156	631	97	192	34	5	27	90	18	.304
1980	Atlanta.........	OF	155	571	79	159	17	3	19	75	11	.278
1981	Philadelphia.....	OF	101	359	62	108	21	3	9	67	15	.301
	Totals..........		1283	4765	720	1375	217	45	154	654	127	.289

MANNY TRILLO 31 6-1 164   Bats R Throws R

Another solid season for slick second baseman . . . Showed consistency with .292 in first half, .282 down stretch . . . Obscured by superstar teammates, but was a NL all-star in 1980 . . . Earned Championship Series MVP honors that year, batting .381 . . . Gold Glove winner in '79 . . . Born Christmas Day, 1950, in Caritito, Venezuela . . . Won fifth game of '80 World Series with a run-scoring single . . . Started pro career in Phillies' system as a 17-year-old catcher . . . Drafted by A's in '69 and eventually swapped to Cubs for Billy Williams before rejoining Phils.

Year	Club	Pos.	G	AB	R	H	2B	3B	HR	RBI	SB	Avg.
1973	Oakland	2B	17	12	0	3	2	0	0	3	0	.250
1974	Oakland	2B	21	33	3	5	0	0	0	2	0	.152
1975	Chicago (NL)	2B-SS	154	545	55	135	12	2	7	70	1	.248
1976	Chicago (NL)	2B-SS	158	582	42	139	24	3	4	59	17	.239
1977	Chicago (NL)	2B	152	504	51	141	18	5	7	57	3	.280
1978	Chicago (NL)	2B	152	552	53	144	17	5	4	55	0	.261
1979	Philadelphia	2B	118	431	40	112	22	1	6	42	4	.260
1980	Philadelphia	2B	141	531	68	155	25	9	7	43	8	.292
1981	Philadelphia	2B	94	349	37	100	14	3	6	36	10	.287
	Totals		1007	3539	349	934	134	28	41	367	43	.264

BAKE McBRIDE 33 6-2 190   Bats L Throws R

Off to a great start last year . . . Batted .333 in April and went into strike with .366 average . . . Tailed off to .227 after play resumed . . . Real name is Arnold Ray . . . Had four straight .300 seasons before joining Phillies in June 1977 . . . Batted .304 in 1980 World Series . . . Had 14 game-winning RBI in '79 . . . Born Feb. 3, 1949, in Fulton, Mo. . . . Rookie of the Year in '74 with Cards . . . Won first game of '80 Series with three-run homer . . . Has hit four inside-the-park homers . . . Baseball and track star at Westminster (Mo.) College, running 9.8 in 100-yard dash . . . Broke into pro ball with .423 average at Sarasota in 1970 . . . A .300 hitter in eight pro seasons.

Year	Club	Pos.	G	AB	R	H	2B	3B	HR	RBI	SB	Avg.
1973	St. Louis	OF	40	63	8	19	3	0	0	5	0	.300
1974	St. Louis	OF	150	559	81	173	19	5	6	56	30	.309
1975	St. Louis	OF	116	413	70	124	10	9	5	36	26	.300
1976	St. Louis	OF	72	272	40	91	13	4	3	24	10	.335
1977	St. L.-Phil.	OF	128	402	76	127	25	6	15	61	36	.316
1978	Philadelphia	OF	122	472	68	127	20	4	10	49	28	.269
1979	Philadelphia	OF	151	582	82	163	16	12	12	60	25	.280
1980	Philadelphia	OF	137	554	68	171	33	10	9	87	13	.309
1981	Philadelphia	OF	58	221	26	60	17	1	2	21	5	.271
	Totals		974	3538	519	1055	156	51	62	399	173	.298

BO DIAZ 29 5-11 190   Bats R Throws R

Emerged as one of the biggest surprises in baseball last year, earning a spot on the all-star team with hitting that led AL catchers . . . His nine game-winning RBI were tops at Cleveland . . . Born March 23, 1953, in Cua, Venezuela . . . Came to Philadelphia in three-way deal last November that landed Lonnie Smith in St. Louis . . . Began career in Red Sox farm system in 1971 and came to the Indians in 1978 with pitchers Rick Wise, Mike Paxton and infielder Ted Cox in exchange for Dennis Eckersley . . . Has been a legend in his native Venezuela . . . Set a Venezuela League home-run record of 20 while leading Caracas to winter league playoffs in 1979-80 . . . Nicknamed "The Cannon" because of his arm . . . Hobby is music.

Year	Club	Pos.	G	AB	R	H	2B	3B	HR	RBI	SB	Avg.
1977	Boston.........	C	2	1	0	0	0	0	0	0	0	.000
1978	Cleveland.......	C	44	127	12	30	4	0	2	11	0	.236
1979	Cleveland.......	C	15	32	0	5	2	0	0	1	0	.156
1980	Cleveland.......	C	76	207	15	47	11	2	3	32	1	.227
1981	Cleveland.......	C	63	182	25	57	19	0	7	38	2	.313
	Totals..........		200	549	52	139	36	2	12	82	3	.253

LARRY BOWA 36 5-10 155   Bats S Throws R

Bounced back with best season since 1978 . . . Batted .268 in the first half and improved to .302 down the stretch . . . Also finished fast in '80, batting .288 in the second half and sparkling in postseason games . . . Batted .316 in '80 playoffs and .375 in World Series while fielding flawlessly . . . Set World Series record by starting seven double plays . . . Born Dec. 6, 1945, in Sacramento, Calif. . . . Best fielding shortstop, statistically, in major-league history . . . Only six errors in '79, setting single-season mark of .991 . . . Two Gold Gloves . . . Led league with 13 triples in '72 . . . Batted .333 in '78 playoffs . . . Has played in five All-Star Games.

Year	Club	Pos.	G	AB	R	H	2B	3B	HR	RBI	SB	Avg.
1970	Philadelphia.....	SS-2B	145	547	50	137	17	6	0	34	24	.250
1971	Philadelphia.....	SS	159	650	74	162	18	5	0	25	28	.249
1972	Philadelphia.....	SS	152	579	67	145	11	13	1	31	17	.250
1973	Philadelphia.....	SS	122	446	42	94	11	3	0	23	10	.211
1974	Philadelphia.....	SS	162	669	97	184	19	10	1	36	39	.275
1975	Philadelphia.....	SS	136	583	79	178	18	9	2	38	24	.305
1976	Philadelphia.....	SS	156	624	71	155	15	9	0	49	30	.248
1977	Philadelphia.....	SS	154	624	93	175	19	3	4	41	32	.280
1978	Philadelphia.....	SS	156	654	78	192	31	5	3	43	27	.294
1979	Philadelphia.....	SS	147	539	74	130	17	11	0	31	20	.241
1980	Philadelphia.....	SS	147	540	57	144	16	4	2	39	21	.267
1981	Philadelphia.....	SS	103	360	34	102	14	3	0	31	16	.283
	Totals..........		1739	6815	816	1798	206	71	13	421	288	.264

STEVE CARLTON 37 6-5 210   Bats L Throws L

His pitching leaves him speechless . . . It also leaves batters talking to themselves . . . Until he ran into Steve Rogers and the Expos in the playoffs, it was nearly a perfect season . . . 4-0 with a 2.36 ERA in April and 4-0 in May . . . 9-1 with a 2.80 ERA before the strike and a merely mortal 4-3 thereafter . . . Struck out the side in the first inning against the Expos early in the season to become first lefty to fan 3,000 men . . . On Sept. 21 at Montreal, he whiffed 12 to break Bob Gibson's NL strikeout record of 3,118 . . . Born Dec. 22, 1944, in Miami . . . Lost twice in NL East Division playoffs to drop postseason record to 4-5 . . . Phils only scored one run in those two losses, however . . . One of four three-time winners of Cy Young Award . . . Six career one-hitters, one under NL mark.

Year	Club	G	IP	W	L	Pct.	SO	BB	H	ERA
1965	St. Louis	15	25	0	0	.000	21	8	27	2.52
1966	St. Louis	9	52	3	3	.500	25	18	56	3.12
1967	St. Louis	30	193	14	9	.609	168	62	173	2.98
1968	St. Louis	34	232	13	11	.542	162	61	214	2.99
1969	St. Louis	31	236	17	11	.607	210	93	185	2.17
1970	St. Louis	34	254	10	19	.345	193	109	239	3.72
1971	St. Louis	37	273	20	9	.690	172	98	275	3.56
1972	Philadelphia	41	346	27	10	.730	310	87	257	1.98
1973	Philadelphia	40	293	13	20	.394	223	113	293	3.90
1974	Philadelphia	39	291	16	13	.552	240	136	249	3.22
1975	Philadelphia	37	225	15	14	.517	192	104	217	3.56
1976	Philadelphia	35	253	20	7	.741	195	72	224	3.13
1977	Philadelphia	36	283	23	10	.697	198	89	229	2.64
1978	Philadelphia	34	247	16	13	.552	161	63	228	2.84
1979	Philadelphia	35	251	18	11	.621	213	89	202	3.62
1980	Philadelphia	38	304	24	9	.727	286	90	243	2.34
1981	Philadelphia	24	190	13	4	.765	179	62	152	2.42
	Totals	549	3978	262	173	.602	3148	1354	3463	3.00

TUG McGRAW 36 6-0 184   Bats R Throws L

Still ranks with best in baseball . . . Thrives on pressure . . . Won Game 4 of playoffs, yielding one hit in three innings . . . Woeful first half with 1-4 record, 4.09 ERA, but finished strong and had ERA under 2.00 in the second half . . . NL lifetime leader with 174 saves . . . Among dwindling ranks of clubhouse characters . . . Unlike most of his teammates, he cooperates with the media . . . Born Aug. 30, 1944, in Martinez, Calif. . . . Coined "You Gotta Believe" slogan which inspired Mets in 1973 . . . 2-1 with 2.05 ERA in two World Series . . . After coming off disabled list, July 17, 1980, he allowed only three earned runs in 52 innings (0.52) to key pennant drive . . . Won one game and saved two others in '80 World Series.

Year	Club	G	IP	W	L	Pct.	SO	BB	H	ERA
1965	New York (NL)	37	98	2	7	.222	57	48	88	3.31
1966	New York (NL)	15	62	2	9	.182	34	25	72	5.37
1967	New York (NL)	4	17	0	3	.000	18	13	13	7.94
1969	New York (NL)	42	100	9	3	.750	92	47	89	2.25
1970	New York (NL)	57	91	4	6	.400	81	49	77	3.26
1971	New York (NL)	51	111	11	4	.733	109	41	73	1.70
1972	New York (NL)	54	106	8	6	.571	92	40	71	1.70
1973	New York (NL)	60	119	5	6	.455	81	55	106	3.86
1974	New York (NL)	41	89	6	11	.353	54	32	96	4.15
1975	Philadelphia	56	103	9	6	.600	55	36	84	2.97
1976	Philadelphia	58	97	7	6	.538	76	42	81	2.51
1977	Philadelphia	45	79	7	3	.700	58	24	62	2.62
1978	Philadelphia	55	90	8	7	.533	63	23	82	3.20
1979	Philadelphia	65	84	4	3	.571	57	29	83	5.14
1980	Philadelphia	57	92	5	4	.556	75	23	62	1.47
1981	Philadelphia	34	44	2	4	.333	26	14	35	2.66
	Totals	731	1382	89	88	.503	1028	541	1174	3.07

DICK RUTHVEN 31 6-3 190   Bats R Throws R

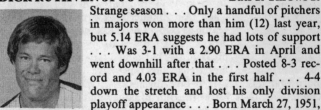

Strange season . . . Only a handful of pitchers in majors won more than him (12) last year, but 5.14 ERA suggests he had lots of support . . . Was 3-1 with a 2.90 ERA in April and went downhill after that . . . Posted 8-3 record and 4.03 ERA in the first half . . . 4-4 down the stretch and lost his only division playoff appearance . . . Born March 27, 1951, in Sacramento, Calif. . . . Won playoff clincher in relief against Astros in 1980 . . . Phils' No. 1 draft choice in '73, but played with Braves before being reacquired in '78 . . . Won 19 of first 24 decisions with Phillies in 1978-79 before elbow problems surfaced . . . Finished '79 season 1-5 and had elbow surgery . . . Played at Fresno State in California.

Year	Club	G	IP	W	L	Pct.	SO	BB	H	ERA
1973	Philadelphia	25	128	6	9	.400	98	75	125	4.22
1974	Philadelphia	35	213	9	13	.409	153	116	182	4.01
1975	Philadelphia	11	41	2	2	.500	26	22	37	4.17
1976	Atlanta	36	240	14	17	.452	142	90	255	4.20
1977	Atlanta	25	151	7	13	.350	84	62	158	4.23
1978	Atlanta-Philadelphia	33	232	15	11	.577	120	56	214	3.38
1979	Philadelphia	20	122	7	5	.583	58	37	121	4.28
1980	Philadelphia	33	223	17	10	.630	86	74	241	3.55
1981	Philadelphia	23	147	12	7	.632	80	54	162	5.14
	Totals	241	1497	89	87	.506	847	586	1495	4.05

TOP PROSPECTS

BOB DERNIER 25 6-0 160   **Bats R Throws R**
An American Association all-star in '81 before joining parent
club . . . Outfielder batted .302 in Triple-A and had three hits in
four at-bats with Phils . . . Born Jan. 5, 1957, in Kansas City,
Mo. . . . Stole 77 bases in 1979 and 74 in '80 . . . Is 7-for-11 as a
major leaguer and could further crowd outfield picture.

LEN MATUSZEK 27 6-2 190   **Bats L Throws R**
Another American Association all-star . . . Plays first and third
. . . Batted .315 with 21 homers at Oklahoma City and .273 in 13
games with Phils . . . Skilled fielder . . . A .305 Triple-A hitter
in 1980 . . . Born Sept. 27, 1954, in Toledo, Ohio.

MANAGER PAT CORRALES: Returns to managing after one-
year absence . . . Led Rangers to 83-79 record as rookie manager in '79, but club slipped to 76-85 in 1980 . . . Pat went to front office when Don Zimmer took over club . . . First season as skipper produced numerous ups and downs . . . Club was 10-30 after the All-Star break in '79, but rallied to win 21 of 31 down the stretch and finish five games back . . .
Born March 20, 1941, in Los Angeles . . . Grew up in Fresno,
Calif., with Dick Ellsworth, Jim Maloney and Dick Selma, all
former major-league pitchers . . . Was a promising catching
prospect, but couldn't escape roomie John Bench's shadow at
Cincinnati . . . Began career with Phillies and also played with
Cardinals and Padres . . . Batted .309 at Des Moines in '61, .304
at Little Rock in '64 and .316 at Indianapolis in '72 . . . Became
a coach for the Rangers in '75 after managing one year in the
minors.

GREATEST CATCHER

A toughie because there are no superstars. Bob Boone was a
pillar in the Seventies and Stan Lopata had some bright moments in the Fifties, including 32 homers and 95 RBI in '56, but

it would be tough to argue with the selection of Spud Davis, an outstanding hitter of the Thirties.

Davis, who joined the Phillies in 1928, batted .342, .313, .326, .336 and .349 in five successive seasons, 1929-33, and led league with 78 assists in '31. Davis, who also played with the Cards, Reds and Pirates, posted a lifetime .308 average in almost 20 years as a big leaguer.

ALL-TIME PHILLIE SEASON RECORDS

BATTING: Frank O'Doul, .398, 1929
HRs: Mike Schmidt, 48, 1980
RBIs: Chuck Klein, 170, 1930
STEALS: Sherry Magee, 55, 1906
WINS: Grover Alexander, 33, 1916
STRIKEOUTS: Steve Carlton, 310, 1972

Steve Carlton needs 38 wins to reach the 300 mark.

PITTSBURGH PIRATES

TEAM DIRECTORY: Chairman of the Board: John Galbreath; Pres.: Daniel Galbreath; Exec. VP: Harding Peterson; Dir. Scouting: Murray Cook; Dir. Minor Leagues: Branch Rickey III; VP-Marketing/Pub. Rel.: Jack Schrom; Publ. Dir.: Ed Wade; Trav. Sec.: Charles Muse; Mgr.: Chuck Tanner. Home: Three Rivers Stadium (53,869). Field distances: 335, l.f. line; 375, l.c.; 400, c.f.; 375, r.c.; 335, r.f. line. Spring training: Bradenton, Fla.

SCOUTING REPORT

HITTING: The Lumber Company was reduced to a toothpick factory last year, as age produced dry rot in a once-feared batting order. Were it not for Bill Madlock's batting title with a gaudy .341 average, the Bucs really would have been hurting at the plate. As it was, nobody else batted above .300, except for rookie catcher Tony Pena, who broke in at .300. Mike Easler hit .286, but managed just seven homers. The team average was .257 and the prospects for improvement were slim, because Dave Parker isn't.

With the exception of Madlock and Pena, all the Pirates tailed off last year and The Family seems headed for divorce court. Omar Moreno still gets on base, but nobody knocks him in. The situation could improve if Parker regains his former magic and if Jason Thompson sufficiently adjusts to the NL to boost a .242 average, but Parker and Thompson both were trade bait over the winter.

PITCHING: Surprisingly, the Bucs pitched the ball better than they hit it last season, though a 3.56 team ERA isn't sensational. There is no big winner, but enough good arms to do the job if a once-formidable bullpen can shut the door. Kent Tekulve fashioned a 2.49 ERA, but didn't help the club with only three saves. He must bounce back, as must starters Jim Bibby, John Candelaria and Don Robinson, who combined for eight victories. Newcomer Tom Griffin, the ex-Giant, will help.

Eddie Solomon, Odell Jones and Rick Rhoden pitched well in spurts and could improve. So could Rod Scurry, who became the top left-hander out of the bullpen upon Grant Jackson's departure. Enrique Romo topped the relievers with nine saves. The overall pitching has to improve if the Bucs are to return to the first division because it's apparent the batting order no longer is menacing.

Three-time bat king Bill Madlock signed sky-high pact.

FIELDING: No individual leaders, but still decent, as last year's .979 percentage suggests. Moreno, who made only one error in 309 chances, ranks with the best center fielders and Pena made a strong showing behind the plate. Everyone knows of Parker's great arm, but he wasn't reaching balls like he used to during his problem-plagued 1981. Traded Tim Foli was a decent shortstop, but players like him and the departed Phil Garner only look good when everyone around them is meshing. Now youngsters Dale Berra and Vance Law will get their chance in the middle of the infield. Veterans Bill Robinson and Willie Montanez are slicker first basemen, but the job belongs to Thompson.

OUTLOOK: Not good. The Pirates haven't grown old gracefully and simply haven't been the same since their fade of 1980. Manager Chuck Tanner once had the knack of surviving injuries and making the best use of his entire roster, but that isn't happening anymore because depth and quality aren't as evident. The Pirates sorely miss what Willie Stargell used to provide on and off the bench and are a shadow of their former selves. The Bucs sorely need a facelift, not merely some cosmetic changes, or else the improving Mets and Cubs might find somebody else to occupy the cellar in the NL East.

PITTSBURGH PIRATES 1982 ROSTER

MANAGER Chuck Tanner
Coaches—Harvey Haddix, Joe Lonnett, Al Monchak, Bob
        Skinner

PITCHERS

No.	Name	1981 Club	W-L	IP	SO	ERA	B-T	Ht.	Wt.	Born
26	Bibby, Jim	Pittsburgh	6-3	94	48	2.49	R-R	6-5	250	10/29/44 Franklinton, NC
47	Camacho, Ernie	Portland	2-3	38	31	4.74	R-R	6-1	180	2/1/56 Salinas, CA
		Pittsburgh	0-1	22	11	4.91				
45	Candelaria, John	Pittsburgh	2-2	41	14	3.51	L-L	6-7	232	11/6/53 New York, NY
49	Cruz, Victor	Portland	2-1	24	19	4.13	R-R	5-9	215	12/24/57 Dominican Republic
		Pittsburgh	1-1	34	28	2.65				
51	Cuen, Eleno	Portland	3-8	77	36	6.55	R-R	6-2	200	8/18/54 Mexico
—	DeLeon, Jose	Buffalo	12-6	159	158	3.11	R-R	6-3	210	12/20/60 Dominican Republic
—	Griffin, Tom	San Francisco	8-8	129	83	3.77	R-R	6-3	210	2/22/48 Los Angeles, CA
22	Jones, Odell	Portland	12-6	153	135	3.53	R-R	6-3	174	1/13/53 Tulare, CA
		Pittsburgh	4-5	54	30	3.33				
34	Long, Robert	Portland	15-3	157	97	2.98	R-R	6-3	178	11/11/54 Jasper, TN
		Pittsburgh	1-2	20	8	5.85				
52	Mohorcic, Dale	Portland	5-3	98	39	4.35	R-R	6-3	205	1/25/56 Maple Hts., OH
25	Perez, Pascual	Portland	1-2	31	11	4.94	R-R	6-2	162	5/17/57 Dominican Republic
		Pittsburgh	2-7	86	46	3.98				
29	Rhoden, Rick	Pittsburgh	9-4	136	76	3.90	R-R	6-3	195	5/16/53 Boynton Beach, FL
43	Robinson, Don	Pittsburgh	0-3	38	17	5.92	R-R	6-4	231	6/8/57 Ashland, KY
15	Romo, Enrique	Pittsburgh	1-3	42	23	4.50	R-R	5-11	185	7/15/47 Mexico
—	Sarmiento, Manny	Pawtucket	7-5	96	99	2.34	R-R	5-11	170	2/2/56 Venezuela
19	Scurry, Rod	Pittsburgh	4-5	74	65	3.77	L-L	6-2	180	3/17/56 Sacramento, CA
44	Solomon, Eddie	Pittsburgh	8-6	127	38	3.12	R-R	6-3	190	2/9/51 Perry, GA
27	Tekulve, Kent	Pittsburgh	5-5	65	34	2.49	R-R	6-4	175	3/5/47 Cincinnati, OH

CATCHERS

No.	Name	1981 Club	H	HR	RBI	Pct.	B-T	Ht.	Wt.	Born
35	Alexander, Gary	Pittsburgh	10	1	6	.213	R-R	6-2	200	3/27/53 Los Angeles, CA
—	Harper, Brian	S. Lake City	192	28	122	.350	R-R	6-2	195	10/16/59 Los Angeles, CA
		California	3	0	1	.273				
—	Holland, John	Buffalo	81	19	53	.250	R-R	6-1	195	9/14/58 Florence, SC
16	Nicosia, Steve	Pittsburgh	39	2	18	.231	R-R	5-10	185	8/6/55 Paterson, NJ
58	Ortiz, Adalberto	Portland	93	2	46	.269	R-R	5-11	174	10/24/59 Puerto Rico
6	Pena, Tony	Pittsburgh	63	2	17	.300	R-R	6-0	175	11/20/57 Dominican Republic

INFIELDERS

No.	Name	1981 Club	H	HR	RBI	Pct.	B-T	Ht.	Wt.	Born
4	Berra, Dale	Pittsburgh	56	2	27	.241	R-R	6-0	190	12/13/56 Ridgewood, NJ
2	Law, Vance	Portland	86	5	43	.277	R-R	6-2	185	10/1/56 Boise, ID
		Pittsburgh	9	0	3	.134				
5	Madlock, Bill	Pittsburgh	95	6	45	.341	R-R	5-11	180	1/12/51 Memphis, TN
14	Montanez, Willie	Mont.-Pitt.	21	1	6	.210	L-L	6-1	193	4/1/48 Puerto Rico
3	Ray, Johnny	Tucson	183	5	83	.349	B-R	5-11	170	3/1/57 Chouteau, OK
		Pittsburgh	25	0	6	.245				
11	Smith, Jim	Portland	97	10	51	.251	R-R	6-3	185	9/8/54 Santa Monica, CA
8	Stargell, Willie	Pittsburgh	17	0	9	.283	L-L	6-3	225	3/6/41 Earlsboro, OK
10	Thompson, Jason	Pittsburgh	54	15	42	.242	L-L	6-4	220	7/6/54 Hollywood, CA
50	Vargas, Hediberto	Buffalo	115	25	84	.272	R-R	6-4	205	2/23/59 Puerto Rico

OUTFIELDERS

No.	Name	1981 Club	H	HR	RBI	Pct.	B-T	Ht.	Wt.	Born
24	Easler, Mike	Pittsburgh	97	7	42	.286	L-R	6-1	196	11/29/50 Cleveland, OH
55	Frobel, Doug	Buffalo	120	28	78	.251	L-R	6-4	196	6/6/59 Canada
12	Lacy, Lee	Pittsburgh	57	2	10	.268	R-R	6-1	175	4/10/48 Longview, TX
18	Moreno, Omar	Pittsburgh	120	1	35	.276	L-L	6-3	175	10/24/52 Panama
39	Parker, Dave	Pittsburgh	62	9	48	.258	L-R	6-5	220	6/9/51 Jackson, MS
28	Robinson, Bill	Pittsburgh	19	2	8	.216	R-R	6-3	197	6/26/43 McKeesport, PA
37	Rodriguez, Jose	Buffalo	65	13	34	.277	R-R	6-1	173	2/25/58 Dominican Republic
		Portland	15	0	2	.246				

PIRATE PROFILES

BILL MADLOCK 31 5-11 180   Bats R Throws R

Won third batting title and became only sixth player in major-league history to do it with two teams . . . Played only 82 games, so drew criticism for backing into bat crown with limited appearances down the stretch . . . Lifetime average of .316 tops among active players . . . Batted .326 in first half and soared to title with .355 second half (50-for-141) . . . Born Jan. 12, 1951, in Memphis, Tenn. . . . Batted .325 in April, .350 in May and .386 in August . . . Ranked fourth in slugging percentage (.495) and only Mike Schmidt had a better on-base average than Mad Dog's .413 . . . Batted .375 in 1979 World Series, helping pennant rush after coming to Pittsburgh in midseason swap with S.F. . . . Candid comments wore out welcome with Giants and he prodded for a trade to escape Candlestick cold . . . Spurned free-agent market to re-sign with Pirates after 1981 season.

Year	Club	Pos.	G	AB	R	H	2B	3B	HR	RBI	SB	Avg.
1973	Texas	3B	21	77	16	27	5	3	1	5	3	.351
1974	Chicago (NL). . . .	3B	128	453	65	142	21	5	9	54	11	.313
1975	Chicago (NL). . . .	3B	130	514	77	182	29	7	7	.64	9	.354
1976	Chicago (NL). . . .	3B	142	514	68	174	36	1	15	84	15	.339
1977	San Francisco . . .	2B-3B	140	533	70	161	28	1	12	46	13	.302
1978	San Francisco . . .	2B-1B	122	447	76	138	26	3	15	44	16	.309
1979	SF-Pitts.	3B-2B-1B	154	560	85	167	26	5	14	85	32	.298
1980	Pittsburgh	3B-1B	137	494	62	137	22	4	10	53	16	.277
1981	Pittsburgh	3B-1B	82	279	35	95	23	1	6	45	18	.341
	Totals		1056	3871	554	1223	216	30	89	480	133	.316

DAVE PARKER 30 6-5 220   Bats L Throws R

Former hero turned into goat by impersonating a blimp during 1981 season . . . Seemed likely to be swapped away by Bucs . . . Batted .286 in first half, but added 20 pounds during strike layoff and was putrid (.228) in second half . . . Used to be best hitter in baseball . . . Now not even No. 1 on Pirates . . . Born June 9, 1951, in Cincinnati . . . Started to stir fans' wrath during injury-plagued 1980 in which he dropped under .300 for first time in six years . . . Tremendous talent who won back-to-back batting titles in 1977-78 . . . Batted .345 in '79 World Series . . . MVP of All-Star Game in 1979 for great throw

. . . Won third Gold Glove that year for sterling outfield play in right . . . Eager to shed fat-cat reputation.

Year	Club	Pos.	G	AB	R	H	2B	3B	HR	RBI	SB	Avg.
1973	Pittsburgh	OF	54	139	17	40	9	1	4	14	1	.288
1974	Pittsburgh	OF-1B	73	220	27	62	10	3	4	29	3	.282
1975	Pittsburgh	OF	148	558	75	172	35	10	25	101	8	.308
1976	Pittsburgh	OF	138	537	82	168	28	10	13	90	19	.313
1977	Pittsburgh	OF-2B	159	637	107	215	44	8	21	88	17	.338
1978	Pittsburgh	OF	148	581	102	194	32	12	30	117	20	.334
1979	Pittsburgh	OF	158	622	109	193	45	7	25	94	20	.310
1980	Pittsburgh	OF	139	518	71	153	31	1	17	79	10	.295
1981	Pittsburgh	OF	67	240	29	62	14	3	9	48	6	.258
	Totals		1084	4052	619	1259	248	55	148	660	104	.311

MIKE EASLER 31 6-1 196　　　　　Bats L Throws R

Didn't become fulltime big leaguer until age 28, but is making up for lost time . . . Batted .350 in May and entered strike batting .317 . . . Slumped to .256 when play resumed . . . Blossomed as a parttime player in '80 and was regular most of '81 . . . Has hit at all levels, but was labelled a good Triple-A hitter until his .338 with 1980 Bucs . . . Born Nov. 29, 1950, in Cleveland . . . American Association batting king with .352 mark at Tulsa in '76 . . . Nicknamed "Line Drive" . . . Proved he could play after Astros, Red Sox and Angels gave up on him . . . Roberto Clemente Award winner as Pirates' MVP in '80 . . . Merely adequate as outfielder, but who cares?

Year	Club	Pos.	G	AB	R	H	2B	3B	HR	RBI	SB	Avg.
1973	Houston	OF	6	7	1	0	0	0	0	0	0	.000
1974	Houston	PH	15	15	0	1	0	0	0	0	0	.067
1975	Houston	PH	5	5	0	0	0	0	0	0	0	.000
1976	California	DH	21	54	6	13	1	1	0	4	1	.241
1977	Pittsburgh	OF	10	18	3	8	2	0	1	5	0	.444
1979	Pittsburgh	OF	55	54	8	15	1	1	2	11	0	.278
1980	Pittsburgh	OF	132	393	66	133	27	3	21	74	5	.338
1981	Pittsburgh	OF	95	339	43	97	18	5	7	42	4	.286
	Totals		339	885	127	267	49	10	31	136	10	.302

TOM GRIFFIN 34 6-3 210　　　　　Bats R Throws R

Rejuvenated pitcher's eight wins with Giants were his high since 1976 . . . Became a full-time starter in spring and was 4-5 in the first half and 4-3 following resumption of season . . . Outstanding August (3-1, 2.06), which included first shutout since mid-70s . . . Also registered first complete game since 1976 and was club strikeout leader . . . Born Feb. 22, 1948, in Los Angeles . . . NL Rookie Pitcher of the Year in 1969 with Houston . . . Signed as free agent by S.F. in spring of 1979

. . . Dealt to Pirates for promising young first baseman-outfielder Doe Boyland during 1981 winter meetings.

Year	Club	G	IP	W	L	Pct.	SO	BB	H	ERA
1969	Houston	31	188	11	10	.524	200	93	156	3.54
1970	Houston	23	111	3	13	.188	72	72	118	5.76
1971	Houston	10	38	0	6	.000	29	20	44	4.74
1972	Houston	39	94	5	4	.556	83	38	92	3.26
1973	Houston	25	100	4	6	.400	69	46	83	4.14
1974	Houston	34	211	14	10	.583	110	89	202	3.54
1975	Houston	17	79	3	8	.273	56	46	89	5.35
1976	Hou.-S.D.	31	112	9	6	.600	69	79	100	4.10
1977	San Diego	38	151	6	9	.400	79	88	144	4.47
1978	California	24	56	3	4	.429	35	31	63	4.02
1979	San Francisco	59	94	5	6	.455	82	46	83	3.93
1980	San Francisco	42	108	5	1	.833	79	49	80	2.75
1981	San Francisco	22	129	8	8	.500	83	57	121	3.77
	Totals	395	1471	76	91	.455	1046	754	1375	4.00

TONY PENA 24 6-0 175   Bats R Throws R

An outstanding rookie season, gradually
knocking Steve Nicosia out of catching job
. . . Batted .271 in first half and sealed job
with .314 second half . . . Has improved with
age . . . Lackluster career in low minors, but
batted .313 in Double-A in '79 at Buffalo,
belting 34 homers . . . Next year was a .329
hitter with Portland of the Pacific Coast
League . . . Born Nov. 20, 1957, in Monte Cristi, Dominican Republic . . . Good speed for a catcher, belting 14 triples in 1980
. . . Began pro career as outfielder . . . Switched to third base
and then behind the plate . . . Did not play high school ball, but
signed with Bucs off sandlots at age 17.

Year	Club	Pos.	G	AB	R	H	2B	3B	HR	RBI	SB	Avg.
1980	Pittsburgh	C	8	21	1	9	1	1	0	1	0	.429
1981	Pittsburgh	C	66	210	16	63	9	1	2	17	1	.300
	Totals		74	231	17	72	10	2	2	18	1	.312

OMAR MORENO 29 6-3 175   Bats L Throws L

Used .291 second half to finish with respectable season . . . Batted .261 first half . . .
Sharp drop in stolen bases after career-high 96
in 1980 . . . A .333 hitter in 1979 World Series
. . . Excellent center fielder, but had been
overshadowed by Phillies' Garry Maddox until last year . . . Born Oct. 24, 1952, in Puerto
Armuelles, Panama . . . Began pro career at
age 16 and batted .290 for Bradenton in '69 . . . Played in all 103
games last year and has streak of 368 going despite dislocated

finger suffered in 1980 . . . Set Pirates' stolen-base record with 71 in '78 and has broken it twice . . . Had 59 steals in first four seasons and erupted with 78 in 1973.

Year	Club	Pos.	G	AB	R	H	2B	3B	HR	RBI	SB	Avg.
1975	Pittsburgh	OF	6	6	1	1	0	0	0	0	1	.167
1976	Pittsburgh	OF	48	122	24	33	4	1	2	12	15	.270
1977	Pittsburgh	OF	150	492	69	118	19	9	7	34	53	.240
1978	Pittsburgh	OF	155	515	95	121	15	7	2	33	71	.235
1979	Pittsburgh	OF	162	695	110	196	21	12	8	69	77	.282
1980	Pittsburgh	OF	162	676	87	168	20	13	2	36	96	.249
1981	Pittsburgh	OF	103	434	62	120	18	8	1	35	39	.276
	Totals..........		786	2940	448	757	97	50	22	219	352	.257

JASON THOMPSON 27 6-4 220   Bats L Throws L

Sluggish NL debut, batting .171 in first half . . . But turned it around after strike with .321 average and eight homers . . . Topped club in homers and tied Moreno with six game-winning RBI . . . Obtained in spring swap with Angels and immediately was traded to Yankees, but Bowie Kuhn voided deal . . . With Willie Stargell and Bill Robinson fading, Kuhn probably did Bucs a favor . . . Fits Pirates' slugging mold . . . Born July 6, 1954, in Hollywood, Cal. . . . Joined Angels in midseason trade with Detroit in 1980 and batted .317 with 17 homers for them . . . Hit 14 homers in first 16 games for Tigers after recall from minors in '76 . . . Attended Cal State Northridge.

Year	Club	Pos.	G	AB	R	H	2B	3B	HR	RBI	SB	Avg.
1976	Detroit.........	1B	123	412	45	90	12	1	17	54	2	.218
1977	Detroit.........	1B	158	585	87	158	24	5	31	105	0	.270
1978	Detroit.........	1B	153	589	79	169	25	3	26	96	0	.287
1979	Detroit.........	1B	145	492	58	121	16	1	20	79	2	.246
1980	Det.-Calif.	1B	138	438	69	126	19	0	21	90	2	.288
1981	Pittsburgh	1B	86	223	36	54	13	0	15	42	0	.242
	Totals..........		803	2739	374	718	109	10	130	466	6	.262

EDDIE SOLOMON 31 6-3 190   Bats R Throws R

A bargain for Bucs after failing in Atlanta . . . Has 15-9 record and sub-3.00 ERA over two years . . . Was 5-3 with a 2.85 ERA in first half, 3-3 over second half . . . Stuck it to former Braves teammates in '80, holding them scoreless in 12⅔ innings . . . Born Feb. 9, 1951, in Perry, Ga. . . . Originally signed by Dodgers, but bounced around before landing in Atlanta rotation . . . Nicknamed "Buddy Jay" . . . Involved in deal which sent Burt Hooton from Cubs to L.A. . . . Might be

on verge of shaking journeyman label . . . Injuries on others on
staff gave him chance to start and he's made most of it.

Year	Club	G	IP	W	L	Pct.	SO	BB	H	ERA
1973	Los Angeles	4	6	0	0	.000	6	4	10	7.50
1974	Los Angeles	4	6	0	0	.000	2	2	5	1.50
1975	Chicago (NL)	6	7	0	0	.000	3	6	7	1.29
1976	St. Louis	26	37	1	1	.500	19	16	45	4.86
1977	Atlanta	18	89	6	6	.500	54	34	110	4.55
1978	Atlanta	37	106	4	6	.400	64	50	98	4.08
1979	Atlanta	31	186	7	14	.333	96	51	184	4.21
1980	Pittsburgh	26	100	7	3	.700	35	37	96	2.70
1981	Pittsburgh	22	127	8	6	.571	38	27	133	3.12
	Totals	174	664	33	36	.478	317	227	688	3.81

RICK RHODEN 28 6-3 195   Bats R Throws R

Made poor swap with Dodgers (for Jerry
Reuss in '79) look a little better by becoming
Bucs' big winner last year . . . Won first six
starts and was 6-1 with a 3.28 ERA in first half
. . . Split six decisions after the strike . . . 3-0
with a 2.17 ERA in April and 3-0, 2.83 in May
. . . Solid .630 major-league winning percent-
age . . . Born May 16, 1953, in Boynton
Beach, Fla. . . . That he reached majors is a minor miracle . . .
Victim of osteomyelitis as a youth, wore a brace until he was 12
. . . Was budding Dodger star, but sat out most of 1979 with
bone chips in right shoulder after joining Bucs . . . Proved he
belonged back in bigs by going 6-3 with a 2.94 ERA at Portland
in '80 before recall.

Year	Club	G	IP	W	L	Pct.	SO	BB	H	ERA
1974	Los Angeles	4	9	1	0	1.000	7	4	5	2.00
1975	Los Angeles	26	99	3	3	.500	40	32	94	3.09
1976	Los Angeles	27	181	12	3	.800	77	53	165	2.98
1977	Los Angeles	31	216	16	10	.615	122	63	223	3.75
1978	Los Angeles	30	165	10	8	.556	79	51	160	3.65
1979	Pittsburgh	1	5	0	1	.000	2	2	5	7.20
1980	Pittsburgh	20	127	7	5	.583	70	40	133	3.83
1981	Pittsburgh	21	136	9	4	.692	76	53	147	3.90
	Totals	160	938	58	34	.630	473	298	932	3.55

JIM BIBBY 37 6-5 250   Bats R Throws R

Staff ERA leader was 4-3 in first half, 2-0 in
second . . . NL Player of the Week, May
18-25, with .500 batting average, 0.56 ERA
and 32 consecutive outs over two games . . .
Has lost only 20 games for Bucs in four years,
winning 45 . . . Pitched well in 1979 post-sea-
son play, but had no decisions . . . Topped
NL pitchers in won-lost percentage in '79 and
'80 . . . Born Oct. 29, 1944, in Franklinton, N.C. . . . Brother of

ex-NBA guard Henry Bibby . . . Has 33-11 record since becoming full-time starter with Bucs in '79 . . . Fired a no-hitter for Texas against Oakland in '73 . . . Played basketball at Lynchburg College . . . Signed as a free agent by Pirates in 1978 and club has no regrets.

Year	Club	G	IP	W	L	Pct.	SO	BB	H	ERA
1972	St. Louis	6	40	1	3	.250	28	19	29	3.38
1973	St. Louis	6	16	0	2	.000	12	17	19	9.56
1973	Texas	26	180	9	10	.474	155	106	121	3.25
1974	Texas	41	264	19	19	.500	149	113	255	4.74
1975	Tex.-Clev.	36	181	7	15	.318	93	78	172	3.88
1976	Cleveland	34	163	13	7	.650	84	56	162	3.20
1977	Cleveland	37	207	12	13	.480	141	73	197	3.57
1978	Pittsburgh	34	107	8	7	.533	72	39	100	3.53
1979	Pittsburgh	34	138	12	4	.750	103	47	110	2.80
1980	Pittsburgh	35	238	19	6	.760	144	88	210	3.33
1981	Pittsburgh	14	94	6	3	.667	48	26	79	2.49
	Totals	303	1628	106	89	.544	996	662	1454	3.61

TOP PROSPECTS

BOB LONG 27 6-3 178   **Bats R Throws R**
Was sensational with 15-3 record and 2.98 ERA at Portland last year before going 1-2 with Bucs . . . Struggled in first two minor-league seasons before being taught to throw underhanded in 1978 (8-4, 2.81 ERA at Salem) . . . Born Nov. 11, 1954, in Jasper, Tenn. . . . Shortstop Vance Law, Vern's son, also might make his move after three straight Triple-A seasons (.277 at Portland in '81) . . . Born Oct. 1, 1956, in Boise, Idaho.

MANAGER CHUCK TANNER: "Chuckles" was doing less of that last year as club dropped from contending status . . . Finished last in second half and it appeared time has come for phasing out some oldtimers and malcontents . . . Extremely patient manager . . . Known for utilizing entire roster and keeping clubs fresh for the stretch . . . It hasn't happened last two years . . . Club no longer battling Expos and Phillies for division supremacy . . . Born July 4, 1929, in New Castle, Pa. . . . Hailed for great job with White Sox and Dick

Allen in '72 . . . Swapped by A's Charlie Finley to Bucs for Manny Sanguillen after '76 season . . . Placed second in 1977-78, scaring Phillies with 37-12 stretch run in '78 . . . Went all the way in '79 . . . One of most personable and cooperative skippers in the game . . . A former outfielder . . . Homered on first at-bat as Milwaukee rookie in '55 and it was downhill thereafter.

GREATEST CATCHER

Subject to controversy because there is no clear-cut favorite. In that case, the moderns rate an edge because they are vivid on the mind. Of the oldies, Al Lopez surely deserves mention because his 1,918 games caught is a major-league mark. But Lopez played with four different clubs and was with the Bucs only from 1940-46, and war-year stats usually are inflated.

As a result, the all-time Bucs' backstop is Manny Sanguillen. He couldn't hold Lopez' glove, but Manny could hit. He averaged .299 in a dozen seasons with Pittsburgh and had four plus-.300 years, topped by a hefty .328 mark in '75. He also topped NL catchers with 72 assists in '71 and has the distinction of having been traded for present manager Chuck Tanner.

ALL-TIME PIRATE SEASON RECORDS

BATTING: Arky Vaughan, .385, 1935
HRs: Ralph Kiner, 54, 1949
RBIs: Paul Waner, 131, 1927
STEALS: Omar Moreno, 96, 1980
WINS: Jack Chesbro, 28, 1902
STRIKEOUTS: Bob Veale, 276, 1965

ST. LOUIS CARDINALS

(Note: At press time, Ozzie Smith had not been signed.)

TEAM DIRECTORY: Chairman of the Board-Pres.: August A. Busch, Jr.: GM-Mgr.: Whitey Herzog; Senior VP: Stan Musial; Dir. Play. Per.: Lee Thomas; Dir. Pub. Rel.: Jim Toomey; Trav. Sec.: C.J. Cherre. Home: Busch Memorial Stadium (50,100). Field distances: 330, l.f. line; 414, c.f.; 330, r.f. line. Spring training: St. Petersburg, Fla.

SCOUTING REPORT

HITTING: It never seems to be a problem for this club, which batted .265 last year. Garry Templeton will be missed, but Lonnie Smith adds punch to the outfield following the departed Lezcano's disappointing 1981. Dane Iorg (.327), Keith Hernandez (.306), Ken Oberkfell (.293) and George Hendrick (.284) all hit with authority last season and Darrell Porter figures to improve a .224 mark.

Bruce Sutter hurled Cards out of many hairy situations.

If there is a weakness, it's a lack of power. Only the Padres and the Astros belted fewer homers last year and Hendrick, with 18 homers, was the only legitimate longball threat. Hernandez and Porter, however, should be able to provide more homers this year. But it's a solid lineup, one which has to hide only Ozzie Smith's puny average. The Cardinals, or make that Whitey Herzog, may live to regret the swapping of Templeton, a gifted athlete who batted .288 despite his emotional problems last season.

PITCHING: A big question mark. Bruce Sutter's performance disguised a weak staff and it doesn't figure to be any stronger minus the traded Lary Sorensen and Silvio Martinez, swapped to Cleveland. Ex-Padre Steve Mura could develop in new surroundings, but the only reliable returning starters are Bob Forsch (10-5, 3.19) and John Martin (8-5, 3.41), unless free-agent Joaquin Andujar returns. Thank heavens for Sutter, whose 25 saves last year gave the Redbirds what they desperately needed, a bullpen stopper. Youngsters like Andy Rincon and John Fulgham could provide a bonus, but it isn't likely. The Cards are a club with serious pitching problems that could prove fatal in their pursuit of a pennant.

FIELDING: The Cards topped the NL with a .981 percentage last year and there's no need to expect a dropoff with Ozzie Smith at shortstop. Smith was the most effective shortstop in the NL, rating tops in assists (442), total chances (658), fielding percentage (.976) and outrageous salary demands. Tom Herr was the best second baseman, leading in assists (374), total chances (590), double plays (74) and percentage (.992), so he and Ozzie could form an awesome DP duo. Oberkfell is no Ken Reitz at third, but Hernandez ranks with the slickest first basemen, so the infield is solid. It had better be, considering that pitching.

OUTLOOK: A tough team to figure. The Cardinals were the biggest winner in the NL East last season, thanks to Sutter, but they don't seem to be in Montreal's class. Herzog obviously did something right with his facelifting and the youth movement could continue to pay off if outfielders Smith and David Green, the key man in the Rollie Fingers swap, come through. Lonnie steps into Templeton's leadoff role and will have some big shoes to fill for a second straight year after supplanting Greg Luzinski at Philly. The strengths are hitting and fielding. Two out of three isn't bad and you obviously can survive in the NL East without super pitching. But a wobbly staff figures to be the club's ultimate downfall, Sutter notwithstanding.

ST. LOUIS CARDINALS 1982 ROSTER

MANAGER Whitey Herzog
Coaches—Chuck Hiller, Hub Kittle, Hal Lanier, Dave Ricketts, Red Schoendienst

PITCHERS

No.	Name	1981 Club	W-L	IP	SO	ERA	B-T	Ht.	Wt.	Born
40	Bair, Doug	Cin-St. L.	4-2	55	30	5.07	R-R	6-0	180	8/22/49 Defiance, OH
—	Citarella, Ralph	Arkansas	8-9	125	81	3.81	R-R	6-0	180	2/7/58 Colonia, NJ
		Springfield	0-0	7	2	3.86				
49	DeLeon, Luis	Springfield	8-7	99	96	2.54	R-R	6-1	153	8/19/58 Puerto Rico
		St. Louis	0-1	15	8	2.40				
31	Forsch, Bob	St. Louis	10-5	124	41	3.19	R-R	6-4	200	1/13/50 Sacramento, CA
41	Fulgham, John	St. Louis			disabled list		R-R	6-2	205	6/9/56 St. Louis, MO
36	Kaat, Jim	St. Louis	6-6	53	8	3.40	L-L	6-5	195	11/7/38 Zeeland, MI
47	LaPoint, Dave	Springfield	13-9	172	129	3.20	L-L	6-3	205	7/29/59 Glens Falls, NY
		St. Louis	1-0	11	2	4.09				
34	Littell, Mark	Springfield	1-2	19	6	3.72	L-R	6-3	210	1/17/53 Cape Girardeau, MO
		St. Louis	1-3	41	22	4.39				
33	Martin, John	Springfield	2-2	37	25	1.45	B-L	6-0	190	4/11/56 Wyandotte, MI
		St. Louis	8-5	103	36	3.41				
—	Mura, Steve	San Diego	5-14	139	70	4.27	R-R	6-2	188	2/12/55 New Orleans, LA
46	Rincon, Andy	Arkansas	0-2	8	6	7.04	R-R	6-3	195	3/5/59 Pico Rivera, CA
		Springfield	1-3	22	17	6.45				
		St. Louis	3-1	36	13	1.75				
32	Shirley, Bob	St. Louis	6-4	79	36	4.10	R-L	5-11	185	6/25/54 Cushing, OK
—	Stanton, Mike	Cleveland	3-3	43	34	4.40	R-R	6-2	200	9/25/52 St. Louis, MO
48	Stuper, John	Springfield	6-14	161	59	4.93	R-R	6-2	200	5/9/57 Butler, PA
42	Sutter, Bruce	St. Louis	3-5	82	57	2.63	R-R	6-2	190	1/8/53 Lancaster, PA

CATCHERS

No.	Name	1981 Club	H	HR	RBI	Pct.	B-T	Ht.	Wt.	Born
—	Bjorkman, George	Springfield	82	28	66	.254	R-R	6-2	190	8/26/56 Ontario, CA
11	Brummer, Glenn	Springfield	18	1	8	.234	R-R	6-0	185	11/23/54 Olney, IL
		St. Louis	6	0	2	.200				
15	Porter, Darrell	St. Louis	39	6	31	.224	L-R	6-0	193	1/17/52 Joplin, MO
23	Sanchez, Orlando	St. Louis	14	0	6	.286	L-R	6-0	185	9/7/56 Puerto Rico
18	Tenace, Gene	St. Louis	30	5	22	.233	R-R	6-0	190	10/10/46 Russelton, PA

INFIELDERS

No.	Name	1981 Club	H	HR	RBI	Pct.	B-T	Ht.	Wt.	Born
12	Calise, Mike	Springfield	104	26	87	.234	R-R	6-1	200	3/16/57 Norwalk, CT
7	DeSa, Joe	Springfield	145	12	73	.292	L-L	5-11	170	7/27/59 Honolulu, HI
—	Gonzalez, Joe	St. Petersburg	124	0	39	.268	B-R	5-10	155	1/21/60 Dominican Republic
14	Gonzalez, Julio	St. Louis	7	1	3	.318	R-R	5-11	165	12/25/53 Puerto Rico
37	Hernandez, Keith	St. Louis	115	8	48	.306	L-L	6-0	185	10/20/53 San Francisco, CA
28	Herr, Tom	St. Louis	110	0	46	.268	B-R	6-0	175	4/4/56 Lancaster, PA
10	Oberkfell, Ken	St. Louis	110	2	45	.293	L-R	6-1	185	5/4/56 Highland, IL
—	Paris, Kelly	Springfield	78	6	31	.267	B-R	6-0	175	10/17/57 Encinada, CA
5	Ramsey, Mike	St. Louis	32	0	9	.258	B-R	6-1	170	3/29/54 Roanoke, VA
—	Santana, Rafael	Arkansas	76	0	19	.227	R-R	6-1	165	1/31/58 Dominican Republic
		Springfield	4	1	2	.500				
1	Smith, Ozzie	San Diego	100	0	21	.222	B-R	5-10	150	12/26/54 Mobile, AL

OUTFIELDERS

No.	Name	1981 Club	H	HR	RBI	Pct.	B-T	Ht.	Wt.	Born
27	Green, David	Springfield	116	10	67	.270	R-R	6-3	165	12/4/60 Nicaragua
		St. Louis	5	0	2	.147				
25	Hendrick, George	St. Louis	112	18	61	.284	R-R	6-3	195	10/18/49 Los Angeles, CA
19	Iorg, Dane	St. Louis	71	2	39	.327	L-R	6-0	180	5/11/50 Eureka, CA
21	Landrum, Tito	St. Louis	31	0	10	.261	R-R	5-11	175	10/25/54 Joplin, MO
—	McGee, Willie	Nashville	125	7	63	.322	R-R	6-0	160	12/2/58 San Francisco, CA
29	Roof, Gene	Springfield	112	11	44	.348	B-R	6-2	180	1/13/58 Mayfield, KY
		St. Louis	18	0	3	.300				
—	Smith, Lonnie	Philadelphia	57	2	11	.324	R-R	5-9	170	12/22/55 Chicago, IL

CARDINAL PROFILES

OZZIE SMITH 27 5-10 150   **Bats R Throws R**

Now a Card after being traded for Garry Templeton . . . Started strong for Padres in '81 with .259 first half, but slumped to .183 rest of way . . . Went 34 straight games without an error and teamed with second baseman Juan Bonilla to form one of the best double play combinations in majors . . . Born Dec. 16, 1954, in Mobile, Ala., home of boyhood heroes Henry Aaron and Willie McCovey . . . Won first Gold Glove in 1980, establishing major-league mark for assists by a shortstop with 621 . . . Glenn Wright of the Pirates held old mark of 601 in 1924 . . . Attended Cal Poly San Luis Obispo (Calif.) . . . Played only one year of minor-league ball and was runnerup to Bob Horner for NL rookie honors in 1978.

Year	Club	Pos.	G	AB	R	H	2B	3B	HR	RBI	SB	Avg.
1978	San Diego	SS	159	590	69	152	17	6	1	46	40	.258
1979	San Diego	SS	156	587	77	124	18	6	0	27	28	.211
1980	San Diego	SS	158	609	67	140	18	5	0	35	57	.230
1981	San Diego	SS	110	450	53	100	11	2	0	21	22	.222
	Totals		583	2236	266	516	64	19	1	129	147	.231

KEITH HERNANDEZ 28 6-0 185   **Bats L Throws L**

Used a great second half to regain .300 form and push lifetime average to within percentage points of .300 . . . Batted .272 in first half and zoomed to .341 after the strike . . . Played in all of Cards' games . . . Was disenchanted during winter of 1980-81 when it seemed Ted Simmons would play first base and he would have to shift to outfield . . . Trade of Simmons settled that . . . Born Oct. 20, 1953, in San Francisco . . . Father Tony was outfielder in Cardinals system . . . Batting champion in '79 and in contention for a repeat in '80 . . . Co-MVP winner with Willie Stargell in '79 . . . A .500 hitter in high school and a three-sport standout . . . Gets job done without much fanfare . . . In Steve Garvey mold.

Year	Club	Pos.	G	AB	R	H	2B	3B	HR	RBI	SB	Avg.
1974	St. Louis	1B	14	34	3	10	1	2	0	2	0	.294
1975	St. Louis	1B	64	188	20	47	8	2	3	20	0	.250
1976	St. Louis	1B	129	374	54	108	21	5	7	46	4	.289
1977	St. Louis	1B	161	560	90	163	41	4	15	91	7	.291
1978	St. Louis	1B	159	542	90	138	32	4	11	64	13	.255
1979	St. Louis	1B	161	610	116	210	48	11	11	105	11	.344
1980	St. Louis	1B	159	595	111	191	39	8	16	99	14	.321
1981	St. Louis	1B	103	376	65	115	27	4	8	48	12	.306
	Totals		950	3279	549	982	217	40	71	475	61	.299

GEORGE HENDRICK 32 6-3 195   Bats R Throws R

Gets job done with *no* fanfare . . . Still won't talk to press, but is a dynamite hitter . . . His 18 homers last year were 10 more than any teammate . . . Batted .277 with 10 homers in first half and hit .291 when play resumed . . . A steal for St. Louis, coming from Padres in exchange for Eric Rasmussen . . . Didn't blossom as a hitter until he came to NL in swap with Cleveland . . . Began career as non-descript reserve outfielder with powerhouse A's of early '70s . . . Another gem Charles Finley let get away . . . Born Oct. 18, 1949, in Los Angeles . . . Belted three home runs in one game for Indians in '73 . . . Has .600 average in three All-Star Games.

Year	Club	Pos.	G	AB	R	H	2B	3B	HR	RBI	SB	Avg.
1971	Oakland	OF	42	114	8	27	4	1	0	8	0	.237
1972	Oakland	OF	58	121	10	22	1	1	4	15	3	.182
1973	Cleveland	OF	113	440	64	118	18	0	21	61	7	.268
1974	Cleveland	OF	139	495	65	138	23	1	19	67	6	.279
1975	Cleveland	OF	145	561	82	145	21	2	24	86	6	.258
1976	Cleveland	OF	149	551	72	146	20	3	25	81	4	.265
1977	San Diego	OF	152	541	75	168	25	2	23	81	11	.311
1978	SD-St. Louis	OF	138	493	64	137	31	1	20	75	2	.278
1979	St. Louis	OF	140	493	67	148	27	1	16	75	2	.300
1980	St. Louis	OF	150	572	73	173	33	2	25	109	6	.302
1981	St. Louis	OF	101	394	67	112	19	3	18	61	4	.284
	Totals		1327	4775	647	1334	222	17	195	719	51	.279

KEN OBERKFELL 25 6-1 185   Bats L Throws R

Solid season at third base, replacing Reitz and missing only one game . . . Just missed third straight .300 campaign . . . Batted .283 in first half, .301 thereafter . . . Made successful switch from second base, where he topped NL with .985 fielding percentage in '79 . . . Born May 4, 1956, in Highland, Ill. . . . "Obie" knocked veteran Mike Tyson out of job in '79 and has been a standout at plate and afield ever since . . . Signed as free-agent bargain by Cards in '76 . . . Broke in with a bang, batting .352 at Johnson City and .351 at St. Petersburg in '75, attracting attention . . . Missed six weeks of '80 season following collision with Steve Garvey.

Year	Club	Pos.	G	AB	R	H	2B	3B	HR	RBI	SB	Avg.
1977	St. Louis	2B	9	9	0	1	0	0	0	1	0	.111
1978	St. Louis	2B-3B	24	50	7	6	1	0	0	0	0	.120
1979	St. Louis	2B-3B-SS	135	369	53	111	19	5	1	35	4	.301
1980	St. Louis	2B-3B	116	422	58	128	27	6	3	46	4	.303
1981	St. Louis	2B-3B	102	376	43	110	12	6	2	45	4	.293
	Totals		386	1226	161	356	59	17	6	127	12	.290

TOM HERR 25 6-0 175   **Bats S Throws R**

Another infield standout . . . Took over Oberkfell's second-base job, didn't miss a game and had an outstanding first full season in bigs . . . Topped club in steals and triples . . . Batted .277-.260 in two halves . . . Proved he was ready for majors with .312 average in first 37 games at Springfield in 1980 . . . Batted .337 with Cards that September and earned starting call in '81 . . . Born April 4, 1956, in Lancaster, Pa. . . . Attends U. of Delaware . . . Showed great speed in minors . . . Had 50 thefts at St. Petersburg in '77 . . . Collected first major-league hit off Mickey Lolich in only second official at-bat . . . On 1978 Texas League All-Star squad . . . Four-sport whiz as a prep.

Year	Club	Pos.	G	AB	R	H	2B	3B	HR	RBI	SB	Avg.
1979	St. Louis	2B	14	10	4	2	0	0	0	1	1	.200
1980	St. Louis	2B-SS	76	222	29	55	12	5	0	15	9	.248
1981	St. Louis	2B-SS	103	411	50	110	14	9	0	46	23	.268
	Totals..........		193	643	83	167	26	14	0	62	33	.260

DARRELL PORTER 30 6-0 193   **Bats L Throws R**

Rejoined Whitey Herzog last year and had tough adjustment to NL . . . Battled injuries and .173 average in first half, but hiked mark to .246 after the strike . . . A four-time AL All-Star . . . Batted .333 and .357, respectively, in '77 and '78 Championship Series under Herzog at Kansas City . . . Born Jan. 17, 1952, in Joplin, Mo. . . . A superstar in '79 . . . Became only second catcher in AL history with more than 100 walks, runs and RBI in same season, duplicating Mickey Cochrane's feat . . . Slipped in '80 after missing spring training while participating in an alcohol rehabilitation program . . . Brewers' No. 1 selection in 1970 draft . . . All-American quarterback as an Oklahoma prep.

Year	Club	Pos.	G	AB	R	H	2B	3B	HR	RBI	SB	Avg.
1971	Milwaukee	C	22	70	4	15	2	0	2	9	2	.214
1972	Milwaukee	C	18	56	2	7	1	0	1	2	0	.125
1973	Milwaukee	C	117	350	50	89	19	2	16	67	5	.254
1974	Milwaukee	C	131	432	59	104	15	4	12	56	8	.241
1975	Milwaukee	C	130	409	66	95	12	5	18	60	2	.232
1976	Milwaukee	C	119	389	43	81	14	1	5	32	2	.208
1977	Kansas City.....	C	130	425	61	117	21	3	16	60	1	.275
1978	Kansas City.....	C	150	520	77	138	27	6	18	78	0	.265
1979	Kansas City.....	C	157	533	101	155	23	10	20	112	3	.291
1980	Kansas City.....	C	118	418	51	104	14	2	7	51	1	.249
1981	St. Louis	C	61	174	22	39	10	2	6	31	1	.224
	Totals..........		1153	3776	536	944	158	35	121	558	25	.250

DANE IORG 31 6-0 180   Bats L Throws R

Rhymes with gorge . . . Team batting leader in '81 as an outfielder-first baseman . . . Batted .304 in first half and did even better after the strike, matching Hernandez' .341 . . . Could be trade bait because so many promising young outfielders are coming up . . . Has been club's most reliable pinch-batter . . . Born May 11, 1950, in Eureka, Calif. . . . American Association batting champ with a .371 mark for Springfield in '78 . . . All-American at Brigham Young before beginning sensational minor-league career . . . As a pro rookie, he batted .367 for Walla Walla in '71 . . . Has batted .300 in eight of 11 pro seasons . . . A Utah sporting goods salesman in off-season.

Year	Club	Pos.	G	AB	R	H	2B	3B	HR	RBI	SB	Avg.
1977	Phil.-St. L.	1B-OF	42	62	5	15	2	0	0	6	0	.242
1978	St. Louis	OF	35	85	6	23	4	1	0	4	0	.271
1979	St. Louis	OF-1B	79	179	12	52	11	1	1	21	1	.291
1980	St. Louis	OF-1B-3B	105	251	33	76	23	1	3	36	1	.303
1981	St. Louis	OF-1B	75	217	23	71	11	2	2	39	2	.327
	Totals		336	794	79	237	51	5	6	106	4	.298

BRUCE SUTTER 29 6-2 190   Bats R Throws R

The main reason Cards had best record in NL East . . . Did exactly what he was expected to do . . . Made club instant contender and was most effective reliever in league with 25 saves . . . 14 of his saves came in second half . . . Set NL record with 37 saves for Cubs in '79 . . . Had been rumored going to St. Louis for two years before Cards gave up Ken Reitz, Ty Walker and Leon Durham for him in December 1980 . . . Born Jan. 8, 1953, in Lancaster, Pa. . . . Totaled 158 saves in six seasons as consistently outstanding reliever . . . Split-finger fastball dips sharply at plate and baffles most hitters . . . American Leaguers included in that lot . . . Has appeared in last four All-Star Games, notching two wins and two saves, not allowing a run and yielding only two hits in 6⅔ innings.

Year	Club	G	IP	W	L	Pct.	SO	BB	H	ERA
1976	Chicago (NL)	52	83	6	3	.667	73	26	63	2.71
1977	Chicago (NL)	62	107	7	3	.700	129	23	69	1.35
1978	Chicago (NL)	64	99	8	10	.444	106	34	82	3.18
1979	Chicago (NL)	62	101	6	6	.500	110	32	67	2.23
1980	Chicago (NL)	60	102	5	8	.385	76	34	90	2.65
1981	St. Louis	48	82	3	5	.375	57	24	64	2.63
	Totals	348	574	35	35	.500	551	173	435	2.43

JIM KAAT 43 6-5 195   Bats L Throws L

Rates special mention because of his longevity and persistence . . . Oldest player in majors . . . This year becomes pitcher with most years of service in majors, 24 . . . Kitty one of few major leaguers to play in four decades . . . Contract purchased from Yankees in 1980 and made contribution by figuring in 23 St. Louis victories in two years . . . Born Nov. 7, 1938, in Zeeland, Mich. . . . Only Gaylord Perry has more career wins among active pitchers . . . Won 16 consecutive Gold Gloves (1962-77) . . . With 812 games, he ranks sixth all-time . . . His 16 home runs are most by an active pitcher . . . AL Pitcher of the Year in '66 . . . Fired 10-inning shutout over Mets in '80, first blanking since '78.

Year	Club	G	IP	W	L	Pct.	SO	BB	H	ERA
1959	Washington	3	5	0	2	.000	2	4	7	12.60
1960	Washington	13	50	1	5	.167	25	31	48	5.58
1961	Minnesota	36	201	9	17	.346	122	82	188	3.90
1962	Minnesota	39	269	18	14	.563	173	75	243	3.14
1963	Minnesota	31	178	10	10	.500	105	38	195	4.20
1964	Minnesota	36	243	17	11	.607	171	60	231	3.22
1965	Minnesota	45	264	18	11	.621	154	63	267	2.83
1966	Minnesota	41	305	25	13	.658	205	55	271	2.74
1967	Minnesota	42	263	16	13	.552	211	42	269	3.05
1968	Minnesota	30	208	14	12	.538	130	40	192	2.94
1969	Minnesota	40	242	14	13	.519	139	75	252	3.50
1970	Minnesota	45	230	14	10	.583	120	58	244	3.56
1971	Minnesota	39	260	13	14	.481	137	47	275	3.32
1972	Minnesota	15	113	10	2	.833	64	20	94	2.07
1973	Minn.-Chi. (AL)	36	224	15	13	.536	109	43	250	4.38
1974	Chicago (AL)	42	277	21	13	.618	142	63	263	2.92
1975	Chicago (AL)	43	304	20	14	.588	142	77	321	3.11
1976	Philadelphia	38	228	12	14	.462	83	32	241	3.47
1977	Philadelphia	35	160	6	11	.353	55	40	211	5.40
1978	Philadelphia	26	140	8	5	.615	48	32	150	4.11
1979	Philadelphia	3	8	1	0	1.000	2	5	9	4.50
1979	New York (AL)	40	58	2	3	.400	23	14	64	3.88
1980	New York (AL)	4	5	0	1	.000	1	1	8	7.20
1980	St. Louis	49	130	8	7	.533	36	33	140	3.81
1981	St. Louis	41	53	6	6	.500	8	17	60	3.40
	Totals	812	4418	278	234	.543	2407	1050	4493	3.44

BOB FORSCH 32 6-4 200   Bats R Throws R

Registered lowest ERA since 1975 and was club's most reliable starter . . . Posted 6-2 record and 3.15 ERA in first half and was 4-3 down the stretch . . . Was in an 11-win rut for three straight years after lone 20-win season in 1977 . . . Lost nine straight in tough-luck '78 . . . Fired no-hitter against Phillies that April . . . Born Jan. 13, 1950, in Sacramento, Calif.

. . . Brother of Angels' ace Ken . . . A good hitter, he batted .295 in 1980 . . . He and Ken are only brother act to pitch no-hitters in majors . . . Was all-league third baseman as pro rookie in '68, but began pitching in '70 . . . One year later, he was 11-7 with a 3.13 ERA at Cedar Rapids.

Year	Club	G	IP	W	L	Pct.	SO	BB	H	ERA
1974	St. Louis	19	100	7	4	.636	39	34	84	2.97
1975	St. Louis	34	230	15	10	.600	108	70	213	2.86
1976	St. Louis	33	194	8	10	.444	76	71	209	3.94
1977	St. Louis	35	217	20	7	.741	95	69	210	3.48
1978	St. Louis	34	234	11	17	.393	114	97	205	3.69
1979	St. Louis	33	219	11	11	.500	92	52	215	3.82
1980	St. Louis	31	215	11	10	.524	87	33	225	3.77
1981	St. Louis	20	124	10	5	.667	41	29	106	3.19
	Totals	239	1533	93	74	.557	652	455	1467	3.51

LONNIE SMITH 26 5-9 170   Bats R Throws R

Three-team swap in November brought this fleet outfielder from Philadelphia via Cleveland to St. Louis . . . Sporting News Rookie of the Year in '80 . . . Batted .256 for Phillies in first half last year and soared to .383 after strike for overall .324 that kept Garry Maddox on bench during playoffs . . . Got chance in '79 when Greg Luzinski was injured . . . Born Dec. 22, 1955, in Chicago . . . Phillies' No. 1 selection in 1974 draft . . . 33 steals in '79 is most ever by a Phillies rookie . . . Averaged .308 and 39 steals in six minor-league seasons . . . Stole 56 bases at Spartanburg in '75 and 66 for Oklahoma City in '78.

Year	Club	Pos.	G	AB	R	H	2B	3B	HR	RBI	SB	Avg.
1978	Philadelphia	OF	17	4	6	0	0	0	0	0	4	.000
1979	Philadelphia	OF	17	30	4	5	2	0	0	3	2	.167
1980	Philadelphia	OF	100	298	69	101	14	4	3	20	33	.339
1981	Philadelphia	OF	62	176	40	57	14	3	2	11	21	.324
	Totals		196	508	139	163	30	7	5	34	60	.321

TOP PROSPECTS

GEORGE BJORKMAN 25 6-2 190   Bats R Throws R

A real sleeper . . . Cards didn't protect him after '80 season and he was drafted by Giants . . . They gave him back and he blossomed into American Association all-star catcher . . . Blasted league-leading 28 homers for Springfield after never hitting more than nine in a season previously . . . Born Aug. 26, 1956, in Ontario, Cal. . . . Cards also high on outfielders Gene Roof (.300 in 60 at-bats with Cards after .348 season at Springfield) and David Green (19 triples in 1980, .270 at Springfield), the key youngster obtained from Milwaukee in the Rollie Fingers deal.

MANAGER WHITEY HERZOG: Survived a stormy season in which he doubled as manager and GM . . . Replaced Ken Boyer in 1980 and went 38-35 down the stretch . . . Club's 59-43 record was best in NL East, but no playoffs because Cards finished second in both races . . . At 30-20, Cards had fewest losses in NL during first half, but 34-21 Phillies played more games and won by one and one-half games . . . Born Nov. 9, 1931, in New Athens, Ill. . . . Rode crest of Kansas City's success with three straight division crowns, 1976-78 . . . Manager of the Year in '76 . . . Former major-league outfielder . . . Originally signed by Yankees . . . In the finest St. Louis tradition of Frank "Trader" Lane, made sweeping changes, dealing 13 players and adding 10 during December 1980 winter meetings.

GREATEST CATCHER

Ted Simmons rates the honors because of longevity and excellence, concluding his 12-year Cardinals career with a .298 average before going to Milwaukee. Simmons batted over .300 six times for St. Louis, including a .332 mark in '75. He knocked in more than 90 runs six times.

He also established a career record for National League switch-hitters with 172 home runs. Underrated defensively because of his hitting prowess, Simmons twice topped the league's catchers in putouts and assists.

No St. Louis catcher was in his class as a hitter—not even Joe Garagiola—though Walker Cooper was productive during the war years.

ALL-TIME CARDINAL SEASON RECORDS

BATTING: Rogers Hornsby, .424, 1924
HRs: Johnny Mize, 43, 1940
RBIs: Joe Medwick, 154, 1937
STEALS: Lou Brock, 118, 1974
WINS: Dizzy Dean, 30, 1934
STRIKEOUTS: Bob Gibson, 274, 1970

MAJOR LEAGUE YEAR-BY-YEAR LEADERS

NATIONAL LEAGUE MVP

Year	Player, Club
1931	Frank Frisch, St. Louis Cardinals
1932	Chuck Klein, Philadelphia Phillies
1933	Carl Hubbell, New York Giants
1934	Dizzy Dean, St. Louis Cardinals
1935	Gabby Hartnett, Chicago Cubs
1936	Carl Hubbell, New York Giants
1937	Joe Medwick, St. Louis Cardinals
1938	Ernie Lombardi, Cincinnati Reds
1939	Buck Walters, Cincinnati Reds
1940	Frank McCormick, Cincinnati Reds
1941	Dolph Camilli, Brooklyn Dodgers
1942	Mort Cooper, St. Louis Cardinals
1943	Stan Musial, St. Louis Cardinals
1944	Marty Marion, St. Louis Cardinals
1945	Phil Cavaretta, Chicago Cubs
1946	Stan Musial, St. Louis Cardinals
1947	Bob Elliott, Boston Braves
1948	Stan Musial, St. Louis Cardinals
1949	Jackie Robinson, Brooklyn Dodgers
1950	Jim Konstanty, Philadelphia Phillies
1951	Roy Campanella, Brooklyn Dodgers
1952	Hank Sauer, Chicago Cubs
1953	Roy Campanella, Brooklyn Dodgers
1954	Willie Mays, New York Giants
1955	Roy Campanella, Brooklyn Dodgers
1956	Don Newcombe, Brooklyn Dodgers
1957	Hank Aaron, Milwaukee Braves
1958	Ernie Banks, Chicago Cubs
1959	Ernie Banks, Chicago Cubs
1960	Dick Groat, Pittsburgh Pirates

Year	Player, Club
1961	Frank Robinson, Cincinnati Reds
1962	Maury Wills, Los Angeles Dodgers
1963	Sandy Koufax, Los Angeles Dodgers
1964	Ken Boyer, St. Louis Cardinals
1965	Willie Mays, San Francisco Giants
1966	Roberto Clemente, Pittsburgh Pirates
1967	Orlando Cepeda, St. Louis Cardinals
1968	Bob Gibson, St. Louis Cardinals
1969	Willie McCovey, San Francisco Giants
1970	Johnny Bench, Cincinnati Reds
1971	Joe Torre, St. Louis Cardinals
1972	Johnny Bench, Cincinnati Reds
1973	Pete Rose, Cincinnati Reds
1974	Steve Garvey, Los Angeles Dodgers
1975	Joe Morgan, Cincinnati Reds
1976	Joe Morgan, Cincinnati Reds
1977	George Foster, Cincinnati Reds
1978	Dave Parker, Pittsburgh Pirates
1979	Keith Hernandez, St. Louis Cardinals
	Willie Stargell, Pittsburgh Pirates
1980	Mike Schmidt, Philadelphia Phillies
1981	Mike Schmidt, Philadelphia Phillies

AMERICAN LEAGUE MVP

Year	Player, Club
1931	Lefty Grove, Philadelphia Athletics
1932	Jimmy Foxx, Philadelphia Athletics
1933	Jimmy Foxx, Philadelphia Athletics
1934	Mickey Cochrane, Detroit Tigers
1935	Hank Greenberg, Detroit Tigers
1936	Lou Gehrig, New York Yankees
1937	Charley Gehringer, Detroit Tigers
1938	Jimmy Foxx, Boston Red Sox
1939	Joe DiMaggio, New York Yankees
1940	Hank Greenberg, Detroit Tigers
1941	Joe DiMaggio, New York Yankees
1942	Joe Gordon, New York Yankees
1943	Spud Chandler, New York Yankees
1944	Hal Newhouser, Detroit Tigers
1945	Hal Newhouser, Detroit Tigers
1946	Ted Williams, Boston Red Sox
1947	Joe DiMaggio, New York Yankees

Detroit's Denny McLain won 31 and was AL MVP in 1968.

Year	Player, Club
1948	Lou Boudreau, Cleveland Indians
1949	Ted Williams, Boston Red Sox
1950	Phil Rizzuto, New York Yankees
1951	Yogi Berra, New York Yankees
1952	Bobby Shantz, Philadelphia Athletics
1953	Al Rosen, Cleveland Indians
1954	Yogi Berra, New York Yankees
1955	Yogi Berra, New York Yankees
1956	Mickey Mantle, New York Yankees
1957	Mickey Mantle, New York Yankees
1958	Jackie Jensen, Boston Red Sox
1959	Nellie Fox, Chicago White Sox
1960	Roger Maris, New York Yankees
1961	Roger Maris, New York Yankees
1962	Mickey Mantle, New York Yankees
1963	Elston Howard, New York Yankees
1964	Brooks Robinson, Baltimore Orioles
1965	Zolio Versalles, Minnesota Twins
1966	Frank Robinson, Baltimore Orioles
1967	Carl Yastrzemski, Boston Red Sox
1968	Dennis McLain, Detroit Tigers
1969	Harmon Killebrew, Minnesota Twins
1970	Boog Powell, Baltimore Orioles
1971	Vida Blue, Oakland A's
1972	Dick Allen, Chicago White Sox
1973	Reggie Jackson, Oakland A's
1974	Jeff Burroughs, Texas Rangers
1975	Fred Lynn, Boston Red Sox
1976	Thurman Munson, New York Yankees
1977	Rod Carew, Minnesota Twins
1978	Jim Rice, Boston Red Sox
1979	Don Baylor, California Angels
1980	George Brett, Kansas City Royals
1981	Rollie Fingers, Milwaukee Brewers

NATIONAL LEAGUE
Batting Champions

Year	Player, Club	Avg.
1876	Roscoe Barnes, Chicago	.403
1877	James White, Boston	.385
1878	Abner Dalrymple, Milwaukee	.356
1879	Cap Anson, Chicago	.407
1880	George Gore, Chicago	.365
1881	Cap Anson, Chicago	.399
1882	Dan Brouthers, Buffalo	.367
1883	Dan Brouthers, Buffalo	.371
1884	Jim O'Rourke, Buffalo	.350
1885	Roger Connor, New York	.371
1886	Mike Kelly, Chicago	.388
1887	Cap Anson, Chicago	.421
1888	Cap Anson, Chicago	.343
1889	Dan Brouthers, Boston	.373
1890	Jack Glassock, New York	.336
1891	Billy Hamilton, Philadelphia	.338
1892	Cupid Childs, Cleveland	.335
	Dan Brouthers, Brooklyn	.335
1893	Hugh Duffy, Boston	.378
1894	Hugh Duffy, Boston	.438
1895	Jesse Burkett, Cleveland	.423
1896	Jesse Burkett, Cleveland	.410
1897	Willie Keeler, Baltimore	.432
1898	Willie Keeler, Baltimore	.379
1899	Ed Delahanty, Philadelphia	.408
1900	Honus Wagner, Pittsburgh	.380
1901	Jesse Burkett, St. Louis Cardinals	.382
1902	C.H. Beaumont, Pittsburgh Pirates	.357
1903	Honus Wagner, Pittsburgh Pirates	.355
1904	Honus Wagner, Pittsburgh Pirates	.349
1905	J. Seymour Bentley, Cincinnati Reds	.377
1906	Honus Wagner, Pittsburgh Pirates	.339
1907	Honus Wagner, Pittsburgh Pirates	.350
1908	Honus Wagner, Pittsburgh Pirates	.354
1909	Honus Wagner, Pittsburgh Pirates	.339
1910	Sherwood Magee, Philadelphia Phillies	.331
1911	Honus Wagner, Pittsburgh Pirates	.334
1912	Heinie Zimmerman, Chicago Cubs	.372
1913	Jake Daubert, Brooklyn Dodgers	.350
1914	Jake Daubert, Brooklyn Dodgers	.329

Year	Player, Club	Avg.
1915	Larry Doyle, New York Giants	.320
1916	Hal Chase, Cincinnati Reds	.339
1917	Edd Roush, Cincinnati Reds	.341
1918	Zack Wheat, Brooklyn Dodgers	.335
1919	Edd Roush, Cincinnati Reds	.321
1920	Rogers Hornsby, St. Louis Cardinals	.370
1921	Rogers Hornsby, St. Louis Cardinals	.397
1922	Rogers Hornsby, St. Louis Cardinals	.401
1923	Rogers Hornsby, St. Louis Cardinals	.384
1924	Rogers Hornsby, St. Louis Cardinals	.424
1925	Rogers Hornsby, St. Louis Cardinals	.403
1926	Bubbles Hargrave, Cincinnati Reds	.353
1927	Paul Waner, Pittsburgh Pirates	.380
1928	Rogers Hornsby, Boston Braves	.387
1929	Lefty O'Doul, Philadelphia Phillies	.398
1930	Bill Terry, New York Giants	.401
1931	Chick Hafey, St. Louis Cardinals	.349
1932	Lefty O'Doul, Brooklyn Dodgers	.368
1933	Chuck Klein, Philadelphia Phillies	.368
1934	Paul Waner, Pittsburgh Pirates	.362
1935	Arky Vaughn, Pittsburgh Pirates	.385
1936	Paul Waner, Pittsburgh Pirates	.373
1937	Joe Medwick, St. Louis Cardinals	.374
1938	Ernie Lombardi, Cincinnati Reds	.342
1939	Johnny Mize, St. Louis Cardinals	.349
1940	Debs Garms, Pittsburgh Pirates	.355
1941	Pete Reiser, Brooklyn Dodgers	.343
1942	Ernie Lombardi, Boston Braves	.330
1943	Stan Musial, St. Louis Cardinals	.330
1944	Dixie Walker, Brooklyn Dodgers	.357
1945	Phil Cavarretta, Chicago Cubs	.355
1946	Stan Musial, St. Louis Cardinals	.365
1947	Harry Walker, St. L. Cardinals-Phila. Phillies	.363
1948	Stan Musial, St. Louis Cardinals	.376
1949	Jackie Robinson, Brooklyn Dodgers	.342
1950	Stan Musial, St. Louis Cardinals	.346
1951	Stan Musial, St. Louis Cardinals	.355
1952	Stan Musial, St. Louis Cardinals	.336
1953	Carl Furillo, Brooklyn Dodgers	.344
1954	Willie Mays, New York Giants	.345
1955	Richie Ashburn, Philadelphia Phillies	.338
1956	Hank Aaron, Milwaukee Braves	.328
1957	Stan Musial, St. Louis Cardinals	.351
1958	Richie Ashburn, Philadelphia Phillies	.350

Ernie Lombardi won batting crowns in 1938 and in 1942.

Year	Player, Club	Avg.
1959	Hank Aaron, Milwaukee Braves	.328
1960	Dick Groat, Pittsburgh Pirates	.325
1961	Roberto Clemente, Pittsburgh Pirates	.351
1962	Tommy Davis, Los Angeles Dodgers	.346
1963	Tommy Davis, Los Angeles Dodgers	.326
1964	Roberto Clemente, Pittsburgh Pirates	.339
1965	Roberto Clemente, Pittsburgh Pirates	.329
1966	Matty Alou, Pittsburgh Pirates	.342
1967	Roberto Clemente, Pittsburgh Pirates	.357
1968	Pete Rose, Cincinnati Reds	.335
1969	Pete Rose, Cincinnati Reds	.348
1970	Rico Carty, Atlanta Braves	.366
1971	Joe Torre, St. Louis Cardinals	.363
1972	Billy Williams, Chicago Cubs	.333
1973	Pete Rose, Cincinnati Reds	.338
1974	Ralph Garr, Atlanta Braves	.353
1975	Bill Madlock, Chicago Cubs	.354
1976	Bill Madlock, Chicago Cubs	.339
1977	Dave Parker, Pittsburgh Pirates	.338
1978	Dave Parker, Pittsburgh Pirates	.334
1979	Keith Hernandez, St. Louis Cardinals	.344
1980	Bill Buckner, Chicago Cubs	.324
1981	Bill Madlock, Pittsburgh Pirates	.341

AMERICAN LEAGUE
Batting Champions

Year	Player, Club	Avg.
1901	Napoleon Lajoie, Philadelphia Athletics	.422
1902	Ed Delahanty, Washington Senators	.376
1903	Napoleon Lajoie, Cleveland Indians	.355
1904	Napoleon Lajoie, Cleveland Indians	.381
1905	Elmer Flick, Cleveland Indians	.306
1906	George Stone, St. Louis Browns	.358
1907	Ty Cobb, Detroit Tigers	.350
1908	Ty Cobb, Detroit Tigers	.324
1909	Ty Cobb, Detroit Tigers	.377
1910	Ty Cobb, Detroit Tigers	.385
1911	Ty Cobb, Detroit Tigers	.420
1912	Ty Cobb, Detroit Tigers	.410
1913	Ty Cobb, Detroit Tigers	.390
1914	Ty Cobb, Detroit Tigers	.368
1915	Ty Cobb, Detroit Tigers	.370
1916	Tris Speaker, Cleveland Indians	.386
1917	Ty Cobb, Detroit Tigers	.383
1918	Ty Cobb, Detroit Tigers	.382
1919	Ty Cobb, Detroit Tigers	.384
1920	George Sisler, St. Louis Browns	.407
1921	Harry Heilmann, Detroit Tigers	.393
1922	George Sisler, St. Louis Browns	.420
1923	Harry Heilmann, Detroit Tigers	.398
1924	Babe Ruth, New York Yankees	.378
1925	Harry Heilmann, Detroit Tigers	.393
1926	Heinie Manush, Detroit Tigers	.377
1927	Harry Heilmann, Detroit Tigers	.398
1928	Goose Goslin, Washington Senators	.379
1929	Lew Fonseca, Cleveland Indians	.369
1930	Al Simmons, Philadelphia Athletics	.381
1931	Al Simmons, Philadelphia Athletics	.390
1932	David Alexander, Detroit Tigers-Boston Red Sox	.367
1933	Jimmy Foxx, Philadelphia Athletics	.356
1934	Lou Gehrig, New York Yankees	.365
1935	Buddy Myer, Washington Senators	.349
1936	Luke Appling, Chicago White Sox	.388
1937	Charlie Gehringer, Detroit Tigers	.371
1938	Jimmy Foxx, Boston Red Sox	.349
1939	Joe DiMaggio, New York Yankees	.381
1940	Joe DiMaggio, New York Yankees	.352

Year	Player, Club	Avg.
1941	Ted Williams, Boston Red Sox	.406
1942	Ted Williams, Boston Red Sox	.356
1943	Luke Appling, Chicago White Sox	.328
1944	Lou Boudreau, Cleveland Indians	.327
1945	Snuffy Stirnweiss, New York Yankees	.309
1946	Mickey Vernon, Washington Senators	.353
1947	Ted Williams, Boston Red Sox	.343
1948	Ted Williams, Boston Red Sox	.369
1949	George Kell, Detroit Tigers	.343
1950	Billy Goodman, Boston Red Sox	.354
1951	Ferris Fain, Philadelphia Athletics	.344
1952	Ferris Fain, Philadelphia Athletics	.327
1953	Mickey Vernon, Washington Senators	.337
1954	Bobby Avila, Cleveland Indians	.341
1955	Al Kaline, Detroit Tigers	.340
1956	Mickey Mantle, New York Yankees	.353
1957	Ted Williams, Boston Red Sox	.388
1958	Ted Williams, Boston Red Sox	.328
1959	Harvey Kuenn, Detroit Tigers	.353
1960	Pete Runnels, Boston Red Sox	.320
1961	Norm Cash, Detroit Tigers	.361
1962	Pete Runnels, Boston Red Sox	.326
1963	Carl Yastrzemski, Boston Red Sox	.321
1964	Tony Oliva, Minnesota Twins	.323
1965	Tony Oliva, Minnesota Twins	.321
1966	Frank Robinson, Baltimore Orioles	.316
1967	Carl Yastrzemski, Boston Red Sox	.326
1968	Carl Yastrzemski, Boston Red Sox	.301
1969	Rod Carew, Minnesota Twins	.332
1970	Alex Johnson, California Angels	.329
1971	Tony Oliva, Minnesota Twins	.337
1972	Rod Carew, Minnesota Twins	.318
1973	Rod Carew, Minnesota Twins	.350
1974	Rod Carew, Minnesota Twins	.364
1975	Rod Carew, Minnesota Twins	.359
1976	George Brett, Kansas City Royals	.333
1977	Rod Carew, Minnesota Twins	.388
1978	Rod Carew, Minnesota Twins	.333
1979	Fred Lynn, Boston Red Sox	.333
1980	George Brett, Kansas City Royals	.390
1981	Carney Lansford, Boston Red Sox	.336

NATIONAL LEAGUE
Home Run Leaders

Year	Player, Club	HRs
1900	Herman Long, Boston	12
1901	Sam Crawford, Cincinnati Reds	16
1902	Tom Leach, Pittsburgh Pirates	6
1903	Jim Sheckard, Brooklyn Dodgers	9
1904	Harry Lumley, Brooklyn Dodgers	9
1905	Fred Odwell, Cincinnati Reds	9
1906	Tim Jordan, Brooklyn Dodgers	12
1907	Dave Brian, Boston	10
1908	Tim Jordan, Brooklyn Dodgers	12
1909	Jim Murray, New York Giants	7
1910	Fred Beck, Boston	10
	Frank Schulte, Chicago Cubs	10
1911	Frank Schulte, Chicago Cubs	21
1912	Heinie Zimmerman, Chicago Cubs	14
1913	Gavvy Cravath, Philadelphia Phillies	19
1914	Gavvy Cravath, Philadelphia Phillies	19
1915	Gavvy Cravath, Philadelphia Phillies	24
1916	Dave Robertson, New York Giants	12
	Cy Williams, Chicago Cubs	12
1917	Gavvy Cravath, Philadelphia Phillies	12
	Dave Robertson, New York Giants	12
1918	Gavvy Cravath, Philadelphia Phillies	8
1919	Gavvy Cravath, Philadelphia Phillies	12
1920	Cy Williams, Philadelphia Phillies	15
1921	George Kelly, New York Giants	23
1922	Rogers Hornsby, St. Louis Cardinals	39
1923	Cy Williams, Philadelphia Phillies	41
1924	Jack Fournier, Brooklyn Dodgers	27
1925	Rogers Hornsby, St. Louis Cardinals	39
1926	Hack Wilson, Chicago Cubs	21
1927	Cy Williams, Philadelphia Phillies	30
	Hack Wilson, Chicago Cubs	30
1928	Jim Bottomley, St. Louis Cardinals	31
	Hack Wilson, Chicago Cubs	31
1929	Chuck Klein, Philadelphia Phillies	43
1930	Hack Wilson, Chicago Cubs	56
1931	Chuck Klein, Philadelphia Phillies	31
1932	Chuck Klein, Philadelphia Phillies	38
	Mel Ott, New York Giants	38
1933	Chuck Klein, Philadelphia Phillies	43

Year	Player, Club	HRs
1934	Rip Collins, St. Louis Cardinals	35
	Mel Ott, New York Giants	35
1935	Wally Berger, Boston Braves	34
1936	Mel Ott, New York Giants	33
1937	Joe Medwick, St. Louis Cardinals	31
	Mel Ott, New York Giants	31
1938	Mel Ott, New York Giants	36
1939	Johnny Mize, St. Louis Cardinals	28
1940	Johnny Mize, St. Louis Cardinals	43
1941	Dolph Camilli, Brooklyn Dodgers	34
1942	Mel Ott, New York Giants	30
1943	Bill Nicholson, Chicago Cubs	29
1944	Bill Nicholson, Chicago Cubs	33
1945	Tommy Holmes, Boston Braves	28
1946	Ralph Kiner, Pittsburgh Pirates	23
1947	Ralph Kiner, Pittsburgh Pirates	51
	Johnny Mize, New York Giants	51
1948	Ralph Kiner, Pittsburgh Pirates	40
	Johnny Mize, New York Giants	40
1949	Ralph Kiner, Pittsburgh Pirates	54
1950	Ralph Kiner, Pittsburgh Pirates	47
1951	Ralph Kiner, Pittsburgh Pirates	42
1952	Ralph Kiner, Pittsburgh Pirates	37
	Hank Sauer, Chicago Cubs	37
1953	Eddie Mathews, Milwaukee Braves	47
1954	Ted Kluszewski, Cincinnati Reds	49
1955	Willie Mays, New York Giants	51
1956	Duke Snider, Brooklyn Dodgers	43
1957	Hank Aaron, Milwaukee Braves	44
1958	Ernie Banks, Chicago Cubs	47
1959	Eddie Mathews, Milwaukee Braves	46
1960	Ernie Banks, Chicago Cubs	41
1961	Orlando Cepeda, San Francisco Giants	46
1962	Willie Mays, San Francisco Giants	49
1963	Hank Aaron, Milwaukee Braves	44
	Willie McCovey, San Francisco Giants	44
1964	Willie Mays, San Francisco Giants	47
1965	Willie Mays, San Francisco Giants	52
1966	Hank Aaron, Atlanta Braves	44
1967	Hank Aaron, Atlanta Braves	39
1968	Willie McCovey, San Francisco Giants	36
1969	Willie McCovey, San Francisco Giants	45
1970	Johnny Bench, Cincinnati Reds	45
1971	Willie Stargell, Pittsburgh Pirates	48

Year	Player, Club	HRs
1972	Johnny Bench, Cincinnati Reds	40
1973	Willie Stargell, Pittsburgh Pirates	44
1974	Mike Schmidt, Philadelphia Phillies	36
1975	Mike Schmidt, Philadelphia Phillies	38
1976	Mike Schmidt, Philadelphia Phillies	38
1977	George Foster, Cincinnati Reds	52
1978	George Foster, Cincinnati Reds	40
1979	Dave Kingman, Chicago Cubs	48
1980	Mike Schmidt, Philadelphia Phillies	48
1981	Mike Schmidt, Philadelphia Phillies	31

AMERICAN LEAGUE
Home Run Leaders

Year	Player, Club	HRs
1901	Napoleon Lajoie, Philadelphia Athletics	13
1902	Ralph Seybold, Philadelphia Athletics	16
1903	John Freeman, Boston Red Sox	13
1904	Harry Davis, Philadelphia Athletics	10
1905	Harry Davis, Philadelphia Athletics	8
1906	Harry Davis, Philadelphia Athletics	12
1907	Harry Davis, Philadelphia Athletics	8
1908	Sam Crawford, Detroit Tigers	7
1909	Ty Cobb, Detroit Tigers	9
1910	Garland Stahl, Boston Red Sox	10
1911	Frank (Home Run) Baker, Philadelphia Athletics	9
1912	Frank (Home Run) Baker, Philadelphia Athletics	10
1913	Frank (Home Run) Baker, Philadelphia Athletics	12
1914	Frank (Home Run) Baker, Philadelphia Athletics	8
	Sam Crawford, Detroit Tigers	8
1915	Bob Roth, Cleveland Indians	7
1916	Wally Pipp, New York Yankees	12
1917	Wally Pipp, New York Yankees	9
1918	Babe Ruth, Boston Red Sox	11
	Clarence Walker, Philadelphia Athletics	11
1919	Babe Ruth, Boston Red Sox	29
1920	Babe Ruth, New York Yankees	54
1921	Babe Ruth, New York Yankees	59
1922	Ken Williams, St. Louis Browns	39
1923	Babe Ruth, New York Yankees	43

Year	Player, Club	HRs
1924	Babe Ruth, New York Yankees	46
1925	Bob Meusel, New York Yankees	33
1926	Babe Ruth, New York Yankees	47
1927	Babe Ruth, New York Yankees	60
1928	Babe Ruth, New York Yankees	54
1929	Babe Ruth, New York Yankees	46
1930	Babe Ruth, New York Yankees	49
1931	Babe Ruth, New York Yankees	46
	Lou Gehrig, New York Yankees	46
1932	Jimmy Foxx, Philadelphia Athletics	58
1933	Jimmy Foxx, Philadelphia Athletics	48
1934	Lou Gehrig, New York Yankees	49
1935	Hank Greenberg, Detroit Tigers	36
	Jimmy Foxx, Philadelphia Athletics	36
1936	Lou Gehrig, New York Yankees	49
1937	Joe DiMaggio, New York Yankees	49
1938	Hank Greenberg, Detroit Tigers	46
1939	Jimmy Foxx, Boston Red Sox	35
1940	Hank Greenberg, Detroit Tigers	41
1941	Ted Williams, Boston Red Sox	37
1942	Ted Williams, Boston Red Sox	36
1943	Rudy York, Detroit Tigers	34
1944	Nick Etten, New York Yankees	22
1945	Vern Stephens, St. Louis Browns	24
1946	Hank Greenberg, Detroit Tigers	44
1947	Ted Williams, Boston Red Sox	32
1948	Joe DiMaggio, New York Yankees	39
1949	Ted Williams, Boston Red Sox	43
1950	Al Rosen, Cleveland Indians	37
1951	Gus Zernial, Philadelphia Athletics	33
1952	Larry Doby, Cleveland Indians	32
1953	Al Rosen, Cleveland Indians	43
1954	Larry Doby, Cleveland Indians	32
1955	Mickey Mantle, New York Yankees	37
1956	Mickey Mantle, New York Yankees	52
1957	Roy Sievers, Washington Senators	42
1958	Mickey Mantle, New York Yankees	42
1959	Rocky Colavito, Cleveland Indians	42
	Harmon Killebrew, Washington Senators	42
1960	Mickey Mantle, New York Yankees	40
1961	Roger Maris, New York Yankees	61
1962	Harmon Killebrew, Minnesota Twins	48
1963	Harmon Killebrew, Minnesota Twins	45
1964	Harmon Killebrew, Minnesota Twins	49

Year	Player, Club	HRs
1965	Tony Conigliaro, Boston Red Sox	32
1966	Frank Robinson, Baltimore Orioles	49
1967	Carl Yastrzemski, Boston Red Sox	44
	Harmon Killebrew, Minnesota Twins	44
1968	Frank Howard, Washington Senators	44
1969	Harmon Killebrew, Minnesota Twins	49
1970	Frank Howard, Washington Senators	44
1971	Bill Melton, Chicago White Sox	33
1972	Dick Allen, Chicago White Sox	37
1973	Reggie Jackson, Oakland A's	32
1974	Dick Allen, Chicago White Sox	32
1975	George Scott, Milwaukee Brewers	36
	Reggie Jackson, Oakland A's	36
1976	Graig Nettles, New York Yankees	32
1977	Jim Rice, Boston Red Sox	39
1978	Jim Rice, Boston Red Sox	46
1979	Gorman Thomas, Milwaukee Brewers	45
1980	Ben Oglivie, Milwaukee Brewers	41
	Reggie Jackson, New York Yankees	41
1981	Bobby Grich, California Angels	22
	Eddie Murray, Baltimore Orioles	22
	Dwight Evans, Boston Red Sox	22
	Tony Armas, Oakland A's	22

CY YOUNG AWARD WINNERS

(Prior to 1967 only one pitcher won an overall major league award.)

Year	Player, Club
1956	Don Newcombe, Brooklyn Dodgers
1957	Warren Spahn, Milwaukee Braves
1958	Bob Turley, New York Yankees
1959	Early Wynn, Chicago White Sox
1960	Vernon Law, Pittsburgh Pirates
1961	Whitey Ford, New York Yankees
1962	Don Drysdale, Los Angeles Dodgers
1963	Sandy Koufax, Los Angeles Dodgers
1964	Dean Chance, Los Angeles Angels
1965	Sandy Koufax, Los Angeles Dodgers
1966	Sandy Koufax, Los Angeles Dodgers

AMERICAN LEAGUE

Year	Player, Club
1967	Jim Lonborg, Boston Red Sox
1968	Dennis McLain, Detroit Tigers
1969	Mike Cuellar, Baltimore Orioles
	Dennis McLain, Detroit Tigers
1970	Jim Perry, Minnesota Twins
1971	Vida Blue, Oakland A's
1972	Gaylord Perry, Cleveland Indians
1973	Jim Palmer, Baltimore Orioles
1974	Jim Hunter, Oakland A's
1975	Jim Palmer, Baltimore Orioles
1976	Jim Palmer, Baltimore Orioles
1977	Sparky Lyle, New York Yankees
1978	Ron Guidry, New York Yankees
1979	Mike Flanagan, Baltimore Orioles
1980	Steve Stone, Baltimore Orioles
1981	Rollie Fingers, Milwaukee Brewers

NATIONAL LEAGUE

Year	Player, Club
1967	Mike McCormick, San Francisco Giants
1968	Bob Gibson, St. Louis Cardinals
1969	Tom Seaver, New York Mets
1970	Bob Gibson, St. Louis Cardinals
1971	Ferguson Jenkins, Chicago Cubs
1972	Steve Carlton, Philadelphia Phillies
1973	Tom Seaver, New York Mets
1974	Mike Marshall, Los Angeles Dodgers
1975	Tom Seaver, New York Mets
1976	Randy Jones, San Diego Padres
1977	Steve Carlton, Philadelphia Phillies
1978	Gaylord Perry, San Diego Padres
1979	Bruce Sutter, Chicago Cubs
1980	Steve Carlton, Philadelphia Phillies
1981	Fernando Valenzuela, Los Angeles Dodgers

NATIONAL LEAGUE
Rookie of Year

Year	Player, Club
1947	Jackie Robinson, Brooklyn Dodgers
1948	Al Dark, Boston Braves
1949	Don Newcombe, Brooklyn Dodgers
1950	Sam Jethroe, Boston Braves
1951	Willie Mays, New York Giants
1952	Joe Black, Brooklyn Dodgers
1953	Junior Gilliam, Brooklyn Dodgers
1954	Wally Moon, St. Louis Cardinals
1955	Bill Virdon, St. Louis Cardinals
1956	Frank Robinson, Cincinnati Reds
1957	Jack Sanford, Philadelphia Phillies
1958	Orlando Cepeda, San Francisco Giants
1959	Willie McCovey, San Francisco Giants
1960	Frank Howard, Los Angeles Dodgers
1961	Billy Williams, Chicago Cubs
1962	Kenny Hubbs, Chicago Cubs
1963	Pete Rose, Cincinnati Reds
1964	Richie Allen, Philadelphia Phillies
1965	Jim Lefebvre, Los Angeles Dodgers
1966	Tommy Helms, Cincinnati Reds
1967	Tom Seaver, New York Mets
1968	Johnny Bench, Cincinnati Reds
1969	Ted Sizemore, Los Angeles Dodgers
1970	Carl Morton, Montreal Expos
1971	Earl Williams, Atlanta Braves
1972	Jon Matlack, New York Mets
1973	Gary Matthews, San Francisco Giants
1974	Bake McBride, St. Louis Cardinals
1975	John Montefusco, San Francisco Giants
1976	Pat Zachry, Cincinnati Reds
	Butch Metzger, San Diego Padres
1977	Andre Dawson, Montreal Expos
1978	Bob Horner, Atlanta Braves
1979	Rick Sutcliffe, Los Angeles Dodgers
1980	Steve Howe, Los Angeles Dodgers
1981	Fernando Valenzuela, Los Angeles Dodgers

AL's Gary Peters and NL's Pete Rose were top rookies in 1963.

Twins' Tony Oliva: twice batting champ and top '64 rookie.

AMERICAN LEAGUE
Rookie of Year

Year	Player, Club
1949	Roy Sievers, St. Louis Browns
1950	Walt Dropo, Boston Red Sox
1951	Gil McDougald, New York Yankees
1952	Harry Byrd, Philadelphia Athletics
1953	Harvey Kuenn, Detroit Tigers
1954	Bob Grim, New York Yankees
1955	Herb Score, Cleveland Indians
1956	Luis Aparicio, Chicago White Sox
1957	Tony Kubek, New York Yankees
1958	Albie Pearson, Washington Senators
1959	Bob Allison, Washington Senators
1960	Ron Hansen, Baltimore Orioles
1961	Don Schwall, Boston Red Sox
1962	Tom Tresh, New York Yankees
1963	Gary Peters, Chicago White Sox
1964	Tony Oliva, Minnesota Twins
1965	Curt Blefary, Baltimore Orioles
1966	Tommie Agee, Chicago White Sox
1967	Rod Carew, Minnesota Twins
1968	Stan Bahnsen, New York Yankees
1969	Lou Piniella, Kansas City Royals
1970	Thurman Munson, New York Yankees
1971	Chris Chambliss, Cleveland Indians
1972	Carlton Fisk, Boston Red Sox
1973	Al Bumbry, Baltimore Orioles
1974	Mike Hargrove, Texas Rangers
1975	Fred Lynn, Boston Red Sox
1976	Mark Fidrych, Detroit Tigers
1977	Eddie Murray, Baltimore Orioles
1978	Lou Whitaker, Detroit Tigers
1979	John Castino, Minnesota Twins
	Alfredo Griffin, Toronto Blue Jays
1980	Joe Charboneau, Cleveland Indians
1981	Dave Righetti, New York Yankees

WORLD SERIES WINNERS

Year	A. L. Champion	N. L. Champion	World Series Winner
1903	Boston Red Sox	Pittsburgh Pirates	Boston, 5-3
1905	Philadelphia Athletics	New York Giants	New York, 4-1
1906	Chicago White Sox	Chicago Cubs	Chicago (AL), 4-2
1907	Detroit Tigers	Chicago Cubs	Chicago, 4-0-1
1908	Detroit Tigers	Chicago Cubs	Chicago, 4-1
1909	Detroit Tigers	Pittsburgh Pirates	Pittsburgh, 4-3
1910	Philadelphia Athletics	Chicago Cubs	Philadelphia, 4-1
1911	Philadelphia Athletics	New York Giants	Philadelphia, 4-2
1912	Boston Red Sox	New York Giants	Boston, 4-3-1
1913	Philadelphia Athletics	New York Giants	Philadelphia, 4-1
1914	Philadelphia Athletics	Boston Braves	Boston, 4-0
1915	Boston Red Sox	Philadelphia Phillies	Boston, 4-1
1916	Boston Red Sox	Brooklyn Dodgers	Boston, 4-1
1917	Chicago White Sox	New York Giants	Chicago, 4-2
1918	Boston Red Sox	Chicago Cubs	Boston, 4-2
1919	Chicago White Sox	Cincinnati Reds	Cincinnati, 5-2
1920	Cleveland Indians	Brooklyn Dodgers	Cleveland, 5-2
1921	New York Yankees	New York Giants	New York (NL), 5-3
1922	New York Yankees	New York Giants	New York (NL), 4-0-1
1923	New York Yankees	New York Giants	New York (AL), 4-2
1924	Washington Senators	New York Giants	Washington, 4-2
1925	Washington Senators	Pittsburgh Pirates	Pittsburgh, 4-3
1926	New York Yankees	St. Louis Cardinals	St. Louis, 4-3
1927	New York Yankees	Pittsburgh Pirates	New York, 4-0
1928	New York Yankees	St. Louis Cardinals	New York, 4-0
1929	Philadelphia Athletics	Chicago Cubs	Philadelphia, 4-2
1930	Philadelphia Athletics	St. Louis Cardinals	Philadelphia, 4-2
1931	Philadelphia Athletics	St. Louis Cardinals	St. Louis, 4-3
1932	New York Yankees	Chicago Cubs	New York, 4-0
1933	Washington Senators	New York Giants	New York, 4-1
1934	Detroit Tigers	St. Louis Cardinals	St. Louis, 4-3
1935	Detroit Tigers	Chicago Cubs	Detroit, 4-2
1936	New York Yankees	New York Giants	New York (AL), 4-2
1937	New York Yankees	New York Giants	New York (AL), 4-1
1938	New York Yankees	Chicago Cubs	New York, 4-0
1939	New York Yankees	Cincinnati Reds	New York, 4-0
1940	Detroit Tigers	Cincinnati Reds	Cincinnati, 4-3
1941	New York Yankees	Brooklyn Dodgers	New York, 4-1
1942	New York Yankees	St. Louis Cardinals	St. Louis, 4-1
1943	New York Yankees	St. Louis Cardinals	New York, 4-1
1944	St. Louis Browns	St. Louis Cardinals	St. Louis (NL), 4-2
1945	Detroit Tigers	Chicago Cubs	Detroit, 4-3
1946	Boston Red Sox	St. Louis Cardinals	St. Louis, 4-3
1947	New York Yankees	Brooklyn Dodgers	New York, 4-3
1948	Cleveland Indians	Boston Braves	Cleveland, 4-2
1949	New York Yankees	Brooklyn Dodgers	New York, 4-1
1950	New York Yankees	Philadelphia Phillies	New York, 4-0

Year	A. L. Champion	N. L. Champion	World Series Winner
1951	New York Yankees	New York Giants	New York (AL), 4-2
1952	New York Yankees	Brooklyn Dodgers	New York, 4-3
1953	New York Yankees	Brooklyn Dodgers	New York, 4-2
1954	Cleveland Indians	New York Giants	New York, 4-0
1955	New York Yankees	Brooklyn Dodgers	Brooklyn, 4-3
1956	New York Yankees	Brooklyn Dodgers	New York, 4-3
1957	New York Yankees	Milwaukee Braves	Milwaukee, 4-3
1958	New York Yankees	Milwaukee Braves	New York, 4-3
1959	Chicago White Sox	Los Angeles Dodgers	Los Angeles, 4-2
1960	New York Yankees	Pittsburgh Pirates	Pittsburgh, 4-3
1961	New York Yankees	Cincinnati Reds	New York, 4-1
1962	New York Yankees	San Francisco Giants	New York, 4-3
1963	New York Yankees	Los Angeles Dodgers	Los Angeles, 4-0
1964	New York Yankees	St. Louis Cardinals	St. Louis, 4-3
1965	Minnesota Twins	Los Angeles Dodgers	Los Angeles, 4-3
1966	Baltimore Orioles	Los Angeles Dodgers	Baltimore, 4-0
1967	Boston Red Sox	St. Louis Cardinals	St. Louis, 4-3
1968	Detroit Tigers	St. Louis Cardinals	Detroit, 4-3
1969	Baltimore Orioles	New York Mets	New York, 4-1
1970	Baltimore Orioles	Cincinnati Reds	Baltimore, 4-1
1971	Baltimore Orioles	Pittsburgh Pirates	Pittsburgh, 4-3
1972	Oakland A's	Cincinnati Reds	Oakland, 4-3
1973	Oakland A's	New York Mets	Oakland, 4-3
1974	Oakland A's	Los Angeles Dodgers	Oakland, 4-1
1975	Boston Red Sox	Cincinnati Reds	Cincinnati, 4-3
1976	New York Yankees	Cincinnati Reds	Cincinnati, 4-0
1977	New York Yankees	Los Angeles Dodgers	New York, 4-2
1978	New York Yankees	Los Angeles Dodgers	New York, 4-2
1979	Baltimore Orioles	Pittsburgh Pirates	Pittsburgh, 4-3
1980	Kansas City Royals	Philadelphia Phillies	Philadelphia, 4-2
1981	New York Yankees	Los Angeles Dodgers	Los Angeles, 4-2

1981 WORLD SERIES

LOS ANGELES DODGERS

Batter	AVG	G	AB	R	H	2B	3B	HR	RBI	GW RBI	SH	SF	HB	BB	SO	SB	CS	E
Baker	.167	6	24	3	4	0	0	0	1	0	0	1	0	1	6	0	0	0
Castillo	.000	1	0	0	0	0	0	0	0	0	0	0	0	0	0	0	0	0
Cey	.350	6	20	3	7	0	0	1	6	1	0	0	1	3	3	0	0	0
Forster	.000	2	0	0	0	0	0	0	0	0	0	0	0	0	0	0	0	0
Garvey	.417	6	24	3	10	1	0	0	0	0	0	0	0	2	5	0	0	0
Goltz	.000	2	0	0	0	0	0	0	0	0	0	0	0	0	0	0	0	0
Guerrero	.333	6	21	2	7	1	1	2	7	0	0	0	1	2	6	0	0	0
Hooton	.000	2	4	1	0	0	0	0	0	0	0	0	0	0	3	0	0	0
Howe	.000	3	2	0	0	0	0	0	0	0	0	0	0	0	1	0	0	0
Johnstone	.667	3	3	1	2	0	0	1	3	0	0	1	0	0	2	0	0	1
Landreaux	.167	5	6	1	1	1	0	0	0	0	0	0	0	0	0	0	0	0
Lopes	.227	6	22	6	5	1	0	0	0	0	0	0	0	2	1	0	0	6
Monday	.231	5	13	1	3	1	0	0	2	0	1	0	0	4	3	4	0	6
Niedenfuer	.000	2	0	0	0	0	0	0	0	0	0	0	0	3	6	0	0	0
Reuss	.000	2	3	0	0	0	0	0	0	0	0	0	0	0	0	0	0	0
Russell	.240	6	25	1	6	0	0	0	2	0	1	0	0	1	2	1	1	1
Sax	.000	2	1	0	0	0	0	0	0	0	0	0	0	0	0	0	0	0
Scioscia	.250	3	4	1	1	0	0	0	0	0	1	0	1	0	0	0	0	0
Smith, L.	1.000	1	1	0	1	0	0	0	0	0	0	0	0	0	0	0	0	0
Smith, R.	.000	1	1	0	0	0	0	0	0	0	0	0	0	1	0	0	0	0
Smith, T.	.500	2	2	0	1	0	0	0	0	0	0	0	0	1	0	0	0	0
Stewart	.000	2	0	0	0	0	0	0	0	0	0	0	0	0	0	0	0	1
Thomas, L.	.000	1	2	0	0	0	0	0	1	0	0	0	1	0	0	0	0	0
Thomas, R.	.000	6	0	0	0	0	0	0	0	0	0	0	0	2	0	0	0	0
Thomas, T.	.000	5	7	2	0	0	0	0	0	0	0	0	1	2	0	0	0	0
Valenzuela	.000	1	3	0	0	0	0	0	0	0	0	0	1	0	0	0	0	0
Welch	.000	1	0	0	0	0	0	0	0	0	0	0	0	0	0	0	0	0
Yeager	.286	6	14	2	4	1	0	2	4	2	0	1	0	2	0	0	0	0
PH Hitters	.364		11	4	4	1	0	1	5	1	0	1	0	1	1	0	0	0
TOTALS	.258		198	27	51	6	1	6	26	3	4	2	2	20	44	6	1	9

Pitcher	W	L	ERA	G	GS	CG	SHO	SV	IP	H	R	ER	HR	HB	BB	SO	WP
Castillo, R.	0	0	9.00	1	0	0	0	0	1.0	0	1	1	0	0	5	0	0
Forster, L.	0	0	.00	2	0	0	0	0	2.0	1	0	0	0	0	3	0	0
Goltz, R.	0	0	5.40	2	0	0	0	0	3.1	4	2	2	1	0	1	2	0
Hooton, R.	1	1	1.59	2	2	0	0	0	11.1	8	3	2	1	0	9	3	0
Howe, L.	1	0	3.86	3	0	0	0	1	7.0	7	3	3	1	0	1	4	0
Niedenfuer, R.	0	0	.00	2	0	0	0	0	5.0	3	2	0	0	0	1	0	0
Reuss, L.	1	1	3.86	2	2	1	0	0	11.2	10	5	5	1	0	3	8	0
Stewart, R.	0	0	.00	2	0	0	0	0	1.2	1	0	0	0	0	2	1	0
Valenzuela, L.	1	0	4.00	1	1	1	0	0	9.0	9	4	4	2	0	7	6	0
Welch, R.	0	0	Inf.	1	0	0	0	0	0.0	3	2	2	0	0	1	0	0
Totals	4	2	3.29	18	6	2	0	1	52.0	46	22	19	6	0	33	24	0

GAME 1
at NEW YORK
Tuesday, October 20

Los Angeles 0 0 0   0 1 0   0 2 0   3 5 0
New York . . . . . 3 0 1   1 0 0   0 0 x   5 6 0
REUSS, Castillo (3), Goltz (4), Niedenfuer (5), Stewart (8) and Yeager,
GUIDRY, Davis (8), Gossage (S) (8) and Cerone.
HR: New York (1)—Watson
  Los Angeles (1)—Yeager
T—2:32, A—56,470

GAME 2
at NEW YORK
Wednesday, October 21

Los Angeles 0 0 0   0 0 0   0 0 0   0 4 2
New York . . . . . 0 0 0   0 1 0   0 2 x   3 6 1
HOOTON, Forster (7), Howe (8), Stewart (8), and Yeager-Scioscia (8),
JOHN, Gossage (S) (8) and Cerone.
HR: None
T—2:29, A—56,505

GAME 3
at LOS ANGELES
Friday, October 23

New York 0 2 2   0 0 0   0 0 0   4 9 0
Los Angeles . . . . . 3 0 0   0 2 0   0 0 x   5 11 1
Righetti, FRAZIER (3), May (5), Davis (8), and Cerone;
VALENZUELA and Yeager-Scioscia (3).
HR: Los Angeles (1)—Cey;
  New York (2)—Watson and Cerone.
T—3:04; A—56,236

NEW YORK YANKEES

Batter	AVG	G	AB	R	H	2B	3B	HR	RBI	GW RBI	SH	SF	HB	BB	SO	SB	CS	E
Brown, L.	.000		0	1	0	0	0	0	0	0	0	0	0	0	0	0	0	0
Brown, R.	.000		0	0	0	0	0	0	0	0	0	0	0	1	1	0	0	0
Brown, T.	.000	4	1	1	0	0	0	0	0	0	0	0	0	0	1	0	0	0
Cerone	.190	6	21	2	4	1	0	1	3	0	0	0	0	4	2	0	0	0
Davis	.000	4	0	0	0	0	0	0	0	0	0	0	0	0	0	0	0	0
Foote	.000	1	1	0	0	0	0	0	0	0	0	0	0	0	1	0	0	0
Frazier	.000	3	2	0	0	0	0	0	0	0	0	0	0	1	0	0	0	0
Gamble	.333	3	6	1	2	0	0	0	0	0	0	0	0	0	1	0	0	0
Gossage	.000	3	1	0	0	0	0	0	0	0	0	0	0	0	0	0	0	0
Guidry	.000	2	5	0	0	0	0	0	0	0	1	0	0	0	3	0	0	1
Jackson	.333	3	12	3	4	1	0	1	1	0	0	0	0	0	2	0	0	0
John	.000	3	2	0	0	0	0	0	0	0	1	0	0	0	0	0	0	0
LaRoche	.000	1	0	0	0	0	0	0	0	0	0	0	0	0	0	0	0	0
May	.000	3	1	0	0	0	0	0	0	0	0	0	0	0	0	0	0	0
Milbourne, L.	.200		10	2	2	2	0	0	2	1	0	0	0	2	0	0	0	2
Milbourne, R.	.300		10	0	3	0	0	0	1	0	1	0	0	2	0	0	0	0
Milbourne, T.	.250	5	20	2	5	2	0	0	3	1	1	0	0	4	0	0	0	2
Mumphrey, L.	.091		11	0	1	0	0	0	0	0	0	0	0	2	1	0	0	0
Mumphrey, R.	.500		4	2	2	0	0	0	0	0	0	0	0	1	1	1	0	0
Mumphrey, T.	.200	5	15	2	3	0	0	0	0	0	0	0	0	3	2	1	0	0
Murcer	.000	4	3	0	0	0	0	0	0	0	1	0	0	0	0	0	0	0
Nettles	.400	3	10	1	4	1	0	0	0	0	0	0	0	1	1	0	0	1
Piniella	.438	6	16	2	7	1	0	0	3	0	0	0	0	0	1	1	0	0
Randolph	.222	6	18	5	4	1	1	2	3	0	0	1	0	9	0	1	1	0
Reuschel	.000	2	2	0	0	0	0	0	0	0	0	0	0	0	1	0	0	0
Righetti	.000	1	1	0	0	0	0	0	0	0	1	0	0	1	0	0	0
Robertson	.000	1	0	0	0	0	0	0	0	0	0	0	0	0	0	0	0	0
Rodriguez	.417	4	12	1	5	0	0	0	0	0	0	0	0	1	2	0	0	0
Watson	.318	6	22	2	7	1	0	2	7	1	0	1	0	3	0	0	0	0
Winfield	.045	6	22	0	1	0	0	0	1	0	0	0	0	5	4	1	0	0
PH Hitters	.250		8	0	2	0	0	0	1	0	1	0	0	0	2	0	0	0
TOTALS	.238		193	22	46	8	1	6	22	2	5	2	0	33	24	4	1	4

Pitcher	W	L	ERA	G	GS	CG	SHO	SV	IP	H	R	ER	HR	HB	BB	SO	WP
Davis, R.	0	0	23.14	4	0	0	0	0	2.1	4	8	6	1	0	5	4	0
Frazier, R.	0	0	17.18	3	0	0	0	0	3.2	9	7	7	0	0	3	2	0
Gossage, R.	0	0	.00	3	0	0	0	2	5.0	2	0	0	0	1	2	5	0
Guidry, L.	1	1	1.93	2	2	0	0	0	14.0	8	3	3	3	0	4	15	0
John, L.	1	0	.69	3	2	0	0	0	13.0	11	1	1	0	0	8	0	
LaRoche, L.	0	0	.00	1	0	0	0	0	1.0	0	0	0	0	0	2	0	
May, L.	0	0	2.84	3	0	0	0	0	6.1	5	2	2	1	0	1	5	0
Reuschel, R.	0	0	4.91	2	1	0	0	0	3.2	7	3	2	0	0	3	2	0
Righetti, L.	0	0	13.50	1	1	0	0	0	2.0	5	3	3	1	1	2	1	0
TOTALS	2	4	4.24	22	6	0	1	2	51.0	51	27	24	6	2	20	44	0

GAME 4
at LOS ANGELES
Saturday, October 24

New York 2 1 1   0 0 2   0 1 0   7 13 1
Los Angeles . . . . .0 0 2   0 1 3   2 0 x   8 14 2
Reuschel, May (4), Davis (5), FRAZIER (5), John (7) and Cerone;
Welch, Goltz (1), Forster (4), Niedenfuer (5), HOWE (7) and
Scioscia-Yeager (7).
HR: Los Angeles (1)—Johnstone;
    New York (2)—Randolph and Jackson.
T—3:32, A—56,242

GAME 5
at LOS ANGELES
Sunday, October 25

New York 0 1 0   0 0 0   0 0 0   1 5 0
Los Angeles . . . . .0 0 0   0 0 0   2 0 x   2 4 3
GUIDRY, Gossage (8) and Cerone;
REUSS and Yeager.
HR: Los Angeles (2)—Guerrero and Yeager.
T—2.19, A—56,115

GAME 6
at NEW YORK
Wednesday, October 28

Los Angeles 0 0 0   1 3 4   0 1 0   9 13 1
New York 0 0 1   0 0 1   0 0 0   2 7 2
HOOTON, Howe (S) (6) and Yeager;
John, FRAZIER (5), Davis (6), Reuschel (6), May (7), LaRoche (9)
and Cerone.
HR: Los Angeles (1)—Guerrero
    New York (1)—Randolph
T—3.09, A—56,513

1981 Official
National League Records

(Compiled by Elias Sports Bureau)

COMPOSITE STANDINGS
EASTERN DIVISION

Club	WON	LOST	PCT	GB	vs Eastern Division						vs Western Division					
					STL	MTL	PHIL	PITT	NY	CHI	CIN	LA	HOU	SF	ATL	SD
St. Louis	59	43	.578	--		9	6	8	5	4	5	5	4	3	3	7
Montreal	60	48	.556	2	6	--	7	10	9	7	4	2	2	2	7	4
Philadelphia	59	48	.551	2½	7	4	--	7	7	10	2	3	6	4	5	4
Pittsburgh	46	56	.451	13	3	3	5	--	6	10	2	1	4	3	3	6
New York	41	62	.398	18½	6	3	7	3	--	8	3	1	3	2	3	2
Chicago	38	65	.369	21½	5	4	2	4	5	--	1	6	1	5	2	3

WESTERN DIVISION

Club	WON	LOST	PCT	GB	vs Western Division						vs Eastern Division					
					CIN	LA	HOU	SF	ATL	SD	STL	MTL	PHIL	PITT	NY	CHI
Cincinnati	66	42	.611	--	--	8	9	5	10	8	0	5	5	4	7	5
Los Angeles	63	47	.573	4	8	--	8	7	7	6	5	5	3	5	5	4
Houston	61	49	.555	6	4	4	--	9	8	11	2	5	4	2	6	6
San Francisco	56	55	.505	11½	5	5	6	--	7	7	2	5	3	7	4	5
Atlanta	50	56	.472	15	6	7	4	5	--	9	4	3	4	2	3	3
San Diego	41	69	.373	26	2	5	3	6	6	--	3	2	2	4	5	3

TIE GAMES: New York @ Pittsburgh, April 22, 8½ innings (2-2)
St. Louis @ Chicago, April 29 (2nd game), 11 innings (2-2)
Chicago @ Atlanta, May 10, 14 innings (5-5)
Chicago @ New York, October 1, 8½ innings (2-2)

STANDINGS OF CLUBS AT CLOSE OF FIRST HALF – JUNE 11

EAST	Won	Lost	Pct	GB	WEST	Won	Lost	Pct	GB
Philadelphia	34	21	.618	-	Los Angeles	36	21	.632	-
St. Louis	30	20	.600	1½	Cincinnati	35	21	.625	½
Montreal	30	25	.545	4	Houston	28	29	.491	8
Pittsburgh	25	23	.521	5½	Atlanta	25	29	.463	9½
New York	17	34	.333	15	San Francisco	27	32	.458	10
Chicago	15	37	.288	17½	San Diego	23	33	.411	12½

STANDINGS OF CLUBS AT CLOSE OF SECOND HALF – OCTOBER 4

EAST	Won	Lost	Pct	GB	WEST	Won	Lost	Pct	GB
Montreal	30	23	.566	-	Houston	33	20	.623	-
St. Louis	29	23	.558	½	Cincinnati	31	21	.596	1½
Philadelphia	25	27	.481	4½	San Francisco	29	23	.558	3½
New York	24	28	.462	5½	Los Angeles	27	26	.509	6
Chicago	23	28	.451	6	Atlanta	25	27	.481	7½
Pittsburgh	21	33	.389	9½	San Diego	18	36	.333	15½

DIVISIONAL PLAYOFFS: Montreal defeated Philadelphia 3 games to 2
Los Angeles defeated Houston 3 games to 2

CHAMPIONSHIP SERIES: Los Angeles defeated Montreal 3 games to 2

BATTING

INDIVIDUAL BATTING LEADERS

Batting Average	:	.341	Madlock, Pitt.
Slugging Average	:	.644	Schmidt, Phil.
Games	:	110	Garvey, L.A. & Smith, S.D.
At Bats	:	450	Smith, S.D.
Runs	:	78	Schmidt, Phil.
Hits	:	140	Rose, Phil.
Total Bases	:	228	Schmidt, Phil.
Singles	:	117	Rose, Phil.
Doubles	:	35	Buckner, Chi.
Triples	:	12	Reynolds, Hou. & Richards, S.D.
Home Runs	:	31	Schmidt, Phil.
Runs Batted In	:	91	Schmidt, Phil.
Game Winning RBIs	:	14	Concepcion, Cin.
Sacrifice Hits	:	18	Reynolds, Hou.
Sacrifice Flies	:	8	Maddox, Phil.
Hit by Pitch	:	7	Dawson, Mtl.
Bases on Balls	:	73	Schmidt, Phil.
Intentional Bases on Balls	:	18	Schmidt, Phil.
Strikeouts	:	105	Kingman, N.Y.
Stolen Bases	:	71	Raines, Mtl.
Caught Stealing	:	14	Moreno, Pitt.
Most Grounded into Double Plays	:	18	Knight, Cin.
Fewest Grounded into Double Plays	:	1	Moreno, Pitt.
(Minimum 319 Plate Appearances)			(468 plate appearances)
Longest Batting Streak	:	23	Howe, Hou. May 1 - 25
			Smith, Phil. Aug. 29(2g) - Oct. 4

During the 1981 season 426 players participated in regular season games

TOP FIFTEEN QUALIFIERS FOR BATTING CHAMPIONSHIP
(*Bats Lefthanded #Switch Hitter)

Player & Club	BAT	SLUG	G	AB	R	H	TB	2B	3B	HR	RBI	GW	BB	SO	SB
Madlock, Bill, Pitt.	.341	.495	82	279	35	95	138	23	1	6	45	5	34	17	18
Rose, Peter, Phil.#	.325	.390	107	431	73	140	168	18	5	0	33	5	46	26	4
Baker, Johnnie, L.A.	.320	.445	103	400	48	128	178	17	3	9	49	8	29	43	10
Schmidt, Michael, Phil.	.316	.644	102	354	78	112	228	19	2	31	91	10	73	71	12
Buckner, William, Chi.*	.311	.480	106	421	45	131	202	35	3	10	75	11	26	16	5
Griffey, G. Kenneth, Cin.* ..	.311	.409	101	396	65	123	162	21	6	2	34	3	39	42	*12
May, Milton, S.F.*	.310	.383	97	316	20	98	121	17	0	2	33	8	34	29	1
Brooks, Hubert, N.Y.	.307	.411	98	358	34	110	147	21	2	4	38	2	23	65	9
Concepcion, David, Cin.	.306	.409	106	421	57	129	172	28	0	5	67	14	37	61	4
Hernandez, Keith, St.L.*	.306	.463	103	376	65	115	174	27	4	8	48	10	61	45	12
Cromartie, Warren, Mtl.*	.304	.419	99	358	41	109	150	19	2	6	42	8	39	27	2
Raines, Timothy, Mtl.#	.304	.438	88	313	61	95	137	13	7	5	37	3	45	31	71
Salazar, Luis, S.D.	.303	.403	109	400	37	121	161	19	6	3	38	3	16	72	11
Dawson, Andre, Mtl.	.302	.553	103	394	71	119	218	21	3	24	64	9	35	50	26
Kennedy, Terrence, S.D.*	.301	.385	101	382	32	115	147	24	1	2	41	6	22	53	0

ALL PLAYERS LISTED ALPHABETICALLY

Player & Club	BAT	SLUG	G	AB	R	H	TB	2B	3B	HR	RBI	GW	BB	SO	SB
Aguayo, Luis, Phil.	.214	.298	45	84	11	18	25	4	0	1	7	1	6	15	1
Alexander, Doyle, S.F.	.176	.255	24	51	5	9	13	4	0	0	6	0	2	12	0
Alexander, Gary, Pitt.	.213	.404	21	47	6	10	19	4	1	1	6	1	3	12	0
Alexander, Matthew, Pitt.#	.364	.364	15	11	5	4	4	0	0	0	0	0	1	3	
Allen, Neil, N.Y.	.200	.600	43	5	0	1	3	0	1	0	0	0	0	4	0
Alvarez, Jose, Atl.	----	----	1	0	0	0	0	0	0	0	0	0	0	0	0
Andujar, Joaquin, Hou.-St.L.# ..	.000	.000	21	23	0	0	0	0	0	0	0	0	1	12	0
Armstrong, Michael, S.D.	----	----	10	0	0	0	0	0	0	0	0	0	0	0	0
Ashby, Alan, Hou.#	.271	.369	83	255	20	69	94	13	0	4	33	4	35	33	0
Asselstine, Brian, Atl.*	.256	.384	56	86	8	22	33	5	0	2	10	3	5	7	1

Player & Club	BAT	SLUG	G	AB	R	H	TB	2B	3B	HR	RBI	GW	BB	SO	SB
Aviles, Ramon, Phil.	.214	.250	38	28	6	7	1	0	0	3	0	3	5	0
Backman, Walter, N.Y.∅	.278	.333	26	36	5	10	12	2	0	0	4	7	1
Bahnsen, Stanley, Mtl.	.111	.111	25	9	0	1	1	0	0	0	0	0	4	0
Bailor, Robert, N.Y.	.284	.346	51	81	11	23	28	3	1	0	8	2	8	11	2
Bair, C. Douglas, Cin.-St.L.	.167	.667	35	6	1	1	4	0	0	1	3	0	0	4	0
Baker, Johnnie, L.A.	.320	.445	103	400	48	128	178	17	3	9	49	8	29	43	10
Barranca, German, Cin.*	.333	.333	9	6	2	2	2	0	0	1	0	0	0	0
Bass, Randy, S.D.*	.210	.313	69	176	13	37	55	4	1	4	20	2	20	28	0
Bedrosian, Stephen, Atl.	.000	.000	15	2	0	0	0	0	0	0	0	0	0	1	0
Bench, Johnny, Cin.	.309	.489	52	178	14	55	87	8	0	8	25	6	17	21	0
Benedict, Bruce, Atl.	.264	.363	90	295	26	78	107	12	1	5	35	4	33	21	1
Berenyi, Bruce, Cin.	.190	.262	21	42	4	8	11	3	0	0	1	0	2	18	0
Bergman, David, Hou.-S.F.*	.252	.391	69	151	17	38	59	9	0	4	14	1	19	18	2
Berra, Dale, Pitt.	.241	.319	81	232	21	56	74	12	0	2	27	2	17	34	11
Bevacqua, Kurt, Pitt.	.259	.407	29	27	2	7	11	1	0	1	4	0	4	6	0
Bibby, James, Pitt.	.143	.321	14	28	4	4	9	2	1	3	1	1	11	0
Biittner, Larry, Cin.*	.213	.279	42	61	1	13	17	4	0	0	8	0	4	4	0
Bird, J. Douglas, Chi.	.100	.100	12	20	0	2	2	0	0	0	0	1	11	0
Blackwell, Timothy, Chi.∅	.234	.342	58	158	21	37	54	10	2	1	11	1	23	23	2
Blue, Vida, S.F.*	.200	.257	18	35	4	7	9	2	0	0	1	0	3	10	0
Boggs, Thomas, Atl.	.152	.174	25	46	2	7	8	1	0	0	3	0	6	0
Boitano, Danny, N.Y.	---	---	16	0	0	0	0	0	0	0	0	0	0	0	0
Bonds, Bobby, Chi.	.215	.380	45	163	26	35	62	7	1	6	19	1	24	44	5
Bonilla, Juan, S.D.	.290	.344	99	369	30	107	127	13	2	1	25	3	25	23	4
Boone, Daniel, S.D.*	.500	.500	37	4	0	2	2	0	0	0	0	0	0	0	0
Boone, Robert, Phil.	.211	.295	76	227	19	48	67	7	0	4	24	2	22	16	2
Bowa, Lawrence, Phil.∅	.283	.339	103	360	34	102	122	14	3	0	31	4	26	17	16
Boyland, Dorian, Pitt.*	.000	.000	9	6	0	0	0	0	0	0	0	0	1	3	0
Bradford, Larry, Atl.	1.000	1.000	25	1	1	1	1	0	0	0	0	0	0	0	0
Bradley, Mark, L.A.	.167	.333	9	6	2	1	2	1	0	0	0	0	0	3	0
Braun, Stephen, St.L.*	.196	.283	44	46	9	9	13	2	1	0	2	0	15	7	1
Breining, Fred, S.F.	.000	.000	45	11	0	0	0	0	0	0	0	0	1	7	0
Brenley, Robert, S.F.	.333	.489	19	45	5	15	22	2	1	1	4	0	6	4	0
Briggs, Dan, Mtl.*	.091	.091	9	11	0	1	1	0	0	0	0	0	0	3	0
Brooks, Hubert, N.Y.	.307	.411	98	358	34	110	147	21	2	4	38	2	23	65	9
Brown, Scott, Cin.	.000	.000	10	1	0	0	0	0	0	0	0	0	0	0	0
Brummer, Glenn, St.L.	.200	.233	21	30	2	6	7	1	0	0	2	1	2	0
Brusstar, Warren, Phil.	---	---	14	0	0	0	0	0	0	0	0	0	0	0	0
Buckner, William, Chi.*	.311	.480	106	421	45	131	202	35	3	10	75	11	26	16	5
Burris, B. Ray, Mtl.	.189	.189	22	37	4	7	7	0	0	0	2	1	4	12	0
Butler, Brett, Atl.*	.254	.317	40	126	17	32	40	2	3	0	4	1	19	17	9
Bystrom, Martin, Phil.	.118	.118	9	17	0	2	2	0	0	0	0	0	10	0
Cabell, Enos, S.F.	.255	.326	96	396	41	101	129	20	1	2	36	9	10	47	6
Camacho, Ernie, Pitt.	.000	.000	7	4	0	0	0	0	0	0	0	0	0	1	0
Camp, Rick, Atl.	.000	.000	48	12	1	0	0	0	0	0	0	0	0	6	0
Candelaria, John, Pitt.*	.231	.231	6	13	0	3	3	0	0	0	3	0	0	1	0
Capilla, Douglas, Chi.*	.000	.000	42	3	0	0	0	0	0	0	0	0	0	0	0
Carlton, Steven, Phil.*	.134	.224	24	67	5	9	15	2	2	0	4	1	2	16	0
Carter, Gary, Mtl.	.251	.444	100	374	48	94	166	20	2	16	68	7	35	35	1
Castillo, Robert, L.A.	.444	.667	34	9	1	4	6	2	0	0	2	0	1	2	0
Caudill, William, Chi.	.143	.143	30	14	0	2	2	0	0	1	0	2	6	0
Cedeno, Cesar, Hou.	.271	.382	82	306	42	83	117	19	0	5	34	5	24	31	12
Cey, Ronald, L.A.	.288	.474	85	312	42	90	148	15	2	13	50	9	40	55	0
Chambliss, C. Christopher, Atl.*	.272	.403	107	404	44	110	163	25	2	8	51	9	44	41	4
Christenson, Larry, Phil.	.100	.100	20	30	2	3	3	0	0	0	1	1	1	16	0
Clark, Jack, S.F.	.268	.460	99	385	60	103	177	19	2	17	53	11	45	45	1
Collins, David, Cin.∅	.272	.381	95	360	63	98	137	18	6	3	23	2	41	41	26
Combe, Geoffrey, Cin.	---	---	14	0	0	0	0	0	0	0	0	0	0	0	0
Concepcion, David, Cin.	.306	.409	106	421	57	129	172	28	0	5	67	14	37	61	4
Cromartie, Warren, Mtl.*	.304	.419	99	358	41	109	150	19	2	6	42	8	39	27	2
Cruz, Hector, Chi.	.229	.468	53	109	15	25	51	5	0	7	15	1	17	24	2
Cruz, Jose, Hou.*	.267	.425	107	409	53	109	174	16	5	13	55	12	35	49	5
Cruz, Victor, Pitt.	.000	.000	22	4	0	0	0	0	0	0	0	0	0	3	0
Cubbage, Michael, N.Y.*	.213	.325	67	80	9	17	26	2	2	1	4	1	9	15	0
Curtis, John, S.D.*	.077	.077	28	13	1	1	1	0	0	0	2	0	0	6	0
Davis, Charles, S.F.∅	.133	.133	8	15	1	2	2	0	0	0	0	1	2	2
Davis, Jody, Chi.	.256	.361	56	180	14	46	65	5	1	4	21	2	21	28	0
Davis, Mark, Phil.*	.091	.091	9	11	2	1	1	0	0	0	1	0	2	2	0
Davis, Richard, Phil.	.333	.479	45	96	12	32	46	6	1	2	19	1	8	13	1
Dawson, Andre, Mtl.	.302	.553	103	394	71	119	218	21	3	24	64	9	35	50	26
DeJesus, Ivan, Chi.	.194	.233	106	403	49	78	94	8	4	0	13	1	46	61	21
DeLeon, Luis, St.L.	.000	.000	10	1	0	0	0	0	0	0	0	0	0	0	0
Dernier, Robert, Phil.	.750	.750	10	4	0	3	3	0	0	0	0	0	0	2	1
Dillard, Stephen, Chi.	.218	.345	53	119	18	26	41	7	1	2	11	2	8	20	0
Driessen, Daniel, Cin.*	.236	.386	82	233	35	55	90	14	0	7	33	5	40	31	2
Durham, Leon, Chi.*	.290	.460	87	328	42	95	151	14	6	10	35	2	27	53	25
Easler, Michael, Pitt.*	.286	.431	95	339	43	97	146	18	5	7	42	6	24	45	4
Eastwick, Rawlins, Chi.	.000	.000	30	2	0	0	0	0	0	0	0	0	0	2	0
Edelen, B. Joe, St.L.-Cin.	.200	.200	18	5	0	1	1	0	0	0	0	0	0	1	0
Edwards, David, S.D.	.214	.321	58	112	13	24	36	4	1	2	13	2	11	24	3

Player & Club	BAT	SLUG	G	AB	R	H	TB	2B	3B	HR	RBI	GW	BB	SO	SB
Eichelberger, Juan, S.D.	.087	.087	25	46	1	4	4	0	0	0	0	0	0	21	0
Engle, Richard, Mtl.*	---	---	1	0	0	0	0	0	0	0	0	0	0	0	0
Espinosa, Arnulfo, Phil.	.200	.200	14	20	0	4	4	0	0	0	2	0	0	8	0
Evans, Barry, S.D.	.323	.376	54	93	11	30	35	5	0	0	7	1	9	9	2
Evans, Darrell, S.F.*	.258	.417	102	357	51	92	149	13	4	12	48	4	54	33	2
Falcone, Peter, N.Y.*	.182	.318	35	22	1	4	7	0	0	1	5	1	0	4	0
Ferguson, Joe, L.A.	.143	.214	17	14	2	2	3	1	0	0	1	1	2	5	0
Fiala, Neil, St.L.-Cin.*	.200	.200	5	5	1	1	1	0	0	0	1	0	0	2	0
Fireovid, Stephen, S.D.#	.143	.143	5	7	0	1	1	0	0	0	0	0	0	4	0
Flannery, Timothy, S.D.*	.254	.343	37	67	4	17	23	4	1	0	6	2	2	4	1
Fletcher, Scott, Chi.	.217	.304	19	46	6	10	14	4	0	0	1	0	2	4	0
Flynn, R. Douglas, N.Y.	.222	.292	105	325	24	72	95	12	4	1	20	2	11	19	1
Foli, Timothy, Pitt.	.247	.297	86	316	32	78	94	12	2	0	20	1	17	10	7
Foote, Barry, Chi.	.000	.000	9	22	0	0	0	0	0	0	0	0	3	7	0
Forsch, Robert, St.L.	.122	.146	20	41	0	5	6	1	0	0	3	1	1	10	0
Forster, Terry, L.A.*	.000	.000	21	2	0	0	0	0	0	0	0	0	0	0	0
Foster, George, Cin.	.295	.519	108	414	64	122	215	23	2	22	90	13	51	75	4
Francona, Terry, Mtl.*	.274	.326	34	95	11	26	31	0	1	1	8	0	5	6	1
Frias, Jesus, Mtl.	.250	.278	25	36	6	9	10	1	0	0	3	0	1	3	0
Fryman, Woodrow, Mtl.	.000	.000	35	5	0	0	0	0	0	0	0	0	0	1	0
Garber, H. Eugene, Atl.	.000	.000	35	5	0	0	0	0	0	0	0	0	0	1	0
Garcia, Alfonso, Hou.	.272	.331	48	136	9	37	45	6	1	0	15	0	10	16	2
Gardenhire, Ronald, N.Y.	.271	.292	27	48	2	13	14	1	0	0	3	0	5	9	2
Garner, Philip, Pitt.-Hou.	.248	.310	87	294	35	73	91	9	3	1	26	4	36	32	10
Garvey, Steven, L.A.	.283	.411	110	431	63	122	177	23	1	10	64	6	25	49	3
Gates, Michael, Mtl.*	.500	1.500	1	2	1	1	3	0	1	0	1	0	0	1	0
Geisel, J. David, Chi.*	.000	.000	11	3	0	0	0	0	0	0	0	0	1	2	0
Giles, Brian, N.Y.	.000	.000	9	7	0	0	0	0	0	0	0	0	0	3	0
Goltz, David, L.A.	.059	.059	26	17	0	1	1	0	0	0	2	0	1	9	0
Gomez, Luis, Atl.	.200	.200	35	35	4	7	7	0	0	0	1	0	6	4	0
Gonzalez, Julio, St.L.	.318	.500	20	22	2	7	11	1	0	1	3	1	1	3	0
Gorman, Thomas, Mtl.*	---	---	9	0	0	0	0	0	0	0	0	0	0	0	0
Green, David, St.L.	.147	.176	21	34	6	5	6	1	0	0	2	0	6	5	0
Griffey, G. Kenneth, Cin.*	.311	.409	101	396	65	123	162	21	6	2	34	3	39	42	12
Griffin, Michael, Chi.	.154	.154	16	13	0	2	2	0	0	0	0	0	0	8	0
Griffin, Thomas, S.F.	.195	.293	22	41	1	8	12	1	0	1	5	1	2	12	0
Gross, Gregory, Phil.*	.225	.304	83	102	14	23	31	6	1	0	7	0	15	5	2
Grote, Gerald, L.A.	.000	.000	2	2	0	0	0	0	0	0	0	0	0	1	0
Guerrero, Pedro, L.A.	.300	.464	98	347	46	104	161	17	2	12	48	4	34	57	5
Gullickson, William, Mtl.	.152	.174	22	46	1	7	8	1	0	0	1	0	3	13	0
Gwosdz, Douglas, S.D.	.167	.250	16	24	1	4	6	2	0	0	3	0	3	6	0
Hall, Albert, Atl.#	.000	.000	6	2	1	0	0	0	0	0	0	0	0	1	1
Hall, Melvin, Chi.*	.091	.364	10	11	1	1	4	0	0	1	2	0	1	4	0
Hanna, Preston, Atl.	.250	.250	20	4	0	1	1	0	0	0	1	0	0	1	0
Hargesheimer, Alan, S.F.	.260	.356	40	73	9	19	26	1	0	2	8	1	11	17	5
Harper, Terry, Atl.	.182	.227	17	22	1	4	5	1	0	0	0	0	0	13	0
Harris, Greg, N.Y.#	.000	.000	20	2	0	0	0	0	0	0	0	0	1	1	0
Hausman, Thomas, N.Y.	.000	.000	20	2	0	0	0	0	0	0	0	0	1	0	0
Hayes, William, Chi.	---	---	1	0	0	0	0	0	0	0	0	0	0	0	0
Heep, Daniel, Hou.*	.250	.281	33	96	6	24	27	3	0	0	11	2	10	11	0
Henderson, Stephen, Chi.	.293	.411	82	287	32	84	118	9	5	5	35	3	42	61	5
Hendrick, George, St.L.	.284	.485	101	394	67	112	191	19	3	18	61	10	41	44	4
Hernandez, Guillermo, Chi.*	---	---	13	0	0	0	0	0	0	0	0	0	0	0	0
Hernandez, Keith, St.L.*	.306	.463	103	376	65	115	174	27	4	8	48	10	61	45	12
Herndon, Larry, S.F.	.288	.415	96	364	48	105	151	15	8	5	41	4	20	55	15
Herr, Thomas, St.L.#	.268	.345	103	411	50	110	142	14	9	0	46	4	39	30	23
Hodges, Ronald, N.Y.*	.302	.419	35	43	5	13	18	2	0	1	6	0	5	8	1
Holland, Alfred, S.F.	.063	.063	47	16	1	1	1	0	0	0	3	0	1	8	1
Hooton, Burt, L.A.	.190	.262	23	42	3	8	11	3	0	0	3	0	4	13	0
Horner, J. Robert, Atl.	.277	.460	79	300	42	83	138	10	0	15	42	6	32	39	2
Hostetler, David, Mtl.	.500	1.000	5	6	1	3	6	0	0	1	1	0	0	2	0
Householder, Paul, Cin.#	.275	.420	23	69	12	19	29	4	0	2	9	1	10	16	3
Howard, Michael, N.Y.#	.167	.208	14	24	4	4	5	1	0	0	3	1	4	6	2
Howe, Arthur, Hou.	.296	.404	103	361	43	107	146	22	4	3	36	3	41	23	1
Howe, Steve, L.A.*	.000	.000	41	1	0	0	0	0	0	0	0	0	1	1	0
Howell, Jay, N.Y.	.000	.000	10	2	2	0	0	0	0	0	0	0	1	0	0
Hrabosky, Alan, Atl.	.000	.000	24	1	0	0	0	0	0	0	0	0	0	0	0
Hubbard, Glenn, Atl.	.235	.349	99	361	39	85	126	13	5	6	33	3	33	59	4
Hume, Thomas, Cin.	.000	.000	51	4	0	0	0	0	0	0	0	0	0	1	0
Hutton, Thomas, Mtl.*	.103	.103	31	29	1	3	3	0	0	0	2	0	2	1	0
Iorg, Dane, St.L.*	.327	.424	75	217	23	71	92	11	2	2	39	5	7	9	2
Ivie, Michael, S.F.-Hou.	.254	.339	26	59	3	15	20	5	0	0	9	2	2	12	0
Jackson, Grant, Pitt.-Mtl.#	.000	.000	45	2	0	0	0	0	0	0	0	0	0	1	0
Jacoby, Brook, Atl.	.200	.200	11	10	0	2	2	0	0	0	1	0	0	3	0
Johnson, Anthony, Mtl.	.000	.000	2	1	0	0	0	0	0	0	0	0	0	0	0
Johnson, Wallace, Mtl.#	.222	.444	11	9	1	2	4	0	1	0	3	1	1	1	0
Johnstone, John, L.A.*	.205	.349	61	83	8	17	29	3	0	3	6	1	7	13	0
Jones, Odell, Pitt.	.200	.200	13	10	0	2	2	0	0	0	0	0	0	3	0
Jones, Randall, N.Y.	.118	.118	13	17	0	2	2	0	0	0	0	0	0	9	0
Jones, Ruppert, S.D.*	.249	.370	105	397	53	99	147	34	1	4	39	5	43	66	7

Player & Club	BAT	SLUG	G	AB	R	H	TB	2B	3B	HR	RBI	GW	BB	SO	SB
Jorgensen, Michael, N.Y.*	.205	.352	86	122	8	25	43	5	2	3	15	1	12	24	4
Kaat, James, St.L.*	.375	.500	41	8	2	3	4	1	0	0	2	0	1	0	0
Kennedy, Junior, Cin.	.250	.273	27	44	5	11	12	1	0	0	5	0	1	5	0
Kennedy, Terrence, S.D.*	.301	.385	101	382	32	115	147	24	1	2	41	6	22	53	0
Kingman, David, N.Y.	.221	.456	100	353	40	78	161	11	3	22	59	6	55	105	6
Knepper, Robert, Hou.*	.149	.255	22	47	3	7	12	2	0	1	3	0	0	15	0
Knicely, Alan, Hou.	.571	1.429	3	7	2	4	10	0	0	2	2	0	0	1	0
Knight, C. Ray, Cin.	.259	.370	106	386	43	100	143	23	1	6	34	7	33	51	2
Kravec, Kenneth, Chi.*	.000	.000	25	15	1	0	0	0	0	0	0	0	2	8	0
Krug, Gary, Chi.*	.400	.400	7	5	0	2	2	0	0	0	0	0	0	0	0
Krukow, Michael, Chi.	.180	.220	25	50	5	9	11	2	0	0	3	0	0	1	0
Kuhaulua, Fred, S.D.*	.111	.111	5	9	0	1	1	0	0	0	3	0	0	13	0
LaCorte, Frank, Hou.	.333	.333	37	3	0	1	1	0	0	0	1	0	0	5	0
LaCoss, Michael, Cin.	.000	.000	20	19	0	0	0	0	0	0	0	0	0	8	0
Lacy, Leondaus, Pitt.	.268	.385	78	213	31	57	82	11	4	2	10	2	11	29	24
Landestoy, Rafael, Hou.-Cin.#	.153	.188	47	85	8	13	16	1	1	0	5	1	17	9	5
Landreaux, Kenneth, L.A.*	.251	.367	99	390	48	98	143	16	4	7	41	4	25	42	18
Landrum, Terry, St.L.	.261	.370	81	119	13	31	44	5	4	0	10	1	6	14	4
Lapoint, David, St.L.*	.000	.000	3	5	0	0	0	0	0	0	0	0	0	3	0
Larson, Daniel, Phil.	.111	.111	5	9	2	1	1	0	0	0	0	0	0	2	0
Lavelle, Gary, S.F.*	.273	.364	34	11	1	3	4	1	0	0	1	0	1	3	0
Law, Vance, Pitt.	.134	.164	30	67	1	9	11	0	1	0	3	1	2	15	1
Lea, Charles, Mtl.	.133	.133	16	15	1	2	2	0	0	0	0	0	1	7	0
Leach, Terry, N.Y.	.000	.000	21	1	1	0	0	0	0	0	0	0	0	1	0
Leary, Timothy, N.Y.	.000	.000	1	1	0	0	0	0	0	0	0	0	0	0	0
Lee, Mark, Pitt.	.500	.500	12	2	0	1	1	0	0	0	0	0	0	1	0
Lee, William, Mtl.*	.364	.500	31	22	1	8	11	0	0	1	2	0	0	4	0
Lefebvre, Joseph, S.D.*	.256	.439	86	246	31	63	108	13	4	8	31	0	35	33	6
Leibrandt, Charles, Cin.	.000	.000	7	8	0	0	0	0	0	0	0	0	2	4	0
Lemaster, Johnnie, S.F.	.253	.287	104	324	27	82	93	9	1	0	28	2	24	46	3
Leonard, Jeffrey, Hou.-S.F.	.290	.510	44	145	21	42	74	12	4	4	29	1	12	25	5
Lezcano, Carlos, Chi.	.071	.071	7	14	1	1	1	0	0	0	2	0	0	4	0
Lezcano, Sixto, St.L.	.266	.393	72	214	26	57	84	8	2	5	28	3	40	40	0
Linares, Rufino, Atl.	.265	.375	78	253	27	67	95	9	2	5	25	3	9	28	8
Littell, Mark, St.L.*	.250	.250	28	8	0	2	2	0	0	0	2	0	0	2	0
Littlefield, John, S.D.	.000	.000	42	1	0	0	0	0	0	0	2	0	0	2	0
Lollar, W. Timothy, S.D.*	.167	.333	24	18	2	3	6	0	0	1	1	0	2	5	0
Long, Robert, Pitt.	.000	.000	5	4	1	0	0	0	0	0	0	0	1	2	0
Lopes, David, L.A.	.206	.285	58	214	35	44	61	2	0	5	17	2	22	35	20
Loucks, Scott, Hou.	.571	.571	10	7	2	4	4	0	0	0	0	0	1	3	0
Lucas, Gary, S.D.*	.100	.100	57	10	1	1	1	0	0	0	1	0	0	2	0
Lum, Michael, Atl.-Chi.*	.217	.319	51	69	6	15	22	1	0	2	7	0	7	7	0
Lyle, Albert, Phil.*	.400	.400	48	5	2	2	2	0	0	0	0	0	1	1	1
Lynch, Edward, N.Y.	.143	.190	17	21	0	3	4	1	0	0	1	0	4	10	0
Maddox, Garry, Phil.	.263	.337	94	323	37	85	109	7	1	5	40	5	17	42	9
Madlock, Bill, Pitt.	.341	.495	82	279	35	95	138	23	1	6	45	5	34	17	18
Mahler, Richard, Atl.	.148	.185	34	27	0	4	5	1	0	0	2	0	0	4	0
Maldonado, Candido, L.A.	.083	.083	11	12	0	1	1	0	0	0	0	0	0	5	0
Manuel, Jerry, Mtl.	.200	.455	27	55	10	11	25	5	0	3	10	1	6	11	0
Marshall, Michael G., N.Y.	---	---	20	0	0	0	0	0	0	0	0	0	1	0	0
Marshall, Michael P., L.A.	.200	.320	14	25	2	5	8	3	0	0	1	0	1	4	0
Martin, Jerry, S.F.	.241	.336	72	241	23	58	81	5	3	4	25	3	21	52	6
Martin, John, St.L.#	.212	.333	18	33	2	7	11	2	1	0	8	1	2	14	0
Martinez, Silvio, St.L.	.200	.257	18	35	1	7	9	2	0	0	2	0	1	12	0
Martz, Randy, Chi.*	.214	.214	34	28	0	6	6	0	0	0	2	1	3	13	0
Matthews, Gary, Phil.	.301	.451	101	359	62	108	162	21	3	9	67	9	59	42	15
Matula, Richard, Atl.	.000	.000	5	1	0	0	0	0	0	0	0	0	0	1	0
Matuszek, Leonard, Phil.*	.273	.364	13	11	1	3	4	1	0	0	1	0	3	1	0
May, Milton, S.F.*	.310	.383	97	316	20	98	121	17	0	2	33	8	34	29	1
Mazzilli, Lee, N.Y.#	.228	.358	95	324	36	74	116	14	5	6	34	4	46	53	17
McBride, Arnold, Phil.*	.271	.385	58	221	26	60	85	17	1	2	21	2	11	25	5
McCormick, Donald, Phil.	.250	.250	3	4	0	1	1	0	0	0	0	0	0	1	0
McGlothen, Lynn, Chi.*	.083	.167	20	12	1	1	2	1	0	0	0	0	0	3	0
McGraw, Frank, Phil.	.000	.000	34	1	0	0	0	0	0	0	0	0	0	0	0
McWilliams, Larry, Atl.*	.100	.100	6	10	0	1	1	0	0	0	0	0	1	7	0
Mejias, Samuel, Cin.	.286	.327	66	49	6	14	16	2	0	0	7	2	2	9	1
Miller, Dyar, N.Y.	.333	.333	23	3	0	1	1	0	0	0	0	0	0	0	0
Miller, Edward, Atl.#	.231	.269	50	134	29	31	36	3	1	0	7	2	7	29	23
Mills, J. Bradley, Mtl.*	.238	.286	17	21	3	5	6	1	0	0	1	0	2	1	0
Milner, Eddie, Cin.*	.200	.400	8	5	0	1	2	1	0	0	1	0	1	1	0
Milner, John, Pitt.-Mtl.*	.237	.393	65	135	12	32	53	6	0	5	18	2	17	9	0
Minton, Gregory, S.F.#	.000	.000	55	12	1	0	0	0	0	0	0	0	0	3	0
Mitchell, Robert, L.A.*	.125	.125	9	8	0	1	1	0	0	0	0	0	1	4	0
Moffitt, Randall, S.F.	---	---	10	0	0	0	0	0	0	0	0	0	0	0	0
Monday, Robert, L.A.*	.315	.608	66	130	24	41	79	1	2	11	25	6	24	42	1
Montanez, Guillermo, Mtl.-Pitt.*	.210	.260	55	100	8	21	26	0	1	1	6	4	5	11	0
Montefusco, John, Atl.	.067	.133	26	15	1	1	2	1	0	0	0	0	0	5	0
Morales, Julio, Chi.	.286	.339	84	245	27	70	83	6	2	1	25	3	22	29	1
Moreland, B. Keith, Phil.	.255	.383	61	196	16	50	75	7	0	6	37	6	15	13	0
Moreno, Jose, S.D.#	.229	.271	34	48	5	11	13	2	0	0	6	0	1	8	4

Player & Club	BAT	SLUG	G	AB	R	H	TB	2B	3B	HR	RBI	GW	BB	SO	SB
Moreno, Omar, Pitt.*	.276	.362	103	434	62	120	157	18	8	1	35	6	26	76	39
Morgan, Joe, S.F.*	.240	.377	90	308	47	74	116	16	1	8	31	3	66	37	14
Moskau, Paul, Cin.	.000	.000	27	6	0	0	0	0	0	0	0	0	0	1	0
Mura, Stephen, S.D.	.136	.159	24	44	2	6	7	1	0	0	4	0	2	7	0
Murphy, Dale, Atl.	.247	.390	104	369	43	91	144	12	1	13	50	3	44	72	14
Nahorodny, William, Atl.	.231	.308	14	13	0	3	4	1	0	0	2	1	1	3	0
Nicosia, Steven, Pitt.	.231	.337	54	169	21	39	57	10	1	2	18	2	13	10	3
Niedenfuer, Thomas, L.A.	---	---	17	0	0	0	0	0	0	0	0	0	0	0	0
Niekro, Joseph, Hou.	.176	.196	24	51	1	9	10	1	0	0	6	0	2	10	0
Niekro, Philip, Atl.	.077	.077	22	52	1	4	4	0	0	0	1	0	3	11	0
Nolan, Joseph, Cin.*	.309	.407	81	236	25	73	96	18	1	1	26	4	24	19	1
Noles, Dickie, Phil.	.105	.105	13	19	1	2	2	0	0	0	1	0	0	7	0
North, William, S.F.#	.221	.298	46	131	22	29	39	7	0	1	12	2	26	28	26
O'Berry, P. Michael, Cin.	.180	.252	55	111	6	20	28	3	1	1	5	0	14	19	0
Oberkfell, Kenneth, St.L.*	.293	.372	102	376	43	110	140	12	6	2	45	4	37	28	13
Oester, Ronald, Cin.#	.271	.398	105	354	45	96	141	16	7	5	42	4	42	49	2
Office, Rowland, Mtl.*	.175	.175	26	40	4	7	7	0	0	0	0	0	4	6	0
Orosco, Jesse, N.Y.	.000	.000	8	2	0	0	0	0	0	0	0	0	0	2	0
Otten, James, St.L.	.000	.000	24	3	0	0	0	0	0	0	0	0	0	0	0
Owen, Lawrence, Atl.	.000	.000	13	16	0	0	0	0	0	0	0	0	1	4	0
Parker, David, Pitt.*	.258	.454	67	240	29	62	109	14	3	9	48	3	9	25	6
Parrish, Larry, Mtl.	.244	.384	97	349	41	85	134	19	3	8	44	4	28	73	0
Pastore, Frank, Cin.	.114	.136	22	44	1	5	6	1	0	0	1	0	1	13	0
Pate, Robert, Mtl.	.333	.333	8	6	0	2	2	0	0	0	0	0	1	0	0
Pena, Adalberto, Hou.	.500	.500	4	2	1	1	1	0	0	0	0	0	0	0	0
Pena, Alejandro, L.A.	.000	.000	14	6	0	0	0	0	0	0	0	0	0	6	0
Pena, Antonio, Pitt.	.300	.381	66	210	16	63	80	9	1	2	17	4	8	23	1
Perconte, John, L.A.*	.222	.444	8	9	2	2	4	0	1	0	1	1	2	2	1
Perez, Pascual, Pitt.	.136	.227	18	22	3	3	5	0	1	0	0	0	0	10	0
Perkins, Broderick, S.D.*	.280	.398	92	254	27	71	101	18	3	2	40	5	14	16	0
Perry, Gaylord, Atl.	.250	.354	24	48	5	12	17	2	0	1	7	0	0	10	0
Pettini, Joseph, S.F.	.069	.103	35	29	3	2	3	1	0	0	2	0	4	5	1
Phillips, Michael, S.D-Mtl.*	.214	.262	48	84	6	18	22	1	0	1	6	0	5	18	1
Pittman, Joseph, Hou.	.281	.341	52	135	11	38	46	4	2	0	7	2	11	16	4
Pladson, Gordon, Hou.	---	---	2	0	0	0	0	0	0	0	0	0	0	0	0
Pocoroba, Biff, Atl.*	.180	.213	57	122	4	22	26	4	0	0	8	2	12	15	0
Porter, Darrell, St.L.*	.224	.408	61	174	22	39	71	10	2	6	31	4	39	32	1
Porter, Robert, Atl.*	.286	.357	17	14	2	4	5	1	0	0	4	0	2	1	0
Power, Ted, L.A.	.000	.000	5	3	0	0	0	0	0	0	0	0	0	3	0
Price, Joseph, Cin.	.000	.000	41	3	0	0	0	0	0	0	0	0	0	1	0
Proly, Michael, Phil.	.000	.000	35	7	0	0	0	0	0	0	0	0	0	3	0
Puhl, Terry, Hou.*	.251	.354	96	350	43	88	124	19	4	3	28	8	31	49	22
Pujols, Luis, Hou.	.239	.308	40	117	5	28	36	3	1	1	14	2	10	17	1
Puleo, Charles, N.Y.	.000	.000	4	2	0	0	0	0	0	0	0	0	0	2	0
Raines, Timothy, Mtl.#	.304	.438	88	313	61	95	137	13	7	5	37	3	45	31	71
Ramirez, Mario, S.D.	.077	.077	13	13	1	1	1	0	0	0	1	0	2	5	0
Ramirez, Rafael, Atl.	.218	.303	95	307	30	67	93	16	2	2	20	1	24	47	7
Ramos, Roberto, Mtl.	.195	.293	26	41	4	8	12	1	0	1	3	1	3	5	0
Ramsey, Michael, St.L.#	.258	.282	47	124	19	32	35	3	0	0	9	4	8	16	4
Ransom, Jeffrey, S.F.	.267	.333	5	15	2	4	5	1	0	0	0	1	1	1	0
Ratzer, Steven, Mtl.	.000	.000	12	2	0	0	0	0	0	0	0	0	0	0	0
Ray, John, Pitt.#	.245	.353	31	102	10	25	36	11	0	0	6	0	6	9	0
Reardon, Jeffrey, N.Y.-Mtl.	.000	.000	43	5	0	0	0	0	0	0	0	0	0	2	0
Reed, Jerry, Phil.	---	---	4	0	0	0	0	0	0	0	0	0	0	0	0
Reed, Ronald, Phil.	.500	.667	39	6	1	3	4	1	0	0	1	0	0	1	0
Reitz, Kenneth, Chi.	.215	.281	82	260	10	56	73	9	1	2	28	4	15	56	0
Reuschel, Ricky, Chi.	.080	.080	16	25	1	2	2	0	0	0	1	0	1	7	0
Reuss, Jerry, L.A.*	.196	.196	22	51	3	10	10	0	0	0	3	0	0	18	0
Reynolds, G. Craig, Hou.*	.260	.402	87	323	43	84	130	10	12	4	31	4	12	31	3
Rhoden, Richard, Pitt.	.188	.229	21	48	4	9	11	2	0	0	7	0	1	7	0
Richards, Eugene, S.D.*	.288	.407	104	393	47	113	160	14	12	3	42	4	53	44	20
Rincon, Andrew, St.L.	.231	.308	5	13	1	3	4	1	0	0	5	0	1	6	0
Ripley, Allen, S.F.	.133	.133	19	30	0	4	4	0	0	0	2	0	0	5	0
Roberts, David, N.Y.*	.250	.250	7	4	1	1	1	0	0	0	1	0	1	1	0
Roberts, David, Hou.	.241	.352	27	54	4	13	19	3	0	1	5	0	3	6	1
Robinson, Don, Pitt.	.250	.250	17	12	1	3	3	0	0	0	1	0	1	4	0
Robinson, William, Pitt.	.216	.318	39	88	8	19	28	3	0	2	8	0	5	18	1
Roenicke, Ronald, L.A.#	.234	.234	22	47	6	11	11	0	0	0	0	0	6	8	1
Rogers, Stephen, Mtl.	.145	.164	23	55	5	8	9	1	0	0	3	1	2	21	0
Romo, Enrique, Pitt.	.000	.000	33	4	0	0	0	0	0	0	0	0	0	1	0
Roof, Eugene, St.L.#	.300	.400	23	60	11	18	24	6	0	0	3	0	12	16	5
Rooney, Patrick, Mtl.	.000	.000	4	5	0	0	0	0	0	0	0	0	1	0	0
Rose, Peter, Phil.#	.325	.390	107	431	73	140	168	18	5	0	33	5	46	26	4
Rowland, Michael, S.F.	1.000	1.000	9	1	0	1	1	0	0	0	1	0	0	0	0
Royster, Jeron, Atl.	.204	.269	64	93	13	19	25	4	1	0	9	1	7	14	7
Ruhle, Vernon, Hou.	.250	.292	20	24	1	6	7	1	0	0	3	1	6	11	0
Runge, Jerry, Atl.	.259	.296	10	27	2	7	8	1	0	0	2	0	4	4	0
Russell, William, L.A.	.233	.282	82	262	20	61	74	9	2	0	22	3	19	20	2
Ruthven, Richard, Phil.	.140	.200	23	50	2	7	10	3	0	0	5	1	2	14	0
Ryan, L. Nolan, Hou.	.216	.235	21	51	3	11	12	1	0	0	1	0	5	18	0

Player & Club	BAT	SLUG	G	AB	R	H	TB	2B	3B	HR	RBI	GW	BB	SO	SB
Sadek, Michael, S.F.	.167	.250	19	36	5	6	9	3	0	0	3	1	8	7	0
Salazar, Luis, S.D.	.303	.403	109	400	37	121	161	19	6	3	38	3	16	72	11
Sambito, Joseph, Hou.*	.000	.000	49	5	0	0	0	0	0	0	0	0	0	3	0
Sanchez, Orlando, St.L.*	.286	.367	27	49	5	14	18	2	1	0	6	2	2	6	1
Sanderson, Scott, Mtl.	.114	.171	22	35	2	4	6	2	0	0	6	2	9	18	0
Sandberg, Ryne, Phil.	.167	.167	13	6	2	1	1	0	0	0	0	0	0	1	0
Sax, Stephen, L.A.	.277	.345	31	119	15	33	41	2	0	2	9	1	7	14	5
Schmidt, Michael, Phil.	.316	.644	102	354	78	112	228	19	2	31	91	10	73	71	12
Scioscia, Michael, L.A.*	.276	.331	93	290	27	80	96	10	0	2	29	5	36	18	0
Scott, Michael, N.Y.	.073	.073	23	41	4	3	3	0	0	0	1	0	3	18	0
Scott, Rodney, Mtl.#	.205	.250	95	336	43	69	84	9	3	0	26	3	50	35	30
Scott, Tony, St.L.-Hou.#	.264	.359	100	401	49	106	144	18	4	4	39	3	20	54	18
Scurry, Rodney, Pitt.*	.158	.158	27	19	1	3	3	0	0	0	0	0	2	10	0
Searage, Raymond, N.Y.*	1.000	1.000	26	1	0	1	1	0	0	0	0	0	0	0	0
Seaver, G. Thomas, Cin.	.200	.273	23	55	3	11	15	1	0	1	6	0	8	16	0
Shirley, Robert, St.L.	.136	.136	28	22	0	3	3	0	0	0	1	0	0	7	0
Show, Eric, S.D.	---	---	15	0	0	0	0	0	0	0	0	0	0	0	0
Sinatro, Matthew, Atl.	.281	.375	12	32	4	9	12	1	1	0	4	2	5	4	1
Smith, Billy, Hou.	.000	.000	10	2	0	0	0	0	0	0	0	0	0	0	0
Smith, Billy, S.F.#	.180	.230	36	61	6	11	14	0	0	1	5	0	9	16	0
Smith, Bryn, Mtl.	.000	.000	7	1	0	0	0	0	0	0	0	0	0	0	0
Smith, C. Reginald, L.A.#	.200	.314	41	35	5	7	11	1	0	1	8	3	7	8	0
Smith, Christopher, Mtl.#	.000	.000	7	7	0	0	0	0	0	0	0	0	0	0	0
Smith, David, Hou.	.250	.250	42	8	0	2	2	0	0	0	0	0	0	4	0
Smith, Kenneth, Atl.*	.333	.667	5	3	0	1	2	1	0	0	0	0	1	1	0
Smith, Lee, Chi.	.000	.000	40	9	0	0	0	0	0	0	0	0	0	7	0
Smith, Lonnie, Phil.	.324	.472	62	176	40	57	83	14	3	2	11	3	18	14	21
Smith, Osborne, S.D.#	.222	.256	110	450	53	100	115	11	2	0	21	4	41	37	22
Solomon, Eddie, Pitt.	.163	.163	25	43	3	7	7	0	0	0	3	2	0	15	0
Sorensen, Lary, St.L.	.065	.087	23	46	1	3	4	1	0	0	0	0	0	21	0
Sosa, Elias, Mtl.	1.000	1.000	32	2	0	2	2	0	0	0	1	0	0	0	0
Soto, Mario, Cin.	.068	.068	25	59	4	4	4	0	0	0	0	0	1	24	0
Speier, Chris, Mtl.	.225	.290	96	307	33	69	89	10	2	2	25	4	38	29	1
Spilman, W. Harry, Cin.-Hou.*	.241	.259	51	58	9	14	15	1	0	0	4	0	5	10	0
Sprowl, Robert, Hou.*	.167	.167	15	6	0	1	1	0	0	0	1	0	0	2	0
Stargell, Wilver, Pitt.*	.283	.350	38	60	2	17	21	4	0	0	9	0	5	9	0
Staub, Daniel, N.Y.*	.317	.466	70	161	9	51	75	9	0	5	21	4	22	12	1
Stearns, John, N.Y.	.271	.333	80	273	25	74	91	12	1	1	24	4	24	17	12
Stennett, Renaldo, S.F.	.230	.264	38	87	8	20	23	0	0	1	7	0	3	6	2
Stewart, David, L.A.	.400	.800	32	5	2	2	4	0	1	0	1	0	1	0	0
Stimac, Craig, S.D.	.111	.111	9	9	0	1	1	0	0	0	0	0	0	3	0
Strain, Joseph, Chi.	.189	.203	25	74	7	14	15	1	0	0	1	0	5	7	0
Sularz, Guy, S.F.	.200	.200	10	20	0	4	4	0	0	0	2	0	2	4	0
Sutcliffe, Richard, L.A.*	.182	.182	14	11	2	2	2	0	0	0	2	1	2	3	0
Sutter, H. Bruce, St.L.	.000	.000	48	9	0	0	0	0	0	0	1	0	0	4	0
Sutton, Donald, Hou.	.137	.137	23	51	1	7	7	0	0	0	3	0	5	12	0
Swan, Craig, N.Y.	.000	.000	5	3	0	0	0	0	0	0	0	0	0	1	0
Swisher, Steven, S.D.	.143	.143	16	28	2	4	4	0	0	0	0	2	11	0
Sykes, Robert, St.L.#	.000	.000	22	2	0	0	0	0	0	0	0	1	2	0
Tabler, Patrick, Chi.	.188	.267	35	101	11	19	27	3	1	1	5	1	13	26	0
Taveras, Franklin, N.Y.	.230	.290	84	283	30	65	82	11	3	0	11	0	12	36	16
Tekulve, Kenton, Pitt.	.000	.000	45	2	0	0	0	0	0	0	0	0	0	1	0
Templeton, Garry, St.L.#	.288	.393	80	333	47	96	131	16	8	1	33	1	14	55	8
Tenace, F. Gene, St.L.	.233	.403	58	129	26	30	52	7	0	5	22	2	38	26	0
Thomas, Derrel, L.A.#	.248	.321	80	218	25	54	70	4	0	4	24	2	25	23	7
Thompson, Jason, Pitt.*	.242	.502	86	223	36	54	112	13	0	15	42	6	59	49	0
Thompson, V. Scot, Chi.*	.165	.209	57	115	8	19	24	5	0	0	8	1	7	8	2
Thon, Richard, Hou.	.274	.337	49	95	13	26	32	6	0	0	3	0	9	13	6
Tiant, Luis, Pitt.	.188	.313	9	16	0	3	5	2	0	0	4	0	1	3	0
Tidrow, Richard, Chi.	.000	.000	51	5	0	0	0	0	0	0	0	0	2	0	0
Tolman, Timothy, Hou.	.125	.125	4	8	0	1	1	0	0	0	0	0	0	1	0
Tracy, James, Chi.*	.238	.302	45	63	6	15	19	2	1	0	5	0	12	14	1
Trevino, Alejandro, N.Y.	.262	.275	56	149	17	39	41	2	0	0	10	2	13	19	3
Trillo, J. Manuel, Phil.	.287	.395	94	349	37	100	138	14	3	6	36	4	26	37	10
Tufts, Robert, S.F.*	.000	.000	11	1	0	0	0	0	0	0	0	0	0	0	0
Turner, John, S.D.*	.226	.419	33	31	5	7	13	0	0	2	6	0	4	3	0
Tyson, Michael, Chi.#	.185	.272	50	92	6	17	25	2	0	2	8	2	7	15	1
Unser, Delbert, Phil.*	.153	.203	62	59	5	9	12	3	0	0	6	0	13	9	0
Urrea, John, S.D.	.250	.250	38	4	0	1	1	0	0	0	0	0	0	0	0
Vail, Michael, Cin.	.161	.161	31	31	1	5	5	0	0	0	3	0	0	9	0
Valentine, Ellis, Mtl.-N.Y.	.208	.359	70	245	23	51	88	11	1	8	36	6	11	49	0
Valenzuela, Fernando, L.A.*	.250	.281	25	64	3	16	18	0	1	0	7	2	1	9	0
Venable, W. McKinley, S.F.*	.188	.313	18	32	2	6	10	0	2	0	1	0	4	3	3
Virgil, Osvaldo, Phil.	.000	.000	6	6	0	0	0	0	0	0	0	0	0	2	0
Vukovich, George, Phil.*	.385	.500	20	26	5	10	13	0	0	1	4	1	1	0	1
Vukovich, John, Phil.	.000	.000	11	1	0	0	0	0	0	0	0	0	0	1	0
Walk, Robert, Atl.	.143	.143	12	7	1	1	1	0	0	0	0	0	0	3	0
Wallach, Timothy, Mtl.	.236	.344	71	212	19	50	73	9	1	4	13	1	15	37	0
Waller, E. Tyrone, Chi.	.268	.451	30	71	10	19	32	2	1	3	13	0	4	18	2
Walling, Dennis, Hou.*	.234	.367	65	158	23	37	58	6	0	5	23	4	28	17	2

Player & Club	BAT	SLUG	G	AB	R	H	TB	2B	3B	HR	RBI	GW	BB	SO	SB
Washington, Claudell, Atl.*	.291	.425	85	320	37	93	136	22	3	5	37	3	15	47	12
Weiss, Gary, L.A.#	.105	.105	14	19	2	2	2	0	0	0	1	1	1	4	0
Welch, Robert, L.A.	.222	.267	23	45	3	10	12	0	1	0	2	0	1	16	0
Welsh, Christopher, S.D.*	.146	.171	22	41	4	6	7	1	0	0	1	0	2	15	0
Whisenton, Larry, Atl.*	.200	.200	9	5	1	1	1	0	0	0	0	0	2	1	0
White, Jerome, Mtl.#	.218	.353	59	119	11	26	42	5	1	3	11	3	13	17	5
Whitson, Eddie, S.F.	.091	.091	22	33	2	3	3	0	0	0	1	0	3	13	0
Wieghaus, Thomas, Mtl.	.000	.000	1	1	0	0	0	0	0	0	0	0	0	0	0
Wiggins, Alan, S.D.#	.357	.357	15	14	4	5	5	0	0	0	0	0	1	0	2
Wilson, William, N.Y.#	.271	.372	92	328	49	89	122	8	8	3	14	2	20	59	24
Wise, Richard, S.D.	.040	.080	18	25	1	1	2	1	0	0	1	0	1	11	0
Wohlford, James, S.F.	.162	.250	50	68	4	11	17	3	0	1	7	2	4	9	0
Woods, Gary, Hou.	.209	.264	54	110	10	23	29	4	1	0	12	2	11	22	2
Yeager, Stephen, L.A.	.209	.337	42	86	5	18	29	2	0	3	7	0	6	14	0
Youngblood, Joel, N.Y.	.350	.531	43	143	16	50	76	10	2	4	25	2	12	19	2
Zachry, Patrick, N.Y.	.158	.158	24	38	1	6	6	0	0	0	2	0	3	12	0

CLUB BATTING

Club	BAT	SLUG	G	AB	R	H	TB	2B	3B	HR	RBI	BB	SO	SB	LOB	SHO
Philadelphia	.273	.389	107	3665	491	1002	1424	165	25	69	453	372	432	103	793	4
Cincinnati	.267	.385	108	3637	464	972	1402	190	24	64	429	375	553	58	789	8
St. Louis	.265	.377	103	3537	464	936	1334	158	45	50	431	379	495	88	747	4
Los Angeles	.262	.374	110	3751	450	984	1403	133	20	82	427	331	550	73	776	5
Pittsburgh	.257	.369	103	3576	407	920	1321	176	30	55	384	278	494	122	717	7
Houston	.257	.356	110	3693	394	948	1313	160	35	45	369	340	488	81	795	9
San Diego	.256	.346	110	3757	382	963	1299	170	35	32	350	311	525	83	769	11
San Francisco	.250	.357	111	3766	427	941	1343	161	26	63	399	386	543	89	797	9
New York	.248	.356	105	3493	348	868	1245	136	35	57	325	304	603	103	726	12
Montreal	.246	.370	108	3591	443	883	1328	146	28	81	407	368	498	138	722	5
Atlanta	.243	.349	107	3642	395	886	1270	148	22	64	366	321	540	98	731	12
Chicago	.236	.340	106	3546	370	838	1205	138	29	57	348	342	611	72	721	17
TOTALS	.255	.364	644	43654	5035	11141	15887	1881	354	719	4688	4107	6332	1108	9083	103

PITCHING

INDIVIDUAL PITCHING LEADERS

Earned Run Average	:	1.69	Ryan, Hou.
Won & Lost Percentage	:	.875	Seaver, Cin. (14-2)
Games Won	:	14	Seaver, Cin.
Games Lost	:	14	Mura, S.D. & Zachry, N.Y.
Appearances	:	57	Lucas, S.D.
Games Started	:	25	Krukow, Chi., Soto, Cin. & Valenzuela, L.A.
Complete Games	:	11	Valenzuela, L.A.
Games Finished	:	44	Minton, S.F.
Saves	:	25	Sutter, St.L.
Shutouts	:	8	Valenzuela, L.A.
Innings	:	192	Valenzuela, L.A.
Hits	:	182	Perry, Atl.
Batsmen Faced	:	763	Carlton, Phil.
Runs	:	94	Ruthven, Phil.
Earned Runs	:	84	Ruthven, Phil.
Home Runs	:	13	Soto, Cin. & Zachry, N.Y.
Sacrifice Hits	:	14	Mura, S.D.
Sacrifice Flies	:	9	Zachry, N.Y.
Bases on Balls	:	77	Berenyi, Cin.
Intentional Bases on Balls	:	15	Lucas, S.D. & Tidrow, Chi..
Hit Batsmen	:	7	Griffin, S.F.
Strikeouts	:	180	Valenzuela, L.A.
Wild Pitches	:	16	Ryan, Hou.
Balks	:	5	Boone, Eichelberger, S.D. & Sorensen, St.L.
Games Won, Consecutive	:	8	Valenzuela, L.A. April 9 - May 14
			Carlton, Phil. April 13 - May 31
Games Lost, Consecutive	:	9	Boggs, Atl. April 26(2g) - June 11

During the 1981 season 171 pitchers participated in regular season games

TOP FIFTEEN QUALIFIERS FOR EARNED RUN AVERAGE LEADERSHIP
(* Throws Lefthanded)

Pitcher & Club	ERA	W	L	PCT	G	GS	CG	GF	SV	SHO	IP	H	BFP	R	ER	HR	SH	SF	TBB	IBB	HB	SO	WP	BK
Ryan, L. Nolan, Hou.	1.69	11	5	.688	21	21	5	0	0	3	149	99	605	34	28	2	5	3	68	1	1	140	16	2
Knepper, Robert, Hou.*	2.18	9	5	.643	22	21	6	0	0	5	157	128	617	41	38	5	5	8	38	1	2	75	3	0
Hooton, Burt, L.A.	2.28	11	6	.647	23	23	5	0	0	2	142	124	571	42	36	3	5	8	33	2	4	74	3	0
Reuss, Jerry, L.A.*	2.29	10	4	.714	22	22	8	0	0	2	153	138	608	44	39	6	6	6	27	2	3	51	1	0
Carlton, Steven, Phil.*	2.42	13	4	.765	24	24	10	0	0	1	190	152	763	59	51	9	3	4	62	3	1	179	9	4
Blue, Vida, S.F.*	2.45	8	6	.571	18	18	1	0	0	0	125	97	513	40	34	7	9	3	54	4	1	63	7	0
Valenzuela, Fernando, L.A.*	2.48	13	7	.650	25	25	11	0	0	8	192	140	758	55	53	7	9	3	61	4	1	180	5	0
Seaver, G. Thomas, Cin.	2.55	14	2	.875	23	23	6	0	0	1	166	120	671	51	47	10	9	8	66	8	3	87	0	1
Sutton, Donald, Hou.	2.60	11	9	.550	23	23	6	0	0	3	159	132	624	51	46	6	13	6	29	3	4	104	5	0
Gullickson, William, Mtl.	2.81	7	9	.438	22	22	3	0	0	2	157	142	640	54	49	3	5	2	34	4	4	115	3	1
Mahler, Richard, Atl.	2.81	8	6	.571	34	14	1	10	2	0	112	109	478	41	35	5	8	3	43	2	1	54	3	0
Niekro, Joseph, Hou.	2.82	9	9	.500	24	24	5	0	0	2	166	150	676	60	52	8	6	6	47	4	2	77	7	1
Alexander, Doyle, S.F.	2.90	11	7	.611	24	24	4	0	0	1	152	156	646	51	49	11	5	4	44	2	2	77	4	0
Sanderson, Scott, Mtl.	2.96	9	7	.563	22	22	4	0	0	0	137	122	560	50	45	10	7	4	31	2	1	77	2	0
Burris, B. Ray, Mtl.	3.04	9	7	.563	22	21	4	0	0	0	136	117	554	56	46	9	6	6	41	3	3	52	6	1

ALL PITCHERS LISTED ALPHABETICALLY
(* Throws Lefthanded)

Pitcher & Club	ERA	W	L	PCT	G	GS	CG	GF	SV	SHO	IP	H	BFP	R	ER	HR	SH	SF	TBB	IBB	HB	SO	WP	BK
Alexander, Doyle, S.F.	2.90	11	7	.611	24	24	4	0	0	1	152	156	646	51	49	11	5	2	44	2	2	77	4	1
Allen, Neil, N.Y.	2.96	7	6	.538	43	0	0	35	18	0	67	64	286	26	22	4	10	3	26	8	0	50	3	0
Alvarez, Jose, Atl.	0.00	0	0	---	1	0	0	1	0	0	2	0	6	0	0	0	0	0	0	0	0	2	0	0
Andujar, Joaquin, Hou-St.L.	4.10	8	4	.667	20	11	0	4	0	0	79	85	336	41	36	6	2	2	23	1	0	37	2	1
Armstrong, Michael, S.D.	0.00	0	0	.000	10	0	0	3	0	0	12	14	58	9	8	1	2	0	11	2	0	9	0	1
Bahnsen, Stanley, Mtl.	4.96	2	1	.667	25	3	0	4	1	0	49	54	208	27	27	7	1	1	24	4	0	28	1	0
Bair, C. Douglas, Cin-St.L.	5.07	4	2	.667	35	0	0	20	0	0	55	55	234	34	31	5	2	0	19	4	0	30	3	0
Bedrosian, Stephen, Atl.	4.50	1	2	.333	15	1	0	5	0	0	24	15	106	14	12	2	0	1	15	2	1	9	0	0
Berenyi, Bruce, Cin.	3.50	9	6	.600	21	20	5	0	0	3	126	97	544	55	49	9	3	4	77	0	2	106	7	2
Bibby, James, Pitt.	2.49	6	3	.667	14	14	2	0	0	1	94	79	385	30	26	4	3	4	26	1	0	48	1	0
Bird, J. Douglas, Chi.	3.60	4	5	.444	12	12	2	0	0	0	75	97	305	34	30	5	1	2	16	3	1	34	2	2
Blue, Vida, S.F.*	2.45	8	6	.571	18	18	1	0	0	0	125	97	513	40	34	7	9	3	54	4	1	63	7	0
Boggs, Thomas, Atl.	4.09	3	13	.188	25	24	2	1	0	0	143	140	606	72	65	11	13	7	54	4	3	81	4	0

Boitano, Danny, N.Y.	5.63	2	1	.667	15	0	0	4	0	0	16	21	76	10	10	2	0	1	5	0	2	8	0	0
Boone, Daniel, S.D.*	2.86	1	0	1.000	37	0	0	8	2	0	63	63	262	23	20	2	2	2	21	7	1	43	1	5
Bradford, Larry, Atl.*	3.67	2	0	1.000	25	0	0	11	1	0	27	26	113	13	11	1	2	2	12	0	0	14	0	0
Breining, Fred, S.F.	2.54	5	2	.714	45	1	0	15	1	0	78	66	326	28	22	4	9	5	38	8	2	37	3	3
Brown, Scott, Cin.	2.77	1	0	1.000	10	0	0	3	0	0	13	16	53	4	4	0	0	1	1	1	0	7	0	0
Brusstar, Warren, Phil.	4.50	0	1	.000	14	0	0	1	0	0	12	12	60	6	6	0	0	1	10	4	1	8	0	0
Burris, B. Ray, Mtl.	3.04	9	7	.563	22	21	4	0	0	0	136	117	554	56	46	9	6	6	41	3	3	52	6	1
Bystrom, Martin, Phil.	3.33	4	3	.571	9	9	1	0	0	0	54	55	227	21	20	3	1	1	16	1	1	24	0	1
Camacho, Ernie, Pitt.	4.91	0	1	.000	7	3	0	2	0	0	22	23	96	13	12	0	1	2	15	1	0	11	2	3
Camp, Rick, Atl.	1.78	9	3	.750	48	0	0	33	17	0	76	68	304	17	15	5	5	1	12	3	1	47	0	2
Candelaria, John, Pitt.*	3.51	2	2	.500	6	6	0	0	0	0	41	42	168	17	16	3	1	1	11	1	0	14	0	0
Capilla, Douglas, Chi.*	3.18	1	0	1.000	42	0	0	16	0	0	51	52	225	20	18	1	3	3	34	3	2	28	6	1
Carlton, Steven, Phil.*	2.42	13	4	.765	24	24	10	0	0	1	190	152	763	59	51	9	12	4	62	3	1	179	9	4
Castillo, Robert, L.A.	5.29	2	4	.333	34	1	0	15	5	0	51	50	220	31	30	5	3	2	24	4	0	35	0	0
Caudill, William, Chi.	5.83	1	5	.167	30	10	0	4	0	0	71	87	331	50	46	9	5	4	31	2	2	45	3	1
Christenson, Larry, Phil.	3.53	4	7	.364	20	15	0	3	1	0	107	108	446	48	42	8	2	8	30	3	1	70	3	2
Combe, Geoffrey, Cin.	7.50	1	0	1.000	14	0	0	6	0	0	18	27	85	15	15	3	1	1	10	1	0	9	0	0
Cruz, Victor, Pitt.	2.65	1	1	.500	22	0	0	4	1	0	34	33	144	10	10	6	3	0	15	4	1	28	1	0
Curtis, John, S.D.*	5.10	2	6	.250	28	8	0	8	0	0	67	70	293	41	38	11	4	3	30	2	1	31	3	0
Davis, Mark, Phil.*	7.74	1	4	.200	9	9	0	0	0	0	43	49	194	37	37	7	2	4	24	0	0	29	1	1
DeLeon, Luis, St.L.	2.40	0	1	.000	10	0	0	2	0	0	15	11	59	4	4	1	1	0	3	2	0	8	0	0
Eastwick, Rawlins, Chi.	2.30	0	1	.000	30	0	0	9	1	0	43	43	183	16	11	2	3	2	15	3	0	24	1	1
Edelen, B. Joe, St.L.-Cin.	5.70	2	0	1.000	18	0	0	6	0	0	30	34	125	19	19	3	2	1	3	1	1	15	1	1
Eichelberger, Juan, S.D.	3.51	8	8	.500	25	24	3	1	0	1	141	136	615	60	55	5	8	4	74	5	3	81	5	5
Engle, Richard, Mtl.*	18.00	0	0	---	1	0	0	0	0	0	2	6	13	4	4	0	0	0	1	0	0	2	0	0
Espinosa, Arnulfo, Phil.	6.08	2	5	.286	14	14	2	0	0	0	74	98	327	52	50	11	2	6	24	2	1	22	1	0
Falcone, Peter, N.Y.*	2.56	5	3	.625	35	9	3	5	1	1	95	84	397	32	27	3	8	4	36	4	0	56	2	1
Fireovid, Stephen, S.D.	2.77	0	1	.000	5	4	0	0	0	0	26	30	110	8	8	2	0	1	7	0	0	11	0	1
Forsch, Robert, St.L.	3.19	10	5	.667	20	20	1	0	0	0	124	106	501	47	44	7	7	4	29	3	4	41	3	1
Forster, Terry, L.A.*	4.06	0	1	.000	21	0	0	6	0	0	31	37	137	14	14	1	2	0	15	3	0	17	3	0
Fryman, Woodrow, Mtl.*	1.88	5	3	.625	35	0	0	16	7	0	43	38	172	16	9	1	0	3	14	1	1	25	0	0
Garber, H. Eugene, Atl.	2.59	4	6	.400	35	0	0	17	2	0	59	49	251	23	17	2	2	0	20	9	0	34	1	1
Geisel, J. David, Chi.*	0.56	2	0	1.000	11	2	0	4	0	0	16	11	66	3	1	0	0	2	10	1	0	7	0	0
Goltz, David, L.A.	4.09	2	7	.222	26	8	0	3	1	0	77	83	319	35	35	4	4	2	25	3	0	48	2	1
Gomez, Luis, Atl.	27.00	0	0	---	1	0	0	1	0	0	1	3	8	3	3	0	0	0	2	0	0	0	0	0
Gorman, Thomas, Mtl.*	4.20	0	0	---	9	0	0	4	0	0	15	12	63	7	7	0	1	1	6	2	1	13	2	0

Pitcher & Club	ERA	W	L	PCT	G	GS	CG	GF	SV	SHO	IP	H	BFP	R	ER	HR	SH	SF	TBB	IBB	HB	SO	WP	BK
Griffin, Michael, Chi.	4.50	2	5	.286	16	9	0	4	1	0	52	64	228	27	26	4	5	5	9	0	0	20	2	2
Griffin, Thomas, S.F.	3.77	8	8	.500	22	22	3	0	0	1	129	121	557	62	54	8	5	2	57	8	7	83	5	2
Gullickson, William, Mtl	2.81	7	9	.438	22	22	3	0	0	2	157	142	640	54	49	3	5	2	34	8	1	115	1	0
Hanna, Preston, Atl	6.43	2	1	.667	20	1	0	10	0	0	35	45	164	27	25	2	4	5	23	4	2	22	6	0
Hargesheimer, Alan, S.F.	4.26	1	2	.333	6	3	0	1	0	0	19	20	80	9	9	3	1	0	9	2	0	6	0	2
Harris, Greg, N.Y.	4.43	3	5	.375	16	14	0	2	0	0	69	65	300	36	34	8	4	1	28	2	2	54	3	0
Hausman, Thomas, N.Y.	2.18	0	1	.000	20	0	0	12	2	0	33	28	130	9	8	2	2	1	7	1	2	13	2	0
Hernandez, Guillermo, Chi.*	3.86	0	0	---	12	0	0	5	0	0	14	14	62	7	6	2	2	1	8	1	0	13	1	0
Holland, Alfred, S.F.*	2.41	7	5	.583	47	0	0	23	7	0	101	87	431	31	27	3	4	5	44	11	2	78	4	1
Hooton, Burt, L.A.	2.28	11	6	.647	23	23	5	0	0	4	142	124	571	42	36	3	5	5	33	2	2	74	6	0
Howe, Steve, L.A.*	2.50	5	3	.625	41	0	0	25	8	0	54	51	227	27	15	3	2	4	18	7	2	32	3	3
Howell, Jay, Chi.	4.91	2	0	1.000	10	2	0	2	0	0	22	23	97	13	12	2	3	1	10	0	2	10	0	0
Hrabosky, Alan, Atl.*	1.06	1	1	.500	24	0	0	9	1	0	34	24	131	7	4	7	4	2	9	9	0	13	3	0
Hume, Thomas, Cin.	3.44	9	4	.692	51	0	0	20	13	0	68	63	281	27	26	3	5	2	31	9	1	27	1	0
Jackson, Grant, Pitt.-Mtl.*	3.77	4	4	.500	45	0	0	16	4	0	43	44	189	19	18	5	3	3	19	5	0	21	2	1
Jones, Odell, Pitt.	3.33	4	5	.444	13	13	1	0	0	0	54	51	232	25	20	3	5	3	23	6	1	30	1	0
Jones, Randall, N.Y.*	4.88	1	8	.111	22	12	0	5	0	0	59	60	229	36	32	8	4	3	17	1	0	14	2	1
Kaat, James, St.L.*	3.40	6	6	.500	41	1	0	22	1	0	53	63	233	25	20	3	5	3	23	8	1	8	1	0
Knepper, Robert, Hou.*	2.18	9	5	.643	24	22	6	0	0	5	157	128	617	41	38	5	6	3	38	4	0	75	8	0
Kravec, Kenneth, Chi.*	5.08	1	6	.143	13	13	2	0	0	0	78	80	356	48	44	5	10	6	39	6	4	50	1	2
Krukow, Michael, Chi.	3.69	9	9	.500	25	25	2	0	0	1	144	146	622	68	59	11	7	7	55	6	6	101	4	1
Kuhaulua, Fred, S.D.*	2.48	1	0	1.000	11	2	0	2	0	0	29	28	119	10	8	1	1	0	9	1	2	16	1	1
LaCorte, Frank, Hou.	3.64	4	2	.667	37	0	0	22	5	0	42	41	184	18	17	1	1	1	21	3	1	40	6	0
LaCoss, Michael, Cin.	6.12	4	7	.364	20	13	1	0	0	1	78	102	354	55	53	7	4	4	30	4	1	22	1	0
LaPoint, David, St.L.*	4.09	1	0	1.000	5	2	0	2	0	0	11	27	45	13	5	1	1	1	2	1	0	4	0	1
Larson, Daniel, Phil.	4.18	3	0	1.000	13	4	0	0	0	0	28	27	122	13	13	3	4	2	15	0	1	15	2	0
Lavelle, Gary, S.F.*	3.82	2	6	.250	31	0	0	16	2	0	66	58	269	33	28	4	3	6	23	4	0	45	1	2
Lea, Charles, Mtl.	4.64	5	4	.556	12	11	2	0	0	2	64	63	267	33	33	3	6	3	26	0	1	31	4	1
Leach, Terry, N.Y.	2.57	1	1	.500	21	1	0	3	0	0	35	26	139	11	10	2	2	0	12	1	0	16	1	0
Leary, Timothy, N.Y.	0.00	0	0	---	1	1	0	0	0	0	2	0	7	0	0	0	0	0	1	0	0	3	1	0
Lee, Mark, Pitt.	2.70	0	2	.000	12	0	0	4	0	0	20	17	83	6	6	1	5	0	5	1	0	5	1	0
Lee, William, Mtl*	2.93	5	6	.455	31	24	6	0	0	1	89	90	365	33	29	6	8	1	14	2	2	34	2	1
Leibrandt, Charles, Cin.*	3.60	1	1	.500	7	7	0	0	0	0	30	28	128	12	12	0	2	3	15	2	0	9	0	0
Littell, Mark, St.L.	4.39	1	3	.250	28	0	0	13	2	0	41	36	186	21	20	2	3	0	31	7	0	22	2	0
Littlefield, John, S.D.	3.66	2	3	.400	42	0	0	13	2	0	64	53	259	28	26	5	4	0	28	5	1	21	1	0

Pitcher	ERA	W	L	Pct.	IP	H	R	ER	BB	SO	WP	Bk
Lollar, W. Timothy, S.D.*	6.08	2	8	.200	77	85	56	52	51	38	7	4
Long, Robert, Pitt.	5.85	2	4	.333	20	23	14	14	10	8	0	0
Lucas, Gary, S.D.*	2.00	7	7	.500	90	78	26	20	36	53	1	1
Lyle, Albert, Phil.*	4.44	9	6	.600	75	85	40	37	33	29	3	2
Lynch, Edward, N.Y.	2.93	4	5	.444	80	79	32	35	21	27	3	1
Mahler, Richard, Atl.	2.81	8	6	.571	112	109	35	41	43	54	3	1
Marshall, Michael G., N.Y.	2.61	3	2	.600	26	26	10	10	8	8	2	1
Martin, John, St.L.*	3.41	8	5	.615	103	85	43	39	26	36	0	3
Martinez, Silvio, St.L.*	3.99	2	5	.286	97	95	48	43	39	34	2	1
Martz, Randy, Chi.	3.67	5	7	.417	108	103	44	44	49	32	2	0
Matula, Richard, Atl.	6.43	0	0	---	7	11	5	5	2	0	3	0
McClothen, Lynn, Chi.	4.75	2	8	.200	55	71	32	29	28	26	0	2
McGraw, Frank, Phil.*	2.66	2	4	.333	44	35	13	13	14	26	2	0
McWilliams, Larry, Atl.*	3.08	2	1	.667	38	31	13	13	8	23	0	2
Miller, Dyar, N.Y.	3.32	1	0	1.000	38	49	20	14	15	22	2	0
Minton, Gregory, S.F.	2.89	4	5	.444	84	84	28	27	36	29	0	0
Moffitt, Randall, S.F.	8.18	0	0	---	11	15	10	10	2	11	0	0
Montefusco, John, Atl.	3.51	2	3	.400	77	75	30	30	27	32	2	2
Moskau, Paul, Cin.	4.91	2	1	.667	55	54	30	30	32	70	2	1
Mura, Stephen, S.D.	4.27	5	14	.263	157	156	72	66	50	12	0	0
Niedenfuer, Thomas, L.A.	3.81	3	1	.750	26	25	11	11	6	77	4	0
Niekro, Joseph, Hou.	2.82	9	9	.500	166	150	58	52	47	62	2	0
Niekro, Philip, Atl.	3.11	7	7	.500	139	120	60	48	56	34	3	0
Noles, Dickie, Phil.	4.19	2	2	.500	58	57	30	27	23	18	2	2
Orosco, Jesse, N.Y.*	1.59	1	0	1.000	17	13	4	9	6	6	0	0
Otten, James, St.L.	5.25	0	0	---	13	16	9	21	20	29	3	1
Pastore, Frank, Cin.	4.02	4	9	.308	132	125	59	59	35	81	3	1
Pena, Alejandro, L.A.	2.88	1	1	.500	25	18	8	8	11	14	0	0
Perez, Pascual, Pitt.	3.98	2	7	.222	86	92	50	38	34	46	5	1
Perry, Gaylord, Atl.	3.93	8	9	.471	151	182	83	66	24	60	1	0
Pladson, Gordon, Hou.	9.00	0	0	---	4	9	4	4	3	3	0	0
Power, Ted, L.A.*	3.21	1	3	.250	14	16	6	5	7	7	3	0
Price, Joseph, Cin.*	2.50	6	1	.857	54	42	19	15	18	41	0	1
Proly, Michael, Phil.	3.86	2	1	.667	63	66	29	27	19	19	2	1
Puleo, Charles, N.Y.	0.00	0	0	---	13	8	8	0	8	8	1	0
Ratzer, Steven, Mtl.	6.35	1	1	.500	17	23	14	12	7	4	1	1

Pitcher & Club	ERA	W	L	PCT	G	GS	CG	GF	SV	SHO	IP	H	BFP	R	ER	HR	SH	SF	TBB	IBB	HB	SO	WP	BK
Reardon, Jeffrey, N.Y.-Mtl.	2.19	3	0	1.000	43	0	0	33	8	0	70	48	279	17	17	5	3	3	21	4	2	49	1	0
Reed, Jerry, Phil.	7.20	0	1	.000	3	0	0	2	0	0	5	7	27	4	4	1	0	0	1	0	1	4	1	0
Reed, Ronald, Phil.	3.10	5	3	.625	39	0	0	22	2	0	61	54	251	26	21	5	6	1	6	8	4	40	5	1
Reuschel, Ricky, Chi.	3.45	4	7	.364	13	13	1	0	0	0	86	87	358	40	33	4	5	0	17	3	4	53	5	0
Reuss, Jerry, L.A.*	2.29	10	4	.714	22	22	8	0	0	2	153	138	608	44	39	6	5	3	23	4	3	51	5	1
Rhoden, Richard, Pitt.	3.90	9	4	.692	21	21	4	0	0	0	136	147	588	66	59	8	6	2	27	3	2	76	6	1
Rincon, Andrew, St.L.	1.75	3	1	.750	5	5	1	0	0	1	36	27	133	8	7	0	7	0	5	1	1	13	1	1
Ripley, Allen, S.F.	4.05	4	4	.500	19	14	0	1	0	0	91	103	396	45	41	5	5	1	27	2	3	47	6	0
Roberts, David, N.Y.*	9.60	0	3	.000	5	2	0	1	0	0	15	26	76	18	16	4	0	0	10	4	0	5	0	0
Robinson, Don, Pitt.	5.92	0	0	.000	16	2	0	7	0	0	38	47	182	27	25	7	3	0	17	7	0	17	3	0
Rogers, Stephen, Mtl.	3.41	12	8	.600	22	22	7	0	0	3	161	149	652	64	61	7	4	2	23	4	2	87	1	0
Romo, Enrique, Pitt.	4.50	1	3	.250	33	0	0	14	9	0	42	47	186	27	21	5	7	3	41	7	1	23	1	1
Rowland, Michael, S.F.	3.38	0	1	.000	9	1	0	0	0	0	16	13	66	7	6	1	1	1	18	2	1	8	0	0
Ruhle, Vernon, Hou.	2.91	4	6	.400	20	15	1	3	0	0	102	97	412	36	33	9	4	0	6	0	1	39	0	0
Ruthven, Richard, Phil.	5.14	12	7	.632	23	22	5	0	0	1	147	162	648	94	84	10	8	2	20	4	3	80	6	1
Ryan, L. Nolan, Hou.*	1.69	11	5	.688	21	21	5	0	0	3	149	99	605	34	28	4	5	7	54	4	3	140	16	0
Sambito, Joseph, Hou.*	1.83	5	5	.500	49	0	0	32	10	0	64	43	255	17	13	4	6	4	22	5	2	41	2	0
Sanderson, Scott, Mtl.	2.96	9	7	.563	22	22	4	0	0	0	137	122	560	60	45	10	7	4	31	5	2	77	2	0
Scott, Michael, N.Y.	3.90	5	10	.333	23	23	1	0	0	0	136	130	551	65	59	11	5	2	34	1	1	54	2	2
Scurry, Rodney, Pitt.*	3.77	4	4	.500	27	0	0	10	1	0	74	74	329	33	31	8	1	5	40	11	1	65	3	0
Searage, Raymond, N.Y.*	3.65	1	0	1.000	26	0	0	7	1	0	37	34	156	16	15	2	3	2	17	3	0	31	4	0
Seaver, G. Thomas, Cin.	2.55	14	2	.875	23	23	6	0	0	1	166	120	671	51	47	9	6	2	66	8	3	87	5	2
Shirley, Robert, St.L.*	4.10	6	4	.600	23	11	0	5	1	0	79	78	342	41	36	6	9	9	34	3	5	36	1	1
Show, Eric, S.D.	3.13	1	1	.500	15	0	0	4	3	0	23	17	92	9	8	3	6	0	9	3	1	36	0	0
Smith, Billy, Hou.	3.00	1	1	.500	10	1	0	1	0	0	21	20	81	7	7	1	2	0	3	0	0	9	2	0
Smith, Bryn, Mtl.	2.77	1	0	1.000	7	0	0	1	0	0	13	14	53	4	4	2	3	0	2	1	0	9	0	0
Smith, David, Hou.	2.76	5	3	.625	42	0	0	22	8	0	75	54	305	26	23	2	6	2	23	8	2	52	4	0
Smith, Lee, Chi.	3.49	3	6	.333	40	1	0	12	5	0	67	57	280	31	26	4	5	0	31	8	0	50	7	1
Solomon, Eddie, Pitt.	3.12	8	6	.571	22	17	2	1	1	0	127	133	521	49	44	10	5	3	22	2	1	38	3	2
Sorensen, Lary, St.L.	3.28	7	7	.500	23	23	3	0	0	1	140	149	579	59	51	5	7	7	26	4	1	52	1	5
Sosa, Elias, Mtl.	3.69	2	2	.333	32	0	0	17	3	0	39	46	170	18	16	4	3	3	8	3	0	18	1	0
Soto, Mario, Cin.	3.29	12	9	.571	25	25	10	0	0	4	175	142	717	69	64	13	3	4	61	3	1	151	4	3
Sprowl, Robert, Hou.*	5.90	0	1	.000	15	1	0	4	0	0	29	40	138	20	19	1	1	2	20	1	0	14	3	0
Stewart, David, L.A.	2.51	4	3	.571	32	0	0	6	6	0	43	40	184	13	12	1	2	2	14	5	2	29	0	0
Sutcliffe, Richard, L.A.	4.02	2	2	.500	14	6	0	5	0	0	47	41	197	24	21	5	1	0	16	2	2	16	0	0

Sutter, H. Bruce, St.L. ...... 2.63 3 5 .375 48 0 0 36 25 0 82 64 329 24 24 5 7 3 24 8 1 57 0 1
Sutton, Donald, Hou. ...... 2.60 11 9 .550 23 23 6 0 0 0 159 132 624 51 46 6 13 6 29 3 1 104 1 0
Swan, Craig, N.Y. 3.21 2 0 1.000 5 3 0 0 0 0 14 14 50 5 6 0 1 1 9 1 0 9 0 0
Sykes, Robert, St.L.* 4.62 2 0 .500 22 4 0 7 0 0 37 37 160 20 19 4 2 0 18 1 3 14 0 3
Tekulve, Kenton, Pitt. 2.49 5 5 .500 45 0 0 27 3 0 65 61 268 19 18 5 4 2 17 1 1 34 2 1
Tiant, Luis, Pitt. 3.95 5 5 .500 9 9 1 0 0 0 57 54 242 31 25 3 1 0 19 2 0 32 0 0
Tidrow, Richard, Chi. 5.04 3 10 .231 51 0 0 30 9 0 75 73 328 45 42 6 11 1 30 15 0 39 1 1
Tufts, Robert, S.F.* 3.60 0 0 ---- 11 0 0 0 0 0 15 20 74 9 6 1 1 1 6 1 0 12 1 1
Urrea, John, S.D. 2.39 2 2 .500 38 0 0 16 2 0 49 43 215 14 13 1 3 3 28 0 0 19 2 2
Valenzuela, Fernando, L.A.* 2.48 13 7 .650 25 25 11 0 0 0 192 140 758 55 53 11 9 0 61 4 0 180 4 4
Walk, Robert, Atl. 4.60 1 4 .200 12 8 0 1 0 0 43 41 189 22 22 6 2 0 23 0 0 16 1 2
Welch, Robert, L.A. 3.45 9 5 .643 23 23 2 0 0 1 141 141 601 56 54 11 5 1 41 3 0 88 2 1
Welch, Christopher, S.D.* 3.77 6 7 .462 22 19 4 2 0 0 124 122 512 55 52 9 5 2 41 2 0 51 1 1
Whitson, Eddie, S.F. 4.02 4 9 .400 22 22 2 0 0 0 123 130 534 61 55 10 6 2 47 5 0 65 3 1
Wise, Richard, S.D. 3.77 4 8 .333 18 18 0 0 0 0 98 116 419 44 41 10 2 1 19 4 0 27 2 1
Zachry, Patrick, N.Y. 4.14 7 14 .333 24 24 3 0 0 0 139 151 616 78 64 13 11 9 56 1 4 76 1 1

CLUB PITCHING

Club	ERA	G	CG	SHO	SV	IP	BFP	H	R	ER	HR	HB	TBB	IBB	SO	WP	BK
Houston	2.66	110	23	19	25	990	4034	842	331	293	64	11	300	24	610	36	4
Los Angeles	3.01	110	26	19	24	997	4099	904	356	333	54	14	302	38	603	19	1
San Francisco	3.28	111	8	9	33	1009	4302	970	414	368	57	24	393	56	561	36	13
Montreal	3.30	108	20	12	23	975	4008	902	394	357	58	18	268	21	520	28	2
Atlanta	3.45	107	11	4	24	968	4078	936	416	371	62	11	330	31	471	25	6
New York	3.55	105	7	3	24	926	3951	906	432	365	74	13	336	35	490	26	10
Pittsburgh	3.56	103	11	5	29	942	4029	953	425	373	60	15	346	51	492	32	11
St. Louis	3.63	103	11	5	33	943	3910	902	417	380	52	15	290	45	388	22	11
San Diego	3.72	110	9	6	23	1002	4297	1013	455	414	64	17	414	59	492	30	19
Cincinnati	3.73	108	25	14	20	966	4065	863	440	400	67	12	393	40	593	27	7
Chicago	4.01	106	6	2	20	957	4165	983	483	426	59	21	388	60	532	42	8
Philadelphia	4.05	107	19	5	23	960	4086	967	472	432	72	14	347	45	580	32	16
TOTALS	3.49	644	176	103	301	11635	49024	11141	5035	4512	719	185	4107	505	6332	355	108

OFFICIAL 1981 AMERICAN LEAGUE AVERAGES

compiled by SPORTS INFORMATION CENTER

STANDING OF CLUBS AT CLOSE OF 1981 SEASON

FIRST HALF

AMERICAN LEAGUE WEST

	Won	Lost	Pct.	Games Behind
Oakland	37	23	.617	
Texas	33	22	.600	1½
Chicago	31	22	.585	2½
California	31	29	.517	6
Kansas City	20	30	.400	12
Seattle	21	36	.368	14½
Minnesota	17	39	.304	18

AMERICAN LEAGUE EAST

	Won	Lost	Pct.	Games Behind
New York	34	22	.607	
Baltimore	31	23	.574	2
Milwaukee	31	25	.554	2
Detroit	31	26	.544	3½
Boston	30	26	.536	4
Cleveland	26	24	.520	5
Toronto	16	42	.276	19

SECOND HALF

	Won	Lost	Pct.	Games Behind
Kansas City	30	23	.566	
Oakland	27	22	.551	1
Texas	24	26	.480	4½
Minnesota	24	29	.453	6
Seattle	23	29	.442	6½
Chicago	23	30	.434	7
California	20	30	.400	8½

	Won	Lost	Pct.	Games Behind
Milwaukee	31	22	.585	
Boston	29	23	.558	1½
Detroit	29	23	.558	1½
Baltimore	28	23	.549	2
Cleveland	26	27	.491	5
New York	25	26	.490	5
Toronto	21	27	.438	7½

DIVISIONAL PLAYOFFS: New York defeated Milwaukee 3 games to 2   Oakland defeated Kansas City 3 games to 0

CHAMPIONSHIP SERIES: New York defeated Oakland 3 games to 0

BATTING

TOP FIFTEEN QUALIFIERS FOR BATTING CHAMPIONSHIP
(3.1 Plate Appearances Times Games Played By Team)

*Bats Lefthanded   †Switch Hitter

Batter and Club	AVG	G	AB	R	H	TB	2B	3B	HR	RBI	GW RBI	SH	SF	HB	TBB	IBB	SO	SB	CS	GI DP	SLG	OBP
Lansford, Carney, Bos	.336	102	399	61	134	175	23	3	4	52	7	1	2		34	3	28	15	10	6	.439	.391
Paciorek, Tom, Sea	.326	104	405	50	132	206	28	2	14	66	13	1	7	4	35	3	50	13	10	10	.609	.385
Cooper, Cecil, Milw.*	.320	106	416	70	133	206	35	1	12	60	11	1	5	2	28	4	30	5	4	16	.495	.367
Henderson, Rickey, Oak	.319	108	423	89	135	185	18	4	6	35	7	0	4	4	64	4	68	56	22	7	.437	.411
Hargrove, Mike, Clev.*	.317	94	322	43	102	129	21	0	2	49	4	4	5	5	60	5	16	5	6	14	.401	.432
Brett, George, K.C.*	.314	89	347	42	109	168	27	7	8	43	6	4	7	3	27	7	23	14	6	7	.484	.365
Zisk, Richie, Sea	.311	94	357	42	111	173	12	1	16	43	4	0	1	3	28	3	63	0	4	8	.485	.366
Oliver, Al, Tex.*	.309	102	421	53	130	173	29	1	0	55	8	4	0	2	24	10	28	9	2	17	.411	.349
Remy, Jerry, Bos.*	.307	88	358	55	110	121	9	1	0	31	4	13	3	0	36	2	30	9	2	6	.338	.371
Mumphrey, Jerry, N.Y.†	.307	80	319	44	98	137	11	5	1	32	5	5	2	0	24	7	27	13	9	8	.429	.356
Carew, Rod, Cal.*	.305	93	364	57	111	136	17	2	2	21	1	10	2	4	45	4	45	16	9	8	.374	.381
Grich, Bobby, Cal.	.304	100	352	56	107	191	14	2	22	61	8	3	3	4	44	4	71	2	4	5	.543	.381
Wilson, Willie, K.C.†	.303	102	439	54	133	160	10	7	1	32	7	4	5	13	18	0	42	34	16	6	.364	.336
Lemon, Chet, Chi.	.302	94	328	50	99	161	23	6	9	50	4	5	4	13	33	0	48	5	8	10	.491	.388
Almon, Bill, Chi.	.301	103	349	46	105	131	10	2	4	41	2	2	3	2	21	0	60	16	6	4	.375	.344

INDIVIDUAL BATTING
(All Players Listed Alphabetically)

*Bats Lefthanded   †Switch Hitter

Batter and Club	AVG	G	AB	R	H	TB	2B	3B	HR	RBI	GW RBI	SH	SF	HB	TBB	IBB	SO	SB	CS	GI DP	SLG	OBP
Adams, Glenn, Minn.*	.209	72	220	13	46	62	10	0	2	24	3	0	2	0	20	4	26	0	0	10	.282	.275
Aikens, Willie, K.C.*	.266	101	349	45	93	160	16	0	17	53	6	0	5	1	62	12	47	0	8	11	.458	.382
Ainge, Danny, Tor	.187	86	246	20	46	56	6	2	0	14	0	4	1	1	23	1	41	8	5		.228	.259
Allen, Kim, Sea	.000	19	3	1	0	0	0	0	0	0	0	0	0	0	2	1	0	2	1	0	.000	.000

*Bats Lefthanded †Switch Hitter

Batter and Club	AVG	G	AB	R	H	TB	2B	3B	HR	RBI	GW RBI	SH	SF	HB	TBB	IBB	SO	SB	CS	GI DP	SLG	OBP
Allenson, Gary, Bos.	.223	47	139	23	31	54	8	0	5	25	2	1	1	—	23	0	33	0	6	6	.388	.337
Almon, Bill, Chi.	.301	103	349	46	105	131	10	2	4	41	2	3	2	—	21	1	60	16	6	4	.375	.344
Anderson, Jim, Sea.	.204	70	162	12	33	46	7	3	0	19	1	2	1	—	17	0	29	3	5	5	.284	.283
Armas, Tony, Oak.	.261	109	440	51	115	211	24	3	22	76	11	—	2	2	19	6	115	0	1	6	.480	.295
Ashford, Tucker, N.Y.	.—	3	..	0	0	0	0	0	0	0	0	0	0	0	0	0	0	0	0	0	.—	.—
Auerbach, Rick, Sea.	.155	38	84	12	13	19	0	3	0	6	0	1	1	—	4	1	15	0	0	1	.226	.202
Ayala, Benny, Balt.	.279	44	86	12	24	35	2	3	2	13	2	—	1	1	11	0	9	0	1	2	.407	.367
Babitt, Shooty, Oak.	.256	54	156	10	40	47	1	3	0	12	0	6	1	1	13	0	13	5	4	2	.301	.314
Baines, Harold, Chi.*	.286	82	280	42	80	135	11	7	10	41	4	—	3	—	12	2	41	6	2	6	.482	.320
Baker, Chuck, Minn.	.182	40	66	6	12	18	1	—	0	6	0	2	—	—	1	0	8	0	0	1	.273	.194
Balboni, Steve, N.Y.	.286	4	7	2	2	5	1	—	0	2	0	—	—	—	—	0	4	0	0	0	.714	.375
Bando, Chris, Clev.†	.213	21	47	3	10	13	3	0	0	6	2	—	1	—	2	0	2	1	0	—	.277	.245
Bando, Sal, Milw.	.200	32	65	10	13	23	4	—	2	9	0	—	1	—	6	1	19	0	3	1	.354	.268
Bannister, Alan, Clev.	.263	68	232	32	61	77	11	2	0	17	2	1	1	—	16	2	19	16	2	1	.332	.310
Barfield, Jesse, Tor.	.232	25	95	7	22	35	3	0	2	9	0	—	3	—	4	0	19	2	3	4	.368	.270
Baumgarten, Ross, Chi.*	.—	21	0	0	0	0	0	0	0	0	0	0	0	0	0	0	0	0	0	0	.—	.—
Baylor, Don, Cal.	.239	103	377	52	90	161	18	1	17	66	11	—	7	6	42	1	51	3	3	13	.427	.326
Beamon, Charlie, Tor.*	.200	8	15	1	3	4	1	0	0	1	0	—	2	—	2	0	4	0	0	0	.267	.294
Belanger, Mark, Balt.	.165	64	139	9	23	33	3	2	1	10	1	5	—	—	12	0	25	2	1	4	.237	.242
Bell, Buddy, Tex.	.294	97	360	46	106	154	16	1	10	64	9	—	10	3	42	10	30	3	2	6	.428	.373
Bell, George, Tor.	.233	60	163	19	38	57	7	2	2	12	2	—	0	—	5	1	27	3	3	1	.350	.256
Beniquez, Juan, Cal.	.181	58	166	18	30	44	5	3	2	13	3	—	4	1	15	0	16	2	4	6	.265	.253
Bernazard, Tony, Chi.†	.276	106	384	53	106	146	14	4	6	34	7	—	9	1	54	0	66	2	4	5	.380	.368
Bochte, Bruce, Sea.*	.260	99	335	39	87	121	16	0	6	30	3	—	1	2	47	2	53	1	3	5	.361	.354
Bomback, Mark, Tor.	.—	21	0	0	0	0	0	0	0	0	0	0	0	0	0	0	0	0	0	0	.—	.—
Bonnell, Barry, Tor.	.220	66	227	21	50	77	7	4	4	28	4	—	3	—	12	0	25	4	3	8	.339	.263
Bonner, Bob, Balt.	.296	10	27	6	8	10	2	0	0	2	0	—	1	—	0	0	4	1	0	2	.370	.321
Bosetti, Rick, Tor.-Oak.	.197	34	66	9	13	15	2	0	0	5	0	1	—	—	5	0	9	0	2	0	.227	.254
Bosley, Thad, Milw.*	.229	42	105	11	24	26	2	0	0	6	0	—	—	—	6	0	13	2	1	2	.248	.270
Brett, George, K.C.*	.314	89	347	42	109	168	27	7	6	43	6	—	0	4	27	14	23	14	6	7	.484	.365
Brookens, Tom, Det.	.243	71	239	19	58	82	10	2	4	25	5	4	4	1	14	0	43	5	3	5	.343	.290
Brouhard, Mark, Milw.	.274	60	186	19	51	69	6	3	3	20	2	2	2	—	7	0	41	1	1	7	.371	.308
Brown, Bobby, N.Y.†	.226	31	62	5	14	15	1	0	0	6	0	—	1	—	5	0	15	4	2	1	.242	.284
Brown, Darrell, Det.†	.250	16	4	4	1	1	0	0	0	0	0	—	0	—	0	0	1	1	0	0	.250	.250
Brunansky, Tom, Cal.	.152	11	33	3	5	14	3	0	2	6	0	—	0	—	8	0	10	1	0	0	.424	.317

Player	AVG	G	AB	R	H	2B	3B	HR	RBI	SH	SF	HP	BB	SO	SB	CS	GDP	vs L	vs R
Budaska, Mark, Oak.†	.156	9	32	3	5	1	0	0	4	0	1	0	2	5	0	0	1	.188	.250
Bulling, Terry, Sea	.247	62	154	15	38	6	0	0	21	7	2	0	15	20	0	0	2	.305	.341
Bumbry, Al, Balt.*	.273	101	392	61	107	17	6	2	27	10	4	2	51	51	22	15	6	.337	.360
Burleson, Rick, Cal	.293	109	430	53	126	13	3	5	33	2	4	2	38	27	6	6	17	.372	.360
Burroughs, Jeff, Sea	.254	89	319	32	81	18	1	11	41	0	5	3	64	32	1	1	13	.395	.339
Butera, Sal, Minn	.240	62	167	13	40	7	0	0	22	3	1	1	14	18	0	2	9	.293	.328
Campaneris, Bert, Cal.	.256	55	82	11	21	2	1	0	5	1	1	0	6	10	0	2	2	.341	.299
Carew, Rod, Cal.*	.305	93	364	57	111	28	2	1	45	2	2	0	45	21	6	9	7	.374	.381
Castillo, Marty, Det.	.125	6	8	0	1	0	0	1	2	0	0	0	1	1	0	0	0	.125	.125
Cerone, Rick, N.Y.	.268	101	381	41	102	30	4	14	85	5	2	4	18	36	1	4	10	.396	.303
Castino, John, Minn	.244	71	234	23	57	12	2	2	21	2	2	0	21	21	0	1	9	.342	.280
Chalk, Dave, K.C.	.224	27	49	2	11	2	0	0	5	1	0	1	5	4	2	2	2	.286	.283
Charboneau, Joe, Clev	.210	48	138	14	29	11	1	6	18	0	1	3	18	38	1	2	8	.362	.248
Clark, Bobby, Cal	.250	34	88	12	22	3	1	1	19	0	0	4	7	17	5	2	5	.432	.305
Clark, Bryan, Sea.*	—	2	0	0	0	0	0	0	0	0	0	0	0	0	0	0	0	—	—
Concepcion, Onix, K.C.	.320	30	0	0	0	0	0	0	0	0	0	0	0	0	0	0	0	.495	.367
Cooper, Cecil, Milw.*	.320	106	416	70	133	35	6	12	60	0	5	0	30	36	4	5	16	.235	.263
Corcoran, Tim, Minn.*	.176	22	51	4	9	0	1	0	4	0	1	0	7	6	0	0	3	.000	.200
Corey, Mark, Balt.	.000	10	8	2	0	0	0	0	0	0	0	0	2	2	0	0	0	—	—
Cowens, Al, Det.	.261	85	253	27	66	18	0	11	18	3	1	1	22	36	3	5	3	.348	.322
Cox, Jeff, Oak.	.231	5	13	2	3	0	0	1	0	0	0	0	4	4	0	0	0	.308	.231
Cox, Larry, Tex.	.300	16	50	6	15	4	0	0	5	0	1	2	10	5	0	0	3	.500	.364
Cox, Ted, Tor.	.246	68	134	12	33	9	0	4	12	3	1	0	12	12	0	2	4	.381	.380
Crowley, Terry, Balt.*	.256	94	352	51	90	25	2	12	24	1	4	2	40	40	2	0	6	.324	.335
Cruz, Julio, Sea.†	.263	96	369	41	97	24	4	2	38	4	3	0	18	27	43	10	3	.369	.318
Dauer, Rich, Balt.	.000	1	2	0	0	0	0	0	0	0	0	0	0	0	0	0	0	.000	.000
Davis, Bob, Cal	.050	17	20	0	1	0	0	0	2	2	0	0	0	7	0	0	1	.100	.136
Davis, Mike, Oak.*	.263	100	346	49	91	14	2	3	55	8	5	0	41	32	13	12	23	.454	.343
DeCinces, Doug, Balt	.215	92	251	24	54	10	1	8	15	3	5	1	32	36	1	3	18	.335	.306
Dempsey, Rick, Balt	.238	73	227	20	54	11	0	7	27	8	3	2	17	13	2	7	11	.379	.302
Dent, Bucky, N.Y.	.313	63	182	25	57	6	0	5	38	7	3	2	23	11	1	2	19	.533	.362
Diaz, Bo, Clev.	.290	72	269	33	78	19	3	5	19	0	2	2	28	29	0	6	9	.346	.334
Dilone, Miguel, Clev.†	—	27	0	0	0	0	0	0	0	0	0	0	0	0	0	0	0	—	—
Dotson, Richard, Chi	.249	93	317	47	79	14	2	11	41	46	2	3	35	0	1	1	11	.379	.351
Downing, Brian, Cal	.125	17	40	7	5	1	0	0	2	0	0	2	4	0	0	0	3	.125	.146
Doyle, Brian, Oak.*	.291	31	86	8	25	5	1	0	11	4	5	1	2	9	0	0	1	.326	.294
Drumright, Keith, Oak.*	.250	13	16	4	4	0	0	0	0	1	0	0	0	0	0	0	0	.250	.294
Duran, Dan, Tex.*	.224	68	134	16	30	3	0	0	10	2	0	3	19	41	2	1	2	.306	.325
Dwyer, Jim, Balt.*																			

*Bats Lefthanded †Switch Hitter

Batter and Club	AVG	G	AB	R	H	TB	2B	3B	HR	RBI	GW RBI	SH	SF	HB	TBB	IBB	SO	SB	CS	GI DP	SLG	OBP
Dybzinski, Jerry, Clev	.298	48	57	10	17	17	0	0	0	6	1	5	0	0	5	0	8	7	1	0	.298	.355
Dyer, Duffy, Det	—	2	2	0	0	0	0	0	0	0	0	0	0	0	0	0	0	0	0	0	—	—
Edler, Dave, Sea	.141	29	78	7	11	14	3	0	0	5	0	0	0	0	1	0	13	0	3	2	.179	.256
Edwards, Marshall, Milw.*	.241	40	58	10	14	17	3	0	0	4	0	2	0	1	0	0	8	6	1	1	.293	.241
Ellis, John, Tex.	.138	23	58	4	8	14	1	0	1	4	0	0	2	0	1	0	10	0	0	1	.241	.219
Engle, Dave, Minn.	.258	82	248	29	64	101	14	0	5	32	4	1	2	1	13	0	37	0	1	10	.407	.298
Essian, Jim, Chi.	.308	27	52	6	16	19	3	0	0	5	0	1	0	0	4	0	5	0	0	2	.365	.357
Evans, Dwight, Bos.	.296	108	412	84	122	215	19	4	22	71	6	0	3	1	85	10	85	3	2	8	.522	.418
Faedo, Lenny, Minn.	.195	12	41	3	8	10	2	0	0	6	1	1	0	0	1	0	5	0	0	0	.244	.214
Fahey, Bill, Det.*	.254	27	67	5	17	22	2	0	1	9	0	2	0	0	4	1	4	0	1	1	.328	.275
Ferguson, Joe, Cal	.233	12	30	5	7	11	1	0	1	5	1	1	1	0	9	0	5	0	0	1	.367	.410
Firova, Dan, Sea.	.000	13	2	3	0	0	0	0	0	0	0	0	0	0	0	0	8	0	0	0	.000	.000
Fischlin, Mike, Clev	.233	22	43	3	10	11	1	0	0	5	0	1	0	3	0	1	6	3	2	0	.256	.283
Fisk, Carlton, Chi.	.263	96	338	44	89	122	12	0	7	45	5	1	5	12	38	0	37	3	3	9	.361	.358
Foote, Barry, N.Y.	.208	40	125	12	26	48	14	1	2	10	4	0	1	5	8	1	21	0	2	2	.384	.256
Ford, Dan, Cal.	.277	97	375	53	104	165	14	1	15	48	4	0	5	2	23	0	71	2	0	16	.440	.328
Funderburk, Mark, Minn.	.200	8	15	2	3	4	1	0	0	2	0	0	1	0	0	0	1	0	0	0	.267	.294
Gaetti, Gary, Minn	.192	9	26	4	5	11	0	0	2	3	0	0	0	0	2	0	6	0	0	0	.423	.192
Gamble, Oscar, N.Y.*	.238	80	189	24	45	83	8	0	10	27	3	0	2	1	35	4	23	0	2	4	.439	.360
Gantner, Jim, Milw.*	.267	107	352	35	94	116	14	1	2	33	3	3	1	1	29	0	29	3	6	6	.330	.328
Garcia, Damaso, Tor.	.252	64	250	24	63	76	8	1	1	13	1	3	3	0	9	1	32	13	6	6	.304	.278
Garcia, Danny, K.C.	.143	12	14	4	2	2	0	0	0	0	0	1	0	0	0	0	2	0	0	0	.143	.143
Gedman, Rich, Bos.*	.288	62	205	22	59	89	15	0	5	26	0	3	1	0	9	1	31	0	0	9	.434	.321
Geronimo, Cesar, K.C.*	.246	59	118	14	29	39	0	2	2	13	1	2	0	0	11	2	16	6	1	3	.331	.310
Gibson, Kirk, Det.*	.328	83	290	41	95	139	11	3	8	40	5	1	1	2	18	1	64	17	5	9	.479	.371
Goodwin, Danny, Minn.*	.225	59	151	18	34	48	6	1	2	17	1	1	1	2	16	0	32	3	1	9	.318	.299
Graham, Dan, Balt.*	.176	55	142	7	25	34	7	1	0	11	0	0	4	1	13	1	32	0	0	3	.239	.245
Gray, Gary, Sea.	.245	69	208	27	51	99	7	1	13	31	3	0	0	4	4	1	44	2	4	5	.476	.259
Grich, Bobby, Cal.	.304	100	352	56	107	191	14	2	22	61	8	0	3	4	40	4	71	2	4	5	.543	.381
Griffin, Alfredo, Tor.†	.209	101	388	30	81	112	19	6	1	21	5	5	4	1	17	1	38	8	12	6	.289	.244
Gross, Wayne, Oak.*	.206	82	243	29	50	89	7	1	10	31	3	3	4	2	34	0	28	2	1	6	.366	.308
Grote, Jerry, K.C.	.304	22	56	4	17	25	3	1	1	9	0	4	2	1	2	0	2	0	1	0	.446	.350
Grubb, John, Tex.*	.231	67	199	26	46	66	9	1	3	26	3	1	1	1	23	1	25	0	3	6	.332	.317
Hairston, Jerry, Chi.†	.280	9	25	5	7	11	1	0	1	6	1	0	0	1	2	0	4	0	0	0	.440	.357
Hancock, Garry, Bos.*	.156	26	45	4	7	10	3	0	0	3	0	1	0	1	1	0	4	0	2	2	.222	.191

Player	AVG	G	AB	R	H	2B	3B	HR	RBI	SLG	OBP
Hargrove, Mike, Clev.*	.317	94	322	43	102	21	0	2	49	.401	.432
Harlow, Larry, Cal.*	.207	43	82	13	17	1	0	0	4	.220	.337
Harper, Brian, Cal.	.273	4	11	1	3	0	0	0	0	.273	.273
Harrah, Toby, Clev	.291	103	361	64	105	12	4	5	44	.388	.403
Harris, John, Cal.*	.247	36	77	5	19	3	0	1	9	.403	.275
Hassey, Ron, Clev.*	.232	61	190	8	44	4	0	3	25	.268	.301
Hatcher, Mickey, Minn	.255	99	377	36	96	23	1	0	37	.350	.287
Hayes, Von, Clev.*	.257	43	109	19	28	8	2	2	17	.394	.352
Heath, Mike, Oak	.236	84	301	26	71	7	3	8	30	.346	.270
Hebner, Richie, Det.*	.226	78	226	19	51	8	6	2	28	.345	.314
Henderson, Dave, Sea.	.167	59	126	17	21	3	0	6	13	.333	.266
Henderson, Rickey, Oak	.319	108	423	89	135	18	4	6	35	.437	.411
Hill, Marc, Chi.	.000	16	6	0	0	0	0	0	0	.000	.000
Hisle, Larry, Milw.	.230	27	87	11	20	6	0	2	11	.414	.295
Hobson, Butch, Cal.	.235	85	268	27	63	7	0	4	36	.336	.326
Hoffman, Glenn, Bos.	.231	78	242	28	56	10	1	2	20	.285	.271
Hosley, Tim, Oak.	.095	18	21	2	2	0	0	0	5	.238	.174
Howell, Roy, Milw.*	.238	76	244	37	58	13	0	6	33	.373	.309
Hrbek, Kent, Minn.*	.239	24	67	5	16	4	0	4	6	.358	.301
Hurdle, Clint, K.C.	.329	28	76	12	25	5	0	1	15	.553	.427
Iorg, Garth, Tor.*	.242	70	215	17	52	11	0	1	10	.293	.269
Ireland, Tim, K.C.†	—	4	0	1	0	0	0	0	0	—	—
Jackson, Reggie, N.Y.*	.237	94	334	33	79	17	1	15	54	.428	.331
Jackson, Ron, Minn.-Det.	.270	85	270	29	73	17	1	3	40	.396	.318
Johnson, Bobby, Tex.	.278	6	18	2	5	0	0	0	5	.611	.316
Johnson, Cliff, Oak.	.260	84	273	40	71	8	0	9	59	.476	.336
Johnson, Lamar, Chi.	.276	41	134	10	37	7	1	5	15	.351	.302
Johnston, Greg, Minn.*	.125	5	16	2	2	0	0	0	0	.125	.222
Jones, Bobby, Tex.*	.265	78	34	2	9	5	0	0	19	.559	.286
Jones, Lynn, Det.	.259	71	174	19	45	5	1	0	19	.322	.332
Kearney, Bob, Oak	—	1	0	0	0	0	0	0	0	—	—
Keatley, Greg, K.C.	—	2	0	0	0	0	0	0	0	—	—
Kelleher, Mick, Det.	.221	61	77	10	17	4	0	1	16	.273	.286
Kelly, Pat, Clev.*	.213	48	75	8	16	4	0	0	14	.307	.337
Kemp, Steve, Det.*	.277	105	372	52	103	18	0	10	49	.419	.393
Klutts, Mickey, Oak	.370	15	46	9	17	4	0	2	11	.696	.396
Krenchicki, Wayne, Balt.*	.214	33	56	7	12	4	0	2	6	.286	.267
Kuiper, Duane, Clev.*	.257	72	206	15	53	6	0	0	14	.286	.285
Kuntz, Rusty, Chi.	.255	67	55	15	14	2	0	0	4	.291	.339

*Bats Lefthanded †Switch Hitter

Batter and Club	AVG	G	AB	R	H	TB	2B	3B	HR	RBI	GW RBI	SH	SF	HB	TBB	IBB	SO	SB	CS	GI DP	SLG	OBP
Lansford, Carney, Bos	.336	102	399	61	134	175	23	3	4	52	7	1	2	2	34	3	28	15	10	6	.439	.391
Laudner, Tim, Minn	.163	14	43	4	7	15	2	0	2	5	0	0	0	1	3	1	17	0	0	0	.349	.234
LeFlore, Ron, Chi	.246	82	337	46	83	101	10	4	0	24	2	1	1	0	28	0	70	36	11	0	.300	.306
Leach, Rick, Det*	.193	54	83	9	16	24	3	1	1	11	2	1	1	0	16	1	15	0	5	5	.289	.323
Lemon, Chet, Chi	.302	94	328	50	99	161	23	6	9	50	4	5	0	13	33	0	48	6	8	10	.491	.388
Lickert, John, Bos	—	1	0	0	0	0	0	0	0	0	0	0	0	0	0	0	0	0	0	0	—	—
Lisi, Rick, Tex	.313	9	16	6	5	5	0	0	0	1	0	0	0	0	0	0	4	0	1	0	.313	.450
Littleton, Larry, Clev	.000	26	23	2	0	0	0	0	0	1	0	0	0	0	3	0	6	0	0	0	.000	.115
Loviglio, Jay, Chi	.267	14	15	5	4	4	0	0	0	2	0	1	0	0	1	0	0	2	2	2	.267	.313
Lowenstein, John, Balt*	.249	83	189	19	47	72	7	1	6	20	4	0	1	0	22	1	32	7	6	8	.381	.330
Lubratich, Steve, Cal	.143	7	21	2	3	4	1	0	0	4	0	0	0	0	0	0	2	1	0	0	.190	.143
Luzinski, Greg, Chi	.265	104	378	55	100	180	15	1	21	62	11	0	2	3	58	8	80	0	1	10	.476	.367
Lynn, Fred, Cal*	.219	76	256	28	56	81	8	1	5	31	6	0	3	1	38	5	42	1	2	7	.316	.327
Macha, Ken, Tor	.200	37	85	4	17	19	2	0	0	6	0	1	1	0	8	0	15	1	2	3	.224	.269
Mackanin, Pete, Minn	.231	77	225	21	52	73	7	1	4	18	4	0	3	0	7	0	40	0	1	4	.324	.258
Maler, Jim, Sea	.348	12	23	1	8	9	1	0	0	2	0	0	0	0	2	0	1	0	0	0	.391	.423
Manning, Rick, Clev*	.244	103	360	47	88	121	15	0	3	33	3	2	0	0	40	0	57	25	3	4	.336	.320
Manrique, Fred, Tor	.143	14	28	1	4	4	0	0	0	2	0	2	0	0	1	0	12	0	1	1	.143	.172
Martinez, Buck, Tor	.227	45	128	13	29	51	8	1	4	21	3	0	1	1	11	0	16	1	0	6	.398	.293
May, Lee, K.C.	.291	26	55	3	16	19	7	0	0	7	2	0	3	0	3	0	14	0	1	2	.345	.328
Mayberry, John, Tor*	.248	94	290	34	72	131	6	1	17	43	8	0	8	1	44	2	45	1	0	7	.452	.363
McHenry, Vance, Sea	.222	15	18	3	4	4	0	0	0	2	0	0	2	0	1	0	4	0	1	0	.222	.263
McKay, Dave, Oak†	.263	79	224	25	59	84	11	1	4	21	4	0	5	2	16	0	43	4	1	1	.375	.318
McRae, Hal, K.C.	.272	101	389	38	106	154	23	2	7	36	11	0	2	5	34	3	33	3	4	11	.396	.334
Mendoza, Mario, Tex	.231	88	229	18	53	61	6	1	0	22	1	14	1	2	7	0	25	2	0	9	.266	.257
Meyer, Dan, Sea*	.262	83	252	26	66	87	10	1	3	22	1	0	2	1	10	1	16	4	3	6	.345	.293
Milbourne, Larry, N.Y.†	.313	61	163	24	51	65	7	1	1	12	2	2	1	1	9	2	14	2	5	3	.399	.353
Miller, Rick, Bos*	.291	97	316	38	92	119	17	2	2	33	4	4	0	1	28	2	36	3	0	1	.377	.351
Molinaro, Bobby, Chi*	.262	47	42	7	11	17	1	0	0	4	1	0	2	0	8	1	11	10	6	1	.405	.392
Molitor, Paul, Milw	.267	64	251	45	67	84	11	0	2	19	1	5	0	3	25	0	29	9	3	4	.335	.341
Money, Don, Milw	.216	60	185	17	40	53	7	2	2	14	1	3	1	1	19	0	27	1	0	4	.286	.293
Moore, Charlie, Milw	.301	48	156	16	47	64	8	1	1	9	0	3	0	2	12	0	13	1	3	2	.410	.351
Moore, Kelvin, Oak	.255	14	47	5	12	17	2	0	1	9	0	0	0	0	5	0	15	1	0	0	.362	.327
Morales, Jose, Balt	.244	38	86	6	21	30	3	0	2	14	6	0	0	0	3	0	13	0	2	6	.349	.270
Morrison, Jim, Chi	.234	90	290	27	68	108	8	1	10	34	6	9	0	2	10	0	29	3	0	9	.372	.265

Player															
Moseby, Lloyd, Tor.*	.233	100	378	36	88	135	16	2	9	43	28	86	11	.357	.280
Motley, Darryl, K.C.	.232	42	125	15	29	39	4	0	2	8	9	15	3	.312	.278
Mulliniks, Rance, K.C.*	.227	24	44	6	10	13	3	0	0	5	6	10	0	.295	.261
Mumphrey, Jerry, N.Y.†	.307	80	319	44	98	137	6	5	6	32	24	27	10	.429	.356
Murcer, Bobby, N.Y.*	.265	50	117	14	31	55	8	0	5	24	12	15	0	.470	.333
Murphy, Dwayne, Oak.*	.251	107	390	58	98	159	6	0	21	60	73	91	24	.408	.372
Murray, Eddie, Balt.†	.294	99	378	57	111	202	21	2	22	78	40	43	2	.534	.363
Narron, Jerry, Sea.*	.222	76	203	13	45	59	14	0	0	17	16	35	1	.291	.285
Nettles, Graig, N.Y.*	.244	103	349	46	85	139	5	1	15	46	47	49	1	.398	.335
Nettles, Jim, Oak.*	—	1	0	0	0	0	0	0	0	0	0	0	0	—	—
Newman, Jeff, Oak	.231	68	216	17	50	71	12	0	3	15	28	28	0	.328	.262
Nichols, Reid, Bos	.188	39	48	13	9	11	0	0	0	3	6	6	2	.229	.220
Nordhagen, Wayne, Chi	.308	65	208	19	64	92	8	0	6	33	10	25	1	.442	.342
Norman, Nelson, Text	.231	7	13	1	3	3	0	0	0	0	1	2	0	.231	.286
Oates, Johnny, N.Y.*	.192	10	26	4	6	6	0	0	0	1	6	2	0	.231	.250
Oglivie, Ben, Milw.*	.243	107	400	53	97	158	14	1	14	72	37	49	2	.395	.316
Oliver, Al, Tex.*	.309	102	421	53	130	173	29	1	4	55	21	28	0	.411	.349
Orta, Jorge, Clev.*	.272	88	338	50	92	127	14	3	5	34	21	43	2	.376	.317
Otis, Amos, K.C.	.269	99	328	49	100	155	22	1	9	57	31	59	7	.417	.328
Ott, Ed, Cal.*	.217	104	405	50	132	72	8	2	22	22	17	42	7	.279	.268
Paciorek, Tom, Sea.	.326	75	258	9	56	26	8	0	14	66	35	50	10	.509	.385
Page, Mitchell, Oak.*	.141	34	92	3	13	11	2	1	0	13	7	29	2	.283	.202
Pagel, Karl, Clev.*	.267	14	15	4	4	11	0	0	1	4	1	1	0	.733	.421
Papi, Stan, Det	.204	40	93	8	19	32	2	0	3	12	4	18	0	.344	.229
Parrish, Lance, Det	.244	96	348	39	85	137	18	2	10	46	34	52	0	.394	.312
Parsons, Casey, Sea.*	.227	27	47	6	11	14	1	1	0	4	2	6	0	.298	.250
Patek, Fred, Cal	.234	16	32	3	11	14	0	0	1	5	5	6	0	.531	.353
Patterson, Mike, Oak.-N.Y.	.313	84	306	6	14	17	1	1	0	9	0	28	8	.395	.353
Perez, Tony, Bos	.252	63	207	35	77	121	11	0	9	39	27	13	0	.319	.174
Peters, Rick, Det†	.256	21	22	26	53	66	7	0	1	15	29	22	6	.227	.292
Phelps, Ken, K.C.*	.136	82	179	5	3	5	0	0	1	1	2	3	0	.227	.331
Picciolo, Rob, Oak	.268	60	66	23	48	71	5	0	5	18	13	22	5	.397	.222
Piniella, Lou, N.Y.	.277	33	66	16	44	68	9	0	5	18	4	11	0	.428	.287
Poquette, Tom, Bos.-Tex.	.152	80	264	2	10	11	1	0	0	7	1	9	1	.167	.100
Powell, Hosken, Minn.*	.239	5	99	30	63	86	11	0	4	25	17	31	4	.326	.298
Pruitt, Ron, Clev	.000	47	76	0	0	0	0	0	0	0	0	8	6	.000	.306
Pryor, Greg, Chi	.224	95	297	4	17	18	1	0	0	5	2	38	5	.237	.299
Putnam, Pat, Tex.*	.266	46	100	33	79	124	17	0	8	35	17	17	2	.418	—
Quirk, Jamie, K.C.*	.250			8	25	32	7	0	0	10	6		5	.320	—

*Bats Lefthanded †Switch Hitter

Batter and Club	AVG	G	AB	R	H	TB	2B	3B	HR	RBI	GW	SH	SF	HB	TBB	IBB	SO	SB	CS	GI DP	SLG	OBP
Randle, Len, Sea.†	.231	82	273	22	63	86	9	3	4	25	2	6	3	1	17	4	22	11	6	10	.315	.278
Randolph, Willie, N.Y	.232	93	357	59	83	109	14	3	2	24	4	5	3	0	57	0	24	14	5	10	.305	.338
Remy, Jerry, Bos.*	.307	88	358	55	110	121	9	1	0	31	4	13	1	0	36	7	30	9	2	6	.338	.371
Rewering, Dave, Oak.-N.Y.*	.233	76	206	20	48	69	5	2	4	17	4	1	3	1	22	1	32	0	2	4	.335	.310
Rice, Jim, Bos.	.284	108	451	51	128	199	18	4	17	62	6	0	7	3	34	3	76	0	0	14	.441	.338
Ripken, Cal, Balt	.128	23	39	1	5	5	1	0	0	0	0	1	0	0	1	0	8	0	0	1	.128	.150
Rivers, Mickey, Tex.*	.286	99	399	62	114	148	21	3	2	26	3	3	3	1	24	3	21	9	5	4	.371	.328
Roberts, Leon, Tex.	.279	72	233	26	65	98	17	0	4	31	2	1	3	0	25	2	38	3	1	8	.421	.351
Robertson, Andre, N.Y.	.263	10	19	5	5	6	1	0	0	0	0	0	0	0	1	0	3	1	0	0	.316	.263
Rodriguez, Aurelio, N.Y.	.346	27	52	6	18	26	2	0	2	8	0	3	1	0	2	0	10	0	2	12	.500	.370
Roenicke, Gary, Balt	.269	85	219	31	59	84	16	0	3	20	3	1	2	2	23	1	29	1	0	1	.384	.344
Romero, Ed, Milw	.198	44	91	6	18	24	3	0	1	10	1	5	2	0	4	0	9	0	2	4	.264	.232
Rosello, Dave, Clev	.238	43	84	11	20	27	4	0	1	7	0	2	0	0	5	0	12	0	0	3	.321	.297
Royster, Willie, Balt	.000	4	4	0	0	0	0	0	0	0	0	0	0	0	0	0	2	0	0	0	.000	.000
Rudi, Joe, Bos.	.180	49	122	14	22	43	3	0	6	24	1	1	1	2	11	0	29	0	0	5	.352	.242
Sakata, Lenn, Balt	.227	61	150	19	34	53	9	0	5	15	2	0	2	1	11	0	18	4	1	5	.353	.284
Sample, Billy, Tex	.283	66	230	36	65	90	11	1	4	25	4	1	0	1	17	0	21	4	3	3	.391	.350
Schmidt, Dave, Bos.	.238	15	42	6	10	17	1	0	0	3	0	0	3	0	7	0	17	0	0	0	.405	.283
Sconiers, Daryl, Cal.*	.269	15	52	6	14	20	0	2	1	9	2	0	1	0	7	0	10	0	0	1	.385	.283
Serna, Paul, Sea	.255	30	94	11	24	38	2	0	4	9	0	0	0	3	0	11	2	2	3		.404	.293
Sexton, Jim, Oak.†	.000	7	3	2	0	0	0	0	0	0	0	0	0	0	2	0	1	0	0	0	.000	.000
Shelby, John, Balt.†	.000	7	1	2	0	0	0	0	0	0	0	0	0	0	0	0	0	2	0	0	.000	.000
Sheridan, Pat, K.C.*	.000	3	1	0	0	0	0	0	0	0	0	0	0	0	0	0	1	0	0	0	.000	.000
Simmons, Ted, Milw.†	.216	100	380	45	82	143	13	1	14	61	12	0	6	3	23	2	32	0	1	10	.376	.266
Simpson, Joe, Sea.*	.222	91	288	32	64	87	11	1	3	30	1	6	2	0	15	6	41	12	3	21	.302	.263
Singleton, Ken, Balt.†	.278	103	363	48	101	158	16	1	13	49	7	2	2	1	61	6	59	0	0	21	.435	.382
Smalley, Roy, Minn.†	.263	56	167	24	44	74	7	1	7	22	6	0	2	0	31	5	24	0	0	8	.443	.379
Smith, Ray, Minn.	.200	15	40	4	8	12	1	0	1	6	0	1	0	0	5	0	3	0	0	2	.300	.200
Sofield, Rick, Minn.*	.176	41	102	9	18	20	0	1	0	5	0	0	1	0	8	0	22	3	2	0	.196	.236
Spencer, Jim, N.Y.-Oak.*	.188	79	234	20	44	64	8	0	13	25	3	0	3	0	19	3	27	1	1	5	.274	.249
Squires, Mike, Chi.*	.265	92	294	35	78	87	9	0	0	22	2	13	5	0	22	0	17	7	2	6	.296	.316
Stanley, Fred, Oak	.193	66	145	15	28	32	4	0	0	7	0	8	1	0	15	0	23	2	0	5	.221	.269
Stapleton, Dave, Bos.	.285	93	355	45	101	150	17	1	7	22	5	2	2	1	21	1	22	0	4	11	.423	.326
Stein, Bill, Tex	.330	53	115	21	38	50	6	0	2	22	3	3	1	0	7	3	15	0	2	0	.435	.369
Stieb, Dave, Tor.	—	29	0	1	0	0	0	0	0	0	0	3	0	0	0	0	0	0	0	0	—	—

Player	PCT	G	AB	R	H	TB	2B	3B	HR	RBI	SH	SF	HP	BB	IBB	SO	SB	CS	GDP	SLG	OBP
Summers, Champ, Det.*	.255	64	165	16	42	59	8	0	3	21	3	0	2	19	3	35	1	1	0	.358	.342
Sundberg, Jim, Tex.	.277	102	339	42	94	124	17	2	3	28	6	2	3	50	6	48	1	5	5	.366	.372
Sutherland, Leo, Chi.*	.167	11	12	2	2	2	0	0	0	1	0	0	0	2	0	1	0	0	0	.167	.333
Thomas, Gorman, Milw	.259	103	363	54	94	179	22	0	21	65	0	5	1	50	2	85	3	2	7	.493	.352
Thornton, Andre, Clev.	.239	69	226	22	54	84	12	0	6	30	0	2	1	23	1	37	0	1	5	.372	.309
Tolleson, Wayne, Tex.†	.167	14	24	6	4	4	0	0	0	1	1	0	0	6	0	3	3	1	0	.167	.200
Trammell, Alan, Det.	.258	105	392	52	101	128	15	3	2	31	3	3	1	49	2	31	10	3	10	.327	.345
Turner, Jerry, Chi.*	.167	10	12	1	2	2	0	0	0	0	0	0	0	1	0	3	0	0	0	.167	.231
Upshaw, Willie, Tor.*	.171	61	111	15	19	36	3	1	4	19	0	1	0	11	2	16	0	2	2	.324	.252
Valdez, Julio, Bos.†	.217	17	23	2	5	5	0	0	0	3	1	0	0	0	0	4	0	0	0	.217	.217
Velez, Otto, Tor.	.213	80	240	32	51	97	11	1	11	28	0	2	2	55	5	60	0	3	2	.404	.366
Veryzer, Tom, Clev.	.244	75	221	13	54	58	4	0	0	14	10	1	0	8	0	10	1	1	5	.262	.280
Wagner, Mark, Tex.	.259	50	85	15	22	31	3	0	2	14	3	0	1	13	0	13	1	0	2	.365	.389
Walker, Chi.-Bos.†	.353	6	17	1	6	6	0	0	0	0	0	0	0	0	0	0	0	0	2	.353	.389
Walton, Reggie, Sea.	.000	12	6	1	0	0	0	0	0	0	0	0	0	0	0	2	0	0	0	.000	.143
Ward, Gary, Minn.	.264	85	295	42	78	106	21	1	3	29	2	1	3	28	0	48	5	2	4	.359	.328
Washington, Ron, Minn.	.226	28	84	8	19	24	2	0	1	5	3	0	0	4	0	14	1	1	3	.286	.270
Washington, U.L., K.C.†	.227	98	339	40	77	104	19	1	2	29	4	1	2	41	0	43	10	5	2	.307	.311
Wathan, John, K.C.	.252	89	301	24	76	94	9	3	0	32	4	2	1	23	0	23	11	4	12	.312	.317
Watson, Bob, N.Y.	.212	59	156	15	33	60	6	0	7	19	0	2	0	24	2	17	0	0	4	.385	.295
Wells, Greg, Tor.	.247	32	73	7	18	23	5	0	0	6	0	0	0	5	0	12	0	0	2	.315	.250
Werner, Don, Tex.	.250	2	8	1	2	2	2	0	0	2	0	0	0	0	0	2	0	0	0	.250	.269
Werth, Dennis, N.Y.	.109	34	55	7	6	7	1	0	0	6	0	1	3	12	0	12	4	0	5	.127	.343
Whitaker, Lou, Det.*	.263	109	335	48	88	125	14	4	5	36	3	2	3	40	3	42	5	3	3	.373	.343
White, Frank, K.C.	.250	94	364	35	91	137	17	1	9	38	3	3	3	19	0	50	4	5	5	.376	.287
Whitmer, Dan, Tor.	.111	7	9	1	1	2	1	0	0	1	0	0	0	0	0	2	0	0	2	.222	.200
Whitt, Ernie, Tor.*	.236	74	195	16	46	58	9	0	1	16	0	5	1	20	1	30	0	2	4	.297	.311
Wilfong, Rob, Minn.*	.246	93	305	32	75	101	11	0	3	19	7	1	0	29	3	43	5	2	2	.331	.311
Williams, Dallas, Balt.*	.500	2	2	0	1	1	0	0	0	0	0	0	0	0	0	0	0	0	0	.500	.500
Wills, Bump, Tex.†	.251	102	410	51	103	126	13	2	2	41	9	1	1	32	0	49	12	8	8	.307	.307
Wilson, Willie, K.C.†	.303	102	439	54	133	160	10	7	1	32	7	1	0	18	0	42	34	8	0	.364	.336
Winfield, Dave, N.Y.	.294	105	388	52	114	180	25	1	13	68	0	7	1	43	5	41	11	3	13	.464	.366
Wockenfuss, John, Det.	.215	70	172	20	37	68	4	0	9	25	1	2	1	28	2	22	0	1	7	.395	.325
Woods, Al, Tor.*	.247	85	288	20	71	89	15	0	1	21	5	1	1	17	4	31	5	4	7	.309	.293
Wynegar, Butch, Minn.†	.247	47	150	11	37	42	5	0	0	10	0	2	0	37	3	9	0	0	9	.280	.327
Yastrzemski, Carl, Bos.*	.246	91	338	36	83	120	14	1	7	53	0	6	0	49	10	28	0	2	10	.355	.341
Yost, Ned, Milw.	.222	18	27	4	6	15	0	0	3	5	0	0	0	3	0	6	0	1	1	.556	.300
Yount, Robin, Milw	.273	96	377	50	103	158	15	5	10	49	6	4	0	22	2	37	4	4	4	.419	.317
Zisk, Richie, Sea	.311	94	357	42	111	173	12	1	16	43	0	3	2	49	3	63	3	0	8	.485	.366

DESIGNATED HITTERS
(Individual Statistics — Players Listed Alphabetically)

*Bats Lefthanded †Switch Hitter

Batter & Club	AVG	G	AB	R	H	TB	2B	3B	HR	RBI	GW RBI	SH	SF	HB	TBB	IBB	SO	SB	CS	GI DP	SLG	OBP
Adams, Minn.*	.193	62	212	13	41	55	8	0	2	20	1	0	2	0	18	4	26	0	1	10	.259	.257
Ainge, Tor.	.000	1	1	0	0	0	0	0	0	0	0	0	0	0	1	0	0	0	1	0	.000	.500
Allen, Sea	.000	2	1	0	0	0	0	0	0	0	0	0	0	0	0	0	1	0	0	0	.000	.000
Ayala, Balt.	.265	27	68	9	18	25	1	0	2	8	0	0	1	0	7	0	7	0	0	2	.368	.342
Baines, Chi.*	.000	1	3	0	0	0	0	0	0	0	0	0	0	0	0	0	1	0	0	0	.000	.000
Baker, Minn	.000	1	3	0	0	0	0	0	0	0	0	0	0	0	0	0	2	0	0	0	.000	.000
Balboni, N.Y.	.000	1	2	0	0	0	0	0	0	0	0	0	0	0	0	0	1	0	0	0	.000	.000
Bando, Milw.	.000	2	4	0	0	0	0	0	0	0	0	0	0	1	0	0	0	0	0	0	.000	.200
Bando, Clev.†	.200	2	5	0	1	2	1	0	0	0	0	0	0	0	0	0	0	0	0	0	.400	.200
Baumgarten, Chi.*	.000	1	0	0	0	0	0	0	0	0	0	0	0	0	0	0	0	0	0	0	.000	.000
Baylor, Cal.	.233	97	356	51	83	153	17	1	17	64	10	0	6	7	41	1	48	3	3	11	.430	.324
Beamon, Tor.*	.300	4	10	3	3	3	0	0	0	2	0	0	0	0	1	0	1	0	0	0	.400	.364
Bell, Tor.	.150	8	20	3	3	3	0	0	0	0	0	0	0	0	0	0	1	3	0	0	.150	.150
Beniquez, Cal	.000	1	3	0	0	0	0	0	0	0	0	0	0	0	0	0	0	0	0	0	.000	.000
Bochte, Sea.*	.000	3	7	1	0	0	0	0	0	0	0	0	1	0	0	0	0	1	0	0	.000	.000
Bosetti, Tor.1-Oak.2	.500	7	2	1	1	1	0	0	0	0	0	0	0	0	0	0	0	0	0	0	.500	.500
Bosley, Milw.*	.222	7	27	3	6	11	3	1	0	5	0	0	0	1	1	0	7	0	0	2	.407	.250
Brouhard, Milw	.000	2	1	0	0	0	0	0	0	0	0	0	0	0	0	0	0	0	0	0	.000	.000
Brown, N.Y.†	.000	1	1	1	0	0	0	0	0	0	0	0	0	0	0	0	0	1	0	0	.000	.000
Brown, Det.†	.156	9	32	3	5	6	1	0	0	4	0	0	0	0	4	0	10	0	0	2	.188	.250
Budaska, Oak.†	.000	1	3	0	0	0	0	0	0	0	0	0	0	1	0	0	0	0	0	0	.000	.250
Burroughs, Sea	.750	1	4	1	3	3	0	0	0	1	0	0	0	0	0	0	0	0	0	0	.750	.750
Butera, Minn.	.000	2	4	1	0	0	0	0	0	0	0	0	0	0	1	0	0	0	0	0	.000	.200
Carew, Cal.*	.250	2	4	1	1	1	0	0	0	0	0	1	0	0	0	0	0	0	0	0	.250	.400
Charboneau, Clev	.242	14	33	3	8	8	0	0	0	4	0	0	0	0	5	0	4	0	0	1	.242	.342
Cooper, Milw.*	.273	5	22	1	6	7	1	0	0	0	0	0	0	0	0	0	1	1	0	0	.318	.273
Corcoran, Minn.*	.429	3	7	1	3	3	0	0	0	2	0	0	0	0	0	0	0	0	0	0	.571	.500
Cox, Tor	.000	1	0	0	0	0	0	0	0	0	0	0	0	0	0	0	0	0	0	0	.000	1.000
Crowley, Balt.*	.257	42	109	12	28	46	6	0	4	20	3	1	1	0	23	3	8	0	0	3	.422	.386
Davis, Oak.*	.000	3	8	0	0	0	0	0	0	0	0	0	0	0	1	0	3	0	0	0	.000	.111
Dempsey, Balt.	.000	1	1	0	0	0	0	0	0	0	0	0	0	0	0	0	0	0	0	0	.000	.000

Player	Pct.	G	AB	R	H	HR	RBI	SLG	Pct.
Diaz, Clev.	.000	3	3	0	0	0	0	.000	.250
Dilone, Clev.	.242	11	33	5	8	0		.242	.324
Downing, Cal.	.222	5	18	1	4	0		.222	.333
Drumright, Oak.*	.286	5	21	2	6	0		.381	.286
Dwyer, Balt.*	.000	1	0	0	0	0	0	.000	1.000
Dybzinski, Clev	.000	1		0	0	0	0	.000	.000
Edwards, Milw.*	.000	1		0	0	0	0	.000	.000
Ellis, Tex.	.000	1	2	0	0	0	0	.000	.500
Engle, Minn.	.000	1		0	0	0	0	.000	.000
Foote, N.Y.	.214	4	14	0	3	0		.286	.000
Funderburk, Minn	.000	1	1	0	0	0	0	.000	.000
Gaetti, Minn.	.191		68	9	13			.360	.324
Gamble, N.Y.*	.556							.556	
Garcia, Tor.	.000				0	0		.000	.333
Gibson, Det.*	.259	9	27	2	7			.333	
Goodwin, Minn.*	.125	5	16	2	2	0		.125	.286
Graham, Balt.*	.095	6	21	1	2	0		.095	.125
Gray, Sea.	.213	15	61	8	13			.410	.174
Gross, Oak.*	.000		1	0	0	0	0	.000	.226
Hancock, Bos.*	.091	4	11	1	1			.091	.000
Hargrove, Clev.*	.556		9	1	5			.778	.167
Harper, Cal.	.000		3	0	0	0		.000	.714
Harrah, Clev.	.333		6	1	2			.500	.000
Harris, Cal.*	.000		3	0	0	0		.000	.429
Hassey, Clev.*	1.000		1	0	1			1.000	.000
Hatcher, Minn.	.246	21	61	10	19			.311	.000
Hayes, Clev.*	.125	11	24	1	3			.125	1.000
Hebner, Det.*	.238	24	84	11	20			.429	.313
Hisle, Milw.	.143	2	7	1	1			.143	.364
Hobson, Cal	.125	4	8	0	1	0		.125	.304
Hosley, Oak	.240	13	50	9	12			.340	.333
Howell, Milw.*	.160	8	25	4	4			.200	.125
Hrbek, Minn.*	1.000	1	1	0	1			2.000	.283
Iorg, Tor.	.171	33	105	7	18			.276	.222
Jackson, N.Y.*	.421	6	19	2	8			.579	.331
Jackson, R., Minn.	.250	8	8	1	2			.250	.450
Johnson, Chi.	.273	68	245	35	67			.478	.250
Johnson, Oak.									.343
Jones, Det.	.000	4	6	0	0	0	0	.000	.250

*Bats Lefthanded †Switch Hitter

Batter & Club	AVG	G	AB	R	H	TB	2B	3B	HR	RBI	GW RBI	SH	SF	HB	TBB	IBB	SO	SB	CS	GI DP	SLG	OBP
Kelly, Clev.*	.245	18	49	6	12	18	3	0	1	10	1	0	1	0	8	2	2	2	0	2	.367	.351
Kemp, Det.*	.389	12	36	8	14	19	2	0	1	5	1	0	0	0	9	1	6	1	0	0	.528	.511
Krenchicki, Balt.*	.000	1	0	1	0	0	0	0	0	0	0	0	0	0	0	0	0	0	0	0	.000	.000
Kuntz, Chi.	.000	5	2	0	0	0	0	0	0	0	0	0	0	0	0	0	1	0	0	0	.000	.000
Lansford, Bos	.316	16	57	9	18	28	4	0	2	8	0	0	0	0	3	0	9	1	0	0	.491	.361
Laudner, Minn.	.000	2	6	0	0	0	0	0	0	0	0	0	0	0	1	0	4	0	0	0	.000	.143
Leach, Det.*	.000	2	1	1	0	0	0	0	0	0	0	0	0	0	0	0	0	0	0	0	.000	.000
Loviglio, Chi	.000	2	1	1	0	0	0	0	0	0	0	0	0	0	2	0	0	1	0	0	.000	.667
Lowenstein, Balt.*	.400	4	5	0	2	2	0	0	0	1	0	0	0	0	0	0	0	1	0	0	.400	.400
Luzinski, Chi	.265	103	378	55	100	180	15	0	21	62	11	0	3	2	57	10	80	0	0	10	.476	.365
Macha, Tor.	.200	2	5	0	1	1	0	0	0	0	0	0	0	0	1	0	1	0	0	0	.200	.333
Mackanin, Minn.	.059	6	17	0	1	1	0	0	0	1	0	0	0	0	1	0	3	0	0	0	.059	.111
Maler, Sea	.400	2	5	0	2	3	1	0	0	0	0	0	0	0	0	0	0	0	0	0	.600	.500
Manrique, Tor.	1.000	1	1	0	1	1	0	0	0	0	0	0	0	0	0	0	0	0	0	0	1.000	1.000
May, K.C.	.111	4	18	1	2	2	0	0	0	3	0	0	0	0	0	0	6	0	0	0	.111	.111
Mayberry, Tor.*	.250	10	32	5	8	13	2	0	1	3	0	0	0	0	4	1	7	0	0	0	.406	.351
McHenry, Sea	.000	1	0	0	0	0	0	0	0	0	0	0	0	0	0	0	0	0	0	0	.000	.000
McRae, K.C.	.270	97	374	35	101	146	23	2	6	33	4	0	4	2	33	3	31	0	4	10	.390	.333
Meyer, Sea.*	.143	3	7	1	1	1	0	0	0	0	0	0	0	0	1	0	1	0	0	0	.143	.250
Milbourne, N.Y.†	.200	3	5	1	1	2	0	0	0	0	0	0	0	0	1	0	0	3	0	0	.200	.333
Molinaro, Chi.*	.333	4	6	2	2	5	0	0	1	2	0	0	0	0	0	0	1	0	0	0	.833	.429
Molitor, Milw.	.350	16	60	9	21	27	3	0	1	5	0	0	1	0	6	1	8	4	2	0	.450	.418
Money, Milw.	.143	2	7	0	1	2	1	0	0	0	0	0	0	0	0	0	2	0	0	0	.286	.250
Moore, Milw.	.263	6	19	3	5	5	0	0	0	2	0	0	0	0	2	0	4	0	0	0	.263	.333
Morales, Balt.	.221	22	68	5	15	22	1	0	2	11	3	0	0	2	6	0	8	0	0	4	.324	.243
Morrison, Chi	.000	1	1	1	0	0	0	0	0	0	0	0	0	0	0	0	0	0	0	0	.000	.000
Murcer, N.Y.*	.284	33	102	13	29	50	6	0	5	20	3	0	0	0	10	2	12	0	1	3	.490	.348
Murphy, Oak.*	.000	1	2	0	0	0	0	0	0	0	0	0	0	0	3	0	0	0	0	0	.000	.600
Nettles, N.Y.*	.333	4	15	1	5	5	0	0	0	3	0	0	0	0	0	0	3	0	0	0	.333	.333
Nichols, Bos	.000	7	0	1	0	0	0	0	0	0	0	0	0	0	0	0	0	0	0	0	.000	.000
Oglivie, Milw.*	.261	6	23	4	6	8	0	0	0	3	0	0	1	0	2	0	3	3	0	0	.348	.292
Oliver, Tex.*	.307	101	420	53	129	172	29	1	4	54	8	0	0	1	24	10	28	3	1	17	.410	.348
Otis, K.C.	1.000	1	1	0	1	1	0	0	0	0	0	0	0	0	0	0	2	0	0	1	1.000	1.000
Page, Oak.*	.136	29	88	8	12	22	1	0	3	12	0	0	0	0	7	0	29	2	0	0	.250	.200
Pagel, Clev.*	.000	1	1	0	0	0	0	0	0	0	0	0	0	0	0	0	0	0	0	0	.000	.000

Player	AVG	G	AB	R	H	2B	3B	HR	RBI	BB	SO	SB	OBP	SLG
Papi, Det.	.300	3	10	3	3	0	0	0	0	0	9	4	.300	.300
Parrish, Det.	.250	5	12	3	3	1	0	0	5	0	5	0	.417	.526
Patterson, Oak.	.000	2	6	0	0	1	0	0	2	0	0	0	.000	.143
Perez, Oak.	.220	23	82	18	18	6	0	0	26	2	17	3	.317	.297
Peters, Det.†	.242	19	62	15	15	9	0	0	17	0	9	1	.274	.397
Phelps, K.C.*	.250	4	8	2	2	0	0	0	2	1	2	0	.250	.250
Piniella, N.Y.	.265	19	49	13	13	2	0	0	25	2	2	2	.345	.510
Powell, Minn.*	.214	8	28	6	6	0	0	0	7	1	7	0	.267	.250
Pruitt, Clev.	.000	1	1	0	0	0	0	0	0	0	0	0	.000	.000
Revering, Oak.*	.000	2	6	2	0	0	1	0	1	0	2	0	.000	.000
Rodriguez, N.Y.	.333	6	6	0	2	0	0	0	1	0	1	0	.333	.333
Rosello, Clev.	.333	3	3	0	1	0	0	0	0	0	0	0	.333	.500
Rudi, Bos.	.185	21	81	10	15	2	0	3	29	3	10	0	.358	.250
Sconiers, Cal.*	.462	3	13	2	6	2	0	0	11	0	2	0	.846	.462
Sexton, Oak.†	.000	1	1	0	0	0	0	0	0	0	0	0	.000	.000
Simmons, Milw.†	.231	22	91	10	21	3	0	3	35	3	10	0	.385	.278
Singleton, Balt.†	.284	30	109	12	31	7	0	3	47	7	12	1	.431	.381
Smalley, Minn.†	.211	15	38	7	8	0	0	1	12	8	7	0	.316	.302
Stapleton, Bos.	.462	3	13	8	6	0	0	1	8	0	0	0	.692	.462
Stieb, Tor	.000	1	0	0	0	0	0	0	0	0	0	0	.000	.000
Summers, Det.*	.241	37	112	10	27	6	0	3	40	7	10	0	.357	.320
Thomas, Milw.	.217	6	23	2	5	1	0	0	6	2	2	0	.261	.250
Thornton, Clev.	.253	53	182	20	46	11	0	5	71	25	20	3	.390	.327
Upshaw, Tor.*	.152	15	46	5	7	2	0	0	13	3	7	0	.283	.204
Velez, Tor.*	.206	74	233	30	48	10	2	0	91	25	13	6	.391	.360
Walton, Sea	.000	3	0	0	0	0	0	0	0	0	0	0	.000	.000
Ward, Minn	.200	2	5	0	1	0	0	0	2	0	0	0	.400	.333
Watson, N.Y.	.222	6	9	1	2	1	0	0	2	2	0	0	.222	.417
Wells, Tor	.500	3	8	2	4	0	0	0	5	0	1	0	.625	.500
Werner, Tex	.250	2	8	1	2	0	0	0	2	0	1	0	.300	.250
Werth, N.Y.	.125	4	8	0	1	0	0	0	1	0	1	0	.500	.125
Wills, Tex.†	.333	8	3	0	1	0	0	0	1	0	0	0	.333	.333
Winfield, N.Y.	.000	1	1	0	0	0	0	0	0	0	0	0	.000	.000
Wockenfuss, Det	.216	39	88	10	19	2	0	3	40	13	17	2	.455	.343
Woods, Tor.*	.333	2	3	0	1	0	0	0	1	0	0	0	.333	.333
Wynegar, Minn.†	.286	9	28	1	8	9	0	0	9	3	1	0	.321	.355
Yastrzemski, Bos.*	.225	48	187	21	42	6	0	1	63	28	15	5	.337	.326
Yount, Milw.	.077	9	13	0	1	1	0	0	1	1	2	0	.077	.143
Zisk, Sea.	.312	93	356	42	111	12	28	43	173	62	28	8	.486	.367

PITCHING

TOP FIFTEEN QUALIFIERS FOR EARNED-RUN LEADERSHIP
(One Inning Times Games Played By Team)

*Throws Lefthanded

Pitcher and Club	W	L	PCT	ERA	G	GS	CG	GF	SHO	SV	IP	H	TBF	R	ER	HR	SH	SF	HB	TBB	IBB	SO	WP	BK
McCatty, Steve, Oak	14	7	.667	2.32	22	22	16	0	4	0	186	140	741	50	48	12	8	6	2	61	1	91	0	0
Stewart, Sammy, Balt	4	8	.333	2.33	29	3	0	18	0	4	112	89	463	33	29	8	4	3	0	57	1	47	1	2
Lamp, Dennis, Chi	7	6	.538	2.41	27	10	3	5	0	0	127	103	514	41	34	4	1	1	3	43	1	71	4	1
John, Tommy, N.Y.*	9	8	.529	2.64	20	20	7	0	0	1	140	135	580	50	41	10	8	2	3	39	0	50	6	2
Burns, Britt, Chi.*	10	6	.625	2.64	24	23	5	0	1	0	157	139	651	52	46	14	5	6	6	49	0	108	6	1
Gura, Larry, K.C.*	11	8	.579	2.72	23	23	12	0	2	0	172	139	680	61	52	11	9	1	1	35	0	61	3	0
Guidry, Ron, N.Y.*	11	5	.688	2.76	23	21	0	1	0	1	127	100	497	41	39	7	8	5	4	26	0	104	6	0
Forsch, Ken, Cal	11	7	.611	2.88	20	20	10	0	0	0	153	143	616	54	49	9	7	8	5	27	2	55	0	3
Blyleven, Bert, Clev.	11	7	.611	2.89	20	20	9	0	2	0	159	145	644	52	51	9	3	3	5	40	1	107	5	1
Leonard, Dennis, K.C.	13	11	.542	2.99	26	26	9	0	0	2	202	202	837	79	67	15	6	5	6	41	0	107	5	0
Langford, Rick, Oak	12	10	.545	3.00	24	24	18	0	0	2	195	190	823	81	65	14	8	8	1	58	2	84	1	0
Petry, Dan, Det	10	9	.526	3.00	23	22	7	1	2	0	141	115	583	53	47	10	9	1	2	57	1	79	4	3
Wilcox, Milt, Det	12	9	.571	3.04	24	24	8	0	1	0	166	152	686	61	56	10	8	5	6	52	3	79	4	0
Morris, Jack, Det	14	7	.667	3.05	25	25	15	0	1	0	198	153	798	69	67	14	8	9	2	78	11	97	2	2
Medich, Doc, Tex	10	6	.625	3.08	20	20	0	4	0	0	143	136	585	51	49	8	8	2	2	33	5	65	1	0

INDIVIDUAL PITCHING
(All Players Listed Alphabetically)

*Throws Lefthanded

Pitcher and Club	W	L	PCT	ERA	G	GS	CG	GF	SHO	SV	IP	H	TBF	R	ER	HR	SH	SF	HB	TBB	IBB	SO	WP	BK
Aase, Don, Cal.	4	4	.500	2.35	39	0	0	31	0	11	65	56	265	17	17	4	1	1	0	24	2	38	1	0
Abbott, Glenn, Sea.	4	9	.308	3.95	22	20	1	0	0	0	130	127	530	64	57	14	6	4	0	28	1	35	1	0
Agosto, Juan, Chi.*	0	0	—	4.50	2	0	0	1	0	0	6	5	22	3	3	1	0	0	0	2	0	3	0	0
Allard, Brian, Sea.	3	2	.600	3.75	7	7	1	0	0	0	48	48	191	22	20	5	2	0	3	20	0	20	0	0
Andersen, Larry, Sea.	3	3	.500	2.65	41	0	0	23	0	5	68	57	273	27	20	4	0	3	0	18	2	40	0	0
Aponte, Luis, Bos.	1	0	1.000	.56	7	0	0	3	0	1	16	11	57	3	1	1	0	1	0	3	0	11	0	0
Arroyo, Fernando, Minn.	7	10	.412	3.94	23	19	2	1	0	0	128	144	542	66	56	11	5	2	5	34	1	39	3	0

Augustine, Jerry, Milw.*	2	2	.500	4.28	27	2	0	9	0	2	61	75	272	30	29	4	2	1	1	18	3	26	3	0
Babcock, Bob, Tex	1	1	.500	2.17	16	0	0	7	0	0	29	21	117	7	7	2	3	1	1	16	1	18	0	0
Bailey, Howard, Det.*	1	4	.200	7.30	9	5	0	2	0	0	37	45	165	31	30	4	1	2	3	13	2	17	3	0
Bannister, Floyd, Sea.*	9	9	.500	4.46	21	20	5	0	2	0	121	128	522	62	60	14	2	0	3	39	0	85	7	1
Barker, Len, Clev	8	7	.533	3.92	22	22	9	0	3	0	154	150	660	72	67	7	6	4	1	46	0	127	5	0
Barlow, Mike, Tor.	0	0	--	4.20	12	0	0	7	0	0	15	22	78	11	7	1	1	2	4	6	1	5	0	0
Barrios, Francisco, Chi	1	3	.250	4.00	8	7	1	0	0	0	36	45	170	23	16	3	1	0	1	14	1	12	1	0
Baumgarten, Ross, Chi.*	5	9	.357	4.06	19	19	2	0	1	0	102	101	435	56	46	9	4	2	1	40	3	52	4	2
Beard, Dave, Oak	1	1	.500	2.77	8	0	0	7	0	3	13	9	53	5	4	1	0	1	1	4	1	15	0	0
Beattie, Jim, Sea	3	2	.600	2.96	13	9	0	3	0	1	67	59	275	24	22	2	1	0	2	18	0	36	2	1
Berenguer, Juan, K.C.-Tor	2	13	.133	5.24	20	14	1	4	0	0	91	84	405	62	53	11	2	7	5	51	1	49	2	0
Bernard, Dwight, Milw	0	0	--	3.60	6	0	0	1	0	0	5	5	27	3	2	0	0	2	0	6	1	1	0	0
Bird, Doug, N.Y.	5	1	.833	2.72	17	4	0	3	0	0	53	58	229	19	16	5	2	4	0	16	3	28	0	0
Black, Harry, Sea.*	0	0	--	.00	2	0	0	0	0	0	1	2	7	0	0	0	0	0	0	3	1	0	1	0
Blyleven, Bert, Clev.	11	7	.611	2.89	20	20	9	0	1	0	159	145	644	52	51	9	3	3	5	40	1	107	3	1
Boddicker, Mike, Balt	0	0	--	4.50	2	0	0	1	0	0	6	6	25	4	3	1	0	0	0	2	0	2	2	0
Bomback, Mark, Tor	5	5	.500	3.90	20	11	0	3	0	0	90	84	377	42	39	6	3	3	1	35	2	33	6	1
Bordi, Rich, Oak	0	0	--	.00	2	0	0	2	0	0	2	1	8	0	0	0	0	0	0	1	0	0	0	0
Brennan, Tom, Clev.	2	2	.500	3.19	7	6	1	0	0	0	48	49	205	20	17	5	2	0	0	14	1	15	0	0
Brett, Ken, K.C.*	1	1	.500	4.22	22	0	0	13	0	2	32	35	144	16	15	2	3	2	1	14	4	7	0	0
Burgmeier, Tom, Bos.*	4	5	.444	2.85	32	0	0	21	0	6	60	61	255	23	19	5	6	0	4	17	4	35	0	0
Burns, Britt, Chi.*	10	6	.625	2.64	24	23	5	0	1	0	157	139	651	52	46	14	5	6	6	49	1	108	1	1
Butcher, John, Tex	1	2	.333	1.61	5	3	1	1	1	0	28	18	106	6	5	0	1	0	0	8	1	19	0	0
Caldwell, Mike, Milw.*	11	9	.550	3.94	24	23	3	0	0	0	144	151	609	70	63	18	10	4	1	38	4	41	3	1
Campbell, Bill, Bos	1	1	.500	3.19	30	0	0	23	0	7	48	45	208	23	17	5	2	2	0	20	4	37	2	0
Cappuzzello, George, Det.*	1	1	.500	3.44	18	3	0	5	0	1	34	28	146	14	13	2	0	0	2	18	2	19	4	0
Castro, Bill, N.Y.	1	1	.500	3.79	11	0	0	6	0	0	19	26	86	13	8	2	2	0	0	5	1	4	0	0
Clancy, Jim, Tor	6	12	.333	4.90	22	22	2	0	0	0	125	126	556	77	68	12	2	4	5	64	0	56	12	0
Clark, Bryan, Sea.*	2	5	.286	4.35	29	9	1	5	0	2	93	92	421	54	45	3	9	4	1	56	4	52	7	3
Clay, Kenny, Sea	2	7	.222	4.63	22	14	0	2	0	0	101	116	445	62	52	10	2	3	3	42	3	32	5	1
Clear, Mark, Bos.	8	3	.727	4.09	34	0	0	20	0	9	77	69	346	36	35	11	4	0	2	51	2	82	6	0
Cleveland, Reggie, Milw	2	3	.400	5.12	35	0	0	10	0	1	65	57	274	41	37	5	4	1	1	30	2	18	6	0
Comer, Steve, Tex	8	2	.800	2.57	36	1	0	22	0	6	77	70	330	25	22	1	4	4	1	31	8	22	2	0
Cooper, Don, Minn	1	5	.167	4.27	27	2	0	11	0	0	59	61	262	33	28	9	4	2	1	32	4	33	1	2
Corbett, Doug, Minn	2	6	.250	2.56	54	0	0	45	0	17	88	80	377	29	25	5	3	5	0	34	13	60	2	0
Crawford, Steve, Bos	0	5	.000	4.97	14	11	0	2	0	0	58	69	257	38	32	10	3	4	3	18	0	29	2	0
D'Acquisto, John, Cal	0	0	--	10.89	6	0	0	1	0	0	19	26	95	24	23	2	1	4	1	12	0	8	1	0
Darwin, Danny, Tex	9	9	.500	3.64	22	22	6	0	2	0	146	115	601	67	59	12	8	3	6	57	5	98	1	0
Davis, Ron, N.Y.	4	5	.444	2.71	43	0	0	22	0	6	73	47	285	22	22	6	4	3	0	25	3	83	1	1

*Throws Lefthanded

Pitcher and Club	W	L	PCT	ERA	G	GS	CG	GF	SHO	SV	IP	H	TBF	R	ER	HR	SH	SF	HB	TBB	IBB	SO	WP	BK
Denny, John, Clev	10	6	.625	3.14	19	19	6	0	0	0	146	139	623	62	51	9	2	5	3	66	3	94	1	0
DiPino, Frank, Milw.*	0	0	—	.00	2	0	0	2	0	0	2	0	10	0	0	0	0	0	0	0	0	3	0	0
Dotson, Richard, Chi	9	8	.529	3.77	24	24	5	0	0	0	141	145	599	67	59	13	4	4	4	49	0	73	3	0
Drago, Dick, Sea	4	6	.400	5.50	39	0	0	24	0	4	54	71	240	33	33	4	4	5	0	15	5	27	2	5
Easterly, Jamie, Milw*	3	3	.500	3.19	44	0	0	16	0	0	62	46	253	23	22	9	6	4	2	34	4	31	0	0
Eckersley, Dennis, Bos	9	8	.529	4.27	23	23	8	0	2	0	154	160	649	73	73	9	5	6	3	35	2	79	2	0
Erickson, Roger, Minn	3	8	.273	3.86	14	14	1	0	0	0	91	93	399	48	39	7	7	6	0	31	4	44	3	0
Espinosa, Nino, Tor.	0	1	.000	9.00	1	1	0	0	0	0	1	4	6	1	1	0	0	0	0	1	0	0	0	0
Farmer, Ed, Chi	3	3	.500	4.58	42	0	0	25	0	10	53	53	243	33	27	5	4	2	0	34	1	42	3	0
Felton, Terry, Minn.	0	0	—	54.00	1	0	0	1	0	0	1	4	10	6	6	1	0	0	0	6	0	1	0	0
Figueroa, Ed, Oak.	0	0	—	5.63	2	1	0	0	0	0	8	8	37	6	5	1	0	0	2	6	0	1	0	0
Fingers, Rollie, Milw	6	3	.667	1.04	47	0	0	41	0	28	78	55	297	12	9	7	3	4	1	13	2	61	6	0
Flanagan, Mike, Balt.*	9	6	.600	4.19	20	20	0	0	0	0	116	108	482	54	54	11	3	5	2	37	2	72	2	0
Ford, Dave, Balt.	1	2	.333	6.53	15	2	0	4	0	0	40	61	185	33	29	7	2	5	0	10	2	12	1	0
Forsch, Ken, Cal	11	7	.611	2.88	20	20	10	0	2	0	153	143	616	54	49	9	8	5	2	27	2	55	0	0
Frazier, George, N.Y	0	1	.000	1.61	16	0	0	9	0	3	28	26	117	7	5	3	2	2	1	11	0	16	1	0
Frost, Dave, Cal	1	8	.111	5.55	12	9	0	0	0	0	47	44	200	30	29	3	2	2	1	19	1	16	0	0
Galasso, Bob, Sea	1	1	.500	5.38	13	0	0	4	0	0	32	44	136	19	17	3	2	1	1	13	0	14	3	0
Gale, Rich, K.C	6	6	.500	5.79	19	15	4	0	0	0	102	107	440	63	61	14	1	6	1	38	0	47	0	0
Garland, Wayne, Clev.	3	7	.300	3.40	12	10	2	0	0	0	85	89	264	40	36	8	6	4	1	14	0	15	3	0
Garvin, Jerry, Tor.*	3	6	.333	4.50	35	2	0	11	0	2	56	46	221	30	28	8	6	3	1	23	2	26	0	1
Gleaton, Jerry Don, Sea.*	4	7	.364	4.76	20	13	2	3	0	0	85	88	369	50	45	10	3	4	3	38	2	31	3	0
Glynn, Ed, Clev.*	0	0	—	1.13	4	0	0	0	0	0	8	8	30	6	1	2	1	0	0	4	0	4	1	1
Gossage, Rich, N.Y	3	2	.600	.77	32	0	0	30	0	20	47	22	173	8	4	2	1	2	0	14	7	48	6	0
Griffin, Mike, N.Y	0	0	—	2.25	2	2	0	0	0	0	4	5	18	1	1	2	0	0	0	0	0	4	3	0
Guidry, Ron, N.Y.*	11	5	.688	2.76	23	21	11	0	0	0	127	100	497	41	39	12	1	1	1	26	0	104	3	0
Gura, Larry, K.C.*	11	8	.579	2.72	23	23	12	0	2	0	172	139	680	61	52	11	9	6	0	35	8	61	0	0
Haas, Moose, Milw	11	7	.611	4.47	22	22	6	0	0	0	137	146	583	68	68	10	6	6	0	40	6	64	3	0
Hammaker, Atlee, K.C.*	1	3	.250	5.54	12	0	0	5	0	0	39	44	169	24	24	8	2	1	0	12	0	11	1	0
Hassler, Andy, Cal.*	4	3	.571	3.72	42	0	0	21	0	3	76	72	315	29	27	6	6	2	0	33	4	44	0	0
Havens, Brad, Minn.*	3	6	.333	3.58	13	12	1	0	0	0	78	76	323	33	31	6	3	5	0	24	0	43	1	0
Heaverlo, Dave, Oak	1	0	1.000	1.50	6	0	0	2	0	0	6	7	27	2	1	0	7	2	0	3	1	1	1	0
Hickey, Kevin, Chi.*	0	2	.000	3.68	41	0	0	14	0	0	39	39	188	18	16	0	0	2	0	18	5	17	1	0
Hobbs, Jack, Minn*	0	0	—	3.00	4	0	0	1	0	0	6	5	29	2	2	0	0	0	0	6	1	1	1	0
Honeycutt, Rick, Tex.*	11	6	.647	3.30	20	20	8	0	0	0	128	120	509	47	47	12	6	0	2	17	1	40	1	0

Pitcher	W	L	Pct.	ERA
Hough, Charlie, Tex	4	1	.800	2.96
Hoyt, Lamarr, Chi	9	3	.750	3.56
Hurst, Bruce, Bos.*	2	0	1.000	4.30
Jackson, Darrell, Minn.*	3	3	.500	4.36
Jackson, Roy, Tor	1	2	.333	2.61
Jefferson, Jesse, Cal.	2	4	.333	3.62
Jenkins, Fergie, Tex	5	8	.385	4.50
John, Tommy, N.Y.*	9	8	.529	2.64
Johnson, John Henry, Tex.*	3	1	.750	2.63
Jones, Jeff, Oak	4	1	.800	3.39
Jones, Mike, K.C.*	6	3	.667	3.20
Keough, Matt, Oak	10	6	.625	3.41
Kern, Jim, Tex	1	2	.333	2.70
Kingman, Brian, Oak	3	6	.333	3.96
Kinney, Dennis, Det.*	0	1	.000	9.00
Kison, Bruce, Cal	0	0	—	3.48
Koosman, Jerry, Minn.-Chi.*	4	13	.235	4.02
LaRoche, Dave, N.Y.*	4	1	.800	2.49
Lacey, Bob, Clev.-Tex.*	0	0	—	7.77
Lamp, Dennis, Chi	7	6	.538	2.41
Langford, Rick, Oak	12	10	.545	3.00
Leal, Luis, Tor.	7	13	.350	3.67
Leonard, Dennis, K.C.	13	11	.542	2.99
Lerch, Randy, Milw.*	7	9	.438	4.30
Lewallyn, Dennis, Clev	0	0	—	5.54
Lopez, Aurelio, Det.	5	2	.714	3.62
Luebber, Steve, Balt	0	1	.000	7.41
Mahler, Mickey, Cal*	0	0	—	.00
Martin, Renie, K.C	4	5	.444	2.76
Martinez, Dennis, Balt	14	5	.737	3.32
Martinez, Fred, Cal.	0	0	—	3.00
Martinez, Tippy, Balt.*	3	3	.500	2.90
Matlack, Jon, Tex.*	4	7	.364	4.15
May, Rudy, N.Y.*	6	11	.353	4.14
McCatty, Steve, Oak	14	7	.667	2.32
McClure, Bob, Milw.*	0	0	—	3.38
McGaffigan, Andy, N.Y	0	0	—	2.57
McGlothen, Lynn, Chi	0	0	—	4.09

*Throws Lefthanded

Pitcher and Club	W	L	PCT	ERA	G	GS	CG	GF	SHO	SV	IP	H	TBF	R	ER	HR	SH	SF	HB	TBB	IBB	SO	WP	BK
McGregor, Scott, Balt.*	13	5	.722	3.26	24	22	8	0	3	0	160	167	664	63	58	13	7	6	1	40	5	82	3	1
McLaughlin, Byron, Oak.	0	0	—	11.25	11	0	0	4	0	0	12	17	61	15	15	1	0	1	0	9	0	3	1	0
McLaughlin, Joey, Tor.	1	5	.167	2.85	40	0	0	26	0	10	60	55	249	24	19	2	6	8	2	21	5	38	1	0
Medich, Doc, Tex.	10	6	.625	3.08	20	20	4	0	2	0	143	136	585	51	49	8	8	2	0	33	5	65	2	0
Mercer, Mark, Tex.*	0	0	—	4.50	7	0	0	2	0	0	8	7	36	4	4	1	0	0	0	7	0	4	0	0
Minetto, Craig, Oak.*	0	0	—	2.57	8	1	0	2	0	0	7	7	31	2	2	1	0	1	0	7	0	8	0	0
Mirabella, Paul, Tor.*	0	0	—	7.20	8	1	0	0	0	0	15	20	73	16	12	2	0	0	1	7	0	4	0	0
Monge, Sid, Clev.*	3	5	.375	4.34	31	0	0	20	0	4	58	58	244	31	28	9	0	3	0	21	2	41	2	2
Moore, Donnie, Milw	0	0	—	6.75	3	0	0	1	0	0	4	4	19	3	3	0	0	0	0	2	0	4	1	0
Moreno, Angel, Cal.*	1	3	.250	2.90	8	4	1	1	0	0	31	27	131	10	10	2	0	1	0	14	0	12	1	0
Morris, Jack, Det	14	7	.667	3.05	25	25	15	0	1	0	198	153	798	69	67	14	8	9	2	78	11	97	3	2
Mueller, Willie, Milw	0	0	—	4.50	4	0	0	1	0	0	2	4	10	1	1	0	0	0	0	0	0	1	0	0
Murray, Dale, Tor.	1	0	1.000	1.20	11	0	0	6	0	0	15	12	62	2	2	0	0	2	0	5	1	12	0	0
Nelson, Gene, N.Y.	3	1	.750	4.85	8	7	0	0	0	0	39	40	179	24	21	5	0	2	1	23	1	16	2	2
Norris, Mike, Oak.	12	9	.571	3.75	23	23	12	0	2	0	173	145	721	77	72	17	6	7	2	63	2	78	14	5
O'Connor, Jack, Minn.*	3	2	.600	5.91	28	0	0	11	0	0	35	46	173	27	23	3	3	0	0	10	0	16	0	0
Ojeda, Bob, Bos.*	6	2	.750	3.14	10	10	0	0	0	0	66	50	267	25	23	6	1	3	2	25	2	28	1	0
Owchinko, Bob, Oak.*	4	3	.571	3.76	29	15	0	2	0	0	39	34	164	15	14	2	3	4	3	19	0	26	0	0
Palmer, Jim, Balt	7	8	.467	3.76	22	22	5	0	0	0	127	117	532	60	53	14	4	4	0	46	1	43	3	1
Parrott, Mike, Sea.	3	6	.333	5.08	24	12	6	6	0	0	85	102	378	51	48	3	0	4	0	28	1	35	1	1
Paschall, Bill, K.C.	0	0	—	4.50	2	0	0	1	0	0	7	7	40	1	1	0	0	0	0	6	0	2	0	0
Patterson, Reggie, Chi	0	1	.000	14.14	6	1	0	2	0	0	7	14	53	11	11	2	0	2	0	6	0	2	1	0
Petry, Dan, Det	10	9	.526	3.00	23	22	7	1	2	0	141	115	583	53	47	10	9	2	4	57	0	79	3	1
Porter, Chuck, Milw	0	0	—	4.50	3	0	0	1	0	0	6	6	20	2	2	0	0	1	0	1	0	1	0	0
Quisenberry, Dan, K.C.	1	4	.200	1.74	40	0	0	35	0	18	62	59	254	16	12	2	5	4	1	15	4	20	1	0
Rainey, Chuck, Bos.	1	2	.333	2.70	11	2	0	0	0	0	40	39	171	21	12	2	1	0	2	13	1	20	1	0
Rau, Doug, Cal.*	0	1	.000	9.00	3	0	0	0	0	0	10	14	45	10	10	2	0	0	0	4	0	3	0	0
Rawley, Shane, Sea.*	4	6	.400	3.97	46	0	0	28	0	8	68	64	295	31	30	4	3	1	4	38	6	77	2	0
Redfern, Pete, Minn	9	8	.529	4.06	24	23	3	0	0	0	142	140	601	70	64	12	6	4	0	52	1	50	8	1
Renko, Steve, Cal	8	4	.667	3.44	22	15	0	5	1	0	102	93	424	40	39	7	3	6	1	42	2	77	2	1
Reuschel, Rick, N.Y.	4	4	.500	2.66	12	11	1	0	1	0	71	75	282	24	21	4	1	2	0	10	2	22	0	0
Righetti, Dave, N.Y.*	8	4	.667	2.06	15	15	0	0	0	0	105	75	422	25	24	5	1	0	1	38	0	89	1	0
Robinson, Dewey, Chi	1	0	1.000	4.50	4	0	0	2	0	0	4	5	18	2	2	0	0	0	0	3	1	6	0	0
Rothschild, Larry, Det	0	1	.000	1.50	5	0	0	2	0	0	6	4	27	1	1	0	1	0	0	6	1	1	0	0
Rozema, Dave, Det	5	5	.500	3.63	28	9	2	12	0	2	104	99	419	42	42	12	2	2	3	25	8	46	2	2

Pitcher	W	L	Pct.	ERA
Rucker, Dave, Det.*	0	2	.000	6.75
Sanchez, Luis, Cal.	0	2	.000	2.91
Saucier, Kevin, Det.*	0	2	.667	1.65
Schatzeder, Dan, Det.*	6	8	.429	6.08
Schmidt, Dave, Tex.	0	1	.000	3.09
Schneider, Jeff, Balt.*	0	0	—	4.88
Slaton, Jim, Milw.	4	5	.417	4.38
Spillner, Dan, Clev	5	5	.500	3.15
Splittorff, Paul, K.C.*	10	8	.556	4.36
Stanley, Bob, Bos.	3	3	.500	3.82
Standon, Mike, Clev	3	3	.500	4.40
Stein, Randy, Sea.	0	1	.000	11.00
Stewart, Sammy, Balt	4	8	.333	2.33
Stieb, Dave, Tor.	11	10	.524	3.18
Stoddard, Bob, Sea.	2	1	.667	2.57
Stoddard, Tim, Balt.	4	7	.364	3.89
Stone, Steve, Balt.	2	2	.500	4.57
Tanana, Frank, Bos.*	7	10	.286	4.02
Tobik, Dave, Det	2	2	.500	2.70
Todd, Jackson, Tor.	7	7	.222	3.95
Torrez, Mike, Bos.	10	3	.769	3.69
Travers, Bill, Cal.*	1	0	1.000	8.10
Trout, Steve, Chi.*	8	7	.533	3.46
Tudor, John, Bos.*	4	3	.571	4.56
Ujdur, Jerry, Det.	4	3	.571	6.43
Underwood, Tom, N.Y.-Oak.*	4	6	.400	3.64
Verhoeven, John, Minn.	1	1	.500	3.98
Veselic, Bob, Minn.	0	0	—	3.13
Vuckovich, Pete, Milw	14	4	.778	3.54
Waits, Rick, Clev.*	8	10	.444	4.93
Wehrmeister, Dave, N.Y	0	0	—	5.14
Whitehouse, Len, Tex.*	0	1	.000	18.00
Wilcox, Milt, Det.	12	9	.571	3.04
Williams, Al, Minn	6	10	.375	4.08
Willis, Mike, Tor.*	0	0	.000	5.91
Witt, Mike, Cal	8	9	.471	3.28
Wright, Jim, K.C.*	2	3	.400	3.46
Zahn, Geoff, Cal.*	10	11	.476	4.42

ALL-TIME MAJOR LEAGUE RECORDS

National	American

Batting (Season)

Average

.438 Hugh Duffy, Boston, 1894   .422 Napoleon Lajoie, Phila., 1901
.424 Rogers Hornsby, St. Louis, 1924

At Bat

699 Dave Cash, Phila., 1975   705 Willie Wilson, Kansas City, 1980

Runs

196 William Hamilton, Phila., 1894   177 Babe Ruth, New York, 1921
158 Chuck Klein, Phila., 1930

Hits

254 Frank J. O'Doul, Phila., 1929   257 George Sisler, St. Louis, 1920
254 Bill Terry, New York, 1930

Doubles

64 Joseph M. Medwick, St. L., 1936   67 Earl W. Webb, Boston, 1931

Triples

36 J. Owen Wilson, Pitts., 1912   26 Joseph Jackson, Cleve., 1912
     26 Samuel Crawford, Detroit, 1914

Home Runs

56 Hack Wilson, Chicago, 1930   61 Roger Maris, New York, 1961
     (162-game schedule)
     60 Babe Ruth, New York, 1927

Runs Batted In

190 Hack Wilson, Chicago, 1930   184 Lou Gehrig, New York, 1931

Stolen Bases

118 Lou Brock, St. Louis, 1974   96 Ty Cobb, Detroit, 1915

Bases on Balls

148 Eddie Stanky, Brooklyn, 1945   170 Babe Ruth, New York, 1923
148 Jim Wynn, Houston, 1969

Strikeouts

189 Bobby Bonds, S.F., 1970   175 Dave Nicholson, Chicago, 1963

Pitching (Season)

Games

106 Mike Marshall, L.A., 1974   88 Wilbur Wood, Chicago, 1968

Innings Pitched

434 Joseph J. McGinnity, N.Y., 1903   464 Edward Walsh, Chicago, 1908

Victories

37 Christy Mathewson, N.Y., 1908   41 Jack Chesbro, New York, 1904

Losses

29 Victor Willis, Boston, 1905   26 John Townsend, Wash., 1904
     26 Robert Groom, Wash., 1909

Strikeouts
(Lefthander)

382 Sandy Koufax, Los Angeles, 1965   343 Rube Waddell, Phila., 1904

(Righthander)

303 J.R. Richard, Houston, 1978   383 Nolan Ryan, Cal., 1973

Bases on Balls

185 Sam Jones, Chicago, 1955   208 Bob Feller, Cleveland, 1938

Earned-Run Average
(Minimum 200 Innings)

1.12 Bob Gibson, St. L., 1968   1.01 Hubert Leonard, Boston, 1914

Shutouts

16 Grover C. Alexander, Phila., 1916   13 John W. Coombs, Phila., 1910

TV/RADIO ROUNDUP

NETWORK COVERAGE

ABC-TV: The American and National League Championship Series, the All-Star Game, Monday Night Baseball and several late-season Sunday afternoon games will be shown by ABC.

NBC-TV: The World Series, selected prime-time games and the Saturday Game of the Week are scheduled by NBC. Joe Garagiola and Tony Kubek once again will be the network's top team and Bob Costas will be a part of the alternate team.

USA CABLE NETWORK: The USA Game of the Week will be shown on Thursday nights.

AMERICAN LEAGUE

BALTIMORE ORIOLES: Chuck Thompson, Bill O'Donnell and Tom Marr call the action over radio station WFBR (1300). Brooks Robinson joins Thompson and O'Donnell on WMAR-TV (Channel 2).

BOSTON RED SOX: Ken Coleman and Jon Miller broadcast over radio station WITS (1510). Ned Martin handles television on WSBK (Channel 38).

CALIFORNIA ANGELS: Bob Starr describes the action on KMPC radio (710) and KTLA-TV (Channel 5).

CHICAGO WHITE SOX: Ken Harrelson and Don Drysdale will be the television crew for Sportsvision cable (Channel 60) and WGN-TV (Channel 9), with Jimmy Piersall doing the pre-game and post-game shows. Radio arrangements were incomplete at press time.

CLEVELAND INDIANS: Herb Score and Nev Chandler are behind the mike for WWWE (1100) and a three-state radio network. Joe Tait and Bruce Drennan work the telecasts on WUAB-TV (Channel 43).

DETROIT TIGERS: Ernie Harwell and Paul Carey broadcast on a 50-station radio network originating with WJR (760).

George Kell and Al Kaline do the honors for WDIV-TV (Channel 4) and a seven-station network.

KANSAS CITY ROYALS: Five-state TV network originates with WDAF-TV (Channel 4), as Al Wisk and Danny Trease call the shots. Fred White and Denny Matthews share radio time on a network headed by KMBZ (980) and WIBW (580).

MILWAUKEE BREWERS: Bob Uecker and a colleague unnamed at press time handle play-by-play on WISN (1130). Steve Shannon will do the games for WVTV-TV (Channel 18).

MINNESOTA TWINS: Bob Kurtz and Larry Osterman telecast on KMSP-TV (Channel 9) and Frank Quilici and Herb Carneal call the plays on an 18-station radio network headed by WCCO (830).

NEW YORK YANKEES: Frank Messer, Phil Rizzuto and Bill White share duties on a TV network headed by WPIX-TV (Channel 11). Fran Healy joins the same crew on a radio network originating with WABC (770).

OAKLAND A's: Bill King, Lon Simmons and Wayne Hagin do the play-by-play on KFSO radio (560), while King and another voice unnamed at press time handle the job for KHBK-TV (Channel 44).

SEATTLE MARINERS: Dave Niehaus and a partner unnamed at press time describe the action for KVI radio (570) and KSTW-TV (Channel 11).

TEXAS RANGERS: Eric Nadel, Merle Harmon and Mark Holtz key the broadcasting team that will work the games for WBAP radio (820) and KXAS-TV (Channel 5).

TORONTO BLUE JAYS: Tom Cheek and Jerry Howarth do the radio play-by-play on HEWPEX Sports Network, originating on flagship station CJCL (1430). The CTV Network television coverage features Don Chevrier, Tony Kubek and Fergie Olver behind the mike.

NATIONAL LEAGUE

ATLANTA BRAVES: WSB radio (750) and WTBS-TV (Channel 17) are the anchor stations for the Braves' network. Ernie Johnson, Pete Van Wieren, Darrel Chaney and Skip Caray provide the coverage.

CHICAGO CUBS: Harry Caray, Milo Hamilton, Vince Lloyd and Lou Boudreau do it on WGN-TV (Channel 9), WGN radio (720) and a 13-station network.

CINCINNATI REDS: Bill Brown and Ray Lane are on WLWT-TV (Channel 5), while Joe Nuxhall and Marty Brennaman call 'em as they see 'em over WLW radio (700).

HOUSTON ASTROS: KENR radio (1070) and KRIV-TV (Channel 26) are the flagship stations. Gene Elston, Dewayne Staats and Larry Dierker handle TV and Elston and Staats double up on radio.

LOS ANGELES DODGERS: Vin Scully, Ross Porter and Jerry Doggett broadcast over KABC radio (790) and KTTV-TV (Channel 11). Spanish coverage of the World Champions is provided by Jaime Jarrin and Rudy Hoyas on KTNQ radio (950).

MONTREAL EXPOS: The English-speaking audience listens and watches Dave Van Horne and Duke Snider work the games for CFCF radio (600) and the CBC-TV network. Jacques Doucet and Claude Raymond say it in French for radio on CKAC (730), while Raymond Lebrun and Jean-Pierre Roy do French play-by-play for CBC-TV's network.

NEW YORK METS: Ralph Kiner is among the three commentators who will handle TV coverage on WOR (Channel 9) and Bob Murphy is a member of the broadcasting team on WMCA radio (570).

PHILADELPHIA PHILLIES: Harry Kalas, Richie Ashburn, Andy Musser, Chris Wheeler, and Tim McCarver describe the action on WCAU radio (1210) and WPHL-TV (Channel 17).

PITTSBURGH PIRATES: Lanny Frattare, Jim Rooker and John Sanders line up for KDKA radio (1020) and KDKA-TV (Channel 2).

ST. LOUIS CARDINALS: Jack Buck, Mike Shannon and Dan Kelly are on KMOX radio (1120) and are joined by Jay Randolph on KSDK-TV (Channel 5).

SAN DIEGO PADRES: Jerry Coleman and Dave Campbell handle the play-by-play for KFMB radio (760) and are joined by Ted Leitner on KFMB-TV (Channel 8).

SAN FRANCISCO GIANTS: Action can be heard on radio station KNBR (680) and can be seen on KTVU-TV (Channel 2). David Glass and Hank Greenwald team up on radio and Gary Park will be joined by a partner on the TV side.

OFFICIAL 1982 AMERICAN LEAGUE SCHEDULE

BOLD = **SUNDAY**   ( ) = HOLIDAY   * = NIGHT GAME   TN = TWI-NIGHT DOUBLEHEADER   (2) or [2] = DOUBLEHEADER

	AT SEATTLE	AT OAKLAND	AT CALIFORNIA	AT TEXAS	AT KANSAS CITY	AT MINNESOTA	AT CHICAGO
SEATTLE		April 9*,10,11 [2] Aug. 2*,3*,4	April 13*,14*,15* July 29*,30*,31* Aug. 1	June 7*,8*,9* Sept. 10*,11*,12	June 11*,12*,13 Sept. 13*,14*,15*,16*	April 6*,7*,8 Aug.13*,14*,15	July 2*,3,[4] Sept. 27*,28*,29*
OAKLAND	April 16*,17*,18 Aug. 9*,10*,11*		April 23*,24*,25 July 26*,27*,28*	June 24*,25,26*,27* Sept. 27*,28*,29*	June 28*,29*,30* Sept. 1*,2*,3	April 13*,14*,15 Aug. 6*,7,8	June 7*,8*,9* Sept. 16*,17*,18*,19
CALIFORNIA	April 19*,20*,21* Aug. 6*,7,8*	April 6*,7*,8* Aug.13*,14,15,16*		June 29*,30* July 1 Sept. 23*,24*,25,26	July 2*,3*,[4] Sept. 27*,28*,29	April 9*,10*,11* Aug.9*,10*,11*	June 10*,11*,12,13 Sept. 13*,14*,15*
TEXAS	June 14*,15*,16*,17* Sept. 17*,18*,19	July 2*,3,[4] Sept. 20*,21*,22*	June 21*,22*,23* Oct. 1*,2,3		May 21*,22*,23 Aug. 30*,31* Sept. 1*	June 18*,19,20 Sept. 13*,14*,15*,16	May 17*,18*,19* Sept. 2*,3*,4*,5
KANSAS CITY	June 18*,19*,20* Sept. (6),7*,8*	June 21*,22*,23 Sept. 24*,25,26	June 24*,25*,26*,27 Sept. 20*,21*,22*	May 28*,29*,30 Aug. 23*,24*,25,26*		June 7*,8*,9*,10* Sept. 17*,18,19	May 24*,25*,26* Aug. 27*,28*,29
MINNESOTA	April 22*,23*,24*,25 July 26*,27*,28	April 19*,20*,21 Aug. 29*,30*,31 Aug. 1	April 16*,17*,18 Aug. 2*,3*,4*,5	June 11*,12*,13 Sept. (6),7*,8*	June 14*,15*,16* Sept. 10*,11*,12		June 21*,22*,23* Sept. 24*,25*,26
CHICAGO	June 25*,26*,27* Sept. 20*,21*,22*,23*	June 15*,16*,17 Sept. 10*,11,12	June 18*,19,20 Sept. (6),7*,8*	June 4*,5*,6 Aug. 16*,17*,18*	May (31)* June 1*,2* Aug. 19*,20*,21*,22	June 28*,29*,30* July 1*,2* Oct. 1*,2*,3	

MILWAUKEE	May (31)* June 1*,2* Aug. 20*,21*.**22***	June 4*,5.**6** Aug. 17*,18*,19	May 27*,28*,29.**30** Aug. 23*,24*	April 23*,24*.**25** July 26*,27*,28*	May 10*,11*,12* July 23*,24*.**25**	April 30* May 1,2 July 19*,20*,21*	May 13*,14*,15*.**16** July 5*,6*
DETROIT	May 25*,26* Aug. 26*,27*,28*.**29***	May 28*,29,**30**.[2] Aug. 23*,24	May (31) June 1*,2* Aug. 20*,21*.**22**	May 10*,11*,12* July 9*,10*.**11***	April 9*,10*.**11** Aug. 2*,3*,4*	April 27*,28* July 15*,16*,17*.**18**	April 29,**30*** May 1,2 July 7*,8*
CLEVELAND	May 10*,11*,12* July 9*,10*.**11**	May 6*,7*.**8,9**	May 13*,14*,15*.**16** July 7*,8*	April 20*,21*,22* Aug. 13*,14*.**15***	April 23*,24*.**25** Aug. 9*,10*.**11***	April 24*,25*.**26*** Aug. 27*,28*.**29**	May 21*,22*.**23** Aug. 30*,31* Sept. 1*
TORONTO	June 21*,22*.23 Sept. 24*,25*.**26**	June 18*,19.**20** Sept. (6),7*.**12**	June 15*,16*,17* Sept. 10*,11*.**12**	April 29*,30* May 1.2 July 13*,14*	April 29*,30* May 1.2 July 7*,8*	July 2*,3*.[4] Sept. 20*,21*,22*	May 4*,5* July 22*,23*.**24,25**
BALTIMORE	May 13*,14*. 15*.**16*** July 7*,8*	May 10*,11*,12 July 9*,10*.**11**	May 6*,7*,8*.**9**	May 25*,26*,27* Aug. 20*,21*.**22**	April 13*,14* July 29*,30*,31* Aug. **1**	June 4*,5*.**6** Aug. 17*,18*,19*	April 16*,17*.**18** Aug. 9*,10*,11*
NEW YORK	May 6*,7*,8*.**9***	May 13*,14*,15.**16** July 7*,8*	May 10*,11*,12* July 9*,10*.**11**	April 12*,13*,14* July 30*,31* Aug. 1*	May 17*,18*,19* Sept. 3*,4.**5**	May 28*,29.**30** Aug. 30*,31* Sept. 1*	April 20*,21* Aug. 12*,13*,14*.**15**
BOSTON	May 27*,28*,29*.**30*** Aug. 23*,24*	May (31) June 1*,2* Aug. 20*,21.**22**	May 13*,14*,15.**16** July 5*,6*	May 6*,7*,8*.**9** July 7*,8*	May 13*,14*.15,16 July 5*,6*	May 10*,11*,12* July 23*,24*.**25**	April 6,8 July 29*,30*,31*. Aug. **1**

ALL-STAR GAME AT MONTREAL, JULY 13

CHICAGO WHITE SOX VS. CHICAGO CUBS **HALL OF FAME GAME AT COOPERSTOWN, AUGUST 2**

OFFICIAL 1982 AMERICAN LEAGUE SCHEDULE

BOLD = SUNDAY ( ) = HOLIDAY * = NIGHT GAME TN = TWI-NIGHT DOUBLEHEADER (2) or [2] = DOUBLEHEADER

	AT MILWAUKEE	AT DETROIT	AT CLEVELAND	AT TORONTO	AT BALTIMORE	AT NEW YORK	AT BOSTON
SEATTLE	May 21*,22,**23** Aug.30*,**31*** Sept.1*	June 4*,**5,6** Aug.16*,17*,18*	April 27*,28*,29* July 23*,**24,25**	June 29*,30* July 1 Oct.1*,**2,3**	May 3*,4* July 15*,16*,17*,**18**	April 30* May 1*,**2** July 19*,20*,21*	May 18*,19*,20* Sept.3*,**4,5**
OAKLAND	May 25*,26* Aug.26*,27*,28*,**29**	May 18*,19*,20* Sept.3*,**4,5**	April 30* May 1,**2** July 19*,20*,21*	June 11*,12,**13,14** Sept.14*,**15***	April 27*,28*,**29** July 23*,**24,25**	May 3*,4* July 15*,16*,17*,**18**	May 21*,22,**23** Aug.30*,**31***
CALIFORNIA	May 18*,19*,20 Sept.3*,**4*,5**	May 21*,22,**23** Aug.31 Sept.1*,**2***	May 3*,4* July 15*,16*,17,**18**	June 8*,9* Sept.16*,17*,18,**19**	April 30* May 1*,**2** July 19*,20*,21*	April 27*,28*,29* July 23*,**24*,25**	May 24*,25* Aug.26*,27*,28,**29**
TEXAS	April 16*,17,**18** Aug.9*,10*,11‖	May 4*,5* July 23*,**24,25[2]**	April 10,**11** Aug.2*,3 TN,4*	April 27*,28* July 15*,16*,17,**18**	May (31)* June 1*,**2** Aug.27*,28*,**29**	April 6,8 Aug.5*,**6*,7,8**	April 30* May 1,**2** July 19*,20*,21*
KANSAS CITY	May 3*,4*,**5** July 9*,10*,**11**	April 19*,20*,**21** Aug.13*,14,**15**	April 16,17,**18** July 26*,27*,28*	May 7*,**8,9** July 19*,20*,21*	April 5,7* Aug.5*,**6*,7,8**	June 4*,5*,**6** Aug.16*,17*,18*	April 27*,28* July 15*,16*,17,**18**
MINNESOTA	May 6*,7*,**8,9** July 7*,**8**	May 13*,14*,**15,16** July 5,6*	May (31)* June 1*,**2*** Aug.20*,21,**22**	June 25*,26,**27** Sept.28*,29*,30*	May 18*,19*,20* Sept.3*,**4*,5**	May 21*,22*,**23** Aug.24*,25*,**26***	May 3*,4*,**5*** July 9*,**10,11**
CHICAGO	April 27*,28* July 15*,16*,17*,**18**	May 7*,**8,9** July 19*,20*,21*	April 28*,29,**30** Aug.23*,24*,**25***	May 10*,11*,12* July 9*,10*,**11**	April 23*,24*,**25** July 26*,27*,28*	April 9*,10,**11** Aug.3 TN,4*	April 12,14,15 Aug.6*,**7,8**

MILWAUKEE
June 11*,12*,13 / Sept. (6), 7*, 8*
June 17*,18*,19*,20* / Sept. 13*,14*,15*
April 13,14,15 / Aug. 6*,7*,8
April 9,10,11 / Aug. 2,3*,4*
June 14*,15*,16* / Oct. 1*,2*,3
June 29*,30* / July 1* / Sept. 9*,10*,11*,12
June 25*,26,27,28* / Sept. 28*,29*,30*

DETROIT
June 11*,12*,13 / Sept. (6),7*,8*
April 6,8 / July 29*,30*,31 / Aug. 1[2]
June 14 TN,15*,16* / Oct. 1*,2,3
April 12,13*,14* / July 30,31 / Aug. 1
June 24*,25*,26*,27 / Sept. 20*,21*,22*
April 22*,23*,24,25 / July 26*,27*,28*
April 21*,22*,23* / Sept. 10*,11,12

CLEVELAND
April 6,8 / July 29*,30*,31 / Aug. 1[2]
June 8,9 TN / Sept. 24*,25,26
June 4*,5,6[2],7 / Aug. 16*,17*
June 24*,25*,26*,27 / Sept. 20*,21*,22*
June 11*,12,13 / Sept. 13*,14*,15*

TORONTO
April 20*,21*,22* / Aug. 12*,13*,14*,15
May 18*,19*,20* / Sept. 3*,4,5
April 6,8 / Aug. 5*,6*,7,8[2]
May 21*,22,23,24 / Aug. 30,31 / Sept. 1
May 28*,29*,30 / Aug. 24*,25*,26*
May 25*,26* / Aug. 20*,21*,22,23*
April 16,17,18,19 / July 26*,27*,28*

BALTIMORE
June 7*,8*,9*,10 / Sept. 24*,25*,26
July 2*,3*,[4] / Sept. 28*,29*,30*
June 21*,22*,23* / Sept. 9*,10*,11,12
May 21*,22,23,24 / Aug. 30,31 / Sept. 1
June 18*,19*,20 / Sept. (6),7*,8*
April 20*,21* / Aug. 13*,14,15,16*

NEW YORK
June 21*,22*,23* / Sept. 17*,18*,19
April 16*,17*,18 / Aug. 9*,10*,11*
July 2*,3*,[4] / Sept. 28*,29*,30*
May (31)* / June 1*,2*,3* / Aug. 27*,28,29
June 11*,12*,13 / Sept. 13*,14*,15*,16*
June 8*,9*,10* / Sept. 24*,25,29,27*

BOSTON
July 2*,3*,[4] / Sept. 20*,21*,22*
June 29,30* / July 1* / Sept. 16*,17,18,19
April 23*,24,25 / Aug. 9*,10*,11*
May 9*,10,11 / Aug. 2*,3 TN,4*
April 9*,10,11 / Aug. 2,3 TN,4
June 14*,15*,16* / Oct. 1*,2,3

ALL-STAR GAME AT MONTREAL, JULY 13

CHICAGO WHITE SOX VS. CHICAGO CUBS
HALL OF FAME GAME AT COOPERSTOWN, AUGUST 2

OFFICIAL 1982

EAST

	AT CHICAGO	AT MONTREAL	AT NEW YORK
CHICAGO.............		June 11*, 12*, **13** Aug. 9*, 10*, 11* Sept. 17*, 18, **19**	April 20*, 21* Aug. 12*,13*,14, **15,15** Sept. 29*, 30*
MONTREAL..........	June 17, 18, 19, **20** July 27, 28 Sept. 10, 11, **12**		April 16*, 17, **18** June 21*,22*,23*,24* Sept. 20*, 21
NEW YORK...........	April 9, 10, **11**, 12 Aug. 3, 4, 5 Sept. 22, 23	April 23, 24, **25** June 29*, 30* July 1* Sept. 14*, 15*, **16***	
PHILADELPHIA....	June 14, 15, 16 Aug. 6, 7, **8** Sept. 6, 7, 8	April 19, 20, 21 Aug. 12*,13*,14, **15** Sept. 22*, 23*	April 13, 14, 15 July 2*, 3*, **4** Sept. 24*, 25, **26**
PITTSBURGH........	April 23, 24, **25** June 28, 29, 30 July 1 Sept. 20, 21	April 13, 15 June 25*,25*,26*,**27** Sept. 24*, 25, **26**	June 7*, 8*, 9* July 29*, 30*, 31* Aug. **1** Sept. 27*, 28*
ST. LOUIS.............	April 13, 14, 15 June 25, 26, 26, **27** Oct. 2, **3**	June 7*, 8*, 9* July 29*, 30*, 31* Aug. **1** Sept. 27*, 28*	June 11*, 12*, **13** Aug. 9*, 10*, 11* Sept. 17*, 18*, **19**
ATLANTA.............	May 11, 12 July 15, 16, 17, **18**	May 17*, 18*, 19* Sept. 3*, 4*, **5**	May 31 June 1*, 2* Aug. 27*, 28*, **29**
CINCINNATI.........	April 27, 28 July 9, 10, 10, **11**	May 28*, 29, **30** Aug. 30*, 31* Sept. 1*	May 17*, 18*, 19* Sept. 3*, 4*, **5**
HOUSTON.............	May 7, 8, **9** July 19, 20, 21	May 31* June 1*, 2* Aug. 26*, 28, **29**	May 28*, 29*, **30** Aug. 30*, 31* Sept. 1*
LOS ANGELES......	May 28, 29, **30** Aug. 17, 18, 19	May 6, 7*, 8, **9** July 7*, 8*	May 13*, 14*, 15*, **16** July 5*, 6*
SAN DIEGO...........	May 31 June 1, 2 Aug. 20, 21, **22**	May 13*, 14*, 15, **16** July 5*, 6*	May 10*, 11*, 12* July 9*, 10*, **11**
SAN FRANCISCO..	June 4, 5, **6** Aug. 23, 24, 25	May 10*, 11*, 12* July 9*, 10*, **11**	May 6*, 7*, 8, **9** July 7*, 8*

*NIGHT GAME   HEAVY BLACK FIGURES DENOTE SUNDAY
                     NIGHT GAMES: ANY GAME STARTING AFTER 5:00 p.m.

NATIONAL LEAGUE SCHEDULE

EAST

	AT PHILADELPHIA	AT PITTSBURGH	AT ST. LOUIS
CHICAGO.............	June 7*, 8*, 9* July 29*, 30*, 31* Aug. **1** Sept. 27*, 28*	April 16*, 17, **18** June 21*, 22*, 23* Sept. 13*, 14*, 15*	May 3*, 4*, 5 July 2*, 3*, **4** Sept. 24*, 25, **26**
MONTREAL..........	April 9*, 10*, **11** Aug. 2*, 3*, 4*, 5 Sept. 29*, 30*	April 6, 8* July 2*, 2*, 3*, **4** Oct. 1*, 2*, **3**	June 14*, 15*, 16* Aug. 6*, 7*, **8** Sept. 6*, 7*, 8*
NEW YORK...........	April 6*, 7* June 25*,26*,26*,**27** Oct. 1*, 2*, **3**	June 14*, 15*, 16* Aug. 6*, 7*, **8** Sept. 6*, 7*, 8*	June 18*,18*,19*,**20** July 27*, 28* Sept. 10*, 11*, **12**
PHILADELPHIA....		June 17*,18*,19, **20** July 27*, 28* Sept. 10*, 11*, **12**	April 16*, 17, **18** June 21*,22*,23*,24 Sept. 20*, 21*
PITTSBURGH........	June 11*, 12*, **13** Aug. 9*, 10*, 11* Sept. 17*, 18*, **19**		April 10, **11**, 12 Aug. 2*, 3*, 4*, 5* Sept. 22*, 23*
ST. LOUIS.............	April 23*, 24, **25** June 28*, 29*, 30* Sept. 13*, 14*, 15*	April 20*, 21* Aug.12*,13*,14*,**15,15** Sept. 29*, 30*	
ATLANTA.............	May 28*, 29, **30** Aug. 30*, 31* Sept. 1*	May 3*, 4*, 5* July 23*, 24*, **25**	May 7*, 8*, **9** July 19*, 20*, 21*
CINCINNATI.........	May 31* June 1*, 2* Aug. 27*, 28*, **29**	May 13*, 14*, 15, **16** July 7*, 8*	May 10*, 11* July 15*,16*,17, **18**
HOUSTON..............	May 17*, 18*, 19* Sept. 3*, 4, **5**	April 29*, 30* May 1*, **2** July 5*, 6*	April 26*, 27*, 28 July 23*, 24, **25**
LOS ANGELES......	May 10*, 11*, 12* July 9*, 10*, **11**	May 31* June 1*, 2* Aug. 20*, 21*, **22**	June 4*, 5*, **6** Aug. 23*, 24*, 25*
SAN DIEGO...........	May 6*, 7*, 8*, **9** July 7*, 8*	June 4*, 5*, **6** Aug. 23*, 24*, 25*	May 28*, 29*, **30** Aug. 17*, 18*, 19*
SAN FRANCISCO..	May 13*, 14*, 15*, **16** July 5*, 6*	May 28*, 29*, **30** Aug. 17*, 18*, 19*	May 31* June 1*, 2* Aug. 20*, 21*, **22**

JULY 13 — ALL-STAR GAME AT MONTREAL
AUGUST 2 — HALL OF FAME GAME at COOPERSTOWN, CHICAGO WHITE SOX VS. CHICAGO CUBS

OFFICIAL 1982

WEST

	AT ATLANTA	AT CINCINNATI	AT HOUSTON
CHICAGO.............	April 29*, 30* May 1*, **2** July 5*, 6*	April 5, 7* July 23*, 24*, **25**, 26*	May 13*, 14*, 15*, **16** July 7*,8*
MONTREAL...........	June 4*, 5*, **6** Aug. 17*, 18*, 19*	May 21*, 22*, **23** Aug. 23*, 24*, 25*	May 24*, 25*, 26* Aug. 20*, 21, **22***
NEW YORK...........	May 24*, 25*, 26* Aug. 20*, 21*, **22**	June 4*, 5*, **6** Aug. 17*, 18*, 19*	May 21*, 22*, **23*** Aug. 23*, 24*, 25
PHILADELPHIA....	May 21*, 22, **23** Aug. 23*, 24*, 25*	May 24*, 25*, 26* Aug. 20*, 21*, **22**	June 4*, 5*, **6*** Aug. 17*, 18*, 19*
PITTSBURGH........	April 26*, 27*, 28* July 9*, 10*, **11**	May 7*, 8*, **9** July 19*, 20*, 21*	May 10*, 11* July 15*, 16*, 17*, **18**
ST. LOUIS.............	May 13*, 14*, 15*,**16** July 7*, 8*	April 30* May 1, **2**, **2** July 5*, 6*	April 6*, 7*, 8* July 9*, 10*, **11**
ATLANTA.............		April 12*, 13*, 14 June 25*, 26*, **27** Sept. 17*, 18*, **19**	April 16*, 17*, **18** June 14*, 15*, 16* Sept. 20*, 21*, 22*
CINCINNATI.........	April 20*, 21*, 22* July 2*, 3*, **4*** Sept. 10*, 11*, **12**		April 23*, 24*, **25** July 27*, 28*, 29* Oct. 1*, 2*, **3**
HOUSTON.............	April 9*, 10*, **11** June 28*, 29*, 30* Sept. 13*, 14*, 15*	May 4*, 5 Aug. 13*, 14*, **15**, 16* Sept. 24*, 25, **26**	
LOS ANGELES......	June 22*, 23*, 24* July 30*, 30*, 31 Aug. **1** Sept. 8*, 9*	June 18*, 19, **20**, 21* Aug. 2*, 3*, 4 Sept. 6*, 7*	April 12*, 13*, 14* June 25*, 26, **27*** Sept. 10*, 11, **12***
SAN DIEGO...........	April 23*, 24*, **25** July 27*, 28*, 29* Sept. 24*, 25*, **26**	June 22*, 23*, 24* July 30*, 31*, 31* Aug. **1** Sept. 8*, 9*	June 18*, 19,* **20***, 21* Aug. 2*, 3*, 4 Sept. 6*, 7*
SAN FRANCISCO..	June 18*, 19*, **20**, 21* Aug. 2*, 3*, 4 Sept. 6*, 7*	April 9*, 10, **11** June 15*, 16*, 17 Sept. 21*, 22*, 23	June 22*, 23*, 24* July 30*, 31*, 31* Aug. **1*** Sept. 8*, 9

*NIGHT GAME   **HEAVY BLACK FIGURES DENOTE SUNDAY**
NIGHT GAMES: ANY GAME STARTING AFTER 5:00 p.m.

NATIONAL LEAGUE SCHEDULE

WEST

	AT LOS ANGELES	AT SAN DIEGO	AT SAN FRANCISCO
CHICAGO............	May 18*, 19*, 20* Aug. 27*, 28*, **29**	May 24*, 25*, 26* Sept. 3*, 4*, **5**	May 21*, 22, **23**, 23 Aug. 31* Sept. 1
MONTREAL..........	April 30* May 1, **2** July 19*, 20*, 21*	May 3*, 4* July 15, 16*, 17*, **18**	April 27*, 28, 29* July 23*, 24, **25**
NEW YORK..........	May 3*, 4* July 15*, 16*, 17*, **18**	April 27*, 28*, 29 July 23*, 24*, **25**	April 30* May 1, **2, 2,** July 20*, 21
PHILADELPHIA....	April 27*, 28*, 29* July 23*, 24*, **25**	April 30* May 1*, **2** July 19*, 20*, 21*	May 3*, 4* July 15*, 16*, 17, **18**
PITTSBURGH........	May 24*, 25*, 26* Sept. 3*, 4*, **5**	May 21*, 22*, **23** Aug. 30*, 31* Sept. 1*	May 18*, 19, 20 Aug. 27*, 28, **29**
ST. LOUIS..............	May 21*, 22*, **23** Aug. 30*, 31* Sept. 1*	May 18*, 19*, 20 Aug. 27*, **29, 29**	May 24*, 25*, 26 Sept. 3*, 4*, **5**
ATLANTA..............	June 7*, 8*, 9* Aug. 5*, 6*, 7*, **8** Sept. 29*, 30*	April 6*, 7 Aug. 12, 13*, 14*, **15** Oct. 1*, 2*, **3**	June 11*, 12, **13, 13** Aug. 9*, 10*, 11 Sept. 27*, 28*
CINCINNATI.........	June 10*, 11*, 12*, **13** Aug. 9*, 10*, 11* Sept. 27*, 28*	June 7*, 8*, 9* Aug. 5*, 6*, 7*, **8** Sept. 29*, 30	April 16*, 17, **18** June 28*, 29*, 30* Sept. 13*, 14*, 15*
HOUSTON..............	April 19*, 20*, 21* July 2*, 3*, **4** Sept. 17*, 18*, **19**	June 10, 11*, 12*, **13** Aug. 9*, 10*, 11* Sept. 27*, 28*	June 8*, 9 Aug. 5*, 6*, 7, **8, 8** Sept. 29*, 30*
LOS ANGELES......		April 15*, 16*, 17*, **18** June 14*, 15*, 16* Sept. 21*, 22*	April 23*, 24*, **25** July 26*, 27*, 28* Oct. 1*, 2, **3**
SAN DIEGO...........	April 9*, 10, **11** June 28*, 29*, 30* Sept. 13*, 14*, 15*		April 13, 14* June 25*, 26, **27** Sept. 16*, 17*, 18, **19**
SAN FRANCISCO..	April 6, 7* Aug. 12, 13*, 14*, **15** Sept. 24*, 25, **26**	April 19*, 20*, 21* July 2*, 2*, 3*, **4** Sept. 10*, 11*	

JULY 13 – ALL-STAR GAME AT MONTREAL

AUGUST 2 – HALL OF FAME GAME at COOPERSTOWN, CHICAGO WHITE SOX VS. CHICAGO CUBS

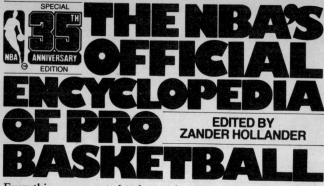

THE NBA'S OFFICIAL ENCYCLOPEDIA OF PRO BASKETBALL

EDITED BY ZANDER HOLLANDER

Everything you wanted to know about pro basketball in one splendid volume:

A definitive reference work, an absorbing history and a pictorial treasury:

From the first pro game in 1896 through the championship game of 1981, this mammoth work contains:

• Lifetime year-by-year records of more than 2,000 players who have appeared in the BAA, NBA and/or ABA • Reviews of every NBA season • Profiles of the greatest NBA players • Histories of the Original Celtics, Harlem Globetrotters • Official Rules • More than 200 action photos, including a 16-page color insert

"If I had to sum it up in a word, I'd say it's a 'slamdunk'"
— From the foreword by Lawrence F. O'Brien, Commissioner, NBA

"We have long needed an encyclopedia like this for anyone who has played and watched the game."
— Nat Holman, Original Celtic

An Associated Features Book

(#H407—$24.95) hardbound volume